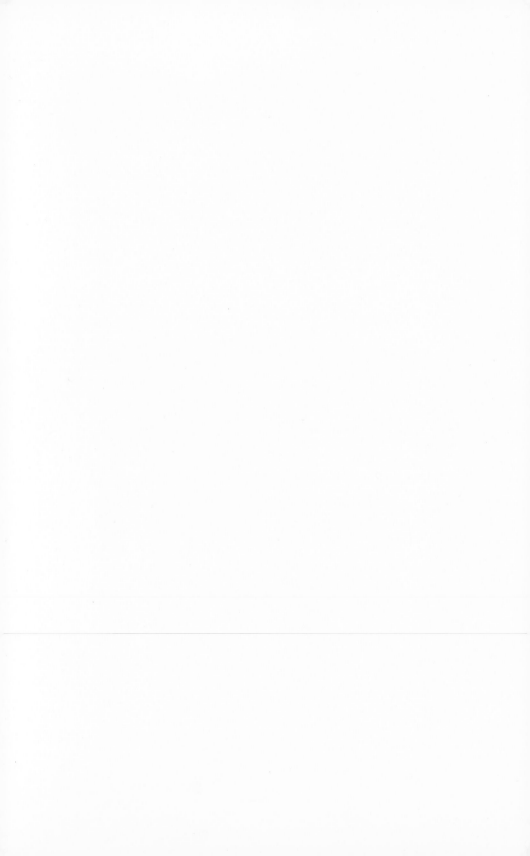

HELLENES & HELLIONS

HELLENES & HELLIONS

MODERN GREEK CHARACTERS
IN AMERICAN LITERATURE

ALEXANDER KARANIKAS

UNIVERSITY OF ILLINOIS PRESS

URBANA : CHICAGO : LONDON

© 1981 BY THE BOARD OF TRUSTEES OF THE UNIVERSITY OF ILLINOIS
MANUFACTURED IN THE UNITED STATES OF AMERICA

Library of Congress Cataloging in Publication Data
Karanikas, Alexander
  Hellenes and hellions.
  Bibliography: p.
  Includes index.
  1. American fiction—History and criticism. 2. Greek Ameri-
cans in literature. 3. Greeks in literature. 4. Greek Americans.
I. Title.
PS374.G73K3   813'.0935203893   80-27482
ISBN 0-252-00792-1

FOR MY THREE DAUGHTERS

Marianthe Vaia
Diana Christine
Cynthia Maria

PUBLICATION OF THIS BOOK HAS BEEN MADE POSSIBLE IN PART
THROUGH THE SPONSORSHIP OF THE FOLLOWING:

Anthony A. Antoniou

Van C. Argiris

Dr. and Mrs. Kostis T. Argoe

Andrew A. Athens

Anna Barra

Nicholas H. and Angelyn Boolookas

Michael G. Cheronis

Frederick F. Cohn

John P. Daros

The Honorable Spyridon Dokianos

Julius L. Echeles

James P. Economos

Nicholas C. Giovan

Dr. and Mrs. Nicholas Glyptis

*In fond memory of Reverend and Presbytera
Constantine Harvalis*

Greek Women's University Club

Hellenic Council on Education

David Horwatt—Center for Television in the Humanities

James G. Kallas

Frank S. Kamberos

John J. Karagiannes

Paul Karanikas

Mr. and Mrs. William Karanikas

Petros N. Kogiones

John D. and Peter D. Maniatis

Mrs. Frank Maritsas

Metron Steel Corporation

Louis Mitchell

Charles C. Moskos, Jr.

National Bank of Greece S.A.

Carl D. Nipp

Order of Ahepa

Helen Zeese Papanikolas

Demetri Parry

Elena Savoy

Dean Stavrakas

United Hellenic American Congress

George M. Zuganelis

CONTRIBUTIONS FROM THE FOLLOWING INDIVIDUALS HAVE PROVIDED
FURTHER NEEDED SUPPORT IN MEETING PUBLICATION COSTS:

S. D. Apostol

Mary Christy

Christ Kametas

Leon Marinakos

Dr. John N. Nicholson

Daphne Soter

Mr. and Mrs. Sam Stavrakas

Theodora Vasils

CONTENTS

PREFACE

RESEARCH for *Hellenes and Hellions* began several years before the bicentennial period, which, with its emphasis on our nation's cultural pluralism, merged with the ongoing civil-rights movement and helped to make ethnic and native American studies an important new trend in education. For more than a decade the federal government has aided significantly by providing funds and personnel for a wide range of ethnically-oriented activities. Many of the novels relevant and valuable for my purpose had long languished in oblivion on secluded library stacks. Some had to be rescued from storage and imminent discard. From the beginning my work involved the recurring satisfaction of finding literary treasure in unexpected places. Existing bibliographies and indexes offered only limited help, since no thorough scholarship existed on the presence of Greek characters in American fiction. A group of friends and avid readers supplemented my search with new and often exciting titles. Relevant titles may still be hiding on the shelves; yet, even without them, one can certainly conclude that the Greek experience in America has been depicted frequently and, at times, movingly in our imaginative literature.

The shifting choice of a suitable subtitle for *Hellenes and Hellions* may well illustrate the developing intent and scope of my study. At first the subtitle *Greek Stereotypes in American Literature* was uppermost in my mind. The protests of the Italian-Americans, angered by their image on *The Untouchables*, that forced the popular television program off the air made me consider that perhaps American fiction also contained ethnic slurs, put-downs, and slanders aimed at Greeks for reasons of xenophobia, negative humor, or even simple annoyance. When a Greek character represented some form of evil, some weakness, some failure, he naturally took something away from one's platonic conception of Greek ethnicity. After much reading, however, I found no consistent or extensive stereotyping of the modern Greek—a fact that greatly interested the Greek-American audiences whom I addressed. Listeners often asked for lists of my sources so they could read the books themselves. They were anxious, it seemed, to explore the images of Greeks created by others and now permanently imbedded in our literature. These listeners were also looking for a record of their immediate ethnic history to learn more about the world of their fathers before that world was gone forever. The question-and-answer periods after the lectures showed that my listeners were also seeking to update and otherwise refine their identity as Greeks in a society that often homogenized the particular into the common and sought to make everyone both equal and the same.

Many of the more richly detailed and consciously ethnic works discussed in *Hellenes and Hellions* belong to the category of the Greek-American novel or the Greek-immigrant-in-America novel, but a subtitle based upon them would reflect only part of the much broader scope of the study. These works—and those about second-generation Greeks—may be the most central and meaningful in what they record about the Greek experience in America. Most of them deal with tensions of an inherited culture that is in the process of being eroded, of becoming Americanized. A good example of a work devoted exclusively to such novels is Rose Basile Green's *The Italian-American Novel: A Document of the Interaction of Two Cultures*. Both the Greek and Italian novels (not to mention all other ethnic and minority literatures) serve once again as reminders of the enormously rich diversity that informs our multilingual, multicultural society.

These Greek-American novels, along with their other values, also reveal the manner in which the American Dream penetrated the donor country to lure away so many of its most intrepid spirits. For this lure to occur, something had to be wrong with modern Greece and something had to be right with America. Even the hardship and heartbreak that resulted from the overselling or misrepresentation of the dream did not deter new waves of immigrants. These novels, in motivating their heroes, often juxtapose the poverty and stagnation of the donor country against the dynamism of America, the dead end against the open door, despair against aroused hope. Thus the novels about Greeks crossing the Atlantic become useful sources of immigration history.

Greeks left their fatherland in droves to disperse throughout the world. Those who chose America dispersed to all its regions, where they engaged in many occupations. The early Greeks concentrated more in some regions and occupations than in others.

The resultant settings of various ethnic novels, among them the Greek, help to infuse the abstraction *America* with very concrete meanings, with the real facts of life. They represent a form of local color more often than not urban, and realistic in spite of the romanticism of the voyage to and the putting down of roots in a new land. Hence Greek-American novels, like those of other established minorities, supplement the research of social scientists in their continuing study of our unique society.

The Greek-American novel that deals with immigrants includes at least the hero's first stages of adjustment and acculturation. Among the themes natural to this type of novel are the strain on familial relationships; the painful backward glance toward those left behind; the alienation of the individual as he faces loneliness and estrangement in a new environment; the response of the receiving community, sometimes peaceful, sometimes violent, depending upon specific circumstances; the intensification of personal problems even within the ethnic enclave; the loyalty to ethnic heritage in conflict with pressures to change or abandon old customs; the ups and downs of class mobility as the immigrant succeeds or fails; and the multiform issues that arise between the first and second transplanted generations. The Greek experience in fiction builds upon these and other themes that are more or less common to all immigrant groups.

Depending upon the author's degree of ethnic consciousness and knowledge, the Greek-American novel also serves to record essential features of Hellenism. What does it mean to be a modern Greek? and How much Greek, how much American? are questions posed and partly answered by many an ethnic novel—not because of quaintness but because of a serious belief that customs once stable will eventually weaken and possibly disappear. In such novels Hellenism is an important source of subject matter, character development, formal structure, and thematic unity. Characters have been shaped to a great extent by their Greek heritage, geographic locality, family history, church, awareness of classical myths, pride in the glory of ancient Greece, revolutionary heroes of 1821, and all the legends and archetypes of an illustrious past.

Although important, Greek-American novels cannot by themselves supply an adequate subtitle for *Hellenes and Hellions*; many other works with modern Greek characters also need to be accommodated. Another subtitle that occurred to me, *The Greek Experience in American Literature*, was suggested by a national bicentennial symposium, The Greek Experience in America, held at the University of Chicago in October 1976 under the sponsorship of the Modern Greek Studies Association, for which I served as cochairman. But this, likewise, seemed inadequate and misleading. Neither did a variant of this work as a subtitle, because *Greek experience* could include everything from a novel about Alexander the Great to one about a Greek-Christian gladiator under Rome or one about an empress of Byzantium. Another scholar may well produce another volume that describes novels and short stories which have had a Hellenizing influence on America—fiction with characters who derive from the three great Greek historic periods that antedate the modern.

The term *modern* determines the time span relevant to the subject matter of *Hellenes and Hellions*. For most historians *modern Greece* means the nation that was reborn in the Greek Revolution of 1821–29 after nearly four hundred years of Ottoman rule. The term *modern Greeks*, therefore, means the people associated historically, ethnically, culturally, and emotionally with Greece, whether living inside or outside its borders. From modern Greece itself, from the so-called "unredeemed Greek lands," and from other countries came the Greek immigrants who settled and eventually prospered in America. Their experience has been recorded in a variety of studies, notably in *The Greeks in the United States* by Theodore Saloutos and in *Greek Americans: Struggle and Success* by Charles C. Moskos, Jr. The Greek-Americans are a relatively small ethnic community; they number somewhere between one and two million. Since the majority of the early immigrants arrived after 1890, the Greeks here are only in their fourth generation.

The time span for *Hellenes and Hellions* consists roughly of the one hundred fifty years between 1825 and 1975. Once involved in what became for me a fascinating subject, I decided to go all the way and examine, for its ethnic significance, every piece of American fiction that depicted a modern Greek character. I expected to find a fairly small hillock of material and found instead a sizable mountain. The result, after a decade of work, is *Hellenes and Hellions*, with its finally chosen subtitle of *Modern Greek Characters in American Literature*. Many books described within its seventeen chapters have genuine literary value; some have little or no value, and are merely potboilers that exploit the sensational. I have tried to deal openly and fully with all of them, since all express some attitude about modern Greeks.

One of my conclusions has already been stated—that the Greek experience in America has often been vividly, concretely, and movingly depicted in our literature. Relevant novels proliferated during the 1960s and 70s, perhaps in consort with the rapid growth of a Greek-American middle class, perhaps because *Zorba the Greek*, *Never on Sunday*, and other Greek highlights captured the American imagination. As the new fiction moves closer to the present, Greek characters, especially those created by non-Greek writers, no longer live in Greek Town nor interact mainly with other Greeks. Second- and third-generation Greeks in fiction suffer problems that derive less from ethnic isolation and identity and more from their own personality and situation. Thus the ethnicity factor goes from being primary in the immigrant novel to being secondary in novels about Greeks for whom the United States is a native land. Whatever Hellenism remains for them, it is not an alien culture to be deplored, concealed, or nourished among bigots, but a legacy perpetuated with pride and pleasure. In their ultimate meaning, the Greek-American novels embody the success story of an ethnic minority that is unusually responsive to the American Dream.

Even if no modern Greek had landed here, the impact of Hellenism upon our culture and institutions would still have been vast. If the early adventurers and colonists had any learning, they had a classical education based upon the Greeks from Homer to Epicurus. The debt owed by all the arts and sciences to ancient Greece, that prompted Shelley to declare "We are all Greeks now," applies as much to America as to England. The Greek revolution of the 1820s prompted a lively and widespread interest in the rebirth of Hellas. The coming of the Greek immigrant added what may be called a physical component to the cultural Hellenism that was already here as a fundamental aspect of Western civilization. *Hellenes and Hellions* constitutes a literary overview of that new ethnic dimension. It is my hope that this study will add a modest new dimension to American literature by stressing the presence within it of a dynamic and complex set of Greek characters.

I am grateful to the following persons for their help in finding relevant titles: Kostis T. Argoe, professor emeritus of history, City Colleges of Chicago; Andrew T. Kopan, department of educational foundations, DePaul University; Charles C. Moskos, Jr., department of sociology, Northwestern University; Joan P. Johnson, Anna Barra, Dion Cheronis, Rachel Dalven, John Curtis Johnson,

Theano Papazoglou-Margaris, Helen Michalaros, James B. Stronks, Theodora Vasils, and Meyer Weinberg. I greatly appreciate the help rendered by Ruth Peaslee, head of children's services, and Gerry Stigberg of the Oak Park Library. I wish to thank the staffs of the Newberry Library and the Library of the University of Illinois at Chicago Circle for their generous assistance. I also thank the president and the board of trustees of the University of Illinois for granting me two sabbatical leaves to facilitate my research and writing. I am especially grateful to my wife Helen and to my three daughters for their understanding of the problems involved and for their patience in helping me see the project to its conclusion.

Alexander Karanikas

OAK PARK, 1980

HELLENES & HELLIONS

၂၅၂၅၂၅၂၅၂၅၂

1

၂၅၂၅၂၅၂၅၂၅၂

NINETEENTH-CENTURY ATTITUDES

EARLY ATTITUDES in America toward the Greeks derived largely from similar attitudes abroad, especially in England. In his *Fair Greece, Sad Relic* (1973) Terence Spencer documents these attitudes as they existed in England since the fall of Constantinople in 1453.[1] The Elizabethans, for example, believed that Greeks tended to be drunkards, "merry Greeks," or "mad Greeks," an idea encouraged by the popularity of Greek wines in the West (p. 36). Ben Jonson distinguished between "Roman gravity and Greek levity." The sixteenth century, as evidenced in *Euphues* and elsewhere, regarded Greeks as faithless cheats and sharpers. Spencer writes that the stereotype of the Greek as a dissipated person hardly survived after the seventeenth century, but that *Greek* meaning a *sharper* remained a cant term for English writers into the nineteenth century. "It was with the considerable disadvantage, therefore, of a derogatory name, that the Greek nation re-entered the consciousness of Europe. Naturally, Englishmen soon discovered the characteristics implied by the label. The Greeks were (at worst) frivolous, drunken, and deceitful; or (at best) they were gay, convivial, and acute" (p. 40). Even Greek women were reputed, without proof, to be lewd. Despite these alleged views, respect for the ancient Greeks never diminished.

For nearly four hundred years the Christian powers of Europe made no effort to help liberate their fellow Christians, the Greeks, from Moslem bondage. The attitude prevailed in the West that the Greeks, although Christians "in servitude to the wicked and dangerous Turks," deserved their fate because they had so terribly degenerated from their ancestors. "It was God's judgment upon a decadent people" (p. 44). Their nearest Latin (Catholic) neighbors despised the Greeks as schismatics; they had, after all, split off from Rome to establish their own Eastern Orthodox Church at Constantinople. No doubt many a Roman Catholic felt grateful to the Turks for having destroyed a rival Catholic empire. Another curious attitude toward the Greeks prevailed, according to Spencer. Virgil had called the Trojans the *Teucri*, a word very close to *Turchi*, the Italian for *Turk*. The association of Trojan and Turk made many believe "that the Turkish conquest of Greece was in some way a revenge for the Grecian conquest of Troy about two and half thousand years before" (p. 9). Others who wanted to hate the modern Greeks had no need of linguistic coincidence from distant history. They simply blasted off against their moral nature, as Jean de Thévenot did in 1655: "The *Greeks* are covetous, perfidious, and treacherous, great Pederasts, revengeful to extremity, but withal very superstitious, and great Hypocrites; and, indeed, they are so despised by the Turks, that they value not even a *Greek* that turns Turk" (p. 44).

During the eighteenth century these and other negative attitudes changed to "eager speculation and controversy whether the Greeks inherited any of the virtues of their ancestors, whether their language could be purified, and whether they would owe their liberation to the kindly, but interested, arms of Russia, France, or England, or to their own exertions" (p. 171). Many Philhellenes before Lord Byron visited Greece and wrote about its inhabitants. A great stirring toward nationhood occurred among the Greeks themselves—through an increase in education, the growth of Greek centers abroad, and two abortive and bloody uprisings against their Turkish oppressors. Spencer cites what he terms a "second renaissance" in the later eighteenth century, with Greece again a focus of classical studies. Writers engaged in a serious debate comparing the modern Greeks with the ancients. Once the Greeks gained their freedom, many westerners believed, they would eventually cultivate industry, sensibility, and integrity. By 1800 the Philhellenism that Byron soon was widely to inspire had already appeared. The whole world sensed that great events impended in Greek lands.

Nineteenth-century American estimates of the modern Greeks did not result from extensive personal contact with Greek immigrants. They simply had not arrived yet. According to historian Theodore Saloutos, only 303 such immigrants arrived from 1820 to 1880. More might have entered unrecorded or under another ethnic designation. From 1891 to 1910 the number rose to 183,498, however, a figure that indicated a swift and large diaspora.[2] The earliest of the Greek settlers in the colonial period, at New Smyrna and St. Augustine, made no impact upon the American conscience.[3] Neither did the scattered adventurers and traders, including Juan de Fuca, a navigator, allegedly Greek, who named the straits between Vancouver and the state of Washington. Despite this initial paucity of Greeks, however, the precepts of Hellenism enjoyed a considerable practical application during the American revolutionary period. For historical example, rationale, and tradition, our founding fathers depended heavily on ancient Greece and Rome. Their classical education had given them models of science, philosophy, architecture, oratory, literature, and the arts worthy of the new republic they had risked so much to form.

The best study of the American experience of Greece during 1775–1865 is Stephen A. Larrabee's *Hellas Observed* (1957).[4] In it the author "recounts the story of the increasing knowledge of Greece gained by Americans who went there in various capacities, as travelers, fighters for Greek independence, relief agents, missionaries, consuls and scholars."[5] Their knowledge was transmitted in numerous books about Greece, published here or in England and available to American readers. Taken as a whole, this material contains an elaborate body of attitudes toward the modern Greek and his newly restored but tattered nation. These attitudes refer almost exclusively to the Greeks in Greece. Several decades later their grandsons were to crowd Ellis Island. These grandsons were to encounter, in addition to friends or enemies on the job, the predisposition toward them created in part by books and articles about their fatherland. Larrabee's resumé and analysis of the earliest of them comprise the substance of his valuable study.

To a great extent the Philhellenism of Thomas Jefferson derived from his admiration of ancient Greece. Yet, as we learn from *Hellas Observed*, Jefferson also enjoyed as respected friends a number of Parisian Greeks while he served as minister to France from 1784 to 1789. Among them was John Paradise, described by Jefferson as "a Graecian and honest man by birth, a gentleman and man of learning by education," who came to live in Williamsburg, Virginia.[6] Others included Count Carberry (Charvounis) of Cephalonia, the royal physician; a Greek lady of exceptional beauty, Madame de Tott; and, most important, Adamantios Korais, or Coray, the scholar-patriot who with the poet Rhigas Pheraios aroused the revolutionary spirit of the modern Greeks. On at least one occasion Jefferson entertained Korais at Chaillot. In 1789 the prospects for an independent Greece appeared dim to the future president. The great powers that plotted to dismember the Ottoman Empire had little sympathy or use for the political rebirth of the Greeks.

Those Americans like Jefferson who favored a restored Hellas did so primarily in the interest of natural human rights—to liberate from bondage the very people whose ancestors invented democracy. For many the breakup of the Ottoman Empire also meant free trade and access to markets and raw materials hitherto difficult to obtain. Others desired a new kind of Christian crusade against the Moslem infidel. As Larrabee notes, the first American novel to call for Greek national revival was Hugh Henry Brackenridge's *Modern Chivalry*, published in various editions from 1793 to 1815. The quixotic hero Captain Farrago invokes Greece before a company of militiamen: "O Poetic and philosophic country, where my mind ranges every day; whence I draw my best thoughts; where I converse with the schools of wise men, and solace myself with the company of heroes, thou art lost in servitude, and great must be the revolution which can extricate thee thence."[7] When the Greek revolution thus forecast finally broke out in 1821, a "Greek fever" of support swiftly spread throughout America.

The extensive and passionate reaction of our poets in backing the Greeks is recorded in *American Poets and the Greek Revolution (1821–1828): A Study in Byronic Philhellenism* (1971) by Marios Byron Raizis and Alexander Papas.[8] The greatest of these poets was William Cullen Bryant; the most popular, Fitz-Greene Halleck. Raizis and Papas quote from one of Bryant's speeches in which he says of the Greeks: "Nothing ignoble or worthless can spring from so generous a stock. It was in Greece that civilization had its origin, and the grand impulse which she communicated to the human mind will never cease to the end of time" (p. 28). His Greek poems include "The Massacre at Scio" (1824), "The Song of the Greek Amazon" (1825), "The Grecian Partisan" (1825), "The Conjunction of Jupiter and Venus" (1826), and "The Greek Boy" (1828). Bryant loved the Greek heritage, the Greek language, and by extension the modern Greeks. "With his poetry and speeches on Greece and his imposing and influential personality as a public figure," Raizis and Papas write, "Bryant perhaps did more than any other poet in America to give moral support to Greece's struggle and influence public opinion favorably toward the Greeks" (p. 29).

Fitz-Greene Halleck became the most popular of the Philhellenic poets by virtue of his ode "Marco Bozzaris," dedicated to one of the Greek revolution's finest heroes. The poem immediately earned Halleck a national reputation. The modern Greek warrior was turned into legend: this was the fate of Bozzaris leading his brave "Suliote band" against a mighty horde of Turks. The action that resulted in his death stirred the American imagination. "He fell in a night attack upon twelve thousand Turks, under Mustapha Pasha, encamped in the plain near Carpenesi in northern Greece— the same location of ancient Plateae where Pausanias had fought the Persian invaders—on August 20, 1823. That Greek attack was an attempt to prevent the Ottomans' advance toward southern Greece. Bozzaris hastened with twelve hundred men and fought Mustapha's army in the plain below him" (p. 77). Unfortunately the renowned leader "received a random shot which killed him instantly." Of the many eulogies written in his memory, "Marco Bozzaris" by Halleck made the greatest impression upon America. The ode rises in feeling to say:

> For thou art Freedom's now, and Fame's:
> One of the few, the immortal names,
> That were not born to die.[9]

The embattled Greek of the American poets was a Christian David pitted against a cruel Moslem Goliath. He was also Achilles and Odysseus at the walls of Troy, Leonidas holding back the Persians at Thermopylae, and many another classical hero born anew and fighting to be free.

The Greek revolution and its aftermath elicited various dramas and narratives in which the Greek appears as victim, hero, or both. The earliest play was *The Grecian Captive, or the Fall of Athens* by Mordecai M. Noah. It was performed at the New York Theater in 1822. In *Turkish Barbarity* (1828) M. Ketch writes about Sofia Mazro, a Greek lady of Missolonghi. The following year appeared *The Personal Narrative of the Sufferings of J. Stephanini, a Native of Arta, in Greece*. At the time the Turks still held the author's family as slaves. Other works on the plight of the Greeks included *Narrative of a Greek Soldier* (1830) by Petros Mengous and *The Grecian Exile* (1845) by Christophoros Plato Castanis. Hiram Powers's famous statue *The Greek Slave* is dated 1843. The Greek cause apparently proved popular on the American stage. Among his many works John Howard Payne wrote *Ali Pacha; or, The Signet Ring* (1823) and *Oswaldi of Athens* (1831). Arthur Hugh Quinn compares *Ali Pacha* with Noah's *The Grecian Captive* because in both dramas the fierce Ali holds Greek girls prisoner, and both girls are sought by their lovers. Another dramatist, S. S. Steele, wrote *The Grecian Queen* (1844). One might logically expect that the Greek hero most

honored in our literature during the nineteenth century, Marco
Bozzaris, would also be depicted on the stage. At least three plays
fulfill this expectation: Oliver B. Bunce's *Marco Bozzaris* (1850), N.
Derring's *Bozzaris* (1851), and Augustus Julius Requier's *Marco Bozzaris* (1860). All three of these plays, however, could not equal the
impact made upon America by Halleck's famous ode. Nevertheless
these "Greek plays" complemented the many "Greek poems" that
helped to solidify public opinion in favor of the Christian Greeks
against the Moslem Turks. Plays, poems, sermons, speeches, editorials, and resolutions in Congress fired up the "Greek Fever"
that Larrabee records in *Hellas Observed*.[10]

Noah's pioneer play, *The Grecian Captive*, contributed to this feeling even though its one and only performance proved unsuccessful. What Captain Farrago had hoped for in Brackenridge's *Modern
Chivalry*—the freedom of Athens—Noah dramatizes as having occurred when one of his characters, Kiminski, exhorts his audience:

> Behold a glorious termination to all our painful struggles!
> Greece is free! The land of the great, the home of the brave.
> The queen of the Arts has broken the bonds of tyranny and
> slavery—and a glorious day succeeds to a long night of peril
> and calamity—Now to merit freedom by the establishment of
> just laws—a free and benevolent spirit to all.[11]

The play itself lacks any genuine ethnic quality. As Noah's biographer Isaac Goldberg observes, the characters are "virtually Americans, and Greece itself is described in terms but slightly altered
from the famous line of the virginal Star Spangled Banner."[12] He
does credit Noah with anticipating historic events by having Athens restored to Greece in his drama. That its first and only performance was a fiasco may have also, in its way, anticipated history;
for the liberty that the Greeks struggled so hard to attain turned
into the fiasco of a monarchy headed by a Bavarian king, Otho.
The producers of *The Grecian Captive*, in pursuit of verisimilitude,
brought a real elephant upon the stage. Luckily the huge ungainly
beast did not crash through the floor, but the elephant "so rocked
the castle on his back, the Grecian general nearly lost his balance."[13]
Then, to make matters worse, the elephant, not house-broken, introduced "an unexpected hydraulic experiment . . . to the great
astonishment and discomfiture of the musicians." Mordecai Noah's
play may have ended on a sour note, but his political sentiments

were pure; and he did, despite the stilted blank verse, celebrate the rise of a free Greece.

The first fictional American to visit Greece appeared three years after *The Grecian Captive.* He was the all-American sailor boy, Jack Halyard, in William S. Cardell's *Story of Jack Halyard, the Sailor Boy; or, The Virtuous Family* (1825).[14] A further mention of this book appears in the chapter on Greeks in children's literature; for *Jack Halyard* was an early book with *American* subject matter "designed for American children, in families and schools."[15] To help support his destitute family, Jack signs on the merchant ship *The Fair Trader* in New York bound for Constantinople. While in Greek waters he spends some hours exploring the island of Paros. He visits a Greek home where he has to depend "on sign language until an interpreter arrived who knew both French and modern Greek." Jack then observes the process of sponge fishing "with the sharp eyes of a Yankee jack of several trades"; he admires the Aegean scenery; and he concludes with an "historical reverie" that, Larrabee feels, is "worthy of one with more formal education."[16] The sentiments of a trusty Jack Halyard, archetype of the American sailor, were those of philhellenes from Jefferson to Edward Everett, the scholar and orator whom Larrabee calls the leading philhellene of the Greek revolution.

Many travelers prior to the revolution visited enslaved Greece and reported back to their countrymen. Most went out of curiosity and touched at Greek ports as part of a romantic grand tour of the Levant. Some like the young Nicholas Biddle went searching for, among other things, traces of the classical heritage. But not until the actual rebellion began, in 1821, did interested Americans have to commit themselves to support or not to support the Greek cause. The Greeks represented a past of undeniable greatness, they were Christians, they challenged tyranny. All these positive factors, however, did not prevent a number of Americans from being against them. Their reasons are detailed in some of the primary sources used by Larrabee in *Hellas Observed.* He regards George B. English as the chief of the American philo-Turks; after leaving our marines, English served as a general of artillery in the army of the pasha of Egypt. He may be regarded, one might suppose, as a janissary of Yankee descent.

The pressures for commitment made an immediate issue of the modern Greek character. Were the Greeks as degenerate as some of their detractors averred? Were they as worthy of freedom as their friends claimed? Samuel Gridley Howe, the American doctor who was surgeon-in-chief to the Greek fleet, addressed himself to these questions in *An Historical Sketch of the Greek Revolution* (1828).[17] He writes in his preface that American public opinion depends too much upon faulty, hasty, and incomplete travelogues. Very often the visitor "flies rapidly over the country . . . he has for a servant, a *Franco-Greek*, who has learned the vices of Europe with the languages, and who steals from him on all occasions; he trades with the Greek merchant, who lives only by chicanery, and who cheats him in every bargain; his *cicerone* is a Greek, who practices a thousand frauds upon him; wherever he turns, he finds some sharp-witted Greeks to take advantage of his ignorance, to gull his credulity, and to fleece him without robbing him; and he indignantly condemns the whole race, as base and trickish."[18] American merchants, naval officers, and other guests, Howe says, also meet only the "most degraded and despicable" Greeks; and they too pronounce their verdict against the entire nation.

Howe himself finds the modern Greek character flawed in some respects. Such flaws, he believes, are due to the long centuries of Turkish oppression. Despite them Howe admires the modern Greeks. He is surprised at finding "*so much* national spirit; and *so much* virtue among them, than there was so little; and he has seen enough of them, to justify him looking confidently for the day, when they will shew themselves worthy of their glorious descent."[19] From his years of service in Greece, Howe draws up a balance sheet of Greek virtues and vices. Only seclusion from "European vice" and from the "immediate gripe" of despotism has "preserved in any degree the virtues of the Greeks; and to know the worth of the people, one must dwell with the peasantry in their retired hamlets; wander with the Kleftes in the mountains; or rove with the half-piratical sailors, among the remote islands of the Aegean." There, Howe believes, one will find the Greeks "shrewd, inquisitive, lively, enterprising, industrious, temperate, hospitable, and pious, in their way; ardently attached to their native land; eager for their own, and their children's education; and often with a rude, but sterling sense of humor; he will find them also, fickle minded, vain, blustering, and deceitful."[20] The effect of environment, Howe also claims, results in regional differentiation. Thus the mountain Greek is brave, hardy, active, lively, adventurous, gay, hospitable, generous, and fickle. The Albanian Greek is enterprising, persevering, unsocial, and cruel. The Moriote is cringing, greedy, hypocritical, timid, industrious, temperate, and kind. And the Greek merchant is shrewd, enterprising, cunning, and tricky. Samuel Gridley Howe drew this image of the modern Greek in 1828 toward the close of the Greek revolution. Thirty years later, in 1868, he writes on behalf of Cretan refugees who needed aid after the Cretan revolution of 1866. In his latest defense of the Greek character, vis-à-vis the Turkish, Howe alludes to some of the "laws" governing race which the ethnologists had devised in the interim.

Shortly after Howe's history appeared, Henry A. V. Post, a member of the New York Greek Committee, published a book which detailed even further the American estimate of the Greek people. In *A Visit to Greece and Constantinople* (1830) he devotes a chapter to the character of the modern Greeks.[21] Their eulogists, he writes, consider them a nation of heroes and patriots, and true descendants of their illustrious ancestors; while their detractors "have stigmatized them as a race of cowardly and misbegotten slaves, without one drop of the pure Hellenic blood in their veins, unworthy of the common rights of humanity, fit only to writhe beneath the lash of the taskmaster, and to drudge at the bidding of an unfailing despot"(p. 254). Like Howe, Post blames the shallow impressions of travelers for most of the negative image. They regard the Greek in his servile status as an object of contempt, forgetting that he could survive only by being selfish, greedy, and deceitful. The Turk, being rich and lordly, inspired admiration. Many adventurers arrived in Greece expecting to fight in epic classical battles, but found a harsh and often tedious reality, with no profit and no glory. Danger and death abounded. Thus disappointed and even disgusted, "they turned their backs upon the cause, and joined in the hue and cry against the tame-spirited, craven-hearted, unprincipled, degenerate Greeks" (p. 257). Even the Philhellenes often soured on the Greeks because of wrong expectations: instead of being received with open arms as champions and deliverers, instead of being rewarded with honors, pay, and power, instead of being deferred to, listened to, and offered command, they met with undisguised suspicions.

In an eloquent passage Post justifies the coldness of Greeks toward outsiders, because "from the Franks they had received little else but insults, and empty promises, and treacherous friendship; the perfidy of Russia towards them they had not forgotten; their affecting appeals to the governments of Europe had been received

with a cold and heartless indifference; the travellers who had visited them had treated them, in many instances, with worse than
Turkish insolence; the dissolute renagadoes of France, Italy, and
Germany, who had been among them since their insurrection, had
shown themselves overbearing, grasping, ambitious of power and
influence—had rendered themselves infamous by their ungodly
and profligate lives—had ridiculed their religion, abused their
hospitality, debauched their women, and fomented discord among
them" (p. 258). For all these misdeeds the partial charities of the
foreigners could in no way compensate.

Like others who tend to accept the alleged degeneracy of the
Greeks, Post locates the reason in their long slavery. When freed,
the galley slave will walk unsteadily and wildly at first. The modern
Greek is like "an unfortunate and degenerate son of a sire once
honoured and revered" (p. 261). Now he needs help in order to be
regenerated; though debased, the Greek wants to learn, for he is
active, intelligent, and willing, unlike the Turk who "shuts out the
light of knowledge" as he would a "pestilence" from his house (p.
262). Despite the scars of tyranny, Post observes that the Greeks
"are a more amiable and estimable people, more hospitable, more
generous, and less disposed to take advantage of travellers, than
their neighbors the Italians," with respect to the lower classes (p.
265). Post has never known an Italian to give a drink of water without expecting money for it, whereas the Greeks refuse compensa-
tion. In Greece Post never felt endangered even when robbery and
murder were rampant; from servants he got nothing but honesty
and fidelity. The Greek can be shrewd, intelligent, enterprising.
"What is called roguery, is in many instances nothing more than a
fair and legitimate triumph of superior cunning and artifice." But
these are the qualities that Americans admire in Yankee sharpers
and swindlers; the only difference is that "the Greek possesses it
[cunning] in greater perfection, and knows how to employ it with
greater tact and skill" (p. 266). As for bravery, modern Greece has
provided examples of "heroism as noble and courage as daring as
any recorded in history" (pp. 270–71). If all the Greeks under Ottoman rule rebelled, as the sultan himself has declared, they could
bring about "the annihilation of our religion and of our empire."
Thus Post rests his case for continued American support for the
Greek cause.

After the Greek kingdom was established in 1832, with King
Otho of Bavaria on the throne, American travelers continued to

visit, discover the land and its people, and record their impressions. Although most of them concentrated on touring famous sites, they also described modern Greeks whom they met and the customs they practiced. The second volume of Nathaniel Parker Willis's *Pencillings by the Way* (1835) deals at length with his Grecian tour.[22] A learned observer and, to judge by his prolific output, an inveterate voyager, Willis arrived in Corfu filled with classical allusions. At Zante he met Count Dionisio Solomos, whom he calls in his book "almost the only modern Greek poet." As one reads Willis's description of Solomos, one thinks of the physical attributes of Byron, Shelley, Keats, and other young romantics. "He is an excessively handsome man," Willis writes of Solomos, "with a large dark eye, almost effeminate in its softness. His features are of the clearest Greek chiseling, as faultless as a statute, and are stamped with nature's most attractive marks of refinement and feeling. I can imagine Anacreon to have resembled him" (p. 68). Throughout his stay Willis is repeatedly impressed by the splendor of the Greek men.

The women he meets in Corfu, then under British rule, are not beautiful, he says; but they have "the melancholy, retired expression of face which one looks for, knowing the history of their nation" (p. 69). Willis scolds the more fashionable Greek ladis for having abandoned their national costume in favor of the European style, which they wear badly; but he likes the servant girls "with their hair braided into the folds of their turbans" and their open-laced bodices and sleeves. Before his tour ends, he does meet handsome women, including one at Mycenae who brought them water, and to whom they gave the remnants of their meal. At Aegina he interviews the lady whom Byron immortalized. "The 'Maid of Athens,' in the very teeth of poetry," Willis exclaims after meeting her, "has become *Mrs. Black of Egina*! The beautiful Teresa Makri—of whom Byron asked back his heart—of whom Moore and Hobhouse, and the poet himself have written so much and so passionately—has forgotten the sweet burden of the sweetest of love-songs, and takes the unromantic name of a Scotchman!" (p. 110). He finds her a very pretty woman, modest and timid, who speaks to them in Italian with a very sweet voice. She offers them sweetmeats, the usual Greek compliment to visitors. "She is a little above the middle height, slightly and well formed, and walks weakly, like most Greek women, as if her feet were too small for her weight" (p. 114). Her skin, Willis goes on, is dark and clear, and she has "a colour in her cheek and lips that looks to me con-

sumptive." The "Maid of Athens," it would seem, has some features of the pre-Raphaelite woman, or perhaps the ideal beauty
of Poe's Lygeia. Willis notes her white and regular teeth, and her
forehead and nose that "form the straight line of the Grecian
model," one of the few instances he has seen of it. "Her eyes are
large and of a soft, liquid hazel, and this is her chief beauty" (p.
115). After his meeting with her, Willis concludes that Byron was
amply justified in regarding her the way he did.

While still in Corfu, Willis sees clothes in a Greek tailor's shop that
he regards as better than the current miserable European fashions.
Whereas some travelers think the men's kirtle or fustanella ridiculous, Willis does not. "The easy and flowing juktanilla [fustanella],
the unembarrassed leggins, the open sleeve of the collarless jacket
leaving the throat exposed, and the handsome close-binding girdle
seem to me the very dress dictated by reason and nature." His praise
of the men's costume is in keeping with his admiration for the men
themselves. Later, while taking an evening walk on the plain of Ar-
gos, Willis mingles with the crowds of Greeks there, and agrees with
Byron that they are a "gallant-looking people." They are very affectionate, he states, and usually walk hand in hand, or sit with arms
over each other's shoulders, or walk in picturesque attitudes and
beauty of dress like heroes on a stage. "I saw literally no handsome
women, but the men were magnificent, almost without exception"
(p. 115). There, too, he meets the brother of Mavromichaelis, the
assassin of Capodistrias, the first president of Greece, who was regarded as a tyrant. The brother was about seventeen, very handsome, tall and straight as an arrow, with the eye of a falcon. The
short twilight of Greece "thickened upon us," Willis writes, "and the
white, swaying juktanillas of the Greeks striding past had the effect
of spirits gliding by in the dark" (p. 106).

Many travelers to Greece kept alert for curious local customs
that revealed aspects of the modern Greek character. Willis is
no exception. In Corfu he witnesses a religious ceremony that
strongly marks the Greeks as superstitious. At the summit of the
Pnyx he learns the legend of the "sliding stone" which indicates
that Greeks value sons more than they value daughters. In fact he
remarks on another occasion that by the "universal custom" of the
country, "the females of Greece are suffered to grow up in ignorance. One who can read and write is rarely found" (p. 149). The
incident at Corfu which bespeaks superstition occurs when the

mummified body of St. Spiridon is paraded through the streets before the whole populace.

> The saint was dried at his death, and makes a neat, black mummy, *sans* eyes and nose, but otherwise quite perfect. He was carried by four men in a very splendid sedan, shaken from side to side with the motion, preceded by one of the bands of music from the English regiments. Sick children were thrown under the feet of the bearers; half-dead people brought to the doors as he passed, and every species of disgusting mummery practiced. The show lasted about four hours, and was, on the whole, attended with more marks of supersition than anything I found in Italy. (pp. 74–75)

During his Greek stay Willis met a son of Marco Bozzaris who acted as the king's aide—a fine resolute youth of eighteen.[23] Another traveler to Greece, John L. Stephens, met and described the widow of Bozzaris.[24] She was under forty, "tall and stately," dressed in black with a white handkerchief on her head "giving the Madonna cast to her dark eyes and marble complexion." Stephens writes that she looked the widow of a hero, one "worthy of her Grecian mothers, who gave their hair for bowstrings, their girdle for a sword-belt, and, while their heartstrings were cracking, sent their young lovers from their arms to fight and perish for their country" (p. 7). Near the grave of Bozzaris, Stephens discovers a grotesque scene—"a pyramid of skulls" of men who had fallen in the last attack upon Missolonghi, "piled up near the blackened and battered wall" they had defended. King Otho had promised to erect a memorial sepulcher for them when he came of age. Meanwhile the skulls remain at every traveler's mercy, "and the only remark that our guide made," Stephens recalls, "was a comment upon the force and unerring precision of the blow of the Turkish sabre, almost every skull being laid open on the side nearly down to the ear" (p. 7).

Stephens expresses mixed feelings about the Greeks in his travel book. He dislikes the "rude funeral" that he happens to witness. He finds the entire burial rite very dreary and the priest "one of the most miserable of that class of 'blind teachers' who swarm in Greece" (p. 27). Like Willis and others he criticizes the "disgusting mummeries of the Greek church" and asserts that he does not wonder why the Turks hold Christians in contempt, since, with only the Greeks as examples, the Turks "see nothing of the pure and sublime principles our religion inculcates" (p. 30). On the positive side he admires the Greeks for having learned how to make good coffee from their Turkish masters. Stephens notices that their new rulers, the Bavarians, habitually mock and insult the Greeks; he observes also that "the Greeks had already learned both their intellectual and physical superiority over the Bavarians," one example being that of the Maniote insurgents who humiliated a party of Bavarian soldiers. Like Willis, Stephens praises the Greek men. There are none finer, he asserts, with good figures, and something "rakish and piratical" in their appearance.

Some American travelers to Greece seem at times to be reflecting the new "science" of ethnology in their comments upon Greek "racial traits." It is perhaps the Reverend Walter Colton in his *Visit to Constantinople and Athens* (1836) who most thoroughly contrasts the alleged characteristics of the modern Greeks and Turks.[25] The restless energy of the former impresses if not appalls him. At Napoli he notices a crowd of Greeks listening to a blind fiddler—a surprising testament to his power, "for the Greek is of so restless a disposition, that you would suppose it impossible even for an angel's lyre to charm him into more than a momentary quietude" (p. 225). Greek men, less commanding in presence than the Turks, are slightly above medium height,

> and of a symmetrical, sinewy formation. They work, walk, and converse with energy; every motion bespeaks muscular vigor; every word betrays a sleepless, inquisitive mind. The face is strikingly indicative of their character. Their thin lips reveal the quickness of their passions; while their restless, darting eyes disclose the fickleness of purpose, versatility of thought, and treacherous instability of faith. (p. 297)

Colton's extended summary of traits resists paraphrase; parts of it also express some unintentional humor. Most of his detailed listing is unproved and unprovable assertion, given without the suspect charts and statistics of the somber ethnologists. For example the Greeks act more from caprice than from conviction, more from impulse than reflection. Their conduct has a "recklessness of consequences" that plunges them into trouble; but their ingenuity in extricating themselves never fails them. They are most brave when facing the greatest odds; with a small fire ship or concealed torpedo they will make a suicidal rush into the very center of a

hostile fleet. The Greek prizes marriage because of the social esteem it bestows. After several pages of Greek versus Turk dichot-
omies, Colton concludes that the Greek is intellectually superior
while the Turk is morally so. More than a decade later, in 1868, Dr.
Samuel Gridley Howe will compile a further contrasting list of
Greek and Turkish "racial characteristics;" but before that, other
American travelers will also contribute to the nineteenth-century
image of the modern Greeks.

When William Cullen Bryant visits Greece in 1852 and 1853, he
wonders as the earlier Philhellenes had done whether or not the
modern Greeks are the same as the ancients with their "fine harmony of intellectual faculties."[26] Bryant feels they are clever and
ingenious but also "they are restless and mercurial beyond almost
any other family of mankind." He is not there long, yet he hears
from others that the Greeks have an avid thirst for education. They
make many sacrifices in order to learn; thus in twenty years hardly
a Greek would be unable to read and write. Dr. Hill, who runs a
school, tells him that a Greek child, if given the choice of a toy or a
book, "invariably chooses the book" (p. 222). He disagrees when
Hill expresses fear that, as the Greeks shed their superstitions, they
will also lay aside all reverence for religion, "and all the restraints
which religion imposes." The government schools, according to
Hill, have made the Greek character worse instead of better. But,
Bryant writes, he has confidence in a people who submit to priva-
tions in order to acquire knowledge. "They are learners in the
school of self-denial, which is the basis of all virtue, and the only
school in which an elevated character is ever formed" (p. 223).

A mostly negative but superficial view of modern Greeks is that
of J. Ross Browne, a "General in the Bobtail Militia," who wrote
Yusef, or The Journey of the Frangi (1853). The first thing he reports
about Piraeus is the "absolute absurdity" of being surrounded by
a legion of boatmen, porters, and hack-drivers "in petticoats."[27]
They were wearing the juktanilla or fustanella that Willis and others deemed fetching. To Browne, though, the Greek men with
their "pomp of mustaches, whips, and petticoats" are "the most
irresistibly ludicrous sight" he has seen in many a day. Other travelers found Athens rather dismal and cluttered with debris—at
least soon after the revolution. Browne glances at the people and
writes: "The population is about seventeen thousand, principally
degenerate Greeks" (p. 89). A hotel in Athens costs him three
francs a day "and no reduction made for vermin." The peasant

folk arrive into town in sheepskins which, like themselves, they do
not wash "more than once or twice" in a lifetime. In the end the
men receive a compliment from Browne which is denied the
women. "The ordinary classes of Greek women to be seen about
the streets," he writes, "are about the most uncouth and miserable-
looking beings one meets anywhere in this part of the world. I
looked in vain for the Maid of Athens." The compliment he pays
the Greek men struggles to surface from Browne's thick and gluey
bias: "In all their rags, however, and in all their filthiness, these
degenerate sons of glory are fine-looking fellows, with bold,
prominent features, eagle eyes, and commanding forms. Some of
the handsomest men I ever saw were Greeks, dressed in the Albanian costume" (p. 90). Browne pens a small but interesting detail:
when they meet he is frowned upon by Otho, the king of Greece,
dressed in the "Greek costume."

David F. Dorr in *A Colored Man Round the World* (1858) reports
briefly about Greece.[28] He finds Athens a sepulcher of past glory.
Dorr cites Alexander's conquest of Egypt as the "greatest triumph"
of man because the Greeks adorned themselves with the spoils—
the results of the black man's genius. On a matter already mentioned, the former slave offers his version of the famous "sliding
stone" at Pnyx. Twenty years earlier Willis had been told that a
slide down the rock by a pregnant woman meant the birth of a son.
Dorr in his book states the belief that the Pnyx guarantees female
fertility. He sees humor in the stone rather than Greek superstition. The country's total population, he writes, is not quite one million; thus America's black slaves would make four kingdoms the
size of Greece.

A later visitor to the Levant, S.G.W. Benjamin, entitles his book
*The Turk and the Greek: or, Creeds, Races, Society, and Scenery in Turkey,
Greece, and the Isles of Greece* (1867).[29] The author spent some of his
youth in Greece. Like many of his predecessors, he adds to his
personal anecdotes and descriptions various comments about the
character and condition of the modern Greeks. Beginning at Constantinople, Benjamin describes how the Greek and Turkish cultures mingle in that holy city of Byzantium. The antiquities attrib-
utable to the Greeks predominate. Of the great Orthodox church
of St. Sophia, he writes: "The Greeks have a tradition that a priest
who was administering the sacrament when the Turkish host burst
into the sacred edifice, was snatched away by an angel and concealed within a crypt in the walls of the building, where he pa-

tiently abides the day when the departure of the Mohammedan will summon him forth from his hiding-place, to complete the mass which he was performing" (p. 7).

Although Benjamin cautions travelers in strange lands not to make quick and easy judgments, he seems to make some himself in matching moral traits and ethnic backgrounds. For example he has a very low opinion of the Franks (Europeans) living in Constantinople. "Like the Creoles of Mexico," he states, "they usually retain the vices of the countries from whence their fathers came, with the low morals of their Greek or Armenian mothers." Benjamin adds: "It is to be said in their favor that their women are often very pretty and piquant in their manners, especially they of the lower classes whose mothers were Greeks" (pp. 22–23). The author does not pause to give the basis of his judgment, for either the negative or the positive qualities of Greek women. Of those oppressed by the Ottomans, Benjamin regards the Bulgarians as "most promising," followed by the Armenians. "Less vivacious, acute, versatile, and handsome than the Greeks, they however display more uniform self-respect, common sense, and sincerity" (p. 73). The Bulgarians, he finds, "thirst" after progress, knowledge, and freedom.

In June the author begins a two-month stay on Scio, the lovely island that suffered a massacre during the Greek revolution. The Sciotes who belong to the Greek church are very bigoted and generally illiterate. In fact their features are not very Greek. "Many of them have a Jewish cast of countenance, and it is by no means rare to hear them spoken of by other Greeks as a sort of mixed race, containing very little Greek blood" (p. 180). They are more Greek than not; and the peasants are more Hellenic than the upper classes, with a dialect of their own. Benjamin mentions Koray's "Papa Trécchas," a satire on "the illiterate clergy of the Greek Church." He meets Sciotes who escaped or otherwise talk about the Turkish massacre. One of them was ransomed by an American, studied medicine in the United States, and returned to practice on Scio. The magnitude of the catastrophe is described: "In six weeks, out of a population of 100,000 nearly 70,000 had been slain or carried into slavery, while most of those remaining escaped to other islands, and Scio was virtually depopulated" (p. 190). Now Scio has nearly recovered, with much fewer but rather contented people— more than ever devoted to their superstitions and corrupt church.

After Scio, Benjamin journeys by boat to Syra and then to Athens. "It was with strange, tumultuous emotions," he writes, "that I once more beheld my native land" (p. 207). Native, the reader recalls, since the author's father served as a missionary in Greece and Turkey and lay buried in Constantinople. For that reason Benjamin is fluent in the "musical Hellenic tongue" and knows the Greek traditions very well. About the Greeks themselves he has mingled feelings. They are still backward but are vital compared to the sleepy Turks. In the Agorá or marketplace with a friend, Mr. Constantine, he easily imagines himself back with St. Paul who wrote: "All the Athenians and strangers which were there spent their time in nothing else, but to tell, or to hear some new thing" (p. 207). No essential change has occurred, except that the bright spark of genius, which died during the Dark Ages, "has not yet been rekindled."

Benjamin echoes the praise of earlier travelers for the refusal of the Greeks to give up their native dress for the European. The dress is usually Albanian, adopted by the Greeks before the revolution and, according to Benjamin, "the finest dress ever worn by any people." He finds sightseeing among the splendid ruins of Athens a welcome relief "from the whirl and din of this age of steam," but he spares the reader long descriptions of familiar landmarks. Conditions for travel outside Athens have improved, but brigandage still exists in places, and lodgings are primitive. At one time the brigands or *klephts* played a role against the Turks similar to that of Robin Hood against the Normans. It was "a singular blending of religion, patriotism, and lawless freedom," that made the mountains of Greece swarm with *klephts* just prior to the revolution. "In the Turkish Empire," Benjamin says, "brigandage is a result of weakness, a sign of dissolution, while in Greece it is a relic of past ages destined, we hope, before long to disappear" (p. 224). He asks that the Greeks be given time to recover from the licentiousness of the Romans, the "monkery" of the Dark Ages, and their enslavement by the Turks. To keep vilifying them only obscures the historic causes for their current condition.

A more careful look discovers "different grades of vice and virtue even among the Greeks; at Constantinople and Smyrna they are less manly and more corrupt than in the interior of Asia Minor or among the mountains of Macedonia and Lakonia" (p. 225). Benjamin defends the modern Greeks against charges of cowardice, citing the many heroes of the revolution, and "the persistence of the Cretans in their present struggle." The Greeks are moving forward, despite the slow pace, in agriculture "for which the Greeks have a native genius," in commerce, and in education. They have also newly purified their language. But the trait which promises most for the future of Greece "is the longing for national unity which fires every Hellenic heart from Zante to Trebizond" (p. 230). The Slavs, Italians, and the Germans are responding to a similar nationalist demand of the age. Nationalism often makes the Greek haughty and even a little ridiculous in the eyes of others. He acts as if his illusions of grandeur are real, or on the verge of being realized. These are some of the "trifles" bringing discredit upon Greece:

> The bare-footed and bare-headed urchins of Athens are christened after the sages and warriors of ancient Greece, and as soon as they attain to years of discretion they commence the national habit of gasconade, talking of what their ancestors have done, and of what they themselves are destined to accomplish. They are constantly planning expeditions across the frontier, and on the slightest pretext make a dash into Turkish territory, discharge their *tuféks* [guns], and return to retail their exploits in the cafés of Athens. (p. 232)

Yet a genuine passion for national unity does exist, for bringing all the Greeks together, in a form to elicit praise and admiration—a prospect that Benjamin predicts "in spite of their numerous and very grave defects."

He anchors these defects primarily in the modern Greek's bondage to the Greek church. No doubt the author's missionary father sought in vain to liberate the Greeks from this religious bondage and to turn them into good obedient Protestants. Yet for nearly four hundred years the Greeks had defended their persecuted, primitive, and perhaps uncouth church against efforts of Turkish annihilation. What the Turks had tried to accomplish with terror the Protestant missionaries sought to effect with kindness and condescension. Be that as it may, Benjamin feels that the Greek church at present, in forbidding freedom of thought, lowers the moral tone of the Greeks. The church desires Hellenic unity in order "to prevent greater liberty of conscience." If the Greek shows his allegiance, "he receives full absolution for all the crimes he chooses to commit; and it is just here that the missionaries take their stand" (p. 236). They preach the "absolute necessity of reducing religion to practice, of infusing moral principle into the character of Greek and Armenian, Jew and Mohammedan; moral principle, without which no people can permanently prosper, that is one great thing lacking among all classes and nations of the Levant" (p. 237). Benjamin continues: "While the Greek Church controls the execution of the civil laws, and forbids the people to think for themselves, casting those who question its authority into noisome dungeons, Greece cannot and will not make any genuine progress" (p. 238). That the missionaries have had some success testifies to the goodwill of the poeple, who "have inherited the beauty and, to some extent, the heroism and genius of their immortal ancestors; they are acute, genial, and courtly in their manners—"but only if the Greeks drastically change their church, or leave it, will they possess "truth, honesty, moral courage, order, and freedom." Then art and science will thrive, and "Greece will again become a power in the world."

After making these remarks, Benjamin writes a chapter about Crete and the Cretans, whose struggle for freedom he admires. He sketches the island's history from the days of the Byzantine conquest to the present. The author believes that unity of Crete with Greece would be beneficial to both, that "Crete under the Turk is like a prisoner chained to a dead man," whereas under Greek rule the Cretans will develop new energies—if the Greek church allows them religious freedom. "Cretan Christianity," Benjamin states, "is of a very low order." Indeed during the last war the Turkish women captives were often butchered lest "the Christian warriors incur the perilous sin of intercourse with unbaptized females!" (p. 267). The writer concludes his book with the prospect of future greatness among the Cretans, once they are free.

Two years after the Cretan rebellion of 1866, Dr. Samuel Gridley Howe wrote *The Cretan Refugees and Their American Helpers*, addressed to those who had contributed aid.[30] The aging Philhellene makes another staunch defense of the Greek cause. He echoes a Jeffersonian idea when suggesting that, if the Greeks had been demoralized by slavery, the Turks suffered the "greater demoralization attendant upon the exercise of tyranny" (p. 7). Jefferson's view had applied to Negro slavery in America. To gather added support for the Cretan refugees, Howe draws another ethnic contrast between Greeks and Turks to the detriment of the latter, whom he stigmatizes as invaders. Between the two "races" he sees a death-grapple going on. Through the ages the Greeks have been sustained by a religion that, though "disfigured by superstition," kept the essential features of Christianity; the Turks, on the other hand, have a religion which degrades and weakens them. "The Greeks sanctified the marriage relation by monogamy; the Turks polluted it by polygamy. The Greeks were reticent and chaste; the Turks, loose and licentious. The Greek women were prolific; the Turkish, sterile. The Greeks were industrious and thrifty; the Turks, lazy and wasteful" (p. 8). The author makes additional contrasts, adding that the hostility toward the Turks helped to perpetuate with "remarkable purity" the old Greek blood—never adulterated enough to have lost its native traits. Howe evokes the new ethnology by contradicting Falmerier and others who dispute the purity of Greek blood; he claims that they overlook "the great law that when two alien races mingle, the purer overcomes or absorbs the other. In virtue of this law, the Slavonian invaders of Greece, in the sixth century, the two hundred thousand Albanian invaders of the sixteenth century, and the later Turkish invaders, have been vanquished by their victims" (p. 9). For evidence to support his thesis Howe points to the appearance and intelligence of the mountaineers in Crete and rugged sections of Greece. Even among the Greeks the Cretans are preeminent. They enjoy physical beauty, mental vivacity, fine skins, delicate features, and large lustrous eyes.

Some of the many travelers who visited Greece, like Howe and Benjamin, had long and intimate contact with the Greek people. The reader can logically have more confidence in their reports than in those written by hasty visitors such as Stephens, Colton, and Dorr. Howe dedicated his life to the Greek cause as surgeon general of the Greek navy, while Post dedicated his time and reputation as a member of the New York Greek Committee. Of the nine travelers cited here two were also poets, Willis and Bryant, and both contributed much more than travelogues to help the Greeks reclaim their heritage. Stephen A. Larrabee sums up *Hellas Observed*: "What the travelers, missionaries, naval personnel, commercial and consular agents, Philhellenes, students and scholars, and others (including a few Philo-Turks) wrote about their experiences in Greece was widely read by the general public in America as well as by persons of classical taste, students, and scholars."[31]

After long anticipation Herman Melville arrived on Greek soil in December 1856. Earlier, in *Moby-Dick*, he had lauded Kanaris, the revolutionary naval hero. Although "weary in spirit" and perhaps afraid of being "written-out," Melville jotted down extensive comments about his stimulating sojourn in Greece and the Levant.[32] In the book that resulted, *Journal up the Straits*, one finds laconic descriptions of Greeks.[33] "Guide boys on the bridge. Greeks, beautiful faces, lively, loquacious. Never wearied leaning over the balustrate & talking with them" (p. 30). On another occasion Melville writes: "Picturesqueness of the whole. Variety of it. Greek trousers, sort of cross between petticoats & pantaloons. Some with white petticoats & embroidered jackets. Fine forms, noble faces. Mustache & C." (p. 9). His ship sailed along the coast of the Morea and stopped at the island of Syra. Returning from the Holy Land, he toured Thessalonika, sailed among the Aegean islands, and spent some days in Athens. On Christmas day, in Syra, Melville noted: "The Greek, of any class, seems a natural dandy. His dress, though a laborer, is that of a gentleman of leisure. This flowing & graceful costume, with so much of pure ornament about it & so little fitted for labor, must needs have been devised in some Golden Age."[34]

Later, in his long narrative poem, *Clarel* (1876), Melville's modern Greek characters assume allegorical significance.[35] His knowledge of the archetypes deriving from traditional Hellenism, both myth and history, makes it natural for Melville to choose Greeks as the symbolic figures he needs. *Clarel*, as Walter E. Bezanson suggests, documents a major crisis in western civilization—"the apparent smash-up of revealed religion in the age of Darwin." To serve his philosophic purpose Melville has his hero, the American youth Clarel, journey through the Palestinian ruins accompanied by a curious group of pilgrims. The seven allegorical figures who are Greek include Agath, an old pilot, whom Bezanson designates as A MAN OF DISASTERS; the Banker, of Greek-English background, who represents MAMMONISM; the Celibate, a Greek monk who stands for A SUPERIOR TYPE OF INNOCENCE; Christodulus, the abbot of Mar Saba and a symbol of UNQUESTIONING BELIEVER; the Cypriote, a handsome boy who epitomizes UNTROUBLED YOUTH; Glaucon, a rich Smyrniote and archetype of IRRESPONSIBLE AND HAPPY YOUTH; and the Lesbian, a man of MIDDLE-AGED EPICURE-ANISM. The most important of these characters is Agath, a "timoneer" or pilot who has a sad and moving tale to tell.[36] *Clarel* has all the essential ingredients for an allegory: the journey to a place of importance (holy in this case), the necessary perils, the symbolic characters, the hero (Agath) who bears the thematic burden, and listeners for what he has to say.

Bezanson relates Agath to the world of *The Encantadas* and an important Melvillian sequence of characters "that includes Jarl

(*Mardi*), the Dansker (*Billy Budd*), and Daniel Orme (in the late sketch "Daniel Orme")." All of them, including Agath the Greek, are "weird, oracular old sea-dogs." Melville's "man of disasters" also belongs to a cycle of monomaniacs that includes Celio, an Italian expatriate with an unsightly hump; Mortmain, a bitter and evil Swede; and Ungar, a victim of war. These men are in *Clarel*, and all are *hommes déracinés*, alienated and alone (p. 86). Agath joins the pilgrims at Mar Saba (St. Saba), a fifth century Greek monastery in the Judah wilderness. This event occurs in part 3 of *Clarel*, regarded by Bezanson as the *Purgatorio* to the *Inferno* of part 2. Agath is "an old Greek pilot" schooled by the inhuman sea and beaten by men (4. 13. 7). Illiterate and by preference uncommunicative about his private tragedies, Agath survives in a brutal world by animal tenacity (61). On his way to Mar Saba he is suddenly assaulted and stripped by Ammonite robbers, for disaster must pursue a "man of disasters." The monks take Agath in so he can recuperate from his wounds.

During Melville's Palestinian travels he visited Mar Saba—a place of "wild grandeur"— where great buttresses supported the monastery over a ravine six hundred feet deep, and where he went to accept "the frugal and somewhat dirty hospitality of the sixty-five Greek monks then dwelling there." In *Clarel* Mar Saba becomes the purgatory of another pilgrim's spiritual journey—toward the youth Clarel's recognition of his own Passion, the acceptance of the "tragic view of life," a life without Paradise. Yet withal he must go forward to his own ultimate and inescapable Gethsemane (76). Agath's example, like that of Job, teaches the young Clarel how to endure hard blows.

Importuned to speak, Agath, with "weird and weatherbeaten face / Bearded and pitted, and fine vexed / With wrinkles of cabala text," tells of his disaster (3. 12. 32–34). In a vessel ironically christened *The Peace of God* he left Egypt fleeing the plague, bound for Venice with a cargo of rusted cannon to be melted and cast anew. Before embarking he befriended a Moorish castaway who carried with him a strong box filled with poisoned swords. Lodged in the cabin just below the compass, the Moor's box with its metal so distorted the instrument that Agath sailed blindly into a great storm. The evil crew got drunk and fought. Agath understood why the compass spun so crazily when he heard "the clattering blades" from the strong box; but too late to control the ship, it smashed on the rocks. Agath regarded the Moor as "a black lieutenant of Lucifer," and he suggested the evil occurred because of "arms in sheaf," an old superstition of the sea that Agath mentions but disavows. Melville invests the old mariner with symbolic power by other means than shipwreck and sole survival. Thus, as Bezanson notes, "a great devil-bird once attacked him at the mast-head, stealing his cap . . . and tapping his brain, driving him into the sea where a shark followed him" (p. 531). Agath has on his arm a tattoo of the crucifixion, indicating that he, too, is a "bleeding man upon the tree." "The Holy City, sighted from the mountains by Mar Saba, leads him to cry out as if from a mast-head: 'Wreck, ho! the wreck—Jerusalem" (4. 1.176), and his analogy for Palestine is a long account of a bleak volcanic island, where the only life that survives is the "giant, languorous tortise, encased against all danger" (p. 531). That Agath the timoneer, the pilot, the symbolic guide and steerer by the stars, should consider Jerusalem to be a *wreck* serves graphically to underline Bezanson's judgment that *Clarel* documents "the apparent smash-up of revealed religion in the age of Darwin."

Melville's other Greek characters, though important, lack the force of Agath's suffering and mania to survive. The Banker has joined the pilgrims not from any religious conviction but to kill time while awaiting the consummation of a business deal in Beirut. Far off in Thessalonica the Banker owns the kind of rich country-estate that Melville describes in his journal. "The Banker is a bitter caricature of MAMMONISM" whose terrible fear of death, symbolized by the Dead Sea, forces him to abandon the pilgrimage. With him rides Glaucon, his future son-in-law, a wealthy and irresponsible rake who sings comical songs and makes "flippant remarks about the Holy Land" (p. 539). A fourth Greek in *Clarel* is the Celibate, a monk living in Mar Saba. A superior type of innocent, as Bezanson terms him, he inspires Clarel with "a temporary ascetic ideal to live 'in the pure desert of the will'" (p. 533). Blind Christodulus, the abbot, typifies unquestioning belief in God, as indicated by his name, which means "Servant of Christ." The fifth Greek in Melville's allegory is the Cypriote whom the pilgrims meet as he descends toward the Jordan River; there he will dip his lady's burial shrouds, a superstitious cleansing and precautionary rite. His solemn errand contrasts sharply with his own nature which is jolly and untroubled. A long since dead Greek mentioned in *Clarel* is the monk Habbibi, whose cell at Mar Saba is visited by two of the pilgrims. "The inscriptions on the cell walls," Bezanson writes, "indicate that he was a MONOMANIAC, obsessed by the terrors of life, the preying of man on man, and of man on himself." The final Greek character in Melville's poem, the Lesbian, brings supplies to the monastery of Mar Saba. Although aware of life's sorrows, he lives for the pleasures of today. For example, he greets the end of Agath's tragic tale with a joke and a draught from his flagon. "Two passages in the *Journal* . . . suggest his background: a rich description of Mytelene, and a comment on the Greek as a natural dandy" (p. 539).

Thus Melville in both *Clarel* and *Journal up the Straits* makes important use of his Greek experience. Always alert to transcendental significance, he compares the Greek with the Pacific islands of his early romances, *Omoo* and *Typee*. He finds that the Greek islands "have lost their virginity' whereas the latter "are fresh as at their first creation." Delos is "of a most barren aspect" and "peculiarly sterile" (15). In those two works and in *The Encantadas*, Melville anticipated the potent wasteland images of Eliot, Pound, and other twentieth-century writers. Through the character of Rolfe in *Clarel*, he explains the ritual of washing the shrouds in holy water; and at the same time he stresses the pagan hold on modern Greek Christians.

> A custom of old precedent,
> And curious too in mode 'tis kept,
> Showing how under Christian sway
> Greeks still retain their primal bent,
> Nor let grave doctrine intercept
> That gay Hellene lightheartedness
> Which in the pagan years did twine
> The funeral urn with fair caress
> Of vintage holiday divine. (3.4.6–13)

The same character of Rolfe, who most nearly speaks for Melville, compares South Sea Island rituals with the Greek games that occur during the acceptance of the Easter fire. Rolfe refers to "that tattooed Greek/The Polynesian" when discussing the paganism of both peoples. The celebration of Greek Easter that Melville describes is unusually wild. The light of God's descent arrives at the Church of the Holy Sepulchre in Jerusalem. "In a frenzy of excitement the pilgrims struggle to light their own torches from the flame until there is a blaze of thousands of them. The bishop is carried out in an assumed faint, and wild panic descends on the pilgrims. The sacred fire is carried by horsemen to the Greek convent in Bethlehem" (p. 624). In *Clarel* Melville has the Easter flame transported to Mar Saba.

Thus the modern Greeks provided Melville the traveler with many exciting personal encounters; and they provided Melville the poet with allegorical types for *Clarel*. They were on Walt Whitman's mind, too, for he mentions them in "Proud Music of the Storm" (1869).

> At Eleusis, home of Ceres, I see the modern Greeks dancing,
> I hear them clapping their hands as they bend their bodies,
> I hear the metrical shuffling of their feet.[37]

Unfortunately for another great writer, Mark Twain, the Greeks did not measure up to his expectations. In the same year as Whitman's poem the young and brash Twain's *The Innocents Abroad* was published.[38] The author's inveterate search for comic effect may partly account for his negative and superficial attitudes.

At Piraeus, port city of Athens, the ship containing Clemens's party must either depart or be quarantined for the customary eleven days. Violating the quarantine at the peril of being arrested, Twain and three companions sneak ashore in a small boat and head for Athens. On the way they steal "a score of bunches of large, white, delicious grapes" and are driven off by a "Ho!" from a mysterious shape in the vineyard. From atop the Acropolis, which Twain admires, they have a beautiful view of Athens by moonlight. Later, on the long road back to the harbor, Mark Twain throws a stone at a dog but misses. He also steals more grapes.

Leaving the next day, Twain compares ancient and modern Greece with only contempt for the latter. "Greece is a bleak, unsmiling desert, without agriculture, manufacture, or commerce, apparently." He cannot fathom what supports its poverty-bound people. The "manly people" of old Marathon are "only a tribe of unconsidered slaves to-day" (p. 62). Twain applies terms like *mendacity* and *ingenious rascals* to the modern Greeks. For eight months of the year they loaf because they have nothing to borrow or confiscate. The "tinsel throne" on which George I sits, in his new and splendid palace, only mocks the "sorrowful rags and dirt" of modern Greece. Mark Twain's ship moves on toward the capital of the Ottoman Empire, which impresses him favorably. "Constantinople," he declares, "makes a noble picture" (p. 66). Like some other hasty observers, Twain finds the richer Turks more pleasant to gaze upon than the impoverished Greeks. Had he truly explored Turkey, he might also have found many poor, illiterate, and backward Turks.

The romance was another genre, besides poems, plays, and travelogues, that revealed American attitudes toward the modern Greeks. Four examples from four countries including the United States testify to the fact that Greece, the Greek revolution, and continued oppression of the "unredeemed Greeks" lay heavily on the western conscience. In *The King of the Mountains* (1861), French author Edmond About wrote a popular tale, read widely in America, about a powerful Greek brigand, Hadgi-Stavros.[39] Indeed the "Greek brigand" became a stock character in later nineteenth-century literature. Anthony Hope, an English author, wrote *Phroso* (1896), set on the Greek island of Neopalia.[40] The young Lord Charles Wheatley buys Neopalia from an elder of the Stefanopoulos clan, but he must fight off a couple of resourceful villains before he can have both the island and "Phroso," the lovely Lady Euphrosyne. In 1897 Edwin A. Grosvenor translated *Andronike, The Heroine of the Greek Revolution*, written by the Greek novelist Stephanos Theodoros Xenos.[41] The attention of the world had again turned to Greece, Grosvenor writes, referring to the disastrous Graeco-Turkish War. The story of "romance and adventure ends with the new Greek queen kissing Andronike on the forehead, and Andronike declaiming: "I thank thee, Almighty! I thank thee, Panaghia! Greece is a kingdom! Greece alive again!""

Hallie Ermine Rives, the prolific American writer of romances, based *The Castaway* (1904) on the life of George Gordon, Lord Byron.[42] At last the most influential of all Philhellenes entered our literature as the protagonist of a novel. The story opens in Greece, which Byron has been touring and savoring with his English friend, John Hobhouse. The year is 1810, Byron is only twenty-two, but already a peer by virtue of the title bequeathed to him at the death of an uncle. A mile away from them rise the minarets of Missolonghi, a town linked forever with Byron's name. An "uncouth and savage body-guard" of several "Suliotes in woolen kirtles and with shawl girdles stuck with silver-handled pistols" attend the English travelers. For a year the two friends have been roughing it in Albania and Greece, while back in England the critics have been blasting away at Byron. In his saddlebag are new verses expressing his great love for Greece, and his hope for her political rebirth. He writes near the town of Missolonghi:

The isles of Greece, the isles of Greece!
Where burning Sappho loved and sung,
Where grew the arts of war and peace,—
Where Delos rose, and Phoebus sprung!
Eternal summer gilds them yet,
But all, except their sun, is set.
.   .   .   .   .

And musing there an hour alone,
I dreamed that Greece might still be free;
For, standing on the Persians' grave,
I could not deem myself a slave. (p. 4)

The day is the Muslim feast of Ramazan—"a long fast for lovers, whose infractions were punished rigorously with *bastinado* and with the fatal sack." Such an infraction occurred, Hobhouse relates in London, when the wild Trevanion (in real life the notorious Trelawny) seduced a Greek girl of Turkish citizenship; and Byron, with pistol bared and bribes paid, saved her from death by drowning. While the craven Suliote guards fled, Hobhouse reported, Byron accosted the Turks bearing the girl sewed up in a sack. Trevanion knew the punishment for making love during Ramazan; therefore he cowardly left the girl in the lurch—a child of only fifteen, with "great almond eyes" sunken with fear. This tale contributes to the legend growing up around Byron during his absence from England. When he fails to rescind the bitter satire *English Bards and Scotch Reviewers*, he returns home even more notorious.

The time passes and the "castaway," Byron, continues to write, including poems calling for Greek independence. Calumny follows him even on the continent. Some of it is spread by the rogue Trevanion, whom Byron had befriended in Greece—"a youth who had vanished suddenly from Missolonghi during the feast of Ramazan" (p. 170). In Switzerland, Trevanion accuses Byron of stealing Jane Clermont from him. The novel details Byron's tribulations and exploits in Italy where he romances the Countess Teresa Gamba. Into the action comes the Greek Prince Mavrocordato of Wallachia. Not far from Byron lurks the villain Trevanion, who hates him bitterly and wants "to blacken and blister" the poet's reputation. Teresa's brother Pietro tries to kill Byron with a Malay kriss, but he recovers. For love of him Teresa drinks poison, and luckily Byron returns in time to save her. They elope. The Shelleys also appear prominently in *The Castaway*. Meanwhile Mavrocordato is closely watching the events in Greece leading to revolution.

Although Trevanion is his outspoken enemy, Byron protects him from seizure by British marines, since Trevanion had earlier deserted his ship, the *Pylades*. A while later, Shelley drowns. Friends of Shelley cremate his body, which burns except for his heart. Trevanion retrieves the heart from the ashes.

From a member of the Greek Revolutionary Committee of London comes a message asking Lord Byron to meet with Prince Mavrocordato. Greece and fate beckon the poet. The London Greek committee, perhaps because of Hobhouse, has chosen Byron to be its official representative in Greece. Ypsilantes had invaded Wallachia and declared Greece free. Byron will sell some properties and give the proceeds for the revolution. But the spokesman for the London committee asks for more:

> The revolution needs now only a supreme leader. Your lordship is known and loved by the Greek people as is no other. The petty chieftains, whose inveterate ambitions now embroil a national cause, for such a rallying-point would lay aside their quarrels. With your great name foreign loans would be certain. Such is the unanimous opinion of the committee in London, my lord. (p. 381)

Such a role in such a cause Byron cannot refuse. The new and final, and most glorious, chapter in his life begins. At Genoa he stocks the brig *Hercules* for the forthcoming voyage. As they near Leghorn, a man swims aboard, a bullet through his arm. It is Trevanion, escaped from the *Pylades*. Byron lets him stay on his own vessel.

The Greeks receive Byron as a savior; and the more he is admired the more is Trevanion's hatred rekindled. The Pietro Gamba who once could have murdered Byron is now his friend. In Missolonghi, with Marco Bozzaris dead, only the arrival of Byron can hold the rival chieftains together. The fate of western Greece now rests in Byron's hands. Byron, as the novel avers, "foresaw that Greece's greatest enemy was not the Turks, but her own dissensions." In an effort to help destroy Byron, the "puppet of Mavrocordato," the evil Trevanion joins a dissident Suliote chieftain, Ulysses. He has come to Greece, Byron says, to aid a nation, not a faction. "Ulysses cursed in his beard and sent Trevanion, for whom he had found more than one cunning use, to seduce the Suliote forces camped within the insurgent lines" (p. 402). Most of Byron's money has gone for the Greek cause. The rainy season makes Missolonghi a "pestilential mudbasket" that fails to dampen Byron's spirit. He insists on living no better than his Suliotes, eating their meager fare and sleeping on damp mats. Greeks warn him about contracting the dreaded marsh fever.

Two Greek leaders, one of them Lambro, are bringing a message for Byron in Missolonghi. The emissary sent ahead is brother to the girl whom Byron years before had saved from being drowned—after the betrayal by Trevanion. Byron gets the message: an invitation from the revolutionaries of the Morea for him *"to wear the crown of Greece!"* (p. 421). Byron, to Lambro's astonishment, refuses the proffered crown. Touched, Lambro remains to fight with him. More and more the illness which has seized him weakens and finally kills Byron. The Countess Teresa arrives to comfort him in his final moments. Because of Byron the embattled Greeks unite and win their hard-fought liberty. The scoundrel Trevanion, evil to the end, is shot through the heart by the brother of the girl whom he had betrayed during the feast of Ramazan.[43]

Other romances set in Greece appeared at the turn of the century. Many American travelers after Melville toured Greece and recorded their impressions in books and articles. After the 1880s enough Greek immigrants settled here to compose a new and identifiable ethnic minority. The only nineteenth-century American writer of classic stature who was of Greek descent, Lafcadio Hearn, never used a Greek character in his fiction. Hearn was born on the island of Lefkas of an Irish father and a Greek mother, Rosa Tessima. He referred to her as "Grecian" or "predominantly Greek," although it is possible she was Maltese, or Maltese with a Greek background. One of Hearn's biographers, Vera McWilliams, suggests that he strengthened his ties with the ancient Greece that he worshiped by stressing the nationality of his mother. His collections of literary essays are filled with allusions to classical Hellenism. Hearn had no apparent interest in the Greeks of reborn Greece, perhaps because he left Lefkas at an early age and never returned. After the age of seven he never saw his parents. Soon, however, Stephen Crane, Jack London, George Horton, Demetra Vaka Brown, and others began making literary use of modern Greeks who were already in process of becoming Greek-Americans.

2

THE FIRST GREEKS
IN AMERICAN FICTION

THE GOLDEN PROMISES of the gay nineties together with en-
demic poverty and the Balkan war lured many Greek immigrants
to Ellis Island. They arrived in increasingly large numbers. The
movement coincided with the spread of naturalism in American
literature. It is not surprising that Stephen Crane and Jack London
responded to the Hellenic presence. Crane covered the Graeco-
Turkish War of 1897 as a correspondent. Though no Byron as
poet, he was romantic in his personal life. Crane wrote no "Maid
of Athens," yet he lived a love story in the midst of the war: he was
to marry the girl who followed him to Athens, Cora Taylor, a journalist credited with being the first female war-correspondent.
When he left Greece, Crane brought out with him two refugee
Greek boys; one of them, Andoni Ptolemy, served the Cranes for
a time as butler.[1]

In a biography of Cora Crane, Lillian Gilkes succinctly describes
Crane's Greek experience in the chapter "Grecian Lark: War and
Romance." She also briefly recounts the causes of the war, the
popular support won by the Greeks, and their final defeat after
the Battle of Velestinos. Crane's sympathies were entirely Greek.
The defeat, effected in part by the treachery of the great powers,
left the brilliant writer dispirited and gravely ill with dysentery. He
would die three years later after covering the Spanish-American
War in Cuba. From his few weeks in Greece (the war lasted a
month) Crane gathered the impressions for "Death and the Child"
and the plot for a potboiler, *Active Service*. Among his letters is one
written in December 1897 to his American agent, in which he
states: "I have made a proposition to McClure that he advance
£200 on the first of January for the book rights of my new Greek
novel—not yet begun."[2] The novel referred to was *Active Service*,
for which Crane apparently had high hopes.

In "Death and the Child" Crane's powers to evoke a scene, sustain a mood, and create a character remind one of the aesthetic

successes he achieved in writing *The Red Badge of Courage*, "The Blue Hotel," "The Bride Comes to Yellow Sky," and "The Open Boat." The "child story," as he called it, transcends the immediate action and makes, at the end, a statement on the nature of man. The story deals with the retreat of a people and the last stand of an army in the face of an implacable foe—a subject filled with dramatic possibilities. Ernest Hemingway's famous account of the retreat from Caporetto in *A Farewell to Arms* may owe something to the earlier short story by Crane, to whom Hemingway was admittedly indebted. Finally, the "child story" set in embattled Greece has a character in Peza who undergoes a crisis similar to that which the protagonist meets and overcomes in *The Red Badge of Courage*.

"Death and the Child" opens with a description of terrified peasants fleeing in confusion down a mountain trail.[3] The Turks are advancing. Image after powerful image expresses the riotous panic. Walking against the stream in search of the battle is a youth moved to great pity by the refugees. It is Peza, the hero of the story. He waits for a lieutenant of infantry to catch up with him; and when he does Peza cries out that he, a correspondent from Italy, is actually a Greek who wants to fight for his country. "I came here merely because my father was a Greek, and for his sake I thought of Greece—I loved Greece" (p. 393).

The character of Peza provides the first major paradox. An untrained civilian, he determines to join the Greek soldiers. The second paradox, or aesthetic contrast, is the innocent child abandoned on the mountain. Below him in the valley swirls the battle. In their panic his parents grabbed an old pipe but forgot "their first-born." The child plays with sticks. Later in the day, when the noise of battle nears, he begins to weep—a "strange, tiny figure seated on a boulder, surveying them [the struggling men] while the tears streamed. It was as simple as some powerful symbol" (p. 407).

The bulk of the story concerns Peza and his sudden notion to join the battle. As he moves forward through scenes of death and suffering, he undergoes subtle changes of attitude—from initial romanticism involving pity for the wounded to thoughts of his own self-preservation to final ignominious flight to save his skin. Death images abound to motivate Peza's awakening to the horrors of war. "It was as if Peza was a corpse walking on the bottom of the sea, and finding there fields of grain, groves, weeds, the faces of men, voices" (p. 398). In a while Peza feels no more sorrow at seeing wounded men, pity apparently having "a numerical limit." Peza is dumbfounded to see a soldier whose jaw has been shot half away. When asked to help, he cannot. Afraid, he does not dare touch the "specter."

The climax occurs when Peza arrives at the front lines; driven by pride, he tells a young officer in Greek that he wants to fight for the fatherland. The officer tells Peza to arm himself from a pile of dead men covered with blankets. Revolted at the prospect, he hesitates. A soldier strips a bandoleer of cartridges from a corpse and gives it to him. "Peza, having crossed the long cartridge belt on his breast, felt that the dead man had flung his two arms around him" (p. 406). He is given a rifle, another relic of a dead man. "Thus he felt, besides the clutch of a corpse about his neck, that the rifle was as unhumanly horrible as a snake that lives in a tomb" (p. 406). Peza had landed among peasants, but he was "a young student who could write sonnets and play the piano quite well." An "old blockhead" sits coolly gnawing on hard bread while Peza is "being throttled by a dead man's arms." The head of a corpse stares at Peza with two "liquid-like eyes." Peza is "being drawn by these dead men, slowly, firmly down, as to some mystic chamber under the earth, where they could walk, dreadful figures, swollen, and blood-marked. He was bidden; they had commanded him; he was going, going, going" (p. 407).

Peza bolts for the rear. Some think he has been wounded; others who know the truth jeer after him and feel good about their own bravery. The soldier with the bread, the "old blockhead," calmly puts it aside and kneels in the trench ready to resume battle. The story now shifts again to the child crying on the mountain. Upon hearing a rattle of stones, he forgets mother and hunger and walks to stand over the heaving disheveled form of Peza. After a silence the little boy asks, "Are you a man?" In that simple question the story rises to its destined allegorical meaning. Crane reinforces the meaning by having the child repeat, "Are you a man?" (p. 408). Peza stares at the child with glassy eyes, gasping like a fish. "Palsied, windless, and abject," Crane concludes, "he confronted the primitive courage, the sovereign child, the brother of the mountain, the sky, and the sea, and he knew that the definition of his misery could be written on a wee grass-blade" (p. 408).

If Stephen Crane wrote at the top of his powers in "Death and the Child," he unfortunately composed near the bottom in *Active Service*.[4] The novel was done hastily for money. Perhaps the only original aspect of *Active Service* is its Greek setting. Otherwise the novel bears the obvious earmarks of a melodrama whose hero, first a scalawag, undergoes a moral conversion for the love of a beautiful damsel in distress. The setting could have been greatly enriched by the usual details of local color, but it was not. Nor does Crane adequately develop a single Greek character.

The heroine of *Active Service* is Marjory Wainwright, whose hand has been asked in marriage by Rufus Coleman, the Sunday editor of the *New York Eclipse*. Her father, a classics professor, disapproves strongly. As Coleman says to her, "I know as well as you do that your father is taking you to Greece in order to get rid of me" (p. 449). Undaunted, Coleman requests expenses and permission to go to Greece and report the imminent war with Turkey. On the steamer bound for England, he meets an actress friend named Nora Black who eventually follows him to Greece as a war-correspondent. Critics have pointed out that parallel in the fiction with Cora Taylor's behavior.

In Athens the hero Coleman learns from the American minister that the Wainwrights have gone to Nikopolis, a town on the Turkish side of the war, where they are in danger. Rufus Coleman determines to rescue his beloved Marjory. Discussing the enthusiasm of Coleman's dragoman for the mission, Crane offers some gratuitous comments on the Greek character. Coleman, in being pleased by the servant's response, "had not been told that any of the more crude forms of sentiment arouse the common Greek to the highest pitch, but sometimes, when it comes to what the Americans call a 'show down,' when he gets backed toward his last corner with a solitary privilege of dying for those sentiments, perhaps he does not always exhibit those talents which are supposed to be possessed by a bulldog. He often, then, goes into the cafes and takes it all out in oratory, like any common Parisian" (p. 469). The dragoman lies to everyone about his master, who wears a natty khaki uniform. The Greek tells all that Coleman is a great English gentleman come to join the cavalry. When the Greek soldiers try to hug and kiss him as a comrade in arms, Coleman eludes their affection. As Coleman and his servant approach the danger zone, the dragoman turns inefficient and craven. "It was a mere basic inability to front novel situations which was somehow in the dragoman; he retreated from everything in a smoke of gibberish and gesticulation" (p. 471). The Greek has a curious love for his wages. Without him to interpret, Coleman cannot proceed. Crane does not seem to ponder why a Greek dragoman, for forty francs a day, should risk his life for a rich American's quixotic quest for love and journalistic fame.

On the war-strewn way to Nikopolis the hero notes a detail that in Crane's hand becomes one of the finest touches in an otherwise mediocre novel: "Before them on the road was here and there a fez from a fled Turkish soldier and they lay like drops of blood from some wounded leviathan" (p. 484). By a mischance owing mainly to the dragoman's ineptness, Rufus Coleman sleeps through a sudden retreat of the Greek forces and wakes to find himself in a chaotic state of affairs; but he is able to succeed in his mission: he runs into the Wainwright party and brings it safely out of danger. Now the actress Nora Black, special writer for the New York *Daylight*, appears, but she does not approach being a romantic rival to Marjory Wainwright for Coleman's attention.

Safe now, the students in Wainwright's class deride the Greek foods they are expected to eat. Crane has his hero express more derogatory thoughts about some of the Greek people. "The manhood of Greece had gone to the frontier, leaving at home this rabble of talkers, most of whom were armed with rifles for mere pretension. Coleman loathed them to the end of his soul" (p. 535). Professor Wainwright changes his mind and blesses the coming marriage between Coleman and Marjory. In the midst of the universal joy Crane makes a final derogatory comment on the modern Greek character. The dragoman furiously berates a countryman. "But at every word the manager seemed to grow more indifferent, more callous. In reality, it is thus that Greek meets Greek" (pp. 589–90). *Active Service* ends with the lovers talking together in a secluded glen.

Stephen Crane did not know modern Greek. In neither the short story nor the novel does he have any Greek word transliterated or used for aesthetic purpose. He mentions that Professor Wainwright understands ancient Greek perfectly, but never once does the classics expert venture a Greek word. One must conclude from this and other factors that Crane, despite his genius, had scant knowledge or apparent interest in Greek ethnicity and culture. One may wonder, though, why his brilliant sense of the concrete and his customarily suggestive language failed him in this instance, when Greece was a new and exotic world for him to observe.

George Horton, another *fin de siècle* American poet and novelist, did have a great interest in matters Greek. As an avid and lifelong

Hellenist, he intimately knew the country, the people, and the language. He could write in modern Greek. Primarily a diplomat, he served as minister to Greece from 1893 until 1898 when President McKinley relieved him of his office. In 1899 he became literary editor for the Chicago *Times Herald* and then conducted the Art and Literary Review supplement for Hearst's *Chicago American*. Through his novels he brought many Greek characters into American literature. Strongly pro-Greek, Horton vehemently criticized the great powers for consistently siding with the Moslem Turks against the Christian Greeks. He returned to important diplomatic duties during the world war and its aftermath. As the American consul general there, he witnessed the burning of Smyrna in 1922. The fact that *Athene*, the leading "American Magazine of Hellenic Thought," devoted its summer 1946 issue to George Horton indicates the high esteem in which he is held by the Greek-American community. The editor wrote: "*Athene* hopes that the time will come soon when the people of Greece will honor 'their' Horton, their 'Kyr Yiorgi' as the Greeks of Chicago affectionately used to call him, by erecting a monument to him in some secluded spot near his beloved Acropolis." [5]

Horton began his literary career as a poet. His *Songs of the Lowly* (1891) won the praise of such authors as Walt Whitman, Eugene Field, and Andrew Lang. Throughout his poetry Horton alludes to Hellenism, both classical and modern. Of most relevance here is the long narrative "Aphroessa: A Legend of Modern Greece" (1897).[6] Its theme touches upon the fact that the country people of Greece "still believe in Nereids, as they have from time immemorial." The protagonist of "Aphroessa" is a shepherd boy, the "graceful Spiridon" of Argolis. So immersed is he in the adoration of nature that he has no eyes for the "athletic maidens of the villages," including the gentle Marigó. The young nature-lover happens to see a Nereid maiden, Aphroessa, who captivates him with her fatal beauty. One afternoon in August she reappears and leads him on a chase through the woods. For a brief time Spiridon has power over the phantom by having grabbed her magic veil; but she cozens him to give it back. The false creature then vanishes forever "from the eyes of men," and Spiridon is found dead beside a spring. Horton's last book of poetry, *Poems of an Exile* (1931), includes the tribute "To My Wife," praising her courage both at "beleaguered Salonique" and later at Smyrna. Horton calls her "the proud heroic daughter of an old heroic race" who stayed "through

fire and slaughter in a pestilential place," and at "martyred Smyrna, when the hideous Turk came down / To give courage to your sisters, you refused to quit the town."[7]

Horton's main contribution to belles lettres was a series of novels that began with *Constantine: A Tale of Greece under King Otho* (1897).[8] The author ostensibly hears the story told by an old Greek sea captain at a café on Poros. In his notes Horton mentions the Greek belief in the terrible Three Fates. He also explains the custom of the *koumbaros*, the "Best Man" at weddings and baptisms, "a relationship . . . more sacred in Greece than that of blood" (p. vii). *Nounos* means "godfather" and *moerologion* means "death song." The plot of *Constantine* involves the betrayal by a *nounos*, a man named Spiridon, of his sacred trust to be the surrogate father of his ward. At the start the narrator gives a brief view of Poros, introduces some Greeks, and says he often sits at a seashore café, among the bubbling narghiles and coffee aromas, where he has "told of the wonders of New York and Chicago, and listened in turn to tales of Greek life" (p. 12). He meets Constantine at the Poros monastery, a "human wreck," old, bent, and ragged; and when he expresses wonder about the reason for this condition, the old Greek captain tells Constantine's sad story to the narrator.

It goes back to 1835. Two young friends, Loukas and Spiridon, build a schooner in the Cyclades. On a voyage back from Russia with a wheat cargo, Loukas dies; but not before he whispers a secret to his friend and *koumbaros*, Spiridon. To be a *koumbaros* under the circumstances means that his friend must act as father to the still unborn child of Loukas. The *moerologion* or widow's lament is sung for the departed. The scene shifts to Poros and the birth of Loukas's child, a son, whom Spiridon names Constantine. The mother dies. A feast is given to propitiate the dreaded Three Fates, then comes the baptism when Spiridon arrives and gives the name. His duties as the *nounos* are described. These are the duties which Spiridon betrays.

He marries a girl, Loukia, with a good *proeka* or dowry; but his real wealth derives from the secret whispered to him by Constantine's father. With the help of a seaman, Barbandone, Spiridon discovers a great trunk filled with gold, jewels, and other valuables at the bottom of a cistern at the house of Loukas. Time passes. Spiridon, his wife, and Constantine settle in Athens in a fine house with a beautiful garden. Barbandone, now a prosperous wine merchant, wants to but cannot read the bundle of papers taken from the trunk. Spiridon has a daughter, Aneza, who grows lovelier and vainer as the years go by. Constantine falls in love with her. From Germany, where he studies law, he sends love letters to Aneza. She writes back, to report that his *nounos* Spiridon has died.

At home in Athens, unable to continue his studies, Constantine confronts his bitchy stepmother, who forbids his marriage to Aneza, on grounds that he merely seeks her wealth. He meets Barbandone, who offers him the job of managing a roadhouse. Another year passes. Aneza decides to marry an impoverished rake, Christo. Very distraught, the rejected lover Constantine rushes to Barbandone, who shows him the stolen papers. They explain that many years earlier the father of Loukas had sold a cargo of wheat to a beseiged Spanish town. The treasure resulted from the sale and from the capture of a pirate ship. From grandfather to father to son, to Constantine, the fortune should have passed, but the thieving *nounos*, Spiridon, kept it for himself. Now the stepmother has it. Rejected and betrayed, the violent Constantine almost chokes Barbandone, curses all, and disappears. He undergoes a long period of madness and then recovers. Twenty years later, an old and resigned man, he happens upon a picnic attended by Aneza near the Poros monastery. He asks the matron with the festive group, "Am I not Constantine . . . and are you not Aneza?" (p. 232). She never goes to Poros again.

This depressing novel was followed by one not any happier, *A Fair Brigand* (1897).[9] The hero is Joseph Chandler Brown, a recent Harvard graduate and "expert in Argive bronzes," who goes to Athens on a year's fellowship to the archaeological institute. He studies a collection of Argive bronzes found during an excavation. After two years in Berlin, where he earns a doctorate, he returns to Athens to continue his research and to publish a book. Anderson, a friend, induces Brown to climb Mount Olympus. They take a "dirty little Greek steamer" to Volo. Even though both Americans speak modern Greek, they are badly deceived on their way by foot to Larissa. Their guide for the climb turns out to be the arch brigand Demetrios Takis. With his accomplices at a prearranged location he kidnaps Brown and Anderson, takes them to a remote brigand village, and holds them for ransom.

The brigands carry the short Gras rifles admired by Greek mountaineers. Anderson says that "all Greeks are brigands." Throughout he has a jocular attitude, while Dr. Brown remains glum, worried about the acids in which his bronzes are soaking.

The bandit Takis, dressed as a dandy, learns from the American consul in Athens that Brown's aunt has plenty of money; and he therefore sets the ransom at fifty thousand francs, or $5,000. The Greek authorities tell the consul that Brown and Anderson "are in the hands of the cruelest and shrewdest brigand in Greece" (p. 48). They are being held at a shepherd's station on Mount Metamorphosis, guarded by a boy, Meetso, a "tall young brigand" in a colorful Albanian costume.

The Americans receive all possible comforts and care as both enforced and honored guests. On Sunday they are conducted to the brigands' church established by Takis on the spot where his beautiful daughter, Kyriakoula, had found an ikon of the Virgin. Takis is a kind of Robin Hood who robs rich foreigners on behalf of his mountain people. The ransom he seeks will be the dowry for Kyriakoula to marry a man of consequence. At the church, however, she casts a longing glance at the expert on Argive bronzes, Dr. Brown himself, the rich captive. Anderson sees her infatuation as a means of their ultimate escape.

Takis appears to admire the Americans, all the while threatening serious harm if the ransom is not paid. "Americans are so enlightened," he cries, "so philhellenic! All Greeks love Americans" (p. 85). Despite these comments Takis is prepared to cut off one of Brown's ears, should his wealthy aunt not cable the money. The brigand is a cruel Robin Hood, whereas his guard Meetso is an egotistic fool, especially when he speaks of his suit for the lovely Kyriakoula. He says of himself: "There is not a handsomer man on Mount Olympus than I am, perhaps not in all Thessaly. I shall wear these fine clothes all the time that Kyriakoula remains here, and I shall again tell her of my love. She can't resist me; I shall talk to her so beautifully, and I shall look so fine and noble" (p. 95). Anderson jokingly asks Meetso if Greeks call their sweethearts by pet names, and Meetso replies yes, "My eyes, my soul, my life, my heart, my little bird, cold water—." The last term means that she is pure and delicious (p. 97).

Until the end Brown is very hesitant to encourage Kyriakoula, since his only love is his Argive bronzes and he does not want a wife. Anderson pursues the matter for their survival. Kyriakoula has been smitten by love at first sight. She becomes the vapid lovesick heroine, pouring forth her soul to Melpo, the servant woman. Melpo reminds Kyriakoula that her father wants her to marry old Poulios, the senator who represents their region in Athens. Takis had become a brigand after killing a man over love for a woman; and when told of this by Melpo, Kyriakoula cries, "To kill a man for love! I could do that!" Later she does. The upshot of the complicated plot is the marriage of Brown and Kyriakoula, the "fair brigand." Yet all does not end well for them. Instead of being a loving husband, he buries himself in his work with the Argive bronzes. Almost totally neglected, Kyriakoula Brown shifts her wild passion to Mortimer Talbot, an attaché in the British embassy. When he learns he will be transferred to St. Petersburg, he boasts to a Russian friend that he has a paramour.

By chance Kyriakoula overhears her lover trying to palm her off as a plaything. "She wants love," Talbot says, "the deep, tragic kind—sighs and threats to commit suicide or pine away and die, and all that sort of thing, you know. It's such fun!" Talbot in effect sets up his own doom when he claims, "She loves desperately, jealously, dangerously" (p. 319). On his last night in Athens, Talbot attends a masquerade party at the French ministry, dressed as an Albanian brigand. Kyriakoula, wounded in spirit, also goes. By this time she is "transformed into a fiend." At a climactic moment during the festivities a white arm flashes high and descends in a "curving gleam of light." At the spot where it happens, the Honorable Mortimer Talbot lies on the floor, "the jeweled hilt of a Turkish knife quivering over his heart." Kyriakoula stands over him. "In her eyes gleamed all the hate of a long line of murderers, and on her lips was the wolf smile of Takis, the brigand" (p. 329). Thus ends the romance.

The author's next novel, *Like Another Helen* (1900), evokes the famous Greek beauty who allegedly caused the Trojan war.[10] The setting is Crete. Horton's Helen is Panayota, the priest's daughter. The "Trojans" are the Turks, especially a fierce brigand named Kostakes who loves Panayota and abducts her for his harem. The closest character to Menelaus is a Bostonian, John Curtis, who wants to report to the world about the Cretan situation. He ardently seeks to rescue Panayota from the Turks. Hero and villain vie for the love of a dolorous and imperiled maiden.

Like Another Helen begins the last week in March 1897 with a caïque leaving Piraeus carrying contraband arms for the Cretan insurgents. The passengers include the protagonist, John Curtis; a Swede named Lindbohm; and a young Cretan student, Michali Papadakes. The Turks have burned the house and the three villages owned by Michali's father. "I am a Cretan," Michali says, "and I go to fight for my country" (p. 9). Curtis at twenty-two imagines himself an ancient Greek "or a Lord Byron." He is a philhellene of the idealistic type that has often been drawn to romantic and tragic Greece. "He [Curtis] had been no mean Grecian at Harvard, and had read 'Loukes Laras' in the modern vernacular. He could speak modern Greek fairly well with the fruit men of Boston" (p. 11).

On its way the caïque is destroyed, presumably by a British cannonade. The three principals swim ashore, with Curtis cutting his foot on the spine of a sea hedgehog. They have landed near the Cretan village of Ambellaki where the curious folk arrive and stare down at them from a cliff. "All the males," Horton writes, "of whatever age, wore high yellow boots, voluminous blue trousers and soft red fezzes, that broke across the crown and fell backwards, ending in a long black tassel" (p. 38). Among the welcomers are the *demarch*, the village mayor, and the *papa* or priest, Maleko Nicolaides. Cretan hospitality begins for Curtis when he is confined for four days in the priest's home. There he meets the "other Helen," Panayota.

He recuperates in time to join the Cretans as they celebrate the first of May by eating roast lamb, drinking, and dancing. Curtis, for his part, sings in Greek his own version of "The Man Who Drinks His Whiskey Clear." The mood suddenly changes for the worst when Papa Nicolaides receives an ultimatum from the evil Kostakes: "bring me Panayota for my harem or I will come with 250 men and destroy all" (p. 87). Curtis responds with a fervid no!

In the ensuing battles with the Turks, Michali has his leg broken by a cannonball. Panayota is captured before she can leap from a cliff. A Greek traitor, Ampates, leads the Turks over the mountain. Kostakes confronts Papa Nicolaides, declares his love for Panayota, and claims that her attitude has caused the fighting. She replies: "I shall find death somehow sooner than dishonor" (p. 142).

The perils of Panayota begin in earnest. She, her father, and other Cretans are led away by Kostakes. The priest escapes and is later killed. John Curtis frees Panayota and then finds Lindbohm. More battles occur, now with the fierce Bashi Bazouks—mounted Turkish irregulars who furnish their own arms and equipment. They have all had some close kin or friend killed; therefore they fight with desperation for revenge and Islam. Panayota's fortunes turn very dire: she becomes the "hopeless prisoner" of six Bashi

Bazouks! Again in the clutch of her "lover" Kostakes, Panayota joins his harem of three wives who, however, soon undertake to help her escape.

Curtis and Lindbohm search for Panayota, who has hidden in a leper's village. The English arrive and hang the brigand Kostakes. At the end of the story an unexpected twist sends Curtis home to Boston while Lindbohm, the true lover, will risk catching leprosy by hurrying back to get Panayota.

In his next novel, *The Tempting of Father Anthony* (1901), Horton wrote a masterpiece that has too long been neglected. The author eschews the melodramatic artifices for a story that flows naturally and honestly from character and situation.[11] One finds in it no dependence on the bizarre, the violent, the shocking, the contrived irony. The character of Anastasi Kriezes, a seventeen-year-old boy of Damala, is a genuine literary creation. Because of family custom, he will become a priest. After reading the "Lives of the Saints," he wants to rise above mere priesthood and be a saint. To his friend Kotsas he confides that he will live in a cave like St. Anthony "and fight with dragons, lions, and elephants" (p. 21). Like a saint he must conquer his own flesh and never sleep. Anastasi puts a crown of thistles on his head, but it hurts so much he takes it off. The two boys leave on a donkey for the cave where Anastasi plans to live. While he stays there, Kotsas must bring him bread. Already irrationally committed, Anastasi feels the need to give away all his wealth; thus he tells Kotsas to present his pet kid to "the poorest man in town" who, after some pondering, he assumes is ninety-year-old Nestor Tombasi, a renowned tippler.

Much of the humor early in the action stems from the trouble Kotsas has in doing the bidding of Anastasi. At home he is questioned about the whereabouts of his missing friend. To get the truth from him, Kotsas's mother pulls his ear, at which point Horton comments, "Many Greek mothers are ignorant of the physiological use of the external portion of the ear, and suppose it designed by a wise Providence as a thing to be yanked" (p. 40). Kotsas finally tells everyone about Anastasi's search for sainthood, but does not reveal his hiding place. He gets into more trouble when he takes Anastasi's kid as a gift to Nestor Tombasi. The old man feels so insulted at being called the poorest man in town that he beats Kotsas, who runs anxiously to Anastasi. At the cavern the saint-to-be Anastasi refuses to see him at first because he thinks Kotsas is the devil in disguise. Then Anastasi not only relents but also tricks his friend into staying with him. Without help Kotsas cannot leave the cave; he is too fat. Tired, the captive boy falls asleep.

While he sleeps, Anastasi confronts his first temptation: from his high vantage he spots two women bathing in a nearby ravine. Undaunted, he yells at them and calls them devils. The poor women flee in great panic and humiliation. Anastasi, proud of his deed, quotes from the "Lives of the Saints" to this effect: "And the devil often visited St. Anthony in the form of a woman, and tempted him" (p. 59). Later, at night, the two ladies Eléne and Katina lead a search party looking for the missing boys. "The moon was full that night—the glorious moon, nowhere so wonderful as in the deep skies of Greece" (p. 66). As the boys watch, they see shapes moving which they imagine to be nereids; actually they are a villager's pigs aroused from their sleep by the searchers. Led by a shepherd who knows of the cave, the party reaches and accosts the boys. Anastasi's mother, the *papadia*, is angry with him for wanting to be a saint and thus "better than his father," who is only a priest. She climbs up a vine and brings them both down. These problems do not turn Anastasi from his purpose. Penniless, he leaves for Poros and the distant monastery of the Life-giving Spring. He is very hungry and thinks of begging, but the lady he meets knows his father, and he is ashamed. Having fallen asleep by the roadside, he is awakened by Eléne and Katina, who offer him biscuits. What kind of devils can these women be, he wonders, who look so nice and treat him so well?

The next section of the novel deals with Anastasi at the monastery. Not only is he a monk but a holy terror to the others. Immediately the arrogant boy finds sin and evil rampant. One monk is a drunkard, another a glutton, the third a gossip. A great victory at the beginning will give him superiority "over these old fathers who have never done anything" (p. 135). Anastasi suffers from an important sin himself—pride. The cook jokingly tries to convince him to be a cook and not a saint. "Good cooks," he says, "are more in demand than saints, these days" (p. 137).

As the reader suspects, the youth sets out to reform the entire monastery, to expunge all sinful self-indulgence, and to make its life austere. He disturbs the universe of the peaceful community; most of the inmates fear and even hate him. The *hegoumenos* or head more or less goes along with him, using him as a gadfly to stir the fat and laggard spirits. During the dinner hour he has Anastasi read from the *Lives of the Saints*, much to the chagrin of the other monks, who do not care to be so often reminded of their short-comings. Eventually the ceremony of ordination is held, and Anastasi will now be known as Father Anthony after his favorite saint.

With new power he grows more tyrannical. "Father Anthony was a thorn of increasing sharpness in the sides of his less earnest brethren." In the monastery he has only one friend, Father Demetrius, and he also fails him when the Lebessi family arrives for a devotional stay. Visitors often came to undergo spiritual exercises for brief sojourns. Among them this time is Theodora Lebessi, who immediately smites Father Demetrius. Theodora (the name means "Gift of God" in Greek) is thirty, which is old for a Greek girl to be still unmarried. Father Anthony, suffused with notions about the devil as a woman, doggedly follows Theodora around in order to protect his fellow priest. He tries very hard to convince Father Demetrius that "all women are the invention of the devil" (p. 161). But to no avail. Theodora and Demetrius become lovers, and Father Anthony spies on them. At one tryst he sees Demetrius press "kiss after kiss upon the upturned mouth" (p. 167). The author has a melodramatic and comic touch: "Then Father Anthony sprang from the oleander bushes and fell upon his knees." He begs Father Demetrius to leave the girl alone, that she is a devil, that he will be damned. Luckily neither lover has a heart attack. That meddling having failed, Father Anthony informs the *hegoumenos* about the amours of Demetrius. The "affair" is ended, but the intense hatred that now surrounds him makes it necessary for Father Anthony to leave.

Father Anthony decides to live in the wilderness as a hermit in order to pursue his career of sainthood. He ends up on the island in a little church, the "Holy Virgin, Averter of Grasshoppers." There he confronts his greatest temptation: from the young girls who go crazy over him. The chief and most determined temptress is Paraskevé Kokkinou. She is beautiful, buxom, and eighteen. She is also rich and spoiled. Marriage, Horton states, is the only honorable course for her to take, since Greece has done nothing or very little to educate girls. The moment Father Anthony sees Paraskevé, he crosses himself for protection and retreats. He cannot escape so easily, however.

She and the other girls make a big fuss to attract him. A handsome young priest living alone in a little church on their island—a very romantic situation! But what a saint! They bring him boiled eggs, preserved oranges, and other goodies, but he throws them away as evil lures. He wants only bread and water. Paraskevé is saddened, but determined. She thinks, "What right has a saint to be so young and beautiful, and have such curly hair?" (p. 205). When Paraskevé goes to him with her friends, Father Anthony tells her to please leave since she is lovely. Paraskevé knows that she is loved.

By chance Father Anthony sees Paraskevé, wearing a red scarf, endangered by an enraged bull. She changes from a simple but enamoured peasant girl to the damsel in distress; and Father Anthony becomes the romantic hero who must save her at all cost. In doing so, he gets two broken ribs, and is cared for at the comfortable home of Paraskevé, who nurses him back to health. Symbolically, he loses his holy book, the *Lives of the Saints*. The final chapter has the *former* Father Anthony, now Anastasi again, married to the beautiful Paraskevé. He has long since left the church and the island of Poros. Now Anastasi lives in Nauplia with Paraskevé and their little daughter. One day his good friend Kotsas arrives to honeymoon with his bride; and he asks Anastasi what happened to his dream of sainthood. Anastasi smiles and replies, "It was only the devil that tempted St. Anthony after all. I was tempted by a real woman" (p. 246).

The Tempting of Father Anthony is a minor classic in the genre of the comic novel. The Greeks in it act like Greeks because George Horton knows his people. His next book, *In Argolis*, expresses even more explicitly his view of the variegated Greek character.[12] Its publication in 1902 may have helped to establish American attitudes toward the new Greek immigrants streaming into the country. The Hortons' stay on Poros resulted from President McKinley's removing him from office; they also had a three-month-old baby, who was too young for the rough Atlantic crossing. Their getting to Poros, their long happy summer, and their leaving are the frame for the author's commentary on the Greek people. In *Home of Nymphs and Vampires* (1929) Horton describes the lore, customs, economy, literature, folk songs, and superstitions of the Greek islands.[13]

The introductory note to *In Argolis* is written by Eben Alexander, Horton's immediate predecessor as United States minister to Greece. Another avid philhellene, Alexander praises Horton as one who knows Greece, "the country itself, its glorious history, its splendid literature, its language old and new, its people and their ways of life."[14] The former minister evokes the classic past but draws attention to the present, and he stresses the need for Americans to know modern Greece better. "We should remember," Alexander writes, "that it is only about seventy years since Greece freed herself from four hundred years of awful slavery, in comparison with which slavery as known in the United States was freedom itself."[15] He praises Horton for limiting himself to recording the "simple life of lovely Poros," the ancient Calauria, where Demosthenes killed himself and where, near the divine sea, the nightingales are always singing.

Horton takes apparent delight in highlighting traits and qualities that he regards as distinctively Greek. For example he has hardly started the book before he explains "the character of Greek profanity."

> It has nothing in it like the short sulphurous thunder-clap of the Anglo-Saxon 'Damn,' neither is it capable of the picturesque effects and imaginative flights attainable in English; but for hair-raising blasphemy, Greek profanity is unapproachable. The commonest oaths of the Greek Christian are insults to Divinity such as captains on the Erie Canal never use when their lines cross; they are hideous outrages of speech such as a Nevada sheep-herder could not use without expecting the earth to open and swallow him. (p. 3)

The occasion is Horton's hiring of "two villainous Greeks" with ramshackle wagons to carry the family luggage from Athens to Piraeus. Throughout *In Argolis* he makes a running comment on the Greek character, especially that of the peasant who in large numbers was leaving for America. The Greek immigrant is soon to begin appearing in our literature; and before he becomes thoroughly "Americanized," he will exhibit many of the traits noted in 1902 in George Horton's lively book.

"Greeks always combine against the foreigner, when their interests are not prejudiced thereby" (p. 9).

Any derangement is regarded by Greeks as owing to cold, but the colder it is outside the greater the dread Greeks have of heated rooms. "A Greek will never draw up cheerfully by your stove or fireplace" (p. 19).

The majority of Greek women over twenty-five are extremely corpulent (p. 23).

"The Greek people are excessively fond of garlic" (p. 24). Horton explains: "Garlic is a phylactery against the evil eye,—an important thing to know in a country where this evil is so prevalent." A kernel of garlic, worn on a ribbon about the neck of a child or a goat, is "most efficacious" (p. 25).

The Greeks maintain a long Easter fast. "I do not believe that any other people on the globe starve themselves for their souls' sake so persistently as do the Greeks" (p. 29).

The Virgin Mary is "the deity *par excellence* of modern Greece, uniting in her person all the attributes of the various heathen goddesses"; and the Greeks have an "interminable line of saints and saintesses" whose "days" they meticulously observe (p. 29).

"From the standpoint of a Greek peasant, a man who is to eat at another's expense in the evening would be guilty of incomprehensible idiocy if he squandered a half penny of his own on food in the meantime" (p. 35).

Describing a funeral on Poros, Horton writes: "Never before had I so fully realized the impressiveness, grandeur, and pomp of which the Greek Church is capable" (p. 60).

"Olives are a favorite article of diet in Greece among the poorer classes" (p. 63).

"Much wine is consumed in Greece, but habitual drunkards are rare" (p. 65).

An almost universal trait in the Greek, according to Horton, is the following: "In his desire to overreach, and to make a small immediate profit, he underestimates the intelligence of his victim" (p. 69).

"I had often been told that the Greek priests encouraged the belief in the evil eye, for the sake of the fees" (p. 74).

It is next to impossible for the Greek girl to marry without a *proeka*, or *dot*—"ready money, or property of some kind, clothing, bedding, furniture, household utensils." Thus girls at birth are "not welcome" to Greek fathers (p. 87).

"A Greek cannot live without his vine or his flowerpot and his view of the sea, but he cares nothing for the condition of his back alley" (p. 91).

The Greeks are very superstitious, especially with respect to Nereids, sea nymphs who originally attended Poseidon, and who can take any shape and can do any harm they wish to anybody at any time" (p. 96).

"Although most Greeks are dark, golden locks and blue eyes are still the poetical dream of nobility in that classic land, as Greek literature abundantly testifies that they have been from earliest times" (p. 100).

To ward off evil, all Greeks make the "talismanic sign of the cross." Many women, also, know magic incantations handed down to them when the previous knower was at death's door. These incantations "are a strange mixture of Christian influence and paganism" (p. 113).

"Greek women make devoted nurses, for the reason that the Greek people in general are passionately fond of children" (p. 116).

"When a man becomes a father in Greece, he acquires immediately a certain standing in the community . . . a dignity and importance which the childless man never enjoys" (p. 116).

"So many people in Greece have seen or heard the Three Fates!" They come on the third night and decide what the new baby's lot will be in life (p. 118).

Priests loom large in the metaphorical speech of the Greek peasants. "Warts are 'priests,' and so are toes protruding through holes in the stockings. A boil on any part of the body is also a 'priest'" (pp. 122–23).

The author describes the "soul-harrowing" church music: "Imagine a number of boys humming through combs over which paper has been stretched, and you have an idea of Greek church music" (p. 130).

"Time is reckoned in Greece by reference to some church festival" (p. 131).

"The majority of the country people of Greece eat meat but once a year" (p. 132).

"When a Greek feels particularly happy, or wishes to express his enthusiasm, he produces an old musket or pistol and discharges it" (p. 137).

At Easter the Greeks burn Judas Iscariot in effigy, in a spirit that reminds Horton of the Fourth of July. "There are enough volleys fired every year at the scarecrow memory of Judas Iscariot to kill all the Turks in Constantinople" (p. 137).

Greek shepherds, who are both "picturesque and filthy," move their flocks to their summer pastures on St. George's Day, April 23. They all eat lamb before they go, the only time they do so each year—the result not of poverty but parsimony.

A doctor has to exhume a body that was knifed to death. "The knife, by the way, is the Greek's favorite weapon, and he is sure to have one concealed somewhere about his person. Don't come to fisticuffs with a Greek" (p. 148).

On traditional Greek hospitality: "After you have been in a Greek's house five minutes, some member of the family invariably appears with a glass of water and a jar of preserved orange leaves, masticha, or small bitter lemons, of which you are expected to take a teaspoonful; or a glass of water and a little pile of Turkish delight, in white and pink cubes; or a glass of water and a cup of Eastern coffee" (p. 186).

Thus writes George Horton about the modern Greeks.

He makes further fictional use of his Greek experience in *The Monk's Treasure* (1905).[16] The romance begins in Chicago where the hero, young Walter Lythgoe, works for his uncle's baking powder company. The elder Lythgoe sends his nephew to Greece to bargain for argols, the natural cream of tartar needed in their factory. Walter's headquarters in the Cyclades will be Ta Castra on the island of Andros; and his contact there is the Reverend Theophilus Ion, a missionary of Greek descent. In Athens he hears about a strange Englishman who "disappears for months at a time and they say he goes and lives among the Greeks in their little villages" (p. 9). The consul takes Walter to Ian McKenzie, who is actually a Scot. McKenzie agrees to accompany him on his searches for argols, but he reserves the right to forage for old manuscripts in various monasteries they happen to visit.

In the long, complicated, and incredible plot Walter Lythgoe becomes deeply involved with the fortunes of Polyxene, ward of the Reverend Ion and his wife. Polyxene is engaged to a man, Spiro Douzinis, whom she does not love. Walter vows to prevent the wedding even though McKenzie warns him of possible danger. Only twenty-five he responds readily to romantic impulses. The first time he hears a nightingale, he thinks: "It became a song of dreams and of mystery, the audible cry of the Greek night's passionate heart, the lyric of unseen trystings, the threnody of sweethearts of old time, the echo of forgotten Sapphics" (p. 72). Polyxene shows him "a queer old trunk, bound in leather," that had once belonged to her grandfather. McKenzie and Walter walk up to the monastery known on Andros as *Agia Brysi*, or Sacred Spring. While there the two discover a charnel house containing the bones of dead monks; and they happen to see the father superior, an old monk, retrieve from the heap of bones a bag filled with a "cataract

of shining, golden, jingling coins"—the "monk's treasure" (p. 148).
In a small hidden apartment Walter the next day finds a hoard of
silver objects each containing an armorial shield with the same
three arrows he had noticed on Polyxene's trunk.

Walter tells McKenzie about the weird discovery, and he specu-
lates: "Polyxene is descended from a baby that was mysteriously
produced by the monks of the same monastery in May of 1822.
Nobody ever knew where he came from and nobody ever has been
able to find out." Walter does find out, however. A major clue is the
same coat of arms on Polyxene's trunk and the hidden silver objects. He and McKenzie calculate the value of the gold coins as
roughly $109,000! Together they journey to Athens where they
discover the startling truth. Later Walter tells Polyxene: "The baby
who was given by the monks to the Abaltis, your grandfather, was
the heir of a noble Italian family, originally from Genoa, but settled
for hundreds of years in the island of Chios." Her great-grand-
father was Giovanni-Maria-Antonio-Ossuni, Duca di Polcavera,
sixth Marchese di Cogoleto. In true melodrama Walter Lythgoe
proclaims to her: "So I have the honor of saluting Signorina Polyxene Ossuni, Duchess of Polcavera, Marchioness of Cogoleto"
(p. 209).

Polyxene now declares she loves Walter, that nothing can come
between them. He decides to rescue the gold and the jewels from
the Greek monks. He also decides to set up shop for argols on the
island of Santorini. But as they steal the treasure for Polyxene,
Walter and McKenzie are attacked by the furious monks. In the
scuffle the monks overpower Walter and lock him in a chamber.
Later he is taken to a high room in the monastery with a lovely
view of the Aegean. Eventually he manages to escape down a
rope—only to be captured by four "tall Greeks with handkerchiefs
tied about their brows." They whisk him to a waiting catboat. "He
who sat at the helm was Spiro, and there was a smile of hellish
triumph and hate upon his face, which was as ghastly pale in the
sulphurous light as the face of a fiend" (p. 311). Polyxene had rejected him as a husband, and he had vowed to kill the American.

Hidden in Spiro's boat is McKenzie, who scatters the rascally
Greeks with an oar. As the novel nears its melodramatic end, the
Greeks turn more villainous and the Anglo-Saxons more noble.
Reference also turns more ethnic, with Walter cited as "the Ameri-
can" and Spiro, for example, as "that jealous Greek" or just "the
Greek." Walter, the knight in shining armor, has rescued the dam-

sel in distress and has uncovered her true identity—one that happily allows her to depart her lowly status as "a Greek peasant girl." Along with her new freedom come a title, duchess, and a fortune in gold and jewels; and she has in Walter Lythgoe a handsome and rich American husband.

The editor of *Athene* magazine writes in his tribute that "Horton's novels rated front page reviews at the turn of the century."[17] A critic in the same issue, C. J. Lampos, apologizes for the "popular" quality of the three novels that he examines; and he points out that the majority of Horton's books were of a much higher level than "best sellers." *Like Another Helen*, he says, created a sensation when it appeared in 1900.[18] The romances that now seem too melodramatic and jejune were indeed the popular reading of the day; and what distinguishes Horton, besides his use of Greek characters, is that in at least one case, *The Tempting of Father Anthony*, he transcends the usual fare and produces a piece of genuine literature. He works at nearly the same level of excellence in *In Argolis* and other writings that introduce the customs and mores of the modern Greeks to the American public. The bulk of Horton's "Greek books" appeared at a propitious moment—when the first great wave of Greek immigrants reached Ellis Island and spread throughout the land.

The name of Demetra Vaka looms large in the history of Greek-American letters. Of Greek descent she belongs to that class of refined Anatolian Greeks who prospered in Turkey despite the latent and ever-explosive animosity. Her autobiography indicates that her family shared all the perquisites of the European aristocracy. Owing to political unrest in Turkey, a fact that always meant trouble for both Greeks and Armenians, her family had to leave. Demetra Vaka arrived in the United States at eighteen, added English to her seven European languages, married Kenneth Brown, and spent a busy life writing, traveling, meeting important people, and helping worthy causes including the Greek war relief during World War II. She wrote more than fifteen books, three of them with her husband and one, *Modern Greek Stories* (1920), with the Harvard scholar Aristides E. Phoutrides. Brought up in Turkey, yet educated on the continent, Demetra Vaka knew both East and West as well as America. Her special field was the Levant, where many old and mysterious cultures blended. Both her first and her last published books are novels. She and her husband joined in writing *The First Secretary* (1907). Her last novel, *Bribed to Be Born*, was written much earlier than its publication date, 1951. The autobiography which she left behind, *A Heart for Any Faith*, also appeared posthumously. It was serialized in several issues of *Athene* magazine soon after she died. The work unfortunately has not appeared in book form.

Throughout her career Vaka by example and precept fought for women's rights. In her first prose work, *Haremlik* (1909), she unveils the deplorable status of Turkish women under the old dispensation, before Kemal Ataturk's revolution began to move the nation forward. There followed a stream of books by Vaka most of which helped to explain the Near East to the West. Some unabashedly expressed her political views. The books include *The Duke's Price* (1910), with Brown; *Finella in Fairy-Land* (1910); *In the Shadow of Islam* (1911); *A Child of the Orient* (1914); *Harem* (1915); *The Grasp of the Sultan* (1916); *The Heart of the Balkans* (1917); *Constantine, King and Traitor* (1918); *In the Heart of German Intrigue* (1918); *In Pawn to a Throne* (1919), with Brown; *The Unveiled Ladies of Stamboul* (1923); and a delightful novel, *Delarah* (1943). Her last work to appear before she died made an eloquent plea for love between the Greeks and the Turks. The titles indicate the range and nature of her interests.

Demetra Vaka's early novel, *The First Secretary*, follows the familiar pattern of having a young American go to Greece where he has adventures.[19] Horton drew his heroes from Boston and Chicago; Vaka draws hers from Detroit. The exotic Levant provides mystery, danger, and love for Stephen Weir, newly assigned in the diplomatic service. He has arrived in Constantinople to be the first secretary in the American embassy. Riding toward the mosque to watch the sultan at his prayers, Stephen notices a Turkish girl with beautiful eyes, wearing the flimsy veil, the *yashmak*. To his surprise she shows him a card on which is written, "I want you to help me" (p. 7). His imagination fired, he must learn who the distressed damsel is, what her problem, and how to aid her—a mission made very difficult by the almost impenetrable social wall behind which Turkish women live.

The girl needing help is Rhasneh, daughter of Takshan Pasha; and she wants to avoid marriage with Haleb Bey, son of Osman Pasha These are Turks of the highest class, who are wealthy and close to the sultan. Rhasneh, having a Christian mother, a liberal father, and Greek friends, enjoys books and a broader outlook than is usual. To learn the identity of the tall handsome stranger,

Rhasneh visits her esteemed Greek friend, Chrysanthy Mavrocor-
thato. Chrysanthy is "a dreamer, a reformer—synonymous terms
in Turkey. She held views on women's rights and equality in a land
where the subject belonged to the far-off interstellar spaces. And
she had a youth's disbelief in what her world had found wise and
proper" (p. 38). Chrysanthy knows of Stephen Weir, the first secretary, and arranges for Rhasneh to have a secret glimpse of him
at a garden party the next night.

Chrysanthy now shocks everyone by eloping with Mr. Staso-
poulo, a teacher. For love she marries beneath her class; and her
father promptly disowns her—which means she has no dowry.
Thus both the Greek and the Turkish girl face parallel problems
with their parents on the issue of marriage. The depth of Rhasneh's feeling is shown by her open defiance of her father, Takshan
Pasha. "Haleb Bey may hold my cold corpse in his arms," she cries,
"but my warm body—never!" (p. 85). By showering gifts upon the
family, the sultan himself will soon demand the lovely Rhasneh for
his royal harem. A quick marriage with Haleb Bey would save her
from this dreadful fate, but Weir is desperately trying to save her
from Haleb Bey. After many tribulations he fulfills the require-
ments of his role as the romantic hero. He receives much help
from the Greek characters, especially from Chrysanthy's little sister
Xeny.

Xeny, a masterful conspirator of fourteen, matures a great deal
as they go from one crisis to another. She comes to understand, in
talking with Rhasneh, that her sister Chrysanthy can be happy with
the man she loves, even though he is not rich. She learns about
goodness in people from Stephen Weir, who promises to take
Chrysanthy and her husband to America and establish them. Xeny
seems immune from the potentially fatal dilemmas that beset her
elders.

When these dilemmas are most knotted, the Mavrocorthatos
have lost a daughter, Chrysanthy, whom they now want back. Stephen Weir languishes in a Turkish jail for disturbing the peace and
striking an officer. Rhasneh has disappeared. And her father, Takshan Pasha, may at any moment be killed by the sultan. By working
together, these Greeks and Turks succeed in escaping their powerful enemies. The Mavrocorthatos bribe the guards, who then release Stephen Weir. Dressed as a woman, Takshan Pasha hides in
the Greek villa. Xeny leads her parents and Stephen to the secret
domicile of Chrysanthy who is now restored to the family's good

graces. Stephen and Rhasneh are finally reunited. Through various other ruses to elude danger, the principals prepare to leave for the United States on Weir's yacht. Chrysanthy has a large dowry, Takshan Pasha a box of bonds, Rhasnah a bag of jewels, and Stephen Weir, the first secretary, has the beautiful Rhasneh.

The action of Demetra Vaka's last novel, *Bribed to Be Born*, occurs before the turn of the century and contains much that helps to define Greek ethnicity from a positive viewpoint.[20] The setting is Constantinople, three days after the coronation of Sultan Abdul Hamid II. Madame Zoë, a great rich lady of Phanar, visits the wife of her nephew—Madame Notaras—a beautiful, liberated blonde girl filled with Parisian notions. After four years of marriage the couple have no children, for Madame Notaras does not wish to jeopardize her figure. Without a son the Notaras line will die. Madame Zoë's mission is to bribe the contrary young wife into bearing children.

Her nephew is "a Byzantine Greek of long lineage," but his wife violates all the canons of Greek etiquette. Madame Zoë bitterly opposed the marriage. Madame Notaras ignores Greek aristocratic manners. Her drawingroom is entirely French, not Greek, and in disarray. "It might be the room of a French courtesan," Madame Zoë sniffs contemptuously" (p. 11). The beautiful girl enters late without apology, dressed in the latest French style; and, instead of kissing the proffered hand, merely shakes it. Madame Zoë comes only from a sense of duty. Insolent to her elder, Madame Notaras says, "Over in Phanar you are not even aware that you are living in the last quarter of the nineteenth century" (p. 12).

Madame Zoë threatens to disinherit her nephew if he remains without issue. This ultimatum greatly shocks Madame Notaras. She comes from an excellent Greek family, though one not of ancient, famous, or aristocratic name. After uttering the dire and cruel threat, Madame Zoë tempts her with a number of rich bribes. "A string of matched Indian pearls would well become your throat," she says softly. "I will give you one that your husband could not possibly afford, at the birth of your first child." At the birth of her second child, Madame Zoë will buy her a new house. If love cannot bridge the gap between them, "little children may." Madame Notaras keenly envies the wealth of her aunt-in-law, and hopes that this wealth would soon be hers. Her mission accomplished, Madame Zoë leaves in a plush sedan chair carried by four strong Anatolian bearers. On the journey home to Phanar, a violent street brawl erupts; but Madame Zoë manages to escape with jewels and skin intact by changing her appearance to that of a poorer woman and ducking into an Armenian shop. On the way again, she smiles as she imagines "the little boy whose mother had been bribed to have him," to carry on "the proud name of Notaras" (p. 17).

The second chapter opens twelve years later. The little *girl*, not boy, bribed to be born, is arriving to stay with Madame Zoë because smallpox ravages Pera, the district chosen for residence by her mother. The child is neglected: her father is often absent in the diplomatic service, while Madame Notaras concentrates on social pleasures. The child arrives with her mind poisoned against Madame Zoë, but she soon learns that here she can ask questions, be instructed, attend company, read books, and be loved. Thus *Bribed to Be Born* deals essentially with a young Greek girl's awakening to a fuller potential. In Demetra Vaka's novel *Delarah* (1943) a Turkish girl undergoes an even more thorough self-realization.[21] For the Greek girl the problem is a vapid, selfish, bitchy mother; for the Turkish, the strong taboo against education of women. Both girls win out.

In the elegant mansion of Madame Zoë the little Miss Notaras blossoms both physically and mentally. The four servants of the house are at her disposal. She can talk, read, argue, and eat all she wants. Against her mother's wishes she has brought along "a battered child's *Iliad*." Madame Zoë is greatly pleased with her. "You are a Notaras, my great-niece," she says. Her hand tightens on that of the girl "whose very existence was the result of her bribery."[22]

When the archbishop of Chalcydon calls, Madame Zoë explains how the child came to be a guest. Her father, Pantelis, brought her because of the smallpox epidemic. Having lived beyond his income, Pantelis had to leave the diplomatic service. He had come to Madame Zoë at fifteen, orphaned; and now he brings his daughter—after eleven years "shrouded in silence." Not that Madame Zoë minds. She loves the child, who in turn regards her as "most wonderful."

A sudden storm erupts that keeps Madame Zoë occupied for days—one of those great "Russian storms" that sweep down from the Black Sea. The occasion demands that she exercise a lot of noblesse oblige. As the saying goes, *enthemou tous ptochous!*—"Remember the poor!" (p. 36). Even little Miss Notaras gathers her toys and clothes to give the needy. Those poor Greeks whom Madame Zoë visits call her *koumbara*.

> When Madame Zoë was young, it had been the custom for the rich Greeks in Turkey to stand as godfathers and godmothers to the children of the poor of their quarter. That made rich and poor *koumbaroi*, spiritually related. It gave the rich the right to come to the homes of the poor, inquire into their welfare and help them, without hurting their self-respect. (p. 37)

The common fear and suffering under the Turkish yoke brings rich and poor Greeks together. After their mission of mercy Madame Zoë and the child return home, thank the Lord at the *ikonostase*, the family shrine, and eat hot soup in the sitting room. (The author explains that the votive light is extinguished on Black Friday and relighted on Easter night.)

For four days the storm continues. The archbishop summons all the rich Greeks together and asks for contributions. Madame Zoë donates her "other large house" on condition that it be equipped as a modern school. The grand lady of Phanar and the child talk. Madame Zoë had once told Disraeli that things would have been better for the subject peoples of the Turks had the British taken Constantinople during the Crimean War. She cautions the child not to dislike the Jews, for they also have been persecuted. "Look at us Greeks, here in Turkey," she says. "We have to bribe and lie to exist, and it has brought out the meanest traits in our nature" (p. 46). Madame Zoë also tells her grand-niece: "Your father belongs to the pro-English party. We of Phanar are pro-Russian" (p. 46). She gives the historical reasons for choosing the Russians. Centuries ago "we Greeks Christianized Russia," and "eventually the Greek race will superimpose itself upon Russia, as it did upon the Latin empire created here by Constantine the Great" (p. 49). The English, on the other hand, would reduce the Greeks and others to the status of "natives."

The Greeks inside Turkey proper, Madame Zoë recalls, fared badly when the mainland Greeks revolted in 1821. She wants the girl to realize why the Turks are hated.

> The Patriarch and all the members of the Holy Synod were hanged, and left to rot upon the gallows, to drive fear into our hearts, so that we should not rise here also. Wealthy men were

killed daily, their possessions confiscated, their children sold into slavery. We lived in such fear that many women went mad. Thousands and thousands of Greeks were brought here from the islands and sold in the slave market, openly, and not a foreign ambassador protested. (p. 58)

Consequently, Greeks inside Turkey and abroad formed a secret society to help the enslaved. Of the great powers only Russia sympathized with the Greeks. Suddenly hundreds of Russians begin returning to Russia, each with passports calling for four or five children. "Those were Greek children bought in the slave markets" (p. 58). Greeks in Austria, England, and France engaged gypsies to go to Constantinople. "Turks did not suspect them, and failed to notice that whereas the caravans arrived with five or six members, they left with twenty or thirty. Those were Greeks, either escaping, or bought in the slave market." Madame Zoë describes how she and her brother also escaped as gypsies, going through the Balkans to Vienna, and what she saw of cruelty convinced her that "God had nothing to do with the making of a Turk" (p. 59).

Now Madame Zoë helps fugitive Greeks escape to freedom. A refugee enters their house, and departs with them disguised as Stephen the butler. They drive to "a small Greek shop specializing in Turkish dishes," which the refugee enters for some *taouk-oksou*, a dessert. The *real* Stephen emerges with the purchase; and when the bright-eyed child notices the exchange, Madame Zoë cautions, "Hush! He is going on a Greek ship tonight, and tomorrow will be out of the power of the Turk" (p. 62). Madame Zoë, the grand lady of Phanar, acts like a true and proud Phanariote who keeps Hellenism alive in the midst of its worst enemies. She also looks ahead to inevitable social changes, and defends a lady of Phanar whom others scorn for stooping to work in her husband's shop.

Toward the end of *Bribed to Be Born* the question arises as to where Miss Notaras will live permanently. Rather than provide a stable home, Madame Notaras prefers going off to the Riviera, Baden-Baden, and Paris to enjoy her fashionable friends. Much to Madame Zoë's joy, the child's father Pantelis decides that she should stay with her grand-aunt, who truly loves her. At the ikons Madame Zoë thanks the Lord for His gift "to an old, lonely woman" (p. 95).

In a memorial article, "Demetra Vaka," Kenneth Brown sums up her essential qualities and declares happy their relationship of forty-four years. He stresses what her literary achievements already proved, that she was an extraordinary person both as artist and thinker. Some of her fiction deserves to be revaluated as contributions both to the growth of understanding between Near East and West and to the increased liberation of women everywhere. With respect to understanding, Brown quotes from a story in the *Delineator*:

> She [Vaka] continually urges that the future of civilization must depend on justice being done to all the nations, large and small, friend and foe. And she believes that justice can only be meted out if we learn to understand the conditions existing in other countries, if we learn to love the good qualities of other races, alien though they may be in habits and religion.[23]

For the Greek-American community Demetra Vaka still remains, after more than three decades, the First Lady of Letters.

The Greek ethnicity abundant in Horton and Vaka thins out to practically nothing in Jack London, one of the earliest authors to bring the new immigrants into American literature. Writers who once sailed the seas, like London and O'Neill, tend to use ethnic types (as are naturally found on board ship) in order to universalize their themes. To judge by London's fiction, the gold rush of the late 1890s lured most of the nationalities, including Greeks, to Alaska. The Russians, of course, had been there for generations; as everyone knows, they sold us Alaska in 1867. What is not so well known is that the first Russian governor of Alaska, Eustratios Delarof, was of Greek descent.[24] In the title story of *The God of His Fathers* (1901), London makes a reference to Greeks in the Arctic when he has a cynical blasphemer, Hay Stockard, tell the missionary Sturges Owen to leave before being killed by Baptiste the Red. "If you go down-stream," Stockard says, "you'll fall in with the Russians. There's bound to be Greek priests among them, and they'll see you safe through to Bering Sea,—that's where the Yukon empties—and from there it won't be hard to get back to civilization."[25] One cannot know from what London writes if the priests are truly Greek or whether they merely represent the Orthodox church.

The author is less ambiguous in another story from the same volume. "The Scorn of Women" has a Greek dancer, Freda Maloof, who plays a leading role in preventing a man from unjustly treating another woman.[26] Her name, a mixture of Nordic and Arabic, might reflect a certain alienation from the Greek community where such a character might originate. If indeed Jack London had a prototype for Freda Maloof, she could have journeyed north to the Klondike from San Francisco. The author had Greek friends there. Or she might have been brought to Dawson by another Greek, Alexander Pantages, later to flourish as a theater tycoon.

Pantages, too, had been in San Francisco where he first acquired some experience with the world of entertainment. For a while he worked in a beer garden. He also became a theater utility-man, then briefly a prize fighter. When gold was struck in the Klondike, Pantages rushed north to seek a quick fortune. That he might have imported dancing girls like Freda Maloof is suggested by what the historian Theodore Saloutos records in *The Greeks in the United States.*

Two things happened in Dawson that were to influence the career of Pantages. He met 'Klondike Kate' Rockwell, and he began to act upon the idea that man will pay cash for entertainment. He had the idea, and the woman had the money. He and two associates bought an amusement place, where he demonstrated his adroitness as a purveyor of entertainment. The miners gladly paid $12.50 a seat for his shows.[27]

Whether or not Freda Maloof had a real prototype, she emerges as a very sympathetic character in "The Scorn of Women." She uses her power to save a girl named Flossie from being jilted by a rich oaf, Floyd Vanderlip. Freda rules in the town while Mrs. Eppingwell, a captain's wife, rules among the select society that attends such functions as the governor's ball. These two strong women from opposite social worlds clash. Of Freda's nationality London expresses some initial doubt; then he accepts her affirmation. "Now Freda was a Greek girl and a dancer. At least she purported to be Greek; but this was doubted by many, for her classic face had over-much strength in it, and the tides of hell which rose in her eyes made at rare moments her ethnology the more dubious."[28] Very soon, however, he accepts the fact of her Greekness. "She never talked of herself, so that it were well to let it go down that when in repose, expurgated, Greek she certainly was" (p. 252).

The arrival in Dawson of a Hungarian "model-woman," Loraine Lisznayi, creates the problem that Freda helps to solve. Loraine offers herself to Vanderlip, a bonanza king with a rich Klondike claim, and he accepts. He has also sent to the states for his girl

Flossie, now on her way to meet him. Dawson buzzes with the scandal. When Freda hears about Floyd's betrayal, she unleashes all her great charm upon him to keep him out of Loraine's clutches until Flossie arrives. Mrs. Eppingwell hears of the betrayal and mistakenly thinks that Freda Maloof is the temptress, not Loraine Lisznayi. After much complication the story ends happily. Flossie arrives, and Floyd gets her, his true love. At the end the society matron, Mrs. Eppingwell, publicly shakes the Greek dancer's hand.

Jack London used another Greek character in *The Mutiny of the Elsinore* (1914).[29] Just as the gold rush attracted ethnic types from the world over, so on a smaller scale does the ocean-going vessel with its motley crew. "This *Elsinore* is truly the ship of souls, the world in miniature; and, because she is such a small world, cleaving this vastitude of ocean as our larger world cleaves space, the strange juxtapositions that continually occur are startling" (p. 164). He peoples the *Elsinore* with a gallery of kooks. "While it might be true . . . that every ship's crew contained several lunatics and idiots, it was a foregone conclusion that our crew contained far more than several" (p. 39). London throughout the novel thinks in terms of Anglo-Saxon, Jew, Maltese, cockney, Italian, Finn, Chinese, and so on. Tony the Greek is usually referred to as "the suicidal Greek." The narrator first hears of him as the "man overboard" who jumped with the intention of getting drowned. When first seen, Tony is swimming *away* from the ship. He is finally rescued and hoisted over the rail of the *Elsinore*. "He was stark naked, covered with blood, and raving. He had cut and slashed himself in a score of places. From one wound in the wrist the blood spurted with each beat of the pulse. He was a loathsome, non-human thing. I have seen a scared orang in a zoo, and for all the world this bestial-faced, mowing, gibbering thing reminded me of the orang" (p. 22). Here the Greek character acts like an animal, a mad ape, on a ship of fools heading for a ludicrous and bloody mutiny. The mutiny is settled by the least likely hero, the narrator, who also falls in love with Margaret West, the captain's daughter.

Tony's job on the *Elsinore* indicates the general folly aboard. When well again, he returns to his post at the tiller! Tony's only other big scene, a second attempt to drown himself, gives London another chance to highlight his bestiality. The problem of finding Tony this second time differs because the *Elsinore* is far out to sea and must turn around. The ship makes this special move to rescue the "crazy Greek" because they are shorthanded. "We can't afford to lose him even if he is crazy," the second mate explains. "He's a good sailor most of the time" (p. 125). This one and only positive value judgment does not deter London from stressing the utter weirdness of Tony as a character.

The narrator describes the efforts to retrieve the mad sailor.

> As we drew close to the Greek he began to scream menacingly at us and to brandish a sheath-knife. His weight sank the ladder until the water washed his knees, and on this submerged support he balanced himself with wild writhing and outflinging of arms. His face, grimacing like a monkey's, was not a pretty thing to look upon. And, as he continued to threaten us with the knife, I wondered how the problem of rescuing him would be solved. (p. 126)

The solution involves violence. The first mate hits the Greek on the head with a boat-stretcher. "The knife fell into the sea," London writes, "and the demented creature collapsed and followed it, knocked unconscious" (p. 127). Later Tony hooks a shark, which he cannot land, and he joins the mutiny in which he plays no significant role. His behavior merely swells a lunatic progress on a voyage where fate turns on folly, men die stupidly, and romantic love triumphs.

The first American novel that deals directly with the Greek as immigrant is Jeannette Lee's *Mr. Achilles* (1912).[30] The book offers the reader more actual Greek ethnicity than anything Jack London wrote. Lee's hero, Achilles Alexandrakis, is also the first Greek protagonist in American literature—that is, from among the immigrants. He owns a fruit stall on Clark Street, in Chicago. He works with his two sons, Alcibiades and Yaxis, who sell from pushcarts. For six months he has been living in the city and not once has anyone asked him about his beloved Athens. As a result, every day Chicago with its gray soot becomes drearier for Achilles. He feels that the Americans might talk with him if they knew that he comes from Athens; therefore he puts up a sign in Greek characters, and his stand becomes known as the Greek Shop. Still nobody asks him about the Parthenon, the Acropolis, Athens. Achilles happens to catch a caterpillar which he puts into a little box, marks it in Greek, *petalouda*, and plans to wait for it to become a butterfly.

The scene in the novel shifts to Betty Harris, twelve-year-old daughter of a packinghouse millionaire. Her music lesson has been cancelled. Walking home to Lake Shore Drive, she dawdles here and there before pausing at Achilles's fruit stall. He gives her a box of pomegranates, and they talk of things Greek. She recognizes the Greek letters on the caterpillar box. "He was a Greek man," she thinks (p. 17). Finally Betty Harris, a child, asks him about the Parthenon! Achilles responds so lyrically that the child henceforth has a passion to learn all she can about Greece. While she is still there, the caterpillar blossoms into a butterfly. Achilles lets Betty release it. Her carriage shows up, finds her, and takes her home. A new joy, and a new interest in Chicago, arouses Achilles because of his encounter with the child.

At home Betty Harris tells her mother about the "marvelous Greek" named Achilles Alexandrakis, his gift of pomegranates, and his "strange tales of Greece and Athens and the Parthenon—tales at the very mention of which her eyes danced and her voice rippled" (p. 32). She had left her music roll in the fruit shop. On its strap Achilles finds the girl's name and address, and he determines to return it soon. At the Harris home the child has created a revival in Hellenism by her avid interest. An instructor from the University of Chicago is hired, and he is so impressed by Betty that his professor also comes—and decides on the spot to spend the next year in Greece.

In a week Achilles Alexandrakis readies his visit to the elegant Harris address on Lake Shore Drive—a Greek immigrant among Chicago's social elite. "The Greek" asks for Betty Harris, and for some time the fruit peddler and the child talk, absorbed in Greek civilization. On that day the Halcyon Club is meeting at the Harris residence; but the speaker, Professor Addison Trent, is on a steamer headed for Europe. He was to have lectured on the inscriptions of Cnossos, in Crete. Now, to take the professor's place, Mrs. Harris invites Achilles Alexandrakis to speak to the club "on the traditions and customs of modern Greek life" (p. 63). Gladly consenting, Achilles enthralls the audience of bluebloods with his speech—about the glory of Athens, and the Greek people, an image more classical and pastoral than actual and modern. Afterward he receives a check, much to his surprise and shock; he cannot accept money for speaking about Greece, his country.

The main crisis erupts when kidnappers take Betty Harris and hold her for ransom. They do so near Achilles' fruit stand. The car used by them smashes a pushcart and runs down Alcibiades. Achilles vows to find Betty Harris and bring the kidnappers to justice. For many days, after an operation, Alcibiades cannot remember anything; he nearly dies. Only he has any clue that might lead to a solution. The tragedy brings together the Greek immigrant and the American millionaire. The rich Mr. Harris keeps a vigil at the bedside of Alcibiades, reading to him and otherwise helping him to recover. The author keeps referring to "the Greek" rather than using his name, perhaps to emphasize the contrast between him and the powerful Harris. In the intense search for the lost Betty, Achilles Alexandrakis is to have the decisive role. The press throughout America tells of "how Betty had sat in the gay little fruit-shop—and listened to Achilles' stories of Athens and Greece, and of the Acropolis."

The kidnappers give Philip Harris three months in which to pay the huge sum demanded. Seven weeks pass, and still Alcibiades has been unable to speak. Harris is willing to pay, but his new Greek friend, Achilles, prevails with him to refuse—to discourage all potential kidnappers. Finally Alcibiades recovers and remembers everything. Yes, he can recognize the kidnappers; and he knows the direction that their car had taken. All by himself the sane, shrewd, and reserved Achilles pursues his plan to find and rescue Betty Harris. The solution nears when Alcibiades spots the two kidnappers in a car. Quickly Achilles grabs a customer's automobile and follows the culprits without their suspecting. They lead him out into the country and a lonely little house. Finding Betty is one thing, but rescuing and returning her home is another. Resourceful as Odysseus, Achilles succeeds.

The first Greek immigrant to be a character in an adaptation of a classical myth is to be found in "Orpheus, who Made Music in Our Square," in Samuel Hopkins Adams's *Our Square and the People in It* (1917).[31] The "Orpheus" of the tale is a cultivated young Greek named Philipopoulos living in New York. Every midnight he appears at the same spot on the square and plays a flute. He plays *La Bohême*. "Orpheus" had met Toinette, a French girl, in a Spanish class and had fallen in love with her, his "Eurydice." Four months earlier an intern at the hospital told him that she, a heart patient, had died. Now in his Hades of grief, the Greek plays in her memory as he had previously done when she could hear him from her hospital bed. Later "Orpheus" discovers that the intern had made a mistake, that another patient and not Toinette had died. Happily, at the end, the two lovers meet again.

American literature since 1917 has amply recorded where the Greeks settled, what they aspired for and how they worked, how they adapted to circumstance, and how they succeeded or failed. The urban "Greek Towns" formed one of the three main areas of Greek-American distribution; the other two were New England and the West. At first few went South except for the spongers of Tarpon Springs, Florida. The fiction about the Greeks reflects their geographic distribution. It also reveals how these Greeks imported the Greek political, religious, and other current dissensions. From the 1920s on was added the new battle, led by rival fraternal orders, over the crucial issue of Americanization.[32] To what extent, for example, should the Greek children now growing up in the *xenitya*, the foreign land, be or not be compelled to remain Greek—in speech, religion, customs, loyalty, and domestic habits? In some novels and short stories these nagging internal conflicts were to become important sources of plot, characterization, and theme.

3

THE GREEK AS IMMIGRANT

THE GREEK IMMIGRANTS had barely lighted their votive candles in praise of their *Panaghia* for a safe voyage when they were closely scrutinized by hostile and friendly American social scientists. What the Greeks thought of their new home, on the other hand, still had no currency outside the coffeehouses and the press that served Greek Town—papers like the *National Herald* and the *Atlantis*. In time the writers among the Greek immigrants, ethnic pioneers such as Demetrios Callimachos, began through their books to solidify a Greek-American identity and to express attitudes toward the broader society. One of these authors, Seraphim G. Canoutas, eventually came to write *Christopher Columbus: A Greek Nobleman* (1943), in which he laid dubious claim to a Greek discovery of the New World.[1]

Credit for the first "scientific" study of the new ethnic influx goes to Henry Pratt Fairchild for *Greek Immigration to the United States* (1911).[2] His report is generally negative, based on the "fact" that a people can lose their culture but retain their inferior racial traits. The Greek-American historian Theodore Saloutos writes that Fairchild

chose to emphasize the worst features; his general thesis seemed to be that the Greeks were a hopelessly degenerate people who were likely to become the dregs of American Society. He had no knowledge of the Greek language and consequently was unable to use Greek sources; he failed to give any serious attention to the cultural impact of those arriving from "the unredeemed lands," and the contemporary character of his study denied him historical perspective. As was common among writers of the day, Fairchild brought the immigrants through Ellis Island, emphasized their poverty, drew some unfavorable comparisons with the older immigrant stocks, and concluded that they were a far cry from the earlier arrivals in terms of physical qualities, intelligence, and capabilities.[3]

Another American author, Thomas Burgess, was far more sympathetic in a study, *Greeks in America*, that followed Fairchild's by only two years, in 1913; and only one year later Lucy M. J. Garnett published *Greece and the Hellenes*, a book of value in explaining the modern Greeks to an American audience. Of the Burgess volume Saloutos says, "His sources of information were the Greeks themselves, the rank and file as well as the leading members of the larger communities, and secondary works."[4] Burgess saw promise in the Greeks whereas Fairchild had found none.

In time, of course, Greek-American writers began to record both their personal and the collective experience of their *ethnos* in the United States. The best known work of Demetrios A. Michalaros, for example, is *Sonnets of an Immigrant* (1930).[5] For this collection of poems his friend and mentor, Jane Addams of Hull House, wrote the foreword. Michalaros was prominent in the Greek-American community of Chicago as poet, editor, dramatist, and television personality. For many years he conducted a weekly television program, *Greek Panorama*. From 1940 until his death in 1967 Michalaros edited *Athene* magazine, now the most valuable single repository of Greek-Americana for future scholars to consult. Among the honors that he received were a plaque of appreciation from the king of Greece and an award from the Friends of Literature.

Michalaros is one of several Anatolian Greeks who won prominence as writers here; the most famous of the group is the film director and novelist Elia Kazan. "In Old Ionia" by Michalaros eulogizes his hometown of Alachata on the westernmost coast of Asia Minor. The first section of fifteen sonnets deals with the poet's childhood in Ionia. "Wanderlust" describes an episode that contributed to his eventual departure.

> A passenger ship that anchored by the bay
> Intrigued our restless hearts with stories gay
> About a land beyond the Yankee sea. (p. 37)

They are "eager boys" who will obey "adventure's thrilling command" to voyage to "the promised land." When they go, the village gathers to see them leave "the sun-mellowed azure bay."

To say that the sonnets strongly reflect the romance of the odyssey is not to say they misrepresent the degree of excitement it generated. To be a youth, Greek or otherwise, voyaging to the New World must certainly have been a tonic brewed by the gods that helped the immigrants bear the crowded steerage, the rotten food, the diseases, the exploitation, the loneliness, and all their other problems. The sonnets of Michalaros exhibit the expected intoxication: he is thrilled "that foggy dawn" when his ship reaches New York. At Ellis Island a "mighty door of new hope swings ajar" for him, in this "motherland of the free" (p. 41). In Maine, where he lives for a while, he learns Yankee thrift and Yankee lore. Then Michalaros goes to "dear, dear Boston where learning is old / And kindness sprouts unchoked and free" (p. 68). Finally he settles for good in Chicago.

> Chicago! beloved harbor of my hopes
> Most American of cities and most fair,
> Queen of the Lakes, the corn-thriving slopes. (p. 53)
> .   .   .   .
> Chicago, seat of the Builder's throne;
> Breeder of the ultra-modern man. (p. 54)

In her foreword to *Sonnets of an Immigrant* Jane Addams compares Michalaros with Jacob Riis, Mary Anton, and Michael Pupin, who also left records of their arrival and subsequent adjustment. He too shows "the early sense of division which at last becomes the triumphant synthesis" (p. vii). Unlike the writings of other immigrants, however, Michalaros describes none of the stresses and strains of the adjustment. Never lonely, never sad, never maligned, never defeated, he allows no backward glance toward Greece to sully his extraordinary delight in America, the country of his dreams. His sonnets express an ecstatic, romantic, and thoroughly uncritical acceptance of the myth of limitless opportunity. The poem "I Am the Immigrant" also gives some well-deserved praise to the immigrant as the builder of America—he who lifts mountains with his bare hands, digs canals, masses the bricks, and runs the machines. As I build, Michalaros writes, each rivet strengthens the "sinews of my guild" and feeds "the blood corpuscles of my Promethean soul" (p. xv).

The novel by a Greek-American that best dramatizes the exceptional lure of the United States is Elia Kazan's *America America* (1962).[6] In it the author details the grim trials and perils of an Anatolian Greek boy who desperately wants to migrate here. Kazan directed five Pulitzer Prize plays, including *Death of a Salesman* and *A Streetcar Named Desire*, and two Academy Award-winning films, *Gentleman's Agreement* and *On the Waterfront*. His first novel was originally conceived as a dramatic work entitled "Hamal," a term that means *porter* in Turkish. The final published version shows many traces of Kazan's original intention: descriptions that read like stage directions, dialogue set up as in a play, spare sentence fragments, ironic twists and turns that often undercut joy with sorrow.

America America has the richly-detailed ethnicity that is usually denied non-Greek writers who use Greek characters. Kazan's own background is Anatolia (Asiatic Turkey), and he naturally has authentic access to his own ethnic experience. The story he tells begins in 1896. His hero, Stavros Topouzoglou, gathers ice on a mountain near his village of Germeer. He is twenty. Helping him to load a wagon is Vartan Damadian, an Armenian eight years his senior. This passage explains how the two young men are bonded together. *"Once long ago, Anatolia was a part of the Byzantine Empire, inhabited by the Greek and Armenian people of that time. In 1381 this land was conquered by the Turks, and since that day the Greeks and Armenians have lived here as minorities, subject to their Mohammedan conquerors"* (p. 20).

After loading their ice wagon, Stavros and Vartan descend to the village. On the way down they talk about going to America—but first they must sell the ice. The Turks are celebrating the holiday of Bayram, when lambs are slaughtered and portions of them are given to the poor. No such bounty awaits the two friends: the Turks are preparing a massacre of the Armenians because "Armenian fanatics have dared to set fire to the National Turkish Bank in Constantinople" (p. 22). Despite the impending terror, Stavros and Vartan sell their ice on the streets of Germeer.

Vartan will not go to the church where the terrified Armenians have gathered. Instead he goes to the Guitars, a cabaret, saying bitterly: "I will drink with my murderers" (p. 32). Stavros is hustled home by his frantic mother, but he later sneaks out to join Vartan at the Guitars. During their dance Stavros for the first time whispers "America America!" Suddenly the music stops. The two friends run toward the Armenian church which the Turks later set on fire with people trapped inside. In the killing that follows Vartan is shot, and Stavros dares to sit beside his body.

The Greek boy's father, Isaac, must pay the Turkish Wali, a huge bribe to save his son from imprisonment. Stavros leaves to visit his grandmother. From her he gets only a dagger, not the money he needs to reach Constantinople. On the way back Stavros is over-

taken by Hohanness Gardashian, a gaunt tubercular youth consumed by a haunting mania to go to America. Stavros gives him
his shoes. At home his father announces that Stavros will be the
first Topouzoglou to remove to Constantinople, the rest to follow.
A cousin has written: "Let Stavros bring me money to put in my
business and I'll make him my partner" (p. 55). From one corner
of their cellar they dig up their family jewel box. Stavros must also
carry and sell in Constantinople all their smoked meat, two rugs,
and their donkey. Once settled, he must bring his three sisters and
see that they are married well; then his four brothers and set them
up in business; then his mother, to make her final days happy. Both
the money and the jewels are sewn in Stavros's coat. Leading the
heavily laden donkey, having said his farewells, Stavros begins his
long and perilous journey.

The road to Ankara, as Abdul the friendly thief himself says, "is
the home of every mother-selling bandit bastard in Turkey." Stavros enlists Abdul's aid in catching a ferryman who had demanded
money on pain of tipping the boat over during the crossing. The
aid given by Abdul is to win Stavros's confidence so that he will
become easier prey for the *hidden* wealth he carries. At an inn Abdul angers Stavros by consorting with two prostitutes. The Turk
promptly knocks him out and tries to give away some of his possessions. Next day Stavros and his donkey Goochook walk toward
Ankara feeling freed of his enemy; but in the town of Soosehir
trouble awaits. The police arrest Stavros; and there stands Abdul,
accusing him of robbery. Since the accuser can accurately describe
each article, the judge rules in his favor. Before giving up his coat,
Stavros swallows some of the coins from the lining. A while later,
on the road to Ankara again, Abdul riding Goochook at a trot
catches up with Stavros and demands the six coins he had seen the
boy swallow. Earlier he had said about the Greeks: "You have
learned how to bear misfortune, swallow insult and indignity, and
still smile. I envy you" (p. 81). Abdul has misread the boy's will.
While Abdul kneels on his prayer rug, Stavros leaps upon his back
and drives his dagger home again and again. "Something is beginning to toughen in the boy," Kazan writes. "He bends over and
goes through the dead man's pockets. He takes his jewels and all
the money he can find, straightens, looks at the coins in his hand"
(p. 83). This will never happen to him again. Stavros reaches Ankara, finds the railroad station, and buys a ticket to Constantinople.

At the harbor in Constantinople he sees a ship flying the American flag. "America, America!" he shouts. He fights for the work of a *hamal*, a porter or stevedore, and he wins. Contrary to expectations, the Topouzoglou Persian Carpet Company owned by their cousin is a dark and dead establishment. The cousin excuses his failure: "You see I have the wrong goods for the market as it is today" (p. 90). He expects Stavros to go to Persia and buy new rugs, but Stavros says he has no money. "I was a fool and I was robbed" (p. 91). The cousin is furious. He wants to send Stavros away, but decides he might arrange a profitable marriage with a daughter of the rich rug merchant Aleko Sinyosoglou. Stavros leaves, goes to the North German Lloyd Line, and finds that it costs 108 Turkish pounds for third-class fare to America. He lies to his parents, says he did not lose the money (contrary to the cousin's letter), and writes that he has a big plan.

The plan, of course, is to work as a *hamal* and save enough for his passage to America. He works with Garabet in a warehouse. He saves all he can, goes without lunch, picks over garbage, steals milk from a mother donkey—acts which fascinate Garabet. Stavros carries with him his *hamal's* harness. In winter he sleeps in a stack of produce carts. He and Garabet, a cynical man of fifty, become friends. Garabet has his eyes on the Greek boy's growing hoard. On the job the other *hamals* have nicknamed Stavros *America America!* Thus they identify him with his dream. Like the cousin, Garabet feels the quickest way to riches for Stavros is to marry some wealthy man's ugly daughter. In the meantime the older man convinces the youth that he needs a whore. They go to Garabet's hovel where they are greeted by a young woman. While he sleeps, she finds his money belt. "Her fingers extract the coins, one by one" (p. 106).

The next day Stavros accosts Garabet and tries to beat him up for helping the whore steal his seven pounds. The girl, Vartuhi, is Garabet's daughter. Instead of killing Stavros for his effrontery, Garabet visits his daughter's quarters above a cabaret and berates her for robbing his friend. She, in turn, had to give the money to her patron or be cast out into the street. "The patron," Kazan writes, "a large bulky Turk, is at home in his quarters. He is entertaining two members of the Municipal Police in full uniform. They are all eating pastries, dripping honey over their chins, and drinking hot sweet tea out of small glasses." Later Garabet tries to console Stavros. "Tell me. Since you left home, have you met among

Christians, one follower of Christ? Have you met among human beings, one human being?" And Stavros replies, "You!" (p. 111).

We learn that Garabet is a leader in the underground. At a meeting a man declares that "the main victims of the Turkish Empire are the Turkish people" (p. 112). A bomb is concealed in a *hamal's* harness. Suddenly the police move in. They kill right and left. "The carnage is terrible to behold." Stavros, who is there, is tossed upon a wagon loaded with corpses. Barely alive, he falls off and thus escapes being thrown from a cliff into the sea. "Garabet's body goes into the sparkling blue water, breaks through the kelp, rises, floats, then is engulfed" (p. 115). Vartuhi finds Stavros on the road, helps him, vows to pay him back. What he needs, he says, is a blue suit of clothes. He has decided on the alternate route: a wife with a large dowry.

The scene shifts to a Greek Orthodox Church where Stavros and Our Cousin have gone to meet, unofficially, the rich Sinyosoglou men and one of their daughters, Thomna, "a very plain young woman, with a long nose and a sallow face" (p. 120). Negotiations follow between Our Cousin and Aleko Sinyosoglou for the marriage of Stavros and Thomna. His intentions are dishonorable: to secure the 108 pounds needed for the fare to America. The Sinyosoglous find Stavros very attractive; he is to have a position in the Sinyosoglou Carpet Company, a prosperous establishment. He sends the good news back home with a picture of Thomna. His family, of course, does not know of his ulterior motive. While the negotiations continue in the back of the store, Stavros notices a beggar outside. It is Hohanness, to whom he had given his shoes. The Armenian boy is hungry, sick, and exhausted. Stavros takes him to a nearby restaurant. Hohanness coughs a lot. The negotiations over the dowry result in Stavros's being offered 500 pounds. He counters, to their astonishment, by asking for only 110. The Sinyosoglous are puzzled, but they agree to the lesser amount.

As the groom to be, Stavros is strangely quiet and reticent. His cool aloof manner alarms Thomna who is a fine girl. She discusses Stavros with Aleko, her father. He has prepared a plush apartment for the young couple. Stavros is moved; the Sinyosoglous are making it hard for him. Alone in the bridal apartment, the couple talk; and Stavros reveals to Thomna his intention to abandon her and go to America. She hopes his dream will pass, as her father said it would. Thomna wants him to wait a year, but Stavros cannot promise.

A rug buyer from America, Aratoon Kebabian, arrives at the Sinyosoglou Carpet Company. Stavros is introduced to the Kebabians as the future son-in-law. He likes Sophia Kebabian, an independent-minded woman of forty-four who needs love. He helps her carry bundles to their hotel, where he pores over magazines from America. Through Sophia's interest in him, Stavros is able to go to the office of the North German Lloyd Line and buy a ticket to America. At last! He will accompany the Kebabians. Also at the office he finds Hohanness among eight boys whose passage has been secured by a Demos Agnostis. They will be shoeshine boys for him in New York, two years without pay. Hohanness still has a very bad cough. They are going on the same boat, the *Kaiser Wilhelm*. Stavros, in a bare room, has brought Thomna to tell her he is going away for good. In America, he says, feeling sorry for her, "I believe I will be washed clean" (p. 159).

Stavros is Madame Kebabian's lover, her kept man, at least for the voyage. He talks much with Hohanness, who loves him. Hohanness must conceal his cough from Agnostis and the authorities; otherwise he cannot enter the United States. The ship reaches Long Island. Stavros, Hohanness, and others gaze upon American soil for the first time. Stavros tosses Vartan's fez into the water. Aratoon Kebabian meanwhile has wrung the truth about Sophia and Stavros from their maid, Bertha. The old man prepares his revenge. He confronts Stavros and tells him he will no longer be his protector; that means Stavros will be sent back. Then Kebabian says he will fix it so that Stavros will never be allowed to enter America. This so enfuriates the boy that he assaults the old man who cries: "Intent to kill!" The guards beat Stavros limp and drag him off to the ship's hospital, third class. There Hohanness comes to visit him.

The next day a motor launch brings officials of the U.S. health service to examine the immigrants. Hohanness learns that Stavros intends to go overboard and swim for shore, even though he cannot swim. During the physical examination Stavros helps his friend control his cough so that Hohanness passes. But then he has a total collapse. He is dying of consumption. Later Hohanness wants Stavros to take his name, the idea being to sacrifice himself for the friend he loves. "Unseen, Hohanness goes over the rail and lets himself drop into the black waters of the bay" (p. 180). He drowns. As they disembark, Bertha hands Stavros a paper sack from

Mrs. Kebabian containing a straw hat and an envelope with a fifty-dollar bill.

On Ellis Island an official searches for a Stavros Topouzoglou who is wanted for assault. "That fellow died last night," Agnostis says, and reinforces the report with a ten-dollar bill. At that moment and in that place Stavros is reborn: the official writes down his new American name. It is "Joe Arness," a derivative of Hohanness, his benefactor. Back home in Anatolia the Topouzoglou family receives a glowing letter from Stavros and a first contribution, $50. They marvel at the amount, and earned so soon! The prodigal son writes he will bring them all to America in order to enjoy a new chance. "People waiting!" he cries as he shines shoes.[7] The Greek immigrant in Kazan's powerful novel is indentured for two years by what used to be known as the padrone system, which had many abuses before it was abolished.

Nothing that Kazan has written in the four novels since *America America* equals the appeal of Stavros—the archetypical youth who leaves home to seek his fortune, to pass by one devouring dragon, one peril, after another, and then to reach his goal. Kazan followed up *America America* with a much more commercially successful novel, *The Arrangement* (1967). Its protagonist, Eddie Anderson, is also of Greek descent and kin to the Stavros the reader already knows. A best seller for thirty-seven weeks, *The Arrangement* sold nearly a million hardcover copies in the United States and was translated into sixteen languages. Kazan's next two novels, *The Assassins* (1972) and *The Understudy* (1974), had no Greek characters; but of the latter the author said that he, Kazan, was actually the protagonist. In his most recent novel, *Acts of Love* (1978), Kazan selects Greeks again, this time to represent the spongers of Tarpon Springs.

The action of *America America* occurs in 1896. The Greek immigrants that Grace E. Marshall writes about in *Eternal Greece* (1938) also began arriving in the 1890s.[8] They are members of the Sarres family, who typify what many other Greeks also experienced. "The book," Marshall writes, "has grown out of stories told by Greek people around a New World fireplace. The speakers are three brothers, Nikolaos, Demetrios, and Joannes Sarres, who tell informally childhood stories of their family and neighbors . . . in Northern United States and Canada" (p. 3). The world, according to Marshall, owes an immense debt to little Greece. Although poor, its people are dignified, hospitable, and alert. If a nation's intelligence is to be "gauged by its peasants and artisans, Greece rates high, for the humblest discuss intelligently home politics and world affairs." She praises the Greek coffeehouse as a "common man's university and debating society" (p. 2). One may well envy the Greek despite his poverty, for he has learned to live without those luxuries that cause the westerner to "worry over thieves, fire, or stock exchange" (p. 3).

The Sarres family derives from Neohori in the Peloponnesus, where Ibrahim Pasha in 1827 sought to kill the entire population. The three brothers tell what they remember best about growing up as peasants in Greece. They recall little deeds of mischief. They describe mother's great kneading trough and her aromatic bread, cakes, and cookies. "Beautiful loaves for the priest were stamped with the sacred seal, containing, in a circle, the Greek cross and the symbols of the victorious Christ, the Panagia, and the nine orders of sainthood." The New Year's "royal cake" had a coin hidden in it for good luck. Mother also made delicious *trahana*, by boiling "fifty pounds of wheat at a time in a huge kettle of milk over a bonfire" (p. 30). The Sarres family made both the soft and the hard Greek cheese. On the home loom Mother weaved their clothes. They had a pet donkey.

The magic word of their childhood was "America," a land carpeted with "golden fleeces." Every Greek girl dreamed "of a great lover coming from America to take her back to luxury and adventure" (p. 74). Demetrios describes a game which they called "The Americans."

> We marked out a space to represent houses and established the girls in these as the wives and sweethearts; half the boys remained with the girls and the rest disappeared from sight. Then there would be a war-cry, "America," and the second group of boys would come charging up the hill. The defenders would cry out in alarm, "The Americans," and would rush out to the defence. But the women would desert to the Americans, and the game was over. (p. 79)

The game was founded on reality, for the American suitors did have "the best chance with the girls."

Parents felt both fear and pride when their sons left. Letters from America were always an event, especially if they had money or a photograph that indicated the sender's affluence. For the son's

visit home the whole village walked out to meet him; and all mar-
veled at his clothes, jewels, and rounded stomach. The children
picked up American expressions, like "Brooklyn." On the Sunday
of his visit, the rich son, with beaming father at his side, entered
the church for his "crowning opportunity of display." To purchase
his candle the great man from America laid down not one but a
hundred drachmas! Later, during the collection, he astonished all
by giving 500 more. "The next visitor who came home glorified his
family by still larger contributions and thus precedents were built
up" (p. 76). In the 1890s the first of the Sarres family to leave
Greece were several nephews the narrator's father had brought
up. The first of the three brothers to go was Nikolaos, then twelve,
to be followed by Demetrios and finally by Joannes.

Joannes describes his sponsor, Spyro, as a miser who overworked
him at the fruit store. To a country youth like himself, New York
and later Millport seemed crowded and dirty. Out of school he
worked long hours for Cousin Spyro with no recreation and no
money for "frills"—such as mittens and rubbers in winter. Once
when Joannes felt sick, the doctor simply ordered him to throw
away the alarm clock and sleep. He comments about the easy-going
Greeks "who had never had to be on time" or had seen a bitter
winter, now having to work on a strict, grueling schedule in all
kinds of weather. "Many toiled in factories and on railroad em-
bankments under harsh overseers," Joannes recalls, "but never a
complaint went back to Greece. Those old Brooklyns of our boyhood days were good sports for not giving a hint of their sufferings
in their first years abroad" (p. 87). For most of them the quality of
their lives eventually improved. Nikolaos details with keen pleasure how the "Greek restaurant at 14 High Street" served as their
warm and friendly social club.

At the store the Sarres brothers met many fine non-Greeks and
learned much about the United States. A German-American
family invited Joannes to their farmhouse for dinner, but he
feared to eat the baked ham, thinking it might be raw. Demetrios
at last led a revolt against Cousin Spyro's restrictions, and the boys
moved in with other relatives and their wives. To the store came
some of Millport's leading citizens, where they ate fruit and nuts
for lunch. They called themselves the Nut Club. A lawyer helped
the Sarres boys with their English; but they lost some respect for
him when he marched down Main Street in a suffragette parade.
Other lawyers—a bank officer, the president of a factory—and a

tailor made up the Nut Club while it lasted. The greatest philhellene of the group, the lawyer Tim Healy, quoted Thucydides and Aeschylus. "He told us of the interest that this district had felt in the Greek Revolution," Demetrios says, "and pointed out Greek names of several streets in the city, Athens, Euclid, Hydra and the like" (p. 98).

Life went on for the Sarres brothers until the Balkan war broke out in 1912. Nikolaos, together with thousands of other Greeks throughout America, returned home to fight against the Turks. "The lovers of Greece in town," Nikolaos recalls, "fêted and honored us before we left, and Boston came out in crowds to cheer our band of patriots as we marched through the city to the boat" (p. 107). He was wounded in Macedonia; then later he went back to the United States and resumed his work. By now Cousin Spyro had amassed great wealth, with much money to lend and invest. Yet both the Sarres brothers were still poorly paid. Afraid to lose them, Spyro offered to make them his business partners soon. Their father and sister, Eleni, visited them. Before long she married Stavros, a "Brooklyn" she met earlier.

The world war came and went. New York City held a big banquet for returning Greek-American soldiers. In the ensuing years various tragedies struck the Sarres family. Their mother died, as did a sister, Coula; and a younger brother, Costas, contracted typhoid fever that weakened him seriously. Eleni's husband failed in business. On a trip to Greece to visit Father and his new wife, Nikolaos met and married his bride, also named Eleni. He describes their simple wedding. Demetrios, fearing for his health, decided to go to Greece; and he tells about the speed with which several matchmakers set out to secure him a bride. During the absence of Demetrios, Joannes "invented a confection" that became so popular he made enough "to clear up all business obligations." Joannes goes on: "Big capitalists urged us to enlarge our business and put on a national campaign of advertising, but just then an embargo on Smyrna figs limited the supply to such an extent that I had to postpone the plan, and then the depression came" (p. 147). They invested more in people than in business, seeking happiness before wealth. In their fruit and candy store the Sarres brothers continued to study and enjoy American types. Much of the book at this point concerns interesting characters they knew and liked.

The brothers drifted into the Democratic party. By chance Demetrios attended the inauguration of President Roosevelt in 1933, and he describes the experience. Nikolaos talks about the difficulty of "becoming American" when the immigrant is already an adult. "I was born in Greece; and therefore I shall always be partly Greek, but my son hasn't any business to be a Greek. Even though I teach him the Greek language and try to hand on to him all that is good in Greek culture, I want him to be a thorough American" (p. 163). He does not believe that marrying a non-Greek helps to speed up the Americanization process. Joannes, on the other hand, recalls the children of a family from Neohori who settled in the Midwest, married both Greek and American wives, stayed together as a clan, grew very rich (with a chauffeur for their peasant mother), and got along well together. Among the Greeks who failed in America was a well-educated economist for whom there was no proper job in town. The hardy peasant, Joannes feels, can adjust better to the rough-and-tumble of business than a youth brought up with learning and luxuries.

By now Joannes and another brother, Georgios, have established themselves in Garyford, Canada; but Joannes remains tied to America. After the Depression he and Demetrios visit Greece. They had a jolly time, which the brothers take turns in describing. They went back home to Neohori, saw their aged father, renewed old acquaintances. They were shocked to find electric lights and other modern improvements. They participated in a witch-conducted exorcism even though they disbelieved in the practice. They helped a girl regain village acceptance after suffering a touch of tuberculosis; her parents had allowed false rumors of pregnancy to circulate rather than admit the disease. Greek peasants had a dread of tuberculosis, a disease brought on by living in damp homes and lack of a proper diet. The Sarres brothers also organized a banquet, a *glendi*, for Neohori. "The whole thing," Joannes says, dancing, feast and all, was a truly Homeric picture" (p. 189). They met many fine people and visited other places—Syra, Mistra, and elsewhere—before returning to the new world.

The last chapter, "Farewell," has Joannes summarizing his attitudes about modern Greeks and Greece. To America had come "the idealistic and the mercenary, the industrial and the idle, the successful and the unsuccessful," nearly all of them courageous and cheerful and able to blend into the new and more open civilization. The father of the Sarres brothers died a contented and very old man, "a real Greek," the best of the Greek peasantry. As Joannes stood on Mt. Parnassus, he felt that Greece was "something in the scheme of human life, with a unique mission" (p. 212).

The events in both *Eternal Greece* and *America America* occur in the mid-1890s, while those in *Gold in the Streets* (1945) by Mary Vardoulakis begin in 1906. At the time of writing the author was a student at Wellesley College. She won a coveted Dodd, Mead intercollegiate fellowship that meant her novel would be published.

> The daughter of Greek immigrants, she has planned to tell their story—their hopes, experiences, and problems—ever since she spent the four years from 1932 to 1936 in their Cretan homeland and herself experienced, in reverse, the change from the Greek countryside to an American mill town. From her sojourn in Crete sprang the conception of a new type of book about immigrants from Greece, a novel that would carry a specific group of peasants from their pastoral life in Greece over the ocean to a cotton manufacturing town in Massachusetts.[9]

Her Greek-Americans are a "sturdy element" in the ethnic complex of America. She describes both the forces demanding adaptation and the resistance to them by the Cretan immigrants.

Roughly seven-eighths of Kazan's novel describes its hero's efforts to reach America, with the remaining slender portion devoted to Stavros's getting settled in New York as Joe Arness. Vardoulakis devotes only one-fifth to the preliminaries—to the problems of George Vardas in Crete, his reasons for leaving, and the crossing. The bulk of *Gold in the Streets* dramatizes the early growth and development of the Greek-American community in the mill town of Chicopee, Massachusetts. All the Cretans there are peasants to begin with; but gradually, as the needs of the community dictate, a division of labor takes place among them. Most of the former peasants readily make the transition to industrial workers, but a few move into the lower middle class by setting up small businesses—a coffeehouse, a restaurant, a store—to serve the growing ethnic enclave. When a priest arrives to form a church, the foundations for the community have been completed. Infants can be properly baptized, the children can be taught Greek, the youth married, the holy days observed, the dying receive last rites.

When the story opens, George Vardas, the twenty-five-year-old protagonist, journeys to Fortreza for a double purpose—to sell two goatskins of olive oil and to attend court owing to a dispute over land with his cousin Nicholas. Among his other errands he must buy some lye, so his sisters can make a new batch of soap, and some silk thread for their loom. His cousin claims a strip of land on which grow ten prolific olive trees. After hearing the case the judge awards the land to George; and Nicholas remains hostile and unreconciled. The danger of a bloody feud grows between the two cousins. An added reason for their hatred is Nina, the priest's lovely daughter, who is desired by both youths. Still another problem for George is the dowry that he must provide for his sisters Tassa and Stella. Thus he has strong reasons for wanting to join the many young Cretans who are leaving for jobs in America.

At a *kafeneon* in Fortreza, after the trial, George Vardas meets an American agent named Sheehan and his interpreter Drakos. They want to recruit workers for the textile mills of Chicopee. Drakos urges the reluctant Sheehan to dangle his gold watch, an "eloquent symbol" of affluence, before their eyes. The Cretans ask Drakos about the fare. They are already sold on the American dream. After the fall planting, a matchmaker arrives with a formal offer for Tassa—the dowry, five hundred drachmas. George Vardas leaves for America and Chicopee with his two best friends, Petro and Michali. At Ellis Island they enter. Then they continue by ferry, train, and trolley to their destination. Because of their beards and queer Cretan costumes, they have already been ridiculed as "gypsies" by the children.

In Chicopee George, Petro, and Michali stay at the home of Peter Bakos, who welcomes them to America. They secure jobs in the great Fulbright mills. Most of the Greek immigrants live in one section of Chicopee, the hill. Very soon George learns that bad blood exists between the Greek and the Polish workers, who feel their jobs are in danger. Much as they dislike to at first, the Greeks must shave off their beards, abandon their native dress, and avoid "acting foreign." A great moment comes for George when he receives his first check, for $5.52, the equivalent of twenty-five drachmas. He immediately sends two dollars to his mother, and he buys himself a pair of long trousers. He spends his free time at the *kafeneon*, the social center where Michali now works. Without a priest, the Greeks of Chicopee observe Easter as best they can.

In June George and his friend Petro move to a factory tenement,—five rooms that cost five dollars a month. At first they use orange crates for chairs and table. They buy a double bed and a mattress secondhand. Peter Bakos shows them how to use gas for light and cooking so they will not choke themselves. A letter from his mother startles George with the news that his uncle Anastasi was thinking of coming to America with his two dauthers. Michali suggests that George's sister Stella might accompany them. A further surprise is the fact that Nicholas also wants to follow him to America; in that case Nicholas would be less likely to win Nina. More and more it appears that George will not return to Crete in time for the fall plowing. Late in June his uncle Anastasi writes to George asking for directions about the crossing and asking for return of the money that he lent George when he left. George has a month to prepare for the arrival of Anastasi and his daughters Froso and Eleni. In the meantime a tragedy befalls the Greek community of Chicopee: at the foundry Yianni the Cretan is crushed by a steel beam from one of the machines. The boy dies and is buried. "Dying in the *xenitya*, in the black exile. Without priest or prayer, an orphan body thrust in the alien earth" (p. 150). His death is a sobering experience for George Vardas and his compatriots.

Barb' Anastasi arrives, and George meets him and his daughters at the Springfield station. An exchange of news follows. His uncle is astonished to learn that people work on night shifts in America. A welcome party is held for the newcomers. To his great joy George learns that Nina, the priest's daughter, is still unmarried, that his cousin Nicholas did not get her. His joy, however, is soon tempered by the growing tension at the mill; more and more greenhorn Greeks keep arriving at a time when the Poles are demanding higher wages. A new problem confronts George when Nicholas shows up in Chicopee: he, too, has been lured by the vision of "gold in the streets." For the sake of appearances (and the fact that their land quarrel happened back in Crete) George undertakes to help his cousin as much as he can.

Finally the trouble with the Poles erupts. In the wild melee that ensues Barb' Anastasi is badly hurt. He is tripped and falls, hitting his head on the edge of a loom. His Greek compatriots, as the passive Poles watch, carry him to the hill unconscious. They summon a doctor who refuses to accept payment. At such a critical moment the Greeks need a priest. "George embarked on a eulogy of Pappa-Minos of Temenya. As he talked he hoped there was no audible tremor in his voice. The thought of Pappa-Minos in

America, with the possibility of Nina coming to Chicopee, shook him" (p. 176). Decisions are made, letters dispatched. Slowly Barb' Anastasi recovers. His friends celebrate his recovery by drinking *ouzo* and dancing. A young Cretan named Meliotes, a student, announces that he may become a policeman. Michali, another youth, has become a *kafetzi*, the keeper of the coffeehouse. In view of the progress being made by all, George Vardas ponders more and more seriously the idea of having his sister Stella join him. "Unconsciously he had been reserving Michali for Stella. Since their first meeting he had regarded him as a brother, someone for whom he felt particular tenderness and concern" (p. 188).

A letter arrives for George's friend Petro that his ailing son has grown worse, that he might soon die. The crisis for Petro precipitates discssion among the immigrants about their prolonged stay in America. By now they have no illusions. George says if he returns to Crete and finds Drakos, the agent, he will "wring his neck and give him to the eagles to eat. He said nothing about the *Polonezi*, not a word" (p. 201). With Petros on his way back, the scene of *Gold in the Streets* shifts to Anidros and the situation at the Vardas home. Pappa-Minos and Nina arrive with a letter from George strongly urging them to migrate to America. A priest is needed to serve the Greek community there. Another letter from George, this one to his mother, tells about Petro's return with passage money for Stella. She can help him earn the money for Tassa's dowry. To the extreme joy of both Stella and Nina, Papa-Minos will go and take them along with him.

The plot shifts back to Chicopee, where George awaits the reaction of Pappa-Minos to the invitation. Stella writes to tell him they will come. Bakos asks George to act as matchmaker on behalf of his nephew Meliotes; the intended bride is Froso, George's cousin. At first Barb' Anastasi will not hear of giving Froso to "anyone but a Cretan," and he ponders and ponders, then gives his consent. As a policeman Meliotes will be in a strategic position to help his friends, to be the advocate of the Greeks of Chicopee. On his first day at the police station Meliotes faces a problem that concerns his compatriots. Some of the Greek women at the textile mill are among those known to have stolen cloth. They include Froso, who only did what she had seen others doing. Why should the owners "miss a few yards which a poor girl can use to good advantage?" (p. 235). The women are using the linen for sheets. Meliotes passes his first test. The owners will not prosecute, but the cloth taken must be paid for in full. "On my word," Meliotes reports, "I promised that none of my people would be involved again" (p. 237).

Gold in the Streets concludes happily for George Vardas. Pappa-Minos, his daughter Nina, and Stella arrive. They are joyously welcomed. The priest brings the good news that Antoni, Petro's son, has improved and will be taken to the city for an operation. George and Nina meet. Nina works at the mill. Her father and others canvass "the possibilities for a small Greek church either in Chicopee or Springfield." George Vardas needs more money than ever. He may move to Hartford where the mills are paying fifteen dollars a week. George contemplates his future, especially his marriage to Nina, "calmly and with a rare serenity." He can move from one place to another, to search for whatever America might have in store for him. Mary Vardoulakis ends her novel with these words: "His thought suddenly was back in Fortreza. Drakos may still be right, he mused whimsically. His sins may be forgiven. We haven't seen half the streets." The dream, in short, has not run its course; nor has it resulted in despair. It still gleams in the offing, luring men onward with its promise of limitless reward.

Mary Vardoulakis dramatizes in *Gold in the Streets* a basic truth about the early Greek immigrants—that most of them worked for wages in mills, mines, factories, and on the railroads. Her title may be a cliché, but it represents how most Greeks and other immigrants saw America from afar. The gold was real money, not the gilding used by the Romans on special occasions—what some Italian immigrants thought "golden streets" meant. The Cretans of Vardoulakis undergo the difficult and often painful transition from peasants to industrial workers, in an environment that changes from hostility to eventual tolerance. Her subject is immigration, her characters are real, her theme is their becoming rooted in America, her tone is romantic. *Gold in the Streets* has the distinction of being the first truly "Greek-American" novel.

Elmer Grossberg's *Farewell, My Son* (1946) also concerns Greek immigration. Polk Siniakides flees to America where he works, engages in class struggles, fails, and dies.[10] As an example of socialist realism, the novel projects a more just future for which Polk's sacrifice of self represents a necessary stage of historical development. The plot is ordered by the relationship between the "old Greek" and a young admirer, Rudy Myers. For many years Polk lived with the Myers family in New York, first in their restaurant as cook and then as a handyman around the house. Throughout the early chapters Polk is characterized as stupid, stubborn, irascible, foolish—a dumb Greek loser to be scorned and ridiculed. As the story progresses the reader begins to share Rudy's admiration and love for him. The many doubts regarding Polk's value as a human being dissolve in the recognition that he bequeaths to Rudy, at the end, the will to champion the dispossessed.

After an absence of six years Polk returns, and Mrs. Myers happens to see him. They had parted as enemies. His situation resembles that of Silas in Robert Frost's "Death of the Hired Man." Rudy visits the old Greek immigrant in his shabby room. Polk the spiritual father and Rudy, his son, spend a wonderful and meaningful day together. Indeed, the one day constitutes the time present in the novel; and time past, the life story of Polk, is seen through a series of flashbacks. He takes Rudy to the wonders of Coney Island for a long and bittersweet reunion during which the "son" has all his questions answered by his "father." Polk as a young man fled to America to avoid being conscripted into military service by the Turks. Here at first he sold fruit from a pushcart, made some money, but got into trouble by fighting with rival street-vendors. Later he became involved with the unionizing of restaurant workers—an element of social realism based on the fact that the hotel and restaurant workers union had a heavy Greek membership. Thereafter Polk's life is filled with strikes, union meetings, cracked skulls, jail sentences, and selfless devotion, for a time, to the revolutionary work of the American Communist party.

The proletarian politics of Polk Siniakides rests on the simple principle that the common man must unite and struggle for socialism. Polk eventually leaves the party—not because he differs over program but because the comrades laugh at his accent when he tries to speak at a branch meeting. Why other members of Greek descent do not rise to his defense, or why he does not belong to a predominantly Greek branch, is not explained. As a noncommunist, Polk continues to believe in social revolution; and he now seeks to give Rudy the vision of a better society. Rudy, on his part, comes to respect the beaten old Greek on a higher, political level than before. He gets a rare view of the pure and selfless soul in Polk. It was Polk who befriended the Myers family in their need, who gave them money, who bought Rudy his piano and inspired him to be a fine musician. Toward the end of the boardwalk Polk gives to Rudy a ring, symbol of the handing down from father to son of a heritage—in Polk's case the ability and the desire to love mankind. They say goodbye to each other. *"Farewell . . . My Son,"* Polk whispers to himself as he watches Rudy's figure recede into the distance (p. 300). Then Polk falls and dies, within sound of the ceaseless and immortal ocean.

The first writer primarily interested in extracting humor from the lives of Greek immigrants was the artist George Demetrios, in his superb volume of short stories, *When Greek Meets Greek* (1947).[11] At least four other works use the same familiar title.[12] The author says in the foreword that his "episodes," as he describes the stories, involve "A species of men called Greeks who for thousands of years have lived in a peninsula and islands full of mountains and surrounded by the sea, and who travel in every remote corner of this earth; but whether they are in Greece or go to America or elsewhere, like any other species of the human race, they have only one desire, and that is to keep their little souls as long as possible in their human bodies, by food, play, and faith." Some of the twenty-five titles are merely anecdotal, entailing brief actions that make a moral point; others, however, are fully developed short stories suitable for formal analysis. All are expressions of the modern Greek character—a mixture of traits dramatized by Demetrios more often than not to amuse the reader. If evils exist, they are not so serious as to result in tragedy. Demetrios loves his characters as much for their flaws as for their virtues.

"The Greek Lion, Leo" concerns the professional wrestler Leonidas and the art student Mary. He is an honest man, "unlike some Greek wrestlers who pretend to be Turks and wear Turkish red felt caps (fezzes) on the mat, where for the amusement and bewilderment of the American audience they pray to Allah on a carpet." Being honest, he cannot get rich in wrestling; and since the promoters think him colorless, Leo becomes a model for artists. "Leo loved to pose, particularly for sculptors, because he felt that in posing for statues he was linked directly with the ancient Greeks" (p. 157). Through much practice and concentration he develops great muscle control. He befuddles Mary, the art student, by playing tricks on her. One day she faints, he confesses his guilt, and she vows to punish him—by becoming his wife.

John in "The Pig and the Candles" has put his son through medical school by washing dishes in Boston. One day in 1945 he receives a letter from his brother saying that his village back in Macedonia has been destroyed by the Germans. At the coffeehouse

John talks about his village—a happy place where the Greeks and Turks liked each other, where life was simple but peaceful and affectionate. Here in Boston one finds traffic, and confusion, and dishes; yet the old mountaineer has his triumph: a son who will be a doctor.

Another story, also set in Boston, tells about Socrates and Pericles, gamblers who lose everything in the stock market. Socrates is a salad cook, who loves Anastasia and wants to bring her to America. He has twenty savings books with a thousand dollars in each. Pericles, a pastry cook, has a wife and four children in Greece; his ambition is to return and then leave again, for "every man in his poor village had to seek fortune in foreign lands" (p. 181). Just before the market crashes in 1929 they invest heavily in stocks. At first Pericles "wins" so much he has all his teeth pulled in order to have gold ones—as befits a millionaire. Then their stocks turn worthless. Many years later, in 1946, Socrates is still a salad cook but has his Anastasia and a daughter. Pericles still bakes pies, but has no teeth. They both still gamble on stocks, horses, and dogs.

"A Corpse Pays for a Party" describes how an adventurer named Anastasios tricks an intellectual (also a Greek) into contributing fifty dollars for a barbecue party. The adventurers detest work, but they enjoy playing cards and discussing politics. They prefer to sell fruit and peanuts from pushcarts rather than work for others. One day Anastasios gets one of his cronies to play the part of a corpse; he then summons Mr. A., the intended victim, to come and see him. Mr. A. offers to pay for "a decent black box and the funeral expenses" (p. 192). With the money Anastasios throws a big party to which all his friends are invited, including the "corpse," Mr. A., and Professor Z. of Harvard. The professor, suspicious, "demanded to know who was the funeral director" (p. 193). Forced to confess, Anastasios has to spend $50 on another party and show Professor Z. an itemized account of the expenses.

In "A Horse and Cart for a Moving Picture Theatre," Prokopios looks ahead and takes advantage of his chances in Kansas City. There he purchases a dilapidated cart and sells candy bars, peanuts, and fruit at a moving-picture house. Owing to his dependability and persistence he prospers, whereas the theater's business declines. One day the manager asks for an even trade—the theater for the cart. Prokopios hires a girl for the piano, chases out the bums, changes the hours, and shows good pictures, all of which bring in the patrons. Mr. Stuart, who neglects the cart, fails again and wants the theater back. Prokopios gives him advice instead, saying that a business is like a marriage: you have "to stick to your wife, otherwise she gets mad and runs away, or if she is strong, she can beat you up" (p. 200).

Steve (for Stavros) in "The Greek Atheist" is a stonemason of enormous physical strength but very poor judgment. He reads a good deal, becomes an atheist, a socialist, and an American citizen. He tries hard to invent a machine with perpetual motion, to temper a copper razor, and to walk on water with a contraption made of rubber tubes; and he nearly drowns when he tests it. Finally he gets very sick, is taken to the hospital, leaves before he is well, and dies over a basin that holds his blood. In his will Steve writes that he "was wrong about God, *there is* God" (p. 211).

In another anecdote Lycourgos has a small haberdashery wedged in between two larger clothing stores, one owned by a Jew and the other by an Armenian. Both of his competitors put up big signs to attract customers: on one side, SELLING OUT AT TREMENDOUS SACRIFICE, and on the other, MAMMOTH FIRE SALE THIS SATURDAY. Lycourgos is not to be outdone by his wily rivals. "Sol and Adrian were aghast on Saturday morning when they saw between their stores a great sign with the words, MAIN ENTRANCE" (p. 216).

In a delightful vignette, "Pam the Cheat," Epaminondas is not only a liar but "a cheat in card games, in business deals, and in everything he touched." He and a Jewish partner go to jail when a Kosher rabbi discovers they sprayed chickens with paint before selling them. Later, washing dishes in a Greek restaurant, he steals steaks in special pockets inside his overcoat. One evening, just as Pam is about to leave, the proprietor makes him stand near the hot stove and listen to a long story. The butter under his derby is soon running down his face. "Yellow fever," the proprietor says, laughing; then he orders the "dirty crook" never to show his yellow face again.

The three other stories about Greek-Americans in *When Greek Meets Greek* exhibit the same sardonic attitude. In one Xenophon, a former grammar teacher who now runs a coffeehouse in Boston, tries to teach modern Greek to a Harvard professor of classical Greek, an American. In another episode, an immigrant buys a black-and-silver hearse for his village in Greece; but it rots in the cemetery unused because the first corpse "decided" against it by nodding his head up and down in transit. That meant "no" to the villagers whose corpses in the future will continue to be carried to their graves on the shoulders of their relatives. The last story in the book, "Gus Pappas," deals with a restaurant owner who returns to Macedonia to see his old mother. After a week in his village Gus feels a complete stranger. "He missed his cronies, the movies, the American jokes, the newspapers, cigars, ice cream, even the speaking of English, which he had never mastered well but could manipulate with relative ease" (p. 239). Gus Pappas has to explain to an octogenarian why he feels the way he does about America. The old man believes that Greece, too, can be great, like America, if her young men had not been killed "in all those damnable wars" and if they had not gone to live elsewhere. "Young man, America is great from nothing but the work and imagination of the youth of the world. I don't blame you for itching to go back. I would like to go there myself and become a philanthropo-Americanós" (p. 245). On this positive note George Demetrios concludes a fine collection of short stories memorable for its vital depiction of Greek characters.

Neither Demetrios nor Vardoulakis developed what may be regarded as a corpus of fiction. The same is true of another potentially significant writer, Jim Dilles. He did publish one novel, *The Good Thief* (1959), about a Greek working-class family in California.[13] The protagonist, Costa Desmas, works in a packing house that has been on strike. Much of the tension at home results from his inability to play the expected role of provider. Thespina, his wife, is especially critical. At the start of the novel he returns from a hill overlooking San Francisco Bay with a bag of dandelion greens. The Desmas and their four children have little else to eat. For his effort Costa receives the usual scorn.

The strike has persisted for seven weeks, creating hardship for the workers. On occasion Costa and his friend Pericles, from Kalamata, serve as pickets for the union. Otherwise, much to Thespina's annoyance, they sit around the house drinking wine and discussing philosophy. They frequently talk about Greece and invoke the heroic days when the Greeks fought the Turks for their freedom. To Thespina they are lazy windbags using the strike as an excuse for sloth.

Spurred by her sharp tongue, Costa Desmas does try to provide for his family, but he consistently fails. "All Greece knows where to find a Desmas," she rails at Costa. "When he is not drunk and sleeping under an olive tree, then he is drunk and sleeping under a fig" (p. 11). Her caustic remarks sometime seem unfair, because Costa with his many limitations does try to cope. His two sons, Stavro and Louie, fish in the bay, gather driftwood for the stove, and sell bouquets of wild flowers. One day Costa kills a duck which falls into the water. In retrieving it Louie nearly drowns. The duck stinks too much for them to eat it. When Stavro complains, Costa hits him. Thespina says: "The monster who kills poor little boys."

To be a thief is, to Costa Desmas, the lowest of the low. Yet the devil works in mysterious ways, and Costa has the fleeting thought of stealing a lamb from the stockyards. He tries to find a job elsewhere, but without luck. Costa returns home to find Thespina attempting to pull a reluctant steer out of their basement. Costa tethers the creature in a corner and feeds it grass; and he worries lest others learn that a Desmas has been a thief. Stavro and two American boys are the culprits—thieves with good motives. What they must contrive to do is return the steer without anyone being the wiser.

This crisis causes even more trouble between Costa and Thespina. Theirs had been the usual arranged marriage. Never more than perfunctory in their love-making, now they turn their backs to each other in bed. Then still another crisis erupts: with a rifle in hand, the panicky Pericles arrives in Costa's yard to announce that he has just killed his young wife's lover. When the distraught Pericles says he has spared her, Costa replies that he should have killed her too. "First I would have shot her" (p. 167). Pericles intends to run off to the mountains where he hopes to survive as a *klepht*, a brigand. However, before he can get away, the police drive up, see that Pericles is armed, and shoot him. They also hear the steer.

Everything has gone wrong for poor Costa. The police return to question him about Pericles and to inform him that keeping a cow on the premises violates a town ordinance. When he denies having a cow, the cops investigate and find the stolen steer. They recognize the animal as belonging to the packing company. Asked how it got there, Costa claims that he stole it from the stockyard. Under no circumstances would he implicate Stavro and his friends, the real culprits. Since Costa confesses his guilt, the police arrest him and take him to jail. He gets a clean pair of socks from Thespina, whose attitude toward him has softened. Costa gives a few instructions about the garden. "In the trunk in our room there is a little money," he tells her. "Look after them [the children] however you can" (p. 185).

From then on events move very swiftly for Costa Desmas. As a Greek father and a Desmas, he has completely failed. In jail for a crime committed by his son, he sits and broods. Union representatives come to assure him of their strong support. They, too, ask if he stole the steer, and he repeats that he had. Unknown to Costa, certain gears for a publicity campaign are set in motion. Reporters and photographers arrive to ask more questions and to flash his picture. "Had a killer here a few years back," Costa's jailer says. "Public enemy number nine. But the papers never called up about him as much as they call up about you" (p. 200). And no wonder, for a picture of him dejected in his cell appears in a San Francisco paper; and the caption above it reads: STRIKER STEALS STEER FOR STARVING TOTS. The publicity is, of course, dynamite against the packinghouse owners who have refused to grant the union demands. Negotiations are resumed, the strike is won, and Costa Desmas is the hero of the hour. The stolen steer is returned, the charges against Costa dropped, and he goes home to his family.

He goes home after he is paraded around town and cheered, much to his confusion. "Ten minutes before he had been lying in jail on a plywood mattress, a caught thief full of disgrace." The next thing he knows "they were parading him up and down the main street as though he were a hero returned from the wars" (p. 244). He rides high on the back seat of a car, made to smile and wave at the crowds by the union leaders beside him. When the car parade stops triumphantly at Costa's house, Thespina is ready to disperse them with the gun. "She swung with her right and the wooden butt of the rifle smashed against the camera, knocking it out of the photographer's hands and down to the sidewalk" (p. 246). Confronted by her fury, the celebrants depart; and when a lone reporter approaches for one last picture, Thespina and Costa jointly chase him off. They want to be left alone. For a while Thespina refuses to welcome even friends and neighbors. "She was a better jailer than the one at the city hall, Costa thought, and a more righteous one" (p. 248). Working in his garden, Costa Desmas ponders the tragic loss of his good compatriot Pericles. He looks forward to the work at the plant, to better relations with Thespina, and to reconciliation with Stavro and Louie, his fine sons. As the dust jacket states, "This is the story of a few wonderful, lovable people, and all through it there is compassion mixed with subtle humor. For these are the people of the author, Jim Dilles, who lives in California, near San Francisco. Mr. Dilles has written short stories, and now he has written this distinguished novel." Unlike many other immigrant novels, *The Good Thief* avoids all topical allusions that might date the story. It offers no clues, no mention of historical events, no public figures, nor other topical evidence such as allusions to current books or films.

The various ways in which the American Dream affected the lives of Greek immigrants are explored by Harry Mark Petrakis (notably in *The Odyssey of Kostas Volakis*) and by Theano Papazoglou-Margaris in her many short stories. Two of them, translated into English, are discussed in the chapter "The Fiction in *Athene*." That she writes only in Greek keeps her from having an audience outside the Greek-American community; however, she is highly regarded in Greece as a leading chronicler and interpreter of that community. Not only have her books been published in Athens, but one, *The Chronicle of Halsted Street* (1962), won a literary award given by the Greek government—the first time the prize went to a writer living outside of Greece.

The author's life determines to a great extent the locale and subject matter of her stories. Some are set in Constantinople and its environs, others in San Francisco, but most in Chicago. Papazoglou-Margaris belongs to that group of Anatolian Greek writers exiled from their land by war between Greece and Turkey, by the catastrophe of 1922, and by the subsequent exchange of populations. She was born near the site of ancient Troy and reared in Constantinople. She left Anatolia when all the Greek children there were relocated in Greece proper. In 1923 she arrived in New York as the adopted daughter of a Greek family. She acted with various Greek-language groups in plays that emphasized social and revolutionary themes. She has been writing since the week of her arrival. Socially conscious at the time, she was the first Greek woman to write for the socialist *Voice of the Worker*. Besides composing her books of fiction, Papazoglou-Margaris for many years has prepared weekly columns for the *National Herald* and other Greek newspapers.

Once uprooted from the motherland, her immigrants voyage to America for only one reason—to work and "fill their tank with gold." Many fail to succeed because of their weaknesses and the effects of a class society. They remain, or become, victims of forces beyond their control. They also frequently suffer from keenly felt nostalgia. Papazoglou-Margaris deals primarily with the fate of Greek women. A favorite theme is the search for a lost friend or relative, then the shock of discovery due to changes wrought by time. The story often ends with the narrator's listening to a tale of woe. Another theme involves the disrupted bonds between the immigrant and the loved ones left behind. Several stories dramatize the presence of social problems and point the way toward solutions. For the most part the Greek characters are simple nonintellectual types with limited cultural and emotional scope. They have little more than hard work and moral integrity with which to confront the foreign land, the *xenitya*.

Eftihia and Other Stories (1939) embodies episodes of World War I and its aftermath.[14] A Greek woman named Eftihia, in the title story, suffers one loss after another: her father, mother, and her betrothed Evangelos, who leaves for Roumania where he marries. Out of shame Eftihia decides not to marry. Then a poor woman dies at childbirth, leaving five children; and Eftihia takes the baby, baptizes her Pandora, and raises her with great devotion. When Pandora grows up, however, she departs to join her father and other kinfolk in Asia Minor. Eftihia's despair leads to illness, until she gets a baby goat whom she also names Pandora, after her lost "child." When war breaks out in 1915, a boat arrives to evacuate all the Christians from the Turkish village. Unable to take her goat Pandora aboard, she gives her to two German sailors and cries: "I always lose all!"[15] After the refugees are relocated, Eftihia visits the marketplace every Friday when stray beasts are sold. She hopes that her beloved goat Pandora will show up, but the lost animal never does.

In "Easter at Ballikeseri" a group of Greek refugees, led by a Turkish drover, makes a difficult four-day journey to reach a place of safety. "The War Wounded" depicts the sadness of war orphans, thousands of them brought to Constantinople from various places in Turkey. In another story set in Turkey, a grandmother named Katingo seeks a medical cure from miracles rather than from a doctor. The result is death for a hapless child. Of more relevance here are stories by Papazoglou-Margaris that follow Greek refugees and other immigrants to America. Such a story is "Number 38," in which the narrator, upon coming to America, asks around for Constanti. Having liked her mother, Constanti would be a second father for her. One person tells her he may have gone to the Alaska fisheries; others mention the mines in Colorado, the sheep ranches of Montana, the stockyards in Chicago. After many years the narrator stops asking for Constanti. Then, ironically, she finds him—unkempt and wrinkled. She seeks rapport with him by blaming the terrible war for all the separations. She turned into a "bolshevik," she says, to fight against the war. To her surprise Constanti furiously attacks her as an atheist. Her one time dream of acquiring a father turns to dust. Not long after, Constanti is found dead in an alley. His body is placed in the morgue. He receives a pauper's burial, and there is no Greek priest to perform the last rites.

"The Waitress" is one of several stories about the hardships of work for immigrant women. In this case the waitress has a sick son. Despite her grief, she has to smile and be polite even to drunk customers. At last she quits her job and gets only $3.50 severance pay. At home she is tempted to kill her son by giving him an overdose of medicine. "Bitter is life!" she laments. "Bitter the medicine!" But at the last minute she decides otherwise. "Those who make life bitter, they should die," not the innocent child.[16] Papazoglou-Margaris writes another tale of despair about Maria and her daughter Helen, both of whom work in the same dress shop. They are on "piece work" with its merciless tempo. Maria recalls her dreams of coming to America and how they have vanished. The moment arrives when Helen puts a needle through her finger. It bleeds, and she faints. Maria shouts and panics so much that the boss summarily fires her.

In a more substantial story, "Our Neighbor," a young man of thirty goes about without speaking to anyone. His neighbors call him the "unsmiling Lazarus." Finally, when he sees a baby taking his first step, he breaks down and tells his story. In Greece he has a wife and two children, a boy and a girl, whom he has not seen in ten years. He has had many *vasana*, troubles. From his wife he receives a letter begging him to come. "Easter soon," she writes, "and still you have not returned." She begs him, "Come now, my dear, back to our poor home so that its door be opened, that I may be happy again who am deserted, having lost you from my side when I was a young bride."[17] She regards herself a widow, her children orphans. The narrator who hears the letter is very moved. She recalls many other wives left abandoned like that in Greece. This forlorn young man was married at twenty, had two children, and was happy but without work. To find work in America he left his country and his family—ten years gone, and still too poor to purchase a return ticket. The narrator, in an effort to console him, mentions others who were gone for twenty, thirty, and even forty years. Later Lazarus receives another letter, this one from his children. Their mother has died. He must come now or they will perish during the winter. He cannot go, and a year passes. At church he has a memorial read for his wife. One day he asks the narrator to accompany him to the park where he praises nature. Nature's bounty is sufficient for all, yet instead what reigns? Injustice, robbery, evil. "I believe," he says, "that man will someday change our planet." That time will never be for poor "Lazarus." He hangs himself for the two thousand dollars in insurance that will help his son and daughter survive.

Two Greek girls, though good friends, take separate roads in "The Fiancée of the Prince of Wales." This title was given to Lulu in her youth after she dreamed she was going to marry the famous English playboy. Lulu went wild when the prince visited the United States. Both girls work side by side at the textile machines. The narrator hopes to marry a bolshevik leader, and together they will conduct a revolution to help mankind. Then she will give Lulu a nice fur coat for the winter cold. Lulu is not impressed. "I'm not insane to marry a worker," she scoffs.[18] The narrator gives examples of Russian princes, emigrés, who did menial work in Constantinople after the revolution. Besides, she tells Lulu, you are not cut out to be a princess, nor will the prince seek you. This attitude infuriates Lulu, who cries that she will marry a prince and have him "slaughter all you bolsheviks!" That ends their friendship—until that same night when it resumes and Lulu, still dreaming, says that if she marries the Prince of Wales, she will convince him to provide an army for the revolution! Ten years pass, and now the narrator meets Lulu again. Once very pretty, she is fat, dirty, and has unkempt children. As she briefly and shamefacedly relates, she did marry a rich man, one with ten stores. But he lost them all, and she is now on relief. Without thinking, the narrator says the Prince of Wales is now king and still unmarried. Lulu hurries off to get free shoes and clothes for her children.

"For Bread" continues in the same vein of economic hardships and their effect on Greek women. Again the narrator meets a friend after a lapse of years. This one is Hope, whom she knew in San Francisco. Hope was sixteen then, but now at twenty-one she is coarse and aged, compared to her previous youth and innocence. Hope's mother had found a Greek man with a restaurant who liked Hope. They were engaged. He got Hope pregnant and then ran off, a bankrupt. She wanted to kill her baby, a girl. Then she met another man (and is still with him) who after a while brought her customers for prostitution. A procurer, he has other girls like Hope. He is heartless, evil, and a gambler. Hope desperately needs one hundred dollars so she can escape to another city. She wants to save Nitsa, her Greek girlfriend, from also getting trapped in prostitution. At the end the narrator wonders how many girls are like Hope, working "for bread" alone.

The fates of various Greek immigrants are explored in *A Tear for Uncle Jimmy*, the second volume of short stories by Papazoglou-Margaris.[19] The title story is a remembrance that includes a bit of West Coast labor history. The narrator, Nitsa, had left California for Chicago many years earlier. In leaving, she made "Uncle Jimmy" promise to answer her letters promptly, letters which, as it turns out, she never got to write. He had arrived in America even before she was born; he was forty-two then, while Nitsa and her friends were in their early twenties. She felt secure with him; he knew his way around, had won medals in the world war, and spoke English well. Uncle Jimmy organized picnics in the fields of California—from the San Fernando Valley among the almonds to the San Joaquim Valley among the cherry trees. The girls asked him about his war medals; and he chided them for being attracted by the military, since war had destroyed their homes. After many jobs in many places, Uncle Jimmy worked as a second cook in a Greek restaurant, for twelve hours a day, seven days a week. In a unionized American restaurant the hours were eight a day, six days a week, with more pay. To get the same conditions the Greeks and Uncle Jimmy went out on strike. At that time in San Francisco a Greek called Black Jack gathered Greek and Italian immigrants as strikebreakers. American workers throughout the West regarded him a curse. Immigrants straight from Europe did not know what scab or strikebreaker meant. During the course of the seven-month strike Uncle Jimmy got beaten up by Black Jack's men. The workers won their strike; had it been lost, all places with eight hours would have reverted to twelve. As it was, San Francisco became the first city in the nation to win decent conditions for hotel and restaurant workers—an industry that hired thousands of Greeks. Nitsa understands Uncle Jimmy's pride in his labor leadership, but still wonders that he, a war hero, should admit to being beaten by Black Jack. Now, as she thinks back, Uncle Jimmy is old and perhaps dead. "Six sisters Barba Jimmy had, and he provided dowries for all, all he married off; yet water from their hands he never drank, a handkerchief of his they did not wash, not one of his shirts did they iron!"[20] Nor did Nitsa, for her part, ever write him once she left San Francisco.

Two problems that derive from ethnicity arise in "Roots" and "Amen." In the first story a Greek woman named Rita is painfully divided between America and Greece. "Here my body, there my soul," she thinks.[21] As a result she refuses to put down roots in America—no house and no child—until it is too late and she dies. In "Amen" the Greek father Stratos weeps because his daughter Tassie has "died"—that is, she has eloped with Stanley, the Polish boy from down the street. "Dead I can stand her," Stratos says, "but not a Polish woman!"[22] Tassie's mother cries that her absent daughter has poisoned her. In Stanley's house things are no better: his mother laments that Tassie is not even a Catholic. Her daughter Paula adds to her sadness by insisting she will also marry a non-Pole. Two years later the situation has changed in both households. Stratos calls his grandson a *Polonezai*, but does so with affection. The boy is an angel with "Greek eyes." To Stanley's mother now the Greeks are not barbarians. She worries a bit because the child calls her *yiayia*—grandmother—and she wishes that the boy would learn a little Polish. What Stratos did not spend on the wedding he will gladly spend on the baptism and reception.

The rigors of exile, including the constant pressure to get rich, sometimes lead to insanity. "In the Fog" tells the story of George, who ends up as a mental patient. The narrator accompanies Katy to see him. Katy has a card from George's mother asking for money. On their ride to Indiana we learn the story through a series of flashbacks. George has been confined for five years, placed there by his sister Tarsi. Soon after doing so, Tarsi was killed by a train at a crossing. Before that, she arranged with the bank to send George ten dollars a month from the nine thousand dollars he had saved. The money represented his wasted life. He felt trapped in the Indiana town where he worked in the restaurant owned by Tarsi's husband. An American girl, Jean, worked with him. One moonlit night they walked together to the park where, at a happy moment, Tarsi appeared and said: "You idiot, you are lost."[23] And she fired Jean from her job. In reaction George took one thousand dollars from his account, went to Pittsburgh, and lost it all in one night's gambling. In the asylum George is obsessed by several things: by the rest of his money, which he wants to lose so that he can be "reborn" as a man; then by his hated sister Tarsi, whom he believes to be still alive; and by a hair on his nose that he thinks

people are always ridiculing. Several other Greeks stay in the same
hospital. Katy and the narrator arrive and find George still anxious
to spend his money. He gives fifty dollars for his mother in Greece
even though he deems her a *striga*, a witch. The narrator, at the
end, recalls the visit with sadness.

Papazoglou-Margaris in "This Is America" deals with Greek immigrants who turn into missing persons and are never seen or
heard from again. They are the lost souls of the diaspora. The boy
Aristotle is born rich and handsome in Constantinople. His mother
Antiope is the aristocrat, his father is illiterate but wealthy. Aristotle has tutors at home because he might learn bad habits from
other boys. When he grows up he is sent to America—presumably
to Harvard—but he secretly brings a bride, Katerina, who resembles his mother in looks yet is as unlearned as his father. They
settle on New York's East Side in a rat-infested apartment. With
only academic knowledge and no skills, Aristotle cannot find a job.
They have a child. Katerina works as a furrier while he babysits.
To pass the time he gets books from the Main Library and reads.
"This is America," he retorts whenever Katerina complains. They
have another child. They argue. Aristotle confesses to a Kastorian
at a fur shop that he plans to leave his wife and children and begs
him, Kosta, to marry her for the good of all. Then Aristotle disappears, some say to become a hobo. Hobo customs are described.
The narrator of the story meets Aristotle in 1932 in a San Francisco soup line. He is the "maestro" of the singing line—so his musical education had some good use. He is called "Aris" and "Greek
Apollo" and is happy though broke. They work briefly in the Santa
Clara Valley destroying plum trees in order to bring the prices up.
The narrator never sees Aristotle again. After World War II she
reads in the "Address Wanted" column of a Greek-American newspaper a request by Antiope, Aristotle's mother, for knowledge
about him. Other such requests took up half a page in the paper.
How did Aristotle get lost, the narrator wonders. In America, she
feels, perhaps ten thousand blacks pass for white and thus lose
their former identity. Some Greeks who know English well pass for
non-Greeks; they assume different names and pretend to know no
Greek. The narrator instances a cousin, Mitso, who lost himself in
the religious sect known as the Holy Rollers—through shame that
he could not send as much money home as others allegedly did.
He got back his self-esteem through the Holy Rollers who, both
black and white, respected him. "I am a Negro from Alabama,"

Mitso claimed, "with a white father."[24] So, in like fashion perhaps, did Aristotle get lost in America. Maybe he became leader of a religious sect. Maybe a millionaire. Wall Street is near the Bowery; LaSalle Street, near Skid Row. "This is America."

"Two Hours" depicts a Greek mother's worry that her seven-year-old daughter might be hit by an auto or molested on her way to school. The author makes a plea for day-care centers. "In the Margin" concerns Cousin Katsos, who has come to America hoping to become a millionaire but who does not. He excused his failures in business by thinking that he never had the right location. When he gets hit by a car and has a claim, his cousin tries to persuade Katsos not to start a new business. Katsos is a marginal man—too old for the factory, not old enough for social security. He must open a new establishment to give himself work.

In "Tammy and Tam," two cousins named Thanassis have wives who hate and compete with one another for status. Tammy has a business, but Tam works for Ford. Tammy's wife gets a Cadillac. Tam's wife is ashamed her husband is a mere worker. Then a supermarket forces Tammy to go bankrupt, and his wife runs off to California with a Greek-speaking Italian. Tammy suffers a mental breakdown. At last, Tam's wife is reconciled to her fate—being the wife of a good worker.

Bessie in "Refuge" is another strong Greek woman saddled with a worthless husband. She owns and runs a Greek grocery store. A good butcher, she sells lamb and shows non-Greek wives of Greeks how to roast it. Bessie is an attractive woman with a fine personality, but for fifteen years no one has praised her eyes. Her husband Gus always drinks; she always works. Bessie got married at sixteen. By the time she was nineteen she had three daughters. Gus wanted a son, but she demurred, saying: "Here today women manage factories."[25] Bessie is a proud entrepreneur. "She wrote secretly to Nassikas, who was well-known through the Greek-American newspapers for his cheese, and he sent her a small barrel of *feta* which was sold immediately."[26] Her skill infuriates Gus, who beats her. Time passes, and now the gossips speak of Bessie's wealth. Her last daughter wishes to attend college and get married. Bessie will be all alone.

Panayiotis, or "Pit" as he is called, is a loser in "The Spark Dies Out." Like many other immigrants, he arrives "with a small suitcase in his hand and large plans in his head."[27] The story chronicles Pit's life from his arrival before the Graeco-Turkish war of

1897 until well after World War II. He had three sisters for whom he "bought" husbands through dowries. Wars and the great Depression kept him from visiting Greece. "Chicago is now my fatherland," he says, "and I am frightened to go far from her."[28] After gambling on horses and losing, Pit sells his lunchroom to a Chinaman and puts all the money on a race. Again he loses. The next morning he is found dead on the doorstep of his lunchroom; he probably froze to death during the night.

Another aspect of the earlier immigration was the manner in which those with some learning, including knowledge of English, used their advantage to exploit their fellow Greeks. "Stranger to All" touches upon this situation. The central character is a teacher of Greek who eventually dies. He taught Andreas and Mary ten years ago; now they are married, and both are teachers themselves. They invite their old Greek teacher to dinner. The father of Andreas still hates such teachers and others with some learning who deceived and profited from the ignorance of newcomers. Yet in this teacher Andreas and Mary found what they wanted in a father. They call on him only to find out that he has died. The story concludes with his funeral service and burial.

Some of the ethnic-related themes mentioned above recur in the two later books by Papazoglou-Margaris, *The Chronicle of Halsted Street* (1962) and *The Travels of Uncle Plato* (1972). On the whole the stories deal less with the problems of immigration; they are less social- and class-conscious and more domestic in their treatment of Greek characters. Several further enrich our understanding of the Greek-American experience. They dramatize again the disruptions caused by the diaspora, the toll on people taken by time, the heartbreak of separation, the conflicts within the ethnic community, the nostalgia for the lost *patrida*, and various specific dilemmas faced by Greeks trying to succeed. Generally the technique remains the same: the narrator meets someone, or remembers someone, or thinks of something past or present, and then the story unfolds either by flashback or by a dialogue.

In "The Other Eugenia," the leading story of *The Chronicle of Halsted Street*, the narrator comes to Chicago seeking a friend, Eugenia, whom she knew in Constantinople.[29] The narrator left for America after the catastrophe of 1922 when the Turks defeated the Greeks in Asia Minor, burned Smyrna, and killed thousands. She likes Chicago much better than the East Side of New York— perhaps because, as she writes, the Caryatids on the museum

building remind her of Greece. Eugenia had been a pretty "photograph bride" and had crossed over on the ship *Alexander the Great.*
The narrator fails to find her, and many years pass. Then, one day,
she notices near an American school a woman selling hot dogs to
the children. The vendor's name is Eugenia, a Greek from the very
same neighborhood in Constantinople. She is tubby, old, not at all
like the "other Eugenia"; yet she is the same, the lost friend. All
the remembered glamor of her youth is gone. Eugenia tells her
story: she was a deceived bride whose husband had misled her
about his wealth. He had borrowed the money to bring her over
and marry her. The boy she really loved was Fotis, still in Greece
with a thriving shop and family. Eugenia's husband had died nine
years ago. Reconciled to her fate, she likes being a hot-dog vendor
on the street. The school children are her "family." Yet she still
hates her brother for having urged her to leave Greece. The narrator never sees Eugenia again, for she fears that the past in her
mind may be only an illusion.

The book contains two sketches based on letters sent from and
to Greece that involve lost relatives. The narrator in "A Mother's
Letter" has for many years held on to a letter which she had received and opened by mistake. It was for John Papas from Maria
Papadopoulos, his mother, begging him to answer. For thirty years
John Papas has been gone. His sister is now a grandmother; without him the house has been a tomb. His mother remembers him as
a child. The narrator has checked the telephone book and learned
from his Irish landlady that John Papas had been dead for three
years. The landlady gave his trunk to the Salvation Army. The "letter to a sister" is sent to Greece by a friend of the sister's brother in
Chicago. This story reminds one of Balzac's Père Goriot, who impoverished himself for the sake of his selfish daughters. The sister
owes everything she has to Athanasios Agathopoulos, her brother
in America: her dowry, with which she secured a husband; her
comfortable house; money for her son, studying in Athens to become a doctor; and their donkey, which has just died. Another
letter arrives for Athanasios from his greedy sister. In it she asks
for another donkey so they can remember him each day. They also
need more money this month because they want to visit their *yioka*
(bonnie boy) in Athens; and once there they must buy gifts for the
girls. Unknown to his grasping sister, Athanasios Agathopoulos is
a poor fruit-peddler with no possessions besides his horse and cart.
He drives Bucephalos down Adams Street and elsewhere crying

his wares. Athanasios loves his old Arabian horse, and he takes great pride in his work. One day Bucephalos drops dead in the street. Athanasios disappears. Later the narrator and the Irish landlady find him dead in the garage with his peddler's cart and cases of fruit. He was three weeks late in paying for the one room he rented. The letter from his sister is there, along with some ragged clothes, and a suitcase with other letters and photos of his kinfolk in Greece. There also is a newly drawn check to help them once more—the reason why his rent is late. Now they can buy a new donkey and go to Athens.

The Greek girl Maritsa of Constantinople marries an American sailor named Louie in "The Suns of Maritsa." When war breaks out she comes to Summit, Oklahoma, where her second son, Spiro, is born. The war ends, but Louie has died of typhus. Years pass. Maritsa leaves for Chicago where the narrator meets her in Greek Town. At the Freedom Fair during World War II Maritsa makes and sells *ravani*, a delicious Greek nectar cake. Both her sons ("suns" she calls them) are in service. Tragedy befalls them. Not only is Niko killed in Europe, but when Spiro comes home to see his ailing mother he dies in an auto accident. Maritsa's friends place her in a sanitarium, expecting her not to live. Later the narrator meets Maritsa at State and Madison in Chicago. She has two new sons, each about ten or eleven. At the sanitarium she saw pictures in Greek papers of Greek war orphans. With ample funds from sale of the Oklahoma farm and her son's insurance, she went to Saloniki and found two boys to adopt who closely resembled her own lost "suns." She keeps healthy, dresses to look like younger mothers, and warns her boys to be very careful when they cross the street. The narrator feels glad for Maritsa.

Other stories by Papazoglou-Margaris in *The Chronicle of Halsted Street* tend to repeat themes and situations already noted. The title story which concludes the book describes the original Greek Town of Chicago. The author sketches the lives of several Greeks associated with Halsted Street—how the area shaped their destiny. *The Travels of Uncle Plato* continues the author's chronicle of various types of Greek-Americans.[30] Taken as a whole, her fiction provides another record of immigration to our shores—the diaspora as it affected modern Greeks. Among writers of Greek descent, only Harry Mark Petrakis has given as much attention to the creation of fictional Greeks who made the dynamic Windy City their permanent home.

A short story by Paul Gallico, "The Hat," features a unique reason for a Greek's migrating to America and his subsequent success as a theater tycoon similar to that of the legendary Skouras brothers. The author describes the circumstances of its writing and reprints the story in *Further Confessions of a Story Teller* (1961).[31] A young Greek road worker, George Pavlides, drops his hat from a bridge across the Corinth Canal. The hat falls upon the deck of a passing ship and is retrieved by a happy passenger. Pavlides decides to follow wherever the hat, his "old friend," goes, and the search takes him to the United States. Here, as time passes, he goes from being a waiter to owning many restaurants and finally to owning a large chain of theaters. He also marries a tall and beautiful Greek girl, Sophia Karakeno. "Fifteen years from the time he landed in New York, he was a millionaire" (p. 310).

During his rise to power Pavlides forgets the original motive for his odyssey—the hat. In the meantime "an Irish Jew from Dublin," Meyer McManus, has become a film mogul as president of Interworld Pictures. The two giants, Pavlides and McManus, clash when the Greek refuses to buy an Interworld picture called *Body of Love*. "We will not play steenky pictsoors in Pavlides Palaces" (p. 311). Their enmity continues until they reach an impasse when they must meet to resolve their differences. Pavlides has bought "the rights to equip his theaters to show Life-o-Scope," a new dimensional form, whereas the equally intrepid McManus "bought the rights to cameras, sound and reproducing equipment of Life-o-Scope" (p. 312). At their meeting an extraordinary coincidence occurs: Pavlides notices that the hat McManus is wearing is the very same one he lost back on the Corinth bridge many years before! The passenger who retrieved it, his "lucky hat," was none other than Meyer McManus. The two men, both giants of the film industry, become fast friends. To celebrate their new accord, Pavlides donates "one million dollars to Grik orphans tsildrens," and McManus gives "one million dollars to the Hebrew and Irish orphans of the world." To top everything off, Pavlides suggests that "we each give one million dollars to the orphans of the United States of Americans because this is such wonderful countries allows bums like us become millionaires" (p. 315). McManus agrees.

Additional fiction about the Greek immigrants fits well into other categories and is examined in subsequent chapters. Indeed, throughout this volume we are never far from the basic fact that two countries exist, Greece and the United States, and that from one to the other a great migration occurred, an astonishing human drama ready-made, so to speak, for American literature. The second generation that "grew up Greek-American" had immigrant parents with key roles in the relevant novels. Some of the "Greeks with a Southern accent" were immigrants who had to adjust to that particular region. The islanders from the Dodecanese who created the legend of Tarpon Springs were especially clannish and consequently attached to old ethnic customs. The fiction in *Athene*, the many characters in Petrakis, Greeks in mysteries—these and more examples serve to indicate that the novels cited in this chapter are only a part of the total experience of Greek immigrants.

4

GREEKS BETWEEN THE WARS

WORLD WAR I meant both internal conflict and general progress for the Greek Towns of America. The major division stemmed from political conditions in Greece, where the republican forces of Eleutherios Venizelos challenged the royalist oligarchy that had ruled since the revolution. The Royalists behind King Constantine were allegedly pro-German, the Venizelists pro-Allies. Even the Greek language figured in the bitter debates, with the aristocrats championing the *katharevousa*, the purist Greek, and the liberals the demotic. Severe religious tensions, detailed in the history by Saloutos, also rent the Greek-American community.

Alongside these internal growing pains, so to speak, was the Greek immigrant's early indecision about whether to stay here permanently or return to Greece. That more than forty-five thousand did go back to fight during the Balkan Wars of 1912–13 argued persuasively for *return*, especially since so many believed in the Great Idea—the recapture of Constantinople and all the other "Greek lands" still held by Turkey. A few years later, when the United States entered the world war, the fact that Greeks also readily donned khaki argued persuasively for *staying* here, since military service meant American citizenship. Events seemed to be going well for the Greeks both here and abroad. One provision of the Treaty of Sèvres, negotiated between Greek Premier Venizelos and the Great Powers, gave the district of Smyrna to Greece; but the Royalists ousted Venizelos and promptly ordered their armies eastward toward Ankara. Their rout and destruction by Mustafa Kemal Ataturk resulted in the massacre and burning of Smyrna, an event that still haunts the Greek, if not the world, imagination.

The literary reaction of writers in Greece to this trauma, which was naturally much stronger than that in America, is detailed in Thomas Doulis's *Disaster and Fiction: Modern Greek Fiction and the Impact of the Asia Minor Disaster of* 1922 (1977).[1] From the 1930 edition on, Ernest Hemingway's *In Our Time* begins and ends with references to the holocaust. The narrator in "On the Quai at

Smyrna" watches a death scene from an Allied ship in the harbor. "The worst," a Turk tells.him, "were the women with dead babies. You couldn't get the women to give up their dead babies. They'd have babies dead for six days. Wouldn't give them up. Nothing you could do about it. Had to take them away finally."[2] The corpses of humans and animals alike float in the harbor. In "L'Envoi" the narrator speaks with the Greek king, who is under house arrest. The Greek generals responsible for the debacle in Asia Minor, all Royalists, have been executed; and the king is happy not to have been shot himself. "Like all Greeks he wanted to go to America" (p. 213). In a dispatch to the Toronto *Star Weekly*, "A Silent, Ghastly Procession," Hemingway describes the "never-ending staggering march" of the Christian population of Eastern Thrace fleeing toward Macedonia. In "Refugees from Thrace" he adds more facts about the tragic Thracian exodus.[3]

Two recent books, one factual and the other fiction, recall those grim and bloody days. Marjorie Housepian, in *The Smyrna Affair* (1971), gives what the book's jacket terms "the first comprehensive account of the burning of the city and the expulsion of the Christians from Turkey in 1922."[4] She bitterly condemns the western Great Powers for permitting the genocide. In the same year appeared Richard Reinhardt's novel *The Ashes of Smyrna*.[5] Although fiction, it is equally valuable as history and as entertainment—a story of love between a Greek girl and a young Turk. Reinhardt, who lives in California, spent more than eighteen months in Greece and Turkey doing research for the story.

The novel opens on May 15, 1919, with a Greek army under Allied protection occupying Smyrna and its environs. The western educated Abdullah loves Eleni Trigonis, the only daughter of a rich raisin-shipper, but his brother Kenan implacably hates all Greeks. Eleni has no feelings for Abdullah, regarding him only as a Turkish dandy who occasionally visits their house. She thinks instead of an Athenian army officer, Dimitris Kalapothakis, with whom her father has been in correspondence for some time. Eleni first teases Abdullah about marriage, then tells him she is engaged, and finally draws the blind on him. Her father Christos is obsessed with patriotic visions of a greater Greece. "The Moslem conqueror had fallen at last; the Christian Greek would rule again" (p. 17). Trigonis wishes his son George more actively shared his expansionist dream—to make of Smyrna "the New York of the Orient!" On the Villa Trigonis Christos has a huge sign painted: "Smyrna Today—Constantinople Tomorrow!" (p. 20).

The Greek takeover faces a little resistance from Kenan's armed band. The fanatic one-armed Turk is captured by Lieutenant Kalapothakis and is then released, but the Greek officer shoots him in the leg as he runs off. At the villa old Trigonis toasts Dimitris as an ideal Greek soldier, one who will carve out a new Ionia with the Smyrna Legion. His son George fears the prospect, because he knows the Turks will resist. The author describes the gluttony of the victors as they feast in "French fashion" after midnight at Villa Trigonis. He satirizes the Frenchified "cultivation" of Madame Trigonis. The Greeks are pompous, egoistic, puffed up with self-importance.

The chapter also deals with the youth of Christos. He likes an Armenian girl he cannot have, and leaves school to peddle English yarn on commission throughout the Levant. While getting rich, he meets Greeks of the diaspora everywhere—the hidden empire of Greeks awaiting the revival of Byzantium. "He came to know all the provinces and circumstances of this Diaspora: the boisterous Greeks of the Dobruja, the sophisticated Greeks of Bucharest, the Russified Greeks of the Volga, the Italianate Greeks of the Dodecanese, the grasping Greeks of Syria, the bland, disdainful Greeks of Alexandria, with faces like halvah" (p. 52). At this point Christos is engaged in business and whoring and has not yet acquired his consuming nationalism. He does feel a pull toward Greece in 1897 during the brief and unsuccessful war with Turkey. This pull extended far and wide, drawing into the conflict "Greek bootblacks from New York, Greek cooks from Boston and Greek diamond thieves from Amsterdam" (p. 54).

Years pass, and then Eleutherios Venizelos, the rebel from Crete, assumes political power in Greece. At the suggestion of Venizelos, Christos Trigonis establishes himself in Smyrna to unite Anatolian Greeks for the struggle ahead. Coming up to the present, 1919, Reinhardt alternates between Greeks and Turks as his plot unfolds. Abdullah, the son of Hilmi Pasha, turns from abstract Marxist ideology to direct action; he organizes a socialist revolution. He orders five thousand rifles from a mysterious figure called Pefko, which in Greek means *pine*. Eleni Trigonis's intended, Dimitris Kalapothakis, hates the Royalists, whereas her brother George tends to be a pacifist. The author clearly defines the deep political division between Royalists and Venizelists in this period.

The term *Kemalist* and the name *Mustapha Kemal Pasha* begin to reverberate throughout the Levant. Rumors grow about a Greek offensive to capture all of Asia Minor, on grounds that the Smyrna region by itself is untenable. Shamed by Dimitris, George Trigonis volunteers for the Smyrna Legion. Dimitris himself schemes to remain in Smyrna by fabricating a plot against Venizelos that has George a traitor. The Greek armies launch their offensive in July 1920. They take town after town, while Mustapha Kemal seeks to reorganize the Turkish forces at Ankara. There Kenan, a delegate to the national assembly, moves its members by offering his life to Mustapha Kemal as the savior of Turkey.

Elsewhere Turkish irregulars and bandits set themselves up as warlords; they raid villages and commit atrocities. Abdullah's "army" of fifteen or so assorted thugs composes the nucleus of his Marxist agrarian revolution. They stick together only for the gold coins he gives them. A bandit named Lütfi contests Abdullah for leadership of the ragtag army and for his money belt. In the ensuing fight Abdullah cuts Lütfi's throat, and the "soldiers" recognize in Abdullah "a stronger and more ruthless master" (p. 190). Enough armed bands such as his exist to dictate terms to the feeble government at Ankara. Kenan as an emissary of that government urges that all such bands, including his brother Abdullah's, be wiped out. Slowly the Turkish forces gather to assault the Greeks.

During the winter of 1920 the limited campaign in Asia Minor ends with a Greek victory. "Exactly one day after the Allies and Turks finally sign the peace treaty at Sèvres, two assassins—Greeks of the Royalist persuasion—step out of ambush at the Gare de Lyon in Paris and fire point-blank at Eleftherios Venizelos" (p. 211). The republican statesman does not die, but the attempt enflames the hatred between Venizelists and Royalists. Venizelos dissolves parliament and calls for new elections. On October 25, King Alexander dies. The Royalists win the elections, and King Constantine returns to the throne from exile in Switzerland. Venizelos promptly leaves the country.

"To Dimitris, the election was a cataclysm" (p. 223). It means almost immediate resumption of hostilities. He is ordered to Ushak, an exposed unpleasant town on the deepest salient of the army of Anatolia. The new Royalist command quickly demotes tested Venizelist officers. Dimitris has to pledge his loyalty to the king. The Turkish irregulars face surrender either to Kemalist forces or to the Greeks. Kenan, now insane, orders his brother Abdullah killed. Abdullah escapes to the Greeks, who believe they can defeat Mustafa Kemal in a month at most.

At Villa Tregonis a domestic tragedy has occurred: Eleni, unmarried, is pregnant. Her parents assume Dimitris Kalapothakis to be the father. Christos Trigonis, using his political power, has Dimitris returned to Smyrna to marry Eleni—without a dowry. Dimitris refuses to admit guilt, and Eleni refuses to accuse him. Instead, she runs away and marries Abdullah. "The perfect wedding took place at the zenith of the day, in accordance with the regulations of Islam, and was as simple as the Prophet" (p. 272). They must quit Smyrna. In her condition Eleni refuses to bed with her husband. Abdullah calls her "daughter of a pig" when he learns she is pregnant with another's baby. She scornfully asks, "Did you expect to steal a virgin at the Carnival Ball?" (p. 277). They make a difficult four-day journey to Abdullah's ancestral home. There, on the way to the well, Eleni falls to the ground and has a painful miscarriage. She lives among her Turkish relatives in quiet despair, their town under Greek control. Abdullah and Eleni agree on one thing: neither has any place to go.

During spring 1921 the Greeks seek to consolidate their new acquisitions. The stern and often cruel methods of expelling Moslems raise international protests. Trigonis, who is now friendly with Dimitris, has him put in charge of investigating reports of Greek atrocities so as to refute them. Greek warlords destroy, pillage, rape, and kill. The Red Cross and others also investigate the charges. The burning of a village ordered by Dimitris puts the Royalists in a bad light. Greeks arrest and deport Turkish officials to a prison island and organize other Turks into slave-labor battalions. Abdullah, unwilling to hide, faces arrest and enslavement. He dares to take Eleni into town with him; and on their return to the farm, only the arrival of a patrol saves him from castration and death at the hands of Greek thugs. These are days of suffering for all.

> Suffering, indeed: and to what end? Greeks and Turks wrought this suffering on one another, and it neither gained nor taught them anything. Yet those dreamers like himself [Abdullah] who tried to turn this meaningless torment into a revolution failed worst of all, because they were unable to transform their thoughts to passions and their ideologies into love. If one could not make sense of his own life, how could he lead an army? (pp. 304–5)

Puffed up with initial victories, King Constantine takes personal command of his armies and envisages himself as the twelfth Con-

stantine to rule the Empire of Byzantium. George Trigonis distinguishes himself in battle. In August 1921 the Greeks meet stiff
Turkish resistance at the Sakarya River, "the battlefield Mustapha
Kemal had chosen," just short of Ankara. At this time Kenan sinks
into an "extraordinary fast . . . ordained to him in a vision by the
Caliph Ali" (p. 323). News of the great battle at the Sakarya
reaches Christos Trigonis in Smyrna. Eleni writes him that she is
very happy; but he says, "As far as I'm concerned, we have no
daughter" (p. 330). At the battlefront, Greek forces face a mountain in their path—Chal Dagh; Dimitris fights under the hated
Royalists; and the winter of 1922 comes without a decision. The
Greeks retreat from the Sakarya (which they call Sangarius) to
their summer positions. The state treasury in Athens is empty, and
the Great Powers refuse to help. Every month weakens the Greek
effort. George Trigonis, now a sergeant, watches the morale fall;
and Dimitris, first banished to a camp at Mudanya and then sent
back to Smyrna, fulminates against the Royalists.

By June 1922 the supreme command of the army of the Hellenes is in the hands of Lieutenant General George Hadjianestis—
a fanatic martinet believed by the Venizelists to belong in a mental
hospital. A professor named Paleologus says grimly: "We've hired
the town fool to pipe us on our march to doom" (p. 360). He sees
"a Front four hundred and fifty miles long, defended by a few
hungry boys and sheep dogs, with Mustapha Kemal on the other
side." August comes, and the new Turkish savior still bides his time,
perfecting his armies. The entire world awaits his offensive. At the
city of Alashehir, the ancestral estate of Abdullah's family is returned to them; and Eleni goes with them to enjoy its comforts.
The Greeks by now have crumbled, and they retreat before the
powerful Turkish advance. From three hundred fifty miles in the
rear General Hadjianestis issues his commands. The people of
Smyrna hear rumors of military disaster that are soon confirmed,
and refugees pour into the city. The rabidly chauvinistic Metropolitan Chrysostomos goes into a fast of expiation. "The rich, the
hunted and the perfidious" begin to leave Smyrna (p. 390). The
catastrophe of 1922 is in the making.

The retreating Greeks burn the Turkish villages they abandon.
Defeated, they start to arrive in Smyrna. A *hoja* (dervish) warns
Abdullah that he must divorce Eleni or be persecuted by the new
order. Eleni overhears the holy man and runs away. The mad
Kenan rides into Smyrna convinced of his "sacred duty to Islam"

to kill his brother Abdullah. At Villa Trigonis Eleni returns to face the wrath of her father, who wants to dispatch her to the island of Chios but is unable to find passage. The fate of Smyrna is on everyone's mind. Some say foreign battleships will arrive to save the city. Christos Trigonis yells, "Traitors," at the retreating defeated soldiers, betrayed though they were by incompetent Royalist officers. He begs Dimitris to find a boat and save Eleni; but, instead, Dimitris thinks of urging a colonel to lead a coup d'etat. As the Turks move in, the quay at Smyrna becomes impassable. (This is the same quay and the same critical moment that Ernest Hemingway also observes and writes about.)

While Christos Trigonis and Eleni hide in their villa, Turks arrest the Metropolitan Chrysostomos. He becomes the prisoner of General Nuredden Pasha, who gives him over to the Turkish crowd for justice. They tear him to pieces and leave his body naked in an alley. "A pack of dogs as gray as wolves rushed out and buried their ravenous muzzles in his wounds" (p. 438). The long-lasting conflict between Greeks and Turks may be summed up in an exchange between Nureddin Pasha and the Metropolitan before his death:

> "For five hundred years the Sultan has given his protection to his loyal Greek community, but you have repaid him with sedition. When our country was at war with France and England, you encouraged the Greeks on the coastline to spy for the enemy. You urged the Kingdom of Greece to go to war against us. You sent petitions to the Allied governments, begging them to enslave us and dismember our country. When the Greeks came to Smyrna, you welcomed them as liberators."
>
> Chrysostomos answered: "I have no regrets. I have been faithful to my ministry. Is it wrong for me to serve my nation and my people?" (p. 435).

"Even if you have wronged *my* nation and *my* people?" The push by the Royalist Greek armies toward Ankara came at a bad time for the Turks. They had lost much of their remaining empire as a result of the world war just concluded. To retake Smyrna and drive the hated Greeks out was a small but welcome consolation.

The action continues. The mad Kenan arrives in Smyrna with Mustapha Kemal and his staff. He finds the Trigonis house, not in search of Eleni, whom he calls a foul whore, but of his brother

Abdullah, with whom he has a score to settle. George Trigonis, now a lieutenant, has reached the harbor of Dikili. There refugees hope for the arrival of transports. People and animals crowd the town. Rather than leave the animals for the Turks, a Greek commander orders that they be slaughtered; oxen, camels, water buffaloes, horses, sheep, donkeys, goats, "the nursling camels and the piebald dogs that had trotted hundreds of miles between the axles of the wagons . . . were herded to the courtyard of a caravanserai and shot between the eyes" (p. 448). Unable to defeat the Turks, the Royalists, who had initiated the catastrophe, could at least defeat the animals. This final massacre torments George Trigonis "almost to madness," and he wanders weeping through the streets. Then he joins a crew that sets out to burn the port city of Dikili— the "funerary pyre of all their dreams: their Anatolia, their Great Idea, their Byzantium" (p. 451).

The scene shifts to Abdullah, who is looking down upon the rooftops of Smyrna. Suddenly he sees smoke rising from the center of the city. "Nobody knew exactly how or where the first spark had fallen. Apparently, a house had taken fire that morning in Chikir Sokak, a sunken alley in the neighborhood of Basmahane Station, where some Turkish soldiers had gone to confiscate the weapons of Armenian civilians" (p. 456). The city burned swiftly. Mustapha Kemal is shocked, but Kenan enjoys the flames that devour "this parasitic Christian colony" (p. 457). The sinister Pefko begs Kenan for a pass to the suburbs in exchange for information about Abdullah. Abdullah, meanwhile, has run to the Trigonis house looking for Eleni. There he meets her father, who, "Raising the rifle, . . . sighted carefully and shot Abdullah through the head" (p. 467), depriving Kenan of his revenge and fratricide. As hordes of refugees jam the quay of Smyrna, Allied warships sit in the harbor oblivious to the carnage and panic.

On the island of Lesbos, George meets Dimitris, who has become leader of a liberation movement to oust the Royalists from power and punish their military counterparts before the firing squad. Plastiras and Gonatas, two colonels, would seize power and force the king to abdicate.

The final chapter, dated September 27, 1922, describes Smyrna after the great fire. Christos Trigonis has become deranged; his mind has somehow blotted out the debacle. Eleni leads him to the quay to await passage out of Smyrna. There Kenan gives her, as a last, bitter parting gift, the tattered shoes and fez of Abdullah. She weeps at the thought that he had followed her, and takes the bundle with her into her unknown future.

The author of *The Ashes of Smyrna* does not take sides in the conflict. Under stress of war and the passion of old hatreds, both Greeks and Turks commit atrocities. The former, especially the Royalists, hurl forces against the Moslem enemy in a vainglorious dream of total conquest, the Great Idea. The latter, stripped of their once great empire, now have only Anatolia and Constantinople left. The characters represented by George Trigonis and Dimitris Kalapothakis point to the future, to the revolution led by Plastiras and Gonatas and to the trial and execution of the Royalist leaders who were responsible for the catastrophe.

During World War II MacKinlay Kantor wrote a short story about a Greek-American veteran of the first world war. Originally published in the *Saturday Evening Post*, "That Greek Dog" makes the point that a Greek, regarded as an alien by bigots, could be a good, patriotic American.[6] Bill Barbilis owns the Sugar Bowl, whose soda fountain has the "most glittering spigots in town" and ten small tables for his candy and ice-cream trade. Barbilis is proud of his American uniform and chevrons. "People militarily sophisticated, there in Mahaska Falls, could recognize immediately that Mr. Basilio Barbilis had been a sergeant, that he had served with the Forty-Second Division, that he had been once wounded, that he had sojourned overseas for at least eighteen months, and that he had been discharged with honor" (p. 141). In 1920 he befriends a lost puppy "no larger than a quart of ice cream." Barbilis lavishes much love upon the little creature. He demolishes the myth that all Greeks are mercenary, for the dog, named Duboko, pays no rent.

Duboko grows up to be as community-minded as his master, "who was proud to be a Moose, an Odd Fellow, a Woodman, and an upstanding member of the Mahaska Falls Commercial League" (p. 143). Barbilis buys a bugle to play for the new American Legion post, but the noise of his practice annoys the doctor, who lives above the Sugar Bowl and is the story's narrator. Duboko barks along with him, the two making "a Greek chorus, so to speak, complete with strophe and antistrophe." Duboko befriends everyone in town, attends all functions, including weddings and funerals.

Trouble starts for Bill Barbilis and his dog when the Klugges, owners of the rival All-American Kandy Kitchen, decide to drive them away. "Loudly they declared that their failure to enrich them-

selves was due solely to the presence in our community of a
Greek—a black-haired, dark-skinned Mediterranean who thought
nothing of resorting to the most unfair business practices, such as
serving good fudge sundaes" (p. 144). The mature Duboko has a
mighty frame; he is a mastiff with a mixture of German shepherd,
English bull, bloodhound, and great Dane. Everyone calls him
"that Greek dog," and some people say he looks like a Greek. "He
had Greek eyes, Greek eyebrows, and a grinning Greek mouth.
Old Major Wingate proclaimed in his cups that, in fact, he had
heard Duboko bark in Greek" (p. 146). Bill Barbilis's father Spiros,
a slight man with drooping mustachios, arrives from Greece.

In 1923, when the fiery crosses of the Ku Klux Klan "flared in
the darkness of our pastures," the narrator attends one of the
meetings. He realizes that friends have donned hoods to express
hatred for Catholics, Jews, and blacks. When a speaker calls the
dollar bill the "flag of the Jews," Barbilis warns him that the bill has
the United States seal on it. From the fender of a car he addresses
the crowd, which has been harangued by out-of-town organizers.
Barbilis reminds the assembly about Jimmy Clancy, a Catholic
killed in the Loraine sector; and Hyman Levinsky, killed the same
day; and Buzz Griffin, the "colored boy [who] used to shine
shoes. . . . and . . . is wounded in the Ninety-Second Division!" (p.
149). The organizers withdraw, but not before the seeds of poison
have been sown.

These seeds bear fruit in the form of hate notes, signed *Anti-
Greek League*, placed under the door of the Sugar Bowl. They demand that Barbilis leave town because he is not a 100-percent
American. Barbilis claims: "This is my town, and I am American
citizen, and I am bugler in American Legion. I bring my old father
here from Greece to be American, too, and now he has first papers" (pp. 149–50).

When Barbilis leaves for Sioux Falls to visit a sick cousin, four
white-hooded figures abduct old Barbilis in their car, the plates
covered with mud. Duboko runs after the car. The Klansmen take
the elder Barbilis to the dump, where they tie him to a fence. They
plan to flog him, but Duboko roars to the rescue. The narrator
says: "No four members of the Anti-Greek League, however
young and brawny, could justly be matched against a four-footed
warrior who used his jaws as the original Lacedaemonians must
have used their daggers, and who fought with the right on his side,
which Lacedaemonians did not always do" (p. 154). Duboko wins

the battle, but loses his life when the routed Klansmen run him down.

The culprits turn out to be the Klugges and two of their hangers-on at the All-American Kandy Kitchen. Furious, the burly Bill Barbilis throws Earl and John Klugge through their own plate glass windows. Duboko is buried behind the Sugar Bowl. "But the crowd of mourners would have done credit to Athens in the age when her dead heroes were burned," the narrator says, "and all the time that Bill was blowing Taps on his bugle, I had a queer feeling that the ghosts of Pericles and Thucydides were somewhere around" (p. 155). When McKinlay Kantor wrote "That Greek Dog" in 1942, tens of thousands of Greek-Americans were already fighting in another of our wars, and some of their stories would soon appear in American literature.

If Barbilis confronts the bigotry of the Jazz Age, Mavromichaelis in F. Scott Fitzgerald's *The Great Gatsby* (1925) helps to illuminate its spiritual sterility.[7] From his roadside restaurant he witnesses the hit-and-run-accident that kills Myrtle Wilson. Myrtle, the mistress of Tom Buchanan, runs into the road and is struck by Jay Gatsby's car, which is driven by Buchanan's wife Daisy. The victim's husband, George Wilson, sets out to get revenge and ends up killing Gatsby, who was innocent. "The young Greek, Michaelis, who ran the coffee joint beside the ashheaps was the principal witness at the inquest." After a siesta he had gone to a nearby garage, where he had found Wilson, the owner, very sick and pale. The man had his wife Myrtle locked up in their apartment above the garage. A little after seven Michaelis emerged from his work, intending to ask some questions of Wilson, only to hear Myrtle cry, "Throw me down and beat me, you dirty little coward!" Michaelis saw her rush into the road, trying to wave down an approaching car. The car struck and killed her, wavered a moment, and disappeared around the bend.

"Mavromichaelis wasn't even sure of its color—he told the first policeman that it was light green." He and another man reached her, "but when they had torn open her shirtwaist, still damp with perspiration, they saw that her left breast was swinging loose like a flap, and there was no need to listen for the heart beneath" (p. 165). The policeman has some trouble writing down the name *Mavromichaelis*; he is interrupted by angry questions from Tom Buchanan, who wants the particulars.

In a novel whose rich symbolism is carefully managed, the role of Michaelis may well be more important than it seems at first. The death of Myrtle Wilson occurs beside the ash heaps that signify a wasteland. The officer asks Michaelis: "What's the name of this place here?" and receives the reply "Hasn't got any name." Such anonymity tends to universalize the significance of the death setting. A further meaning to Fitzgerald's use of Michaelis may derive from the author's possible conception of Gatsby as a Christ figure. Some critics have explored this possibility by building on the statement that Jay Gatsby sprang "from his Platonic conception of himself. He was a son of God—a phrase which, if it means anything, means just that—and he must be about His Father's business, the service of a vast, vulgar, and meretricious beauty" (p. 168). For the sake of that beauty, the dream of Daisy Fay sought within the great dream of financial success, Gatsby sacrifices himself.

The novel raises the question What kind of God, what kind of Christ, does modern man deserve? Beside the sterile ashheaps, the eyes of Dr. T. J. Eckleburg stare out emptily from the gigantic, neglected billboard. No one knows who the oculist is, for he has abandoned his own sign. Only the persistent stare remains—the brainless, sightless God of the ashheaps who materializes as the enigmatic "Owl Eyes" of Gatsby's mansion. If the religious symbolism pertains, Michaelis may represent the archangel Michael to Dr. Eckleburg's God. In this allegory of American man in the 1920s, Fitzgerald offers little hope of redemption, love, and human loyalty. Everything that is holy by virtue of its integrity smashes to pieces against the hard materialistic malice of the Tom Buchanans or is dissolved by acids within the individual's twisted and diseased imagination, as in the case of George Wilson's motives for the murder of Gatsby. Henry Dan Piper regards Dr. Eckleburg as the "symbol of a world without the idea of God, a kind of anti-God."[8] When Wilson finds that his wife Myrtle has cheated him, he has her confront the eyes of Dr. Eckleburg and says: "God knows what you've been doing. You may fool me but you can't fool God." Piper recalls that after Myrtle's death Wilson tells Michaelis, "God sees everything," before he sets off on his quest for vengeance. "As we might expect," Piper concludes, "he only succeeds in killing the wrong man" (p. 333).

In 1926, the year after *Gatsby* was published, another classic of modern American literature appeared, Hemingway's *The Sun Also Rises*.[9] The protagonist, Jacob Barnes, tells of his exotic but sterile pilgrimage from Paris to Pamplona, Spain, with Robert Cohn, a fellow expatriate, and Lady Brett Ashley, a woman he might have loved had he been normal, but a war injury had rendered him impotent. Early in the novel, at the Café Select, we are introduced to two Greeks: a portrait painter called Zizi, who regards himself as a duke, and Count Mippipopolous, whose title though unexplained appears to be genuine. In Zizi's sole appearance he brings the fat count, who wears an "elk's tooth on his watch-chain," to Lady Ashley and her friends.

Like Barnes and Cohn, Mippipopolous is an expatriate American, having made his money in business in the U.S. It is interesting to note that Hemingway includes him among his gallery of cognoscenti—those who instinctively "belong," who live by the right code, who sympathize with the victims of *nada* (and may themselves be victims), and who face the perils of life with chin up, have a Dionysian love for the sensuous, and can die, when they must, bravely. Mippipopolous is to *The Sun Also Rises* what, to a great extent, Captain Rinaldi is to Hemingway's other notable early work, *A Farewell to Arms*. Both fall well within the code, and both, though relatively minor, serve to illuminate and otherwise enhance the role of the protagonists.

A certain ambiguity concerning both Zizi and Mippipopolous results from our learning about them from Brett Ashley when she is drunk. Barging in upon Barnes, she talks about the count who brought her to his flat. When he asks about Mippipopolous, she readily gives the count her approval, saying, "He's quite one of us." To his question "Is he a count?" she replies that she thinks so. "Deserves to be, anyhow. Knows hell's own amount about people. Don't know where he got it all. Owns a chain of sweetshops in the States" (p. 32). After a sip of brandy and soda she repeats that Mippipopolous lives by their code. "He's one of us, though," she reaffirms. "Oh, quite. No doubt. One can always tell." It turns out, according to Brett, that the count is supporting Zizi's artistic career. The dialogue between Barnes and Lady Ashley goes on:

> "Is Zizi really a duke, too?"
> "I shouldn't wonder. Greek, you know. Rotten painter. I rather liked the count."
> "Where did you go with him?"
> "Oh, everywhere. He just brought me here now. Offered me ten thousand dollars to go to Biarritz with him. How much is that in pounds?"
> "Around two thousand." (p. 33)

Count Mippipopolous is very cosmopolitan, very understanding. Lady Ashley refuses to go with him to Biarritz, to Cannes, and to Monte Carlo, because she knows too many people at all these places. He is "awfully nice" about her rejection and "damn nice" when she admits to being in love with Jake Barnes. Rising above his disappointment he has offered to take them both to dinner. She tempts Barnes with the dozen bottles of Mumms the count has bought, but Barnes declines, since he has to work on the morrow. The rich man, who happens to be Greek, is funding the Lost Generation's search for excitement, love, and meaning while drifting in a rootless, unhistoric time, a time when a Mippipopolous can become a count and a Zizi a duke. The count has no further role to play after wining and dining Lady Brett Ashley in Paris. Soon afterward she leaves with Barnes and several others for the fiesta and bullfights in Pamplona, Spain.

At the turn of the decade, before and after 1930, came the first of the whodunits that used important Greek characters. Credit for the very first goes to Dashiell Hammett and his classic mystery *The Maltese Falcon* (1929). At about this time, also, Thomas Wolfe first brought modern Greeks into southern fiction. These and other related works will be discussed in later chapters.

Another author, James T. Farrell, expresses a cynical view of the immigrant's fate in "The Benefits of American Life."[10] He prefaces the short story with an excerpt from a Greek poem: "Ye orphan sons of Greece, / Scattered hither and beyond, / Persecuted and forlorn / And by all nations beshun" (p. 302). At the age of thirteen Takiss Fillios arrives in the "paradise" of Chicago, to find dirty streets, long hours of work, a relative who exploits him, fear, and loneliness. "He learned that he was considered a dirty Greek greenhorn, and that many Americans would have been just as pleased if he . . . had never come to this land" (p. 303).

Time passes, and he grows up without being much of a success. He cannot learn to save money, but he does learn about the whores in a brothel owned by his cousin and how to dance like the Americans at a dance hall owned by Greek Professor Christopolos. Then the Depression hits and Takiss has a tough time finding work until he sees an advertisement that says *Dance Marathon*. "The word Marathon struck him. Greek" (p. 306). He decides to enter. The author details the nature of the "entertainment," which is in effect a month-long agony for the contestants. Takiss, with his blonde partner Marie Glenn, wins the second place prize of $250. However, he develops a bad cough. He wants to become a celebrity, a famous Greek-American, so he engages in sixteen dance marathons. He earns extra money by doing stunts, dancing, and singing "Yes, We Have No Bananas." The Greek press writes about him and prints his picture. "He had money now, five thousand dollars. He returned to Greece. But the strain of the marathons had ruined his lungs and he had tuberculosis" (p. 311). Ironically, the money America had given him went to the health resort where he sought a cure.

The friendship between a Greek immigrant and a Bohemian, a Japanese boy, and other ethnic types informs the nine stories of Charles Caldwell Dobie's *San Francisco Adventures* first published in 1937 and reprinted in 1969.[11] The stories recount episodes in the life of Josef Vitek, beginning in 1916 and ending twenty years later. During this time "the Greek" works beside Josef in a bakery, the two of them close friends and bachelors.

In the first story entitled "Four Saturdays" the Greek, who is in love, annoys Josef with his constant sighing. On the first Saturday they visit a Greek coffeehouse where the dancer is Miriam, "a Jewess from Constantinople." At the sight of her, Josef quickly falls in love, and he too begins to sigh. When he proposes to Miriam on the third Saturday and is rejected, the Greek mocks him mercilessly. On the fourth Saturday Josef finds his friend at the coffeehouse but not Miriam. The Greek tells him, "She has married one of her own people," and he hates her, for it was she over whom he too had sighed in vain (p. 17).

Although the Greek could be caustic and cruel at times, he could also be compassionate. In "The Gift" Josef helps the Japanese boy Ito, who cleans the bakery and has burned his hand with grease. The others laugh, Josef says, "especially my Greek friend who works beside me" (p. 28). After a week of ostracism Ito returns to work bearing *the gift*, a cherry bough in bloom. An argument ensues over which country has the best blossom. The Greek boasts, "Blossoms in Greece are such as only gods plant" (p. 37). The argument is closed when the boss declares that in springtime blossoms are blossoms everywhere "but there is only one Josef." At this Josef bursts into tears, and his Greek friend kisses him on both cheeks.

In a sad story entitled "Gray Socks," Josef's landlady knits socks for a nephew who is a soldier in France. When his legs are blown off, the Greek must break the news to her. She then decides to knit mittens for his hands instead. "Christmas Cakes" is about ethnic prejudice. A German woman who appears to be hoarding sugar has it taken from her by neighborhood women. When the Greek hears that this sugar—which was being saved to bake a special Christmas cake for Josef's landlady—was taken, he and his comrades contribute money so the woman can buy the sugar and eggs she needs to make her cake.

In "The Elder Brother" the Greek celebrates his nameday with a feast, and the landlady scoffs at the idea that such a "stupid lout" should be named for a saint. At her dinner table, to which she has invited a fortune-teller, the talk of ghosts, gypsies, and vampires frightens both Josef and his Greek friend. As the fortune-teller Elena reads Josef's teacup, cards, and palm, he suspects that she wants him, but he fears vampires and feels "two burning lips" against his throat. Elena attends the Greek's nameday celebration, at which the feast is even better than Josef had imagined. While dancing, Elena shows her teeth; they are small, sharp, and pointed! The Greek monopolizes her all night and then goes home with her—to protect Josef Vitek from becoming her victim. He says he has no heart's blood for Elena to drink, because a "cracked jug" holds little wine.

"The Fallen Leaf" is an old man, once Josef Vitek's baking master in Bohemia, who has failed miserably in America. He now picks the garbage pail near the bakery. When the starving Bohemian is jailed as a vagrant, Josef pledges that he will find his compatriot some work. Despite his Greek friend's initial reluctance, Joseph brings his former master to the bakery and invites him to demonstrate his baker's skill. All evening he works, proud and pleased. The Greek says he deserves a crown of laurel. Then the old man dies, a smile on his lips. Josef comments, "My Greek friend made the sign of the cross in mid-air with an upraised finger" (p. 145).

The Greek has an even stronger role in "St. Christopher and the Devil." The Greek is angry with Tony, his helper, whom he supposes has stolen his St. Christopher medal and gold chain. Near the bakery is a pension run by Basques, where Josef Vitek sometimes eats. At the pension Josef and his friend see Manuela stroking a toad in a glass dish. She is a witch, a stranger whispers, with charms for a lover and death for an enemy. He explains how Manuela's power works through wax and clay figures.

Later, Josef watches horrified as his Greek friend kneads and bakes a likeness of Tony. The Greek makes a deal with Manuela to spell the boy's death, and Josef hires a Sicilian witch to undo her evil spell but to no avail. As Tony lies near death, the boss asks, "Which of you . . . owns that?" holding up the glistening chain and medal. The Greek pales as he realizes his error. He and Josef compel Manuela to withdraw her spell, and Tony revives immediately.

In a gesture of remorse and trust, the Greek makes the sign of the cross, kneels, and slips "the holy image . . . about Tony's neck" (p. 178). In this gesture is repeated the author's pattern of behavior for the Greek as he moves again from evil to benevolence.

During the 1930s modern Greeks began to appear in American plays besides in fiction. Maxwell Anderson's poetic drama *Winterset* (1935) alludes to Greeks but does not bring them on stage. The protagonist, Mio Romagna, has for years been trying to clear his father's name in a long search for truth and justice. When his friend Carr asks what happened when they split up, Mio replies: "Fell in with a fisherman's family on the coast and went after the beautiful mackerel fish that swim in the beautiful sea. Family of Greeks—Aristides Marinos was his lovely name. He sang while he fished. Made the pea-green Pacific ring with his bastard Greek chanties. Then I went to Hollywood High School for a while." [12] The play makes no further reference to Greeks.

In *The Time of Your Life* (1939) William Saroyan gives a Greek newsboy a brief part. He enters Nick's Pacific Street Saloon and asks, "Can you use a great tenor?" The boy is only eleven. He says he wants to sing, not "holler headlines all the time." Nick lets him sing "When Irish Eyes Are Smiling," which to everyone's wonder and delight he does in a swift and beautiful voice. Nick wants to know if he is Irish, and the boy replies, "No, I'm Greek." He comes from Salonica. Nick calls him a great singer and invites him to return in about a year, "Along about November 7th, 1940." [13] The youth happily runs out to peddle his papers. He proves a typical Saroyan point—that people are wonderful. Later in the play a bum named Harry speaks about being in Sharkey's on Turk Street for a cup of coffee. "George the Greek is shooting a game of snooker with Pedro the Filipino." Harry's reminiscence has a counterpoint between the coffee and the Greek's game. "George the Greek takes the cue. Chalks it. Studies the table. Touches the cue-ball delicately. Tick. What happens? He makes the three-ball! What do I do? I get confused." [14] Neither the Greek newsboy nor the pool shark is mentioned again.

In his next play, *Love's Old Sweet Song* (1940), Saroyan uses four

Greek characters.[15] The Armenians and Greeks share a common bond in having been historically the major victims of Turkish atrocity. Three actors of Greek descent appeared in the original Broadway run of *Love's Old Sweet Song*. Of one of them, Saroyan writes, "John Economides, the famous Greek actor, as Pericles Americanos, not only translated my lines into Greek, but brought to his part the comic solemnity and gentle anger which the role called for."[16] In the play Georgie Americanos, the "Greek-American Postal Telegraph messenger," arrives at the home of Ann Hamilton with a telegram purportedly from Boston. He recites from memory the message that Barnaby Gaul will soon arrive to whistle a song under Ann's window, that he had met her once twenty-seven years earlier and has always loved her. Thus the Greek boy plays both Hermes and Cupid. Ann cannot remember Barnaby Gaul. When someone does whistle outside, it is an itinerant pitchman named Jim, who goes along with the romantic idea and plays Barnaby. Then Georgie's rival messenger, Italian Tom Fiora, arrives to tell Georgie that the telegram from Boston was a hoax, a trick played to get even with him. But, hoax or not, the love it portended is taking hold.

The play, being a comedy, has farcical elements, and these involve Greeks. "Demetrios, a small middle-aged Greek with a big black mustache, pushes a lawn-mower into the yard, begins to cut the lawn, suddenly notices the roaring lion, roars back at it" (Act 1). The Greek roars at a statue. "Barnaby Gaul" questions him about his citizenship status; he regards himself an American citizen and is due to receive his final papers the next month. Then Gaul chases him away because the lawn does not need cutting.

The huge family of Cabot Yearling appears; they have fourteen children and another on the way. Needing a home, they choose Ann's. The children break things and eat everything in sight. Georgie Americanos calls them mice and tries to chase them off. The crowded scene is sinister, yet the Yearlings with their *copia* of life are a contrast to Ann's deprived spinsterhood, her empty house and heart. Gaul disappears, and she worries that the "itinerant merchant" who peddles Dr. Greatheart's Five-Star Multi-Purpose Indian Remedy, has gone back to Boston. She wants to sell her house and follow him. But, in spite of threats, the Yearlings refuse to leave. Georgie reveals to Ann that the original telegram was a hoax, but *her* truth about love cannot be affected by a right or wrong name. She now leaves her home and goes to live in that of Stylianos Americanos, Georgie's father. In the meantime, Gaul has returned. He understands why the Yearlings remain; they have no place else to go. Georgie, with an understanding beyond his years, tries to convince "Barnaby Gaul" that he is not a fraud and that he should go to his father's house to get Ann.

Act 3 takes place in the parlor of the Stylianos Americanos home, which Saroyan describes as "typical of the parlors of almost all peoples of the Near East in America. Oriental rug. An old Army rifle, crossing a sword in its sheath, over an enormous photograph of eleven men, ranging in age from 15 to 70, all with mustaches of one sort or another; each in a military uniform or part of one; each holding a gun. American and Greek flags, crossed." He ends with "Also two large photographs of STYLIANOS in wrestler's tights."

Stylianos sits at front center smoking a nargileh. His father, Pericles, enters, and they talk, one in Greek, the other in English. Pericles laments the passage of his life and says he longs to return to Smyrna, a dream made impossible by "the infidel Turks." Ann Hamilton enters, describes her situation, and praises Georgie as "a wonderful, wonderful boy." Demetrios, the cousin, comes in and mentions the lady's troubles, but Stylianos banishes him to the kitchen. He tells old Pericles, "She's in love, Papa," and that explains her confusion. Stylianos brings her wine, and they drink together.

Georgie enters with two items of news for Ann: the Yearlings set her house on fire, and Barnaby did not leave town. Georgie sends Stylianos to retrieve Barnaby from a saloon. At home Stylianos comically employs a variety of wrestling holds in pressuring Barnaby to return to Ann. Finally, Barnaby, after the histrionics, admits he loves Ann. Ann Hamilton rushes into the room. Barnaby has returned! Then the Yearlings pour in looking for one of their girls, one that Barnaby has handed over to the sheriff for safekeeping. With true Greek hospitality Stylianos Americanos invites them all to stay for supper.

Saroyan also uses Greeks, Armenians, and other nationalities in his short stories. In "Laughing Sam" a Greek newsboy, Nick Kouros, teaches a troubled youth named Sam how to sell papers.[17] Success in the street trade, he says, comes from yelling "paper, paper" and "whatever the news is" (p. 7). A character referred to only as "the Greek" has a larger role in "The Crusader," the title referring to a slot machine on which he and some others gamble for low stakes.[18] "The small Greek with the false teeth and the sick eyes was the luckiest of all, and gamest, and the marbles acted well for him, stacking up a high score every time" (p. 203). He wins only when the game is fast, not slow; "high-strung, reckless, and at the same time cautious," he curses even as he wins.

In "The Only Guy In Town," an alcoholic Greek named Peter Karamokoulos dominates the story.[19] Besides drink he has a problem with the memory of his second wife, Nazia, who he hopes is dead. He wants to beat up women who remind him of her. When a sideshow comes to his California town, he ventures to wrestle with a huge Jugoslavian, Bulgov, for the five hundred dollars offered to anyone who can pin him to the mat. Pete threatens to "break every bone" in Bulgov's body while bragging about the warriors and athletes of Athens; but during the fight Bulgov tosses him out of the ring eight times, and finally "a committee of eighteen Greeks" hold a meeting in the tent and "jump on Mr. Karamokoulos and take him home" (p. 86).

The narrator likes Pete even though he considers him to be rather stupid. He sells Pete a newspaper every night and tells him tall tales about Greece, including such farfetched "news" stories as that Greece has conquered Italy on the west and Turkey on the east. Pete at first believes these lies and asks for details—perhaps these illustrious victories involve his relatives. "Read the names, Kid," he says. "Read the names. I worship the heroes of Greece resurrected" (p. 89). When he is told the truth by a friend, he feels like killing the narrator, but he soon gets over his grief that Greece has not yet conquered anybody.

Pete tells his own lies, mainly to women, about the money he is winning "in Chinatown on lottery." Somehow he gets enough cash to open up the "Karamokoulos Hamburger Parlor" on Mariposa Street. He tries to keep the place open day and night without sleep. He marries Ella, his waitress, a "nice tramp," then cracks up, drinks too much, fights with all, and goes repeatedly to jail. At the end he leaves for Frisco, to find "a town his size." The narrator follows: with Pete Karamokoulos gone, everything seems to die. He was "the only guy in town."

In "The Struggle of Jim Patros with Death" in a later collection by Saroyan,[20] the protagonist is a waiter at Omar Khayyam's in San Francisco, a restaurant to which the author refers elsewhere in his fiction. "He [Patros] is a good-natured Greek of forty-four who seems a good deal younger. He is a little under medium size, but not quite small enough to be a small man. He is well-built, and waits table with efficiency and style. He knows how to be helpful without being obtrusive, and his manners are naturally good" (p. 53). Patros gambles, follows the horses daily, and occasionally plays stud poker. He also tells stories about himself, like the time he nearly died in Chester, Pennsylvania, during the influenza epidemic of 1918. Jim Patros relates that, after everyone expected him to die, what finally cured him was heavy bleeding from his nose and chicken broth—gallons and gallons of chicken broth. And perhaps something else—his doctor, who was from Smyrna, attributed his cure to his having gone barefoot in Greece until he was seventeen, when he left for America. "You see, Jim said. From the earth to my feet came the strength of the old country. If I had worn shoes in the old country, I would be dead now, not alive" (p. 15).

The coauthors of the play *My Sister Eileen* (1941), Joseph Fields and Jerome Chodorov, included in its cast a character named Mr. Appopoulos.[21] In Ruth McKenney's original stories he was called Mr. Spitzer. In both works he is the landlord of Ruth and Eileen. McKenney described Spitzer as a "large, handsome, ferocious man who wrote poems and painted pictures when he wasn't terrorizing his female tenants" (p. 197). In the play, Appopoulos is "a squat, powerfully built man" with a "heavy shock of hair, bushy eyebrows," "a complete bully whenever he feels it is safe."[22] Onstage he speaks with a vague foreign accent, "possibly Greek" or East Side.

By being pushy and cunning, Appopoulos rents an undesirable basement apartment in Greenwich Village to the Sherwood sisters, who are newly arrived from Columbus, Ohio. As a character he suffers from the breezy superficiality of most Broadway comedies. The girls scoff at a painting in the apartment from his "blue-green period," but he is either too dense or too thick-skinned to accept their recurring insults. Comedy ensues as the sisters get involved with a variety of stray characters who wander in and out of their easily accessible home. That one of the visitors absconds with the painting makes Appopoulos furious, since he is planning a one-man show. The show has no viewers when held, in spite of a sign advertising "free iced tea," and he gets the lost painting back from the pawnshop. Appopoulos is equally unlucky in making a pass at Eileen. He is a Greek in name only, for he has no ethnic consciousness whatsoever; his name might as well have remained Spitzer.

In Sterling North's collection of fictionalized profiles, *Seven against the Years* (1939), some of the contending social themes of the thirties are captured.[23] North begins his narratives with an episode about a Greek student attending the University of Chicago. The first chapter is called "Nineteen Twenty-Nine," the year that Robert Maynard Hutchins took office as the president; the last is "Nineteen Thirty-Nine," the year that seven friends who had graduated ten years earlier meet for a class reunion. At the outset the whole senior class is being graduated with the exception of Demetrius Dardanus. "Wildeyed and mouthing strange Greek oaths Demetrius beat his fists against the unyielding doors of the Bursar's office" (p. 1). The character of Dardanus is based on Nicholas John Matsoukas, a journalist and publicist long associated with the theaters of the Skouras brothers. His problem at the commencement stems from a twelve-dollar student loan. All about him the university is putting up buildings worth millions.

"Now it was June with enough sunshine to please even a Greek. Sunshine was like retsina, that good, strong resin wine" (p. 2). Demetrius in frustration lies on the steps as Mark Harbord, a friend and reporter, finds him. Demetrius tells the story of an IOU for twelve dollars he won at poker from a boy named Blucher, whose mother is worth about $20 million. Demetrius hoped the bursar would accept the IOU., since Mrs. Blucher is a trustee. But the university loves buildings, not "peoples," and Demetrius does not like snobs.

> The members of the Greek letter fraternities were the Greeks, so that made Demy a barb. But if they were the Greeks, maybe Dardanus could be the American. If they were the snobs, maybe Demetrius could carry the torch of American democracy. The spirit inherent in the speeches of Lincoln and the poetry of Walt Whitman. That first rush of emotion he had known at Ellis Island—this great, beautiful, free country that Americans took for granted, were so casual about, sometimes even spat upon. (p. 4)

Harbord intervenes. He takes Demetrius's case directly to the president, and Demetrius is graduated.

Dardanus's exploits during the intervening decade are recounted in chapter 6 of the book. His story begins on the island of Sphacteria, which guards the harbor of Pylos. The account contains many details of Greek ethnicity. It sketches an authentic

Greek character, with his own peculiarities. If Dardanus liked you, "he would not try to seduce your sister" (p. 198). If he thought you were a genius, you shared his last bowl of stifado and drank from his last bottle of retsina. Being honorable, "Demy the Greek" returned money loaned—in six weeks or maybe a year, but not money borrowed from women, who were, he argued, "fortunate to enjoy his company," and "inferior creatures whose principal use was well known to all Greeks" (p. 198). For two years Dardanus had shivered at the university without a coat, yet no friend went hungry "while Demy had garlic, red peppers, tomatoes, cheese and a shelf of spices above the two-burner gas stove in his attic room" (p. 199).

During his rich, spoiled youth on Sphacteria, Demetrius had feared the Nereids (nymphs) and the Kalikanzaroi. He believed these agents of the devil caused his leg to atrophy, making him limp. At the university he kept repeating, "That's my life," implying fatalism. He got his latest scholarship by showing the big tear in his pants. Dardanus told about his childhood, his irreverence, and petty misdemeanors, and how his father became poor. He sold provisions to British warships using the harbor until an unfaithful servant conspired against him with a secret partner, undersold him, and left him with huge quantities of perishable food. Then, when the world war broke out, the Greek government reserved the island for its own purposes. Twelve-year-old Demetrius "was put aboard a freighter and sent by a circuitous route to America"—to Chicago, where Uncle Stephen put him to work shining shoes. At times he carried an American newspaper "under his arm so that people would think he could read the language as well as anyone" (p. 203). For a while he worked as a water boy on a section gang in Wisconsin. In time he enrolled at the famed University of Chicago.

On one occasion Demetrius Dardanus cornered the Lenten market in octopus to wreak vengeance on Charley Zenos, who owed him $24.65 for clerking Saturday nights in his grocery. Dardanus went to a rival grocer, George Pappadopoulos, and got him to buy up the whole octopus cargo of the Greek steamer *St. Spiridon* due to arrive in New York. "And since Greeks could eat no butter, milk or blooded flesh for forty days it took no prophet to predict that the annual rush for octopi was imminent, for Greeks can make days of fast into days of feasting with their beloved octopus and a few tons of olives" (p. 207). Zenos moans that he is a "ruined Grik," but he invites Dardanus to dinner anyway. Despite Lent it consists of whole roast milk lamb, stifado of hot onions and spices, feta cheese, "rich Greek pastries and thick Turkish coffee." After dinner Dardanus promises to get Pappadopoulos to sell Zenos some of the octopi, then Zenos will pay him the $24.65. Unfortunately the greedy Pappadopoulos refuses. Dardanus tries to have the archbishop issue an edict "against eating octopus soup during Lent," but the archbishop sees through the scheme and with a laugh sends his friend away dissatisfied. Dardanus, despite his cunning, has lost all around. "S'n'fa b'tch, that's life" (p. 210).

Broke on Easter eve, Dardanus does not have twenty-five cents for either a hamburger or a candle at St. Sophia's—to "sit with the others in the darkness awaiting the moment when Christ would incredibly appear, and all the candles would be lighted from the Archbishop's taper" (pp. 211–12). Unable to borrow the small sum, Dardanus steals five nickels from his Aunt Catherine. With it he buys a candle, sits next to his Great Uncle Alex, and gets invited to his wealthy home for roast lamb and wine. "S'n'fa b'tch, that's life," he says. Destiny can be both bad and good—roast lamb and wine after forty days of black bread and octopus soup.

Another great scheme of Demetrius Dardanus involved the promotion of "Grik Day" at the Chicago World's Fair. To get ahead of "another dirty Grik" who planned to have his "Grik Day," Dardanus needed five hundred dollars from his reporter friend, Mark Harbord. "Harbord's chief was sore at Dardanus for palming off a story about a fourth-century Greek manuscript of the New Testament discovered at Colosimo's on which Chicago gangsters swore bloodthirsty oaths before slipping out in big, dark sedans to riddle the opposition with tommy guns. A photographer sent to Colosimo's the day after the story was run could find no Greek manuscript" (pp. 217–18). With such chicanery Dardanus could also have invented a way to penetrate the walls of Troy.

For his "Grik Day" at the Century of Progress, he planned events stemming from the Hellenic heritage. One featured the goddess Aphrodite jumping out of a lily pond to the applause of fifty thousand "Griks."

> Besides his soap-suds Venus, Demetrius planned to show the siege of Troy, the battle of Marathon, the trial of Phryne, Socrates drinking the hemlock, and a Greek strong man from Cephalonia whose specialty was the death-defying cannon act. This Cephalonian pocket Hercules amazed and instructed by supporting a six-hundred-pound bronze cannon of antique

design across the back of his neck. With arms locked firmly around the barrel, with muscles bulging and legs braced, he took a lighted torch between his teeth, turned to light the fuse at the breech of the cannon, and while women fainted and strong men shut their eyes took the recoil as easily as a duck hunter might the kick of a twelve gauge. (pp. 219–20)

If the Cephalonian slipped and sent a foul ball into the bleachers, that was all right with Dardanus. "What's a couple of Griks more or less?" After getting the antique cannon out of hock, he was ready for the big day.

On "Grik Day" at the fair, crowds gathered: Greek merchants and their wives, proud Greek fathers "whose children would be soldiers in the siege of Troy and the battle of Marathon," large Greek mothers all primped and powdered, and "sleek-haired, dapper young men in low, fast cars," there to look at the famed Aphrodite. But it rained. "It rained on the siege of Troy and the battle of Marathon. It rained on Socrates drinking the hemlock and the trial of Phryne. Aphrodite slipped as she was arising from the foam and sprained her ankle, and the fuse fizzled when the Cephalonian pocket Hercules tried to shoot his cannon (p. 222). The event was a disaster; and instead of the anticipated profit of $10,000, Dardanus was left soaked to the skin and coughing, wishing that other "dirty Grik" had put on "Grik Day" at the fair.

At that particular time Dardanus was the jack-of-all-trades for the *Hellenic Gazette*, the Greek newspaper in Chicago. Since the bank held a large mortgage for him, the paper's owner, Heliogabalus, was a Republican, an ardent patriot with a passion for government "of the peoples, by the peoples and for the peoples" (p. 223). Dardanus, a Democrat, actually believed in Lincoln's sentiment. Whereas his boss wrote editorials in Greek for the GOP candidates, Dardanus in his English articles often took exactly the opposite position. Unknown to Heliogabalus, his *Hellenic Gazette* suffered from political schizophrenia.

These days Dardanus was busy and impoverished. "At one and the same time he was playing poker for Nick the Greek, doing publicity for the Greek Orthodox Church, promoting Greek Day at the Chicago's World Fair, and putting every cent he could earn into costumes for the Byzantine choir" (p. 224). Unfortunately, hardly anyone came to the concerts, and Dardanus, coughing blood, had to go to the Municipal Tuberculosis Sanitarium. Within a week he organized a protest riot there to secure better food.

From his hospital bed his columns in the *Gazette* promoted the idea of a free Greek sanitarium to be established in the Southwest. Then the *Gazette* folded, and Dardanus and Heliogabalus celebrated the sad event "with a bottle of raki." Said Dardanus, "S'n'fa b'tch, that's life."

The tenth anniversary reunion of the Class of 1929 briefly brings together such political enemies as Andre O'Sullivan Maloney, who runs a consumer cooperative in Minnesota, and multimillionaire Frederick Oswald Blucher, founder of the Knights of the White Gardenia. Afterward Mark Harbord lunches with Demetrius Dardanus at Peter Anagnosti's Athenian Café, where they have "egg-lemon soup and chicken pelaphy" and discuss the past and future. Dardanus tells of his work on the WPA Writers' Project, in which he had "outlined a book called 'Sons of Ulysses'—a study of Greek-Americans so interesting in design that his plan was to be used as a model for similar books on other national groups throughout the country. But the witch-burners in Washington as a prelude to destroying the whole writers' project were cleansing it of 'aliens' and Demy had failed to take out his final citizenship papers. He had just been notified of his dismissal" (p. 325). Harbord and Dardanus ruminate about tragedy. It is no longer the highborn who are brought to disaster by the gods. No, Dardanus claims, it is the fate of peoples—"We, the peoples . . . of the United States" suffering the economic disaster of the system. Both friends agree: "That's life."

Two years after *Seven against the Years*, another volume appeared with basically the same theme—the fate of a high-school class of 1929 during the Depression. Edward Newhouse's *Anything Can Happen* (1941) contains two episodes devoted to Manny Hirsch, each of which involves George Kyrillis, the Greek owner of a candy-and-cigar store.[24] The setting is Manhattan. But, instead of developing only seven characters as North did, Newhouse profiles thirty in relatively brief sketches. Both sections on Manny Hirsch depict events in the Greek's store, the first when the boys are still in school, the second an unspecified number of years later. We learn little about George Kyrilis compared to North's Dardanus.

Manny, a jokester in high school, puns on the "Ode on a Grecian Urn." "What's a Grecian urn, he said, what's a Grecian urn? Fifteen a week maybe, if he don't own the restaurant" (p. 37). He "runs numbers" for Kyrillis. When Rizzuti, the cop on the block, chases the boys into the candy store, Kyrillis lectures him on their right to gather on the sidewalk as long as they want to without being harassed. In the later episode Manny Hirsch is still running numbers for George Kyrillis. He tries to convince the Greek storekeeper to add a gambling table to his policy racket, but his proposal is refused because of the potential risk. Now cynical and aimless, Manny Hirsch prefaces his smart remarks with "Comes the revolution." Both the resignation in Dardanus's "That's life" and the threat in Manny's "Comes the revolution" typify the critical period of the thirties and its literature of social protest.

During World War II Philip Freund wrote and published the title story of *The Young Greek and the Creole* (1944).[25] Stories in the collection develop ethnic types under the general theme of the romance of life. The man identified as a Creole, Lucian Herve, is a well-established New York sculptor; the Greek, Myron Parahedes, is a restless and impoverished youth who dreams of one day going to South America. The boy has run away from home. "His father had been a defrocked [for alcoholism] Greek Orthodox priest, still known to his fellow-countrymen in Cincinnati as 'Papa' Parahedes" (p. 101). Myron has spent several years on his own. Brief flashbacks summarize both his and the sculptor's past.

They met on the street when the ungainly Greek begged money for a meal. Herve, who admires the Hellenic contribution to art, invited Myron home. The chance encounter reminds Herve of how the great Phidias and other classical sculptors transformed raw and ugly clay into stunningly beautiful figures. He wants to do the same. He employs Myron as a model, and his passion in molding the clay merges with the boy's intense obsession to visit South America.

When the clay figure nears completion, Herve decides to repay Myron by giving him the travel money. But the boy's wanderlust has gotten the better of him, and he has left behind a note: "It doesn't look as though I'm going to South America right away. So I think I'll just drift around and see some more of this country" (p. 111). For months afterward the Creole artist works on the onyx statue, which is bought by a rich patron of an art museum in Rio de Janeiro. Thus, in transmuted form, the Greek boy does go to South America.

At the end the author invokes the Hellenic tradition, as Herve expresses the feeling that he had put both his and the boy's spirit into the stone. "In just the same way, when the young Greeks had stood naked in the sunlight, Phidias had endowed them with divinity; they had been human, but they became divine Apollo, and the people had come to offer them homage" (p. 112).

5

GROWING UP GREEK-AMERICAN

LIKE OTHER ETHNIC GROUPS the Greek immigrants faced the difficulties of adjustment to a new environment. Most arrived with strong emotional ties to the mother country—ties of family, friends, and memories. The stronger the ties, the more divided the personality, the more difficult the adjustment. Many a sociology book has been written on the subject of Americanization, the ultimate victory of the American Dream, whereby the foreigner, through education, hard work, and luck, ends up as a patriotic taxpaying citizen, a good credit risk. Growing up as a hyphenated American has a natural tension that serves well the dramatic needs of fiction. Greek-American writers, as already noted, have made ample use of their ethnic material. Their literary contributions, like those of writers from other ethnic traditions, have only now begun to receive critical and scholarly attention.

What it meant to be Greek, rich, and beautiful in the epoch of the first world war could well be the theme of Ariadne Thompson's *The Octagonal Heart* (1956).[1] In a vivid and evocative style the author recreates her childhood days spent at Parnassus, the family's estate in a suburb of St. Louis. The patriarch of the family was the first Greek Orthodox bishop to be ordained in the United States. Ariadne Thompson's father was a very successful businessman who also served as the Greek consul in St. Louis. Her book chronicles a segment of life far removed from that of the usual immigrant who arrived poor, uneducated, and alone. The tension in *The Octagonal Heart* is never poverty and survival, the problems of taking root faced by most newcomers; instead it is the question of whether or not a Greek girl should become a doctor and whether or not she should marry a non-Greek. In lieu of developing a plot the author recalls the life around the house itself: who lived there, what they did, and "how it [the octagonal house] shaped the heart of childhood." The book begins and ends on the nostalgic note that what once was has gone forever—and that it lives only in recollection.

The author's maiden name was Ariadne Pasmezoglu. In the 1880s her maternal grandfather, a priest, was sent from Athens to found a Greek Orthodox church in Chicago. From St. Louis came Demetrius Jannopoulo to ask that Ariadne's grandfather establish a church in his city. Jannopoulo, who owned a prosperous tent-and-awning company, was a man of wealth, position, and devout faith. As a result of his visit to Chicago he met and married Elene, Ariadne's aunt, in 1892. For a wedding gift he gave his bride a pair of fabulous diamond earrings and built Parnassus on a thirty-acre estate in the suburb of Webster Groves. To indicate the social status of her uncle, Mrs. Thompson writes: "Demetrius and his bride were guests at a ball given in Chicago for Their Royal Highnesses, the Infanta Eulalie and the Infanti Antonia of Spain" (p. 62). King George of Greece had bestowed upon him the Order of the Royal Cross.

Ariadne's paternal grandfather had a lucrative silk-manufacturing business in Smyrna. When her father Hector was born, his mother "threw gold coins to the peasants from her balcony" (p. 99). He attended the American College in Athens; then he left for St. Louis, where Demetrius Jannopoulo, then the Greek consul, promised to take care of him. He did so at a typically high level: Hector Pasmezoglu as a start was given the position at the St. Louis World's Fair of heading the Olympic Games. In a few years the rest of the Pasmezoglu family migrated to America; the Turks burned their home and their factories. In time Hector met Ariadne's mother at Parnassus and married her.

Mama, christened Penelope, was no ordinary Greek girl, certainly not like the thousands who later arrived at Ellis Island with little if any education and no money. "Mama had a beautiful coloratura soprano voice and often sang arias from the great operas with the St. Louis Symphony Orchestra" (p. 37). She was once offered a contract by the Metropolitan Opera of New York, but her husband put his foot down and said no. She put up a lukewarm struggle for women's rights, yet on the whole was happy to love and live with "the handsomest man in St. Louis." He had a certain elegance. He took pride in his collection of five hundred neckties. "He wore sideburns, a dark, ruby ring on his finger, a stickpin in his cravat, and whenever he went out he wore spats and carried a cane" (p. 82). When attending the symphony he sported a top hat and tails and an Inverness cape—a Greek in high style consorting with his rich American peers.

Money does much to make an idyll of Ariadne Thompson's childhood in Missouri. She delights in recording the conspicuous consumption, the many luxuries, that financial well being made possible. Another conspicuous feature of the idyll was its Hellenism, which emerged as a strong mingling of the pagan classical with the Christian. The author refers to Parnassus as her Aunt Elene's little stronghold of Greek culture "thriving on the outskirts of a great American city" (p. 55). In another instance she writes: "Once I heard Papa say that Auntie regarded Greek culture exactly as she regarded her liver; something one could not do without and over which one must keep constant vigil lest it grow sluggish" (pp. 15–16).

The big house itself, named Parnassus after the mountain of the muses, had an octagonal reception hall from which extended wings to create the over-all shape of a Greek cross. Such a mingling of the pagan and Christian consciousness seems to come naturally to Greeks who are both educated about the "glory that was" and devout in their own lives. Even though the folks at Parnassus had a Christian bishop in their midst, they invariably went to the mythology and the classical period for their names. Ariadne had a sister Artemis and a brother Pericles. Her cousins at Parnassus were Aphrodite, Achilles, Demosthenes, and Aristotle. Their huge and amiable Saint Bernard was, of course, Hercules. The children regarded clouds as "Apollo's Flock." The sleigh was Mercury; the two rowboats in the pond, Zephyrus for the wind and Amphritite, the wife of Neptune. The parrot, taught to garble a fragment of "Farmer in the Dell," had the dubious honor of being called the Sybil of Cumae. And thus it went. At times the author as a child had difficulty equating her relatives with the figures after whom they were named. Her Uncle Themistocles, for example, was the soul of gentleness, whereas the real Themistocles was a zealous and aggressive statesman.

Ariadne Thompson saturates her writing with classical and mythological allusions because she had a "Greek upbringing" together with her American education. The personages of the ancient myths are more familiar to her than those of the Mother Goose nursery rhymes. Knowledge of modern Greek also makes it possible for her to flavor her fine book with typical expressions that she translates for the general reader. She often uses a classical frame of reference for various happenings at Parnassus.

Most of *The Octagonal Heart* deals with the people and the special events associated with Parnassus. Celebrities like the lecturer Burton Holmes, the dancer Isadora Duncan, and the singer Helen Traubel visited the house; but the visits had much less effect on the children than did holidays such as Easter and Christmas. The "Greekness" of these holidays is recorded in authentic and concrete detail. And since the period covered begins before the first world war and extends beyond the armistice, the author also refers to outside forces that impinge upon their home. Both cousins Achilles and Demosthenes go to war. Yet the book she has written still remains an idyll of childhood. The Greek foods they eat, the Greek clothes they wear, the Greek customs they observe—these factors and more provide a genuine ethnicity to the chronicle.

The central tension, however, derives from Cousin Aphrodite's conflict with her mother over her ambition to become a doctor and her possibly marrying a non-Greek. If anything violated Ariadne's idyll it was the frequently bitter squabbles that banished Aphrodite weeping to her room. The children all knew the problem: would their cousin Aphrodite really have to marry a Greek? "It seemed to overlay everything, like a vague shadow, at Parnassus" (p. 15). She writes humorously of a corollary matter—the reluctance of Greek mothers generally to inform their daughters about sex. Mama firmly believed such knowledge "was best acquired in the marriage bed, and, until that fatal hour, it should be held in escrow, like a dowry. Meantime it was her intention to guard our virginity as if it were the Kohinoor diamond" (p. 135).

Of most immediate concern was Aphrodite's wish to enter medicine. The decision had to be made soon because she was already attending college. Beautiful and vivacious, she had some renown as the "Goddess of Washington University," a title that impressed her young cousin Ariadne. Her father Demetrius tended to be neutral on the question of a career, but both Aphrodite's mother and her grandfather, the patriarch, strongly opposed. That Aphrodite won out in the end resulted from a visit to Parnassus of the Metropolitan of Greece, the highest ecclesiastical authority in the Orthodox Church. When asked for his opinion, he surprised all by responding, "I consider your daughter's desire very laudable. We are entering an age when women, as well as men, must learn to be self-reliant. Moreover, to be of service to man does not go against God's teachings, rather it goes hand in hand with them. I consider it a credit to your daughter that she desires to take up this profession" (p. 127).

This problem having been decided, Aphrodite had the even

more important choice to make regarding a prospective husband. "You are Greek," her mother would say, "and you will be happiest married to a Greek" (p. 60). The mandatory dictum made Aphrodite weep and wail. Whereas her father Demetrius attempted to blend Greek culture with an American flavor, Aphrodite's mother "was as Greek as the first stone Pyrrha threw behind her from which, according to mythology, sprang the Hellenic race" (p. 62). Her fears that Aphrodite would marry a non-Greek were well founded. At school her willful and beautiful daughter fell in love with a medical student named Armin Hofsommer. Ariadne's mother had foretold the event to Auntie by reading the coffee cups; the grains predicted a handsome husband for Aphrodite— but one not Greek.

In the final chapter, "The Ashes of Parnassus," the author tells how a catastrophic fire burned the octagonal house to the ground. The children conducted a treasure hunt through the ashes for Auntie's diamonds; eventually they were found. The new house that replaced the old could never be the same. In time the whole estate owned by Uncle Demetrius was subsumed "by that new development indigenous to the American countryside known as the subdivision" (p. 12). Gone were the landscaped lawns, the orchards, the rolling pastures, the farmland, the chestnut trees, the huge barn, the chicken pens, the carriage house, the cowsheds, and the main house. "It is all gone now," Ariadne Thompson writes, "lost to us these many years, and there is nothing of it left to see with the eyes or feel with the hand or touch or hear with any part of the body save the heart. But in the heart it has remained, and I will tell you about this house and all the people in it, and how it shaped the heart of childhood" (p. 13).

A Greek family of a lower class and a later year, 1932, are vital elements in *My New Found Land* (1963) by Dean Brelis.[2] The setting is Newport, Rhode Island; the time, the autumn immediately before the election of Franklin D. Roosevelt. Dimitri Chrystofilos, a young Greek, undergoes a crisis in loyalty toward his alcoholic father, John, followed by discovery of his true mother and a rebirth of faith in himself, his father, and people generally. The novel opens with Newport awaiting a visit from Roosevelt and ends a few weeks later on the day after his election. At the railroad station where Dimitri gets the papers for his route, he runs into Bob Buchanan, a Negro whose son has just left prison. Later in the story Dimitri and Bob become partners in a shoe-repair shop.

On his route Dimitri is asked by a rich lady, Mrs. Balfour, to take part in a church pageant to benefit the poor; and he agrees to appear in an Evzone costume wearing the *fustanella*. From there he goes to Mrs. Kaplan's bakery to buy some stale cookies. On the street his drunken father embarrasses him by talking in Greek. The friendly cop on the scene takes the father to the jail to sleep off his drunk—and perhaps to remember who provides the bootleg liquor.

Brelis then describes Dimitri's home life. Xenia, his mother, has strong ethnic feelings. No bread in America, she claims, compares with the bread in Athens from which "you could make a whole meal" (p. 34). For her, Roosevelt is a wise man who wants to overcome the four horsemen of killing, waiting, lies, and sadness. "Surely this Roosevelt family must have Greek blood" (p. 35). Dimitri gets along well with his mother and also with Father George of St. Constantine's. For ten dollars a month his father keeps the church fires going, a job that sometimes falls to Dimitri.

At a place called Greek Wharf, Dimitri's Uncle Stavros maintains a houseboat painted white and blue, the colors of the Greek flag. He lives by catching and selling fish and lobsters off Point Judith, in Narragansett Bay. Dimitri's mother keeps trying to break down his will to remain a bachelor. "She was currently awaiting a letter from Greece with a photograph of the latest prospective bride for Uncle Stavros" (p. 46). Dimitri thinks little of Xenia's matchmaking, and hopes she will fail. Stavros is really only a friend of the family, but Dimitri calls him uncle anyway. He had been one of the first Greeks in Newport, had served in the navy, and received a pension. Yankee fisherman enjoy his homemade wine and the stories he tells about the Aegean. While Dimitri and Uncle Stavros talk, a lobster boat passes which is manned by Baxley, a bootlegger from Block Island.

The author describes the noisy colorful crowds who have gathered at the square to hear Roosevelt. Dimitri, however, does not stay, for he has seen Baxley and fears that the gangster will catch him. Baxley does find Dimitri. "Your old man," he explains, "he bought stolen goods and I want our property back" (p. 56). They search the church, and they discover two cases of whiskey hidden in the coalbin. Father George and Uncle Stavros, arriving, force Baxley to kiss the Greek cross and to tell all about the whiskey. He does, and they let him take it away. The incident ends with Father George's entreating Dimitri not to mention his father's mistake in buying the stolen goods. "Your father wants your respect" (p. 63).

Dimitri then goes to the jail, where he learns the shocking news that Bob Buchanan's son was shot and killed while resisting arrest. His father meant to sell the whiskey and pay the bank, which is threatening to foreclose on the mortgage. Out of jail later in the day, the distraught parent drags himself into the house half-dead, wet, and incoherent. He had tried to drown himself but had failed.

Part 1 of the novel is entitled "Doubts"; part 2, "Partners." Since the illness of Dimitri's father continues, the boy must operate the shoe-repair shop by himself. Dimitri expects to earn a lot on Saturday, a busy day for the shoe-repair shops. Another Greek, Angelo Varelakis, owns the rival Radio Shoe Repair across the street, a prosperous business with modern furniture and machinery.

Dimitri breakfasts at the lunchroom next door owned by a Greek ex-boxer, Spike Drake (Constantine Palakaris) and Lars Olsen. "Lars was the only Swede I had ever met who spoke Greek" (p. 89). Spike is about to violate the Greek community's strictest rule by marrying a non-Greek from New York, and Father George has agreed to officiate. Lars will be the *koumbaros*, the best man. As for the girl Dot, Spike says she has been attending a Greek church, that she is confirmed and "a legitimate Greek Orthodox."

Dimitri, who cannot cope alone at the shop, arranges to go fifty-fifty on the shines with Bob Buchanan. They work well together. Many customers enter the shop for shines and shoe repair.

That night a group of young toughs arrive from the Athletic Club. Bob does not like "that kind of trash." One of them, Big Jim, curses, and as a protection against the bad words Dimitri makes the Greek sign of the cross. The toughs laugh at him. After a busy profitable day Dimitri goes home where his proud mother prepares his bath and soaps his back. Some day, she says, the "good Greek girl" he marries will do this for him. If he marries a non-Greek, she will learn. Xenia gives Dimitri a dollar from his earnings.

Early the next morning Dimitri goes to the church for his Sunday duties, to tend the fires and then assist Father George at the altar. He turns his gaze from the dome and the icon of Christ to look at the saints, all of whom he knows: "Saint George, a curly-haired man with bare arms spearing the dragon; and over next to him, Saint Spyridon performing the miracle of ridding a Greek island of snakes" (p. 126). And so on. Later he hears Father George pounding in his cellar workshop. Removing the canvas, the priest reveals a beautiful model of the Acropolis—in the

Christian period when the cross and the Greek flag flew atop the Parthenon while under Turkish attack.

The priest worries about the meeting after church and the vote on renewal of his contract. Brelis describes the church hall, a made-over barn, where Greek school occupied one room, and "every time there was a christening or a holiday like the one celebrating Greek Independence Day, or a dance to raise money for the church, or a play given by the Greek school children, the hall became a place of excitement and lights, music, and the women in the large kitchen making coffee and sandwiches" (p. 133). The walls have pictures of Greek Revolution heroes, "dark-bearded men with their white kilts and the ancient rifles," and "one picture of the Suliote women, dancing in a circle at the edge of the cliff," who leaped to their deaths ahead of the approaching Turks. The stage has both Greek and American flags and a likeness of Herbert Hoover.

The only issue at the meeting is Father George's competence to continue as priest. For Mrs. Kanelopoulos and others he is not American enough: he speaks no English and does not drive a car. She demands "more of an American feeling in our ways." The women should use their vote more often in church affairs, nor should they sit segregated by themselves. She proposes that Father George listen to some of their requests. "He wears the robes and the tall hat," she complains, "as if Newport were the muddy street of a village in the Peloponnesus" (p. 139). An oldtimer, Stratis, reminds the audience that Father George built their church with his own hands and tools. Finally the priest himself speaks. For months, he says, he has been pondering an invitation from a "handful of Hellenes" living in a small town in Georgia. As had happened in Newport, he wants again to witness "God's beauty in seeing a church rise where there is none," and he will therefore leave (p. 144). He will not stay to own property, learn to speak English, and drive a car to please those who are ashamed of being Greeks.

Soon after the meeting, Angelo Varelakis comes to Dimitri's house and buys their repair shop. Later Uncle Stavros arrives loaded down with lobsters and flowers. He knows of a vacant store on Long Wharf they can rent for a new shop. Dimitri's mother plagues Uncle Stavros about Margarita, the intended bride from Greece. "She is eighteen years old. She has been educated; she can read and write. She sews beautifully and if you are interested, she will send you a sample of her nice pillows. That is very nice, yes, Stavros?" (p. 153). *Margarita* would be a pretty name for his boat, which he now calls *Texas Girl*. Xenia threatens to put the evil eye on that mysterious Texas female.

Part 2 of *My New Found Land* ends on a tragic note. Dimitri attends the pageant rehearsal at the home of the wealthy Balfours, where he has a run-in with their boy, Dexter, over being Greek. Dexter regards the *fustanella* skirt as "sissy pants" and he labels Dimitri a *guinea*. Their tiff makes him ponder his identity. "At home, I was a Hellene, and in the store, when I was running it, a Rockefeller or a Ford, and in my thoughts sometimes I was an Evzone, sometimes a midshipman. And once in a while . . . I was Socrates and Pericles" (p. 159). Mrs. Balfour gives him a card with GREECE to slip over his head. The children there represent fifteen ethnic groups in Newport. At the end of the rehearsal the Balfours bring in their pet bear, Brownie, to do his circus act. When Brownie does his dance, Dexter joins him, and finally gets carried away and slaps the animal on the back. Confused, the bear grabs Dexter by the throat and holds on. In the excitement Dimitri takes Dexter's sword and runs off with it. After some days in the hospital Dexter Balfour dies.

In the last and shortest section, "A Gift," some of Dimitri's problems are resolved. He also learns why his father once uttered the name *Eleni*. Bob Buchanan accepts Father George as his priest even though they speak different languages; together they will journey to Georgia. Bob explains: "That Georgia country seen most everything. But Father George, I reckon, will get some of those crackers talking and thinking. They might treat him good— and then they might not. I'm going in case they figure to give Father George a poor welcome" (p. 174). Dimitri translates for them. Their new shoe-repair shop opens on Greek Wharf to good business, with Dimitri's father sober and working. The young toughs falsely lure Dimitri to the Athletic Club, but he escapes their homosexual intentions. He fights off three of them who intercept him in an alley. He returns Dexter's sword to the Balfour house. At Spike's wedding Mrs. Kanelopoulos reveals to Dimitri that Xenia, his apparent mother, is actually his stepmother and that Eleni, his real mother, is dead.

Dimitri has to adjust himself to the revelation. Uncle Stavros takes him to the cemetery and shows him his true mother's grave. The marble cross brought from Greece is gone, stolen by robbers and never replaced. Uncle Stavros assures him: "I can tell you that Eleni can only be happy in heaven knowing that you are loved by Xenia." (p. 200) At home Xenia is making a batch of *kourambiedes* for Father George and Bob Buchanan. Mrs. Kaplan contributes a bag of fresh hard rolls. Many of Father George's friends, including Dimitri, go to the ferry to see them off. In Father George's workshop Dimitri learns that the model of the Acropolis has been given to him. The priest's note also reads: "You have never been a stranger in this church, Dimitri; and in this new country, be watchful, be faithful, be a pure Greek, loyal to this America, and you will have enriched her as she will enrich you. Adio, and the Lord be forever beside you" (p. 207). Dimitri takes the magnificent gift home. Election Day arrives. Early the next morning his mother Xenia reports the news: Roosevelt has won. "Newport," she says, "is celebrating." As a result of his feeling for America, "our country," Dimitri loads the model Acropolis onto his wagon again and takes it to the American school. "It is theirs, too," he informs his mother (p. 209). He does not care that some of the people there might think him crazy.

The problem of a young Greek girl facing marriage, possibly to a non-Greek, recurs in George Christy's novel *All I Could See from Where I Stood* (1963).[3] The main line of action, however, deals with Stephanos Hermes, a twelve-year-old boy living in the western Pennsylvania town of Commandment Hill on the eve of World War II. The story opens with his spilling the milk Mama has forced upon him. He likes summer despite the heat because there is no Greek school, although his folks threaten to ask Alevrou to keep up the classes. She is a tutor who looks like a ghost, and is called "Flour-Face" by other Greeks, as her name suggests. Stephanos hates everything Greek, including how "turkey-necked Aunt Dimmy was always singing songs in Greek about their beautiful dark eyes" (p. 12). Commandment Hill, a steel mill town, has many ethnic groups: Poles, Croatians, Germans, Italians, blacks, and Greeks. Stephanos likes the "joking Greek grocer" called Afendi, who stocks grape leaves in jars, halvah, Hymettus honey, and oregano. School has ended for summer; it is June 1940. Leaving the library, he meets his sister Molly on the way home.

Molly is sixteen, *sour* sixteen to Stephanos, who remembers her leading the handkerchief dances at her birthday party, the *kalamatianos* and *syrtos* and *tsamikos*. She even slapped the heel of her shoe as older men did when they danced. Mama Hermes is fat from the butter-and-oil drenched Greek cooking, which she cannot give up. "Her two favorite subjects were Greece and Molly. Whenever a lady Mama knew in Greece wrote to her, Mama purred like a cat with the news: some rich Greek-American was either building a library or laying water pipes for her village, or there was a *panegyri* at the Church of the Holy Fathers, or Mama's old-maid cousin, Koula, inherited a little money and someone finally asked to marry her" (p. 19). As for Molly, Mama wants her to marry a boy with curly hair from a good house in the old country, preferably from Chios "where we know the blood." Stephanos has observed that Molly never gets asked to dance at Greek dances whenever the American bands played. Molly, also fat, is cloistered.

Stephanos likes Christopher Stevens who is the All-American Greek Boy. Even Molly concedes he is handsome and that he imitates Parkyakarkus better than anyone else. Too bad, though, that he has Americanized their family name. Mama criticizes Christopher for driving his big black Buick convertible, dating American girls, and being "too modern." His father left his family a lot of money when he died. Christopher paints, plays the guitar, and sings loudly. His mother, in black, has mourned four years. Stephanos also likes Electra Stevens, nicknamed Lekky. She is blonde, tall, and thin. "Greeks were originally blond," Molly told Stephanos; but centuries of slavery darkened them. Every week Christopher throws a party, and Stephanos spies on it.

Told by the boy, the novel embodies his childish scorn, partial comprehension, stubborn attitudes, irrational responses, and frequent satire. He sees his "Greek" bedroom as unbearably strange and un-American, with the holy pictures of Jesus, the saints, cherubs of love, and the blessed Virgin Mary. On his dresser sits a ruby glass with a fat wick that "sputtered in the holy oil." Often at night the votive light frightens him with images on the walls "like monster butterflies, ready to pounce."

A strong prejudice against Greek girls going to college is shown by both Lekky's mother and Mama Hermes. Such girls "learn too much" and they "act so smart that the men have to listen, and who needs a bossy wife?" They also smoke and drink without shame. Gossip in town has it that Lekky Stevens loves a Viennese interne in Pittsburgh whom she will not marry lest she break her mother's heart. Mama Hermes calls Lekky "that whore girl," without any cause, and orders Molly and Stephanos to avoid her. Although twenty-six, Lekky does not rebel against her mother; instead she accedes to the role of a *good Greek girl* who can date only the "right" Greek man.

Stephanos welcomes the reopening of school. Despite his protests Molly goes ahead with plans for his birthday party. Stephanos, filled with childish pique, comes late and unkempt. Molly hits him for his refusal to wash. Then Papa enters drunk and unbuttoned; and he vomits before the astonished guests. Mama Hermes determines to leave home with Molly. Stephanos ponders a lonely house, thinking if Mama leaves: "Who would fix their food: the eggplant dish, *imam baildi*, that Papa liked; the egg-lemon soup Stephanos liked at holidays; the Greek sweets they all liked—*kourambiedes* and *melomacarona*" (p. 112).

Instead of leaving, Mama rushes her plans to marry off Molly. She arranges for them to visit a prospective husband, Michael Lykos (nicknamed Toto), in the upstate town of Prosperity. Mama's fervent prayers have been answered. Toto comes from "fine Greek people," has been in America five years, and saves his money. Actually, Toto is an aging slob. Molly tries to stall Mama but to no avail. They return to Commandment Hill with all the arrangements made.

At the engagement party, held in November, Aunt Dimmy sings old Greek songs that Stephanos thinks make no sense in English. "The Little Vest You're Wearing Was also Sewn by Me," a sick love song called "My Dearest, The Hour's Arriving," and one that goes "Kerno Ton Pono Mou Krasi"—"I Toast The Pain of Love with Wine" (p. 123). For the party desserts are brought from Pittsburgh—"pans of *baclava, kataifi, flogeres.*" Mama is giddy with joy; and at church she crosses herself often and fast, as if she were "practicing some strange kind of finger exercise" (p. 129). For his present Stephanos receives a tie clip in the shape of "a Cretan scimitar" that he wears all day. During the ceremony the priest places a ring on Molly's finger, and Mama Hermes cries happy tears.

Stephanos's hatred for Greekness increases. He hates *avgolemono* soup and *plaki* when his friend Tony Breckenridge can eat hamburgers. He hates Mama talking Greek on the street, he hates Greek school, he hates "Greek blood" and Greek manners. As for the Greek priest, "He evens believes Christopher Columbus was Greek, that's how crazy he is." And Marco Polo, too. To be Greek was simply and deplorably old-fashioned.

Anybody who had a Greek name was always hollered at, especially the Greek boys named for old heroes like Pericles and Aristotle and Socrates and Menelaus. Their mothers and fathers and uncles and aunts constantly screamed, "Why can't you live up to your name?" Who wanted to live up to the people who lived thousands of years ago? Perry Patras and Socky Stavros and Ari Loulas were always getting cracked with the yardstick in Greek school for talking or not listening, and the priest's face would turn red as he rattled that they were a disgrace to their namesake. (p. 143)

In the midst of Stephanos's ethnic-caused woes, a real tragedy occurs: Lekky Stevens commits suicide. The reaction to her death by Mama and some of the other Greek women shows them at their worst—insensitive, backward, crude in their vaunted Greek manners. Mama condemns Lekky's brother Christopher for not crying, calls him a bad Greek man. The men come and go as they please, but Greek girls stay close to their mothers. The gossips blame that *allophilo* (the non-Greek interne) for Lekky's death. The women argue about whom Greek girls should or should not marry. Mama again condemns Lekky for having gone to college, where she acquired "fancy ideas about being independent," because a decent woman "wants a home and a family." Mama is unaware that it is precisely her kind of talk that can destroy a Lekky Stevens.

Many things conspire to destroy a Lekky. Stephanos recalls a horrible argument that she and Christopher had the night she swallowed the pills. Although she had bitterly complained of a headache, he kept up a cruel and loud banging on his cello, driving her off to her room. Now, as Lekky lies in state in the living room of her own home, Christopher will not come to see her. Nor does he attend the home funeral service, thus causing a scandal. Molly explains to Stephanos that the priest will not allow a church funeral since her death was not an act of God. So the priest officiates at the Stevens home—"in a chasuble of gold" and wearing "a tall round headpiece like a black stovepipe, the *kalimafchi* with the hanging black veil in the back" (pp. 154–55). Stephanos will greatly miss Lekky.

Stephanos meets a newcomer from Texas, Kiki Bailey, whom he tells that he is an Eskimo. When Kiki visits Stephanos's house, he asks Papa about their religion at the North Pole. "Are there Greek Eskimos?" Papa replies, no, "We're only Greeks" (p. 187). Surpris-

ingly Kiki shows a keen interest in Greece. Papa speaks about the
peasants on the islands, their love of nature, the beautiful blue
Aegean, the fresh fish, the lamb at Easter, and "especially Mykonos
where there are hundreds of chapels built by fisherman saved
from storms on high seas." Stephanos is bored, but Kiki, as if to
betray him, says that being Greek "beats being an Eskimo." Later,
when Papa asks Stephanos why he is ashamed to be Greek, he replies, for lack of a better answer: "Because we never do anything
right" (p. 191).

The Hermes family now suffers a serious crisis. The Greek radio
program, "Grecian Life," plays *Omorfi Athena*, "Beautiful Athens,"
in honor of Michael Lykos (Toto?), requested by a wife and two
loving children in Athens who miss him and wish him *kali proto-
chronia*—a happy New Year's. Is there another Michael Lykos? The
request for the song had come from a Mrs. Lykos in Athens. Papa
calls Toto, who denies having a wife; but others in Prosperity admit
hearing rumors to the contrary. The ugly truth is finally confirmed. Very sad, Mama learns that Toto did desert his family "to
make a fortune in America." He is what *Lykos* means in Greek, a
wolf.

April arrives, with Easter and spring at hand. Stephanos finds
Greek school unbearable. He makes new friends, and they talk
about the New York World's Fair. Stephanos still cannot understand why Greeks are so special, being poor and starving in Greece
and always writing letters begging for money. Every afternoon at
siesta they quit work, drink *ouzo*, and nap. But Kiki really likes
Greeks better than Eskimos. His father knows "ancient Greek and
recited Homer aloud once to Stephanos." To top it all, Kiki might
go to Greek school too.

At Greek Easter, which Stephanos loves, he is more mixed up
and ambivalent than ever. The Hermes family attends the Holy
Week services, described in some detail here, as in other novels by
Greek-Americans. On Wednesday the bearded priest "made the
sign of the cross from a cotton swab dipped in holy oil over their
foreheads, cheeks, chins," and so on; and some of the women take
the swabs home for invalid relatives. On Thursday night they attend "the lengthy service of the Twelve Tales of Christ, *Ta Dodeka
Evanghelia*." Everyone kneels and bows his head at a "black wooden
cross with a cardboard cutout of Christ, wreathed in lilacs," set up
before the altar. On Good Friday they witness "the mourning of
Christ's crucifixion," when the choir stands around the flower-

covered bier and chants "the unforgettable dirges of death—'En Zoe Entafo' and 'Aksion Este' and 'Eghenai Paso'" (p. 211). On Saturday night, at the stroke of twelve, the priest cries, rejoicing, "Christ is Risen," and he comes forth to spread the holy light. Candle by candle, the flame is passed to all. As red Easter eggs are cracked for good luck, people cry "Christ is risen" and are answered, "He is truly risen" (p. 213).

At the novel's end Stephanos has moved toward a greater tolerance of his Greekness. Among other things he likes Mama's Greek sweets and Papa's Greek memories. He enjoys watching Papa devour the eyes from the lamb's head, biting "succulently into the shiny globular eyeballs." His sister Molly, soon to be graduated from high school, is growing up; and Aunt Dimmy has found somebody handsome, with wavy hair and a car, for her to marry.

The protagonist of *Thieves' Market* (1949) by A. I. Bezzerides is a hotheaded young Greek, Nick Garcos.[4] Unlike Stephanos he does not despise his Greek heritage, but he does hate his mother.

The story begins in the rich agricultural San Joaquin Valley and ends in the brutally cutthroat produce-market of San Francisco, the "thieves' market." Bezzerides has written about Greeks in other fiction and in a Hollywood filmscript about the spongers of Tarpon Springs. Both Nick and his father worked in a fig packing house. After his father dies, hatred crackles between Nick and his mother—for what she did to poor Yanko, who tried so hard to succeed but failed because of her constant bitchery.

> Another memory came on Nick, of his father working in the coal yards of the town and coming home black with dust, of him unloading lumber from the flat cars over in Helbing's Mill; working in the farms, the vineyards and orchards of the valley, working in the packing houses, in the wineries, buying a wagon and a horse and peddling fruits and vegetables in the streets of Fresno, shouting Fresh orangey, peachy, trying hard to make money to buy a farm, to buy a truck, not for himself but for wife and child, to make a foothold for them in the world. And in all this Nick saw his mother's sullen face. (p. 4)

She hoards the four thousand dollars left for them as a legacy from Yanko's insurance. She wants to hold onto Nick as her only chance for security. Yet his contempt for her has no limit.

Nick contrasts their failure with the extraordinary success of the clever Tartarian brothers. Much of this success he attributes to

Ahna, the loving wife of Haig Tartarian who built a fleet of trucks to haul fruit and produce. Ahna kept encouraging him, while Nick's mother criticized poor Yanko. Bezzerides captures well the banter, the sexuality, and the greed of the fig-house workers, among them the "strong women from Germantown and Russiantown and Armeniantown and Woptown" with their jealousies and gossip. When Nick is ten minutes late for work, his boss Ganso banishes him to the tier of boxes near the hot roof; so Nick quits in a huff and goes to see his girlfriend Polly. In her are nascent those qualities of bitchery that more than matured in Nick's mother—a shrewd sense of how to manipulate and rule a man. "The hell with her, Nick thought. I don't need her" (p. 31). Nor does he need his mother, from whom he takes most of the insurance money to buy a used truck.

To haul and sell produce in the San Francisco market Nick Garcos teams up with a partner, Ed Kennedy, a tough unscrupulous man who knows all the dirty tricks of the trade. The rest of *Thieves' Market* details the trials and horrors of buying, delivering, and selling two truckloads (six hundred boxes in each) of Golden Delicious apples which they get from a hapless farmer. Kennedy cheats him out of six hundred dollars which the remorseful Nick gives back. He is represented as strong, well-meaning, and naive—a bumbler, victim, and sucker in the eyes of the thieves. Even his partner plans to skin him alive. On the journey to market Nick manages to get pinned upon his truck, badly bruising his neck, and Kennedy rescues him. But Kennedy himself has a more drastic and fatal trouble: his decrepit truck goes out of control, crashes, and burns, killing him. The apples are left unharmed near the town of Altamount.

Meanwhile, at the San Francisco market on Fulton Street, Nick waits for Kennedy who will make the deal with Figlia, the buyer. Figlia embodies all the cunning of a shyster and crook. He sees a natural-born sucker, Nick, with a load of beautiful apples parked at his platform, and he determines to steal them. From Ed Kennedy he cannot steal, but he knows what Nick does not—that Kennedy is dead. The whole business is based on making a killing whenever one can. Figlia has a hireling slash a tire on Nick's truck to keep the load there. Then he pays a whore, Tex, to occupy Nick an hour or so while Figlia disposes of the load. Because Nick is decent, Tex likes him enough to expose Figlia's scheme; and Nick goes to Figlia, threatens him, and forces him to pay $6.50 a box for the six hundred boxes in his load. After he pays Nick and sells the apples, Figlia hires two thugs to waylay Nick, keep the five hundred dollars in cash for themselves, but return the check to Figlia. He also has other men prepare a truck to retrieve the load of apples left when Kennedy died.

In the melee with the two thugs, the whore Tex grabs Nick's wallet and runs off; but one of the men, Frenchy, catches up to her, and she throws the wallet at a passing train, near the bay. Most of the money and the check float away in the water. Going to Figlia, Nick demands a new check, and he gets some of the cash back from Frenchy. A "swamper" (helper), who wants to drive for Nick, tells him about the death of Kennedy, the load of apples, and Figlia's plan to steal them. The novel ends with Nick and his new friend driving in his truck to Altamount to square things with Figlia, the master thief of the thieves' market.

Another character who tends to despise *Greekness* is Daphne in "The Education of a Queen," a novella by Thalia Selz which appeared in the *Partisan Review* and in *The Best American Short Stories* (1962).[5] Daphne is twelve when her Greek father, a lawyer, brings home a "stray" in the person of Joshua, an artist. She speaks about the guest bed in which the strays slept; it symbolizes the mixed blood of her heritage: her mother is non-Greek. The quilt on the bed is dated 1833, and represents her great great grandmother Otis who drove a wagon from Barnstable on Cape Cod to Ohio alone. The blanket, dated 1897, represents her father's mother, Anastasia Karamoulis, who "had woven it with thumb-pricks, tears, and hate for her husband to keep himself warm and uncomfortable within steerage on his way to make a million grass-green dollars in the States" (p. 555). Her father's strays were mostly Greek, but sometimes Negro or Jewish.

Daphne detests her mother's pretensions about Greekness, as when she asks Joshua, "Are you Greek perhaps? If you are, you'll like our lamb stew I'm sure" (p. 557). Daphne feels nothing *our* about it. She calls her mother as "prissy" as a New England preacher, and says: "Most of all I detest the Greek routine." Her mother regards anything Greek to be peerless. Joshua is not Greek, and little Daphne loves him immediately. Then, to her intense anguish, her father begins to round up the Greek girls for him. Daphne has "no truck" with Greek girls herself, but worries that Joshua might go for the Greekness in one of them, especially Vasiliki. Daphne defines the name in a further denigration of

Greek ethnicity. "It is the feminine form of Basil: in Greek most of us are merely afterthoughts of the male, as it were: female appendages, like an extra set of nipples, on the male name. It means 'little queen'" (p. 568). Vasiliki was already being called a *poutana* by the old hags. Engaged twice already, she did not return the rings and other gifts. She gave a watch to a favorite cousin and one ring to the church. The daughter of a fat sweaty Macedonian, Vasiliki receives slings and arrows from the Daughters of Hera "with their 'teas' and their 'luncheons' and their squealing Demotic 'minutes' and their infernal money-raising" (p. 569). Thus Daphne gets in her digs at middle-class Greek women.

She realizes the uniqueness of her position. Her father, a lawyer, enjoys much respect in the Greek community despite his mixed marriage, free talk, and mockery of the church. "I could afford to be scornful of Greek girls and go my way: I had an American mother, American girlfriends, and an American college waiting for me. My mother had graduated from the same college in 1918—my grandfather in 1892—my great-grandmother in 1869. I was a free agent" (p. 569). Vasiliki is not. At seventeen she is hemmed in by her Greekness. Joshua notices her beautiful bosom and warms to her. He shows her his art objects, boxes with nude figures in them. A traumatic event occurs for Joshua when Vasiliki in her shocked immaturity reports him to the police for his "pornography." Daphne's father has him released from jail. The allegedly lewd boxes which the police confiscate are tossed into the fire at the station by error. Joshua, never too well, becomes seriously ill and goes to the hospital. Vasiliki keeps coming to Daphne's house "to find a good husband at our hands." In the end she does, but the husband is killed at the Battle of the Bulge.

"The Education of a Queen" begins and concludes in the Tyrol with Daphne reminiscing about the past. She remembers her adolescent love for Joshua; she recalls her fondness of Vasiliki, her college affairs, and Joshua's tragic death from pneumonia. Now, as she sheds the tears of memory, she blames her family for the deep hurt that Vasiliki inflicted upon him. "Within that fiery ring of Family—internecine passions, false pride, bitter resentments, pointless loyalties—in that magic area we were for a while doomed to live, not to die. If we had held tightly together, I think that no one, not even Vasiliki, could have hurt him" (p. 687). She cries, too, for her own "murder" of Joshua at the age of twelve. She might have saved him had she been older and wiser. Therefore, within the unhappy context of a mixed Greek and American parentage, Daphne undergoes the "education of a queen."

In "The Death of Anna" Thalia Selz discloses how a Greek woman's ethnic values influence the nature of her dying.[6] In the hospital with uremic poisoning, Anna Pappas ponders her past and stubbornly rejects the idea of death. She worries about her son and daughter, both of whom married non-Greeks. The daughter was divorced and left with two children. Anna worries about her husband Theodore, soon to be alone. Anna suddenly hates God as that Somebody who took her father off to America when she was still tiny, who "killed her mother with nephritis and chased the young Anna out of Greece to scramble for her bread in this crazy America," and who, after her life of penury, "had given her two such ungrateful children" (p. 263). Theodore says they are fine kids; but Anna laments that Angelos, like Sophie, also married an American.

> What she meant was a series of pictures: that nice Greek girl she had picked out for Angelos—crying in the Ladies' room because Angelos stood her up for the St. Constantine's Day Dance; Angelos, with his American bride on his arm, striding laughing up the aisle of a Presbyterian church in Oak Park; the wife Jean spooning pabulum into their baby's mouth; the baby, whose name was Ann, crowing "poon!" in English. Nowhere in the picture did Anna see herself. (p. 265)

As she lies near death, she dreams about the funeral supper; and her many guilts surface. She made too big a fuss when Sophie divorced Bob over his philandering. According to Angelos, Sophie was raised to be cold toward men. Sophie counters by calling Angelos "Mama's sonny-boy Angie" for whom nothing was too good. Also in her dream, Anna blames herself for costing Theodore his clerking job in City Hall—because she poured coffee into her saucer at the mayor's Christmas party. Anna takes the punishing dream as a sign from God. Contritely she admits to herself that she was too stubborn, too selfish—loving Angelos too much, Sophie not at all, and being a bad wife to Theodore. He tries to moderate her guilt feelings toward the end, even though "she had pursued him for more than a hundred seasons with imaginary faults" (p. 269). A slip of the tongue has Theodore telling her to forget the past, and Anna replies: "The past is all I have." Soon afterward she dies.

Grace Metalious, the author of *Peyton Place* (1956), has Greeks in her three novels about small-town life in New Hampshire.[7] Although married to a Greek, she uses very little ethnicity in her characterizations of Michael Rossi in *Peyton Place* and the Pappas family in *The Tight White Collar* (1960). All her important Greeks are educators, as was her husband (whom she eventually divorced). With respect to "growing up Greek" in America, Michael Rossi is already grown up and thoroughly nativized before he arrives to assume his official duties as the principal of the Peyton Place schools. In *Return to Peyton Place* (1959) Rossi gets fired because his stepdaughter Allison MacKenzie publishes a shocking novel called *Samuel's Castle*. The theme of "growing up Greek" applies more to Christopher Pappas in *The Tight White Collar* than to Rossi. In both cases bigotry, xenophobia, and hatred complicate life for the Greeks.

The antagonism toward Rossi begins in the school-board meeting in which his appointment has to be considered and voted upon. "Rossi!" roared Leslie Harrington. "What the hell kind of a name is that?" After told it is "Grecian," and that Rossi worked in a Pittsburgh steel mill, Harrington responds: "A goddamned Greek, and a lousy millworker at that. This Boston agency [for teachers] must be run by screwballs."[8] In mid-April the school board under Harrington hires Rossi, and Peyton Place hates the idea of Greeks coming to join the "colony of Polacks and Canucks." Harrington is biased against "Mr. Independent Greek Rossi" for having to beg him to accept the position. Rossi has a master's degree from Columbia, is well educated and unafraid. Some people regret giving the job to a Greek when other good teachers are available. At thirty-six Rossi is a "massively boned man," six feet four inches tall, and very handsome "in a dark-skinned, black-haired, obviously sexual way, and both men and women were apt to credit him more with attractiveness than intellect. This was a mistake, for Rossi had a mind as analytical as a mathematician's and as curious as a philosopher's."[9] Rossi is also honest, tactless, and given to a "vicious temper" that prompted language he had learned "on the lower East Side of New York City."

Metalious builds up Michael Rossi as a kind of Greek god who attracts Constance MacKenzie, the blonde mother of the heroine Allison MacKenzie. Other than marrying her in book 3 of the novel, Rossi plays a relatively passive role in *Peyton Place*. He is called a "horny Greek" and "that big, black Greek." Despite his delicate position as school principal, he manages to sleep with Constance a dozen or so times before their marriage. Two years pass, they get married, and Peyton Place rocks with scandals that happen to others. In *Return to Peyton Place* Allison comes home with her novel, *Samuel's Castle*. Michael Rossi still stands broad and straight. "Is my Greek god getting a little old and paunchy?" Constance teases him. When the novel appears, all hell breaks loose in Peyton Place because the major characters are local citizens thinly disguised. Rossi defends Allison's book and is fired by the angry school board. "You wrote a good book and got paid for it and became famous," he tells his stepdaughter.[10] Toward the end of the novel Allison has a bad automobile accident in which her lover, the publisher Lewis Jackman, is killed. Rossi's "cheerful presence" helps restore her to health. The story concludes with Allison thinking of another novel. All else may pass away, but people with a talent have their mission: they must work.

Grace Metalious employs considerably more Greek ethnicity in *The Tight White Collar*, her third novel.[11] The plot, which begins around 1940, involves rich and poor, WASPs and "foreigners," as in *Peyton Place*. Two small towns in northern New Hampshire constitute the setting: Cooper Station, which is middle class, and Cooper's Mills, proletarian. The former has a Board of Guardians who supervise what happens in town. Again, as in Peyton Place, someone in authority recommends that an educator of Greek descent be brought into the school system. This time Arthur Everett, the school superintendent, wants to hire Christopher Pappas to teach history at Cooper Station High. The most bigoted member of the board, Doris Delaney Palmer, calls him "that Greek fellow from the mills," and goes on: "He's living in a shack up at the Mills with that wretched wife of his and their two brats and he's teaching physical education at the School for the Feeble-minded over at Marmington." The person who first recommended him, James Sheppard, contradicts the statement and speaks in favor of the Pappases. "They live in a house they rent from Eben Seton for thirty-five dollars a month. The Pappas children are not brats, but attractive, well-behaved, intelligent children. And Mrs. Pappas is far from wretched." Behind the opposing statements are secret causes and motivations which it is the author's purpose to reveal.

The discussion brings out that Chris Pappas was born in Cooper's Mills of parents who ran the fruit store on Main Street. He failed in a previous teaching job because he refused to pass a girl whose influential father then strongly objected, and because a few "pinheads" there, in West Farrington, "claimed that Chris Pappas was a Communist" for saying that some of the world's greatest writers were Russians. Chris also said that the Puritans ran from intolerance "only to become intolerant themselves." One supporter believes that such a "God's Angry Man" might do Cooper Station some good. The ayes win, and Chris Pappas will come to teach their children.

As the reader learns, Chris is up against more than the bigotry of Cooper Station. His wife Lisa, a "Canuck" girl with middle-class illusions, has grown bored with him and their life. At his new place of residence Chris Pappas rents a cottage from Anthony Cooper, the bohemian black sheep of his family. He thinks of seducing Lisa Pappas, and does so in the midst of the controversy over Chris's coming to teach there. That her adultery may deliver Chris to his enemies does not seem to bother Lisa. Pregnant again, she tells Anthony the baby is his, even though she had two sessions with Chris also. When she suggests marriage to Anthony, he is so shocked that he turns against her and Chris; and he will see Doris Delaney Palmer in order to banish the Pappases from Cooper Station. Lisa, a real bitch, betrays Chris in his hour of need. He is sacked, much to Lisa's annoyance, and is paid off as the contract provides. The private citizen who gives the three thousand dollars happens to be Anthony Cooper. Unknown to Lisa and the town, Chris Pappas has received good offers from elsewhere including one from Massachusetts for forty-five hundred dollars a year.

The Tight White Collar concludes with Chris and Lisa in a new environment: Gammon's Landing, Massachusetts, far from the small-town pressures of Cooper Station. Lisa has another girl, Linda. She had feared having a son lest he look like Anthony Cooper; although most Greeks preferred sons, Chris would not tolerate one fathered by someone else. Gradually Lisa begins to feel some love for Chris. They return to Cooper's Mills for her mother's funeral, and stay with Aphrodite and Costas in whose house they make love. At last the once restless and dissatisfied Lisa realizes what a jewel she has in Chris Pappas. After her emotional adventure and the sorrow of her mother's death, she becomes reconciled to a middle-class life with a man who is steady and going places.

Although he regards himself primarily a poet, Konstantinos Lardas has also written excellent fiction, some of which embodies

poetic language, rhythm, and intensity. Lardas was born in Steubenville, Ohio, yet spent enough time in Greece to provide him
with memories and material for several stories. As a youth of four
he lived for a year on the fabled island of Icaria; then he spent
another year in Greece, 1962–1963, on a Fulbright student grant.
Within the Greek experience Lardas finds not only exquisite
beauty, compassion, and love, but also enough savage evil to universalize man's inhumanity to man. What Greeks have sometimes
done to Greeks, when class privileges are at stake, equals what
Greeks and Turks have often done to each other. Stories by Lardas
set on Icaria form one group, the larger, while those in America
form another. One among the former, "The Devil Child" (1961),
became an *Atlantic* first, a literary distinction shared by two other
Greek-Americans, Petrakis and Mountzoures. A book of poetry by
Lardas, *And in Him Too; In Us*, was nominated for a Pulitzer prize
in 1964.

The Pittsburgh area that Lardas knows well, having gone to public schools and college there, then having worked for a decade as a
partner in an industrial painting and roofing company, provides
rich ethnic matter for the long story *A Tree of Man* (1968).[12] First
privately printed in book form, it also appeared in *Spectrum*. A
family memoir, the novella concentrates on the last years of *papou*,
the grandfather, who terraced a wonderful garden on land sloping
down to the B&O railroad tracks. Nikola, the father, had just purchased a large house with excellent plush flower gardens that *papou* wanted to dig up in order to plant vegetables. "Some food
from all this land," he explained. Upon them rained ceaseless soot
from a nearby steel mill, whose blazings ricocheted across the
Monongahela River. When *papou* began wrecking the flowers and
lawn, even their neighbor came to protest: "Our neighbor, silkly-
sheated, and handsome, and Daughter of the Revolution, and
daughter of a minister, who'd asked me, sharply, yesterday, if we,
we Greeks were Christians,—what had she thought of this old
man, of these new Greeks who came, and bore a plague with them
in coming, to destroy" (p. 4). Nikola measured out an area hidden
by the house for *papou's* victory garden, so the "world would never
know that we were peasant herders of vast flocks of goats in the
Aegean, that we were exiled sea-men come from the Icarian Main;
that we were workers in America, in Pittsburgh, in her factories,
on her bridges; and that we earlier had come from the coal mines
of West Virginia, from the Scaife Works of Verona, and from the

restaurants and bakery shops of Steubenville, Ohio" (p. 5). On the side of the chasm allotted him, *papou* over the years brought forth a marvel of crops from his hard-wrought terraces.

He worked in sight of the Anderson Memorial Bridge which "we'd never painted, but held to be our own." They painted countless others in Pittsburgh and elsewhere. With poetic rhythms and images Lardas creates vignettes from his family's past—that part when *papou*, too old for bridges, carves a fruitful beauty on a steep decline. Pride, nostalgia, love, all suffuse and energize the intense prose. Then *papou* dies, and his coffin goes past his gardens on its way "to Wilkinsburg and to the ragged cemetery of the Greeks, which even here in America, was like that tiny cemetery on an Icarian cliff," there to rest forever with his many relatives (p. 6).

For what happens thereafter Lardas pens a lyrical passage.

> The velvet grass is gone. Of the three poplar trees that stood in proud array beside the house, but one remains, the others, hollow grown, have fallen of their weariness and of the lowly worms that, secret, grooved their hearts. The petaled flower that never grew to fly from us in brilliant wings, is cast away, is wholly gone from us. The house is ruined now, but is abiding, warm, and holds his issue yet. His is a jungle now that once was ringed with order. His garden is despoiled now: the plum trees and the figs; the grapevines with the roses grope along the fence, a wilderness of growth; wild planetrees, sumacs flourish here: and heaps of the discarded rotting ropes and paint and thinner drums and lids and cable-rustings to the soil, and stubs of brushes, scrapers, dusters, and broken platforms, stages, flaking, scarring now his gardens, and fallen like a lava flow across the hill, these scars of our old trade, heaped refuse of the many factories and bridges we had cleaned and painted in Kentucky, and Ohio, and New York, in Pennsylvania, Illinois, in Maryland, Virginia. (p. 23)

In stories set on the island of Icaria, Lardas at times uses the Greek boy Tasso, who has returned from the United States. Another character who reappears is Yanni, the evil-possessed "Devil Child."[13] In this story Yanni leads the other children to the wake for Stamatoula, whose pomegranates and lemons they had often stolen. For this act Stamatoula and her sister, Philio, had cursed them. Yanni has written a poem about them which he now sacrilegiously sings and dances. In it he implies that the sisters are witches. From the kitchen door Philio cries out: "Oh Sister, Stamatoula. Still he mocks us." Yanni, the obsessed, runs off into the night. Philio calls: "You evil thing. You devil."[14]

The hatred that emanates from Yanni has at least a momentary cooling in "The Bird," an allegory based on the great flood in the Old Testament. For six days the rains have deluged Icaria. Yanni wants to lead the children to the caves on Mount Pramnos, there to build rafts. The story introduces Tasso, who represents good to Yanni's evil. Tasso is also "the *Amerikano*" born in America, and often teased for that reason. They meet in Yanni's "ravaged home" surrounded by a stone wall "built by Yanni's father to protect his wife, Marika, from the eyes of strangers."[15] Two months before Yanni's birth, the father sailed for America with the idea of returning rich. "Tasso remembered. Yanni's father had abandoned them. He had lost his way without Marika. He had married again in America and had abandoned them. The calendar had been his last gift to Marika and to Yanni. Yanni had never known his father."[16] Much of Yanni's delinquency was no doubt caused by his father's cruel and truant act.

In the story the children more or less re-create the myth of Noah on Mount Ararat. Yanni says the earth will be destroyed by another flood, the result of the present rains; but Tasso says the reason will be fire. Tasso and Kleis, a Greek girl, stand beneath a dripping plane-tree on Yanni's land. Tasso regards himself as an exile from America; and when a raindrop falls upon a pool, Tasso feels the concentric rings can reach out to "touch perhaps Marika's husband" and "send him Yanni's need." He and Kleis fashion out of mud a beautiful gull which Yanni, out of envy for their happiness, stomps to pieces. Tasso and Yanni fight. Then, together, the three of them fashion a new bird more beautiful than before. God, too, had once made creatures out of mud. The white breezes cause the bird's wings to flutter. "And the gull, in startled cawing, rose and flew from them" (p. 392).

Tasso, Yanni, and Kleis appear in a later story, "The Broken Wings" (1972), published in the Martha Foley collection, *Best American Short Stories* (1973).[17] The story opens with Tasso waiting for the funeral procession of Anastasia. A flashback recalls the previous winter when he had to go to Therma for his granny's mineral water. The excitement "made him think of those festive Saturdays in America, when his mother had saved enough coins and given them to him so that he too could go to the movies with his friends" (p. 6). In town Tasso meets Kleis, and together they watch Anastasia's last puppet show. She is pregnant, and her husband has forbidden her to continue. Anastasia's puppets represent King Minos, Daedalus, Icarus, and the minotaur. Feeling a tap on his shoulder, Tasso turns to see Yanni, with face as "sharp and deadly as the face of Minos." His eyes warn Tasso to stay away from Kleis, whom both love. When Anastasia's show has Icarus crying, "Father, Father, I am falling," Tasso remembers his granny's cries of pain and runs off to get her medicine.

Later, lying in ambush, Yanni breaks Tasso's water jug with a rock, and laughs. Anastasia comes along with a lamp and helps Tasso get home. She gives him the Icarus puppet. Soon she will have her own son, her own Icarus. As time passes, Anastasia more and more treats Tasso as her own. She laments that he will someday leave her. "You will return to that strange land," she tells him, meaning America, "where gold is in the streets, where many kings, where many gods abound" (p. 12). One day Yanni and Niko are teasing Tasso with a ball, tossing it back and forth beyond his reach, when Anastasia, now very big with child, leaps up, catches the ball, and hands it to Tasso. Now, with Anastasia dead, he waits for her funeral procession to pass; and, he thinks, she should not have stretched so hard for the ball that day. Tasso sees the coffin, with Anastasia smiling. "And in that smile, he understood the meaning of her name, the name of Stasia, Anastasia, the meaning of the Resurrection."

Three other stories by Lardas are set on Icaria. In "The Usurpation" (1969–70) Tasso has a friend in old Trifon, a surrogate father.[18] One time Tasso says to him: "My father was like you, Trifon. But he worked not under cover of the open skies, but in America, under the blazing heat of corrugated factory roofs. For a long time he worked; until one day, a huge ladle, containing molten steel, exploded, like your charcoal treasures sometimes do, and he was bathed in liquid death" (p. 232). The title refers to a statement by Trifon that Tasso has usurped his heart, his life. Foreshadowing occurs when Trifon tells his adopted son, thinking of Tasso's father: "Fathers should die before their sons are men," to be spared the inevitable heartaches. To everyone's shock, Trifon commits suicide atop a burning charcoal pyre, killed by the gases. Killed by fire just as Tasso's father before him, in America. As the crowd calls "Tasso!" the boy rushes up the great pyre to place a wreath upon the godlike Trifon. "And as they called him from the refuge and the safety of the hill, the great mound, reeling from the weight of the child, released its hold, burst outwards, inwards, downwards, consuming Trifon and his son" (p. 235).

The primitive island-custom of exhuming a corpse after three years, washing the bones, and depositing them in a communal charnal house is highlighted in "The Cypress Trees, the Sun" (1973).[19] Kyra Toula, the mother, wakes up early to get to the cemetery before the priest, Father Manolis, and the village digger; for her son, Taki, lies dead there and the time has come to remove him. Lardas uses flashbacks, the woman's grieving memories, to describe Taki as a sensitive, intelligent, and beautiful youth. To the grave also come Aliki, who loved Taki, and her brother Alexis, Taki's best friend. Together the boys often spent hours and days on Mount Pramnos. The digger opens up the grave. To Kyra Toula's horror, the body has not yet decomposed. She cries, "Son! Son! Not decomposed! Who curses you?"[20] Aliki confesses that she has, but has not meant to curse him forever. After the confession, Father Manolis says, the body will properly decompose in another three years. But, unknown to the others, Alexis also had cursed Taki. The two of them had been lovers, and something had gone wrong—perhaps a tiff over Aliki. Alexis's curse, if indeed a curse holds fast, will "bind him there until Judgment Day." Alexis makes no confession as Aliki had done, but suggests that nature keeps Taki's soul from a state of peace.

One of the most deeply felt and vividly expressed of Lardas's stories is "How Beautiful, the Feet" (1971).[21] Again the death of a loved one governs the action, tone, and theme. The story is a long lament by a sister for a brother's dying and, through his death, a powerful attack on those responsible for crimes against humanity. Others before Lardas (Kazantzakis, Myrivilis, Venezis, Ritsos) have dramatized the long and bitter agonies of the Greek people. Lardas limns them here as the sister mourns for Nikos, dead from consumption, but in effect killed by the Greek Rightists who imprisoned him during the civil war in the forties. A village leader, he had stood with the people against privilege and exploitation, had exposed corrupt politicians, scorned arrogant bishops, opposed the fascist gendarmerie. And, as a result, Nikos had "incurred the wrath of unforgiving men." After invoking past martyrdoms to justice and freedom, Christ, the Armistad slave ship, the Suliote women of Zalongon, Lorca, and others, Lardas ends with the dead Ho lying in state, his feet bare, to symbolize the jungle marches—the naked feet from Christ to Ho—to illustrate the march of all mankind toward the inevitable but long delayed peace.

The early fiction of H. L. Mountzoures appeared in the *New Yorker* and the *Atlantic* before he published *The Empire of Things and Other Stories* (1968).[22] One of the stories in the collection, "The Buoy," was an *Atlantic* first in 1964. Mountzoures concentrated on short stories until he came out with his novel, *The Bridge*, in 1972. Some of the material from his stories reemerged in revised form in the novel; relevant names and events were changed to conform to the greater needs for plot and characterization. *The Bridge* deals with a Greek-American family living in Connecticut. The hero, Philip Neros, holds our attention for over twenty years until at twenty-six he resolves some of the domestic problems that obsess him. Not all the stories in *The Empire of Things* have Greek characters; but several do, with a variety of types and themes.

In "The Beating" two Greek brothers, Nick and Stavros, hate each other. Although they work side by side in their flower shop, they have stubbornly refused to speak for forty years. Their behavior is joked about in the community. Their cousin Mara, an old woman, and her daughter Sophie come fearfully to the shop with a newspaper clipping reporting Stavros hurt. The women ask Nick what has happened, and he replies: "He was beat up." For the first time in his life he reveals some emotion about his brother. He weeps. He tells them Stavros is at his house. The women drive to Nick's house, which they find unkempt; and there Stavros has a "dome of plastered bandage on his head. The swarthy skin of his face was bruised. The area around his eyes was purple, and a long stitched cut stood out over his right eyebrow" (pp. 21–22). When asked to explain he condemns "this violent hell we live in" and says that he and his friend Peter Cavallos had been playing poker at the coffeehouse. As they leave, about two in the morning, two young girls who had previously inquired about a vacant apartment wish to see it right then. Because of their jobs, they have no other time. One of them suggests a drink in Stavros's apartment first. Against his better judgment, he complies—a gesture he regards as innocent. Peter Cavallos is seventy-five and he is sixty-eight; both are old men. No sooner are they inside the apartment than two young men, allies of the girls, burst in, severely beat up both Peter and Stavros, and rob them of their cash—about fifty dollars.

Half an hour later, one of the girls returns with two policemen. "She went to the police station and said there had been a bad fight between the two old Greeks in this house where she was with her boyfriend, and she had left her coat up there. She wanted her coat" (p. 24). The upshot of her stupidity is that the police immediately see the truth—all the blood—and they arrest her. She implicates the other "monsters." Peter is still in the hospital, while Stavros has been released in the care of his brother. Obviously the horrible beating has reversed their relationship of long standing; the facade of hatred has been stripped from the underlying affection. "The doctor put a new bandage on today, a little while ago," Stavros says. "Nick—he washed me" (p. 25). Mara and Sophie invite Stavros to recuperate at their house where he will have constant care and companionship. On the way Mara tells her cousin that Nick cried when he told what happened. "Like a small child. Poor Nick." Stavros, however, does not seem pleased that his suffering has forced a change in the familiar pattern. He touches one of the deep wounds with a clumsy finger. "Come on," he snaps. "Open this goddam door and help me out" (p. 26).

The narrator of "The Buoy" is visiting Greece, and staying with relatives in Ioannina, the capital of Epirus. Although from Connecticut, he has returned to Epirus to learn more about his family and ethnic heritage. There he meets and becomes friends with Costas, a cynical youth with a socialist bent. They argue the politics of freedom at a café near the beach at Previza. They swim, then talk some more. The narrator tells Costas: "You old son of a bitch, you, I love Greece and America and life!" (p. 52). A significant outburst, because the story builds to a confrontation with death. The two friends, one Greek and one Greek-American, share their tragic pasts. Costas talks about the Germans who killed his father as a hostage, and of a big orange grove confiscated by the Greek government. He also bitterly relates how he was tricked into marrying a sluttish girl whom he detests. For firing a gun in the air, not at her, he serves two years in jail. Now he waits for her to commit adultery so he can divorce her. After much talk Costas and the narrator decide to swim far out to a bell buoy in the bay.

After long tedious exertion, the buoy looms before them—elusively near yet unattainable because of a strong antagonistic current. From being "romantic and caressing" the water becomes monstrous, a "cold harpy," while the bell buoy undergoes various metamorphoses. "Suddenly it [the buoy] became a hideous priest smirking at me, an evil old priest with gaps in his teeth where the open metal ribbing was, and he took me into the church. And then,

where two large bolts had been on the face of the buoy, right there
were the tragic eyes of the virgin in the icon" (p. 61). To the narrator the buoy is the *Panaghia*, but to Costas it is first a "stupid cop,"
then God Himself.

> Sometimes the buoy tried to become again for me the Virgin
> and for him the policeman. But Costas was right—first
> through humor and then through delirium and horror, it *was*
> God, it was the Unknown and Uncaring God in His Unknown
> and Uncaring holy water, with the priestesses lying around
> brown and splendid, and far away His ant people crawling
> and sunning on the white strip. (pp. 61–62)

The narrator and Costas, who gets a severe leg cramp, nearly
drown before they are picked up by a fisherman's caïque miles out
to sea.

In "Love and Wisdom" the narrator's Greek mother dies when
he is eleven; his three youngest brothers are placed in a foster
home—a fate that also looms for the Neros children in *The Bridge*.
Now the narrator and his two older brothers are taken to live in
Boston with a distant relative; the woman in charge of them, Ellen
Slocum, reminds one of Abigail in *The Bridge*. Both are kind old
ladies who provide a home with love for their young wards. Also
reminiscent of the novel is the narrator's comment about his parents: "Like other men who had come from Greece to America, he
used his wife harshly without knowing it was wrong. Here in a
strange America, in the Depression, my mother had no family to
turn to for solace or courage" (p. 75). Philip Neros says something
similar about his demented mother in *The Bridge*, that she is terribly alone in her tragic predicament. The order and happiness that
Ellen Slocum brings, however, are short-lived. An "old Greek
woman" replaces her who determines to keep a "Greek house" that
includes regular church attendance and ethnic foods. The boy maneuvers through the welfare office to be sent to the foster home
with his younger brothers—an event closely paralleled with that in
the novel, during which Philip comes under the cruel dominance
of the foster mother, Rolla Lavin. The Philip of "Love and Wisdom" is Terry Vallas. He too never becomes a doctor. The
"mother" he loves, Ellen, dies and is buried in a pauper's grave in
potter's field.

Four other stories in Mountzoures's *The Empire of Things* have
Greek characters. Some, like Terry and Ellen, are characters from

his earlier fiction. Terry is now married to Laura. As they pack to leave their apartment, Terry finds an encyclopedic dictionary, a self-education book given to him a long time before by Ellen. Should he keep it or not? His youth, his past, his maturity are all suggested by the old gift, which he decides to discard.

"Fathers" is told from the point of view of an American boy married to Chloe, a Greek girl. Her father did not attend the wedding because she married a Catholic. Again one hears echoes of *The Bridge* since the mother in that fiction, Thalia Neros, also suffers from obesity; her husband is also gossiped about as having a mistress. In "The Lecture" a college-bred youth named Mike, already twenty-seven, gets talked to by Uncle Panos who worries about his lack of success. The story contrasts those Greeks who grub for money and those who live to enjoy themselves. Mike prefers to write poems, to savor life, to losing everything that he values in the ratrace for money. "A Reunion" treats with commendable subtlety the meeting of two sisters after a separation of thirty-six years. Tom's mother resembles Thalia Neros of *The Bridge*, who has a sister in Greece also named Mary. In "A Reunion" Mary arrives from Greece, rests one day before the ordeal, then the moment comes, the relatives have gathered, the sisters meet. Tom's mother is mentally disturbed. She poignantly remembers her sister Mary— who has crossed the ocean to see her.

The Greek background of Mountzoures emerges fully in his first novel, *The Bridge*.[23] Its hero, Philip Neros, is another example of a Greek growing up in America, in a family beset with severe problems, including his mother's insanity. Philip is only five when the story opens; he is twenty-six at the close when he is still, despite having some hope for the future, embittered and drifting. The picture of Greek-American family life, the quality of parentage, and the difficulty of bridging the generations are grim and foreboding. The title has various symbolic meanings. Perhaps the most visible but least important meaning is that which bridges the gap between immigrant and second-generation Greeks, the abyss between Philip Neros and his parents. Only at the end is the tension eased, when Philip's father Christos utters the word *love* as the reason for having put up with his wife, a madwoman. The name Neros means *water* in Greek; hence the word *bridge* is relevant in the choice of names. The deeper significance of the title evokes Hart Crane's poem "The Bridge," which seeks to express the myth of America, using the Brooklyn Bridge as its powerful referent.

"Hart Crane," Philip muses. "The library yesterday—a long time ago. Hart Crane and the Brooklyn Bridge: his passion for it. Why? I'll find out. I'll go down there and walk across it" (p. 271). Because of construction he cannot walk across; instead he manages to reach the East River shore with the bridge passing above. Philip sits at the end of a rotting wooden dock . . . the bridge huge, "but somehow delicately flying across the river." As he gazes upon the river and the bridge, a vision of his mother rises from the surface, an existentialist revelation that helps to establish his own identity. "He was a point between the sun, the bridge, and the river, and his past came down to this absolute point, the source of mystery, of his life." His mother's vision hovered "in the harmony of the bridge, the sun, and the river." He thought: "My spirit is yours. You died for the American dream. For money and work, my father's cheap labor. You died for others to ascend. I'm you who never died" (p. 273). The vision disappears. The river tries to suck him in, but Philip escapes the fatal seduction. In evoking Crane's poem Mountzoures makes the point that Philip Neros also has a claim to the myth of America.

The Neros family occupies an apartment in a three-story brick building in the Connecticut seacoast town of Pequot. Philip's father comes home only on Sunday. The rest of the week he peddles fruit by truck on Laurel Island. At home Philip learns Greek; at school he learns English. Ethnic details keep emerging. The children pray and make the Greek Orthodox cross before the family shrine. Their mother recalls the blue sky of Greece. She makes *pita* and the sugar-covered cookies called *courabiedes*. She teaches Philip Greek songs. She drinks the bittersweet Greek coffee. They eat *feta* cheese. Philip's father drinks *ouzo*. The family celebrates Easter in traditional fashion. On the negative side is the male chauvinism of the Greek husband, who beats his wife when she is slow with his supper. He keeps making her pregnant without her having any say in the matter. Thalia Neros slaves in the house, ends up with eight children, and goes insane. One reason for her mental collapse is the gossip brought by a "friend" that her husband has been unfaithful to her on the island. More and more Thalia Neros neglects her infants; for a time the boys, Philip included, are sent by the authorities to the Fastheath County Home.

When World War II begins, Papa Neros works in a war plant. Soon he and his brother, Taki, buy a small restaurant. Events move quickly in Philip's life. Among other things the boys shine shoes.

They learn to masturbate. Owing to Thalia's worsening condition, the Neros household turns into a pigsty. Philip fears his mother after she hits him on the head with a knife; with good reason he feels hatred. While sledding he breaks his leg and spends two weeks in the hospital. One day the head nurse informs him that his mother has been sent to the hospital for the mentally ill. All the younger Neros children are now in a foster home. Philip returns home to a surprisingly clean apartment; then his friend Merton tells him the truth: during his hospital stay, because of a fire in their apartment, his parents were arrested for negligence. After being examined, Thalia Neros was declared legally insane and confined. As a news story reports, she had run naked in the hall.

A woman named Abigail Watrous cares for Philip and his older brothers. The relative peace ends when Christos Neros decides to bring Thalia home from the asylum; it seems that he cannot do without sex, despite her condition; but he now uses contraceptives. For Philip his mother's return poses a serious problem: he is too young to remain at home. The welfare officer suggests that he learn a trade at a county technical school a hundred miles away. But he, although only thirteen, has determined to become a doctor. Encouraged by Abigail, whom he loves, Philip begs to join his younger brothers and sisters at the foster home run by the Lavins. The court agrees.

Life at the Lavins soon proves unhappy. Rolla Lavin, the foster mother, is a Hitler. Hitler himself is dead, the great war over. Rolla has the state forbid Abigail to see Philip any more. She derides Philip's desire to be a doctor. She gives the children mediocre food and allows them little or no fun. She becomes more and more cruel toward the Neros children. A neighbor, Mrs. Ross, complains to the authorities that they are beaten, starved, and left out in all kinds of weather. The social worker who investigates the complaint believes Rolla Lavin, and the terrified children do not dare to testify against her. The tyranny continues. Their father, Christos, comes infrequently to visit, to touch their dull hair, squeeze their thin arms, and kiss them. Rolla wants his visits to stop. He upsets them. He's a "sneaky bastard," a "dirty foreigner." Philip protests that his father's a naturalized American, and she replies: "He's a thick, ignorant Greek" (p. 133). One has to agree with her. Either that or Christos is ignorant about Americans and the evil they can do.

Four years pass for Philip under the thumb of Rolla Lavin. Her vulgarity, cruelty, and mockery do not abate. About his wish to be a doctor she says: "You'll never amount to a pisshole in the snow" (p. 139). When she refuses to sign his application papers for college (because her maltreatment of the Neros children may be discovered), Philip decides to return home to his father and mother. A new and happier time opens up for him: he works in the restaurant, The Oasis, and earns money; he has sexual relations for the first time—with a girl named Irene Powers; and he enrolls in Winthrop University in Thornton, "an old colonial town on the Connecticut River, full of Greek revival mansions and slums—foggy in winter, rainy in early spring" (p. 156). Uncle Taki has died and Christos Neros is sole owner of The Oasis. One day he surprises Philip by showing him a house he has bought. In terms of money the Neros family is no longer poor.

Much of the middle part of *The Bridge* concerns Philip's stay at Winthrop University. He majors in English. He sleeps regularly with a girl named Joanna Errin, a student from a neighboring college. He helps his sisters and younger brothers home from Rolla Lavin's. "The girls had lived there sixteen years, the boys twelve. They had never known home. They did not understand Greek" (p. 209). His brother Tommy gets married; and at the reception Philip feels Greek as he watches the Greek dances and hears the clarinets play like shepherd's pipes. His mother Thalia stuffs herself with *avgolemono* soup, *dolmathes*, *pita*, salad, and spring lamb. "Philip loved all his family at this Greek wedding in America" (p. 212). Shortly, he receives his degree from Winthrop. Joanna attends the commencement. His sister Mog, after the ceremony, whispers in his ear: "Father cried."

Time moves on. Philip buys a diamond ring for Joanna, but he is drafted before they can marry. They part, apparently for good. Neither of their families favored the marriage. Stationed on Governors Island, Philip is able to remain in close touch with his home. His sister Dorry writes to say that their mother had been sent again to the mental hospital. She had taken to running outside the house and screaming in Greek. David Miles, a friend that Philip meets in New York, thinks that he suffers from a "wicked Oedipal thing" with respect to his mother. He searches for love and excitement in New York after hours. He goes to bed with a girl who claims she prefers girls. He tells David he wants to write the great Greek-American novel. David half-seriously suggests they make a suicide pact. By now Philip has definitely decided to be a writer. But he feels lost. He has to find out where he is from and where he is heading—"the way to freedom" (p. 260).

Philip's search for his past leads him back to his father. He learns that their village in Greece is Georgias, population about six hundred, near the coast of Epirus opposite from the island of Corfu. "High up on the tallest mountain," Christos Neros says in Greek, "is the Monastery of the Prophet Elias." In his youth the Greeks of Epirus were still fighting the Turks for their final independence. He recalls searching dead Turks for valuables. Christos came to America at seventeen to make money, returned to Greece in 1928, and married Thalia the next year. He describes the wedding to Philip, and the voyage to America. Later Philip tries to talk about the past with his mother. She is distant, desperate, living with the "secret knowledge of the Destroyed" (p. 288).

Released from the army, Philip hitchhikes to Vermont to see Joanna. For three days they enjoy each other, making love; but he still cannot bring himself to marry her. Both have lost their youthful innocence. They part without anger and tears. Philip suddenly realizes that the idea of visiting Greece has been haunting him. He decides to see his cousin Chrysanthe there and search for answers. Before making the trip, he visits the mental hospital, sees his mother, and reads her medical record. Dementia praecox. Gross obesity: 320 pounds. Prognosis: poor. "Philip flew to Athens at the end of June. He took the bus into the city, found a cheap hotel. It was late afternoon and deathly hot and still in the room of marble floors, closed shutters. He slept" (p. 315). One of Philip's reasons for visiting Greece, the land of his fathers, is to work on a novel. He will stay with Chrysanthe, her husband George, and their five-year old daughter Theodora, in Ioannina, Epirus.

Chrysanthe tells him about his mother's sister Mary, of whom he is ignorant. Philip immediately goes to see her. Chrysanthe's husband George, a leftist sympathizer, criticizes America for having an "excessive military power, an overwhelming, meddlesome global economic influence, disproportionate greed and wealth and sick materialism" (p. 324). When Philip agrees, George is surprised, since most Greek-Americans come back and say they "kiss the American soil," they mouth clichés "about equality, justice for all, God bless the United States of America, the land of opportunity!" (p. 324). A new friend that Philip meets, Costas, asks him what life is like for immigrant Greeks, and Philip gives a negative report.

I'll tell you about the Greeks in my hometown. They come to America young, work their balls off in some greasy restaurant to save up thousands of dollars, and this small pile of money becomes an end in itself. They neglect their wives. In fact, there is a real failure in a lot of the marriages. Spiritually. They don't divorce, that would be scandalous—they just live it out desperately. And it's mostly because of what the American dream is to them—being respectable and careful and publicly unpassionate, making money, having a big new car in the garage, cheating a little on the income tax, owning a two-family house and living in half of it, gradually buying more property. It's because of this materialistic dream—and they didn't just make it up themselves, it's what drew them to America in the first place—that these people are spiritually doomed. (p. 326)

When Costas asks how this affects the children, Philip is equally caustic. "Young Greek-Americans are busy making money." They attend church, are rigid, "almost reactionary." In another generation there will be nothing "Greek" left in them, nor will it be "embarrassing to have immigrant Greek blood." It will be snobbish, quaint, to have this exotic touch. "You'll be able to say at a cocktail party, 'I'm part Greek,' and the hostess will say, 'Oh, how lovely. Jack and I were in Greece last spring. It was really—interesting. And so cheap'" (p. 327).

Philip's bitterness stems from some of the unhappy circumstances of his family life, the frailty of his convictions, the shifting of his values. He and Costas visit a whorehouse. He passes out at a wedding reception. Philip goes to the Albanian border and looks through binoculars at Georgias, his father's village, now behind the Communist lines. He feels no roots there, "only a weird Jungian pull." Chrysanthe tells him her life story—how she came to America and married, divorced her husband, and returned to Greece, where she married George and had Theodora. Philip writes on his novel, and the project goes well. Little by little he gathers more information about his relatives and their past. They constitute his ethnic roots. From Chrysanthe he receives a very favorable picture of his father: it was not *his* idea to have so many children. He *did* love his wife. He was a hero to stay with her, to keep his eye on the children, to sustain his dignity. As Philip ponders, a weight seems to lift from his heart.

Before returning to America, he hears that his friend David Miles has committed suicide. Philip's return is hastened by a virus that puts him to bed. The doctor tells him: "Go back to America, to central heating" (p. 353). He goes into a delirium during which highlights and fantasies of his life pass before his consciousness. An epiphany and resolution are reached when he jots down some notes and concludes: "Snapshot of her [his mother] in the square of the Monastery of the Prophet Elias. SALVATION." The delirium serves also to help bring the long book's episodic content into focus.

The illness over, Philip Neros flies to America, to ride home in "Father's new luxurious Oldsmobile." He thinks: "Everything in America seemed luxurious—immediately, instantly smooth and cushioned, futuristically modern, amazingly facile" (p. 365). Back in Pequot he remembers Joanna. He brings his father a bottle of the best cognac. He finds his mother and tells her about Greece, bringing regards. Christmas comes to the reunited Neros family. They have a fir tree as in the old days. In February, with Mother screaming again, Philip and his father have a talk. He asks his father why he has been unable to admit her insanity. "Because I loved her." Thus concludes a novel whose hero, Philip Neros, has an unusually difficult time growing up to be a Greek-American. Many such protagonists face problems, but few are so traumatic and long-lasting.

6

GREEKS WITH A SOUTHERN ACCENT

THE SOUTH is a region where one can hear modern Greek spoken with a distinct southern accent. Although most of the early Greek immigrants settled in the North, Midwest, and West, many went southward and formed stable communities there. Florida had two of the most famous Greek-American towns: New Smyrna, which lasted only about a decade as a Greek colony after its beginning in 1768, and Tarpon Springs, the later and far more enduring sponging center.[1] The leading Greek-American fraternal order had a southern origin. The AHEPA, American Hellenic Educational Progressive Association, was born in 1922 at Atlanta. Thus by the twenties enough Greeks lived in Dixie to warrant a major effort at Americanization, at least among the business and professional class. The role of AHEPA in the Americanization process figures prominently in *The Wing and the Thorn* (1952), a well-written, ethnic-oriented novel by Roxanne Cotsakis, herself an Atlanta resident.[2] To what extent the process succeeds—the problems and tensions it raises—forms a vital part of the saga of John Pantellis, her protagonist. Cotsakis provides the extensive Greek ethnicity that the plot requires.

The reader finds little use of such ethnicity by Thomas Wolfe, the first southern writer to reflect the Greek presence in Dixie, in *Look Homeward, Angel* (1929).[3] Neither here nor in his later work, however, does Wolfe fully develop any Greek character. His initial mention of a Greek occurs in a "brilliant slapdash improvisation," as he calls it, when a Harry Tugman pretends he is reading a society column in the local paper. Among the items he declaims, "A delicious nine-course collation had been prepared by Artaxerxes Papadopolos, the well-known confectioner and caterer, and proprietor of the Bijou Café for Ladies and Gents."[4] Later in *Look Homeward, Angel* Wolfe depicts this café along with other short vignettes that are a cumulative description of spring's arrival.[5]

In *Of Time and the River* (1935) "Greek restaurant men" are mentioned several times.[6] If Wolfe, like so many other writers, measured out his life with coffee spoons, he must have done so in Greek joints. At one point Helen Gant ponders the fact that she knows everyone in Altamont (Ashville, North Carolina). She knows the bankers, lawyers, butchers, and, among others "the Greek restaurant man . . . even the niggers down in Niggertown," but because of the town's status consciousness she has to be careful about showing her friendship. "Mr. Pappas is just a Greek lunchroom proprietor, but he seems to me to be one of the finest people I have ever known, and yet if Junius Pearson saw me talking to him I should try to make a joke out of it—to make a joke of talking to a Greek who runs a restaurant" (p. 228).

Wolfe mentions another Greek by name in *Of Time and the River*. He does so in connection with Bascom Pentland, who had gotten rich by building "small cheap houses" in the suburb of Boston and selling them on long and profitable terms to Irish, Jewish, Negro, Belgian, Italian, and Greek laborers and tradesmen. When they pay him, Pentland engages them in conversation, often to their discomfort. Wolfe chooses an encounter with Makropolos, the Greek, as his example; the result is the first instance in American literature when a writer used in fiction the kind of "Greek dialect" which comedians like George Givot made popular on the radio and in night clubs. Pentland angers Makropolos when he talks poetically about the "isles of Greece" and says he wants to visit the "ruins" of the noblest of ancient civilizations. Wolfe gives the Greek's reaction.

> For the first time a dark flush, a flush of outraged patriotism, began to burn upon the swarthy yellow of Mr. Makropolos's cheek: his manner became heavy and animated, and in a moment he said with passionate conviction: "No, no, no! No ruin! Wat you t'ink, eh! Athens fine town! We got a million pipples dere!" He struggled for a word, then cupped his hairy paws indefinitely: "*You* know? *Beeg!* O, ni-ez!" he added greasily, with a smile. "Everyt'ing good! We got everyt'ing good dere as you got here! *You* know?" he said with a confiding and painful effort. "Everyt'ing ni-ez! Not old! No, no, no!" he cried with a rising and indignant vigor. (p. 183)

Wolfe has Makropolos continue in this vein in an effort to convince Pentland that in Athens one can rent a new house for "fee-fateen dollar" a month. This brief encounter is Wolfe's longest use of a Greek in the novel; yet he conveys a hint at least of the preju-

dice once current in the phrase "greasy Greek." At a later point in
Of Time and the River he evokes the romantic mood of loneliness, a
major theme, and he does so by referring to "the soiled and weary-
looking night-time Greeks, and all the others who inhabit the great
shambles of the night (p. 475). Knowing what we do about the
author's hunting of strange places, we can safely assume that he
spent many a doleful midnight over a coffee cup in restaurants
owned by swarthy Greeks.

The first half of *The Web and the Rock*,[7] is a retelling to a great
degree of *Look Homeward, Angel*, a fact supported by the very minor detail that both books mention the Bijou Café for Ladies and
Gents—yet the town's name has changed from Altamont to Libya
Hill. The hero Euene Gant is now George Webber, but both in
actuality are Thomas Wolfe. One of the persons the lad George
likes is Nebraska Crane, whose father is a police captain and former professional wrestler. All one winter George and Nebraska
had gone to the City Auditorium to watch Mr. Crane face "a whole
series of sinister antagonists—Masked Marvels, Hidden Menaces,
Terrible Turks, Mighty Swedes, Demon Dummies, and all the rest
of them." Wolfe describes the matches in his usual fashion—at
length. One night the terrible black hood was torn off the face of
the Masked Marvel, who turned out to be the young Greek who
"worked behind the counter at the Bijou Café for Ladies and
Gents" down by the railway depot. This creature who "struck stark
terror to the heart" was merely "a rather harmless and good-
natured Greek who cooked hamburger sandwiches for railway
hands."[8] The thrill, however, was the same. Whatever happened to
the Artaxerxes Papadopolos who catered elegant "nine-course col-
lations" for society folk in *Look Homeward, Angel* Wolfe does not say.
Apparently the Bijou Café for Ladies and Gents got declassed by
time and literary circumstance. Be that as it may, *The Web and the
Rock* marks the first time American fiction relates Greeks to the
sport of wrestling. During the twenties and thirties the legendary
figure of the wrestler Jimmy Londos graced many a billboard
throughout the United States.

Thomas Wolfe never developed a Greek character in his volu-
minous work. That is not the case, however, with Carson Mc-
Cullers. The spectacular first novel she wrote at twenty-three, *The
Heart Is a Lonely Hunter* (1940), presented the world with the re-
markably drawn friendship between the two deaf mutes, John
Singer and Spiros Antonapoulos.[9] (McCullers even correctly spells

the suffix: it is *poulos* and not *polos* as Wolfe has it.) The preconditions for the eventual tragedy are set very early in the story when
Antonapoulos, having gone berserk once too often, is sent to an
insane asylum two hundred miles away. His inseparable friend of
ten years' standing, Singer, grieves over his loss; having been
touched by his soul-humbling affliction, he exercises a peculiar
force upon a circle of troubled acquaintances—until he finally
shoots himself. When Antonapoulos sickens and dies, Singer cannot face the rest of his life alone.

The setting is identified only as a town "in the middle of the
deep South." McCullers differentiates between the two mutes:
Singer is quick, intelligent, immaculate, and soberly dressed,
whereas Antonapoulos is an "obese and dreamy Greek" who in
summer wears a "yellow or green polo shirt stuffed sloppily into
his trousers in front and hanging loose behind" (p. 1). "His face
was round and oily, with half-closed eyelids and lips that curved in
a gentle, stupid smile." He is the first mentally retarded Greek to
appear in American literature. He works in a fruit store owned by
his cousin, Charles Parker, a Greek with an anglicized name.
(Wolfe, Warren, and Grau are southern writers whose Greeks in
fiction own restaurants.)

In his cousin's store Antonapoulos makes candies and sweets,
uncrates the fruits, and cleans up the place. Late every afternoon
Singer arrives, and the two friends leave to spend the evening together. Under the disapproving eye of his cousin, Antonapoulos
gathers a bag of foodstuffs to take with him. "For, excepting drinking and a certain solitary secret pleasure, Antonapoulos loved to
eat more than anything else in the world" (p. 2). They share two
rooms in the upstairs of a small house near the business district.
The only words the big Greek ever shapes with his plump hands
are "Holy Jesus," "God," or "Darling Mary." Even within his mute-
ness he is mute, while Singer does all the finger talking. For this
one-sided conversation and the friendship in general Singer has a
desperate need that is overlooked until nearly the end, when he
commits suicide. Those who come to him for succor have no idea
of his own chronic loneliness and despair.

He lives for others, especially for Antonapoulos. Though mute,
Singer "sings" for them a solace that he cannot provide for himself. The afflicted approach him for salvation, yet all the while he
is himself doomed, mainly because he loses the only friend with
whom he can be happy. For that friend Singer will do anything.

Antonapoulos uses an overstuffed sofa while Singer uses a straight plain kitchen chair; the former sleeps in a "large double bed covered with an eiderdown comfort," but Singer has only a narrow iron cot. Antonapoulos cooks all the meals, Singer washes all the dishes. The arrangement works quite well until, ten years after they meet, a drastic change occurs in their relationship. First Antonapoulos gets sick and is never again the same; then he regresses to intractability and ends up committed to an asylum by his cousin. The brunt of the trouble and the expense are borne by Singer.

He takes leave from his work at the jewelry store to nurse Antonapoulos back to health. "The doctor made out a diet for Antonapoulos and said that he could drink no more wine. Singer rigidly enforced the doctor's orders" (p. 4). All day he sits beside the big Greek's bed; he tries to amuse him, but to no avail. Antonapoulos finds fault with everything, fretful because of the diet and cure for alcoholism. Singer tries to amuse him by drawing pictures; instead of helping, one sketch "hurt the big Greek's feelings," so Singer has to draw one making his face young and handsome, his hair bright yellow, and his eyes "china blue."

And still the trouble persists. When they eat in restaurants, Antonapoulos steals items such as lumps of sugar, pepper shakers, and pieces of silverware. For these and other damages Singer always pays. When scolded at home, Antonapoulos responds with a bland smile.

> The months went on and these habits of Antonapoulos grew worse. One day at noon he walked calmly out of the fruit store of his cousin and urinated in public against the wall of the First National Bank Building across the street. At times he would meet people on the sidewalk whose faces did not please him, and he would bump into these persons and push at them with his elbows and stomach. He walked into a store one day and hauled out a floor lamp without paying for it, and another time he tried to take an electric train he had seen in a showcase. (p. 5)

The many court cases involving Antonapoulos soon impoverish Singer. His bank savings go for bail and fines, to free the demented Greek from "such charges as theft, committing public indecencies, and assault and battery." His money gone, Singer even borrows some from his employer. Nothing he does can avoid the final trouble: the cousin, Charles Parker, makes arrangements to have

Antonapoulos put away. Singer writes a note saying, "You cannot do this. Antonapoulos must stay with me" (p. 6). But his wish is not honored. The Greek leaves for the distant institution.

"Singer knew that everything was finished," McCullers writes (p. 7); and for three hundred pages more, she continues to describe Singer's life made lonely at first and then unbearable by the loss of Antonapoulos. The cousin, who "understood the American dollar very well," uses his money and influence to hustle him off. McCullers repeats words such as *bland* and *remote* to indicate how Antonapoulos drifts away mentally. Singer half-dreams about him. "Nothing seemed real except the ten years with Antonapoulos" (p. 8). He packs boxes for him but never receives a reply. He cannot bear to remain in the rooms where Antonapoulos had lived, so he rents a place in an old boarding house; and into his life enters a group of characters drawn to him by their various human needs.

The bulk of *The Heart Is a Lonely Hunter* concerns Singer's relationship with them—the problems they bring to him, the solutions they take away. They include Jake Blount, a drunken, bitter radical; Benedict Copeland, a disillusioned Negro doctor; Biff Brannon, a restaurant owner whose wife dies; and a young girl named Mick Kelly who loses her innocence and faces the harsh dilemmas of adult life. Yet always in Singer's mind looms the hulking blank-faced figure of Antonapoulos. He makes three well planned but unhappy visits to the Greek. During the first, Singer brings "a scarlet dressing-gown, soft bedroom slippers, and two monogrammed nightshirts," but Antonapoulos tosses them down in disgust. He wants food. This dementedly selfish response foreshadows the disillusionment Singer suffers at the end of his visit, when he leaves after having failed to reach his lost friend.

The months of summer and autumn pass. Singer is lonely. He sends Antonapoulos a large box of Christmas presents. He composes many letters which he never mails; they accumulate in his pockets until he destroys them. In one letter he writes: "The way I need you is a loneliness I cannot bear" (p. 184). The time comes when he must return to the asylum, to learn that Antonapoulos has been transferred to the infirmary with nephritis. He sat in bed propped up with pillows. "He wore a scarlet dressing-gown and green silk pajamas and a turquoise ring." Throughout the sad visit McCullers creates a regal impression for the sick Antonapoulos. "Sitting motionless in his bright, rich garments he seemed like some wise king from a legend" (p. 190).

Singer's third and final trip to see Antonapoulos ends with the tragic knowledge that his beloved friend is dead. Six months have passed, months filled for Singer with thoughts of the absent Greek. "Sometimes he thought of Antonapoulos with awe and self-abasement, sometimes with pride—always with love unchecked by criticism, freed of will. When he dreamed at night the face of his friend was always before him, massive and gentle. And in his waking thoughts they were eternally united" (p. 276). At the infirmary Singer learns that Antonapoulos has died. While waiting for the return train, he wanders about town. At the poolroom he has a beer with three other mutes. "He asked if they knew Spiros Antonapoulos. They did not know him. Singer stood with his hands dangling loose" (p. 279). His hands, with which he speaks, are unable to speak any more. Back at home, Singer leaves his luggage in the middle of the station floor, gets a pistol from his place of work, goes to his room, drinks iced coffee, smokes a cigarette, and puts a bullet into his chest. Without Antonapoulos and the thought of him alive, Singer himself cannot live.

The Heart Is a Lonely Hunter was greeted with adjectives such as *grotesque, macabre, compassionate,* and *wise.* Spiros Antonapoulos is one of the unique Greeks in American literature. Only in the eyes of John Singer does he have any real value as a human being; his own cousin, Charles Parker, must logically place him where he belongs—in the asylum. In this novel Carson McCullers plumbs the depths of southern abnormality in much the same way she does in *Reflections in a Golden Eye.* Both are glimpses into differing versions of hell. Singer's hell is the unbearable loneliness of life without Antonapoulos. He commits suicide perhaps in a futile pursuit of his lost friend. That Antonapoulos has so many negative qualities only intensifies the degree of loneliness that the heart is capable of enduring.

The theme of Robert Penn Warren's *The Cave* (1959) is not loneliness but the search the major characters must undergo to find the real behind the illusory in the secret caves of their own being.[10] No specific southern location is given in *The Heart Is a Lonely Hunter*; the action of Warren's novel, however, occurs in Johntown, Tennessee. The Greek restaurant-owner involved has been a loser in Cincinnati, Louisville, and Nashville; and he is convinced, the author states, that "he was going to fail in Johntown, and fail past Johntown, and fail, and fail" (p. 41). "The Greek was not a bad fellow for a Greek in business in Johntown, which was a place not designed to bring out the best qualities in a Greek in business there. Nick Pappy—which was what Johntown had decided was a good enough name for Nicholas Papadoupalous—was not a bad fellow, but he had his troubles" (p. 42). Unless the Greek himself is rather stupid, he would not spell his name as Warren has it—*oupalous*. But then, when it comes to names, Warren calls the place *Johntown* and not the usual *Johnstown* or *Johnton*, which might mean that he has in mind a place to defecate, *john*, and not a person named *John*. It is a uniquely vicious and viscous kind of evil he is probing, and not the holiness associated with one of Christ's leading disciples, so to call the place *Johntown* seems quite fitting.

Nick Pappy owns the only public eating place there, Ye Olde Southern Mansion Café. He is broad-built, burly, with a blue chin, narrow eyes, and shiny bald head. "You knew he would have a black pelt on his belly like a buffalo robe, and have a scrotum like two doorknobs stuck in a chamois bag" (p. 43). He has excessively white hands, square-cut nails, wears a diamond ring on his right hand, and drives the "best car in Kobeck County," a Cadillac in which on Sundays especially he enjoys going about the state with his blond wife beside him. "Then to round out Sunday, his idea [of the good life] would be to come home, to the shotgun bungalow he rented and called home, take off his shoes and hound-tooth tweed, drink a half pint of Jack Daniels on the rocks, and lay his wife" (p. 42).

A dark shadow falls upon the good life of Nick Pappy. His wife Giselle, a former strip tease "artiste," lies in bed all the time, sick and fat, and the blonde fades from her hair. Instead of making love he drinks whiskey before going to bed, and he drives around Tennessee alone. Then Nick Pappy notices his waitress, Dorothy Cutlick, who confronts him for a raise in pay. After some negotiations he lets her stay in the back room of the restaurant, where she silently memorizes Latin declensions during their intercourse. The arrangement turns into another great disappointment, for she leaves him to take a better job at the People's Security Bank. He owes the bank four thousand dollars. In time Mr. Bingham, the man at the bank, calls upon the Greek to help him secure an abortion for, as Nick Pappy assumes, Dorothy Cutlick. He plays his hand well, he can go places in Johntown, and not be a loser again.

Nicholas Papadoupalous is not the protagonist of *The Cave*. That role belongs to Jasper Harrick who lies trapped in a mysterious cavern. The jacket states that "His struggles are reported to the nation by a 'friend' who crawls in after him to exploit the disaster, to cash in on the rescue attempt." One can suspect that Jasper Harrick's cave, which also becomes his tomb, resembles Plato's cave in terms of analogy, as a graphic means by which to cast into relief the hidden essences of the major characters. Most of them worsen as human beings as the tragedy deepens. Ironically it is Nick Pappy, the perennial loser, who emerges as better than the indigenous southerners around him. When he has to choose between making much needed money and saving a life, he abandons the former and blows the whistle on those racketeers who had, for profit, prolonged Jasper Harrick's entrapment.

With Jasper's "friend" Isaac Sumpter, Nick Pappy drives to the scene of the accident to see what can be done. The author has Sumpter envy the Greek and show contempt for him.

> *Johntown,* Isaac Sumpter thought, *the town where Ikey gets his first ride in a Cadillac, and it's the only Cadillac in town, and the Cadillac belongs to a bald-headed Greek who sweats through his seersucker coat and smells like a place where a dray horse stood too long, and who buys the superoctane with proceeds from a hash-haven for truckshovers.* And, stealing a look at the Greek, he thought the Greek was exactly the kind of guy you would expect to have to have a Cadillac so he would feel like a big shot—or maybe even half human. (p. 192)

Already Ike Sumpter is scheming about enriching himself by exploiting the terrible predicament of Jasper Harrick. When they stop for him to buy flashlight batteries, he as a rural correspondent telephones the Nashville *Press-Clarion* to break the story of Harrick's trouble. Sumpter tells Nick Pappy a million people might gather to watch the rescue, that much profit can be made, perhaps a tourist hotel built, providing they move with bold caution. The visitors have to eat, and Nick Pappy can feed them. Tempted by the potential money, he rides back to town to arrange for a telephone line to the cave while Ike Sumpter goes ahead alone ostensibly to find the lost Harrick.

Nick Pappy becomes the handyman doing the greedy entrepreneur's bidding. Sumpter emerges from the cave with a survey that supposedly shows where Jasper lies trapped. The Greek is very sorry for his parents; the mother is a "nice lady" and the father is dying of cancer. Sumpter, on the other hand, thinks only of money.

"You have got the loaves and the fishes," he tells Nick Pappy. "All you need is the multitude" (p. 238).

The crowd of the curious builds rapidly; their worried faces gleam in the bright television lights. At times the crowd, led by the preacher, Ike's father Brother Sumpter, takes on the appearance of a religious revival. The people pray and sing hymns together. They are asked to confess their sins. Some, like the character Jebb Halloway, want to enter the deep cave (symbol for the inmost self), but either they are afraid or are dissuaded by Isaac, who wants no one to reach the trapped man. The rescue of Jasper Harrick would wreck his commercial enterprise. As it becomes clear, Warren utilizes the crisis to reveal and condemn the sacrifice of a human being on the altar of profit. In the midst of the confusion Nick Pappy listens and watches and honestly tries to understand. *"If God makes everything happen,* he thought, *then God certainly would know about that rock on Jasper Harrick's leg, for He had put it there on that leg.* So what was the use of harking on God knowing?" (p. 268). Thus he ponders and casts doubt upon the platitudes uttered by the preacher. He also wonders about the law, for he suspects Lieutenant Scrogg and Isaac Sumpter have made some kind of a deal. Nick Pappy neglects the receipts pouring in. God was keeping him from tending his business. While others are being "saved" by the preacher, the father of Jasper Harrick says, "He will die. In the ground" (p. 272).

Nick Pappy drops everything and goes to the Harrick home to make waffles for the dying old man. He complains to Mrs. Harrick that after six years in Johntown he has still to hear his name correctly pronounced. She in turn reveals that shortly after Jasper was born, her husband abandoned them for three weeks to consort with the whores of Chattanooga. The bond of sadness almost drives them to sex; but they forbear, and Pappy makes waffles instead.

The plot moves forward with glaring light thrown on other secrets in people's lives. The banker's young daughter, Joe-Lea Bingham, confesses before the television cameras that she is pregnant with Jasper's baby. Among those whom the confession shocks is Nick Pappy, who all along has believed the requested abortion is for the Cutlick girl. Actually it is for Bingham's own daughter. Nick Pappy hears and the confession is for him "like losing money," it is like "bleeding to death" (pp. 325–26). Life sets one up only to knock one down.

At the cave Isaac Sumpter and Jebb Halloway emerge from the opening and make an announcement to the effect that Jasper tells them to pray, that he cannot hold on, that it looks as if he is a goner. And Nick Pappy thinks: "*He dies now and I will not pay off that note. That girl confesses to Jesus and he is dying. They is all against me*" (p. 327). Seeing the grief on Mrs. Harrick's face, he cannot stand the guilt he feels for having sought to make money from her son's trouble; and he rises, runs toward the cave, and cries, "I am going in. I will get him out. I will lift the rock!" However, he never makes it to the cave. Lieutenant Scrogg viciously pistol-whips him. In the hubbub somebody other than the conspirators quietly enters the cave to learn the truth. That person is MacCarland Sumpter, the preacher father of Isaac—his father, going in old but strong to deprive him of his "success."

The father does so inadvertently; but more important to Warren's purpose, the preacher Sumpter emerges with a big lie on his lips—that the trapped man Jasper Harrick had denied ever having made any girl pregnant! The furious onlookers realize the preacher lies, and they move forward to "fix him," but Nick Pappy "had raised up from the cave mouth, and had stepped in front of the crouching, white-faced old man." The Greek cries to the potential lynch mob: "Get back or somebody will get killed" (p. 337). Lieutenant Scrogg later credits Nick Pappy with preventing a possible lynching of Brother Sumpter.

> Folks started hooting at that preacher, thinking he was lying about going all the way in to the fellow caught. Then some toughs was gonna fix him. But that Greek, he is built like Zybysko used to be, and is as crazy as a Brahma bull with a cocklebur up his ass hole, and he took the preacher's side. He stood up there, sweating and wall-eyed, and swore somebody was going to get killed. And they might have, if you didn't shoot him from a reasonable distance. It would take an elephant gun to bring him down off his feet the first whack, and, dying or not, if he laid hands on you he would bust somebody. (p. 348)

This act of bravery concludes Nick Pappy's active function in *The Cave*. Again he faces bankruptcy, but his integrity as a human being has not only remained intact but has grown. Not so with Isaac Sumpter whose father has protected him from a murder charge by withholding what he, Brother Sumpter, discovered. He had reached Jasper Harrick to find him already dead, but *still warm,* indicating that his son had deliberately kept food from him to prolong the commercial exploitation. Isaac must leave John-town, but not Nick Pappy. He is reconciled to making the best of things on a more realistic basis. He looks at his sick wife Giselle and wants her to recover. She no longer has to live up to his illu-sions. With some loss of weight she could still be attractive, even with brown hair!

A southerner of Greek descent is barely mentioned in Shirley Ann Grau's fine novel, *The Keepers of the House* (1964). Whereas Nick Pappy in *The Cave* holds an angry mob at bay, in Grau's story Peter Demos is part of a mob that sets out to destroy the Howland House because of a shocking revelation: its previous white owner, now dead, had had five children with a black woman he had actu-ally *married!* William Howland was one of the state's richest men. The present "keeper of the house," Abigail, narrates throughout; and she reaches the point where her grandfather's past becomes a public scandal in the press. "It was a photostat of a certificate of marriage. Between William Howland and Margaret Carmichael."[11] The woman was a Negro. When the news spreads, a mob sets out from town to burn down Howland House. They do fire the barn, but not the house, which Abigail protects. Among many others she names, there "was Peter Demos, who kept the café, and Joe Har-riman from the feed store; Frank Sargeant from the lumber yard. His son, who was one of the bookkeepers at the new mill. Claude King, who ran the Ford agency. . . . They were the good people out there."[12] Among the good people, a Greek who had won status as a southern white—by being allowed to join a lynch mob.

None of these novels by non-Greek southerners tell us very much about the true "Greekness" of their characters. For this knowledge and insight the reader can go to two Greek women, both southerners, who have written ethnic novels: *The Wing and the Thorn* (1952) by Roxanne Cotsakis, already mentioned; and *Enter-ing Ephesus* (1971) by Daphne Athas. Like several other novelists Cotsakis begins the odyssey of her hero in Greece, then brings him across the Atlantic to America where most of the action occurs. Her novel is thus also an "immigrant novel" and one that depicts "growing up Greek" in the U.S. Enough time elapses during the ups and downs of the complicated plot, from 1906 until 1946, to include both the immigrant and the second-generation Greeks. Cotsakis writes with an intimate and thorough knowledge of her characters; she often pauses to explain ethnic household and communal customs not known to the average reader. Some of these customs have already eroded away, and in time many others will also vanish. For this reason they are recounted here in detail.

The boy Yannis lives with his aunt and uncle in Messinia. His parents have died of poverty and illness; also dead is a brother. Yannis feels caged by the "accursed mountains." He sees no future for himself "except to break his back upon the furrows" and then to "stand and watch unseasonable rains wash the raisin crop down the mountainside" while he stands helpless and waits for another hard winter. Yannis therefore determines to emigrate to *Ameriki*; despite the fact that he is a *horiati*, a villager, he is intelligent and can succeed in *Nea Yorki* where there are "ditches to dig and dishes to wash and streets to sweep!" [13] His neighbor Pavlos forges a letter from his brother in America so Yannis can show the authorities at Ellis Island that he has a sponsor. The brother is Michail Mavromatis of Minneapolis. Yannis sells the donkey and his father's share of the farm for passage.

For the young immigrant nearing New York the Statue of Liberty looms out of the night as might a saint, "like Saint Dionisius of Zakynthos whose story all villagers knew. Dionisius' mummy roamed the earth constantly, returning each December 17th to his bier at Zakynthos to replace worn out iron shoes with new ones which devout villagers placed on his tomb annually" (p. 9). To a sailor boy, Spiros, Yannis vows that as soon as he makes his fortune he will return home—a common dream that did not often materialize. At Ellis Island the interpreter gives Yannis his American name—John Pantellis. A clerk puts around his neck a placard with his name and patron's address. John buys a railroad ticket for Minneapolis, but at the station he tears up the ticket and forged patron's letter, hides the placard, and runs off alone into the streets of New York. In the sack that holds all he owns he has a piece of *kefalotiri* cheese. John sings to himself:

> *If you should go to Kalamat'*
> *And fortune comes your way,*
> *Bring me a colored neckerchief*
> *When you return some day.*

Until he chances to find some fellow Greeks, John has a lonely time of it: he gets cheated when he buys an ill-fitting suit; he sleeps on a park bench; he suffers through rain, alone and afraid of the police. Then from a doorway he hears Greek spoken. *"Patrioti!*

Countrymen!" he cries, and rushes upstairs to what turns out to be a *kafenio*. "Men sat at scarred tables, smoking, talking, drinking amber *retsina* wine or loudly slurping thick sweet Turkish coffee. An old man sat dreaming by the window, his hands absently shifting the amber beads of a *koumboloyo* [worrybeads] around a thick waxed string" (p. 17). At the *kafenio* John meets Georgios Panos and Chris Triantafillos, partners who sell fruit from a pushcart. "We're nothing to the Americans," Georgios tells him, but they will work "like the dogs they say we are . . . be greedy as the pigs they think us" (p. 19). John eagerly wants to join them, despite the occasional trouble they have. Yesterday a band of boys grabbed what they could and upset the cart—"bananas black in the gutter, the grapes mashed like for making wine!" Georgios and Chris accept John as a partner. He has forty dollars to invest in the pushcart. They repair to their smelly room on Madison Avenue.

Early next morning they go to the produce market where, using John's money, they load the pushcart with apples, lemons, oranges, grapefruit, and grapes—grapes that make him nostalgic for home. They readily sell their fruit then eat at the *kafenio* midst the "friendly boisterous Greek atmosphere, the smell of dry retsina wine, the soft flowery Greek talk around him" (p. 23). John keeps his money in a tobacco pouch. Very rapidly their business improves; luckily for him John Pantellis has found honest partners. Upon Chris's suggestion they sell vegetables as well as fruit. John learns to make purchases; he arranges displays on a palette-shaped board, with a list of produce on their cart. They find a good regular route and keep a record of customers. Some days they dispose of three or four cartloads. John writes to his uncle and aunt, tells about his progress, and sends them five dollars. They need a better neighborhood, however, with higher types of people. They also need to expand.

Before long they open a fruit-and-vegetable stand and call it the Fresh Shop. "John went down to the Bowery and stole a cat to serve as mouser" (p. 39). They also move to an apartment house owned by a landlord named Joseph Nix. That Christmas the Nixes invite them for eggnog on the same day that Dionisios Petrakis, a friend, invites them to the wedding of their seventeen-year-old daughter to the nearly sixty-year-old Alekos Koutsonikas, proprietor of the Cretan Grill. John does not like it when *proxenitisais*, marriage arrangers, mate two generations in such fashion. Both the Nix apartment and Aletha Nix, the daughter, impress him. The party, however, is cold, "like a wake after a Greek death." Greek hospitality is much warmer. John notes the lack of proper segregation between men and women. He also feels uneasy when Aletha takes him by the arm for a drink. *Farmaki.* "It's poison!" says Georgios about the eggnog. In the music room alone Aletha asks John about Greece. He tries to speak English well, but his words come out comically. "I come to Ameriki to be good American peoples like you Papa!" (p. 47). John regards as indecent Aletha's low-cut dress that reveals the "beginning swell of her breasts." A young man enters the room and kisses her—under the mistletoe. Aletha tries to explain the custom of kissing under the mistletoe at Christmas, but John makes the moral judgment: "Is not nice . . . in my country." She abandons him in disgust, leaving him confused; in the midst of luxury, she appears indecent.

After the Nix party, John and his friends go to the Petrakis flat which, by contrast, they find full of life: children and babies, the feast cooking, the old women together in the parlor, "their ankles decorously crossed under long, full skirts." Everything falls for John into the "familiar pattern of village life" (p. 51). The priest performs the wedding ceremony, chanting the nuptial liturgy, while the packed guests watch. During the wedding supper they drink Mavrodaphne wine and "the milky ladies-punch they called 'soumada.'" John Pantellis regards the Orthodox Church as unchanging. "I believe as I was taught" (p. 53). He is more conservative than Georgios on sex, more rigid than the priest on dynamics of church affairs. He is said to be a "fine Greek" and a "real Greek" by the mothers present who eye him as a potential son-in-law. John's rigidity about remaining Greek conflicts with his earlier wish to become more American than the Americans. The rigidity develops later into a stubborn monomania that causes much domestic tension.

During the next few years John's experiences multiply, yet his sanctimonious character keeps him from adjusting well to America. When dared by Georgios to visit a brothel, he wants to bring along a box of candy for the whore; and, afterwards he wonders if she felt anything for him. Time passes. It is 1912, and John has turned twenty-two. He has held up Joseph Nix as a model American, only to be shocked when, through an error in delivering a basket of fruit, he inadvertently exposes Nix's mistress to his wife. The three Greek *becharides,* bachelors, now cook their own meals: *yachni* of meat and vegetables, *krithari,* rice *pilaf,* "broiling lamb's intestines, lavishly oiled and garlicked," Greek bread, "wild Hymettus honey," salads, Turkish coffee, and rice custard topped with cinnamon (p. 72). More important for their future, they receive a letter from the second cousin of Georgios's father urging them to move South to a place named Auburn. The three partners argue the wisdom of going.

Chris's bride Elayni arrives, an Athenian with "none of the down-cast eyes, the decorum of young women they knew in Greek families." They get married at noon. Another big event for the three friends is the coming of a photograph bride, Dionisia, for Georgios. She appears as a "moon-faced, fuzzy-haired peasant with thick beads around her neck. She was posed with the finger-on-cheek in the manner village photographers found charming" (p. 89). One day John meets Aletha Nix outside the building and takes her to Marchette's, a fine restaurant, for *sampanyi*, champagne. Very soon both are drunk. When they leave they hire a hanson, find a parson, and get married. Her parents are furious; and John cannot understand why, even though Nix calls him a "low-down, no-count, good-for-nothing woP! Why, you filthy, stinking, burgling woP!" (p. 100). Aletha says that she loves John. Her father, however, cries, "If he's your husband, you're not my daughter." And he forces Aletha to choose. She chooses to abandon John and stay with her parents. As a result of this traumatic rejection, John agrees with his partners to sell the Fresh Shop and go South to Auburn. He writes to his uncle for a bride; and for him comes Androula Margaritarou, the Lula he had once fondled. February 6, 1915, is the ninth anniversary of John's arrival in America. The partners buy a restaurant in Auburn. John has gone to night school to learn better English. All of them have a hunger, Georgios says, to drive themselves until they drop. Thus ends the first book of the novel.

The middle book of *The Wing and the Thorn* concerns John Pantellis the father. The time leaps thirty-one years to January 7, 1946, St. John's day. John drives to Agios Georgios Greek Orthodox Church in his big Buick. His pretentious house sticks out like a "festered thumb" in Greek Town; it sports "a frieze of stylized Grecian warriors" holding "spears and torches, alternately puncturing and frying the rears of the warriors in front of them" (p. 114). Another garish touch, in front of the balcony, is "an oversized eagle, his claws firmly wrapped about a planet-shaped ball, inside of which was a light fixture which flooded the steps below with illumination so bright that people shaded their eyes when they came to the front door after dark" (p. 114). A monstrosity, yet a Greek house, too, since it has its pot of basil, a *vasilico* plant, whose sprigs are used for sachets in handkerchief knots, to sweeten the breath, chopped into salads, meatballs, and stews, or tied in bunches to dry for winter cooking. Behind his imposing house John Pantellis has a grape arbor, a pit for barbecuing whole lambs, and a two-car garage that also holds barrels for retsina wine.

He now owns a lucrative insurance business. Lula, being a "Greek wife," has never seen the office. His daughter Maria, nineteen, has not been at his office for five years; the American men there might look at her. She has a brother Laki, eleven. Lula and Maria argue about fixed marriages, a practice still followed by some Greeks. Maria cites her friend Katie Trianon, who was forced to "marry a bum like Teddie," and she vows that "nobody's going to push me into a marriage like hers, believe me!" (p. 122). An added problem is that Maria loves Dimitri Trianon, John's own godson; and according to church law, he is her spiritual brother and thus "forbidden to her in marriage." Before the guests arrive for John's patron saint's day, Lula thinks of the old superstition that people can become paralyzed if they fail to observe a holy day. The best known hex among Greeks, however, is the *matiasma*, the giving and receiving of the evil eye.

Thus the bestower of a compliment must spit to dispel the un-witting granting of the curse. Some Greeks presume "any illness a *matiasma* until proven otherwise." Proof of a *matiasma* follows a set routine:

> The seer would pour oil into clove-spiced water and watch it carefully to determine whether more than normal of the oil went to the bottom of the container. If it did, incantations for unhexing would begin immediately. The victim would be anointed with oily crosses on forehead, cheek, chin, and appendages while recuperative and exorcising prayers were muttered.
>
> No layman knew the dispelling prayers. Sorceresses—for they were always women—kept such words secret until they passed their powers to their successors. And woe unto any who spoke the words to anyone else! (p. 126)

Lula's best dispeller of the *matiasma* is Mrs. Fafouti. The youthful Efthimia Routos is allegedly good at dream divining.

Among the many guests is Dimitri, now twenty-six, out of the service and about to teach philosophy at a military school. He feels that John Pantellis, despite his success, is isolated from America, that he does not live up to AHEPA's ideals. To John, AHEPA is "an organization of Greek-Americans who want to retain their Greek culture in a foreign country." But to Dimitri, AHEPA means to break chains, not to forge them. He blames John for his self-isolation. "You built yourself little caves to hide in and pretended you were chased there" (p. 143).

Other matters intrude. Katie Trianon, Dimitri's sister and daughter of Chris, John's old friend, admits the baby she is having does not belong to her husband, but to an American with whom she had an affair. John Pantellis reacts wildly, he wonders why Chris has not killed her, and he rushes home to ask Lula if Maria knows the facts of life. Lula cries: "You can't shut that child off from the world!" Up to now he has had little to do with Maria's upbringing; now, as always, he pays no attention to Lula's opinion. He readily assumes that Maria has had affairs in secret, and threatens to punish her for deceiving him. Stubbornly he demands that they avoid the Trianons lest they contaminate Maria. Lula is appalled by his gross insensitivity and says: "You have talked up Greece so long and low-rated America so long." He insists: "I am the master in this house," and he orders her: "Now go to Maria!" (p. 152).

By happy contrast Georgios's household is more normal and Georgios more reasonable. He reads *Satyros*, the Greek comic paper, whereas John Pantellis has no sense of humor. Georgios, too, has become rich, owning "the largest florist shop in Auburn." His wife Dionisia has grown fat; she loves the Turkish delight *loukoum*, and she easily forgives Georgios's infidelities. Pitsa, their daughter, is not pretty. "She knew as well as Dionisia that she could never compete for the favor of the young eligible Greek men. They concentrated only on the very beautiful, the greatly dowried, and the comfortably loose girls in the community. Others were wallflowers" (p. 155). Pitsa must find her own husband or "rot in Greek Town." Unlike Lula with Maria, Dionisia has long since informed Pitsa about boys and sex. Dionisia would prefer an American son-in-law to the "spoiled jackasses" among the young Greeks. Yet Pitsa is a good Greek girl who has kept up her native language, knows how to use a Greek typewriter, and regularly assists the priest at church.

Because of church law Maria and Dimitri are, in a sense, star-crossed lovers. John forbids Maria to have anything to do with her friend Katie, who has gone to Florida for a divorce. John had also forbidden Maria to attend college. "A shrew, that's what an educated woman is!" (p. 163). On the "Greek Fourth of July," March 25th, the local AHEPA holds an affair that also includes the auxiliary groups, the Daughters of Penelope and the Maids of Athens, to begin at "eight-thirty Greek time"—meaning any time before ten—in the church basement. John Pantellis, president of the local AHEPA lodge, plans to announce the results of the fund-raising campaign. During the recent war Greeks throughout the country had contributed millions in clothing, food, and supplies to their impoverished countrymen. AHEPA has now, in 1946, raised money to build hospitals for Greek casualties. Besides helping through the church and societies, John has been supporting Lula's family and others in his old village. Yet withal Georgios pities John for being mulish, for not wanting to understand America, for not knowing what a fine family he has.

At the AHEPA affair an unexpected crisis erupts for Maria. While she is dancing with Dimitri, a tall red-headed man enters the hall—a "Christmas tree" in the author's vivid phrase. He is Angelos Telemachos of Chicago, invited by John Pantellis and her godfather. Maria, furious, suspects that plans for a fixed marriage have progressed behind her back. Angelos acts with familiarity and calls her "darling." At the party John orates about the legendary Greek patriot Athanasios Diakos whom the Turks tortured to get him to renounce being a Greek. As daggers cut into his body, Diakos cried: "I was born a Greek and a Greek I shall die!" The Turks killed the brave Diakos by strapping him to a pole and roasting him over a pit of coals. Behind John hang portraits of Diakos, Kolokotronis, Bishop Germanos, and Marco Bozzaris. For these expressions of Greek patriotism Angelos Telemachos has nothing but scorn. He has a poor opinion of his fellow Greeks, having attended an English college in Istanbul.

At the dance a *gero*, old Omiros Koutsos, who owns a hotdog shop on Main Street, plays on a scratched fiddle the *Kalamatiano*, the "traditional dance of the Kalamatan Islanders." Cotsakis relates the dance to one of the most famous episodes of the period before the Greek revolution.

Legend told that the women of Zalongou had danced this same dance in a tragic flight from pursuing Turks. Knowing that capture and rape were imminent—as well as slaughter for their children—the Zalongan women had formed a Kalama-

tiano dancing circle with their children, kissed each other tear-
fully, and followed the intricate pattern down the road and
dropped one by one over the cliffs of Zalongou to death. (p.
184)

These were Suliote women from a wild and mountainous region
of Epirus; the year of their martyrdom was 1801.

After the AHEPA affair at the church, John Pantellis wants to
invite Angelos Telemachos home for a snack. But both Lula and
Maria object—it is 2 A.M. A stiff argument ensues during which
Maria tells her father, "I love Dimitri. I have to marry Dimitri. . . .
I have to! This is one thing I must do no matter what you wish!"
(p. 189). John has everything planned with Angelos: to give him
his daughter, give him the firm, build them a big house, and then
John will travel to Greece. He feels betrayed. "You can't have Dimitri!" he roars, regarding it a sin to marry one's spiritual brother.
In the next chapter Dimitri brings their problem to Papa Anastasis,
who informs him that the church dropped the rule some years
before, around 1941. Dimitri can certainly marry Maria. The
priest blames the older parents for keeping the youth ignorant;
the old still believe in superstitions and "pagan rituals," while the
young are leaving the church. Papa Anastasis believes instruction
classes should be given in English—a revolutionary idea at the
time. When told about the change in church law, John Pantellis
cannot believe it, and opposes it if true. Nevertheless they have an
engagement ceremony, with the wedding of Dimitri and Maria to
be held immediately after Lent. The news of the event spreads,
causing a stir. A moving scene occurs when a young Greek girl
named Mary Demos learns of the church law's being cancelled.
Two months earlier she had wed a fifty-five-year old man; but she
loves her godfather's son, Leonidas.

Greek Easter arrives a week after "American" Easter. The author takes pains to describe the church observances of Holy Week.
The Greek Orthodox Church calculates time by the Julian calendar, which runs thirteen days behind the Gregorian. Besides that
basic fact of time, "Easter had to occur the first Sunday after full
moon following the equinox. Greek Easter also had to follow Pass-
over, and sometimes this threw the holiday several weeks behind
'American Easter'" (p. 212). In the course of Holy Week the
church observes the following rituals: Monday, the betrayal of
Christ; Tuesday and Wednesday, the Crucifixion; Thursday, the
funeral procession; Good Friday, Christ in His tomb; Saturday,
communion and the end of fasting; Easter Sunday, the Resurrec-

tion. Fasting, if rigidly adhered to, means the "omission of all animal matter and oils, which included eggs, butter, milk, and even olive oil except for Shrove Tuesday." But not olives themselves. No doubt from her own memories Roxanne Cotsakis describes the fasting children as "a discontented brood who gnawed disconsolately at peanut butter and banana sandwiches, drank water instead of milk, and looked wistfully at the delectable meat sandwiches their American classmates ate at recess" (p. 214). Fasting supposedly purified one for the taking of communion; however, even fasting did not qualify some for the Eucharist. "People with open wounds and women at menstrual cycles were not supposed to take communion. Neither were those who bore a fellow man a grievance" (p. 214).

After the Saturday night Resurrection services, the Pantellis family plans to eat the traditional Easter breakfast of *avgolemono soup*, "a rich chicken broth filled with rice and topped with a meringue of eggs beaten with lemon juice" (p. 216). Another Greek soup eaten at this time (not mentioned in the novel) is *magaritsa*, a thick mixture of rice with chopped lamb lungs, heart, and entrails. Up very early on Sunday, John will prepare Easter dinner *a la patrida* featuring a whole young lamb roasted over his charcoal pit. He will tie the lamb to a pole and carefully turn it for hours, basting the body every few minutes "with a new dish mop dipped in a sauce of lemon juice, olive oil, salt, pepper, and oreganon spice." Fellow Greeks will come to drink a glass of wine and to "crack" colored eggs for *kali tihi*, good luck, or to nibble on the *giovetsi*—lamb giblets roasting on a smaller spit. Most Greeks in Auburn no longer roast a lamb; but for John Pantellis the old custom means the happiest day of the year.

On Saturday, before the Resurrection, Dimitri and Katie Trianon talk about her problem. She will not marry Paul, the American father of her child, because of his prejudice. "He'd sniff at the strange odors and frown at the Greek talk" (p. 219). Katie herself, confused, also hates the ugly lace curtains, the old furniture, the Greek pictures on the wall, the icon in the front hall. Yet she resents Paul's turning up his nose at Greeks and lets him have it. To Dimitri she admits she is "not at home with Greeks or without them," and he rejoins by saying that, unlike Maria Pantellis, she lacks patience. They can live in both worlds, have both Greek and American friends. Unfortunately for Katie, she slips on a pebble and falls; taken to the hospital, she loses her baby, which is buried after a "postmortem christening" in a corner of the "large Trianon plot in the Greek section of Woodhaven Cemetery where the Auburn Greek Towners buried their dead" (p. 227).

Meanwhile, on Saturday night, the Pantellis family goes to church for the midnight Resurrection service. Other writers besides Cotsakis have also described the ritual. The priest appears in gold and scarlet robes, symbols of holiday joy. Worshippers hold tall yellow candles in the total darkness, the priest has a white candle . . . and the "flame blazed like a meteor" in a dark "which was total except for the pin-points of brilliance from night-lights over the icons" (p. 225). The priest intones: "Come and receive the light!" Three young deacons face the priest at the foot of the altar steps; they light tapers from the white candle, and pass the light on to the congregation, row by row. Led by the priest, the worshippers sing *Christos anesti,* "Christ is risen."

A few days after Easter comes the *koufeta* party in preparation for Maria's wedding with Dimitri. She and her friends gather to tie "the Jordan almonds inside the tulle with a satin ribbon and a sprig of orange blossoms " (p. 229). Katie regards the big job as part of the price of being Greek, and she exclaims: "These passionate Greeks!" The wedding is lavish. For her dowry John Pantellis had given Maria a check for twenty-five thousand dollars even though he still disdains her union with her "spiritual brother." Atop the ceremonial table a silver tray, a gift of the *koumbaros* and best man, holds the bundles of Jordan almonds, "symbols of fruition." Cotsakis details the ritual: the exchange of wreaths, the priest's prayer, advice, reading from the Bible, the locking of hands, the triple crossing of the wreaths, the sips of wine from the golden chalice, the gold rings on fingers, and the procession around the table. No kiss of husband and wife concludes the ceremony. The "outsiders" are struck by the pageantry; and even the Greeks whisper among themselves about the costly flowers, gowns, and other accoutrements. Maria is radiant. "Her dark hair was caught in a pearl-embroidered lace cap and piled in a Grecian coiffure at the back of her head, revealing the classic profile." "Circlets of diamonds" pierce through her ears, the gift of her godfather, while Dimitri's gift is "intricately set pearls in an antique lavalier" which shine "with soft lustre about her throat." For her protection against evil spirits Maria has been instructed by Mrs. Fafouti. "Pinned inside her white satin brassiere was a protective bunch of herbs and bark intended to ward off the curses of evil though admiring eyes" (p.

231). The newlyweds had refused a big wedding reception. They leave early from the catered one held in the church basement. The event has displeased John Pantellis because it contradicted his authority. He has lost face in Greek Town.

The next Greek-American custom described by Cotsakis is a christening, attended by John and Lula, for the six-month-old Farantos baby. The baptismal font, the *kolimbithra*, holds the center of attention in the living room. The ritual calls for the godfather, Dovalos, to swear he will give the child succor and a Christian upbringing. Dovalos spits thrice to show contempt for Satan, and he repeats the Credo: "I believe in one God, the Father Almighty, Creator of heaven and earth." The priest takes the baby, submerges him three times, and chants, "In the name of the Father . . . and of the Son, and of the Holy Ghost" and concludes, "Accept . . . your servant—" Dovalos, who names the baby, "Epaminondas!" The godfather's brother passes out shiny new dimes to each child who screams "Epaminondas is his name!" (p. 235). The priest has one final act to perform. "With cotton dipped in sanctified oil he traced crosses on forehead, nose, chin, palms, heart and face" of the newly named infant.

Georgios has been pleased to see John Pantellis humiliated, after all his high and mighty talk about remaining Greek. Ted Tamparis, Katie's former husband, offers to sell Georgios a stolen pin and bracelet with eighty-four diamonds—over twenty carats—for a bargain price. Pitsa, for whom the hot jewelry is intended, goes out and calls the police, telling them where in Ted's cigar store the jewelry is hidden. Before long the police arrive and arrest him. Pitsa tells Georgios that her husband will "buy my diamonds." At his home John Pantellis gets a phone call and goes to the jail to bail out Ted Tamparis on grounds that "the Greeks must help each other" (p. 254). The *Times-Examiner* has a front page picture and story about John and the priest arranging bail for a Greek criminal. Lula condemns John for defending Tamparis on an ethnic basis. A dog is a dog, no matter what its nationality, and she tells John that "pompous, sanctimonious fools like you" make things hard for others. He laments: "Everything is scattered. Our morals, our thoughts, our children, our religion" (p. 254).

Very boorish during a dinner at the Trianons, John creates much tension by condemning Katie as being "wild." He will not forgive nor forget. Georgios's wife Elayni flares up at John, the so-perfect Greek, accuses him of getting drunk as a lord and marrying "that red-headed Nix girl. And her father kicked him out!" For standing up to John and exposing his scandal, her husband Chris slaps Elayni and calls her "filthy *skila!* Bitch!" As a result of the tension Lula Pantellis suffers a heart attack and dies. After her funeral John plans to move to Greece with his son Laki, whom he does not inform beforehand. He criticizes Maria for not wearing the traditional black, and she replies: "I am as desolate in pink as in black" (p. 269). When John tells Laki they will live in Greece together, the youth violently rebels. "I'm no Greek—I'm an American. I've never seen that old place and I don't want to. I won't go!" (p. 275). As a result John Pantellis will go to Greece alone. Thus ends the second book of *The Wing and the Thorn*.

The final book, "The Man," opens as John lands at the airport in Athens. On the flight he has met a Mr. McBride, an American diplomat, who regards John also as an American. A series of revelations begins that eventually humbles and humanizes him. Gone for forty years, since 1906, John finds that he knows nothing about modern Greece. McBride knows much more. Even as a youth John had not ventured from his village of Messinia and knew little of Greek history. McBride invites John to stay with him and his wife Phyllis who, much to his surprise, speaks fluent Greek and works hard as an archaeologist. She is a blunt argument against his hard-and-fast rule that "a wife's place is in the home." Furthermore she has the audacity to invent a unique theory about the "origin of the alphabet" which is too deep for John's comprehension. Phyllis "looks" as Greek as anyone, although she is of Rumanian ancestry born in Boston. She calls John a "tourist." McBride's cook makes *stifado*—a Greek cook for Americans! A neighbor of the McBride's, in "moral" Greece, is Lampbros Vafiadis, a writer grown rich from a prewar series of pornographic bestsellers. Everywhere the black market flourishes, with no rationing. In America, John says, we had rationing. The question is: who are the *we?* The cook does not regard John a Greek. "Not a Greek?" he asks indignantly (p. 296). Not an American either. She does not know what he is.

John Pantellis finds Greece poor, war-torn. Athens is quiet, like a dead city. He tours it in a jeep provided by the Americans. McBride gets him a plane ride as far as Kalamas; because of his war-relief work, John is a privileged person. If the king returns via the coming plebescite, he may decorate John with the "Order of the Phoenix." Phyllis McBride he cannot understand at all. She flirtingly calls him "Johnny-boy" and wants him to call her "Phyl." John cannot fathom flirting; he is humorless. She baits him by asking had he known many women? The fact is that John has never bothered to know *any* woman; he has never respected women enough. He disparages, too, the custom of siesta which demobilizes all work for part of the afternoon. Phyllis comments, "Which proves you're not Greek anymore!" (p. 306).

More shocks await John Pantellis as he retraces his steps to the village of his youth. Kalamas has changed. "The city was as strange as New York had been to him on arrival," except that Greek is spoken. He meets his nephew, Marko Margaritaros, to learn that he is mixed up with the Communists . . . and hostile to John for being an American capitalist. John's niece Lula wears trousers! At a tavern where they eat, the keeper catches a live hen to kill and cook for them, a practice that John has forgotten. He had sent Marko's father money to buy cows, but the boy snaps: "We received no money for cows." John suspects deception somewhere. In Marko's jeep they drive past the beautiful Taygetus Mountain to Messinia. The village is unrecognizable. Only a few wear the peasant *vlahika* and *fustanella* costumes; the rest wear European clothes. Aristo, his brother-in-law, is a drunk, dirty and shiftless. John insists he will stay in his own house, although it has not been lived in for a long time. "The family stood before the cabin waving goodbye, their silhouettes like cadavers against the bleak stone house" (p. 318).

Needless to say, more grief awaits John Pantellis; and the bulk of the evidence points to his own ignorance about the Greece he has loved only from afar. The house is filthy, the floor gritty with dried manure. Even the mountain air saps his strength. Marko is surly; he will do errands only if John pays for them. All money sent them had been drunk and gambled away by Aristo. John and Marko discuss the Greek Communists, with Marko saying they have "new ideas" about the future. "They fought for Greece just as I did. They are boys like me, men like I will be . . . Greeks like myself. They will change things" (p. 323). John had a brother once, named Marko, who died. He decides to help his nephew Marko with his education. Together they clean the house. John will build a new house for his sister's family; he will also renew the farm, restore the vineyard, buy equipment. And he orders them all not to call Marko a Communist, but a "good Greek."

In his village John speaks with the old priest Papastratos, telling him he is no longer sure he wants to remain. They discuss the Greeks of America as well. "You took 1906 with you and tried to plant it in America," Father Papastratos says, "but you woke up one day to realize it was 1946 there, so you ran away . . . hoping to find 1906 here" (p. 333). The point is that everything changes, and John Pantellis must change also. And he does, much to his credit. Through a lawyer he arranges to pay Marko's school expenses in Athens. He buys animals, supplies, and fuel to renovate the farm. Back with the McBrides on his way to America, John is praised for taking Marko away from the Communists. The American believes they merely "posed" as Greeks while serving as the hard core of the resistance. In "L'Envoi" the McBrides at the airport give John a present for Maria—"Hymettus honey in a peasant-made ceramic jar of streaked blue."

John returns home to the United States with new plans about many things, including his "cold box of a house in Greek Town," built as an act of revenge. "Not for beauty but for revenge. Not for comfort but for spite against fineries he had wanted to surpass. Against the velvets in the Nix house, the elegance of Mrs. Alston . . . against all the hurt and the despair . . . his house had been his revenge." A *wop* they had called him. He finally sees that some of the old Greeks act "like vultures," grasping at life with greedy hands, "devouring even the lives of their young to satisfy their craving." John Pantellis vows he will help Maria and Dimitri anew, and in his own way. "Give them the patience I never had!" From his ability to change has finally emerged a harmony he has never known.

This detailed summary has resulted from the amount and accuracy of ethnic material which Roxanne Cotsakis's novel contains. No other work by a Greek-American writer offers so much information with such meticulous care. Even her fellow southerner, Daphne Athas of Chapel Hill, N.C., gives comparatively few details in *Entering Ephesus*, the only one of her four novels that uses Greek characters. In it she has a family with a Greek father that plummets from wealth in New England to poverty in the South.

> A ratbucket shack on the wrong side of the tracks in Ephesus, U.S.A., is where the Depression-ridden Bishop family finds itself in 1939. Ephesus is a smallish university town in the South, a place that makes the former Bishop wealth and New England house of fourteen rooms and forty-nine windows by the sea seem out of a whole other universe.[14]

For more than a year the father, Pavlos Episcopoulos, has been alone in Ephesus, N.C., trying to recoup after economic disaster in the North. In Ephesus he raises tomatoes without much success, while back in New England his *Mayflower*-descended wife supports the family of three daughters "by the cliché strategem of baking and selling apple turnovers" (p. 13).

The long novel's minimal use of ethnicity is explained in a number of ways, least of all perhaps by the father's marriage to a Yankee girl, Clara Parsons. He himself was born in Khartoum, dropped the name *Paul* because he detested St. Paul, and changed his surname *Episcopoulos* to the Anglicized *Bishop*. "He was Greek but had never been in Greece" (p. 12). Throughout the story he is referred to by the initials P.Q., a device that not only minimizes his Greekness but tends to dehumanize him altogether. "As a student," Athas writes, "P.Q. tried to organize the Greeks of New England, to make them learn English and read American history to get them out of the mills of Lawrence and Lowell, out of the ghettos and raise them up." This activity must have occurred in high school, for on the same page P.Q. mentions that he attended the University of Illinois. Also on the same page we read that P.Q. was "always separated from the rest of the Greeks by his slow-burning egotism and the arrogance of messianic idealism," traits no doubt accentuated by his marrying into "the cream of Yankee society" (p. 12).

P.Q. Bishop has the makings of a marvellous character; unfortunately he is not developed enough; he remains shadowy throughout. That he fails to emerge as a Greek is, of course, unimportant with respect to aesthetic excellence. What is vital, however, is his not having a role large and important enough to fully release his potential as a character. He talks a lot in a novel in which everyone talks too much. That the dialogue is often witty, sharp, and subtle does not compensate for P.Q.'s peripheral impact on the meager action. Yet the basic ingredients are there: one of the earliest Greeks in America, a highly intellectualized Greek (not the usual earthy peasant), a mixture "of opportunist and utopian," a Micawber spouting Plato and Aristotle, a loser all the way.

When Clara Bishop and her daughters—Irene, Urania, and Sylvia—arrive in Ephesus, they find P.Q. renting a former funeral home in the heart of Niggertown. The house belongs to a Mrs. Kanukaris (maiden name Wanda Rupee), the "white-trash widow of a café Greek whom P.Q. had met when he first came to Ephesus and who had died two months later" (p. 16). In over a year, though, P.Q. has not made a single friend among his black neighbors. For an "unprejudiced Greek Yankee" such a studied isolation seems odd. Nor do any of the Bishop girls develop a single black girlfriend in the three-year course of the novel. Their vivacity runs toward smart comments, pointless sex, and status envy.

Entering Ephesus has poignant moments that now and then surface from the inveterate intellectualism. As Thorstein Veblen wrote in *The Theory of the Leisure Class*, few personal experiences are harder for one to take than to fall from a higher to a lower social class. Such a tragic event happens to the Bishops at the worst possible time for the daughters: when they reach the sensitive stage of going from adolescence to early womanhood. Urania says when she learns they will live in Niggertown: "It's a relief to know we have hit rock bottom" (p. 17). One feels pathos for P.Q., with his brilliant mind, delivering laundered linen on a bicycle. Perhaps the emotional high point in this story about maturation comes when the youngest, Sylvia (called Loco Poco), is killed by a truck. For her accidental death the Bishop family receives a check in the amount of fifteen hundred dollars to pay the funeral expenses. A little is left over. Later they give Loco Poco's things away. When asked by Irene about the shoes, P.Q. replies: "I gave them to that old nigger plumber for his kids." The final blow falls at the end when, unable to pay the rent even for the decrepit mortuary, they are evicted and leave to begin anew, this time in a gypsy tent on land they hope to own.

The most "Greek" of southern towns, by far, has been Tarpon Springs, Florida, home of the famed sponge divers. The next chapter surveys the ethnic fiction based upon their lives. Tarpon Springs represents perhaps the most nearly complete and self-sufficient of America's many Greek Towns—not the most affluent nor most populous but the most autarkical. It would seem axiomatic to say that a character from a vital Greek Town shows much more Greekness (a John Pantellis, for example) than does an isolated Greek living among Americans, like Nick Pappy in *The Cave*. The latter has less opportunity either in fiction or in real life to express his ethnic heritage. In the final analysis, however, the degree of ethnicity used for plot structure, characterization, and theme depends upon the author's aesthetic purpose.

THE LEGEND OF TARPON SPRINGS

N O SINGLE GREEK TOWN in the United States has been as romanticized in literature and film as the Florida seacoast sponging community of Tarpon Springs. Nor has such an ethnic entity been so cruelly bankrupted as when the fungoid blight devasted the sponge beds the winter of 1947. Ironically, the January 1947 issue of the *National Geographic Magazine*, prepared earlier, featured a seventeen-page spread on the hitherto thriving enclave, "Sponge Fishermen of Tarpon Springs."[1] Its author, Jennie E. Harris, had no portent of disaster when she wrote her Greek idyll of sponging off Florida's coast. The spongers themselves knew of the encroachments by the blight which first hit the Bahamas about December 1938 and then "spread and reached the rich sponge beds of the West Coast of Florida, Cuba, and Honduras."[2] The price of sponges skyrocketed, and the spongers grew wealthy on the diminished harvest—until 1947 when the disease turned epidemic. The decline of the Greek sponging industry is told in *Strangers at Ithaca* (1962) by George Th. Frantzis, who lived for twenty years among the spongers, and who cast his account more as a narrative epic than as a regularly integrated history. Despite its rambling structure, unscholarly method, and personal sentiment, *Strangers at Ithaca* contains invaluable memorabilia about the unique ethnic settlement of Tarpon Springs. The romanticism is there, certainly, but so is the obverse—the exploitation of the Greek workers by the Sponge Exchange, and the grim trinity of Desolation, Destruction, and Despair caused by the blight. Upon the decline of the sponging industry followed the rise of Tarpon Springs as a tourist attraction, and many a lithe young Greek who might have gone to the depths of the Gulf for sponges now put on diving shows for the gullible strangers.

The customs and superstitions of the Greek spongers have also been studied by devotees of American folklore. As early as 1939 the *Journal of American Folk-Lore* published an item by Eileen Elita

Doering, "A Charm of the Gulf of Mexico Sponge Fishers," in which she states:

> The fishermen will not start out to sea on Tuesday, because they consider it unlucky to start any enterprise on a Tuesday. Neither will they leave port in any new year before Epiphany. When the sponge fishers see the funnel of a cyclone, they carve a cross on the mast of the ship and then stick a knife into it. This saves them from the fury of the storm. The person who performs this charm is committing a sin and must do some form of penance. The fishermen do not hesitate, however, to resort to this charm when in danger.[3]

Doering does not explain that many Greeks are leery about Tuesday because Constantinople fell to the Turks on that weekday in 1453.

At least three articles about Tarpon Springs have appeared in the *Southern Folklore Quarterly*. The first, by J. Frederick Doering, analyzes the mixture of religion and superstition in the blessing of the sponge boats on January 6, the holy day honoring St. Nicholas, patron saint of sailors. Robert A. Georges wrote two articles for the quarterly. The first describes the *vendouze*, "a form of cupping intended to cure colds and pneumonia," as told to him by residents of Tarpon Springs and Savannah. His "The Greeks of Tarpon Springs: An American Folk Group" is a valuable statement on the customs, beliefs, and superstitions of the famous ethnic entity.[4] That the sponge divers lived in constant peril from the vagaries of the sea made them unusually superstitious. That they lived isolated from the rest of Greek-America tended to leave intact their self-contained heritage.

In addition to the literature, several films based on the golden age of Tarpon Springs helped to create the legend of the spongers. Elia Kazan, the Greek-American stage and movie director, made *Sixteen Fathoms Deep* in 1948 for Twentieth-Century Fox. Later Hollywood produced *Beneath the Twelve Mile Reef*, written by A. I. Bezzerides, a film that dramatized the rivalries for love and sponges among the Greek divers. The Bureau of Commercial Fisheries of the United States Fish and Wildlife Service released a fifteen-minute documentary, *Sponge Treasure from the Sea*. Finally a prominent member of the colony, Johnny Gonatas, created a documentary entitled *The Story of the Sponge*. He told the visiting Greek writer Elias Venezis in 1949 that he realized fifty thousand dollars from tourists paying a small admission price. If the fame of Tarpon Springs attracted Hollywood, it also attracted American novelists who found significant characters, themes, and tensions among the spongers.

The first of several novels about Tarpon Springs is *Full Fathom Five* (1948) by Ahmad Kamal.[5] Although the book provides relatively few ethnic details or facts about sponging itself, Kamal knows his subject from having worked on a sponge boat in the Gulf of Mexico. He mentions that the blight has begun to make the fishermen search longer and harder for their prizes. His main interest, however, is not in their methods of earning a living but in a conflict and misunderstanding over love that divides two Greek brothers. *Full Fathom Five* is narrated by one of them, Alek Paradisis.

The story opens far out in the Gulf with Alek working on the family boat, the *General Joseph Finegan*. The non-Greek name of the vessel derives from the fact that Alek's grandfather, Yeannis Paradisis, fought for the Confederacy in the Civil War. "He was with General Joseph Finegan at the Battle of Olustee when on February 20, 1864, General Truman Seymour was defeated and Tallahassee saved from the Federal troops" (pp. 57–58). On his father's side Alek's ancestors go back to 1758 when they settled in Florida, presumably in the New Smyrna colony which failed and dispersed. They came to Tarpon Springs "about 1910 when the sponge industry began to look really good" (p. 58).

Another sponge boat, the *Smyrna*, brings them a letter from Alek's mother who reports that Paul, his young brother, has returned home. The slight plot turns around Alek's trying to marry Paul off to Evee, the girl that he thinks Paul loves. At first he cannot understand what has gone wrong with his brother. Paul is unaccountably irascible, he drinks too much, and he takes drugs. Alek himself has loved Evee for many years; but, being honorable, he does all he can to bring her and Paul together. He even stays out on the ocean on a long trip in dangerous waters. His best friend and crew-mate, the Negro Jonesy, is killed when he dives down to save Alek from sharks.

Angered by Paul's apparent malingering and drug-addiction, Alek more or less compels him to resume diving for sponges, believing that the work and ocean air will rescue him from the doldrums. An accident occurs during one of Paul's dives that sends

Alek down after him without equipment. Lying on the ocean floor, Paul stares at him blankly through the faceplate. On board later Alek, thinking that his brother had been "hopped up," beats him viciously in order to straighten him out. Before long, however, Alek learns the sad truth about Paul. The pills that he takes are morphine to ease his terrible headaches. Even worse, Paul has gone blind. He was blind when helpless in the water, and blind when Alek beat him. Alek already feels guilty for causing the death of Jonesy; now he feels even more guilt for pummeling his blind brother. A final revelation concludes *Full Fathom Five* on a relatively happy note. Up to nearly the end Alek Paradisis has believed that Paul loves Evee, but that the war "changed" him. The truth, however, is that Paul loves a girl named Mary; and she loves him enough to marry him despite his blindness. A more joyful Alek, less violent and more compassionate, is now free to pursue his own true love, Evee.

The most ambitious novel about the Tarpon Springs spongers is *The Islanders* (1951) by Joseph Auslander and Audrey Wurdeman.[6] Social scientists, of course, will refer primarily to prose writers such as Harris and Frantzis. Frantzis in particular has gathered the most important facts. It is interesting to learn, for example, that John M. Cocoris, in 1896, was the first Greek to settle in Tarpon Springs; and that he, more than any other person, established the sponging industry on a modern basis. He and his brothers made a qualitative change by diving rather than hooking sponges from the surface. "The spongers of Tarpon Springs, true Greeks," Frantzis writes, "brought with them . . . their enthusiasm, their culture, their religion, and their manners and customs."[7]

Auslander and Wurdeman pack into *The Islanders* a large amount of the spongers' ethnicity—the customs mentioned by Frantzis. The fictional name they give to the colony is Turtle Run. In another novel, *Bazzaris* (1965) by Don Tracy, the name for Tarpon Springs, or a town like it, is Rovalla. Whether called Tarpon Springs, Turtle Run, or Rovalla, the place referred to is the same: the place where Greek mariners gathered from their ancient lands, had a Golden Age, and lost it when nature turned against them. The action in *The Islanders* occurs after World War II, when the sponges have already sickened, but apparently before the catastrophic blight of 1947. Some Greek youths refuse to further their education, for "the principal of the high school earned less in a whole year than a diver in a single week's haul, and moreover,

Latin phrases and algebraic equations had nothing to do with un-
der-water wisdom."[8]

Being a poet's book, *The Islanders* begins with a cat's view of a
Greek restaurant, the Parthenon Bar and Grill, owned by Christidos and Spiros. Here and there the writing is lyrical and figurative,
especially in descriptive passages. The cat sees the kind of sleazy
Greek restaurant that Harry Mark Petrakis often depicts in his fiction: "spots of congealed gravy under the oven . . . black beetles
and big woolly spiders . . . the scurry of a mouse, the papery rustle
of a cockroach, the drip of a leaky faucet, the gurgle of the pipes
as water is drawn upstairs, to keep Cat alert."[9] Thus the tone is
immediately established that all is not well in the *National Geographic*'s idyll of the spongers. All in all, the authors reflect the
contending forces in Turtle Run: economic stability versus decline,
ethnic tradition versus erosion, puritanism versus liberty, the old
versus the young, a sense of viable community based on sponging
versus rootless alienation.

The family of Christidos, a widower, consists of John, now at
twenty-three an airline pilot, a daughter Zoe, twenty-one, and Stephen, seventeen, a moral weakling and troublemaker. A delin-
quent in school, a thief at home, he wants to join the sponge fleet
to make a lot of money; but Christidos urges him to enter a profession. The moral decay in Stephen, plus the changing times, deprive Christidos of his traditionally austere role, as explained by
Frantzis. "The father is the leader of the family—the paterfami-
lias . . . his every wish is executed with alacrity and speed. The
command and decision of the father is an unalterable law to which
all owe obedience and respect."[10] A major line of action in *The
Islanders* shows how this convention falls apart in even a tightly knit
ethnic enclave such as Tarpon Springs.

The situation differs between Spiros, the partner, and his son
Philip, a hard-working student in medical school. Both fathers,
write Auslander and Wurdeman, "worshipped the god of education; to have a son who is a professional man was the dream, the
rainbow's end, the ultimate ecstasy."[11] The authors speculate about
the countless lambs, chickens, and tripe Spiros had to boil, bake,
and stew in order to have Philip educated. The problem is not
ambition, but the son's choice of a girl.

Both fathers have assumed that Philip and Zoe would marry, yet
at spring vacation he announces he has fallen in love with a girl
who works in the medical library, Frances Slater, not of Greek de-

scent and three years older. The choice displeases Spiros. "How much better, my son, to take for bride the woman chosen by your own people, the pure cool spring from which no lips have drunk, the child carefully reared to be a Greek wife and mother? What do we know, after all, of these foreign American women?"[12] The ethnic factor is here tantamount to "aristocratic breeding" as a basis for choosing a mate. Philip on such a delicate matter as marriage demands the prerogatives of a free American, but his father defends the Greek practice of an arranged marriage and a proven virginal bride. A Greek girl of Tarpon Springs can attend a dance or party only with her family or her fiancé "who expects to find her unkissed and pure when he marries her." Frantzis continues, "This principle of purity bears such weight in the marriage, that even in Greece, today, lack of virginity is grounds for divorce."[13]

The Greek being "a garrulous and gregarious sort of fellow," the Parthenon Bar and Grill provides its partners a chance to talk with many people. Spiros cooks basting lamb with oil and oregano, simmering tripe and suet for soup. On the wall of the restaurant hangs a map of Greece and the Aegean; but the isle of their origin, Symi, is not shown. From such Dodecanese islands as Symi, Halki, Kos, and Kalymnos were lured the spongers of Tarpon Springs. Spiros the cook was not heavy enough to be a diver; he could not clasp the diving stone about his head and jump overboard, to seek "the black-veiled sponges in their rock crannies." Nor was he strong enough to "lie belly-down on the thwarts, snaring the seagrowth with a twist of a trident," nor had he the sturdy legs "of a dredge-caster or a netter."[14] Spiros has had to settle for something less than the glamor and profit of diving.

At the Parthenon a pensioner called the General eats and keeps a tab. Another pensioner, George Pappas, writes bad metrical tragedies under the name of George Gordon Byron. Cursed and disowned by his father, pampered by his mother, Lord Byron wears a seersucker suit, carries Greek and American flags, and a briefcase bulging with books and papers. He features a pince-nez. To the restaurant in poverty-gracious pretense he daily brings two cracked eggs and an overripe orange given him by Vlastos the corner grocer. Lord Byron is a sponger of another kind, and Christidos tolerates him only because he is Greek and would otherwise "beg from the Americans and disgrace us further" (p. 24). Cimon the waiter notes that Lord Byron has "made a science of the business of living without money." Actually Vlastos gives him six cracked eggs a day and the spoiled fruit. Cimon's cousin the florist gives him the daily carnation "which makes a fop out of a fake," the barber trims his hair for nothing, and he cadges cigarettes and beer. Lord Byron affects an Oxford accent and scorns "the vulgar colloquial Greek spoken by a waiter from the Dodecanese" (p. 28). He reads old Greek newspapers. At various homes that Lord Byron visits he gets treated to coffee, *baklava*, and even *ouzo*. At weddings, christenings, and funerals he consoles all who weep— whether for sorrow or for joy. A pain in the neck to Christidos, Lord Byron makes a profession of his "calculated madness."

From March to September, business is poor at the Parthenon because 90 percent of the Turtle Run men and boys are out with the fleet. There follows in the novel an account of sponging methods, which are given in greater detail by Frantzis and Harris. The most historical is Frantzis, who includes the initial and deadly competition between the Greeks and the "Conchs," hook-spongers from the Bahamas whom the Greeks eventually chased away. Auslander and Wurdeman deal with the present. The sponge beds may be found anywhere along the Florida coast from St. Marks to the Anclote Keys. Various ships pursue the method—diving, hooking, or dredging—that is best suited to the equipment, experience of the crew, and condition of ocean floor. The boats engaged in the search and harvest always carry an odd-numbered crew (15, 17, 21), and all save the cook pair off in dinghies. The cook, himself a good seaman, runs the boat and trails behind the dinghies to load on the sponges.

Except for the mechanical diving helmet, all the methods "are as old as Homer," and all seek the best quality and largest number of these "mysterious and complex sea-growths we call the sponge" (p. 32). Some boats use a dredge known as the *kankava*, a net with a heavy iron bar that goes along the ocean floor and scoops up "fish, turtles, unwary octopi, sea-fans, and coral" together with the sponges. In a second method the hooker peers through his sponging-glass, observing the shallow depths, poised to strike down at the sponge with his "trident-like *kamaki*." The third and most prevalent method involves a naked diver leaping headlong, "his diving-stone tilted to angle him down to a remembered crevice rich in the precious sheep's wool, while his partner plays out his guide rope and retrieves the trapezoidal stone which is the diver's rudder and weight; it is all the same so long as the deck is swamped with the soft, black-veiled bodies of the day's catch" (p. 33). At sunset the crew with bare feet stomp out the sponge's life juices that "spurt, thick and milky, from the osculi, and the clinging black veils which shroud them slip off like grape-skins when the grapes are boiled" (p. 33). Then the sponges are threaded with a long steel needle "through the pits of the osculi" to avoid tearing. Depending on size, from about eight to fifty sponges are threaded on one string, and over the side the strings go—"like great primitive necklaces strung out for the wife of Cyclops, to wash in the clean salt water all night, absolving their impurities in the communion of the sea. Out again in the morning, to be beaten free of sand and small stones, and the shreds of gelatinous black, as tenacious as mortal sin, which lurks inside the sponge canals" (p. 33). The sponges are heaped on the deck to dry, while the crew goes off in the dinghies for another day's harvest. The chapter on methods of sponging ends with a lyrical passage on the deaths of sea-creatures. "All prophecy and parable exists in the detritus of the ocean-floor: doubloons are mixed with dead men's dreams, and even the very sand itself consists of sparkling, powdered skeletons" (p. 35).

In *The Islanders* two contentious factions live in Turtle Run: the self-named "true Greeks" from mainland Greece and the Dodecanese and the "Turkish Greeks" from Asia Minor, Egypt, and Corfu. "It is said that in a town of a thousand Greeks, there are fifteen hundred political cliques, because every man forms his own individual party, and at least half of them belong to two" (p. 38). Hence the factions have two Greek Orthodox churches in Turtle Run with opposing ideologies, two Democratic clubs, two lodges with their ladies' auxiliaries, "and two cemeteries to keep their bones forever undefiled, one from another." The "Turkish Greeks" patronize the Olympia Restaurant, the "true Greeks" the Parthenon operated by Christidos and Spiros. To the Parthenon also come the convalescent Greek wounded, sent to American clinics by the Greek government. About a dozen of them stay at a nearby hospital and hotel. They include amputees, brilliant psychotics, and the blind, such as Major Alexis Dragoumis. Most had been wounded on Mount Pindus and the Albanian front. As the novel graphically states, some return to Greece "with new, more-or-less useful metal-and-plastic arms or legs, with marvellously matched artificial eyes, with the curiously bland expression of faces rebuilt by flesh molded from flank and breast and upper arm."

As a result of the war the once rich and aristocratic Alexis has lost both his sight and his wife Lisa. A land mine exploding in

Epirus wrecked his face and blinded him. Through further medical research he hopes to see again; if not, then he will use his revolver on himself. A prisoner of the Nazis, he was freed by the
Allies. Years pass, but there is no sign of Lisa, who had taken their
cash reserve. Alexis prefers not to find her while he is still blind.
With money left from his father's tobacco holdings in Egypt, he
hopes to secure a specialist who can help him. In the meantime he
regularly visits the Parthenon; he is led by Pete Cockinos, a lame
man from Niceros.

Alexis's face has a "perverse splendor," like "a Greek coin run
over by a Roman chariot" (p. 43). At the major's table Lord Byron
is not welcome, but the visiting diplomat Basil Economou is; the
two men discuss books, the theater, politics, and the situation in
Greece. Alexis also likes to have Zoe Christidos around; she has a
velvety and comforting voice, and hands that are "warm, firm, and
vigorous." He wonders about Zoe's beauty, but is afraid to ask
Cockinos.

The engagement between her and Philip ends because of his
friend, Frances Slater. Zoe is surprised but not heartbroken; Philip
had regarded her as his "personal property." She mocks him about
fancy women in big cities. Now she feels free to move about, and
to be looked at by other men. One of them she dislikes heartily:
her employer at the insurance office, Michael Diamantopoulis, a
rich, sweaty, old, bald widower who "was an efficient Greek, which
meant that he was noncharacteristic of his race, for, whatever virtues have been spawned in the Aegean, efficiency is not outstanding among them. If a Greek makes an appointment for the afternoon, he may keep it any time from after lunch to after dinner"
(p. 49). On such occasions the authors seem to feel that Turtle Run
is a Typee or an Omoo and that they are the first white persons to
wander among the aborigines.

Be that as it may, Mr. Diamantopoulis, or Diamond, is very "ag-
gressively American," and he goes every Tuesday to Tampa for the
Rotary Club luncheon. He is also an Elk, an Eagle, a Moose, and a
Woodman of the World. A Methodist by conversion, he gives to
charities on the assumption that "bread cast upon the waters" will
return fourfold. He mouths all the Benjamin Franklin platitudes
about success. Nobody in Turtle Run likes him very much. When
Zoe slaps his face for trying to kiss her, he tears her blouse angrily;
but he is sure her father Christidos will keep her in line for him.
In the meantime he consoles himself with non-Greek prostitutes.

At the rival Olympia Bar and Grill, Lord Byron follows Zoe's brother Stephen Christidos, who likes the beer, jukebox, and pinball machine. He also likes the alcoholic concoctions available there. "Greeks seldom, if ever, sampled these mixtures," preferring beer, ouzo, or brandy depending on their social status. The place is run by city Greeks from Tampa. Lord Byron, who is "weakly male" and attracted to Stephen, "is sufficiently touched with madness as to lose one characteristic—perhaps the chief characteristic—of the rest of our Greeks. He did not worry." Like a sparrow, he eats crumbs where he may; and he talks, and talks

> of the old ways of their people and of the ancient days when lived young Glafkos, the legendary hero of the spongers, whose hands and eyes were shaped by the sea, who was so handsome that the gods were jealous, and who dove, one day, from the cliffs of Symi and never came up. Some say he still lives and dreams at the sea's bottom, clasped in the arms of an ocean goddess who was old before Zeus made heaven and earth. (p. 56)

Lord Byron identifies Stephen with the Glafkos of legend and plans a long ode in his honor. Christidos, however, condemns the friendship between Lord Byron and his lazy son.

For days Major Alexis Dragoumis has been absent from the Parthenon. Cockinos then makes his way down from the hospital alone "because a Greek must talk to his kind, or perish, and though there were plenty of various kinds of Greeks at the hospital, there was none from the island of Niceros save himself" (p. 77). Cockinos explains that Major Dragoumis neither eats nor sleeps. Zoe is curious about him, but holds back from asking questions. Economou knows the harsh truth about the major's wife: she has known for one and a half years where Dragoumis is, but "she wouldn't care to have her rich Italian bed-fellow, or her fine friends, know that Alexis still lives" (p. 81). The authors of *The Islanders* leave the blind major and return to the sponging.

A general poverty has befallen Turtle Run. Many of the sponges, though not all, have "sickened on the ocean floor from some strange disease that left them frail ghosts of themselves, tearing like lettuce at the touch of a sponger's hook." The once busy Sponge Exchange opens only one day a week; and the "vast, acrid-smelling sheds, usually packed to bursting with the yellow-brown dry chitinous skeletons of a million sponges, stood half empty" (p.

82). The sponging boats, which were forbidden to women, were named *Athene, Hera, Persephone*, and so on, themselves women "jealous of their cat-footed cursing, ineffectual little lovers who builded them and manned them; who deserted them for land and who returned because they could not do otherwise, since ships and seas had shaped their lives these centuries past" (p. 83). When they died, the Greek islanders were buried with a photograph of themselves under glass on the headstone. The wealthier ones might be sent back to Greece in their coffins, "salted like herrings" to lie among their relatives on the "sand-grain" of Symi, Halki, Niceros, or Andros. The graveyard of Turtle Run is filled with dead Greeks. The men are buried in their clothes and winding sheets. In good times the corpses were laid in fine stone vaults. If killed underwater by sharks, or by a line cut by a turtle or a jealous rival, the victim was buried in his costly gear, since "the pressure of even ten or fifteen fathoms jammed the pulp of his body up into his helmet" (p. 95). The remains would be a veritable horror to remove. In his more extended account of Greek customs, Frantzis describes the "Xodi," the wailing of the dead that involves loud cries, screaming, pulling of one's hair, even the beating of the body and face with stones—this done by the women only.

The earliest of the Dodecanese islanders arriving in Turtle Run four or five decades earlier slept in crowded clapboard boarding houses built in boom times by small-town Americans, then abandoned. The Greeks, mostly bachelors, moved into them. A number of "city Greeks" also arrived "from Charlotte and Birmingham, hearing that the pockets of the spongers were lined with gold" (p. 88). The innocent uneducated Greeks slept in rows of bare cots. Believing only in gold coins, yet they got regularly cheated by the packers and operators. Only a few of the workers received their full measure of gold for their harvest. A lucky or clever captain might return to the Dodecanese "in a store-bought suit of harsh cheap wool tight in the crotch and armholes," sporting a dollar watch with its yellow metal tarnished, his hair cut and oiled, "reeking of rose or jasmine or gardenia." The proud immigrant wears a "sleazy green silk shirt and emerald sleeveholders" (p. 90). Thus adorned, he returns to the town of his birth for a wife, whose father thinks the bridegroom is a great man in the New World. But something clings to him forever: the smell of the dead sponge.

As time moves ahead to the present, the Greek immigrant survives the pejorative names such as *dago, spick, wop, hunky, sheeny, squarehead, greaser,* and *mick* . . . and he is not so easily cheated because he has some education and knows about strikes. Yet even in good times the spongers were generally poor. The divers were usually in debt. Now, with most of the sponges sick, bad times have fallen upon them. The sponges may be good at twenty fathoms or more, but the young men refuse the risks. Debt holds the divers with the fleet lest they head for the citrus fields inland "and become a new kind of garlic-smelling okie, and to leave the town of Turtle Run as stripped and dead as the skeleton of a sponge" (p. 97). This world of losers appeals to the loafer Stephen Christidos; and for the pseudo-poet Lord Byron it is the world of the mythical Glafkos.

In a minor subplot of *The Islanders* the impecunious General decides to become a leader by unionizing the spongers, a stupid move in view of the conditions in the industry. A labor agitator had previously been sent to Turtle Run, "a Greek, a large damp pink man who talked well and fast in a high eunuch-voice," and whom the town had run out. Nevertheless the General saw how the organizer lived off the fat of the land and felt he might do the same. Another subplot has John Christidos, the "good" son, periodically chucking everything and going on a drunken binge under the name of Johnny Mitchell. Cut out to marry a "nice Greek girl," he takes a whore to his room. The episode illustrates self-debasement and then repentance on the part of a youth whose life is too strictly ordered, and who is threatened by disintegration. A crisis has developed for Lord Byron: Stephen Christidos is slipping away from him as a golden god image; as a result Lord Byron will now seek Major Alexis Dragoumis for his golden idol, to make himself essential to the blind man.

At this point the authors comment generally on Hellenic conceptions of beauty and transience. They write in idealistic terms: "Your Greek is perhaps more finely tentacled than the rest of the human species; the delicate trembling snail-horn perception is heightened in him through thousands of years of observing essential beauty, and exploring essential pity and fear (p. 125).

Plato with his fixed absolutes and Heraclitus with his fluidity also enter their speculations on time and change. "To your Greek," they write, "the fleeting and transient is the imperfect and the unbeautiful; this may well be the reason why, though in ancient times their gods were deathless, their concept of the persistence of human personality after death was vague and wandering" (p. 125). The allusion to death at this point serves as a subtle foreshadowing of events to come.

The relationship between the blind Alexis and Zoe Christidos deepens into a love affair. Although Pete Cockinos believes in strict morality, he feels that Zoe is "good medicine" for his beloved major, and thus will not inform her father. In old Greece such a "wanton" as Zoe would be stoned to death. Regarding Greek attitudes toward such unsanctified liaisons, Auslander and Wurdeman strike a classical definition; how pertinent it is to modern times may be a question for debate.

> Your Greek has a congenital distrust of the amorphous; the shapeless, the formless, the anarchic, the chaotic are numbered among his chief abominations. He is infatuated with definitions; he demands frames about his subject, even though the subject be a sweet-breathed girl lying in fragrant grass. Logic is his law, and he can only function freely and confidently in an ordered cosmos. (p. 150)

Alexis Dragoumis thinks that to have another eye operation and to marry a Greek-American girl form a kind of pattern.

When a tourist enters Turtle Run, he gets a whiff of garlic and sponge-stench, he sees street signs in both English and Greek, a curiously domed church, immaculate streets, and perhaps a grandmother on a porch crocheting, the ball of thread inside a huge conch. He passes stores and coffeehouses. A woman from Halki will shop at a store owned by a man from Halki. She buys *baklava* and *kourabiedes* from a coffeehouse where she bargains through an open door front; no woman can enter there except on pay day nights to drag out a drunken husband. Otherwise he may gamble away all he has in this "garrulous sanctuary." The visiting tourist has some curio shops in which to browse and buy.

At seventeen Stephen Christidos is seriously seeking a job as a diver; but he has previously dived only from an excursion boat—a fake dive with a fake sponge he has with him all the time. Nobody wants to hire him because he knows the half-baked kid to be a bum, hanger-on, and swaggerer—and a shame to his father. Stephen ruefully recalls how his brother John, though only sixteen, had dived and retrieved the Epiphany Cross on the day in honor of St. Nicholas, patron saint of mariners.

All during the fantastically beautiful procession down to the waterfront and beyond, to the jetting spur into the bay and the little raised stone platform from which the visiting bishop would throw the beribboned cross, the procession of priests and church dignitaries in robes of white and gold and purple, and of the mayor and the town officials in their correct black suits, and the whole town trailing after, on foot and in old jalopies decorated with rosettes and colored streamers. (p. 165)

Tourists in droves watch the narrow group of Greek divers naked save for trunks and towels. The winner receives fifteen hundred dollars in Greek gold coins—and public acclaim. When John Christidos won, "he held high the cross; the white dove, symbol of Christ's own baptism, was released across the waters." Other writers, including Harris and Frantzis, also describe this annual ritual of Tarpon Springs.

The death-driven Stephen frequents a forbidden marsh beyond the town limits, a refuge where he escapes from rebuffs and holds mock funerals of huge cockroaches, frogs, sparrows, and other creatures. He runs there in panic when the Widow Samarkos nearly seduces him. He hides "on the graves of his small forgotten victims." He dreads the legend of the man, now dead, who suffered foul play during the ritual of the cross. The man's hand "had been lopped at the wrist but still clung like a crab to the golden standard as the victor waved it at arm's length over the water, and the blood of the defeated stained and muddied the blue surface" (pp. 172–73). Unable to work, Stephen steals larger and larger amounts from his father's restaurant. Without his knowledge, Stephen has been selected by the evil M. Diamond to be an instrument of vengeance against Zoe and the whole Christidos family. Diamond plans to give him work, to catch him stealing, and to have him arrested; or, better yet, to blackmail Zoe into marrying him. The General has also chosen the loafer Stephen to be his convert and flunky, to have him run errands and say: "This is for the General" (p. 196). Finally Lord Byron wants Stephen to dive deep into the "turquoise water-smoke" of the sea, there to become a golden spindle shell, a sort of divinity, a myth. All three of these maimed characters seize upon the worthless Stephen to work out their own foolish schemes.

Lord Byron, the demented poet, goes to the seashore among the gaggles of gulls and buzzards. He talks to a crab as if to a "Sea-

Person." The authors use Lord Byron's aberration as an occasion
to express the Greek's attitude toward the ocean.

> Always, washing in and out of the innermost recesses of the
> thoughts of the people, awake or asleep, broods the omnivo-
> rous and inscrutable sea, the cradle of Poseidon and Christ,
> half-pagan, half-Christian, punitive and capricious, spend-
> thrift and niggard, shaper of their eyes and hands and hearts,
> ruler of their passions and appetites, accepting their homage
> like a courtesan, rejecting their sacrifices like a queen: the life-
> giving, life-sustaining, youth-devouring sea. The Sea giveth
> and the Sea taketh away: blessed be the name of the Sea. (p.
> 201)

This paraphrase from the Bible touches, without a doubt, one of
the enduring elements in Hellenism.

As the novel moves toward its climax, two lines of action, one
positive and the other negative, involve Zoe Christidos and her
brother Stephen. Sorrow reigns in the house of their neighbor Spiros, for Philip has married the American girl Frances instead of
Zoe. Spiros declares that "our oldest son is dead, or worse than
dead. I'll not have his name mentioned in this house from now on"
(p. 210). Spiros imagines Frances's painted face and her lack of
manners and morals. The Americans in general indulge in quarrels, murders, and loose living. The chance for the wicked M. Diamond to attack Zoe through Stephen comes soon; as expected, the
thief steals forty dollars from Diamond's desk, and the old con-
niver knows it. To steal from his own father is one thing, but to
steal from another is unforgivable, and Christidos would lay a
curse upon his son. To prevent this calamity and the scandal, Zoe
will succumb to him. Or so M. Diamond thinks. Zoe, however, informs him that she is getting married soon and will doubtless live
in Greece. From her meager savings she returns the forty dollars
to M. Diamond. Zoe's father is thunderstruck that Major Alexis
Dragoumis, the patrician and patriot, should love the daughter of
a restaurant keeper. He gives them his blessing. By now the major
has learned about his false wife and will sue her for divorce. He
hopes eventually to establish a school on the slope of Mt. Hymettus.

While these events are happening, Stephen has been busy trying
to drive an old car owned by Spiros. Unfortunately he has an accident in which he kills Lord Byron. Before he dies, the poet says:

"Give him my eyes, my eyes. Give them to Major Dragoumis" (p. 255). The major is quickly prepared for the emergency operation to restore his sight. The accident occurred because Lord Byron stepped in front of the car, and Stephen panicked. Later, having gone totally berserk, Stephen streaks naked into the church, climbs up and up to the tower where he clangs the bell. Then he runs off, away from town, to the beckoning sea where he drowns himself— diving at last, for death.

Christidos undertakes to have Lord Byron, his son Stephen's only friend, buried. There are two coffins at the church, but one is empty, for Stephen's body is lost at sea. Frantzis's description of Greek burial customs states that if the body of a drowned sponger remains lost, the family places parts of his clothing (suit, shoes, hat) on a white sheet and then the dirges begin. Auslander and Wurdeman describe the funeral: "Your Greek takes his religion seriously," and go on to say, "Like other highly emotional peoples, he turns to stylization in religion; church services evolve into a miracle play of great beauty and great formality; so is God propitiated, and so, also, is man's soul, which God demands." They translate what the Greek priest intones over the dead. Part of the service goes:

> O God of spirits, and of all flesh, Who has trampled down Death and overthrown the Devil and given Life unto Thy world, do Thou the same, Lord, today, giving rest to the souls of Thy departed servants, Stephen and George, into a place of brightness, a place of verdure, a place of repose, whence all sickness, sorrow and sighing have fled away. Pardon every transgression which they hath committed, whether by word or deed or thought, for Thou art a good God, and lovest mankind. O Lord, there is no man who liveth and sinneth not; Thou only art without sin, and Thy righteousness is to all eternity and Thy word is true. (p. 273)

Stephen's brother John weeps and thinks of going to Mount Athos to become a monk. The people walk to the cemetery where they sing at the grave, "Open, O earth, and receive that which was made from Thee" (p. 296). The priest strews upon the grave common dust from the shell-made road, then sprinkles the dust with holy oil. A vigil lamp burns at the head of the gravesite.

When the novel ends, Major Dragoumis has partial sight after the operation that gave him Lord Byron's eyes. He sees everything with an opalescent fringe. His friend the diplomat, Basil Economou, has obtained the divorce in absentia. Reconciled at last to the death of his son, Christidos regards Stephen as Glafkos, the sea god. At the conclusion the reader is back at the Parthenon Bar and Grill, where all is empty save for the presence of the cat, who listens for the sounds of the night.

As the foregoing amply illustrates, *The Islanders* is richly embroidered with ethnic detail. The authors undercut the basic romanticism of their fictional Turtle Run by limning the evil that surfaces in the community's life. In her article for the *National Geographic*, Jennie E. Harris leaves the romantic idyll inviolate; in fact the ancient Greek heritage serves as the context for her profile on the "Sponge Fishermen of Tarpon Springs." She watches an incoming boat and thinks: "Such a boat entered Aegean ports in the epic days of Homer." She mentions that for centuries the Dodecanese Islands were famous as sponge centers. "Among these . . . were Kos, where Hippocrates, father of medicine, had lived, and Patmos, where the exiled St. John wrote the *Revelation* of the Bible."[15] In the 1870s, before the Greeks arrived, others were hunting sponges in the Gulf of Mexico—when Heinrich Schliemann was finding the ruins of Troy "where, perhaps, beautiful Trojan women once used sponges in perfumed baths."[16] Auslander and Wurdeman also refer to ancient history by recalling that Achilles asked to have a sponge in his helmet, while a Roman soldier held a vinegar-soaked sponge to the parched lips of the crucified Christ.

Don Tracy, the author of *Bazzaris* (1965), goes to the period of the Greek revolution for the title of his novel.[17] For many Greeks the heritage is so vividly alive that Marco Bozzaris fell in battle only yesterday; and a few days before, Achilles died at Troy. As the novel's jacket informs, Tracy lives in Clearwater, Florida, and knows the Greek spongers of nearby Tarpon Springs very well. The hero of *Bazzaris* (the name given to a sponge boat) is a former diver, Fotis Giranopoulis, who becomes the multimillionaire real-estate tycoon known as Pete Gerard. Back in the sponging town of Rovalla, the people remember him as one who abandoned his wife, Eleni, for a visiting movie starlet thus disgracing his family. He revives bitter memories when he unexpectedly appears at Eleni's funeral. Violence results. The blurb on the front jacket reads:

> So begins a compelling novel whose contemporary story is projected against a fascinating old-world background. Here

we discover the little-known world of the Greek-American sponge community. Here we meet the proud, clannish Greeks who came to the Florida coast to dive for the lucrative sponge. These men, and their women, have raw, often brutal passions. Their loyalties are fierce; their rituals primitive.

Tracy has various characters take turns in narrating the story. The sections are in groups of chapters, with each chapter divided into parts. For example, of the five parts of chapter 1, three belong to Pete Gerard and two to Andy Garretson, Rovalla's chief of police. Various flashbacks, bridging past and present, serve to concentrate and intensify the action.

The basis for Pete's vast fortune is the Gerard Land Development Company, a powerful element in Florida's postwar boom. Before leaving for Rovalla, he talked with his brother Gus about his motives for attending the funeral. Pete feels he has honest motives—to mourn his wife's death quietly, to see his aging parents. Gus, however, thinks he wants to be envied as a great success; and he warns Pete against going. Eleni's brothers are vengeful because he ran out on her for a *kseni* (foreign) movie queen. They call him a *Turko* and may kill him. As he approaches Rovalla, Pete Gerard wonders why he has really come. He notices the new junior high school built on land once owned by his father Gregorios Fotis Giranopoulis, which Pete sold from under him by forging his father's name on the deed; then he ran off with Lorey King, a rising movie star. He needed the money to support her.

The occasion for his betrayal of wife and family was the location in Rovalla of a movie troupe making a film about José Gasparilla, *Pirate's Galleon*. Times were bad for the spongers, the blight at its worst, and many young Greeks signed up as extras. Tracy gives no indication that the fictional movie had anything in common with *Sixteen Fathoms Deep* (1948), the movie directed by Elia Kazan that both Frantzis and Venezis mentioned. Pete, as Fotis Giranopoulis, and Lorey King made love—and she allegedly was better at it than Eleni. "She remembered her partner in rapture and somehow she took him where she went, transporting him to a place he had never approached before." That betrayal of Eleni occurred fifteen years before; in the meantime Pete broke up with Lorey who told him to get lost, that she "wouldn't tie herself down to a cheap Greek hustler who made a seedy living at the crap tables" (p. 7). Pete and his brother Gus, with money won in Las Vegas and Hollywood, re-

turned to Florida for a game called "Land Development," speculation in real estate.

He thinks of his weakness as a youth in selling, for only eight
thousand dollars, his father's valuable thirty-two acres to a shyster
named Hackburn. The man, a member of the school board, made
a killing on the deal. "The only thing that Hackburn hated more
than cigarettes were Greeks. Hackburn hated Greeks like some
people hated Jews and Negroes." Perhaps because an irate Greek
father once knifed him, leaving a gimpy leg, for his fooling around
with a Greek girl. Hackburn belonged to the Ku Klux Klan and
had relatives all over the state; thus he could create many problems
for the Greeks until they grew in strength and numbers. He called
them "dirty foreigners, idol worshippers, and queers" (p. 9).

The tavern in Rovalla is crowded for the important occasion, the
funeral of Eleni Somarkitis Giranopoulis, abandoned wife of the
great Pete Gerard. Pete goes directly to the Somarkitis house on
Leros Street. Hostile stares greet him. The coffin with the deceased
Eleni stands in the *tsala*, the parlor, where he courted her after the
arranged match, always with a Somarkitis woman to chaperone.
He thinks back to their wedding in 1944. Now, dead at thirty-six,
she looks like sixty. Once Eleni was beautiful; but she was stupid,
with never an original thought or ambition, owing to her being
brought up to obey her father, brothers, and uncles. He felt her as
much a "dead weight" as the thirty-five-pound stones used in
sponge diving. When the disease hit in 1947, he wanted very badly
to leave Rovalla. "I was the oddball, the Greek who hated the Gulf,
who hated being a Rovalla Greek sponger" (p. 15). Yet he was
trapped with "a stupid Greek wife" who would end up with a
dozen kids no matter how careful he tried to be. Pete realizes he
left home in a shameful way. Moreover he feels that Eleni's seven
brothers "swore out the blood oath" against him "in spite of the
fact that the Church was trying to stamp out the old-country ven-
dettas in Rovalla" (p. 15). Eleni refused all money from him. Pete
Gerard pays his respects at the coffin, and leaves—but not without
a deep knife wound in his back.

From the point of view of Andy Garretson, the sheriff, Pete's
arrival in Rovalla means trouble. Perhaps two thousand men
would like to see him dead, "the labor goons he'd bucked, the competitors he'd sunk by siccing the same goons on them, the husbands with wives who'd gone to the mattress just because he looked
at them" (p. 16). Pete Gerard was the "sonofabitch" who sold

swamps to Yankees for building lots. Despite other handsome Greeks in Rovalla, Pete "got all the poontang," and he took Eleni, the prettiest Greek girl, away from his brother Gus. The sheriff knows the Somarkitis clan mean to kill Pete Gerard, even though Spyros Somarkitis says, "We won't stain Eleni's memory with this filth's blood" (p. 21). Andy Garretson wants Pete to leave town when he sees the wound. "These *chalkiti* are like sharks," he says. "One sniff of blood and they're all over you" (p. 22).

Pete Gerard's brother Gus receives the phone call to retrieve Pete from Rovalla. Before leaving, Gus fornicates with his brother's mistress, Katie MacKinnon. For a time he had wanted Pete to die so he could marry his cast-off wife Eleni. In a flashback we learn that Gus gave Eleni his first love gift when he was only thirteen: a beautiful shell he found forty fathoms down. The shell he gave Eleni could have brought close to five thousand dollars from a collector; it was bigger and more nearly perfect than one found by Sozon Vatikiosis which he presented to the Smithsonian. The next section in *Bazzaris* belongs to Pete's father, Gregorios Fotis Giranopoulis. He had violated Greek custom by bestowing his own name to his first-born son. He goes to the jail to see him now. When Pete ran off with the *kseni*, his mother Thalie cried "the *Thrinos*, the wailing lament for her damned son," a practice forbidden by the church because of its excesses. The senior Fotis describes the *Thrinos* as a "terrible thing," when genuine grief gave way to madness. "In the throes of these orgies, the women mourners tore their clothes and then their flesh while they shrilled weird inhuman cries." The usually gentle Thalie had run through the town "ripping great bloody scratches in her face and breasts, tearing out her hair and biting her tongue and lips until her saliva ran foamy red, because her best-loved son had forsaken us all, our love, and our pride in him, for what lay between a cheap little trollop's legs" (p. 38).

The action moves to Kitsos Giranopoulis, Pete's uncle, as seen from the father's point of view. Kitsos blames the devil for what people do, except in this case he does not forgive Pete his betrayal. Gus arrives to drive Pete back to Clearwater. They walk down Piraeus Street. They pass St. Basil's Church, the cost of which bankrupted the men of Rovalla. Before he leaves, Pete wants to see the old family boat, the *Bazzaris*, now owned by Dimitrios Samoris. It had once sailed to America out of Kalymnos in the Dodecanese Islands. "They headed for a wonderland called Rovalla, Florida,

where the streets had gold paving blocks and a man who knew how
to dive for sponge had only to stay a year, maybe two, and then go
back to Kalymnos, the richest man in the world" (p. 52). The boat
has a double-end felucca design, forty feet long, with a sprit main-
mast and mizzen; her archetype was the Greek *sacoleve* which
sailed the Aegean Sea before the birth of Christ. During the war
between the hook-spongers and the divers, the *Bazzaris* received a
gasoline engine. The boat has not left its mooring since the "Year
of the Disease, 1947."

The fictional character of Dimitrios Samoris reminds one of the
real John M. Cocoris, an early leader of the Greek spongers of
Tarpon Springs. Samoris was a "top chandler" who financed the
sponge fleet when times were good; at one time he was the richest
man in Rovalla—and perhaps on the entire west coast of Florida.
Chandlers such as Samoris employed the *platica* system—the *platica* being the amount of money advanced to the sponge crews, to
the diver, deckhand, cook, engineer, and the lifeline tender so
their families could live until the sponges found could be sold at
auction. All went broke during the 1947 disease except for Samoris, who got out early enough to save his fortune. To Pete Gerard the *Bazzaris* seems to have shrunk. Back at the Clearwater hotel
the first thing he wants is sex with Katie MacKinnon. His orgasm
wipes out the image of Eleni dead in her coffin, the boat *Bazzaris*,
Rovalla. The story continues.

The bigoted school board member, Hackburn, is not alone in
hating the Greeks. James B. Burnside, once chief of police of Rovalla, County of Nestor, Florida, is also extremely biased against
them. He has killed a Greek, Nick Kolokotronis, who would have
knifed him. The Greeks think they own the town—"like the niggers think they own the whole country now." Yet some of his best
friends are Greeks. Burnside thinks this about Pete Gerard: "As
far as I cared, he could lay all the Greek girls he wanted to, but I
didn't want him messing around with white women" (p. 60). Thus
he equates *Greek* with *nigger*, or did so at first, as foreigners with a
religion regarded as Catholic. For the most part the Klan is kept
"too busy with the niggers" to disturb the Greeks. What has gotten
lost, according to Burnside, is the old Rovalla of 1907, the rich
resort town with its fancy hotels and swells, a place with *class*. The
Greeks came and ruined it.

The bigotry of retired Sheriff Burnside is matched by the rigidity of the priest, Father Spyros Ioannis, in demanding that the Greeks remain *pure* Greek. As Burnside sees the history of the sponge industry, it was early turtle-hunters who first found sponges in Rovalla; they followed a turtle into the sponge bed, and word got around to E. R. Raye, who operated "a fleet of Greek and Conch hook-spongers out of Key West then" (p. 62). A large influx followed of Greek divers from the Dodecanese, with the women and children. Many gambled all day and night. The tourists who habitually enjoyed the area now faced "a crowd of foreigners yelling Greek in their ear and the sponge boats so thick in the river that it was worth a fella's neck to try to take his girl out sailing" (p. 63). Now and then he as sheriff heard complaints about rape, but he felt the girls chased after the Greeks. Nor does he believe that half the Greeks were queer; those he has known went for "regular tail." Burnside feels the Greeks refused to become Americanized. He recalls when they had to ride on a special railroad car reserved for Negroes and Greeks. After the 1947 blight, Pete Gerard, then still Giranopoulis, was prepared to leave; and he seized his opportunity when in August of 1949 the film company arrived to produce *Pirate's Galleon*. After Pete ran off with Lorey King, his mother conducted a *Thrinos*. The powerful E. R. Raye forced a law through the City Council banning "this *Thrinos* crap" (p. 69). To the police the ritual was an example of disorderly conduct and disturbance of the peace.

Indicative of how strongly Father Ioannis feels about preserving Greek mores is his calling Pete Gerard a *satanas*, a Satan, for his treatment of Eleni. To return for her funeral only confirms the evil in him. The priest believes in "the ancient doctrines." As he tells parishioners, "I use the St. Basil's Liturgy of Jerusalem instead of the shorter, more convenient version of Chrysostom" (p. 74). More than anyone else he tried to keep Fotis Giranopoulis (Pete) both a sponger and a Greek. One cannot easily escape his heritage despite his alien clothes, manners, language, and "strumpets." He berated the irreligious youth by saying: "You have cuckolded half the non-Greek husbands in town. You have used your excellence in mathematics to win at gambling. You have run down a field with a leather ball simply to gain acclaim from the aliens" (p. 82). The attack by Father Ioannis on football reflects a common antagonism between immigrant parents and sons addicted to strange and foolish games such as football, baseball, and hockey. More than anyone

else, too, it was Father Ioannis who influenced old Thalie Giranopoulis to cry the *Thrinos*, advising it would ease her heart to
mourn according to the old tradition.

Among the various ethnic factors of consequence to the Rovalla
spongers is the manner of preparing octopus for dinner. They
banged, scrubbed, and doused it in seawater at the dock, so "it
would not spoil, turn poisonous, or be touched by the Evil Eye"
before it reached the house. The spongers abided by the "unyielding law" that no woman could ever step foot upon a *kaiki*, a boat.
Greek men in Rovalla seldom got fat, but the women sometimes
did in later life. Both at home and at the coffeehouses the Greeks
liked the three types of Turkish coffee: *skheto* (plain), *metrio* (medium), and *variglyko* (heavy, sweet). During and after the 1947
sponge blight, the Philoptohos Society helped many destitute
Greeks with food and clothing.

The novel *Bazzaris* has two important characters in the rich man,
Dimitrios Samoris, and Pete Gerard's uncle, Kitsos Giranopoulis.
For many years Samoris bankrolled the sponge fleet, often collecting interest as high as 25 percent. He was a chandler who could
finance as many as a hundred boats in each *taksidhi*; six to ten short
trips or *gazes* made up a *taksidhi*. The money advanced to each
diver and crew member was called the *platica*. Sometimes a diver
jumped his *platica* and took off, but most of them who did returned
to work. Samoris arrived from Kalymnos in 1907, helped to establish Greek control of the Sponge Exchange, and withdrew rich before the 1947 blight ruined the others. Now he wants to see Pete
Gerard, hoping he will be a soft touch for a "deal that will avenge
Eleni and Kitsos and all of us"—to pool their money in "bringing
Rovalla back to life" (p. 107). Somewhere in the region of half a
billion dollars, Pete's fortune together with Samoris's much smaller
one could set up the Society for the Rehabilitation of Rovalla.
(Frantzis in *Strangers at Ithaca* recounts the actual efforts made in
Tarpon Springs after 1954 when healthy sponges began to grow
by the millions in the old beds.) What Samoris proposes in *Bazzaris*
is a wild, impractical, and nostalgic scheme to restore the "strange
and wonderful culture that had been transplanted from the Dodecanese Island to the West Coast of Florida, complete with Greek
customs, dress, religion, language, food, superstitions—the whole
way of life" (p. 120). A realtor and director of the Sponge Exchange himself, Frantzis at the end of his book relates efforts he

and others made to establish "The Greek Museum of Tarpon Springs" as a means of preserving Greek culture.

The story of Kitsos Giranopoulis, Pete's uncle, also begins on the island of Kalymnos. As a youth he dived for sponges there in the usual manner, with no helmet or air hose; yet he went down forty fathoms and more. He discovered a bed of sponge called "Turkish Cup," worth eighty dollars a pound, which made his fortune. With the money he and his brother Gregorios ordered "the finest *kaiki* ever built—*Bazzaris*" (p. 127). The builder was an old man, Naipighos, who lived on an unnamed island and died seventeen days after finishing the boat. Kitsos loved *Bazzaris* and Kalymnos, but more and more he listened to the extravagant stories about a new land, Rovalla, and he finally sailed there with Gregorios. They found only a few hook-spongers at first, yet later E. R. Raye moved north to Rovalla with his Greek sponge divers. For his literary purposes Tracy minimizes the existence of Tarpon Springs in order to build up his mythical Rovalla. The counterpart of E. R. Raye could be the real John K. Cheney, the man most responsible for the initial growth of the industry.

Kitsos Giranopoulis scorned the hook-spongers even though they worked harder than divers and required a special talent, an "uncanny combination of knowledge and blind instinct" to bring up a sponge with a cumbersome hook. "The average Greek," the novel states, "would work five times as hard as the Conch and hook up many more sponge" (p. 131). Kitsos nearly failed his first tests as a Rovalla diver due to the difference in technique. On Kalymnos they dived naked, with knife at waist for sharks, a shorthandled hook in hand for detaching sponges, and a net bag for their take. Now in Florida Kitsos had to use the new equipment: the helmet, weighted rubber suit, the leaden boots, laboring under the air compressor and the trailing hose—all according to rules established by E. R. Raye, the boss of the sponging trade. At first Kitsos and his brother worked on the *Bazzaris* the old way, but they saw how the "machine divers" easily outstripped them by far in harvesting sponges. So Kitsos took secret diving lessons in the Chellafia River. He felt imprisoned by the suit; he also believed the greatness of diving had gone, for anyone could dive in the safety of the suit. Yet the new way meant more wealth.

Kitsos learned fast, and with the increase of "Greek power" in the sponging business the time came to wrest the leadership from the American, Raye. Not that he was necessarily bad; indeed he had helped most of the islanders reach the Promised Land. "And it was also true that his controlled auction brought fair prices and that his interest on the loans he had advanced them was not exorbitant, *but he was not Greek*." His boats, too, were not Greek-built, not genuine *kaikia*. Though a benign *ergethoris*, he paid no attention at all "to Greek customs, superstitions, and traditions that stretched back through the centuries to the darkness of civilization's birth" (p. 133). Since Kitsos hated the idea of being indebted to E. R. Raye, he sought out Dimitrios Samoris, who knew of a different way to finance the sponge fleet. Their partnership "began the Greek ascendancy in the port of Rovalla" (p. 140). But the changeover did not take place without violence.

The ensuing "sponge war" turned family against family, brother against brother, and father against son. In Tracy's fictional account the war began with the hookers, who might have been goaded by E. R. Raye. Kitsos Giranopoulis recalls the period of strife.

> The Greeks he'd brought to Rovalla all owed him money; the boats they worked belonged to him; the Exchange was run by his men and through it he could tell a sponger whether he prospered or went broke; everything in Rovalla was run by E.R. Raye until Dimitrios Samoris and I dared challenge his monopoly. Our rebellion, small as it was at first, gave the other Greeks ideas. (p. 162)

When the big shift to Samoris started, E. R. Raye fought back. He raised prices to keep a grip on the market. Mysterious fires broke out at the Samoris boatyard guarded by armed Greeks. Acid was thrown over sponges stored by Samoris. In a six-month period more than a dozen men, hookers and divers, died in "the secret sponge war." The police were kept out of it. A speedboat manned by four men with blackened faces nearly killed Fotis (Pete) by cutting his lifeline. Kitsos found the hooker responsible, a *Symiaki* (from Symi) and beat him up. Raye had a war on his hands that gained him nothing. He finally gave up, sold Dimitrios Samoris his Sponge Exchange and other sponge properties, moved to New York City, and there died.

In his history of Tarpon Springs, *Strangers at Ithaca*, Frantzis does not mention a sponge war in which the Greeks revolted against the monopoly control of John K. Cheney. Apparently no such bloody confrontation occurred in the real colony. Frantzis does document the conflict between the Conch and other Key West hook-spongers and the Greek divers whose eventual victory gave them unlimited access to the Florida sponge beds. Frantzis details other kinds of trouble that disturbed the peace of Tarpon Springs. During Prohibition several types of smugglers operated in the area. One consisted of "moonshiners" who installed stills in secret places and produced "a cheap and harmful drink" mostly for local consumption.[18] The other gang of smugglers was of organized criminals who had their tentacles spread all over the country. Their collaborators in Tarpon Springs sent out small boats into the Gulf to meet large schooners bringing whiskey from Cuba or Nassau. A third kind of crime which flourished in the Tarpon Springs area involved the smuggling in of aliens of all nationalities, particularly Chinese, after passage of the new exclusion laws.

> They would charge the smuggled aliens great sums of money, and if danger appeared anywhere, they threw the creatures overboard into the Gulf where they perished by drowning or provided food for the sharks. This group included some strong men of Tarpon Springs, Americans as well as Greeks, who retained permanent connections with Cuba.[19]

These unusual but historical facts play no role in the novel *Bazzaris*. As it moves toward its conclusion, the focus centers on Pete Gerard's condition, which worsens because he refuses to see a doctor. Publicity about his knife wound would send shock waves throughout the world money-markets, and damage especially the market positon of the Gerard empire. The final pages are devoted to responses on the part of various characters toward Pete's life-and-death crisis.

Kitsos Girandopoulis will take the *Bazzaris* into the Gulf for one last and fatal trip. Pete's brother Gus admits he loves him, even though Pete took Eleni away from him; now Gus prays for his brother to get well. The father, Gregorios, had been glad the Somarkitsis had hurt Pete, but regrets his attitude and regards it a sin. He also regrets having always let Kitsos dominate him and force actions upon his son. The attitudes of other characters throw more light upon the past. Dimitrios Samoris blames himself for being responsible in part for the Giranopoulis tragedy. He admits that he has been a selfish and "wicked man," too busy making money to regard the personal wishes of those around him. He knew that Kitsos maneuvered to keep Fotis (Pete) from going to college on an athletic scholarship; and he also knew it was wrong for Fotis to have married Eleni so young. Kitsos also forced Fotis to become a sponge-diver against his will. Samoris therefore feels a share of the guilt for what Fotis did when he ran off with the starlet.

Father Ioannis, a symbol of vengeance, had wanted Fotis dead, and now he seems to be dying. Yet the sheriff, Andy Garretson, hopes the great Pete Gerard will live to avoid the investigation that his death would require. The knifing had not been reported. After pondering the Samoris plan, Pete turns it down, although he says: "Restorations are very big right now. The tourists are becoming very heritage conscious."[20] He feels that he owes Rovalla nothing. When he comes to, in the hospital at last, he learns that Kitsos has returned safely with the *Bazzaris* after a short quixotic voyage. The news has broken out that Pete Gerard is in critical condition; the Gerard stock falls on the New York Stock Exchange; and his men are flown in to help quiet the potential panic. The novel's *Isterografon*, or afterword, belongs to Kitsos Giranopoulis, the uncle, who admits he could not sail out to drown both the *Bazzaris* and himself. "'Bring me through this,' I screamed at *Bazzaris*, 'and I'll make amends. I'll find Fotis and beg his forgiveness on my knees. For everything, the scholarship, the hate I bore him, the lies I told—everything'" (p. 214). In keeping with his character Kitsos claims that he returned to the hospital to save Fotis's life. "I was the only one who could summon him back. I, Kitsos Giranopoulis" (p. 215). And the novel ends.

The only novel about Tarpon Springs written by a Greek is Elia Kazan's latest, *Acts of Love* (1978).[21] One of its major characters, Costa Avaliotis, had once been a famed sponge-boat captain; and the legendary sponge center serves as setting for much of the plot. The main interest, however, concerns the rich and very confused American girl, Ethel Laffey. Although only twenty-two, she has already enjoyed many affairs in many places; and now, in search of stability, she marries Teddy Avaliotis—a young Greek navy man whose father, Costa, furiously objects. Ethel's marital vows apparently mean nothing since her affairs continue unabated, on the excuse that she wavers between wanting discipline and craving freedom. Teddy, on the other hand, eventually demands authority much like that of Costa's over his mother. Ethel makes a great show about "learning Greek ways" at Tarpon Springs, away from Teddy, all the while sleeping with a rich Greek businessman. Being terribly "wicked," she even allows herself to be rudely seduced by Costa, her sixty-two-year-old father-in-law. Then he, out of a need to punish treachery to his son, chokes her to death. Released from a murder charge on grounds of temporary insanity, Costa Avaliotis walks about Tarpon Springs a larger and more prosperous hero. Teddy soon finds a new and more pliable girl to wed. All these events, even the murder of Ethel, are "acts of love."

In this novel Kazan returns to the use of Greek ethnicity that was absent from his two previous novels, *The Assassins* and *The Understudy*. His interest in Tarpon Springs itself goes back to at least 1948 when he directed on location the film *Sixteen Fathoms Deep*. In *The Arrangement* he has the protagonist, Eddie Anderson, advise his aging father to retire to Tarpon Springs, there to bask in the sun, visit the coffeehouses, and reminisce with the crusty Greek spongers. Those aspects of *Acts of Love* that directly relate to Tarpon Springs may be seen as a kind of epitaph for the whole sponging experience. Everything great and wonderful has long been relegated to the past. Costa Avaliotis represents the ethnic values that governed Tarpon Springs during its heyday: the idolatry of family, the pride in work, the sacredness of honor, the addiction to custom, the respect for God, the punishment of treachery in any form. Under the ancient laws which he must obey to retain his manhood, Costa must kill the woman, Ethel Laffey, who has so wantonly shamed the name of Avaliotis.

Tarpon Springs, the land of heroic Greek legend, fell victim to a phenomenon of nature—the red blight which destroyed the once-lucrative sponge beds. The four novels and other writing on the subject may be more valuable as records of Greek ethnicity than as literary achievements. They present authentic accounts of a social and cultural history which has, in the main, passed from the American scene. Synthetic sponges and other substitutes have all but driven natural sponges off the market. Artists, tourists, and senior citizens find that area of Florida very attractive. The once thriving ethnic enclave of Tarpon Springs still exists, some sponges are still harvested, the annual ritual in honor of St. Nicholas still survives; but the Golden Age of the Greek spongers has long since passed into history, memory, and myth.

ᔕᒲᔕᒲᔕᒲᔕᒲᔕᒲ

8

ᔕᒲᔕᒲᔕᒲᔕᒲᔕᒲ

THE GREEK AS WAR HERO

THE RECORDED HISTORY of Greeks in battle goes back to the Trojan War. Achilles, Odysseus, Leonidas, Themistocles, Philip, Alexander, and others emerged early enough to form archetypes of the warrior, not for Greeks alone but for all mankind. The Greek revolution of 1821–1828 brought forth a fresh gallery of *pallikars*—heroes and martyrs—this time not in struggle with Trojans and Persians but with equally formidable Turks. Many a Greek restaurant, coffeehouse, and home has on its walls highly romanticized paintings of revolutionary heroes such as Kolokotronis, Bozzaris, Katsandonis, Bouboulina, and Kanaris. Their very names bespeak valor. Many poems, articles, songs, and stories eulogize the exploits and sacrifices that wrenched a reborn Greece from the powerful Ottoman empire. Thus the image of the Greek in battle has three major sources: mythological, classical, and modern, not to mention the long Byzantine and intermediary Greek experience with its host of conquests and defeats. The past has bequeathed to the modern concept of the Greek soldier (as held by many Greeks) the cunning of Odysseus, the skill of Achilles, the efficiency of Philip, the wild courage of *klephtic* chieftains, Suliotes, Cretans—all this and more; the Greek like the brave Leonidas is always pitted against savage overwhelming odds. Perhaps the most popularly held trait is that of wild reckless courage supported by great skill and/or strength and endurance.

A recent evocation of the heroes of the Greek revolution is *The Hour of the Bell* (1976) by Harry Mark Petrakis.[1] In it a battle-scarred warrior like Captain Boukouvalas dies in the sure knowledge that folk songs and legends will forever enshrine his name. Even though he is practically at death's door, he makes a final foray on his charger and routs the Turks at a crucial and decisive moment. The grizzled Vorogrivas leads a *klepht* band on Mount Parnassus; in the Greek consciousness mountains are synonymous with freedom. After them the sea, where skill with ships, guns, swords, and fire—and heroes like Kanaris and Bouboulina—helped to defeat the Turks. In this first volume of a projected trilogy Petrakis centers the action on the Battle of Tripolitsa, in 1821, early in the rebellion. The Greeks as victors slaughter, pillage, and loot, as if to avenge on a single day their four hundred years of Turkish enslavement.

During the nineteenth century armed uprisings in Crete and trouble in other unredeemed Greek lands kept alive the image of the modern Greek fighting for freedom. Yet not until World War II did the Greek as war hero enter prominently into American literature. The Greek hero did so in British literature as well. For a time during the height of Nazi conquest about the only encouraging reports came from Greece, whose resistance led by EAM-ELAS daily created new epics of heroism. The writings of Leland Stowe, Robert St. John, and other correspondents still resonate with tributes for the Greeks of the occupation period. The Greek as war hero in our fiction stems from that tragic time. The earlier novels treat of the native Greeks there (not Greek-Americans), but with Americans also involved owing to some contingency or another. Later novels and stories depict Greek-Americans fighting with United States forces wherever they might be; they share the general allegiance to the Stars and Stripes, not to their ethnicity, nor to the *patrida* of their Greek parents. If they show any ethnic pride, it is that they as Greeks can serve their country, America, as well if not better than anybody else. Should they win the Congressional Medal of Honor, as some did, or merit statues in parks, such as George Dilboy of World War I, then of course the recognition by society at large rebounds to the credit of the Greek-American community.

By happenstance and not design a number of novels recreate the chronology of wartime Greece—from the initial invasion, through defeat and occupation, to the rise of the Greek resistance. Not all of these novels belong to American literature. Colin Forbes, an English writer, deals in *The Heights of Zervos* (1970) with the actual day when the German juggernaut under Field Marshall von List sweeps into northern Greece.[2] In another English war novel about Greece, Alistair MacLean's *The Guns of Navarone* (1956), the prize fought over is the powerful German artillery, which "controlled the approaches to the eastern Mediterranean island of Kheros."[3] Other novels about the war period belong to Greek literature, notably *Exodus* (1950) by Elias Venezis and *The Fratricides* (1963) by Nikos Kazantzakis, based on the civil strife after the liberation.

Most of the action in *The Heights of Zervos* occurs on April 6, 1941, when the Germans battle for the mountain. *The Angry Hills* (1955) by Leon M. Uris, also about Greece, begins at the same time, or perhaps a week or two later.[4] "This was April of 1941," Uris writes, "and the floodgates had opened. In the north, the invasion had begun" (p. 9). The protagonist is an American, Michael Morrison, but a number of Greeks, both patriots and quislings, also play vital roles.

Morrison has come to Athens to get a legacy left by his Greek wife, Ellie, killed in an automobile accident on the Golden Gate Bridge. He is a moderately successful novelist. Ellie's death has brought him close to despair with life, but he has a son and a daughter to raise. The intrigue and danger begin for Morrison when he visits "the ancient mansion of Fotis Stergiou," an attorney. After the arrangements for the legacy have been made, Stergiou asks a favor of Morrison—to deliver an important document to a Sir Thomas Whitley, London, on a plane leaving the next morning. Extra precautions are necessary. The minute Morrison leaves the house, Major Howe-Wilken of British Intelligence enters Stergiou's office. The conversation reveals that Howe-Wilken and his associate Soutar are constantly being watched by the Gestapo leader Konrad Heilser. They had no choice but to use Morrison to get an important message to London. He does not know what the letter contains. In time he learns—a list of seventeen names which the Nazis desperately want to have. They are the names of Greeks "planted" in the collaborationist government; ostensibly they are pro-Hitler, but actually they will work with the resistance and with British Intelligence. Having day-to-day access to Nazi military secrets, they can be of immense value to the Allied war effort. From the moment he receives the envelope, Morrison's life is in extreme jeopardy.

The chapters in *The Angry Hills* keep shifting between the "good guys" and the bad, including Greeks in both camps. Zervos, a government clerk, heard of Stergiou's plan and told the Germans. "Heilser slipped into Greece ahead of the German invasion and with Zervos' help got the rat pack working with him. The traitors, the opportunists, the cowards. All of them anxious to throw in with the Germans in time. Heilser and his Greek friends had done their job well" (p. 14). Heilser's spy network is so efficient he knows immediately that he must check out Morrison, who visited Stergiou. This is done by a man named Mosley; he clears Morrison of any suspicion after drinking with him. Drunk, Morrison returns to Stergiou's mansion only to find him murdered. Another man there, dying, tells him he must deliver the envelope. "A plane— leave Tatoi airdrome—midnight—take my credentials." And he adds before he dies, "They'll get you" (p. 23). Drunk and alone in the dark empty streets, Morrison looks at the credentials. They belong to Major Howe-Wilken.

The rest of the thriller is a cycle of perils, surprises, and narrow escapes, not to mention killings. Morrison's getaway plane at Tatoi airdrome is blown up by Stukas, and he manages to catch a train going south from Athens. When the Stukas destroy the train, Morrison escapes to the countryside with the scattered British, Palestinian, and Australian soldiers.[5] They hurry toward the coast where a steamer, the *Slamat*, is to evacuate them. That, too, is bombed and destroyed. These initial events set a pattern of danger that pursues Morrison until the end, when he safely departs Greece with the names memorized. Captured by the Nazis, he knocks himself unconscious when he leaps from a prisoner train. A Greek named Christos takes him to a remote village to recuperate. The girl sent by British Intelligence to aid him, Lisa Kyriakides, is a double agent with orders to kill him if his capture seems imminent. The boat dispatched for his escape is boarded by a German patrol, and Morrison with other escapees is imprisoned. Luckily, he bribes a Greek guard who transmits a message to the underground. Morrison is freed by a daring group of Greek partisans, and eventually he reaches a British submarine. He touches Lisa's shoulder softly "as the coastline of North Africa appeared on the horizon before them."[6] Not only have they made it to freedom, but they have left behind a growing resistance that will plague the German Occupation until the liberation.

A novel by a Greek-American writer depicting events of the Occupation and the resistance is Theodore Vrettos's *Hammer on the Sea* (1965).[7] The time of the story is November 1942. Vrettos involves only Greeks as they organize, fight, and die to liberate their land. Stavro, a former philosophy student, finds himself in a mountain cave with Kapetan Thanasi and his partisans. "Last night they had all gone to Platano. Kapetan Thanasi insisted—communion before each mission" (p. 5). Stavro meets nineteen-year-old

Anna there, living with her uncle, a priest. Their mission is to cut wires at Potami, high on a slope of Mount Taugetos. Young Stavro's initiation to war's savagery comes swiftly and painfully. He cannot give the coup de grace to a dying German boy shot during their mission.

Next day he goes home for a visit with his mother, bringing her a chicken and olive oil. His father's olive trees "looked deprived, unwanted—like an old man sick and about to die" (p. 12). The children on the street are mere skin and bones. At the church Pappa Lambro greets him and says that Anna is still asleep. Every day, the priest says, he begs God to spare Platano from Nazi destruction. For every act of sabotage, the Germans take reprisal. They destroy whole towns. Anna arrives.

The pall of death hangs over all. Little details proclaim the intensity of the people's suffering; for example, old Pelopida protests to Pappa Lambro that he buried the cobbler's son with his clothes on. Uncle Petro questions the wisdom of God, calling him Zeus; and he urges his nephew Stavro to give up "this guerrilla business . . . living in caves like an animal" (p. 23). Then he changes attitude and urges Stavro to take him into the mountains to fight. When two German soldiers come asking for the men of the house, Petro runs scared into the cellar, a coward. Stavro goes to Pappa Lambro's house to learn from Anna that the Germans have taken him. Stavro promises to find him. The abduction of the priest evokes the days when Stavro served as an altar boy. At the plane-tree he sees a horrible sight, a Nazi reprisal.

> Standing directly beneath the tree now, Stavro brought his eyes up—a storm of nausea swelled inside his stomach: the huge tree was burdened with human bodies. They swayed and spun around in the strong wind, their heads tilted sharply to the side as if they had just heard a sound and were trying to make out what it was, from where it came . . . faces waxen in death, eyes bulging out, teeth clenched against lips, heads drooped. (p. 30)

Pelopida is among the victims, but not Pappa Lambro. On the cistern wall the Germans have posted a placard stating that twenty-six males from Platano have been sentenced to death for the murder of three Germans near Potami, and that the following number of Greek males had already been executed: at Tripoli, 107; Sparta, 86; Kalamata, 239; Andritsa, 73; Megalopolis, 94; and Potami, 11.

An old woman screeches "Murderer!" at Stavro, the guerrilla (p. 32).

At the mountain sanctuary Stavro helps bury Pythagora, a comrade in arms. Kapetan Thanasi is hardened to death, but young Kleanthi cries. That night Stavro visits the village and sleeps with Anna; he feels responsible for the death of the hostages. Anna, too, is tormented; and she asks: "What do the Germans want with Greece? She is not beautiful any longer. . . . She is starving, flies crawl over her body, her belly is swollen, her ribs stick out like rosary beads, she faints in the street and no one cares enough to pick her up . . . what do they want with her?" (p. 41). Still no sign of Pappa Lambro. Despairing, Stavro tells Anna to expect nothing from God. At home his Aunt Zacharo lies dead. The priest who reads the rites, Pappa Thoma, heard that Pappa Lambro may be in Kalavryta on a road gang. When Stavro leaves, his Uncle Petro accompanies him.

The action moves from episode to episode. At the cave Stavro castigates Petro as a coward before Kapetan Thanasi. Their next mission is Tigani, to liberate a German train heading north with two thousand Greek prisoners. At Tigani the partisan band informs the people of the strike. Pappa Demetrios leads his congregation to the tracks; and, as the train is about to depart after getting water, the priest and the others block it with their bodies. The partisans chase off the German soldiers. The Greek prisoners escape. The craven Uncle Petro tells Stavro: "We won!" (p. 64).

Spring arrives—1943. Stavro informs Anna he must go to Kalavryta after Pappa Lambro, but Kapetan Thanasi refuses permission. His cowardly Uncle Petro has been a pain in the neck, even mocking Stavro about Anna. The partisans attend church for Easter. The Greeks of Potami have dysentery and suffer from near-famine. "We are a beaten people," Pappa Thoma says, "we do not look like Greeks any longer; our eyes do not burn with hatred when we see the Germans enter our village . . . our spirit is broken, *we are hungry, hungry, hungry!*" (p. 78). The author treats Kapetan Thanasi's band as an isolated military unit, although by early 1943 the Resistance was already highly organized, through the EAM-ELAS coalition, and performing prodigies of heroism and sacrifice that astonished the world and made all Greek-Americans proud.

In front of Pappa Thoma, Stavro calls God a "cannibal" for allowing so much suffering. The priest is shocked. Later Pappa Thoma condemns as a profiteer a man from Stavro's own village,

Barba Spero, the owner of the coffeehouse. Petro vehemently defends Spero when Kapetan Thanasi declares he must die. Petro finds the verdict intolerable, but his nephew Stavro feels that their *kapetan* has to be obeyed. At the coffeehouse Barba Spero explains that he was bringing down two sacks of potatoes from his cousin's farm when some people grabbed the sacks and forced gold sovereigns upon him, making him a profiteer against his will. When another partisan insists upon killing him, Petro kills Spero with the rifle. He and Stavro cannot return to the cave. They go to Kalavryta on a perilous journey to find and rescue Pappa Lambro.

December comes, with hunger and death everywhere. Not far from Kalavryta, Stavro and his uncle find refuge at a monastery. The monks warn them to abandon their goal, that Kalavryta might be the object of a reprisal. Stavro, thinking of Anna, insists on proceeding. In flashback and conversation more of Stavro's tragic life is revealed, including the killing of his father when the Italians first invaded. His brother Stellio also died. The abbot invites Stavro to return to the monastery after the war, saying: "No man can be truly happy unless he believes in God" (p. 108). Throughout the novel Stavro ponders the meaning of religion, seeking a belief he cannot find in the midst of God's betrayal of man. As a student of philosophy he cannot believe in the god who now reigns in Greece, "a god of *evil eyes*, icons, threats of everlasting punishment. I cannot believe in this kind of god . . . I cannot nurse my soul on the milk of a fleshless logos!" (p. 109). Stavro and Petro leave the monastery just before four German trucks appear.

From a distance they hear the sound of machine guns. After the Germans leave, Stavro and Petro return to the monastery to find the monks brutally slaughtered. In the village of Zachlorou they secure a priest and citizens to bury the victims. Again Stavro questions the savage motives of God. Then, by a great coincidence, two other travelers arrive outside the monastery: they are Kapetan Thanasi and Kleanthi, Stavro's friend, who have followed them from southern Greece all the way to Kalavryta to help find Pappa Lambro. They bring Stavro news about Anna; she will have a child. Kapetan Thanasi's promise to keep an eye on Stavro for her seems a slender motivation for him to abandon his area of operations and journey. Kapetan Thanasi has learned from the elders that Petro had been right: old Spero was innocent of profiteering. The priest who was summoned to bury the monks, Papa Yiorgo, accompanies them to Rogous. Stavro and Petro argue with him about

religion. Petro expresses an earthy pagan attitude. At the church
Stavro meets a beautiful fair-haired girl, Tina. She comes to him in
the cemetery after vespers; and they almost fornicate before
Stavro comes to his senses and pushes her away.

They linger too long in Rogous. The Germans break into the
church service. In the ensuing battle Kapetan Thanasi and Stavro
kill nine Germans, but three escape. The people all leave Rogous
since other Germans will soon destroy the village. Stavro stays behind to bury Papa Yiorgo; then he is led to the chapel of the
Prophet Elias by Mitso, a wounded boy. At the church Uncle Petro
had hidden under the Holy Table, having no weapon; still Stavro
regards him as a coward. From their mountain retreat the refugees
can see smoke billowing above their burning homes. Kapetan
Thanasi says they must leave for Kalavryta, but Petro advises delay.
They argue over whether or not Kleanthi should also carry a revolver. The boy feels useless without one. They leave the people
without saying goodbye. They pass the ashes of Rogous, where
Petro pauses to honor the dead. Kapetan Thanasi strongly berates
Stavro and Petro for constantly fighting each other. Stavro, the
philosophy student of twenty-three, is unbending in his attitudes:
questioning the wisdom of God with village priests, hating Uncle
Petro for his cowardice, refusing Kleanthi's eagerly proffered help.

In the city of Kalavryta Stavro asks an old priest about Pappa
Lambro, and is told the priest is dead, worked and starved to death
by the Germans. The priest then leads Stavro to the cemetery and
Pappa Lambro's grave. Again Stavros feels guilt, saying that he
killed the priest who baptized him, married his parents, and buried his brother Stellio. Stavro determines to take the body of Pappa
Lambro back to Platano, even though the distance is over one
hundred kilometers. Petro again demurs, but Kapetan Thanasi
agrees; and the priest, Pappa Yerasimos, offers them food, rest,
and a donkey. In the morning, hope falls from the sky in the form
of leaflets dropped by English planes. GENERAL EISENHOWER'S MES-
SAGE TO THE GREEK PEOPLE. It said in bold letters that Italy has
crumbled; the "soft belly of Hitler's Europe" lay exposed. "Greeks,
be patient a little longer." Germany in her peril will "strike more
savagely than ever before," and will use every deceit to "destroy or
disorganize the active resistance of the Greeks" (p. 169). The leaflet contained instructions as follows: each man must obey his superior, the villages must continue resisting, the peasants should
give food and shelter to guerrilla bands and deny food to the

enemy, maintain the watchwords of unity and discipline. "Greeks, be on your guard . . . we will inform you when the hour strikes for general action" (p. 170).

Stavro, moody and unyielding, trying to transcend fixed attitudes, argues with Uncle Petro over the need to hate Turks, refuses to listen to an atrocity tale. They go to the cemetery before dawn to exhume Pappa Lambro's body; and as they dig, they are surrounded by German soldiers. "The Germans order all inhabitants of Kalavryta to assemble in the schoolhouse," shouts the town crier. Before long, the men are taken off to a cliffside. The schoolhouse, filled with women and children, is burned. When the men are gunned down, Uncle Petro, out of love, protects Stavro with his body. Petro dies bravely. With the help of two mules, Stavro bears the bodies of Uncle Petro, Pappa Lambro, Kapetan Thanasi, and Kleanthi back to Potami, and to Anna. The Germans are pulling out of Greece.

The next novel that continues the chronicle of war-torn Greece is Glenway Wescott's *Apartment in Athens* (1945), one of the earliest books on the subject.[8] The novel dramatizes the severe problems of the Helianos family from the summer of 1941 until 1943. For a greater sense of safety they have left their own house in the suburb of Psychiko for a city apartment owned by a business friend. The family consists of Nikolas, the father and former publisher; Mrs. Helianos, who has heart trouble; twelve-year-old Alex, who is weak of body; and his younger sister Leda, who is weak of mind. In April 1941 the family lost an older son, Cimon, in the battle of Mount Olympus. They are bereaved, impoverished, and frightened. Mrs. Helianos has relatives fighting for freedom in the mountains, a fact known to the Gestapo.

Nikolas Helianos is not a war hero in the usual sense of the word. Unlike Con Reynolds in *Never So Few* he leads no men into battle; unlike Peter Zervas in *The Man with the Black Worrybeads*, he commits no acts of sabotage. Of a timid, intellectual cast, Nikolas wants to survive and grieve quietly; but the war comes home to him when a German officer, Captain Ernest Kalter, is billeted in his household. He takes up more than half their apartment. He eats their meager food. Rather than give the Helianos children his leftovers, he saves them for the dog kept by a fellow officer. The presence of Kalter means much extra work for the whole Helianos family. Furthermore, as a thoroughgoing Nazi and member of the master race, he shows nothing but contempt for his Greek hosts.

"All you Greeks have venereal diseases" is one of his remarks (p. 14). Another is "You Greeks are all thieves by nature" (p. 25). The novel explores the subtle nuances of what it means when a powerful enemy shares an apartment with his victims, at a time when famine, terror, and uncertainty rule the land.

In the spring of 1943 Captain Kalter has a two-week furlough in Germany. When he returns, promoted to major, he seems to be totally changed. The Helianoses ponder his pale and wasted mein; he is listless in exercising his authority, careless about his food, lax in his person, and somewhat compassionate. Before long Kalter reveals the cause of his change—a personal tragedy that has brought him to the brink of suicide. He confides his problems to Nikolas Helianos, his enforced Greek host. Just before he returned home to Germany, his elder son, a fighter pilot, crashed and was killed. Then, before he even got there, his house in Königsberg was destroyed in an air raid; a bomb set it afire, his wife died of severe burns. While she lay unconscious, the major's younger son was killed in Russia. After speaking of his loss, Kalter says he has decided to commit suicide. He loathes living. "It is a psychopathic condition" (p. 128).

Nikolas Helianos tries to commiserate with him and thereby makes a grievous error. Without thinking he says how sad it is that two men, the fuehrer and the duce, have brought them both so much tragedy. Major Kalter reacts violently. "How dare you, you vile Greek," the major shouts, "how dare you say a word against the Fuehrer!" (p. 132). He strikes Helianos in the face, calling him a "stupid subnormal brute" and a "filthy Slav." Kalter loses no time in having the hapless Helianos dragged off to jail. He has committed a grave crime in speaking ill of the fuehrer. The action now concentrates on Mrs. Helianos, her two children, and the troubled Major Kalter. She has another heart attack but survives. She worries much about her husband. Unable to act, she ruminates at length. She allows her temper to flare up at the German when he accuses her son Alex of stealing his key. Then, in the middle of June, "there was a pistol shot, resounding through the apartment. She could tell by the sound exactly what part of the apartment it came from: the sitting room, his room." (p. 167) Major Kalter has been good to his word: he has committed suicide. Lucky for Helianos, he is imprisoned and cannot be accused. Or so his wife thinks.

Able to read German, she glances through Kalter's suicide note, addressed to his friend Major von Roesch; happily for her, he has taken all the blame for his death upon himself. Rather than call the authorities, Mrs. Helianos calls von Roesch, who arrives with a lieutenant and assumes control of the situation. Unknown to her the suicide note is the equivalent of a time bomb set to destroy her husband Nikolas. She read the note too rapidly to understand the instruction to von Roesch: "*Speak to the political bureau of the secret service about it: Lieutenant-Colonel Sertz. Perhaps he will have some method of explaining the circumstances of my death to serve their purpose in some way, in the checking of the Greek resistance. Thus even in death I may still serve a little useful purpose, for the fatherland*" (p. 189). The German officers, however, do not misunderstand the message from the dead. If they so wish, they can have the death reported as a political assassination rather than a suicide. Although Major von Roesch absolves Mrs. Helianos, he claims that Helianos is a malcontent and an intellectual, that members of his family are in the underground. He hints that Helianos may suffer the supreme penalty. Frightened, Mrs. Helianos protests his innocence; and indeed he is innocent. Yet, in the end, Helianos is shot and, inadvertently, becomes a martyr. Mrs. Helianos and her son Alex will now take active part in the fight for freedom.

Apartment in Athens, for all its good intentions, suffers as a novel from an almost total lack of ethnicity. Some research into the actual workings of a Greek household would have greatly enriched the setting, plot, and characterization. The reader gets no concrete images of Athens itself, for that matter—no mention of real neighborhoods, streets, and other locations except for the Acropolis. Had Wescott been more familiar with the routine of a Greek household, the observance of religious holidays, the cuisine, the customs, and so on, he could have shown more graphically how Major Kalter disrupts that routine. The Helianos family has lost a son, Cimon, in the war. Apparently unknown to Wescott, it is a vital rite for a bereaved Greek family to memorialize the departed twice, once forty days after his death and again a year later. Even under the Nazi occupation the Helianoses would have gone to church in order to observe the tradition. That they do not is symptomatic of the author's failure to make the most of his aesthetic opportunities.

Instead of providing concrete ethnic detail, Wescott occasionally generalizes about the Greek nature, in comments that are half-truths at best. "Greeks and other Mediterranean men," he writes, "have not a great many sentiments in their talk or even their thought, but they are almost all familiar with this: the feeling of family, which in extreme instances may be a positive spell in a man's blood." (p. 19) In another curious comment Wescott says of Helianos: "As he was a Greek, it was not in his nature to condemn a woman very severely for a mere error or shortcoming of intellect; and as he was a good man he wanted not to wound her self-esteem if he could help it" (p. 102). Would that all Greek husbands were, indeed, so considerate of their wives. When Major Kalter changes into a stricken man pondering suicide, the author suspects that his weakness baffles Helianos: "It was all too strange for comfort; too sudden and incoherent for a Greek mind" (p. 130). In another instance Mrs. Helianos goes to the kitchen window "with the un-Greek notion" that midday sunshine does her good. These and other comments may be true in part, but they cannot compensate for the lack of realistic ethnic details.

Another type of Greek war hero is Petros Zervas, the protagonist of George N. Rumanes's novel *The Man with the Black Worrybeads* (1973).[9] Set in the strategic port city of Piraeus during the Nazi occupation, presumably 1942, the story provides Petros the chance to display his talents as leader, lover, saboteur, and killer. From being a once affluent black marketeer he becomes a resistance fighter risking his life for Greece. With equal abandon he risks his life for his friends, in acts that border on the irrational. The clicking of his worrybeads is a motif that parallels the inner tension with outer danger. By 1942 nearly two thousand people are dying daily of starvation in Athens and Piraeus alone. Two acts of sabotage occur in the plot; and both of them succeed because of Petros Zervas. First, he leads a group that sinks three tankers loaded with oil for Rommel in Africa; then he helps the RAF smash a German convoy. The Gestapo naturally wants to catch and kill him. Although the action focuses on Petros, the forty-three chapters rotate from character to character like a film.

The head of British Intelligence in Piraeus is an American, Major David Cunningham, who uses the name of Georgios. Three freighters lie anchored in the harbor. Cunningham must find a team of Greek patriots intrepid and cunning enough to destroy them.

On the lookout for recruits among local patriots, Cunningham witnesses a scene of great daring by a group of Greek black marketeers. He is watching "the blue-eyed young Greek" expertly hoisting cargo from the wharf to the deck, when a German army truck crashes into a Greek farmer's donkey cart. In the commotion, Cunningham notices that the blue-eyed Greek unloads the net of supplies into the water *beyond* the deck. To Cunningham's growing astonishment, the Greek leaves his post at the winch, dives overboard, reaches an anchored fishing boat, and begins to haul in the bobbing crates. "What made his performance so stunning was the meticulousness of his planning, his coolness under danger." Cunningham thinks: "No wonder the young Greeks on the dock had been so pleased to see him: men would follow that kind of grin loyally, devotedly" (p. 43). In short, Cunningham believes he has found his man. By the time the Germans realize what has happened, the "fishing boat" is escaping.

The paths of the "blue-eyed Greek" and Trudi Richter, the "German whore," cross when she drives to an isolated alley to sell gas from Colonel Schneider's limousine to the black marketeers. During the siphoning she meets Petros Zervas who gives her a searching look. Suddenly two lights appear at the end of the alley—a German bicycle patrol. Petros decoys them away so that Trudi Richter can escape. In the course of running off, however, Petros falls into the clutches of what he is led to believe are Gestapo agents. They arrest him, handcuff him, undress him, and start to question him—until their mood changes, and the reader knows the false Gestapo agent in charge is Major David Cunningham. He asks Petros if he has noticed the oil tankers in the harbor. The wheels of sabotage begin to turn.

The rest of book 1 of *The Man with the Black Worrybeads*, dated December 1941, deals with the planning and execution of that sabotage. In the course of it Petros Zervas goes off on another dangerous mission: to steal from the main German compound (the former Zacharias villa) the medicines badly needed by an ailing comrade, Spyros Kanares. Where else could medicines be found? The intrepid Petros sneaks into the mansion only to be seen by— Trudi Richter. He has his stiletto at her throat before he realizes who she is. Out of gratitude for having helped her earlier that night, Trudi gives him the medical supplies. He kisses her and she, with unexpected intensity, responds. Before leaving, to swim across the bay, he gives her the details of how to reach the schoolhouse where they can see each other again. At the risk of losing her highly placed protector, her comforts, and possibly her life,

Trudi Richter ventures to the abandoned schoolhouse where she gives herself to Petros Zervas.

The sabotage of the three oil freighters moves forward. Petros and Nico Andreades put together a demolition team that includes eight young Greek boys in their early teens, all strong swimmers, all eager to prove themselves men on behalf of Greece. They are instructed about how to attach, to the ships' hulls below the waterline, the magnetized limpets with their high concentrate of nitroglycerine. The young swimmers, led by Nico, secure the limpets to the freighters and leave for shore. However, in fifteen minutes instead of forty-five the freighters blow up. The flames and flashes reveal the hapless Greek boys in the water. Needless to say, the German soldiers machine-gun them. Petros Zervas watches and curses the British for their deceit. Only Nico Andreades makes it to safety. Believing that Petros has misled the eight boys, Nico solemnly vows to kill him.

The action of book 2 takes place in June 1942. Field Marshall Rommel's "Operation Aïda" has been highly successful, but he needs vast new supplies in order to cross the Nile and capture the Suez Canal. Thus the German lifeline through Piraeus is more vital than ever. In the harbor a large convoy of ships awaits the command to move out across the Mediterranean. British headquarters at the Citadel in Cairo is determined to destroy the convoy by a vast air raid. All available Lancaster and B–17 bombers are organized for the strike. In Piraeus itself Major Cunningham, Petros Zervas, Nico Andreades, and their comrades must man the beacons to guide the bombers to their target. Petros's station is atop Kastela Hill. Should the weather be too murky for the beacons to work, he has a secret additional means of frustrating the German convoy: he prevails upon the old pilot Spyros Kanares to ground the commodore's ship at the mouth of Piraeus harbor, to delay the departure of the convoy long enough for the British bombers to find and smash it. The wily Gestapo chief gets closer and closer to catching the saboteurs. In this pursuit he is unwittingly aided by Petros Zervas himself who, in a bragging mood, reveals the entire plan for the air raid to Trudi Richter.

Fearing she may die in the air raid, Trudi orders a car with which she hopes to reach Athens. In asking for the car she tells the lie that she has a job to do for Lieutenant Colonel Streck. The Gestapo immediately suspects the truth—that she has contact with the Greek resistance, that some new sabotage impends, and that the target is the convoy. Furthermore the Germans have broken part of the British code; they know of an air strike on Piraeus harbor. What they must still learn is the placement of the beacons that will guide the RAF. To make them reveal themselves, the Germans by Streck's order send a decoy Lancaster on a run toward the convoy. The ruse works. From atop Kastela Hill, Petros Zervas sends forth his beacon and waits for the bombs to fall. Instead the decoy radios down his location; and German patrols quickly converge upon the hill to capture him. In the meantime Trudi Richter has been arrested and tortured. When the pain fails to break her, Willy Streck enters the chamber to talk to her, to pretend friendship; but when the phone rings, no doubt with the report from the decoy plane, Streck apologizes and sets her free. The naive and desperate Trudi Richter heads straight for Kastela Hill and Petros Zervas, unaware that Streck's men are following.

On the hill Petros wonders why the British planes have not responded to his beacon. About him a strange drama unfolds. The Gestapo is stalking Trudi Richter who is climbing toward him. From the harbor rolls up the chemical fog released in order to conceal the convoy ships. A platoon of Wehrmacht troops reach the crest and, catching sight of a figure in civilian clothes, open fire with automatic rifles. They have made a grievous error. "And so Willy Streck, lieutenant-colonel of the Gestapo, intimate of Himmler and friend of the top members of the Nazi hierarchy, died on the muddy side of a lonely hill in a drab Greek town" (p. 309). The death of Streck does not lessen the peril confronting Petros Zervas and Trudi Richter. By now, too, the success of the mission seems to be in grave doubt: the Germans are obviously onto them. When Trudi finds him she tells Petros they are surrounded. They must break through the tightening ring. By answering to the name of Brandt, Petros manages to leave the hill with Trudi. As he heads for town, the scene shifts to Spyros Kanares on the *Salvatore Spoleno*. He pilots the vessel so that the outgoing tide rams into a breakwater. Another ship grounds beside it, the two of them effectively blocking the narrow channel. "Spyros, feeling very old and fatigued, raised his hands in surrender. The captain slapped his face and told him he was under arrest" (p. 319). He has done a heroic deed, not for Greece, but for Petros Zervas. It is to him that Spyros feels a greater obligation.

Meanwhile Petros feels that all is not lost, that he can still pull victory out of defeat. He kills a German soldier and dons his uniform. Then he and Nico head for the power station. Nico's hatred for him has not diminished; nor does Petros set him straight about what went wrong during the earlier sabotage. After much danger and killing of German sentries, Petros Zervas reaches and turns on the switch of the large generator. "From one end of the breakwater to the other, the floodlights, the buoy lights, the utility lights on the warehouse walls, the crane lights, the coal depot lights, and the lights over the railroad tracks burst forth in dazzling brightness" (p. 340). Moments later the RAF planes rain their tonnage of bombs on the doomed convoy.

At the instant of his triumph Petros gloats—that he, born a nobody in an orphanage, should be responsible for such a holocaust. Instead of sharing the triumph which, after all, is not personal but for the cause of Greece, Nico Andreades suddenly turns against Petros. "You burned down Piraeus," he cries, and adds, "What's next, Athens?" (p. 348). This incredible lack of understanding on Nico's part serves the author's purpose of having Nico murder Petros Zervas on behalf of mankind. He does so with a Luger taken from the body of a dead German lieutenant. "You don't deserve to live, Petros Zervas," Nico shouts. "I execute you and I condemn your soul" (p. 351). The stiletto that has killed so many slips from one of Petros's hands. Clutched in the other are the black worrybeads which Nico Andreades takes and stuffs into his pocket. At the deserted beach of Anavissos, twenty-five miles from Piraeus, a British submarine surfaces in a small cove. Nico and old Spyros decide to stay, but the others leave: Major Cunningham, Trudi Richter, Elena. "Soon the sun came out of the Aegean Sea and its rays bathed the nearby Temple of Poseidon. The day promised to be fair, fair for everyone, weak or strong, friend or foe. It could have been another beautiful day for Petros Zervas" (p. 360). Far better, would it seem, had he been killed by the enemy than by his oldest friend. The irony is almost too much for the reader to bear.

In the short story "Throuffi" by Alexander Karanikas, the protagonist Throuffi Sideris must keep his aid for the *andartes* (the guerrillas) a deep secret, even from his wife Andonia.[10] He runs the only mill in the remote Macedonian village of Kiparissi. Unknown to all he delivers flour and meal to the *andartes* in the nearby mountains; the village resounds with tales of their heroism, their battles and acts of sabotage against the German occupation. For staying home and working, ostensibly, as usual, Throuffi suffers much scorn and ridicule—as much as George Panagos, a villager whom the Germans have appointed as their local quisling. The patriotic children pelt Throuffi and his donkey with stones. His hostile wife contrasts him with Cosmas Drakos, leader of *andartes*. Father Alexis urges him to fight. "I'm too fat," Throuffi complains, not knowing what else to say. Even Panagos, his fellow "traitor," warns him to leave for the mountains: he has papers proving that Greeks will be sent north as slave labor. Throuffi refuses to go. "It now became the daily practice of young Stergios Drakos, son of the partisan chief Cosmas, to stand at the entrance of the mill where he taunted Throuffi as a coward, made ugly noises with his mouth, and thumbed his nose" (p. 43). At night around their supper table, his wife Andonia gives him the latest reports about the partisan exploits in the mountains.

During the harvest season Throuffi makes countless deliveries to outlying customers preparing for a long winter. "The miller's figure, stooped forward on the cart seat, had a certain magnificence against the twilight sky. His repeated departures from Kiparissi were always those of an exile scorned by his compatriots" (p. 44). In fact Throuffi is secretly carting the flour to the *andartes* so they may survive the winter. His task becomes even more dangerous when a detachment of German troops arrives in Kiparissi led by Major Konrad Kundst. His mission, as he informs the assembled townspeople, is to destroy the "Communist bandits" in the hills. Heil Hitler! The Germans will kill anyone caught aiding them. Using trickery and terror, Major Kundst learns the names of eleven such "bandits" from Kiparissi. His soldiers commit rape and other atrocities. Then one morning Andonia wakes up to discover that Throuffi has not returned from a nighttime delivery. She gets hysterical, visits the distant farm of Likouris, to learn that Throuffi has not been there for three weeks. On her way back to town, she hears the church bells. In the square, before the church, Major Kundst has prepared a gruesome spectacle: Throuffi's severed head on a table! "He has delivered your flour to the bandits, the *andartes!*" It was the patriotic child, Sergios Drakos, who under questioning had revealed that Throuffi took his flour "to places where nobody lived" (p. 49). Weeping, the Kiparissians recognize their latest hero. George Panagos, the reluctant collaborator, goes off to warn the *andartes* not to expect any more flour. The people bury Throuffi at sundown.

Up to this point the Greek characters depicted in war and its often tragic aftermath have been natives of Greece. The first American writer to create a Greek-American as a war hero seems to be Tom T. Chamales in *Never So Few* (1957).[11] Curiously enough, despite the setting in Greece of the various wartime thrillers and mysteries, the ethnic content of these novels is almost always nonexistent. Even Chamales, who was himself of Greek descent, does not give much Greekness to his hero, Con Reynolds. Very early in *Never So Few* the author introduces him with the clearly Greek name of Constantine Theodoros Reynolds, from Chicago. His English friend Danny de Mortimer calls him "that foxy Greek" when he sees him preparing an ambush. As the novel proceeds, however, Con assumes a broader identity; by birth as well as acquired characteristics, so to speak, he becomes universalized. He is a type of the ideal fighting man under certain conditions: jungle warfare behind the Japanese lines in the Kachin country of North Burma. Others wonder and Con himself sometimes asks exactly what and who he is. The only other Greek in *Never So Few* is Gus Regas, whom Chamales denigrates at first and whom he stereotypes to a degree. When the two meet in Calcutta, Regas is pleased that he has finally found a real fighting man and adds he "should have known" it would be a Greek. "A Greek? Con wondered. An American? A Burman? A Kachin? What was he? Really and truly, what was he? French? His mother was French. He had more French in him than anything" (p. 163). By birth he is Greek and French, but Con Reynolds has acquired so much else that he sometimes feels ambiguous, alone and unique. Despite his relative lack of ethnicity, he is the most fully developed Greek-American fictional hero of World War II. To what extent *Never So Few* is autobiographical one can only surmise; however, as the blurb on the back cover of the Signet edition states, "Tom T. Chamales entered the army at eighteen and after training was shipped overseas as a second lieutenant. In Burma he commanded the 3rd Battalion, American Kachin Rangers. He fought behind the Japanese lines for a year and a half and also took part in the invasion of Rangoon."

Chamales begins his novel on December 19, 1943, with Con dictating a message to his radioman about a successful ambush that killed twenty-four Japanese. The setting is the Kachin Hills of North Burma, behind the enemy lines. The country of Burma is composed of regional peoples such as the Kachins, the Karens, and the Shans. Con and the Englishman named Danny de Mortimer lead separate detachments of Kachin scouts. "Six hundred and fifty men between us," Con muses bitterly, "while the American-fed Chinese 38th and 22nd Divisions sat on their ass on the India Burma border. Forty to fifty thousand battle seasoned sons of Nippon against six hundred and fifty Kachin Scouts and eight white men" (p. 9). These are the odds and the setting for the unfolding of Con Reynolds's heroic story. It is, above all, a tribute to the bravery of the Kachins themselves.

As a legendary leader of the only active fighting Allied forces in North Burma, Con Reynolds moves about in the China India Burma theater of operations, the CBI. For consultation, for furlough, for recuperation, he goes to places like New Delhi, Colombo, Ledo, Calcutta, and finally Rangoon—but most of the time he spends in the field, the hills and jungles of the Kachin country, conducting a brutal type of guerrilla combat against the omnipresent enemy. His extended military mission is to maintain pressure on the Japanese, to gather intelligence continuously, to advise on Allied strategy, to harass, kill, and otherwise frustrate the Japanese while an offensive to drive them from Burma gets under way.

The war being a group effort, Chamales develops a number of characters whose fate meshes with that of Con Reynolds. They serve to further explain and enlarge him by their thoughts and actions. In the midst of so much death, Con ponders the ambiguities of life, searching for meaning. In the philosophy of survival with sanity preached by Nautaung the key is *patience*, the ability to wait things out, to act when time has ripened. But the irony of fate also operates in the novel. No matter how wise, daring, and charismatic the hero, he can still be destroyed by chance. For his own integrity and the respect of others, a man responds to the harsh demands of war—yet beyond them always lurks the *nada* of death, the ultimate abyss.

Small things as well as great characterize Con Reynolds. His "goateed lean body" has been toughened by combat and other jungle perils. His pet monkey, Scheherazade, has become alcoholic on American scotch. Danny asks himself: "What was that driving electric quality about Con that never gave him a moment's rest; that throbbed through him intensely, generating that excessive vitality?" (p. 28). Reminiscent of the Hemingway code hero, Con Reynolds consumes large quantities of liquor, gets drunk, but always keeps his balance. The love that he finds in the war zone, like that of Frederick Henry in *A Farewell to Arms*, is not intended to endure. "He loved Margaret Fitch but he never believed that anyone could really love without vanity or material want as Nautaung did, and sometimes he became irritated seeing his own weakness and the weakness of his woman, through the strength of this simple man" (pp. 14–15). Margaret has respectability, and she comes to Calcutta as a Red Cross worker; but her way is not that of the changed Con Reynolds. His true Catherine Barkley is a Hungarian girl, Carlotta Vesari.

More than fame, more than memory, liquor, or love, it is warfare that most fully defines Con Reynolds. He is an expert in guerrilla tactics, in the context of a people's war of liberation. He has an instinct for the moves needed to outwit the enemy; he is cruel and seemingly inhuman when leniency breeds defeat. Con Reynolds orders a beautiful Shan woman executed the moment he knows that she is a Japanese spy. He had earlier rationalized such brutality by saying: "You are living again . . . in a primitive age, so we will live again by a primitive law" (p. 133). As a white man, a *du*, he has the added task of retaining the awe in which he is held by the Kachins under him.

The military action continues into 1944, with the Allied offensive in the making being the main event. That Con Reynolds is called upon to confer with CBI leaders like Generals Stilwell, Merrill, Chennault, and Wingate only adds to his stature. He leads in ambush after ambush, secures many airdrops of supplies, kills a Kachin traitor, and executes seventeen Chinese renegades who steal American goods. This action surprises not only Carla with its cruelty; it also angers Chiang Kai-shek, head of the Kuomintang, who apparently shared in the take. Con Reynolds cannot abide the idea that Chiang, an Allied leader, should be in cahoots with renegades stealing American supplies and selling them to the Japanese. His superiors demand that Con apologize to the Chinese; after all, Chiang's armies are pinning down a million Japanese soldiers. Only after considerable trouble is Con able to return to his post. Severely wounded in battle, he leaves the Kachin country to recuperate, make love with Carla, and receive a new assignment—to collect intelligence in Rangoon prior to an Allied invasion.

A touch of ethnicity enters the narrative when Danny the Englishman is ill with plugged kidneys. He needs to be sweated in order to eliminate the waste. Carla suggests they use not blankets but a cure known as *vendousis*. "Goblets from the dining room," she says, and Con agrees. "Water goblets. Thick ones. We'll give him vendousis. Set fire to cotton in the glass and place the glass on his back. When the cotton burns the air out a vacuum will form, the skin will be sucked up into the glass and the waste drawn out" (p. 232). Con Reynolds knows about vendousis also. He has seen them used before. "In Greece. And once in America when I was a small boy," he said. "My father made my mother give them to him." (p. 233) It is Carla who administers the *vendousis* to Danny. They work, and Danny speedily recovers.

For the most of *Never So Few* the other Greek, Gus Regas, re-ceives a very negative treatment. His being a stereotypical Greek serves as his "cover" for his true identity, his secret mission. Both he and Con have the same first name since "Gus" is the usual Greek nickname for Constantine. Regas is introduced through a Filipino comrade of Con's, José Lau'rel, in a flashback before the war. Lau'rel's girlfriend Nickie was in Hongkong "with a ship's chandler; a puffy skinned short and sloppy fat Greek by the name of Regas. Later he had seen Regas everywhere: fatter, sloppier, looking more distasteful every time they met" (p. 106). Gus Regas, intensely hated by the Filipino, is referred to repeatedly as "the Greek." It is in Calcutta, during the war, that Con Reynolds meets Regas for the first time; on the same occasion he meets Carla Ve-sari. Regas is presented as a shipping magnate, which he is, with an "exaggerated English accent." "He looks something like a com-bination of Sidney Greenstreet and Peter Lorre, Con thought. But this guy was no actor" (p. 164). On the plane to a staff conference in New Delhi, Danny de Mortimer mentions the name *Colonel Pic-colo*. The English colonel, Pearson, has heard of him but does not know who he is. "We'd be in a hell of fix without him. He's the only really dependable source of information from several vital areas. Only God knows where he gets the information he gathers" (p. 182). On board the plane only Father Barrett knows, and he has taken an oath to himself never to divulge the truth. "Hardly a day passed that he didn't pray for the short fat little Greek, Gusto Re-gas; shipper, opium addict, and black marketeer. Inwardly the priest chuckled" (p. 182). Later in the action, when Con and Carla have become friends, she gives only vague information about Re-gas; for example, the refugees "called him Zaharoff of the Orient," referring to the Greek billionaire Sir Basil Zaharoff, the notorious trafficker in munitions. She apparently knows nothing more.

One day Con Reynolds goes on order to Southeast Asia Com-mand Headquarters in Kandy, Ceylon, where Colonel Piccolo has asked to see him. He turns out to be Gus Regas, the "short, sloppy-fat Greek," much to Con's pleased astonishment. As their new relationship takes form, Gus explains that he has been a British subject for years. His family owns one of the world's largest shipping businesses, with a branch even in Tokyo.

"I have a brother who operates a fleet out of Panama. No taxes, sailing from there. And another brother with a fleet out in South America. In this business we get around and have contacts. I began to devote a little time to the Foreign Office when I was quite young, picking up tidbits of information. Before I knew what happened the deal had pyramided on me." (p. 387)

Serving Gus Regas on intelligence missions, Con Reynolds drives himself as if he were in a one-man war, and that he has to get it over with as soon as possible. "As the legend spread within the service, agents began to fear working for him almost as much as they feared the enemy" (p. 523). He takes fantastic chances right along with his men, "using elements of surprise or sheer boldness to accomplish his coups." In two weeks the Allied armies are going to invade Rangoon; a week later, if all goes well, Con Reynolds will marry Carla.

His last mission, arranged with Regas, is to get into Rangoon before the invading forces in order to secure the Bank of China, but only after releasing the forty Kachin prisoners held in the main Japanese stockade. He is going in with a special platoon of Burmese Rifles to prevent the "looting of the main financial institutions." Con expects Rangoon to be evacuated, but fully mined and booby-trapped, like "one big firecracker" set to explode. Con's week of rest is cut short by the sudden news the Japanese are leaving Rangoon. He explains to Carla why he has fought so hard of late: to win a position of influence so that he can guarantee the Kachin people some degree of justice in the peace settlements. His latest duty calls him; they speak their endearments, kiss, and part. Carla never sees Con Reynolds alive again. In Rangoon, as he enters a building, he feels something against his right ankle. "There was a click, click like the ticking of a clock and he saw a piece of string lying curled over one paraboot" (pp. 536–37). The booby trap explodes, and Con Reynolds is dead. Only the legend remains.

Another important war novel with a Greek-American as a major character, if indeed not the protagonist, is Anton Myrer's *The Big*

War (1957). The historian of the military novel in America, Wayne Charles Miller, names Chamales and Myrer as writers who describe the horrors of war but make no real protest against it as a class or political institution.[12] "Indeed," Miller writes, "Chamales . . . seems to take pleasure in showing how brutal his hero, Con Reynolds, can be" (p. 147). Miller reproduces the conversation during which Con wins an argument with his group's doctor on the merits of torturing Japanese soldiers. One of Con's men, Ringa, had extracted information from a prisoner by putting a bamboo splinter up his penis and lighting it. The doctor condemns this "adjustment" to the "realities" of war, but Con Reynolds overpowers him with, "But that goddamn stupid piece of information just happened to have saved the lives of over six hundred Americans and two thousand Chinese. And every Chinese that can fight takes some of it off our guys" (p. 148). The argument, of course, makes the same sense as the reasons for President Truman's atom bombing of Japanese school children at Hiroshima: the action helped to end the war and save "millions of lives."

Miller also finds lacking in Chamales's *Never So Few* "the tension between officers and enlisted men, so frequent in the protest tradition" (p. 148). The soldiers are not saving the world for democracy but are merely out "to accomplish a series of tactical objectives." The poor Kachins are doomed as a small nation no matter what happens. Liberated from the Japanese, they can only fall victim to "the rape and pillage and crooked rule" of the Chinese. "Or even the American." In the face of such a bleak prospect, the soldier must kill and kill, or be himself dead—that and nothing more. Miller finds the same absence of moral indignation in Myrer's *The Big War* in which, even though his heroes die, he does not protest the war other than to depict it as horrible and pointless. Thus Miller attempts to make a distinction between these newer military novels and those that grew out of the first world war.

Anton Myrer's Greek hero is Danny Kantaylis, from a mill town in western Massachusetts.[13] A badly scarred veteran of Guadalcanal, he rejects an offer to go on a bond tour throughout the country, preferring to rejoin his Marine outfit for additional combat. Apart from rounding out a gallery of ethnic types—to show the equality and universality of patriotic sacrifice—Kantaylis says or does nothing "Greek" throughout the novel. The story begins with Corporal Kantaylis in charge of his squad during a three-day bivouac in the Carolinas. Tired and edgy, the men engage in typical barracks talk; they argue and fight over trivial matters. Kantaylis, "his broad, handsome face strangely perplexed and drawn," broods over a letter. His face is "yellowed with malaria and deeply lined" (p. 17). Except for the ugly and mean Capistron, the men respect Kantaylis, not only as a genuine hero but as a squad leader who has never reported them for breaking rules. His intellectual friend Newcombe (a Harvard graduate) reads in Kantaylis's scars "the runes of his suffering" (p. 21).

As a result of something in the letter Kantaylis goes absent without leave. He hitchhikes home to western Massachusetts both to see his family and to marry Andrea Lenaine, pregnant with his baby. There he learns that Andrea fears punishment for their *sin*— a child conceived out of wedlock. After much convincing, Andrea, now his wife, consents to sex; and she will assume that the baby came from this time and not before. Kantaylis explains why he refused the bond tour, even though it meant no further overseas duty. He does not believe in heroes. War is cruddy, and we must kill and kill to finish the rotten business as soon as possible. Kantaylis will not wear his hero's ribbons and medals, but he will return to kill, in "this stupid Goddamn world" (p. 120). He begs Andrea to be sure to tell their child just how stupid and damned the world really and truly is. She feels a shock at this glimpse of the dark within his soul.

The reader next sees Kantaylis in the brig where a sadistic sergeant, Ransome, first taunts him as a "hero" on a rutting spree, then beats him senseless. The sergeant knows that Kantaylis was on Guadalcanal, that he suffers from malaria; but hates him anyway for being a "big-ass" hero. Ransome calls Kantaylis a *dago* as an added insult. Kantaylis can easily kill Ransome, "a gutless stateside garrison commando," but makes no move because he wants to rejoin his squad. Part 1 of *The Big War* ends with Kantaylis finally out of prison.

The scene shifts to a naval landing craft in the Pacific war zone. Kantaylis and his comrades talk while waiting for the invasion of an island held by the Japanese. Kantaylis as a veteran explains about combat; and he tells that he received his many wounds while "stopping a banzai" attack. The bombardments to soften up the island begin. When they come, in part 3, the battle scenes of landing under fire, securing a beachhead, and proceeding through chaos and carnage recall similar scenes from many films of World War II.

Kantaylis, cool under fire, gives courage to a Lt. D'Alessandro who momentarily panics, then recovers to forge ahead. For five days the battle rages. The narrator Newcombe expects that Danny Kantaylis, the men's "talisman and mainstay," will get them past all the tough going. He thinks of the phrase *"Each of you is a leader,"* then remembers the source: Kantaylis.

The old Greek, he thought happily, foolishly, shaking his head. The old Greek NCO himself. Mister X. It was a prayer, a war cry—a still, small affirmation in the face of disaster. Out of all the horror and ignorance and exhaustion, whatever was to come, he had salvaged this much: this one thing he could hold pure as an emerald in the palm of his hand. (p. 347)

The Americans liberate a lot of the Chamorrans caged by the Japanese. Kantaylis plays the role of the Good Samaritan helping whomever he can. He gives food from his rations to Chamorran children. He also tries to give water and a cigarette to a dying Japanese soldier; but another Marine in his group, Helthal, kills one prisoner and tries to kill a second. Kantaylis orders him to go into the jungle after the escapee. He thinks all the men have gone to hell—a bunch of suicidal bastards. In the course of the battles Danny Kantaylis blows up an enemy tank with dynamite; and in the process mortally wounds himself. Newcombe takes over and tries to save Kantaylis, whose eyes are "dazed and sightless," and whose guts are "hanging all over his legs." Four men carry Kantaylis in a stretcher to a field hospital, but already he has died. Newcombe sadly looks at the body and thinks: "A face strangely wizened: gray and shrunken and old. Not Danny at all" (p. 392). It is Newcombe who writes Andrea Kantaylis saying that Danny was a "very rare man" who "lived with rare nobility." The war goes on.

The Greek ethnicity lacking in *Never So Few* and in *The Big War* emerges abundantly in Chamales's second and last novel, *Go Naked in the World* (1959).[14] The war still hangs heavy in the consciousness of Nick Stratton as he tries to find himself in civilian life. At only twenty-three Nick is a major on his way out with a medical discharge. Like Con Reynolds he fought in Burma. In addition, he was in the North African cities of Oran and Cairo and in Greece, where he was almost killed by "the rebel Commie troops" outside of Sparta. The thrust of the novel is inward on the wounded psyche of the hero: what the war did to him, both good and bad, and what he retains of character, attitude, and will to cope with a powerful, crafty, and domineering father—old Pete Stratton, multimillionaire theater magnate and, as Nick regards him, son of a bitch. He wants to shove his success down Nick's throat for Nick's benefit; but Nick needs time to breathe, to heal, and to decide his own future.

Old Pete Stratton achieved the American Dream the hard and devious way, including contacts with Al Capone and the underworld. He ran a famous night club before going into the theater business with the Stratos brothers, Charlie and George. "Now fifty-six theatres in three states," Nick ponders. "The absolute control of over fourteen towns. And the buildings they had bought in the towns" (p. 26). Worth two million dollars at least, Old Pete is both ruthless and generous. All powerful, he wants his only begotten son Nick to become a tycoon after his own image. The ethnic element, the importance of being Greek, courses strongly throughout the novel. For example, when Nick finally gets home, he and his father spit upon each other for good luck. The Greek characters are not only authentic with respect to verisimilitude, but the major ones with rather thin disguises stand for real-life Greeks who strutted across the Chicago scene in the forties. Our interest in them, however, is only as fictional representations, as ethnic constructs in a work of imaginative literature.

They belong to the fantasy world of Nick Stratton, a Greek veteran wounded in body and spirit who has come, as the back cover of the paperbound edition states, "from the desolation of war to the plush, decadent glitter of Chicago's North Shore." Ninety-nine percent of the veterans would have clutched with joy at such a ready-made feast. But not Nick Stratton—he has identity problems that he must resolve on his own. In the true spirit of the Hemingway hero, he gorges himself on the rich food, liquor, and easy sex. When he falls in love, he does so unknowingly with Chicago's highest priced call girl, Nora. Among her past clients is Old Pete himself, who uses Nick's romantic mishap as a weapon to force him to marry a good Greek girl, Pat Rakis. Again unknown to Nick, the proposed marriage with Pat is a cold-blooded scheme by Old Pete to extend his theater empire into the South. Her aging father owns a chain of theaters that will eventually come into Old Pete's control. Even though Pat is a deserving girl, Nick Stratton breaks off the engagement as soon as he learns the truth. Stripped down to his bare self, he goes to the small island he has purchased in the Florida Keys. There, close to the purity and innocence of nature,

Nick writes a novel, and the novel is accepted. His long and agonizing search for true identity has ended. Old Pete Stratton sells
his holdings in the theater business. And Nora, who visits Nick on
his island, mysteriously vanishes, presumably a suicide. But her
body is never found. Nick's self-liberation is finally complete.

The web of ethnicity that Chamales weaves in *Go Naked in the
World* begins with Old Pete's thinking about how his American wife
spends money. "No Greek girl would spend money like she did.
An old country girl knew the value of a dollar" (p. 22). A few pages
later Chamales mentions Greek Town on Halsted Street, where
Old Pete and his cronies reminisce about the time they lived in a
"hay loft over a horse barn." They drink *retsina* and eat of *pacha*—
a soup made of head, brains, feet, and entrails of lamb—octopus,
lamb, olives, goat's cheese, and rice-stuffed cabbage leaves. "Then
sweets, those rich buttery honey sweets which were not really of
Greek heritage but a by-product of the Turkish occupation" (p.
25). Then Turkish coffee, and ouzo, a cordial which was supposed
to have "an aphrodisiacal effect." Nick Stratton has inherited his
father's liking for Greek food, but he does not often frequent the
Greek restaurants on Halsted Street. He prefers lamb cooked on a
skewer by a relative, Old Gus, a wise ancient who keeps goats. Just
as Nautaung in *Never So Few* serves as a spiritual father and guide
for Con Reynolds, so Old Gus does for Nick Stratton. Being outside the scramble for riches, Gus can advise the troubled youth
from a more philosophic vantage. More than that, it was said that
Gus "could spell the evil eye and forecast the future and that Old
Pete never made a deal without consulting him" (p. 81).

Two other vital Greek characters are Pierro Stratton, first cousin
of Nick, and Lou Duck, an unsavory restaurant owner and a crony
of Old Pete's. Pierro enters the novel in process of "blowing on the
hose, forcing the water from one jug into the other, strengthening
the one lung he had left. Pierro Stratton was twenty-nine years old.
His other lung he had left at a beach town in Italy called Anzio"
(p. 35). He also constantly worries about having inherited syphilis
from his father, despite the fact that the positive tests could result
from malaria. A brilliant promising architect, he won a fellowship
in 1937. With six months of it spent in Greece, he returned so
fluent in cultivated Greek that nobody here "wanted to speak in
the native tongue with him" (p. 41). Ironically Pierro hates the idea
of being a Greek, a fact that Nick Stratton knows and turns against
him. Nick deliberately calls him *Greek* in direct address. What

Pierro thinks and says helps to further characterize Nick, Old Pete, and others; but he fares ill before the end. Chamales creates an aura of doom about him from the start. Later in the plot Pierro marries a society girl, Marci Preston, who gives up her acting career for him. Before their first child is born, perfectly normal, Pierro commits suicide. His ailments and phobias were too much for him to bear. Marci names their son Peter for Old Pete.

Lou Duck owns the lucrative Silver Saddle Restaurant near the Drake Hotel where Old Pete and his friends regularly seclude themselves to gamble, drink, and whore. Pierro thinks of him negatively: "Lou Duck, whorehouse operator de luxe, president of the Greek Men's Club of the First Greek Orthodox Church, and millionaire restaurant man" (p. 48). Lou Duck befriends Pierro by planning some buildings for him to design; and he befriends Nick Stratton by revealing to him that Nora is a prostitute. In the case of Lou Duck, Chamales juxtaposes whoredom and religion to indicate how readily society ignores one's seedy past after one becomes very rich. Lou Duck, the Stratos brothers, and Old Pete himself are all crude, vulgar, and cruel people; and Nick, fascinated by their money, position, and power, almost joins them.

With his younger sister Yvonne, Nick has a relationship similar to that between Holden Caulfield and Phoebe in *The Catcher in the Rye*. Nick does not suffer Holden's psychological problems, nor seek in her the same emotional refuge. Nick and Yvonne have a bond, apart from the fierce arguments that Old Pete stirs within the family. They discuss sundry subjects such as parents, God, and Ernest Hemingway. A time seems to come when the Hemingway hero must state the quality of his belief; thus Frederick Henry, asked by Count Greffi, "Are you *Croyant?*" answers affirmatively, "At night," then goes off to his "clean place," the mountains.[15] While Yvonne and Nick discuss how best to handle Old Pete, she asks him, "You do believe in God, don't you?"[16] He replies that every man does, in his own way. He admires Christ's courage, which rises far above the courage needed in "a war, or in a football game, or in a baseball game." Nick admires Hemingway the man for the guts it took to go his own way. "Like Old Pete goes his. That's why Old Pete's admired" (p. 166). By virtue of that same courage Nick must oppose his father's dominance—just as he rejected the regimen of college by leaving it, so now he demands his own way of life. What Hemingway meant by courage, Nick believes, "was the courage it took to separate yourself from society, to give up what you had to give up in order to be capable, or should I say properly trained, in order to be able to face that death. Like Christ. The courage to live alone" (p. 167). This statement may well be the central theme of *Go Naked in the World*—go forward to self-discovery stripped of every emolument, be it parents, position, wealth, power, and even love.

Nick Stratton undergoes that painful divestment until he is, indeed, stripped naked and alone on his isolated island in the Keys. There, like a modern Antaeus, he touches the bare beauty of nature and is renewed as a human being. Before he reaches his "clean place," Nick must completely and absolutely free himself from Old Pete. When Nick accepts a job with his father's company and becomes engaged to Pat Rakis, Old Pete's victory seems assured. But his victory crumbles when Nick cannot stomach the shabby tricks his father plays to gain more power. One of the shabbiest is the proposed marriage with Pat, a fine girl that Nick likes but does not fully love. Her father has "about as much money as any Greek in America and no wife," no one except Pat. "And she was about the most beautiful Greek girl Old Pete had ever seen" (p. 161). Nick Stratton escapes in time from the confinement that the marriage would impose. Another shabby trick played by Old Pete is to use his influence to have Nora arrested as a prostitute. To his father's face Nick angrily declares, "I ought to kill you," and follows up by threatening to expose Old Pete's whoring to his wife unless he clears Nora of all charges. A strong tentacle of his immediate past reaches out to Nick when Nora and he meet again in Florida. Driven from Chicago, she functions as a call girl in Miami; and when Nick finds her she has also become a junkie. Earlier she had admitted that she was a lesbian; before Nick came along, only women could make her feel what she wanted to feel. Nick takes Nora to his island refuge. He starts writing his novel. The final divestment for him is the disappearance from his life of Nora. She walks down to the sea and begins to swim. "The search lasted two weeks but no trace of her was ever found" (p. 402). Nick believes her to be dead—her suicide not only an atonement for her sins but also the result of "a greater love and respect for his own life." His book accepted, Nick goes back home and then to New York for its publication.

Another Greek-American soldier, Sergeant Gus Damianos, appears in *Path for Our Valor* (1963), a novel about paratroopers in peacetime written by Thomas Doulis.[17] The setting is Fort Mosby near Von Steuben, Tennessee, home for the 43rd Airborne Division. Damianos is the sergeant of the guard, who has helped catch an escaped prisoner. The sergeant is tall, heavy, and muscular. The surly captive is questioned. Later in the novel, Damianos is referred to as Greek; but no ethnic details are used to describe him or his actions. Damianos loves to jump and free fall, and he hates those who bring their rivalries and "ambitions into what was his pleasure." He and his buddies make a jump; and when photographs are taken, Damianos is very angry. The press has violated the integrity of his exultation.

At a bar with a friend, Damianos drinks, dances, and then lays a whore. To Sophie he complains that everyone is crowding him. "Pretty soon even civilians will be jumping, acting like it ain't nothing to be a paratrooper" (p. 54). Another big mass jump occurs, with the experienced Sergeant Damianos busy with know-how and leadership. In the drop a Major Jenkins lands in a tree; and Damianos finds him mangled, dead. Later he gets drunk in their usual hangout. He tells his friends that perhaps next time it will be he who dies like the major. The two other leading characters in *Path for Our Glory* are Barrett Clarke, of a rich Philadelphia family, who is bored by life; and Captain Kinnard J. McIlhenny, an unpopular disciplinarian who, demoted to corporal, gets sliced to death by a propeller. Damianos tells Sophie he will not skydive any more. Among his few possessions he has an icon of Saints Constantine and Helen, and an old wedding photo of his parents. His mother died one spring just before Easter; and the National Guard killed his father during a steel strike in Pennsylvania's Monongahela Valley. Gus Damianos had gone to war already bitter and hard. Now, feeling he will die, he buys a $15,000 insurance policy and makes his girlfriend Sophie the beneficiary.

Ahead of the men lies the great Operation Razor Blade. As one phase of preparation for it Sergeant Damianos leads a jump to look over the Crossroads Drop Zone. In the area, during Razor Blade, a thousand "guerrillas" would be seeking ways to escape from the paratroopers. Jealous of a wild doe's freedom, Damianos brutally kills her with his .45; and for the same reason he shoots at a soaring eagle. Thus ends part 1.

Early in the second part Damianos learns from his paramour Sophie that she is pregnant. They ponder their options about the baby. For a year he has been supporting Sophie. The tavern is in his name. When Damianos suggests they marry, she replies that he prefers his freedom over any binding responsibilities. But when he asks her again, she accepts. Damianos talks with his buddies about his marriage, and also about the duration and hardships of Operation Razor Blade. Nikki, the wife of his friend Clarke, arrives in town; but Damianos will not allow Sophie to associate with her because he thinks she is a tramp. The problem with Clarke and Nikki is that she wants him to fail, to wash out, fearing for his life.

Part 3 of the novel begins with a prospectus for Operation Razor Blade. The men prepare. They all leave for the field of maneuver. Having left Sophie behind, Damianos is "overwhelmed by a feeling of loss, of alienation toward what he had for most of his mature life considered his only function." That is, to be a soldier, to fight enemies, "to protect one of the intangibles skillfully explained by those who rarely fought for them" (p. 277). During the maneuver Sergeant Damianos helps a Major Zoltan "capture" General Aarons. In the truck the general notices that Damianos is a Greek name. "First woman I ever laid was a Greek," Aarons says. "Best screw I ever had" (p. 283). He does not remember her name.

Trouble strikes in the form of a strong wind when a mass parachute jump occurs. Damianos by collapsing the chutes saves many men from being dragged to their death or severely injured. Some men are snagged in trees. Several die in the snafu. This tragic jump is the first assault, with a second coming. When it does, a new disaster strikes. A plane crashes. Damianos, sensing his own death, shaves off his beard because he wants to be a clean-shaven corpse. *"My name is Cosmas Damianos, he thought, and my face is a Damianos face"* (p. 330). He and Clarke talk about the maneuver and about freedom. Next day, the third and the last big jump of Razor Blade is to take place.

This jump incurs a third disaster: several men of Damianos's group fall into the path of a disabled Boxcar (carrier plane) and are killed. On the ground a police call is made to retrieve the bodies. Clarke, who had barely escaped death, now refuses to jump again. The men are gathered to locate the dead and disfigured bodies—a gruesome task. Yet, to meet the challenge, General Aarons orders a fourth jump for the thirteen thousand paratroopers involved in Razor Blade. Clarke leaves the formation shouting "No!" and "I will not jump!" (p. 376). Thus he frees himself, as he claims. Handcuffed, he is taken to the stockade. *Freedom, dignity, courage*, and *manhood*—Sergeant Damianos ponders—all these words merge and have meaning as he prepares to skydive again.

These four words stressed by Doulis express, in part, what other authors also attribute in their fiction to the modern Greek as war hero. *Cunning, skill,* and *daring* may be added to them. The literature has obviously done justice to real-life Greeks who, on the one hand, struggled to liberate Greece from Nazi occupation, and, on the other, fought as American soldiers wherever duty called them. The returned Greek veteran, wounded in spirit like the mythical Orestes, also stalks through our literature. A good case is that of Nick Stratton, as we have seen; an even better is Alex Rifakis in Petrakis's novel, *In the Land of Morning.* The Greek woman as war heroine applies only to Greece. No author has depicted a Greek-American girl in a wartime situation suitable to bring out her heroic potential.

9

THE GREEK LOVER

Hᴵˢ ˢᴏᴍᴇᴛᴵᴹᴱ Homeric capacity as lover, sex symbol, or just
plain stud, as depicted in our fiction, must be cited as another of
the modern Greek character's attributes. More often than not,
though, he is just a Greek who happens to be in love. The classical
simile "He looks like a Greek god," an Adonis, still serves as a description of male beauty. The Hellenic tradition with its initially
religious sanction allows for a great deal of libidinous activity.
Without fertility there is no harvest of life, and so the ancient
Greeks honored Dionysus and his satyric hosts with plays and rites
of rampant sexuality. They deified the male organ and called him
Priapus; and when his psyche or glands went askew, they or others
after them termed the condition *priapism*—a mixed blessing at best.
The island of Lesbos named the lesbian proclivity, and its greatest
poet, Sappho, was first to sing its joy. From the goddess Aphrodite
we get the word *aphrodisiac;* from *satyr* the word *satyriasis;* and from
nymph, nymphomania. Odysseus gained a renewal of potency, not
from the horn of a vanishing animal, but from the benevolence of
Athena, the goddess of wisdom. If in our time man's fertility has
gone berserk, resulting in the population explosion, the fault lies
in our forgetting the most famous of Greek maxims, "Everything
in moderation."

Our most celebrated courtesan, Xaviera Hollander, the "Happy
Hooker," regards Greeks as her favorite lovers. Her capsuled
evaluations of how various ethnic types perform include the following: "Gʀᴇᴇᴋs. On a private basis, Greek young men are the
ones I adore most as lovers. They are sensitive, strong, warm, and
exciting. Greeks are rarely circumcised, but they are very clean.
The older, richer Greeks as customers are very charming and sophisticated in bed, and sometimes slightly kinky."[1] In her profession, she writes, *Greek style* is the term applied to anal sex. She dedi-
cates *The Happy Hooker* to Larry and Takis, with Takis introduced
at the courtroom before she (as "New York's most notorious
madam") and her call girls get sent to Riker's Island. She calls him

"my sweet Greek lover, Takis," and later in her autobiography describes some of her pleasant intimacies with him. Xaviera Hollander mentions other Greek lovers in her subsequent writings.

In another bedroom confessional and How to Do It Better book, *I Am Sexual*, the author Janet Baker has a friend who credits Greek lovers for making her a sensual woman.[2] Lora has difficulty finding the right man to marry; so one day she angrily takes out all her savings and flies to Greece. "Well," the author says, "Lora came back from Greece a different woman. She had a smashing tan and was dressed in a floaty Greek peasant dress that made her look very earthy and sexy."[3] According to Baker, American men do not want women who sleep around, the way Greek men do. It is Markos, her first lover, who changes Lora. "What he did, as patiently and lovingly as possible, was to teach her the joys of her own body. Lora found to her delight that she was a very apt pupil and was soon begging Markos to show her how to give him pleasure in return. He had opened up a delicious new world for her."[4] Following Lora's example, Janet Baker goes on to become an expert lover, and to write her book.

The first popular Greek-American sex symbol was Lou Tellegan, star of the silent films. Cy Rice, the biographer of Nick the Greek, describes Tellegan as "a tall, thin, suave, early-day matinee idol of Greek ancestry who was later to establish himself as a great lover in the movies."[5] Lou Tellegan came to be known as the "Cave Man" and the originator of the "Cave Man Embrace." Rice details the mechanics of the famous hug.

> This was performed in a standing position. His right arm would crushingly encircle a cinched waistline while his left hand, fingers spread, descended flatly on top of an elaborate hairdo. The willing but struggling victims of this inescapable wrestler's hold were slowly drawn toward his manly loins and pressed against them. Once the bodies touched, the lips followed suit. It was rib-cracking and spine-tingling. Ladies in the audience gasped and, despite the darkness of the theater, hid their faces behind fans.[6]

The primitive masculinity of Lou Tellegan is far removed from the smooth-headed and more gentle manner of Kojak, the television hero and sex symbol played by Telly Savalas. Even the irrepressible Zorba, archetype of the modern Dionysian hero, does not use the bone-crushing tactics of Tellegan when he makes love. As in so many other matters, so in the pursuit of erotic pleasure, short of crime: one's taste cannot be disputed.

Various authors have created a wide variety of Greek lovers. Some live in America, while others live abroad; and some are men, others women. The two most prodigious examples in the fiction of Petrakis, Leonidas Matsoukas and Antonio Gallos, exhibit epic prowess. Through the power and skill of their passion they surpass all others in satisfying their women. The sexual act is always riotous. Between Matsoukas and the widow Anthoula, as Petrakis writes, "the battle rose to a fevered pitch and in desperation he swept her up, spun her over, her breasts mashed against the sheet, imprisoning the ring, her buttocks hung before him. For a moment their bodies poised suspended on the precipice of the earth, then, holding her thighs like the frame of a chariot, he drove forward and down."[7] Antonio Gallos, the Greek gangster, is also an "avid lecher." While performing, he is no less a lover than Matsoukas. "Despite his age," Petrakis avers, "he retained the haunches and loins of a heavy-balled lion or bull." When Gallos has the widow Asmene in bed, "he turned hard and demanding upon her body, his flesh and bone slapping against her hollows and hills."[8] The lust of strong men for women, and strong women for men, is an aspect of a general lust for life that animates the pages of Petrakis.

The main love interest in Edmund Keeley's first novel, *The Libation* (1958), concerns a Greek girl named Helen and a boy, Timothy Gammon.[9] Actually, they are brother and sister, a fact not known by them until after they have committed an incestuous act. The plot consists of a series of revelations, with time past and present manipulated in the manner of Faulkner's *The Sound and the Fury*. Indeed, as the *New York Times* review states, "In a sense, William Faulkner is the godfather of Edmund Keeley's absorbing first novel. Mr. Keeley's Yoknapatawpha County is modern Greece and his Compsons are the Gammons, who have a 'family curse.'"[10] Their family curse is lust, adultery, illicit passion, incest, at least incest between Helen and Timothy, performed innocently without knowledge of their true blood kinship. Faulkner's Quentin Compson never consummates his incestuous feeling toward his sister Candace. Instead he is shown to suffer a traumatic response toward her loss of virginity to somebody else. After her marriage, he kills himself. Keeley's Benjy is the idiot whose name is Armenian, a refugee boy of the Asia Minor disaster who is adopted by Cassandra, wife of Achilles. She is mistress of Thomas Gammon and mother through him of both Helen and Timothy. *The Libation* is not "a tale told by an idiot," nor in any real sense a Greek adaption of *The Sound and the Fury*. Nor is it, despite its title, adapted from *The Libation Bearers* by Aeschylus—though a curse also pervades the Oresteia and tendencies toward incest there also play a role.

The story by Keeley begins as an idyll of love between Helen and Timothy and ends with her apparent success in reconciling him to the fact that despite their incest, they are still brother and sister; and, as such, they can forget the uneasy past and have a happy future. That past includes more than the childhood love, now matured, of the two siblings. The climax of *The Libation* and much of the relevant action occurs in 1950, but the various flashbacks begin in 1922, with the catastrophe that burned Smyrna and drove the Greeks from Asia Minor. It is soon after that Cassandra, over the objection of Achilles, gets Armenian from some gypsies and adopts him as her own son. Achilles and the American, Thomas Gammon, join as partners in the fur business. Gammon has ventured west, away from the holocaust, with the vision of setting up a new church and proselytizing for members. The old family curse of lust betrays him into recurrent adultery with his partner's willing wife, Cassandra. Her namesake in the Oresteia became Agamemnon's unwilling concubine after the fall of Troy; previously, when she refused Apollo's advances, the god punished Cassandra by making her a prophetess whom no one believed. The adulteress Cassandra in Keeley's novel cuckolds Achilles (no relation to the Homeric hero except for his ultimate wrath) and bears both Timothy and Helen as the fruit of Thomas Gammon's lust.

The ancient archetypes hover about *The Libation* but do not govern its action precisely according to their nature. As Troy burned, so also does Smyrna; and Agamemnon sails west to meet his dire fate as Gammon after Smyrna comes west to meet his. The fur business with Achilles succeeds well as the years pass, and so does his illicit love with Cassandra. Timothy, the first child, is sent to school in America, whereas Helen, the second, remains in Greece. Only Gammon and Cassandra know that the children are brother and sister; certainly not the children themselves and not Achilles. Grown, Timothy returns from America and promptly resumes a more sophisticated love idyll with Helen. As a result Achilles forces the issue when he demands that Thomas Gammon and he discuss

the business of the wedding. Gammon, knowing the marriage taboo because incestuous, argues with Achilles while they are duck-
hunting. While the idiot, Armenian, watches, they grapple for the
shotgun. The gun goes off, and Gammon drops dead. That
Achilles desperately tells Armenian to forget what he has seen implies that he has deliberately murdered Gammon. Armenian retrieves the spent shell. Fearing exposure and arrest, Achilles eventually leaves for the northern border. The duty of informing
Timothy, and through him Helen, of their kinship is left up to
Cassandra. She performs the difficult task in time to prevent the
marriage.

From *The Libation* the reader learns that modern Greeks are vul-
nerable to the same old and dangerous passions that fueled the
classical tragedies. Keeley's second novel, *The Gold-Hatted Lover*
(1961), takes its title and tone from the romanticism of F. Scott
Fitzgerald.[11] Its protagonist, Tom Macpherson, is five years out of
Princeton and a vice-consul in Salonika, Greece. He agrees to host
an August tour for a college friend, Bradley Cole, and his wife
Gloria. As a result the novel gives a tourist's picture of Greece, with
some details about various places of interest, but hardly any about
the people themselves. Tom stays in Athens with Doris, sister of his
best Greek friend there, "a painter of my age with a limitless capacity for talk and whoring." Doris herself has shown "a limitless
capacity for marrying worthless men" (p. 12). At the port of Piraeus where Tom goes to meet the Coles, he sees among the
crowds "eager relatives grappling with returning Greek-Americans, their children screaming for air as they were pinched and
hugged with abandon" (p. 20). The friends are reunited. For their
visit to Crete, Doris finds a Greek girl named Vera Karras to be
their guide. That Cole takes an immediate liking for her provides
a major line of action in the novel.

The trip to Crete develops into a serious marital crisis for the
Coles. Vera Karras does not cause but helps to precipitate the crisis
when Bradley Cole goes away with her and leaves Gloria alone
with Tom Macpherson. Vera shows how modern Greeks haggle
over prices when she bargains for a rented car in Herakleion.
Their driver, Niko, has three daughters by a wife not yet twenty.
They visit a taverna for the bouzouki music. Niko says, "And the
singer is—excuse the expression—a well-known whore. I even remember her from the mountains" (p. 90). They drink a lot of Cretan wine. Throughout the novel they also drink a lot of ouzo. Un-

der the right conditions, Tom learns, ouzo acts like an aphrodisiac—
when taken straight from the bottle on an almost empty stomach,
and with a girl like Gloria available. They return to Athens where
he sleeps with Gloria; then he goes to the island of Poros for some
needed meditation. He scuba dives and fishes. In Athens again, he
finds to his surprise that Bradley and Gloria Cole are together
again. Vera Karras, it turns out, is actually a prostitute.

Tom Macpherson also appears in Keeley's next novel, *The Imposter* (1970), as a friend of the American CIA agent Simon (Sam)
Kean.[12] The novel is more of a thriller than a love story, although
as a typical self-respecting agent Sam also spends time in bed with
women. Part of his purpose in joining the CIA is to expose it from
within; along the way he attempts to make a separate peace with
the organization—that is, to quit on his own. Searching for purpose, he ends up in Greece where he asks his friend Tom Macpherson for help in getting himself set up. Tom has a Greek
named Jim find Sam an apartment in Athens, in the Kolonaki section. The Greek lavishly decorates the place, then organizes an exotic house-warming party at which Sam meets Stella. She makes
her point by scoffing at his attitude toward Greek women, calling
him silly. "About Greek women anyway," she says. "For example,
you think we're all innocent because you read somewhere that girls
in the villages are supposed to stay virgins until they're married."[13]
Sam makes love with Stella, then has to go into hiding because both
Stella and Jim are murdered in his apartment, and he is accused.
His brother Dick arrives from the States to search for him. From
the novel's resolution the reader learns that the victims are both
CIA agents, undoubtedly killed over the Cyprus question. Sam
Kean goes off again, this time with the girl he genuinely loves,
Alison.

Two major characters, the girl English and the man Greek, leave
England for a Greek island and romance in Elsie Lee's *The Passions
of Medora Graeme* (1972).[14] Medora flees the country when Alistair
Pitt-Ramsey announces he will marry another woman. She and Alistair run the designing firm Dollistair. Dr. Simeon Vlados leaves
England to recover from the death of the woman he loves, yet
cannot save. Emotionally upset, Medora accepts an invitation to
sail aboard the *Circe* with some friends. Three weeks later the vessel's engines die near the Greek island of Thanaxos. Captain Pan-
dros says about the island, "Very small, but hokay. Tomorrow we
fix."[15] There Medora disembarks, promptly sprains her ankle, and

is invited to stay with the Vlados family. She meets the young Dr. Simeon Vlados, also from England.

Thanaxos is a flax-producing island with linen its main product and lifeblood. At the moment the electric generator that powers the looms does not work. Simeon attempts to raise money from the relatives of successful but absent islanders who migrated to other lands. He cannot raise enough despite the fact that his friend's father, the Turk Mr. Indronu, gives a large sum. Medora's stay with Simeon, his father Jason, and his mother Lissa, an excellent cook, has the same therapeutic effect it has had on Simeon. Furthermore, she recognizes the woven designs made by some of the island women. She had bought some of their cloth from Feneloni, who has clearly been paying the islanders much too little and reaping great profits. So she arranges to buy directly from Thanaxos and to give the people a fairer price than Feneloni does. Through her American uncle, Medora replaces the generator and secures new looms.

One night when itinerant workers from a nearby island raid Thanaxos, Simeon Vlados rescues Medora from a man who is bent on assaulting her. In the heat of the rescue, Simeon, already overcome by much ouzo and excited by the fight, forces himself on her. Medora is rather compliant; and next day when he awkwardly tries to apologize, she indicates that she enjoyed his love. Their liaison begins. Simeon points out to Medora why Alistair married Lady Gwen Howard and not her, but she cannot enlighten him about his lost love, Diana Landry. Both lovers return to England, Medora because Dollistair is in trouble; and Dr. Vlados to resume his practice.

Because both of them are so busy, they cannot reach each other by phone. After Vlados learns from Diana's husband and doctor that she could, through hysteria, make herself ill, he realizes that he was not responsible for her death. Diana, knowing her husband was remarrying, made herself sick because she would not be able to get his money. Dr. Vlados's surgery on her had been successful, but she was too weak and therefore she died. This knowledge relieves Simeon from his guilt feelings. He then goes to Medora, and they have a civil wedding. Several months later they marry again, in the Anglican church, and again on Thanaxos by the Orthodox priest, Father Anastasis. Medora's friend Suzy Francot is paired off with Xeno Indronu, the nice Turk.

Perhaps the best known of the fictional Greek-American lovers is Eddie Anderson in Elia Kazan's *The Arrangement* (1967).[16] Eddie's Freudian discontents derive in part from the highly "civilized" nature of his status as advertising executive with wealth and obligation. That he is a Greek is clear from the beginning when Kazan gives his real name—Evangelos Topouzoglou. Of his heritage the protagonist says: "I was the eldest son to a man named Seraphim Topouzoglou, who was born in Anatolia and brought to this country by his elder brother, Stavros Topouzoglou, the first of our tribe to cross the Atlantic. Stavros landed on Ellis Island in 1899, and the first thing he did was change his name to Joe Arness" (p. 30).

The plot of Kazan's novel involves much more than the search for sexual happiness, even though sex is central to Eddie's problem. He and his wife Florence have an understanding "that just so long as I didn't make a fool of her with our friends or publicly humiliate her, she'd look the other way" (p. 11). Both are forty-three; they have been married for twenty-one years and live in a beautiful house in Bradshaw Park. They own various status objects such as a fine record collection, two original Picassos, three cars, and a pool. However, Eddie Anderson violates the terms of their "arrangement" by falling in love with Gwendolyn Hunt, a worker in his office. Another sign of impending disaster is his growing loss of interest in his work. In having both Gwen and Florence, Eddie feels "eastern," Levantine, for enjoying several wives is alien to American mores. Regarding Gwen's value in sex, Eddie says, "She *unroutined* it" (p. 19). Regarding himself as a superior lover, he feels that he needs more than a wife to satisfy his sexual needs.

Besides working for the Williams and MacElroy agency, Eddie Anderson as a free-lance writer does "justice pieces" for leading intellectual magazines. He goes on a writing safari to New York, with Gwen along, to prepare an article on a reactionary politician named Chet Collier. The train ride is one long fornication for them. Back at home, however, serious trouble begins when Irene, their black maid, finds in a secret drawer some nude beach photos of Eddie and Gwen. It was Ellen, their eighteen-year-old adopted daughter, who suggested to Irene that she show the photos to Florence, who promptly starts divorce proceedings. To add to his woes, Eddie gets soundly beaten up by Collier over Gwen. Back on the West Coast, he accedes to Florence's wish to see her psychiatrist. For eleven months he tries to stay with her. They read books like the Siddhartha together, but they cannot make love. Bored and nervous, Eddie begins to gamble. Then he drives his Triumph TR4 into a trailer. The accident changes his life.

He speaks his mind, when not childishly silent, on the excuse of "brain damage." He does not want to work, and refuses even to write a magazine article. He buzzes the ad offices of Williams and MacElroy with his Cessna 172. At a welcome back party attended by movie people Eddie gets very drunk, walks home, and has to be helped by the police. At home he calls his brother Michael in Westchester because their father has pneumonia. Their daughter Ellen, too, is troublesome. A spoiled bratty girl, she has had an abortion in Tiajuana. "I hate Radcliffe" is her opinion of college. She wants to be different from both her parents; she wants to be "honest." In the settling of his debts, Eddie gets stripped clean by Florence. In low spirits he flies to New York to see his father, help Ellen, and write an article about a Latino politician, Rojas.

On the same flight he meets Chet Collier, now Gwen's lover. In Spanish Harlem, at a party, he talks with the wife of Rojas and admires her honesty. "Order-professed, chaos-concealed," he thinks, "was the subject that interested me most in the world" (p. 203). He had intended to destroy Rojas as a misleader of his people, a phony; but after talking with Mrs. Rojas, he decides that he himself is the real *puta*, the whore. She tells him that instead of writing literature he was out to destroy others for the entertainment of his readers and the swelling of his bank account. Eddie gets drunk again. He goes to Gwen's apartment only to see her enter with another man. His daughter Ellen dates Collier, his arch foe. Days pass, and Eddie keeps going down. He gets bounced from a Harlem bar, he urinates on an old Zephyr cigarette ad he once dreamed up, and ends in the court of Judge Ben Weinstein, an old college friend. Both belonged to the Communist Party before World War II, during the days of the Popular Front. Even then Eddie wore a Brooks Brothers suit, a "Commie's disguise," so that as a "Commie" he could "represent himself to be just like everyone else, a little ahead, maybe, but not too much, and never as a person dedicated and determined to bring down this body politic." Both he and Weinstein soon left the Communist movement to seek wealth in their respective professions. Eddie sees Weinstein caught like himself in a false arrangement, buried alive under the heavy weight of success, and spiritually dead. All people, Eddie thinks, are divided between the sellers and the sold.

In time he goes to Gwen and to Charles Collier, Chet's brother, to learn much to his surprise that she has a child! The boy looks like him, as Eddie says. This Collier has not been sleeping with Gwen, only taking care of her. Eddie has sex with her again, and again, and he thinks: "This time we did it in simple mutuality, symphonized as the Greeks say" (p. 288). Many tergiversations, mostly leading downward, follow in Eddie Anderson's human relationships. Florence attempts to entrap him back into their old marital arrangement, but to no avail. He goes into and out of a mental hospital. As a symbolic act of severance from his family past, he torches their old house on Long Island. Much time is devoted to the long dying of Eddie's father, Sam Arness. Florence's lawyer Arthur Houghton is taking care of her—which is all she ever wanted. Two happier years pass for Eddie, Gwen, and the child Andy living together on the top floor of her uncle's house. The uncle owns a liquor store in a shopping center. At one point Gwen sadly tells Eddie: "Some day, Eddie, take a chance, love somebody" (p. 541). As the long novel draws to a close, Eddie has finished and sent off his first complete story, one in praise of Florence. After a tiff with Gwen he takes his savings and decides to go off for a while—to Montauk Village, at the very end of Long Island. There he begins to feel some power of his own, some hope, a new exhilaration. Gwen arrives soon, and "The marriage of the monsters was performed by the mayor of Patchogue" (p. 543). Later that evening Gwen reveals that she is pregnant again. They eventually own the liquor store, having bought out her uncle. The baby's coming, Eddie's steady, and he writes a lot. "But I do worry sometimes," he ponders. "Is this what all that drama, that great overthrow was for—this simple living and working, this day to day confluence?" (p. 543).

Even though the ethnicity factor does not obtrude, it nevertheless pervades *The Arrangement*. When summarized, the allusions to Eddie's Greek heritage may seem more important than their actual significance to plot and theme warrants. These allusions create a well-rounded image of what it means for Eddie Anderson to be facing his destiny and dilemma as a wealthy but troubled middle-class Greek-American. For example, Eddie says, "Being Greek, blondness is my fetish. I was given black hair, a little on the oily side, once very thick." The fact that he readily sleeps with Gwen leads him to a moral judgment: "I thought of her as soiled. That's a good Greek middle class word. I'm embarrassed to recall this now" (p. 33). When their affair threatens his marriage and comfortable life, he ponders the gravity of his situation.

> No Italian, no Spaniard, certainly no Frenchman would give up his home, his life's savings, and his wife for a piece of tail. And no Greek, ancient or modern, would discommode himself in the least for any such trifle, no matter how succulent. The Greek would simply accept the fact that a man had to give up a lot of things in life to hold on to the main thing. (pp. 66–67)

Thus Eddie Anderson regards it as un-Greek of him to give up so much for a new girl.

A polygamous Greek lover, Eddie sleeps with Gwen in the morning and with Florence at night—another aspect of the "arrangement" redefined as "the technique of keeping one woman in place while you temporarily carry on with another." A most needed tangible for the success of the adventure is the male sexual organ, which Eddie regards as the "most honest part of man." In his eulogy of it he calls the penis by various names: Bird, Peter, One-eyed Dick, The Erect One, Tumescent Teddy, Joint, El Conquistador, the Member, the Root, Big Peter, Old One-eye, Mindless One, Little Friend, Shiny-Headed One, and Peckerstiff. Eddie does not mention any Greek locutions for the same vital object; although, after all, the Greeks also have several words for it.

A running theme throughout *The Arrangement* is Eddie's relationship to his father—a bittersweet bond, not always happy and not always sad. Eddie reminisces about old Sam Arness, who would come home and follow a certain ritual each time.

> He'd pour himself an *ouzo*, fog it with water, and call for "a little something," his *Mezeh*, the appetizers. My mother had them ready, too, on pain of terrible displeasure. She ran them out to him: sardines perhaps, pistachios always, fat-cheeked Greek olives, soft as plums, and some of the sour, salty, hard cheese which they make in that part of the Turkish highlands from which my father came, the cheese named after the province, *Caesari Payneer*. (p. 223)

That Eddie's father would show "terrible displeasure" if his mother did not jump at the command is an instance of the arrant male chauvinism at the center of the relationship. Many other instances occur, among them Sam's admonition to Eddie: "I told you thousand times, marry Greek girl. I told you. They satisfy stay home" (p. 239). Mother was never listened to seriously and, according to Eddie, she was neglected in matters sexual. Sam Arness ruled as an autocrat at home.

Toward the end of *The Arrangement* the question arises of how the failing Sam Arness should spend his remaining days. Eddie suggests to the Greek priest that Sam, instead of being put into a nursing home, should go to Tarpon Springs. The following comment reflects Kazan's knowledge of the sponging center based upon a personal visit and work there on a film.

> The point, Father, is that Tarpon Springs is full of beat old Greeks who were brought to this country a long time ago to dive for sponges. But now we've developed a synthetic sponge that is cheaper to make and to market. So these fellows down there sit around all day in the coffee houses, play backgammon, and bitch. I think my father would find a lot of congenial company down there, fellows who feel just like he feels—and in Greek, too. (pp. 339–40)

Thus would end the long and busy life of an Anatolian Greek who came to America obsessed with the dream of big success. When Eddie is going through the old family house on Long Island (which he later burns down), he questions the wisdom of his family's having crossed over the Atlantic. The whole passage, he thinks, "had been a failure, not the country's fault perhaps, but the inevitable result of the time and the spirit in the air in those days. The symbols of affluence gained had been empty even by the standards of the market place. The money they had acquired wasn't worth much; they had found that out in 1929." The other material goods they owned, Eddie feels, also meant nothing. "These men who had cried America, America! as the century died had come here looking for freedom and the other human things, and all they had found for themselves was the freedom to make as much money as possible" (p. 430). Thus Eddie Anderson, with his love life momentarily smashed, echoes Kazan's critical view that much is amiss with the bourgeois values that dominate our culture.

Another Greek lover, Charlie Stavros, uses his sexual knowhow as therapy for Janice, the unhappy wife of Rabbit Angstrom in John Updike's *Rabbit Redux* (1971).[17] Stavros sells cars in her father's agency. Janice loves him, she says, "for the way he searches out every nook and cranny in her body and soul and sells them to her as Rabbit never did."[18] Since the point of view focuses upon Rabbit, Updike does not detail the expertise by which Stavros gluts Janice with pleasure. That the loving is offstage and accepted by Rabbit with equanimity diminishes Stavros as a character. He is less a formal antagonist than a partner, a friend, and sharer of the same woman. The first mention of Stavros occurs when Janice suggests to Rabbit that they try the new Greek restaurant which Stavros has recommended. Since Janice knows her way around the place, Rabbit suspects that she and Stavros are lovers. Before the truth comes out, Updike gives the reader a touch of Greek ethnicity by discussing the menu of The Taverna.

In looking the menu over with Rabbit, Janice says: "Everything is more or less lamb. *Kebab* is when it's on a skewer. *Moussaka*, it's mixed with eggplant."[19] Their son Nelson says he hates eggplant. He wants *kalamaria* even though no one knows what they are. "Have the *souvlakia*," his mother suggests. "It's pieces of meat on a skewer, very well done, with peppers and onions between" (p. 43). Nelson says he hates pepper; instead he wants *melopeta*. But Rabbit calls him a dope, that *melopeta* is a dessert. By chance Charlie Stavros arrives and is invited by Janice to join them. *Kalamaria*, he explains, "it's little, like, octopuses cooked in their ink" (p. 44). Nelson finally settles for *keftedes*, meatballs, without the "tomatoey goo." As for Rabbit, he picks a menu item at random: *païdakia*, only to be told by Stavros: "It's marinated lamb, you need to order it the day before, for at least six" (p. 45). Stavros orders *souvlakia* for them in Greek; and while they wait, they argue.

At this point in the novel Rabbit is a superpatriot with a flag on his Falcon. For Charlie Stavros, the Greek-American liberal, Rabbit's sticker means to "screw the blacks and send the CIA into Greece." Rabbit retorts that the Greeks cannot manage the show by themselves. Then he lets Stavros really have it. "And it really burns me up to listen to hotshot crap-car salesmen dripping with Vitalis sitting on their plumped-up asses bitching about a country that's been stuffing goodies into their mouth ever since they were born" (p. 47). Janice, as one might expect, has a very different opinion of Stavros. Besides selling her herself, he murmurs about her parts, "giving them the names Harry [Rabbit] uses only in anger"—and he can make the sex act last forever, whereas her husband cannot hold back. Stavros has another asset besides his "thick sweet toy." "The fur on the back of his shoulders at first shocked her touch, something freakish, but no, that's the way many men still are. Cave men. Cave bears" (p. 53). Janice ruminates about the intimate physical aspects of their love.

After some heated and acrimonious prodding by Rabbit, she admits sleeping with Charlie Stavros, a person that Rabbit says he likes, "an O.K. guy, for a left-wing mealy-mouthed wop" (p. 62). After her admission they have a sophisticated husband-wife talk about each other's infidelities. Their talk ends in sex after which Rabbit sleeps and dreams of driving north with Charlie Stavros in a scarlet Toyota. The fantasy has Stavros discussing his problem: "Lyndon Johnson has asked him to be his Vice-President. They need a Greek." Since Stavros refuses to leave town, "they are negotiating to have at least the summer White House moved to Brewer" (p. 69). In this shrewd nightmare Updike shows Rabbit, the cuckold, elevating his wife's lover to an impossible height above himself. Actually, despite being good for Janice, Stavros has a heart murmur from an early rheumatic fever. That is why, according to Janice, he will never marry. "He has a gift, Charlie does, of making everything exciting—the way food tastes, the way the sky looks, the customers that come in" (p. 70). The essential thing about him is that he loves life. Throughout the story Rabbit, who sets type in a print shop, imagines headlines for sundry occasions. This one reads: "LINOTYPER'S WIFE LAYS LOCAL SALESMAN. *Greek Takes Strong Anti-Viet Stand*" (p. 72). Janice defends Stavros's intelligence, saying he would have gone to college had he not been a Greek. Rabbit—the latter-day Babbitt—lets his bigotry glare in his response: "Don't they let Greeks in now? The nigger quota too big?" (p. 73). Janice calls him sick.

Updike does not further characterize Charlie Stavros, but uses him as a means of getting Rabbit rid of Janice so he can more freely move about in search of his spiritual health. She moves in with Stavros; but at summer's end he wants Rabbit to take her back. He seeks out Rabbit to discuss the problem of what to do with Janice. In effect the Greek salesman wants to "sell" her back to her husband where she properly belongs.

> Rabbit tries to imagine Stavros's room, which Janice described as full of tinted photographs, and instead imagines Janice nude, tinted, Playmate of the month, posed on a nappy Greek sofa, nappy mustard color, with scrolling arms her body twisted at the hips just enough to hide her gorgeous big black bush. The crease of the centerfold cuts across her navel and one hand dangles a rose. The vision makes Rabbit for the first

time hostile. He asks Stavros, "How do you see this all coming out?" (p. 159)

And Stavros replies: "That's what I wanted to ask you." Before the conversation ends, the Greek fixer has begun to convince Rabbit to give his marriage another chance. Knowing he is going to die, Stavros maneuvers to have Janice return to a marriage stronger for having weathered a serious storm. *Redux*, an adjective, according to the book's note, means *led back*, a medical term *indicating return to health after disease*. The sexuality of Charlie Stavros has been Janice's badly needed therapy. He leaves the scene with honor and dignity intact.

One should not surmise from the foregoing accounts that "Greek lover" applies only to male Adonises with Homeric sexual powers. Greek women also get into the act. The fiction of Harry Mark Petrakis has both retiring and bold Greek women; some cling to a still pervasive moral code while others move forward to the new freedoms. The symbol for the former may well be the votive light before the ikons protecting the hearth; the symbol for the latter, the searing spotlight in a Greek taverna beaming on the gyrating belly dancer. Petrakis encompasses both extremes as part of the complicated Greek character, while other writers push the image of the Greek woman into the darkest areas of perversion, debauchery, and decadence—an indulgence of the body reserved for the very rich.

The little girl in *Miri* (1957) by Peter Sourian belongs in the nice but no longer innocent category.[20] The novel is divided into three parts, each seen from the first person point of view by its three principals: Miri, the girl; Josh, the American boy; and Lexy, Miri's cousin. Miri lost her family in the war. Her Uncle Alex, in whose lavish New York home she stays, owns merchant ships. She has come from Greece an orphan, does not speak English very well, is quite shy; but unknown to those around her she slept with a German officer during the occupation, in order to avoid starvation. Both of the boys fall in love with Miri in this low-keyed story of growth, adjustment, and maturation.

The three are college students in the Boston area. Miri, in the company of Josh Bigelow, goes to Boston with a package of Greek food which her aunt put up for Lexy. Josh is very blonde and handsome, whereas Lexy seldom shaves and looks like a slob. Something serious is bothering Lexy. He has an excellent mind but refuses to study. He is a fine runner but he quit the team. He gambles a lot and wins. Josh tells Miri: "He wins a lot. The others say he's too cold-blooded about it, and they get pretty mad at him sometimes. He just never gets reckless. He says it's the Greek in him, but I don't know about that, because he's very superstitious" (p. 22). Miri and Josh have a date. They walk along the river, they discuss respective customs, but they do not make love. They are timid toward each other.

The autumn passes. At Christmas Miri returns home, to fall again, as usual, under her stern uncle's domination. She cannot change and grow as at college, where she is free to be herself. Josh Bigelow attends Greek church with her.

Back at school again, she notices that Lexy has gotten worse— more anarchistic, more irresponsible. He *wants* to lose. By the time of final examinations Josh is in love with Miri, but as yet they have not even kissed. Lexy has decided to return home, because he claims he needs money. He tells Miri he wishes he had been in Greece during the war; and he asks her how her family died. Someday she may tell him.

Miri compares Uncle Alex with her own father. Her uncle "with all his Greek ways" makes her remember the past. Alex is "rich and more cruel" than her father was, yet like him, with the "pinch on the cheeks, the bestial way of eating," and all the charm" (p. 41). Lexy, after being practically disowned, returns home to confront his irate father. Uncle Alex slaps him and calls him a "lizard." The reason for this bitter generation conflict soon comes out, in the section of the novel which belongs to Josh.

Josh met Lexy wearing a rumpled suit, bloodshot and ex-hausted, the first day of college. As the friendship develops, Lexy recounts the scandal that implicated his father. A newspaper had claimed, Lexy tells Josh,

> that my father was a crook, and that he was cheating the gov-ernment, and that he was being indicted, and it went on and on about him and some other Greek shipowners, all sons of bitches, and then besides all that, there was a short editorial . . . about what bums they all were, and me with all my fancy education about the right thing to do, and about people starv-ing all over the world, and the Greeks, too. (pp. 59–60)

Thus with only seventy-five dollars in his pocket Lexy had run away and did not return until now.

At the college Lexy wins the one-hundred-yard dash for the freshman team, visits a whorehouse, plays backgammon with a Mr. Dracatos in his imports store. To Dracatos, Lexy says of Josh: "He's an apprentice Greek." (p. 72) The other rich boys at school are curious about Lexy: he is the son of a shipowner. As time passes, Lexy goes from shame in his father's indictment to being "nearly proud of it, in some treasonable fashion." It is when Lexy says he has to visit his "damned cousin" across the river that Josh Bigelow first meets Miri. Lexy offers him some of the Greek food Miri has brought from home. Josh, after meeting her, ponders about "this Greek girl with her charming accent, and the warmth and gentleness of her, what she could teach me" (p. 81).

At the close of the school year, Josh goes to Lexy's house where he gets a glimpse of Greek home life, not all of it pleasant. Temperamental, Lexy's father gets very angry when the butler brings a bottle of *Metaxa* instead of retsina, a "Greek liquor made of rosin," as Josh describes the well-known wine. The atmosphere at Lexy's house improves rapidly. Josh wishes he could understand them all when they spoke Greek, "wishing I was Greek." Josh plays backgammon and likes retsina. He feels proud when Lexy's father asks him to write a letter to the New Hellas Athletic Club declining to be its president. "You like Greek things, eh?" he says to Josh. Events are going so well, Josh feels sure he wants to marry Miri. She, however, tells him he does not really want her. "You want to marry *this family*" (p. 115).

The novel's point of view finally shifts to Lexy, who admits to himself he has been on "a long boy-hero kick." He used his father's indictment as an excuse to be righteous and angry. "My father seemed to me to be boastful, mean, and stupid" (p. 121). He paid too much attention to other women at the house. "He has always shouted to my mother, and she has sometimes shouted back, but usually ended up in tears." When he has to meet Miri, Lexy expects to see an ugly girl, but she is not. "She just seemed very Greek" (p. 122). That Miri impresses Josh Bigelow helps make Lexy proud to be a Greek. Almost secretly he begins to study Greece. During the war Greece created many heroes, including Miri, "and it seemed to me unjust," he muses, "that a girl like Miri should have the luck to have her family die in the war, to have seen war, when I had no real adventure at all and more than enough family" (p. 123).

Lexy kisses Miri, and finds it not terrible, in view of the fact he once thought all Greek girls unattractive. "The idea of sleeping with one of them seemed unimaginable, just plain impossible. I don't know why." In college Lexy is majoring in engineering, a course of study that can be useful in the family business. His father plans to let Lexy take over his empire when he dies. In time Miri reaches the point of saying to Lexy "I love you." (p. 142) She undresses for him, but at first he forbears. Miri, however, finally reveals that she slept with a man during the hard times in Greece—with a considerate German officer who saved her life. Miri is in a quandary; she loves both Lexy and Josh. What should she do? For one thing, she goes to bed with Lexy.

The affair with Miri proves good for Lexy—for his growing understanding and attachment to his family, and to the Greekness of his family. Now, partly owing to Miri, he feels proud, strong, and confident. He regards his father now as "just about the strongest, most courageous man" in the world. Father and son drink to the future from "two glasses of *Ouzo*, which some good poor New York Greek made in a bathtub and brought to the house every month in a gallon bottle" (p. 152). Sourian must have had Prohibition gin in mind, not ouzo, when mentioning the bathtub. Be that as it may, the novel *Miri* ends with Miri leaving on an early train back to Boston to have dinner with Josh Bigelow. They love each other, too—but they all have a lot of maturing left before the real decisions can be made.

No genuine love, only self-interest, motivates the thirty-five-year old Greek nurse, Major Marjorie Stavropolis, in John D. Spooner's *Three Cheers for War in General* (1968)[21] Many books and films have depicted chaotic military organizations for humorous purposes; not all of these works are purely imaginative. Spooner's funny novel deals with a peacetime Army reserve unit, the 229th General Hospital, which comes under the Boston Subsector Command, the Eleventh Army Corps, the 1700th Hospital Sector, the unit led by Colonel Beauregard, a dentist. As reservists, the characters leave for their regular summer training at Camp Cannon, near Utica, New York. Major Stavropolis has been the colonel's mistress for five years, mainly because she also lusts for the rank of colonel.

In an early reference to her, Colonel Beauregard wonders if he should take her into his tent for a lay. She, in turn, thinks of him as a "little shrunk-up bastard" of dubious sexual prowess.

Major Stavropolis did not have her own apartment until she was thirty-five, and hence little privacy. "Greek families were notoriously large" (p. 31). She is tall, and tough, the kind of nurse who gives "lousy backrubs" and is "stingy with the alcohol." She has the habit of saying: "There's nothing new you could show me, buster." A bit of ethnicity, but not much, crops up here and there. "Her Greek ancestry," Spooner writes, "gave her instinctive knowledge in the ways of pleasing men, inherited from the sunlit days of the golden past along the Aegean" (p. 32). Colonel Beauregard is shocked and surprised at first, then curious and delighted "by the glories that were Greek." The colonel pictures "an olive grove, with the Parthenon in the background and maybe a few goats," when they kiss (p. 96). Major Stavropolis shows that she is "both resourceful and Greek" in carrying around her diaphragm in her brother's discarded cuff link box. She also puts some drops of Arpege into her crotch before donning her silk panties.

Since the novel is humorous, neither the love-making nor anything else is taken too seriously. At camp, where all goes wrong, the men hunger after the Greek nurse's "luscious Aegean breasts." Eventually the reserve hospital unit gets active duty for a punitive foray into the Caribbean. When the reader last sees Major Stavropolis, she has shifted her hopes for a promotion via the bed from Beauregard to a Colonel Harden.

If the novel by Spooner inclines toward the ribald, George Revelli's *Sweet Marpessa* (1973) plunges into the depths of pornography.[22] The ancient revelers in the satyr plays had a religious sanction for their bald antics, but in *Sweet Marpessa* the only sanction is the author's desire to transform relatively "hard porn" into hard cash. The prologue takes the reader to World War II when the Greek shipowners, such as Marpessa's father Bellerophon Andruledarkis, made their initial millions. He was a captain in the Royal Hellenic Navy, yet he has traces of Brooklyn in his accent. "I worked for a time in America," he tells the barkeep at the London Ritz. "As a longshoreman" (p. 3). He has just lost two of his merchant ships at sea and expects the usual huge recompense from Lloyd's and from the British and American governments.

Andruledarkis dictates a letter to Marpessa at Palm Beach. It will arrive in "the Greek diplomatic bag to America," and on his way the messenger will pick up a present for her at Tiffany's. He writes to his "sweet baby Marpessa" that he personally planted the mines that blew up a German destroyer off Norway, and that King George of Greece will give him another medal. To a lieutenant he adds: "If the yellow-bellied sonofabitch ever gets the guts to leave his hideaway in South Africa." He orders Rupert Vassal, a painter, to go to the convent of the All Holy Virgin in Hadhemere and paint a full-length portrait of his wife. She is supposedly mentally ill. While an air raid sounds outside, Andruledarkis fornicates vigorously with his current mistress, Jill.

After the prologue the novel proper opens in Silverglades, the palace of the Marquess and Marchioness of Glastonbury. Their great wealth stems from an American supermarket fortune on the one hand and "unrefrigerated Greek tramp-steamer money on the other." Several years have passed since World War II. The marchioness is—Marpessa Andruledarkis! By a previous marriage she has two sons now in distant prep schools. At thirty she ranks as one of the world's most beautiful women—her nose long, inbred, appropriately Grecian, with narrow nostrils. She is also one of the world's best dressed women. Both of her marriages had been arranged by her father, the second to young Dickie Glastonbury.

They spent their honeymoon in Greece, much of the time with the Greek royal family on islands owned by Andruledarkis. Marpessa speaks English, French, Greek, Italian, and Portuguese. At a soccer match she and her friend, the Princess Jane, meet a soccer star named David Scrivener who has a shocking role to play in the story. The foul-mouthed princess makes lavish use of four-letter words. After the game at Newcastle, Marpessa will make Scrivener "something Greek, a moussaka or something." (p. 18) Princess Jane has a twelve-year old stepson, Dmitri, who also figures in the novel's lurid plot: Marpessa teaches him about sex.

Andruledarkis, now in his sixties, is a man of "violent handsomeness" and immense sexual appetite, who is pictured as strongly incestuous toward Marpessa. He kisses her on the lips, "his manicured hand cradling her breast openly," when she asks to use his yacht at Cannes for an affair that requires discretion. He flaunts a seventeen-year old tart who calls him "Seraph." Andruledarkis wants Rupert Vassall to paint Marpessa again in the nude. When he makes a pass at her, Marpessa says, "Oh, fuddles, Daddy, you Greeks don't know the difference between a daughter and a goat." The daughter is saved from her father by the entrance of his mistress in negligee who raves about his being a "beautiful man." Her favorite line of his is: "Beware of Greeks baring gifts" (p. 32).

Marpessa has a secret and very plush hideaway. There with David Scrivener, she tells him she was named for one of her father's oil tankers that got sunk by U–boats; all the crew drowned, most of them known to Andruledarkis since childhood. "I bring bad luck to people," Marpessa says. As for the meaning of the name: "Marpessa was one of the least interesting people in Greek legend. She was beautiful, courted by Idas and Apollo, and instead of choosing the divine Apollo, chose Idas, who was absolutely nobody among people who were anybody in Greek mythology. She was frightened that Apollo would get tired of her when she grew old" (p. 38). When Scrivener asks her nationality, Marpessa replies she is an American by citizenship, but completely of Greek blood, "except probably for some Turkish, like so many Greeks." They lunch on "taramoslata," which she describes, and on moussaka, which she calls a Greek shepherd's pie. The base of "taramoslata," she explains, "is raw pike roe with all sorts of stuff, like, well, onion, egg yolk, lemon juice, and so on" (p. 39). Not mentioned specifically is olive oil, also an ingredient.

Marpessa's pro forma husband, Dickie Glastonbury, is an expert on guerrilla warfare. He uses her hideaway at night for a foursome that includes a Soviet attaché, a Colonel Lapinsky, George Nestoridis, and Rupert Vassall. It seems the group will engage in a homosexual orgy. Vassall has been to bed with Marpessa; Lapinsky spends time with her later in the story; and Nestoridis, son of another shipowner, wants to seduce her—and Marpessa hopes he will not turn homosexual. Later Vassall calls to say the "whole evening was a Dickie Glastonbury plant," to let the world know that his friendship with a Soviet diplomat (and quite likely a spy) was not a secret.

Marpessa's supposedly ill mother now resides at the convent of Saint Sofia on the island of Chios. She does not accept the fact that her son Nicholas was killed on D–Day. Andruledarkis calls a letter from her gibberish. "For some reason," he says, "gibberish sounds even more like gibberish in Greek" (p. 56). The letter to Marpessa chides him and explains more about the name. "Marpessa was the daughter of Evanus. Neptune lent her his chariot, and it was Zeus, not Evanus, who let Marpessa make her decision between god and mortal. So unlike today, when your father decides such questions himself" (p. 57). When Andruledarkis fondles Marpessa's breast, she hisses at him, angry that he disbelieves her mother's "divine revelation," to the effect that the icon shed ice-cold tears at her birth.

The plot of *Sweet Marpessa* moves in various shifts of scene. At a soccer match Scrivener misses an important point, another sign that Marpessa brings people bad luck. They sleep together, and afterwards they discuss Greeks and their sex habits. "And, you know, David," she says, "Greeks are very funny about sex. Heterosexuality and homosexuality don't mean a thing to them" (p. 83). At his studio, in another scene, Rupert Vassall is painting Princess Jane and her stepson Dmitri in a nude pose. The frank talk about sex embarrasses the young boy. Vassall wonders if he should paint in the boy's erection, but Marpessa has other plans. She sets the nude Dmitri on her lap, cups her hand "over his excited, hairless genitals," and gives him an orgasm. The experience, she says, will keep him from becoming a homosexual like Dickie. On another occasion Marpessa and Scrivener have an automobile accident in which three people die. Back in London from a soccer trip, he entertains in his flat a top model named Carol. He moodily tells her that he needs "a toffee-nosed Greek bitch who said if I ever uttered her name she would set her precious Daddy on me. She would, too" (pp. 122–23). Scrivener knicks Carol's nipple with a knife, and hints he will cut off Marpessa's nipples. Carol screams and leaves in panic.

In Paris the Soviet diplomat Lapinsky escorts Marpessa to a house of offbeat sex run by a Mme. Fontana. The place reeks of "decadent evil." They see a sex show. On the *Xerxes*, at Cannes, Marpessa meets George Nestoridis by surprise and goes to bed with him. Scrivener is being transferred to the Birmingham soccer team, the equivalent of being banished to Siberia. A big question arises: where's Dickie Glastonbury? He seems to have disappeared. Sir Geoffrey Remington tells Marpessa the *Daily Mirror* has rented the studio next to Rupert Vassall in order to overhear their gossip. Marpessa worries about herself. All newspapers have dossiers on celebrities, Sir Geoffrey says, and he has seen hers prepared by "a certain Fleet Street newspaper"—and furthermore David Scrivener has been trying to peddle a series of ghost written articles on "My Secret Life with Marpessa Glastonbury."

The artist Vassall is visited by two British secret agents from Scotland Yard and M15, who ask if he knows the Marquess of Glastonbury, Dickie. They want to know who his friends are. Vassall does not mention Marpessa's hideaway. After the agents leave, Andruledarkis bursts in to demand all the incriminating portraits of Marpessa. Vassall calls him "you incestuous bastard," and they fight. Greatly concerned, Marpessa goes to Dickie's secret place to find Norman Quickfall there, an agent of M15. He informs her that her husband Dickie's in Moscow. He has been an agent of the Soviet KGB for four years, recruited in Vietnam while studying guerrilla tactics there for the Pentagon. Lapinsky of the Red Army was assigned as his contact. Marpessa moans that she brings bad luck. "I suppose I shall have to marry George Nestoridis after all. A Greek! Eck!" (p. 197).

As it happens, Marpessa brings bad luck to herself also. At home she finds David Scrivener, hand in a cast because of a broken wrist. Marpessa's maid Bianca has been sleeping with him. Bianca cries: "The *marchesa* is a whore!" (p. 201). She leaves and will blackmail Marpessa hereafter. The embittered Scrivener says, "I was great until I met you. You made me a has-been, and tonight, for all one knows, you may make me a murderer." (p. 206) Marpessa wants to pray to see if the icon will weep icy tears again, as at her birth. Scrivener ties her up, naked, and hangs her on a hook; then he proceeds to kick a soccer ball at her body with great power and accuracy. Marpessa dies. He cuts off her nipples, knifes her through the navel, and writes a note: "Fuck all Greeks, prominently including Bellerophon Andruledarkis. Only the English are worth a shit." Scrivener then kills himself.

The epilogue to *Sweet Marpessa* attempts to shock the reader even more. It is a year later, and Andruledarkis is speaking with Princess Jane, his mistress. George Nestoridis has married a Swedish au-pair girl with whom Andruledarkis has also fornicated. He also tells Jane how relieved he is that Marpessa has gone. "It was like a dead weight lifted from me. Christ, what a bitch!" Andruledarkis justifies both his present attitude and his former lechery toward his daughter. "She used up everybody," he says of Marpessa. "You, me, the soccer sex maniac, not to mention that poor bastard Vassall" (p. 212). Andruledarkis blames Marpessa for driving her mother to a nunnery. He claims that all he ever loved was— ships. He ends up with Jill, the girl he slept with during the Nazi blitz.

Not so hot or kinky a lover as Marpessa is Rima Azen in C. L. Sulzberger's political novel, *The Tooth Merchant* (1973).[23] The *New York Times* columnist writes an "artfully camouflaged lampoon on war" whose protagonist is an Armenian petty thief and spy, Kevork Sasounian, on a mission for the Turks. They send him to Soviet Armenia, under duress, to report on Beria's underground atomic installations, when Beria still has power, supposedly near the Turkish border. Kevork enters Soviet territory. Soon after, a terrible earthquake cuts him off from his past, family as well as Turks, who may well believe him dead. At a monkey farm used for scientific experiments he meets a stunningly attractive woman. She, too, is of Anatolian heritage. "My father was Circassian," she says, "my mother Greek." (p. 55) She claims ancestry from the Argonauts and the mythical twins Castor and Polydeuces. "My name is Rima Azen," she tells Kevork. Her husband runs the trout fishery for the neighboring Abkhazian Autonomous Republic. Rima speaks Greek with an archaic accent. Kevork speaks Greek and sixteen other languages.

He asks if many Greeks inhabit the region, and the beautiful Rima replies yes, plenty. "There are still a few Hesychasts, the mystic brethren, in the monastery. There are large Greek and Armenian colonies in Sukhumi. And all the way to Novi Aphen. But these are new Greeks. Some came from the Crimea. And some came from Smyrna, after the Turkish massacres" (p. 57). Part of Rima's exotic beauty stems from her being a golden, blue-eyed blonde. While her husband attends a conference, she drives with Kevork back to her home. They eat, then make love—Rima Azen, the Soviet Greek sex object, and Kevork the Armenian Apollo. As he relates, "She made love remarkably well. Her body, stripped of its factory dress, was even whiter, more soft and infinitely more feminine than my experienced eye expected. Her breasts were huge, like Persian melons. Her waist was slender and her thighs were strong. Her navel winked with mischief" (p. 61). Afterwards Rima leads him to a cave safe from her husband should he return earlier than expected. Well supplied, Kevork enjoys many wonderful days there in splendid sensuous isolation.

But the adventure does not end with sex. Rima Azen is more than an Abkhazian official's errant wife; she also serves as the secret custodian of a power handed down from the mythical days of Jason: a huge quantity of dragon's teeth. She makes known her secret to Kevork out of reverence for their love-making. Rima surprises and frightens him when she prepares a furrow and has Kevork plant three of the gnarled brown kernels. Three warriors in antique armor rise from the earth. They threaten Kevork until Rima tosses a pebble among them, after which they fight with and slay each other. A pebble of discord. As they die they scream in ancient Greek. Rima explains, "These are the sons of Cadmus. You have sown the dragon's teeth" (p. 67). And she relates the story of

the old myth and its lingering aftermath. Rima's mother was descended from the original custodians of two large bags of teeth—
"a secret weapon more frightening than any clandestine nuclear
development in Armenia's Sanga Valley" (p. 70). At will Kevork
could raise vast armies and hurl them into battle to serve whatever
cause he fancied. He and Rima make love "sluttishly" again and
again to transcend the death they control.

After seeing Stalin and other Bolshevik bigwigs in Moscow—in
order to "sell" his hoard of dragon's teeth—Kevork returns without success to Rima Azen. He prevails upon her to escape with
him, abandon her husband, and peddle the sacks of teeth elsewhere. They travel by truck and ship to Istanbul, where Kevork
goes to a restaurant run by "a rascally Greek friend" of his, Pandeli
Cobanoglu. A man of parts, Pandeli promises to secure proper
papers for Rima and a caique for Kevork. In order to peddle his
dragon's teeth Kevork leaves her behind in the care of Yusuf, a
shady entrepreneur, and sails for Cyprus on Michali's caique.

Kevork and the Greek captain talk during the trip to Cyprus.
Much of it is tongue-in-cheek on the author's part, as when he has
Michali describe a saint-smuggling expedition when he was fourteen. The Greek refugees in Prokopion, Euboea, wanted back
their Saint John from Cappadocia, which is Armenia. The Greeks
of Cappadocia "are famous for their cleverness," Michali says.
"They can see a flea wink. They can forge a shoe for a gnat. They
are even cleverer than the Armenians" (p. 155). They succeed with
their help in bringing Saint John to Euboea in Greece. Before
reaching Famagusta, they suffer a "wild Meltemi," a storm, that
prompts Michali to offer up a sacrifice. He casts "a pannikin of
wine on the heaving waters" and shouts: "Mermaid, Alexander the
Great still lives and reigns." (p. 158) And, sure enough, the paci-
fied Poseidon quickly stills the waves.

Kevork's cousin Sahag treats him royally in Famagusta, gives
him money, lodging, food, and fine clothes. He also has Kevork
murder Turgot, the Turkish bum who seduced his daughter Araxie and gave her gonorrhea. Despite the risk Kevork fornicates
repeatedly with the luscious Araxie. Pandeli Cobanoglu writes that
Rima Azen is in trouble, that the Turks are after her. Meanwhile
Sahag takes him to the home of Loizides, a Greek friend, where he
meets the English writer Lawrence Durrell and George Seferiadis,
the great poet. Seferiadis sits "in gloomy silence" while Durrell,
gulping both wine and olives, keeps up a learned chatter. It seems

that Loizides is high up in EOKA, the Cypriote terrorist organization then fighting the British "with the aim of joining Cyprus to Greece." It killed "apathetic Greeks" more often than anyone else. Among the EOKA group that Loizides gathers to watch Kevork's demonstration (hoping to sell them the dragon's teeth) is the legendary Dighenis. "Dighenis was a hero of Byzantine poems known to all Greeks of Istanbul and therefore to all Christians, even us, the Armenians. Rumor suggested this new Dighenis was really a certain Colonel Grivas, a right-wing Greek officer who had been born in Cyprus. He was reported to have landed secretly near Tisouri, in the West, a few weeks earlier" (p. 176). After some deliberation, Dighenis refuses to buy Kevork's teeth. The EOKA does not need 500,000 archaic soldiers, speaking an Attic tongue; besides Kevork's price is too high.

A Jewish entrepreneur named Avrahm gets Kevork out of Cyprus on a small plane bound for Israel. Avrahm revises Shakespearean scholarship by claiming that Othello was not a Moor. "The Venetians," he tells Kevork, "would no more send a Negro than a Jew to govern one of their provinces. He was a Greek named Mavro. When he married a local Miss Cordato, he added her name to his. Mavro means black. There is still a Mavrocordato family" (p. 186). Regardless of his color, Othello's "murderous tradition" still thrives on Cyprus. Kevork Sasounian soon leaves the Hellenic world for Israel and Egypt, where he is arrested as an Israeli spy. Freed by Kermit Roosevelt and the American embassy, Kevork has Sulzberger, a newspaperman, take money and a message to a girl named Rima in Istanbul. She is to meet Kevork at an Armenian church in Paris.

To his surprise the Americans as a result of a deal with the Turks have Rima Azen in their custody. Kevork picks up his two sacks of dragon's teeth from his cousin Sahag. In Paris with the teeth, the Armenian salesman demonstrates for NATO generals Norstad and Gruenther. That such world leaders take him seriously makes them ridiculous. In any case, Kevork's next stop is Washington and President Eisenhower and Dulles. The president decides against using the dragon's teeth. The plan looks good on paper, he says, but what we need more of is not soldiers but "motivated machines." On the way back to Paris the cargo plane drops his sacks of dragon's teeth into the Newfoundland Basin—three miles deep. And in Paris Kevork has a new occupation: pimping. Rima Azen is the best of the three girls who run for him on the Rue Godot de

Mauroy. "She earns twice as much as the others." For the Soviet Greek girl it is a bourgeois job.

It would seem from the evidence that American authors like to imagine modern Greeks as great lovers. The writers of Greek descent, like Petrakis and Kazan, naturally tend to exaggerate the sexual powers of their ethnic heroes. In doing so, they enrich and enlarge the myth if not the stereotype of the Greek lover. They know, too, that sexual fantasies of all kinds—the more imaginative (kinky) the better—have enormous appeal for the sex-starved American reader. With the potent professional endorsement of the Happy Hooker, who ought to know, the Greek Lover as an archetype should continue to flourish in our fiction. He takes his rightful place alongside the French Lover, suave and masterful; the Latin Lover, intense and volatile; the Scandinavian Lover, moody and profound; the Black Lover, strong and jocular; and the Jewish Lover, mercurial and brainy, for whom sex is both pleasure and therapy. In short, one finds it difficult to separate fictional truth from fictional nonsense in what authors write about Great Lovers, be they Greek or be they not.

10

THE FICTION IN *ATHENE*

From 1940 until his death in 1967, Demetrios A. Michalaros of Chicago published *Athene*, during all those years the most durable magazine of "Hellenic thought." Within the Greek-American minority, as in other minorities, many journals have come and gone. Each presumably made a contribution to its particular heritage for a time, then disappeared in the limbo of lost enterprise. In the late 1940s *Life of Greece* existed briefly in Boston. Then a magazine for Greek women, *Hellenida*, edited by Iphigenia G. Copadis of Manchester, New Hampshire, was published. For many decades the two leading Greek-language newspapers, the *Atlantis* and the *National Herald*, issued impressive monthly supplements that included Greek matters in their coverage. Greek left-wing and labor elements supported the weekly *Greek-American Tribune* until it died a victim of McCarthyism. What promised to be an exciting and valuable publication, *Greek Heritage*, appeared in the 1960s with Christopher G. Janus as publisher and Kimon Friar as editor. Its five lavishly produced issues may well be collectors' items. Still another quarterly, the *Charioteer*, is also a high-quality publication; it is sponsored by the Parnassus Society of New York, a fact that helps to assure its continuity. Of all these journals and others not mentioned (such as *The Ahepan*, organ of a fraternal organization) only *Athene* concentrated its attention on the Greek-American community—on its traditions that derived from classical Greece, but more immediately on the contributions of its members to all aspects of American life. Special attention was always given to its civic leaders, educators, clergy, scientists, doctors, scholars, writers, poets, and artists. Among these contributions were translations into English of works written by famous Greeks in Greece. Some of the American stories do not use Greek characters, but those that do need to be examined for whatever they can add to the scope of our study.

A large number of aspiring writers responded over the years to the following invitation printed by *Athene* in one of its early issues:

"Wishing to encourage younger writers of Greek descent we print this short story in which the reader will find a rather serious attempt to unfold movie-fashion an original plot. We shall be glad to consider short stories from our younger readers regardless of the background of the plot."[1] The fiction in *Athene* parallels on a limited scale the much broader reflection of the Greek-American experience extant in the novels considered here. In these stories as in the novels the impulse toward the *diaspora* originates in Greece and reaches throughout the world, including particularly the United States. Despite the time of their publication, the relevant stories will be grouped for analysis according to their setting. Those set in Greece will be examined first, then those set in America. They represent in all about a dozen aspects of the Greek ethnic experience.

Peter Gray's eloquent story, "Threnody for Stelios," was reprinted from the *Virginia Quarterly Review* in the January 1942 issue of *Athene*.[2] The author addresses his mourning song to the departed Stelios: "Last May you were married, and now this morning your widow is wailing" (p. 6). With this refrain Gray begins and ends his threnody; in the body of the story he characterizes Stelios and shows what effect his death has on those around him. Stelios had mocked death—a typical habit of the Greek hero from time immemorial. At his wedding feast he had shouted, "We'll die, all of us," believing that he would never die; for the cry was to be sung only at weddings when one was happiest. Yet during the night Stelios has died, and now his bride Matina is weeping and two carpenters are building his coffin. The ritual of his funeral has begun.

Matina must light Stelios's lamp. They cover all the pictures on the wall lest any of their joy escape. Matina hurls the "big gilt mirror" out the window; the bride and bridegroom had stood before it in their wedding clothes. She breaks and scatters all the flower pots, and she burns the wedding garlands. The refrain is repeated, followed by the words "and now the old women are washing your body with wine" (p. 6). His grandmother, whom Stelios once called a miser, slips the gold ring from his finger "to keep safe for Matina." She also breaks off his two gold teeth because she does not believe in "tempting grave robbers." She helps the other women dress the dead Stelios in his wedding clothes—for his marriage with the black earth. The bell tolls for Stelios; and while it does, a procession of mourners arrives at his house to mourn him, to pay their last respects, and to bring him messages to carry with him to the Other World.

The widow Chrysoula, whose husband Lambros died a month before, leads a chorus of mourners at his bier, asking: "Stelio, Stelio, with what dark bride are you going now?" (p. 7). She brings him a red pomegranate and an orange to eat on his way, and more fruit for Lambros. She sends greetings to him through Stelios; she sings a dirge filled with her bitter pain, which is followed by "a tortured frenzy of whooping and screaming in unison." When the wailing subsides, Chrysoula continues with her message: she wants Stelios to tell her husband that she keeps the light burning on his grave. She will read a mass for him in church and "give all the village wheat to eat for your soul." Then she reveals a battle going on with her mother-in-law, who wants back the blankets, the watch, the knife with the gold band, and the gray horse, all of which Chrysoula will return in time. Before the forty days of mourning are over, women are already urging her to remarry; and she wonders out loud, confused, whether or not she should think of Niko, who had been Stelios's good friend.

When Chrysoula is led away, her place at the bier is taken by the mayor, who brings Stelios a large bouquet of pink roses to take to his daughter, now dead for six years. The mayor is still sending her roses and greetings. He tells his departed Nitsa that he gave the church a thousand drachmas for her soul. He and his wife miss her. He sold the olive trees that were her dowry and bought a flock of thirty-two sheep, "and hired lame Aleko to watch them." The mayor informs Nitsa that her cousin Phoula is engaged to marry a lawyer from Patras. "And your mother has given Phoula some of your things for her dowry, some copper pans and bedding. Charon asked for none of your dowry when he took you away" (p. 7).

When the mayor has finished, old Elaine the Drunk pushes her way to the bier, disheveled and ragged as ever. No one can wail better than she, and now she is wailing for Stelios, who sometimes gave her a few drachmas for wine. She will drink wine tonight at his wake. She asks why the church bell rings, why the fruit and the flowers, what the harvest that takes a man? "Who chooses the best man in the village and cuts him down?" (p. 8). Elaine sighs, shudders, regains herself, "steps forward very quietly, somehow beautiful in her tatters, and kisses your lips." Her second kiss is a gift for her own brother. Stelios tastes wine and love on her lips, but she tastes death on his.

The tone of the wailing changes; it grows wilder, stronger. "They are like wolves now, baying their hunger and barking in unison and howling the moon. A mad, animal, night force, yapping and howling around your bier." They howl not only his death, but Death itself. Into this tornado Stratis, the brother of Stelios, cannot enter. He is young, touchy, timid one moment and blustering the next. He loved Stelios jealously. The mourning unbearable, Stratis leaves for the church where the sexton, old Panayotis, is still ringing the bell. He orders Panayotis to go down and leave. Stratis "grabs the clapper and strikes the bell a violent blow, a smashing metal-on-metal dong." When the old man goes, bewildered, Stratis hauls up the ladder, fastens the trap door, then smashes the bell with all his might. "Another shattering blow, and now he can weep, now the tears run" (p. 8).

While the bell tolls and the mourners wail, half-mad Tomas digs Stelios's grave. The two of them once had a savage stone-hurling fight. Now Tomas lifts and dumps rich spadefuls of earth. "He works slowly, his fleshy lips drooping apart and his tongue sticking out." Suddenly he starts to mumble a lullaby with voice hollow and monotonous; the singer rocks a silver cradle for his loved one to sleep, this time the sleep of death. The spade of Tomas strikes through a rotted board. He scratches with his fingers and "collects a little heap of bones." He adds them to the larger pile of bones in the windowless charnel house. "Here are the dry bones of Nitsa the mayor's daughter, the bones of many of your ancestors, of some famous men who fought the Turks, of all the old villagers you've ever heard about, those you've never heard about, all dumped together in this cave darkness." As a boy Stelios and his cousin Loukas had dared to come here and stay long enough to count up to one hundred and fifty. Tomas will get a full day's pay and eat roast lamb and lentils. The threnody by Gray ends with the refrain: "Last May you were married, and now this morning Matina is wailing" (p.9). You mocked at death and now your brother is tolling your knell. You laughed, and now "mad Tomas is digging your grave, Stelio."

"Threnody for Stelios" expresses in taut and evocative language the funeral customs of at least one locality in Greece. These customs of the old country help to explain the Greek immigrant; they are what he has to abandon or modify as he becomes Americanized, a process he cannot escape. Another story in *Athene* by Peter Gray, "The Swallow," is less a reflection of old country mores; nevertheless it is equally eloquent, and almost as moving as it symbolically depicts the loss of another husband.[3] This time it is Aristèna, reputed to be a witch, whose Photis has escaped to the mountains. He has a five hours' headstart on the gendarmes who come to kick open Aristèna's door and ask, "Where is he? Where's your Photis?" (p. 10). From the violence of their arrival and their anger, one can guess at the gravity of the crime committed, yet its specific nature is unrevealed.

Aristèna plays dumb to all their questions and continues to knead the dough while the gendarmes search the house. The captain mentions her reputation as a witch and claims she is not much of one when she admits she has a few remedies for sore throats, fever, and warts. A very superstitious woman, Aristèna feels her loaves will not properly bake with the gendarmes in the house. When they leave, taking a picture of Photis with them, she anathematizes them with a powerful curse: "Forty times the harm that you plan for my Photis!" she whispered, and thrust her open hand at their backs. "Forty times heavier and blacker! Fall in your own snares, rot in your own jails, die of your own bullets, bleed—" (p. 10). Her curse is interrupted by a loud clatter of birds: a flock of starlings are chasing a large brown hawk, who fights back bravely. Aristèna tries to fathom the meaning of the omen; she hopes it is good, but is not sure. "The hawk might even—God forbid—be a sign of Photis running in the mountains and the starlings were the gendarmes after him" (p. 11). She thinks not, since the hawk has flown toward the seashore and not the mountains.

The gendarmes have looked for Photis's boat, but have not found it since it had been sold with its name smeared black. Aristèna shapes the dough into loaves; then she sits staring at the holy ikons and their votive flame, with her thoughts on him in the mountain cave "unharmed and strong, with her eyes tensed on the flame and her thoughts tensed on him until suddenly the flame wrenched apart, tugging at her eyes, and she knew he was indeed safe" (p. 11). Thus before a Christian ikon she employs her powers of magic; in them Aristèna has an intense belief. Before leaving for town with her loaves, she runs her hands over Photis's good suit. Despite what people said, she has not magicked him because one does not "waste potions and charms and spells where they aren't needed." She thinks of magic all the way to the village bakery and back. She looks for signs, but none appear. Just as she reaches her house, she finds a small black bird perched on the handle of the charcoal basket beside the stoop. "She knew at once it was from Photis. It stayed very still, looking at her, and she took it in her hand and held it cupped carefully against her breast. It was an omen about Photis, she knew, a sign for her" (p. 12).

She puts the swallow on the table and lights the lamp. The bird hops off the edge and thuds to the floor; its right wing is injured. "With her finger she stroked his head, glossy like Photis's hair" (p. 12). The bird in its misery and helplessness is very much like Photis, but she is different; she has fought hard against problems with work, intrigue, and magic. Like the stricken swallow, Photis would die unless helped. Aristèna puts the bird in an earthenware pot, safe on the table. For the brew that she plans to make, to cure the hurt wing, she needs some milk which she goes to her neighbor Barbàra to borrow. They talk. Barbàra marvels that Aristèna bothers about a swallow when her Photis is hiding from gendarmes. "Besides," Barbàra says, "a bird that's hurt never gets well; it always dies" (pp. 12–13). But she recognizes that Aristèna can do things that others cannot. "Your mother and grandmother were like that too," she says, indicating that the secrets of home-healing were handed down from generation to generation. With the milk Aristèna mixes brandy and gives the bird to drink, then she applies a compress to the hurt shoulder.

She felt magic very strong in her hands now and in her arms and throat. The bird in his bandage did not move. The magic burned and throbbed in her blood like a fever, stronger than she had ever known it before, and she felt that her hands could pull up trees or strangle gendarmes or massage an invalid to health, but she didn't know what to do with her hands and the force in them. (p. 13)

Over the swallow in the pot marked with sooty crosses Aristèna recites her most powerful charm. She sprinkles salt around the table. To the charm she adds new words: "Sailing ships and floating thistledown and soaring smoke and winking fireflies and whirling confetti and creaking windmills and whizzing bats and flapping flags," plus many other elements, including angels, comets, locusts, winds, echoes, nereids, whirlwinds, skyrockets, and St. Elias. Before going to bed she lights more candles before the ikons and hangs garlic above each door and window. In the morning, however, the swallow is dead. Aristèna's magic has failed. She buries the bird but vehemently tells Barbàra that it flew away, safe and free. As soon as her neighbor leaves, Aristèna departs for town. She goes down to the sea to follow the rocky shore path. "Strong magic often came to her when she went this way and stared intently at the sun on the water. Strong magic would have to come to her. For Photis would be needing something very special that day"

(p. 32). The story ends indeterminately: one does not know whether the special magic will protect Photis from gendarmes or get his soul into heaven when he dies.

The part that Greece and Greeks played in World War II was reflected in *Athene* by means of articles, short stories, poems, and photographs. Many a threnody was undoubtedly sung in real life for the countless thousands who died from combat, bombardment, disease, and famine. The literature of Greek wartime participation is predictably extensive. An early instance is the story "Adventure in April," written by E. L. Elsworth and reprinted from *Chamber's Journal*, an English publication.[4] The time is April 1940, when the Germans have invaded Greece to salvage the defeat suffered by their Italian allies. Old Nico, the café keeper, thinks of his son Costa, who has been gone a year with his regiment, fighting and destroying the "macaronis." He was apprehensive because of the Germans; if they crushed the Greek and British forces, the days of great sorrow would be upon them. At the back of the café, old Maria is cooking a mess of vegetables and oil for themselves and for any travelers who might come their way.

"While Nico sat dreaming, the sound of motor traffic approaching from a great distance crept into his consciousness" (p. 18). As the sound nears he looks up and down the road, but the heavy vehicles are soon crashing through the trees: they belong to the British forces in retreat. They are manned by hot and dusty Englishmen, Australians, and New Zealanders whose first thought is to get away, to leave Greece in boats. Out at sea the British Navy could retrieve them. "With true Greek hospitality," the author writes, "the old couple made the soldiers understand that the café was at their disposal, and that as soon as the food was cooked they should eat what there was" (p. 19). Through one of the soldiers who speaks some Greek, Nico tells them there is only Costa's little boat until Raffina ten kilometres away. As they are speaking a messenger arrives by motorcycle to inform the men that "the Navy will lie up this coast tonight to take off everybody with invasion boats. Keep your men hidden carefully, for the Jerries will surely be over looking for you" (p. 19).

The youth in charge, Sergeant Nicholson, angrily calls back those who went into the sea for a swim. Nico, Maria, and Costa's wife Thomais serve the weary soldiers beans, bread, and retsina wine, "the resin-flavoured wine of Greece." Jack Phillips, the Australian, sits next to Thomais and teases her with talk and gestures;

she understands enough to set her to giggling helplessly. He gives her a thousand drachma note, worth about two pounds, for a kiss, and she shows him her wedding ring. Then Jack, followed by the rest of the soldiers, empties his pocketbook on the table. The pile of money grows before the astonished eyes of their Greek hosts, who need to be convinced the men want them to keep it. After they eat, they take cover along with their hidden vehicles until nightfall. All goes well until the afternoon when a German bomber bombs the abandoned lorries. The terrible blast smashes the café windows. When the plane leaves Thomais helps Sergeant Nicholson with the wounded; she washes the dust off their faces; and she looks everywhere for Jack Phillips, but does not find him.

The afternoon wanes, and night falls. The sergeant sees the signal from the destroyer, and he returns it with his torch. Very quietly the men gather on the beach, the boats loom out of the darkness, ground on the sand, load up, and leave. Before long the destroyer steams silently away. At the café, while trying to sleep, Thomais hears a low, insistent sound, the sound of a man's faint moans. She goes to the doorway and looks out, then sets forth stumbling over the wreckage and rubbish left by the explosion. She hears the cry of "water." At last she finds a man pinned under a twisted mass of iron, and quickly runs back to get Nico and Maria. "Old Nico held the little oil lamp closer to the man's face, and as its feeble rays shone upon the features of Jack Phillips, the girl gave an exclamation, for she thought he was dead" (p. 32). In moments he does die, but not before he is made to understand that his comrades had gotten safely away. "A sweet, faint smile smoothed away the anxiety from his face, and then it faded, and with a fluttering sigh his spirit went out upon the night" (p. 32).

The story "Shambles" by George B. Soorlis dramatizes the effect on an old sea captain of the devastation suffered by his beloved home port of Piraeus.[5] Blind and retired, he lives in New York City with his family, his daughter Domna, her husband, and his grandson Soterakis. Of the fleet that he once owned, Captain Spetseris now has only the *S.S. Soterakis* under repairs in New York Harbor. The rest of his ships have been sunk by the Nazis. He lives happily enough, but often longs to return to Piraeus, when the war ends. A couple of times each month his captain-in-charge, Captain Manolis, brings him progress reports on the *Soterakis* and other news, mainly about the war, that he picks up at the coffeehouses in the Greek colony. Captain Manolis goes to the *Hydra*, built by an old seawolf forty years before, which is "the regular 'home' for many shipowners as well as sea captains in the harbor of New York" (p. 19). There from four young officers of the Greek merchant marine he hears some awful news: they show him a photograph of Piraeus destroyed by Nazi bombs. "It is all a shambles now!" Captain Pantelis, one of the officers, exclaims. "Coal-black shambles! You can hardly recognize any of the streets" (p. 19).

Manolis does not know how to break the news to Captain Spetseris; the dream of his blind old age has been to set foot once more on Piraeus and then die. On a Sunday Captain Manolis visits the Spetseris home in order to tell him. He goes through the back door to consult the captain's wife about the matter. "She was cooking the regular Sunday roast-beef-ala-Piraeus dinner, which the Captain could never part with, despite all the sorrow and hardships" (p. 19). Above the faucet a sugar sack full of *yiaourti* is draining. Evanthe is also preparing cabbage rolls, *lahanodolmades*, called *yiaprakia* by other Greeks. Today she will serve them with yogurt. She and her husband have been devoted to each other a very long time. "There is an old Greek saying that characterizes the impossible when one promises to his beloved: 'The bird's milk for you, my darling,'" which the captain spoke to Evanthe—the best that a lover could provide for his beloved (p. 19). When Captain Manolis enters, she is gloomy; last night's dream portended that something bad would happen to her captain.

In the kitchen Captain Manolis reluctantly tells Evanthe the shocking news about the devastation of Piraeus. Taking out the photo made by an Allied plane, he exclaims: "See, our beloved homes, our proud Piraeus, is all shambles! Coal-black shambles!" The little boy Soterakis overhears them and repeats, "Coal-black shambles" (p.36). Later, at the dinner table, when Captain Manolis tries to withhold the entire story from the old blind seawolf, the boy unexpectedly mentions the picture and demands to hear again about the "coal-black shambles." Immediately the blind Captain Spetseris senses that something is being kept from him. "What picture?" He asks the truth. He has faced many dangers before, like any seaman who is prepared to jump overboard from a sinking ship "with a prayer smiling." Captain Manolis spares him no detail about the fate of Piraeus; but the old man, upon hearing, suffers an apparent heart attack and dies. He has only time enough to kiss his grandson Soterakis goodbye before "his blind eyes closed into everlasting darkness from which there is no return" (p. 48).

Jane Lianos in "The Liberated" dramatizes an incident that occurs shortly after what she calls the Bloody Purge of December 1944.[6] Greece has been liberated from the German occupation only to plunge into a tragic civil war. The narrator is John Avery, an American relief-worker. Out of loneliness in a devastated land he goes to the Crystal Bowl, a restaurant in Athens frequented by other Americans. "I wanted very much to escape from this country, to get away from the blank stares of the starving, the bewildered students fighting for a confused conception of freedom, merciless politicians that reminded you of medieval feudal lords—I wanted to get away from all of it."[7] As he sits in the restaurant, pondering, a tall man in shabby clothes approaches and greets him. It is an old classmate of his from Stanford University, Christo Marinis, class of 1938. Christo had come to America to study and to improve the state of his mind, his stomach, and his country. The two friends talk over coffee. It amazes Avery that Christo dwells upon the pastel colors of Greece during the midst of a political conflict, when people are jailed without reason, inflation controls the economy, and the black market flourishes. "The man talked of patience and pastel coloring" (p. 13).

Several months pass without any further news of Christo Marinis. Then one night in March, Avery is awakened by some quick taps on his door. He is frightened until he learns it is Christo, who desperately needs penicillin and medical care for his little daughter Sophie. To add even more to Christo's agony, his wife had been shot that day by having been caught in crossfire. Without any further word Christo leaves. John Avery begins, at midnight in Athens, a frantic search to find some of the scarce medicine needed for the child's pneumonia. He rushes to the temporary Relief Quarters where his friend Mike refuses to go against orders and turns him down. "It's not only her life, John," Mike says, "but a million others. We can't play favorites" (p. 14). Everywhere he goes, Avery is rejected.

Finally, in despair, he visits the bombed-out house that shelters Christo and his daughter. The door is opened by a young woman in black; other women in long dresses look "like phantoms from another world." He apologizes to Christo for his failure to get the medicine; the bereaved Greek friend thanks him and says it no longer matters. He points to the still body on the bed. All about them now there is weeping. Months earlier Christo Marinis had been optimistic about the future, like a social realist who sees the dream beyond the present nightmare. Now, however, he cries in defeat: "This, all this . . . is the liberation. This is what we have been waiting for—what we fought for. . . . four long bloody years" (p. 41).

"A Messenger" by Theodore P. Vasilopoulos is a war-related tale of the supernatural.[8] The narrator has just returned to America after visiting relatives in Greece. He is impressed among other things by the facile manner in which Europeans tell ghost stories; but he suspects a desire to promote tourism motivates the Scots with their Loch Ness monster, the English with their haunted castles, the Hungarians with their Count Dracula. He finds no such rationale in the case of the Greeks. Two of his six months in Greece, he writes, were spent with relatives in a remote village near Pyrgos. To while away the evening hours there he exchanges ghost stories with them. The elders turn increasingly serious and mute; they cross themselves three times before venturing forth into the darkness. Very superstitious and susceptible, the elders, as the narrator is told, "deplored the sacrilegious attitude of the younger generation" (p. 36).

After a week the narrator decides to meet other kin on the far side of the mountain. He shaves, washes his hair, puts on his best suit, and takes his leave at sundown—to avoid the heat of the day. He has not gone three steps when his cousin brusquely grabs his arm to deter him. She explains her strange action, saying: "You may laugh at our tales of the vrykolakes, or vampires and nereids but we take those things seriously here. I cannot let you go anywhere. The sun has set and you have just washed your hair" (p. 37). When the narrator scoffs at her and the villagers and tries again to say goodbye, they surprise him, tie his hands with ropes, and carry him to a porch chair. Both young and old explain to him the peril from the nereids, the agents of the Evil One with whom they are in constant battle.

> Someone brought incense and candles, and seven centuries went up in smoke. We were back in the Middle Ages. I looked at the young ones, implored them to set me free, but they were silent. They regarded me now, I was certain, as possessed of the devil. They began to wail like something out of the Arabian nights. The candles were lit and placed on the railing on both sides of me. I tried to do something, even laugh, but the

deadly seriousness of the rite of exorcism stifled me. They went about their business with such meticulousness and spite that it put the Spanish Inquisition to shame. (p. 38)

The old crones think him bewitched and prescribe further remedies. One says he must atone for his sins. He screams back at them, calls them "old bastards," and suddenly they disappear. The candles go out, and he sleeps. In the morning he wakes up without his bonds. Still angry at being "kidnapped" by a "mob," he goes off without breakfast to file a complaint at the police station in Pyrgos. The chief listens politely to his story but does nothing. To appease the narrator's anger the chief relates what had happened to him. During the war he was taken as a prisoner and held in the enemy's country. His fellow villagers from the same battalion, upon returning, informed his parents that he was missing in action. The girl to whom he was engaged gave up hope and married another. His parents, however, kept praying for his safe return. "My parents told me that John, a friend of mine from another village, had come to them months later, when my letters had stopped coming, on a dashing white horse, and told them not to despair; that I lived, a prisoner in a foreign country" (p. 39). John, in other words, had been a messenger bearing the good news. Despite the narrator's impatience, the chief of police continues. Last year he went to John's village to pay his respects to John and his kin. On the way he was passed by John on his dashing white horse. He shouted: "Welcome. I shall see you later." Before vanishing in the dusk he added: "Wait for me." At the village he was treated royally by his friend's parents. When he waited all day for John to appear, he told his hosts to give John his regards, that he had to return that night. At his words the old couple burst into tears. "John, my only son," the old man said, "died in the very first battle in Albania, carrying messages for the high command" (p. 39). As a ghostly messenger now, he still carries messages for a High Command— presumably God.

Two stories dealing with educational subjects are "The Scholarship" and "Papa and the Turkish Language." The first was written by Peter Bien, the well-known translator of Nikos Kazantzakis and student of that great author's linguistic achievement. The second, by F. P. Zachariou, diverges in tone from the stories previously noted—nothing dreadful happens. In Bien's fiction a young Greek lad in an agricultural school fails to win a highly coveted scholarship to America.[9] The story opens with Basilis Dimitriathes, the student in question, brushing down his favorite colt Kokinaki in the barn. He tells his bad news to Doc Simos, the American-trained veterinarian, who visits the barn every morning before breakfast. He checks on the students. The doctor, dressed in a checked sports jacket, has little sympathy for Basilis's catastrophe. Others are also refused, he says; then he criticizes the distraught boy for not brushing the colt properly. At home Doc Simos tells his wife in English that if a five-thousand dollar scholarship waited in America "for every Greek village hick who wants one," then who would be left to work the farms? He is a big man now who has forgotten his own peasant origins.

As he labors Basilis recalls how Doc Simos had easily cured the colt Kokinaki of rickets with vitamin D. It was the doctor himself who had recommended him for the scholarship. Basilis has a reverie about his being a veterinarian, too, and being called upon to cure a child with rickets. The noise of a large American threshing machine wrecks his daydream, and he is alert once more to his wondrous surroundings: the beautiful barn, the school, the fat chickens, the prize imported bull that was stronger "than the Cretan bull which Herakles brought to King Euryptheas," and, above all, the agricultural machinery that would someday revolutionize farming in Greece (p. 22). Basilis is skeptical of any quick or profound changes in his own village, with its poverty, its antique methods, and natural disasters—as when the hail ruined his father's peach crop and the bank refused him a loan because of his old debts. Basilis thinks of Thanae, the girl he left behind in Sithirokastron. He thinks of his lazy brothers sitting in the café and playing *tavli*.

The lost scholarship follows another disaster. When Thanae finished school in the village she went to Saloniki to work in a doctor's office. "One letter came at the beginning saying how nice the doctor treated her: how she had beautiful new dresses, new shoes; how she went to the cinema and sometimes even to a restaurant to eat. . . . Then nothing until six months later" (p. 23). At that time Thanae informs Basilis that, though she still loves him, she will marry the doctor because he is very rich and she will never have to work again. She hopes for his sake that he can go to America. With both Thanae and the scholarship denied him, Basilis feels destroyed.

Together with the other students he answers the cook's bell and goes to the main building for lunch. He almost weeps from wondering why such malevolence pursues him—what has he done? The school director calls for silence and announces the six scholarship winners. They stand, receive the applause. The director wishes both winners and losers good luck, and hopes the latter will understand that "even in America scholarship funds are always limited." But Basilis cannot understand. He sees himself growing old in the parched fields of his village. He goes outside and walks and walks; and as he does the poison slowly drains out of him, drop by drop, "as though he were leaving a trail of black heavy oil behind" (p. 44). Then the desire to talk with someone rises up in him strongly—to someone who would understand. Not to his mother, not to Thanae, not to Doc Simos, not to the director. "Suddenly Basilis remembered. He got up, tossing away the rocks he held in his hands, and walked—then ran—towards the barn" (p. 44). There, of course, with his spirits revived, he will talk to Kokinaki, the fine young colt.

In "Papa and the Turkish Language" F. P. Zachariou describes a stubborn Greek boy who refuses, at first, to learn how to read and write Turkish because he already speaks it.[10] The setting is Kouvouklion, at a time when all its people are "Turkish subjects clinging tenaciously to their Greek roots" (p. 10). The stubborn boy is the narrator's father, Papa, who misses school from August till November when the olives ripen. The teacher makes no allowances for late arrivals like Papa; the other boys have already finished the Turkish primer. To deceive the teacher, Papa gets help from a fellow student, a translated passage; but the teacher finds out and slaps him. That night Papa tears his grammar in two, hides it in the hay, and announces he has lost it. But his father compels him to buy another book. This time Papa "wrote tiny Greek characters under the Turkish letters and again he read well" (p. 10).

The suspicious teacher takes Papa's book and shakes it, but nothing falls out. Because of his weak eyesight he cannot see the tiny Greek letters, but he borrows a grammar from another pupil and asks Papa (Petro) to read again. When he fails, he gets another sharp slap; and that night Papa throws the new book into the fire. "My grandfather," Zachariou writes, "was a practical man and did not relish the idea of enriching any publisher of Turkish textbooks" (p. 10). Thus whenever the others get up for the Turkish lesson Papa sits alone doing something else. This standoff lasts for three winters until a new teacher arrives, one who is studying to be a priest. He takes Papa aside and asks, "How is it that you, one of my best students, do not read Turkish?" (p. 10).

Papa's stock answer is that he is Greek, so he does not need Turkish. The new teacher explains the value of an education. He gives Papa a beginner's book and promises to help him acquire the alphabet and grammar. He also recites the famous little rhyme about the moon shining pupils their way to school—when learning was forbidden them by their oppressors. "That was a time when Greek children went to school in fear, at night studying in hidden cellars" (p. 34). At supper Papa announces his decision to learn Turkish. His father, without showing surprise, gives him the money for the new book. When the teacher refuses the money, Papa's father tells him to keep it. Beaming as he pockets the coins, the boy says, "I decide to learn Turkish and already I am rich" (p. 34)

Humor and fantasy feature two works by John Belasco, who served for many years as the New York correspondent for *Athene*. "Robbery at the Acropolis" deals briefly with the Athens chief of police Zabanis and with Captain Tsabogas, charged by His Majesty himself, the king, to find out who has robbed the Hollywood actor John Gilmore of his wallet containing about a thousand dollars.[11] The theft allegedly has occurred at the Acropolis, Athens' biggest tourist attraction. A successful robbery there is an affront to the dignity and reputation of all Greece. To redeem their good name the authorities made a strenuous effort to find the thief and recover the stolen money. Captain Tsabogas and his aides are suspicious of John Gilmore's account since some of the details are not probable. To his sweetheart Irene Williams, daughter of the American ambassador, Gilmore tells the truth—that he was the victim of a pickpocket in a tavern. He does not want the world to laugh at him for having been so easily duped. Instead he embroiders the truth by saying he was held up at the Acropolis, near the cell that once imprisoned Socrates; and when the police confront him with evidence to the contrary, he compounds the first lie with another—that the holdup was a hoax to get material for a film. "I did it just to see with what dispatch and skill you here in Greece went about handling criminals, and I must say I am pleased."[12] The Greek authorities are furious with the American for having fooled them and put them through such strenuous effort. During his trial, however, a strange turn of events tantamount to a deus ex machina occurs to settle the crisis on a happy note. The trial is held in English as a very special occasion at the Acropolis, as in the case of Socrates. A surprise witness arrives and demands to testify; he is a cab driver who gives his name as Nick Pappachristophoropoulos. That afternoon he had found John Gilmore's wallet in the back seat of his cab, honestly lost there by the actor. The judge closes the case with a sentence of mercy; he also states that Greece is deeply indebted to the United States for its many benefactors, and that such a renowned artist as Gilmore honors Greece with his presence. At the suggestion of Captain Tsabogas, the judge marries Gilmore and Irene Williams on the spot. After the ceremony Gilmore is frightened by a roar of guns and thinks a revolution has begun. Irene reassures him, "It's a Greek custom in celebrating weddings. The police department is sanctioning our wedding, thanks to Captain Tsabogas."[13]

In John Belasco's science fiction "Atlas Takes Over" an old man falls asleep during a planetarium show and dreams the entire action.[14] In his reverie a streak of light from Venus shatters a neighboring star; as a result of the celestial disturbance Venus herself moves to a new fixed position relatively close to Earth. The catastrophe has created a serious problem for Earth—a severe drought that calls for imminent evacuation. To plan for the eventuality a mission is sent to Venus "led by professionals who speak the ancient Greek language, because first reports indicated the existence of a culture similar to that of ancient Greece, on planet Venus."[15] The leader of the space mission, Rex Evans, reports back before landing that they can see a beautiful city with a huge stadium "full of people attending some sort of Olympic games." When the spacecraft lands Rex radios Earth again that everything on Venus has a Greek background. He and his crew meet Venusians who look Greek but speak English. "My name is Alexander Armodian, owner of this plantation," one of the Venusians says. When asked about the mystery of the Greek culture, he explains that two centuries before an American space ship had visited Venus, then in a primitive state, and was too damaged to return. Since the Venusians were very backward, the Americans undertook to modernize their society. "Professor Thompson being an admirer of the immortal Aristotle and other great thinkers had selected Greek culture and teachings to bring up the Venusian world under the English language which he so well mastered."[16] During the rest of the story the Earthians visit the City of Olympia where they are welcomed, meet many Venusians, and ask many questions about their way of life. They find Venus based on a mixture of classical myth and reality. Atlas belongs to the Triangle Tower and rules the planet together with Aristotle and a Goddess. At the end the old man wakes, shaken by his dream.

More realistic and down-to-earth is the true story "From Turkish Slave to American Chef" by Nicklas Frankel, as told to M. R. McLaren.[17] The narrative, which reflects an early instance of diaspora, begins in 1889 on the island of Skyros, Greece. The miller warns his wife Katerini to keep a close eye on their infant boy lest some harm come to him. While her husband and two older sons leave for work, Father Alexandros arrives to chat with Katerini and her excited neighbors. The priest's visit distracts her long enough to allow her infant to crawl off by himself to the beach where he is last seen by playing children. A week's frantic search fails to locate him. "Perhaps some pirates stole him," Katerini wails. "One day he will return."[18] Others despair and think the boy was drowned or eaten by a shark. The long search ends.

The pirate who steals him, Captain Mustafa Pasha, is a huge Turk with a pegleg. He kidnaps the boy because his marriage of two years has brought him no son. "So, before the moon changed, the Greek miller's child became a member of his household on a Turkish date grove. They called him Ali" (p. 21). He is placed in the care of Anita, a slave, who is ordered to bring him up as the captain's son. "Never take him outside the walls." Anita, who is sixteen, brings him to her own room in the attic of Mustafa's *seray* (seraglio). There they listen together "to storks clacking their bills on the roof, a sign of good luck; and here she told him folktales and taught him how to do the chores of a houseboy" (p. 21). Years pass.

When Ali is seven, kind-hearted Anita wants him to have a memory of Smyrna such as hers acquired when old Fatima took her there as a child. In Smyrna, two kilometres away, Ali is fascinated by the *pazars* (merchants) with their big supplies of colorful cloth, dressed lambs, huge hampers of fruit, the smell of strong coffee. He asks many questions about the mosque, the school, and so on. Anita warns him never to tell Baba, his pirate "father," about their forbidden journey. His appetite for learning whetted, Ali manages to sneak out to Smyrna again; he tries to attend school with the other boys, but the *hoca* (teacher) sends him home to bathe, wear clean clothes, and fetch the needed money.

Led into the big house by the guard, Ali is so eager to attend school that he forgets the rule never to enter Baba's room, the one in which he received those awful looking men, and no one else. Many of these big men lacked an arm or leg; some had a patch over one eye. Most of them had ugly scars all over their faces and Ali trembled just to think of them. No women ever entered that room; not even Anita was allowed to wield her feather duster there. (p. 22)

When the fierce pirate asks "Why did you come?" Ali blurts out that he needs clothes and money for school; and when asked how he has learned about school and other boys, Ali informs on poor Anita. Furious about having been disobeyed, Mustafa Pasha punishes Anita by having her spend the cold rainy night roped to an olive tree. Ali himself is forever banished from the comfortable big house, and he must live with the adult slaves in their mud huts. Later that night, when the slaves are asleep and the moon is out, Ali with a bread knife frees Anita, whose drenched long black hair and wet clothes cling to her like skin. Her teeth chatter. She thanks him and sneaks back to the house. Ali, pleased with his deed, returns to the slave quarters.

Worried about Anita, Ali now works in the date orchard holding up ladders for the pickers. Three days later he hears the cook tell Abdul, another slave, "Anita is dying." The same Abdul seeks out Ali to ask him what country he comes from; and Ali, in his innocence, replies that he is from Baba's *seray*, and that his father lets him work to earn enough money for school. Upon hearing this, the old slave says, "You're not the master's son. He stole you, just like the rest of us. We never get paid for anything" (p. 23). Ali insists that he is because Anita has so informed him. Abdul points out the difference in color between Ali and his supposed father. "The master is a dark Assyrian. You are all Aryan. Right here in Turkey is where Europe and Asia have met for years. Years ago it was the home of the Hittites, the first men to use iron weapons. Right here, too, are the best pirate hide-outs in the world." Abdul tells Ali he remembers the day Mustafa Pasha brought him. "You were just learning to walk." More than ever Ali must see Anita before she dies, to have her confirm or deny what Abdul has said. At night he steals into the attic where the dying girl confirms Abdul's statement. "He stole me from Spain when I was six," Anita says. "Fatima raised me to be his chamber-maid. She told me, as I am telling you, on her deathbed" (p. 23).

For the next six years Ali works as a slave in the date orchard; he learns about date culture, graduates to ladder climber, and finds he loves to cook. As a matter of fact the cook hopes that Ali will some day replace him in the kitchen. Ali longs to visit the distant lands which the slaves have mentioned as their homes—Spain, Portugal, Greece. One day when a sudden storm disperses the date-pickers, Ali notices the ladders left among the trees. That night in the rain he uses one of them to negotiate the wall and make his escape. He runs until he drops from exhaustion; when he awakes, he can see the ocean on the horizon. Ali waits for night to renew his flight, runs for hours, reaches the ocean, and sleeps on a bed of seaweeds. The seaweed that he eats makes him sick. For hours he suffers a severe stomach ache, until he notices the sails of an approaching ship. Ali prays to Allah that they see him. They do. Before long, faint and ill, he is brought on board.

A huge man addresses Ali in Turkish: "Welcome aboard the Dolphin."[19] The crew, however, speak a tongue unknown to him. Strangely, too, the men carry guns and knives under their wide belts. Ali gorges himself on boiled rice, bananas, ripe olives, and bread, then sleeps for two days and nights. Upon awakening, he discovers that his rescuers are also pirates. Ironically, as one of the crew says, he has "jumped from Pompeii into Vesuvius itself," from one volcano into another. The *Dolphin* has a crew of ten men. In a few days, during the assault on a ship loaded with spices, the captain orders Ali to his bunk, telling him he will have a job to do soon when the pirates raid the land. Ali hopes he will not be expected to kill. As it happens, the captain gives him a gun which he must shoot as a signal if anyone approaches the *Dolphin* when the pirates are gone. That night Ali seizes his golden opportunity to escape for good. He cuts the *Dolphin* loose so that it floats out to sea. He reaches shore in a small boat, while a battle rages beyond him. He runs over rocks until he finds a stone house where the strangers, aroused by the pirates' raid, seclude Ali in a dark cave on a mountainside. Behind him the "heavy iron doors clanked shut" (p. 47).

Some of the people want him shot as a pirate; but others, who note he came unarmed, demur. An elder befriends him and brings bread, cheese, and water. Ali wishes he could understand their language. On the third day, much to his joy, a man arrives who speaks to Ali in perfect Turkish. Through him Ali gives a long recital of his life up to his latest escape. Later that day he is taken before the mayor in a crowded council room. Ali hears strange talk filled with unusual animation. A messenger arrives with a large book. The mayor reads from it solemnly. "Through a back door, an old woman came running, screaming something which sounded like so much gibberish. She ran up to Ali, tore his *aba* from his shoulder, pointed eloquently to the huge mole on his shoulder and showered him with kisses" (p. 47). She keeps repeating, between her tears and laughter, "Nikolas! Nikolas!" The interpreter explains the situation to Ali,—that the elder, Father Alexandros, had demanded the mayor send for the Missing Person File, because a little boy had disappeared at about the time when Ali was a baby. The woman, his *metera*, recognizes her long lost son by the telltale mole. "And your captor is your father," the interpreter's eyes glistened. "These two younger ones are your brothers. Your real name is Nikolas Frankoules" (p. 48). Ali's return to his original home occurs in 1906. Thereafter, until 1915, he learns how to be a Greek, as earlier he had learned how to be a Turk.

By the latter date, however, both of his older brothers, Socrates and Paulos, have migrated to America. "Come to America," they write to Nikolas-Ali. There is no piracy there to require a cave for a fortress, and President Wilson is doing his best to make the world safe for democracy. Thus it happens that Nikolas Frankoules sets sail, crosses the United States, and goes first to San Francisco. He washes dishes in a hotel, enrolls in night school, and makes friends with the chef.

> In 1922, the erstwhile slave married an American girl who took great pride in her husband's steady promotion from vegetable man through fry cook, grill and broiler man, second cook. By now they were living in Chicago and liked the windy city very much. Here their son and daughter were born; here he became a naturalized citizen and simplified the spelling of his name. Here, too, one day he was promoted to The Chef of a small hotel. (p. 48)

As a retired old man reflecting upon his success, Nikolas Frankel, the author, advises all not to complain about high taxes. "God bless America!"

A relatively short anecdote written by Jewel Drinkamer, "The Heart's Tongue," serves to illustrate still another aspect of immigrant life—the loneliness of being unable to communicate, and the joy of finding a fellow countryman.[20] Nicholas Lavrakas arrives at Ellis Island knowing only one person here, a bachelor cousin who lives in a Massachusetts mill town. The newcomer makes his way there by showing his cousin's address on a piece of paper. His cousin gets Nick a job at the mill. The foreman takes him by elevator to the fourth floor, where Nick has to clean tubes and spindles. He knows no English, only *yes* and *no*. He also knows nothing about work hours, elevators, or drinking fountains. "At three o'clock the foreman remembered him. He came up and showed Nick a water fountain in the hall outside the room, took him to the washroom, and offered him a piece of sandwich when he found that Nick had brought no lunch."[21] That night he and George buy bread and sausage for the next day. Before falling asleep he thinks of the olive groves on his island, of the blue sky, and of the dancing waters "on which the tiny fishing boats rocked."

Nick returns to work, and things improve slightly. He finds new ways to clean the tubes, he sees a tree through the "opaque panes of glass," he hears sparrows, and finds at noon that George had added olives to his bread and sausage. The olives make him homesick and lonely. On the third day a second man arrives to join Nick at work. "Nick could not explain it, but somehow the presence of the second man he could not speak to made him even more lonely."[22] They eat lunch in silence. Outside a storm thunders; on this dark day Nick feels desolate. The man indicates he is thirsty, so Nick takes pity on him and leads him out to the drinking fountain. As the man nears the fountain, Nick says in Greek, "Drink, you poor devil." The other man stops in amazement, a great joy breaks over his face. "Fellow countryman," he says, also in Greek; and they "fell on each other's neck and wept."

The dropping of the atomic bomb on Japan at the end of World War II revived interest in a super weapon of the past: Greek fire, the incendiary chemical used very effectively by the Byzantines against enemy ships. C. J. Lampos in his conversation piece, "The Atomic Bomb and Greek Fire," has a Greek character named Christopher Demetrios Papadopoulos who lectures the narrator on "how another great people dealt with a weapon [Greek fire] which in its day was as formidable and decisive" as the atomic bomb.[23] The two men agree that the "colossal discovery" would pose no peril to mankind if international rivalries and hatreds were to be outlawed. Papadopoulos begins his lecture on how Greek fire helped to defend Byzantium and Western Europe from the Saracen invaders. The rest of the story is not fiction but historical writing broken up by brief bits of dialogue. Christopher Demetrios Papadopoulos outlines the conflict between Byzantium and the Saracens, or Arabs, from 634 until 960, very sketchily, but nevertheless highlighting a number of significant naval battles in which Greek fire made the difference. One such battle was the destruction of the Saracen armada in 677—the first Moslem defeat. Another was the routing of a huge Saracen armada "of perhaps 1,800 ships and 180,000 men" that menaced Constantinople in August 717. And so on. Papadopoulos compares the Byzantine empire and the United States on the basis of the secret weapons owned by both. The former was surrounded by barbaric and warlike peoples bent upon its destruction, whereas the United States is the "liberator of mankind" and can use her might for permanent peace. When the narrator asks for more definite ideas, Christopher Demetrios Papadopoulos snaps with comic indignation: "Say, what do you want for three cigarettes?"[24]

The repetition of unusually long Greek names is an obvious effort at levity in several stories. For that reason John Belasco in "Robbery at the Acropolis" gives to the cab driver who finds the American actor's wallet the name of Nick Papachristophoropoulos. In quite a number of novels examined here the Greek character's real name is mentioned once or twice; then it is quickly anglicized, and the original name does not appear again. Paul Nord in "Napoleon Kalmer" has a good deal of fun with another long Greek name. A poet and dramatist, Nord is well known in Greece under the name of Nikos Laides. Of his several stories in *Athene*, "Napoleon Kalmer" is the most ethnic and the most humorous.[25] As in many of his poems, the language of his fiction is clever, witty, and sophisticated, based on considerable erudition.

The narrator, Jimmy Vlachos, is sitting and ruminating at his habitual location—in the Chase Cafeteria on Seventh Avenue, at a spot where he can see much of 42nd Street and the *Time* flashing newstape. As a recent arrival he thinks of how every immigrant since Columbus has had to discover America for himself. This task is made easier for Greeks. "Every other Greek a Greek meets proves quite willing and prompt to put his own experience, acquired the hard way, at the disposal of his compatriot. He does that with a generosity and a 'bonne grace' which is quite characteristic of the race, and what is more, no lucrative issue is involved" (p. 14). To the narrator's table for two comes a man who, after beginning to consume his coffee and Danish pastry, opens up the Greek daily *Atlantis* and pretends to read. Actually he is spying on and sizing up the narrator, who immediately spots him for a Greek. The stranger introduces himself as Archimedes Kalome-

ros, Archie Kalmer for short; but his real last name is Kalomero-
poulos, or Kalomerakis. Since Kalomeros means Bonaparte in Italian, Archie asks Vlachos had he not heard that "the great
Napoleon was a descendant of the Kalomeroses of Magne, in Lak-
edaimon of Peloponnesus, Greece, who had fled the Turks and
had settled down in Corsica? Have you never read the poem by
Alexander Soutsos, who says so? Or don't you know either that
Christopher Columbus was a Greek, and his name was Colombot-
sos, before he discovered America and had his name curtailed?"
(p. 14). To Archie all big men in America are Greeks; he mentions
Arturo Toscanini, George Raft, and Zachary Scott.

For a while longer they speak in Greek. It turns out that although Archie Kalmer washes dishes for a living, he is also a part-
time actor in the Greek-American theater. He feels highly qualified to play a Greek on the American stage, for his broken English
is very much like the phony Greek-accented English of George Givot, the professional entertainer who calls himself The Greek Ambassador. Archie complains, "That Chorch Gavotte ees an American acter who'z a shame for Griks. He ridiculz Griks. While we real
Grik acters starve and dish washes, he makes money with Grik lan-
guich" (p. 15). Next time he sees George Givot playing a theater,
Archie Kalmer will gather a bunch of "Griks" and picket him. He
brags that he has been an extra in various films. "I plaid with Dog-
lass Fairbanks and Merry Bickforth and Norma Searer and with
the Grik acter Gary Kouperos" (p. 16). What most surprises Jimmy
Vlachos is the boast by Archie that he has played Napoleon on the
stage; it turns out that Archie struck a pose in costume and stood
immobile for as long as fifteen minutes "with one of my foots opon
the rock of Staint Elena and with the other foots opon the Atlantic
ocean" (p. 16). Another Greek dishwasher, Karabournazos, challenges Archie's performance, claiming he can play a better Napoleon.

The result is a "Napoleon contest" with both "Grik acters" trying
to outlast each other in striking their immobile stance. Archie
claims that the crowd clapped longer for him than for Karabournazos. A dirty trick by his opponent shows up; the telescope for
Archie to hold is made of iron, that of Karabournazos is cardboard. In a ruckus that ensues Archie mistakenly hits Mrs. Bonaparte with the telescope. She spends two weeks in the hospital,
Karabournazos goes to jail, but Archie the winner goes free. At the
end of the very one-sided conversation, Archie Kalmer sells Jimmy

Vlachos, for the cut rate of fifty cents, a ticket for tomorrow night's Greek theater.

The anglicizing of a difficult Greek name is not the theme of N. Nicolai's ". . . And a Time to Love!"[26] Such a change does occur, however, and it apparently eases the way up the military service for the hero, Alexander Panagiotopoulos. "After the legal change of his unspeakable Greek name, he went to West Point as Alexander Blake" (p. 28). When the story opens, in September of 1948, Major Blake, aged thirty-seven, is a provost marshall stationed with the 10th Constabulary Regiment at Stuttgart, Germany. A sudden ear infection disables him briefly, but long enough for the major to reminisce in a flashback about his earlier years. He recalls his boyhood in Fairmont, West Virginia, where his father owned an import business. "In 1918 his happiness came to a sudden and unexpected end. Within one week the Spanish Influenza took its toll and the only survivors of the tragedy that cost the lives of Nicholas Panagiotopoulos, his two sons and his oldest daughter, were young Alexander, his sister Irene, and his grief-stricken mother." (p. 28). After settling her afairs in Fairmont, she moved the remnants of her family to Washington, D.C., where she had relatives. Alex grew up tall and handsome. He enjoyed the training at West Point, where he met a cadet named Bruce Fairbanks; at his home in Wake Forest he in turn met Cynthia Hughes, with whom he fell in love. A society girl, she had no concept of drab Army life; nor did her mother approve the match. Cynthia returned his ring and married someone else.

Now in Germany, Major Alex Blake is enjoying a fourteen-day furlough that has brought him to the Hotel Weinbauer in the shadow of the Bavarian Alps. He eats alone in the dining room where he, an American, is stared at by the other customers. "That night around four he woke up with a crushing earache which rapidly reduced him to a shivering pain-racked ghost of himself. He groaned; his left ear throbbed unbearably and a huge lump began to appear. He felt like some evil force had deliberately pressed an object the size of a tennis ball into his inner ear" (p. 27). An hour later he buzzes for the landlady, who telephones for a doctor to come from the neighboring town of Hohenschwangau. It turns out that the doctor is Veronika Bader, a lovely young woman who examines him and finds an abscess. She pours warm oil into his ear, but tells him to expect discomfort until it opens. In the afternoon, after he sleeps, Dr. Bader returns with penicillin and an old-fashioned infrared lamp. Before he falls asleep again, he says, "You are the prettiest doctor I've ever seen and I hope to see more of you!" (p. 28).

The next morning Major Blake's ear has cleared. He rises, has breakfast, and gets from the landlady the address of Veronika Bader. He drives there in his big car; looking up, he admires the snow-white mountains and the fairy-like castle, Neuschwanstein, "built by the mad King Ludwig II of Bavaria." The major finds the address of the lovely Dr. Veronika and rings her bell. Her father lets him in. When Veronika arrives with her mother, she is surprised to see her patient so hale and hearty. After a pleasant Kaffeeklatch, Alex convinces her to guide him to the castle of Neuschwanstein. They join a group making the climb; afterwards, on the descent from the impressive structure, they hold hands. The rest of the day Alex and Veronika drive around the countryside. He takes her to Oberammergau where they dine at the officers' club. An unpleasant moment occurs there when a drunken friend, Captain Moore, insults Veronika. "A baby doctor, eh, anyone here for having babies?" Alex and Veronika escape their friends, they dance, and drive back to her town. "In the shadow of her door they turned toward each other and, with their arms entwined, kissed in a wordless, breathless embrace" (p. 31). Before she falls asleep she ponders her future: whether to marry the stranger, Major Blake, or to do what everyone in Munich expects, marry Karl Reinhardt.

The next day when Alex calls, Veronika asks him to help with the haying. They joke about it, he saying that he is "a mountain boy from West Virginia at heart" (p. 31). A pastoral idyll follows: they work, they lunch, they walk in a cloister of trees, they kiss again. Alex declares his love for her. After ten days of dreamlike happiness, he receives an unexpected note from Veronika, who has decided to return to the refuge of her Munich practice. "Dear Alex, you'll forgive me if I go away without saying goodbye to you. Please try to understand and believe me it will be better this way. Veronika" (p. 32). Undaunted, Alex drives to Munich where he finds her house with the brass sign on the door reading "Dr. Veronika Bader, Kinderarztin." Inside, he finds her with a man she falsely claims is her fiancé, Dr. Karl Reinhardt. He, a most honorable man, realizes that she loves the tall American and, although he has loved her for years, bows gracefully out of her life, goes home, and gets drunk. Alex drives back to Stuttgart in deep gloom. The next morning, Sunday, Dr. Reinhardt scolds Veronika for not having gone after Major Blake, the man she loves. With great understanding he gives her the keys to his car. It is now her turn to seek out the object of desire; as she looks at herself in the mirror she panics at the chance he may reject her. "Forgive me, Alex, for having been so stupid; I was afraid to fall in love—it came so quickly!" (p. 60). She reaches Stuttgart in the little BMV. At the huge army post a corporal calls up Major Blake. Someone at the gate, he says, wants to know if he has any use for repentant pediatricians. The major replies that he will be there in a minute. Love has conquered once more.

The ethnic element in N. Nicolai's story is slight. The author mentions some Greek foods,—"dolmades, lamb shishkebab, baklava, corrabiedies"—during the flashback when Major Blake is still Alexander Panagiotopoulos and living in West Virginia. The ethnic content is much more prevalent, however, in "Shortcut to Riverdale," by Alexander Karanikas, and in two stories by Theano Papazoglou-Margaris translated for *Athene* magazine. The story by Karanikas represents a chapter from a novel entitled *Peter Saw the Wind*.[27] The boy protagonist, about fourteen, is Peter Alepogiannis, whose last name has been shortened to Alepos. In the small New Hampshire village of Joppa the father, Lukas, works in a bobbin shop situated on the Piscataquog River. Here the boy learns about bigotry and xenophobia; and in the novel, when a Turkish friend of his is persecuted by the Ku Klux Klan and eventually killed, Peter goes on a personal rampage of revenge that ends with his exposure and sentence to a year in reform school. "Shortcut to Riverdale" involves a confrontation between father and son over the illegal home brewing of *ouzo*. This theme of confrontation is quite common in American literature as a whole; among Greek-American writers it has varying applications, many of them deriving from Greek background.

The story begins with a paean of praise for the Indian-named river that runs behind the Alepos house, the Piscataquog. Peter loves the river for its seasonal changes, its wildlife, its floods, and the swimming hole which the boys frequent all summer. On the way home from a swim with his brother Jimmy and two American friends, Peter finds what he thinks is a good mushroom and tosses it into the pigpen. Father Alepos angrily sends Peter into the mucky pen to retrieve the poisonous toadstool before the pig can eat it. The two sons highly respect their father who has told them many stories of his youth in Macedonia—"about the haunted crags of Mt. Olympus, where voices spoke from the clouds and shadows; about the cataracts that seemed from afar like Persian spears; and about the wolves that roved in packs, as ready to kill a man as eat his lambs" (p. 109). For eleven years he lived among the *klepthes* and the sheep and the Turks. There he met Christina, the "goddess of Mt. Olympus," whom he married and then left because he listened to a factory agent touting jobs in the shoe factories of Lowell and Manchester. The voices said, "Go to America, go to America."

That evening Uncle Sotiri arrives from Manchester feeling sad about conditions in his textile mill—the long hours, low wages, and hostility from other workers. Peter and Jimmy are suspicious when they overhear Father Alepos mention a "new business." Never before has he kept anything from them. Jimmy goes fishing, but Peter climbs to the top of a nearby pine from which he spies on his own parents. Before long he sees Chahnah, the Turkish barber, drive into the yard in his Model T bringing two boxes that turn out to be raisins. When it grows darker Peter descends from the tree and peers in through the kitchen window. His worse suspicions are confirmed: the three men have rigged up a makeshift still; they are to make *ouzo*.

Shocked by his father's criminality—the year is 1929, with Prohibition in effect—Peter runs through the night to find and tell the bad news to his brother. Jimmy is older and more realistic; he does not romanticize the notion of being a "good American," since he can see that the "richest guys are the bootleggers" (p. 112). Unconvinced, Peter declares he will stop his father, but is warned to keep his mouth shut. In a while their uncle leaves. The confrontation between Peter and Father Alepos erupts immediately when Peter wishes to go through the kitchen to the bathroom. His father tells him to go outside, to the pines, and Peter asks, "Why're we makin' *ouzo?*" The secret out, Father Alepos cries, "You've been spying. See what happens in America, Christina, a father can't trust his own sons!" (p. 114). A bitter argument ensues during which Peter defiantly calls his father a gangster. He roars "Out of my sight!" and swings his fist toward his son's head. There follows an explosion and sudden darkness; he has shattered the hanging light bulb. Though untouched, Peter feels soundly beaten, and he weeps before his parents. "Where are you, Christina?" Father Alepos calls to his wife. "Bring us a candle" (p. 114).

More grim in tone and equally ethnic in its content is the story "Theia Giannitsa" by Theano Papazoglou-Margaris.[28] That and another of her stories, "The Nymphs of Lake Michigan," were translated into English from her book *The Chronicle of Halsted Street*, which has been examined more fully in an earlier chapter. The author has produced dozens of stories on many facets of the Greek-American experience. In "Theia Giannitsa" the protagonist has a dollar alarm clock whose "terrible *driing*" sounds every morning at six o'clock. Another of the elderly Greek woman's eccentricities is the way in which she finds a room to rent. The narrator describes how Theia Giannitsa went from door to door looking for a "Greek house" in which to live. At each door she asked, "Greek? You Greek?" and if the answer were no she excused herself and moved on. Out of kindness for the strange visitor the narrator invites her in for coffee; snow is falling, and it is cold. Theia explains that she wants to be near her own people, near Greeks, so that when she dies she will not be buried in an alien cemetery. "Not to be thrown into the grave like a heathen," she says, "the way they did with Dimitraina, God rest her soul" (p. 55).

During their talk Theia Giannitsa reminisces about her past. She has been in America for nearly forty-five years, coming when boatloads of Greek youths were leaving from Patras and Piraeus to escape the poverty of Greece. The girls either had to join the men or remain unmarried. "I'm one of the first Greek women who came to this city," the old lady says, "and in those days it ended at Dante Avenue. Right here where your house is, then it used to be a field where we used to gather dandelions" (p. 55). The narrator sadly thinks of many others like her, "grown old in foreign lands, alone, dragging weary bodies about the streets of America, Canada, Australia" (p. 55). When Theia Giannitsa claims she has enough money saved for her funeral, the narrator asks why she does not return to her motherland—her *patrida*—only to be told that after half a century in America Theia would be even more a stranger there. Her own mother, were she living, would not recognize her withered face. Here, at least, she knows a few old timers who have "shared the same bitter cup of separation." Grown garrulous with her desperate need for a home, Theia Giannitsa talks on and on—about her life here, about the Greek-American community, about the growth of Chicago into a great metropolis. "In the old cemetery there were only a dozen graves of our people and today we have three big cemeteries filled with Greeks. They came to America for a year or two, as I did, to make their pile and go back where mothers, sisters, wives, children waited" (p. 56).

Outside it is turning dark, and the narrator is worried; she has no room for Theia Giannitsa. She interrupts her long discourse by suggesting that Theia rent a room next door, from an Italian lady. There she will hear Greek even when she does not want to, for across from her window Katina of Smyrna is always scolding one or more of her seven children. Convinced, Theia Giannitsa takes the room; and from that day her terrible alarm clock ruins everyone's sleep with its loud ring. Then one morning the alarm does not sound, nor the morning after. Rosina, the landlady, finally breaks into her room and finds her dead. But Theia Giannitsa, the narrator goes on, did not always live alone. She married at twenty, had four children, and was widowed at twenty-six. She could have easily remarried but feared that a stepfather might ill-treat her children. In time, one by one, her children left home. Her first daughter married and died in childbirth a year later; the second married a man of another nationality and settled with him in Oregon where she became a stranger to everything Greek. Theia Giannitsa also had two sons, both of them lost to her. The elder as a result of the war suffered a "living burial" in a veterans' hospital while the younger son, unable to find work, "had gone to Alaska with the fishing boats and was never seen or heard from again." Now poor old Theia Giannitsa is dead, and the narrator wonders how many more days her passing would have gone undetected had it not been for the tin alarm.

Nostalgia, whimsy, and humor play a large part in the fiction of Theano Papazoglou-Margaris. All three of these elements may be found in one of her better-known stories, "The Nymphs of Lake Michigan."[29] It deals with the unsuccessful attempt of John Kouroupis to secure a young wife. After having arrived in America, where his compatriots made him work eighteen hours a day for a piece of bread, John heads for the Northwest to earn good wages working for the railroads. He saves a good amount, comes to Chicago, and eventually owns a fine restaurant. For a long time he had wanted to get married; in his youth he could not afford a wife, for the few Greek girls here were very particular. "Even the scarecrows expected a man to have a 'corner restaurant' and a 'Lincoln car' and a 'bankbook' with lots of dollars" (p. 15). Some Greeks then were bringing brides to America by photograph. Having seen a picture he liked, the groom would "send his picture, and a ring, and the fare, and the bride would arrive at Ellis Island. The groom went with a priest and a best man, and they were married before she set foot in New York" (p. 15). John Kouroupis saw one friend of his badly hooked by the photograph method—stuck with a ton of meat; and another friend received an "emaciated creature," a skeleton that he sent back on the next boat. Not only did he have to reimburse the priest, but the girl's irate cousin beat him black and blue. So John refuses to see a photograph bride, and he will not marry an American girl. "He wanted his children to be pure Greek" (p. 15).

Years pass with John's problem unresolved, although he makes money even during the Depression. When he finally decides to leave America for good, find a bride in Greece, and live out his life there, World War II forces him to cancel his departure until peace returns. However, John Kouroupis is already forty-nine, turning fifty! He must act soon. As he has changed with time, so have conditions among the Greek-Americans. A whole new crop of Greek girls have been born and raised here—and now, with the war, most of the eligible men are away. As luck would have it, a girl of eighteen is thrust upon him by her relatives; they say she is twenty-two and he is prepared to accept it since she has a good figure. His future father-in-law, who is forty-five, feels better if John Kouroupis drops his age even lower, to forty-three. The engagement set, John lives in heavenly bliss dreaming of being the husband of the young Angela. It was her mother who connived to have her say yes, her mother who calmed down her brother Dino, the "dumb American," who raised the roof. The wedding day finally arrives. "Angela was an angel as a bride! She was a nymph on land . . . no! A sea nymph, for they say that Lake Michigan has many sea nymphs. They say that nymphs enchant the people and keep them here, and that is why Chicago has thrived and flourished, for no city in the history of the world ever grew so fast" (p. 16).

The wedding over, five hundred guests are seated at the dinner tables, eating and reveling. Before them stands an enormous wedding cake. "Next to Dino is Gus, the groom's business partner." He barely drinks, but keeps staring at the bride and groom. Then he whispers to Dino that if he wants his sister to be really happy, she should grab the bridegroom's hair and say to him, "Happiness and health to you, my husband" (p. 16). That is the custom in his village. Dino does as he is told, suspecting nothing; and Angela, being a "proper Greek girl," dutifully grabs her husband's hair and tugs. Shocked at the result, she rolls up her eyes and swoons to the floor clutching his hair in her hand. John Kouroupis leaps up frightened and ashamed. The guests scream, for they do not know what has happened. Doctors among them soon revive the hapless Angela, but when she sees her bald husband, now a strange old man, she promptly faints again. Her brother Dino shakes poor John Kouroupis and shouts, "A wig, damn you, you were wearing a wig!" The doctors revive Angela once more. When she opens her eyes, she does not see her husband, for in the commotion he has disappeared for good. Two steps from the aristocratic hotel was the big lake. Where did John Kouroupis go? "A sea nymph from Lake Michigan must have caught him," some say (p. 62).

In nearly each of its 126 issues *Athene* magazine published one or more pieces of fiction among its other contents. The stories mentioned here are those most relevant to our general purpose. Many others, although written by Greek-Americans, eschewed ethnic material in favor of a wide variety of other subjects. The magazine performed what it regarded as a valuable service in publishing the best fiction of modern Greek writers in English translation— authors such as Kostas Ouranis, Alexander Papadiamantis, I. M. Panayotopoulos, Elias Venezis, Stratis Myrivilis, and others whose achievements pertain to Greece and not to the United States. The same is true of a series of stories presented under the heading *Modern Greek Legends*. They were written by Theodore Gianakoulis, who also served as associate editor of *Athene*. Demetrios A. Michalaros, the editor, could never pay any of his many authors. All contributions, including those of Gianakoulis, were labors of love. That Michalaros never lacked for creditable material testifies to the interest of both Greek and non-Greek writers in the past and present of Hellenism. A further proof of this interest was *Greek World*, a successor to *Athene*, a well-edited and lively journal. The eighteen stories examined above dramatize various traits of the modern Greek character. This they do regardless of what else, in aesthetic terms, they may or may not contribute to American literature as a whole.

⧉⧉⧉⧉⧉⧉⧉

11

⧉⧉⧉⧉⧉⧉⧉

THE GREEKS OF PETRAKIS

A MERICA'S LEADING AUTHOR of Greek descent, Harry Mark
Petrakis, has created over the years a large gallery of characters
whose ethnicity is both genuine and pronounced. They represent
a wide variety of types, backgrounds, and occupations, most of
them identified with the older Greek Town of Chicago. Writing in
Greek, Theano Papazoglou-Margaris exploits the same general
setting. She deals more with the Greek as a dweller in a strange
land than does Petrakis. Most of his characters are fairly well established Greek-Americans whose problems derive more from themselves and one another than from their environment. This fact,
however, does not make them any the less Greek; of their ethnic
status the reader is constantly aware.

To recapitulate: as records of human emotions, the Greek-
American novels dramatize the dreams, hopes, fears, loneliness,
failures, and anguish of displacement; then the multiple tensions
of establishment, Americanization, and conflict between the ex-
tending generations. Beyond the factual history is the psychological realism, the drama of romantic voyagers being stripped of their
illusions by the harsh necessities of the New World. Alongside the
physical displacement, then, is the emotional correlative, the dark
or light inner experience made visible by the writer. Among the
themes natural to the immigrant/ethnic novel are the social conditions in the donor country, the various strains on familial relationships, the response of the receiving community, the alienation and
xenophobia, the intensification of personal problems, the pull between ethnicity and Americanization, the nostalgia for what has
been lost, and the vicissitudes of class mobility affecting the immigrant.

These and other themes inform the fiction of ethnic-oriented
authors. For Harry Mark Petrakis the Greek experience serves as
a major source of formal structure, plot and character development, and thematic unity. Much of the dramatic tension turns
upon the Greekness of this or that personage. For example the

Greek boy in *Lion at My Heart* rebels against a stern father who damns him for marrying an Irish girl.[1] Their domestic battle constitutes the entire plot. When a Greek boy or girl is the protagonist and a parent the antagonist, the climax involves acceptance or rejection of some ethnic factor, or a recognition of a deeper truth, or a workable compromise. Whom to marry, what occupation to pursue, how to treat Mother, how much to love Greece—these and other issues infuse the aesthetic tensions with ethnic and often social significance. At the disposal of the Greek-American authors, too, is the Hellenic heritage. To a great extent their characters have been shaped by this heritage; thus it is natural for a writer like Petrakis to allude to Greek mythology, the Greek classical period, and recent Greek history. More than that, it is natural for him to compose allegories and thinly veiled adaptations of mythic structures that make a strong impact upon the modern Greek mind.

From his Greek heritage, from the Greek immigrant experience, and from his own life and imagination, Petrakis has created a vigorous group of Greek characters. They include a wide range of moral traits, both positive and negative; and since Petrakis rarely pits a good Greek against a bad American or member of some other ethnic group, the evil needed for conflict, tension, and suspense has to reside in bad Greeks. The fiction of Petrakis is filled with bad Greeks, or twisted Greeks, or foolish Greeks—if one takes as a standard the idealized Greek that some of his readers might expect of him. His fiction is also filled with emotional Greeks. They are mostly Dionysians, creatures of the heart, of the passions. They are not Apollonians, creatures of the mind, reserved and logical. Or, one might say, the logic of their passions leads them into aberrant and, at times, "un-Greek" modes of behavior.

For example, the father in *Lion at My Heart*, Angelo Varinakis, is exposed by the priest as a philandering hypocrite. In the same exchange the priest admits that he goes to a woman to help assuage his loneliness. Unmarried Greek Orthodox priests are not supposed to fornicate. Another priest, the embittered Father Grivas, confesses that he lives on hatred, a most un-Christian obsession. For the most part Greek businessmen are greedy, ignorant, and bigoted; they grow fat on profits, in one instance, while people die in Viet Nam. Unless they are widowed or nubile, Greek women are often depicted as sexless and bitchy, crones with poisoned tongues. A Greek husband like Matsoukas in *A Dream of Kings*, despite his apparently genuine love for his son, cheats on his wife, cheats at dice, and disgraces himself generally.[2] Petrakis shows some Greek youths as hippies—as "hairy apparitions" who loaf, smoke hashish, and come to a church social wearing sneakers "studded with stars." These are signs that the Greeks in America are a decadent race—gluttonous, money-hungry, shallow in their emotional lives and lacking in a standard of excellence. Thus is the ethnic-oriented writer driven to seek evil within his own nationality, in order to balance the good, to create a tension, to fashion a plot, and to advance a theme.

The Greek experience in America provides for Petrakis a general structure, a form, within which to create his fiction. His characters live in Greek Town, U.S.A., and they move in actions both comic and tragic, so conceived as in many cases to have symbolic and universal value. Classical and later Hellenism is available, of course, to all mankind; but for a Greek writer like Petrakis, Hellenism has a special relevance since many of its aspects influenced every stage of his own life. Thus the myths, legends, and archetypes associated with Hellenism take on a personal and almost an intuitive meaning. In his reminiscence, *Stelmark* (1970), Petrakis, himself a second-generation Greek, expresses well the power of his inherited tradition.[3] It was an enigma for him in his childhood, he writes, to feel a strong nostalgia for Crete, a land he had never seen but had known in his blood through his family. "The songs, tales, ballads, and proverbs passed from my parents to me."[4] He learned all the myths, as told to him, "steeped in blood." The Cretans who had come to Chicago abounded with energy—the "white-haired old men from Sfakia dancing on the holidays," "stiff and brittle" but moving with "awesome grace"; the lovely Cretan girls all of whom would eventually "settle in the inexpicable embrace of death." Considering the origin of Petrakis's parents, one is not surprised that his only "immigrant novel," *The Odyssey of Kostas Volakis* (1963), should concern a hero from Crete.

Petrakis contrasts the legend ("fair land in the midst of Homer's wine dark sea") with the reality of Crete, the village "a parched and poor habitation of stone and clay huts with tiny windows." Poverty stalks the land: a few "thin and wretched flocks of sheep" graze on "arid patches of grass"; the chickens are "scraggy," the dogs wild, dirty, and fierce from hunger.[5] The village has endured massacres and famines, and from it now the young men are leaving for America. Kostas Volakis, too, will go to join them. Illiterate son of a herdsman, he is "strong as a Minoan bull" and grateful for being alive after having fought the Bulgarians in the world war. He marries Katerina not for love but for her dowry, which buys his passage to America, to Chicago. For their departure the blind minstrel Limakis, an omen-bearer, sings a lament.

> Farewell, Kostas,
> Farewell, Katerina.
> Go with God
> and sow your children
> on the strange wild earth
> of another land.
> Do not forget those you leave.(p. 4)

With some exceptions—the teeming crowds on the sidewalk all "dressed in strange and resplendent grandeur"—their first impressions of Chicago are very negative: the steel mills a region of "grayness and gloom," the railroads a "maze of tracks and shacks." Their patron Stathis Glavas says that in the mills "men work like tiny bugs beside the giant furnaces." He had once seen a man crushed to death by an iron mold. In Chicago, according to Glavas, "trust only the children under six years of age. When an older child approaches, smile to show you are friendly, but be on your guard. When an adult comes near, particularly an African or a Sicilian, prepare to defend yourself against assault. And when a policeman calls to you, hold tightly to your pocketbook" (p. 6). The cynicism of Glavas is reinforced by the automobiles that seem monstrous to Katerina, by the ominous merchants of Maxwell Street, and by their fourth-floor, windowless tenement room the size of a prison cell. He has come, Kostas Volakis thinks, from the place of his "despair" to the place of his "destiny."

The novel traces its hero's destiny from the year of his arrival, 1919, until 1954 when a climactic reconcilation occurs between Kostas and his son Alex, who is in the penitentiary for having killed his brother Manuel. Kostas's odyssey encompasses the usual process of Americanization, the class mobility (from herdsman to restauranteur), and the long drawn-out domestic life with its variable joys and sorrows. In time the Volakis family rises above the depressing poverty with which it began; but its destiny is marked by a tragedy befitting the pen of an Aeschylus. Eventually the couple have five children: Aeneas, Rhodanthe, Alex, Manuel, and Angela. Aeneas, the first-born son, sickens and dies. Alex, the second son, grows up emotionally disturbed. In a fit of jealous rage he strikes Manuel with a poker and kills him. Thus all three sons are lost to Kostas Volakis. Only after many years does he relax his solemn vow never again to see, in prison, his bitterly disowned Alex.

At the geographic level Chicago has been the Ithaca for the odyssey of Kostas; but at the symbolic level, as the priest Father Marlas affirms, "Every man's life is an odyssey; it does not matter if the body remains rooted in one place, for it is the heart and the spirit that journey to Ithaca" (p. 251). To foreshadow the troubles ahead for Kostas, and to stress the perils of survival, Stathis Glavas says: "I have seen many like you come and go. Their dreams are bubbles that burst upon the rocks of this fierce land. They come wild to walk upon the streets of gold and find ghettos and jungles in which the ruthless and clever feed upon the helpless and weak" (p. 14). Their patron's naturalistic vision is meant in part to subdue the newcomers to his will; by instilling the fear of hunger and defeat he can more easily exploit them in his restaurant. Their hours are so long, the work so hard, and the rewards so meager that at night, alone in their room, Kostas and Katerina bitterly argue the wisdom of their coming to America. Now in their adopted Ithaca, they must live and die according to the dictates of their fate.

The element of fate, of *moira* or *kismet*, hovers about the characters of Petrakis. Another and more explicit set of determinants is the many archetypes or universals which they represent. Not all his characters, of course, are symbols or analogues; otherwise Petrakis would write nothing but allegories, adaptations, and parodies, to mention the more derivative genres. Yet his use of archetypal persona is a central feature of his literary strategy. Such a use is abetted by his own ethnic heritage, which is filled with well-known mythological and historical types.

Petrakis's first novel, *Lion at My Heart* (1959), features an unremitting struggle between Angelo Varinakis and his son Mike over the boy's love for an Irish girl, Sheila Cleary. The father, who fiercely loves Mike, as fiercely loves being a Greek; and he prefers to lose his son rather than moderate his cultural identity. A second son, Tony, narrates the growing alienation between his father, the lion, and his equally stubborn brother. The oedipal displacement of the father by the son turns on a radical difference over the virtues of being Greek. In order to defend his love Mike Varinakis increasingly disowns his ethnicity. At one point he speaks to his brother in self-justification: "Ever since we were kids we eat and sleep and grow on the glory of Greece. All around us we got nuts like Simonakis [an extreme nationalist] haughty as hell because two thousand years ago they knocked hell out of some Persians and knocked hell out of each other and a guy named Socrates got poisoned and a guy named Odysseus got lost" (p. 41). For his part the father does not flinch from cursing his disobedient son. The curse seems to work: Sheila's premature baby is born dead. His son Mike condemns him as a butcher. The father goes to Gerontis's coffeehouse where, drunk but unbending, he roars, "I am Angelo Varinakis and I make steel like Joe Magarac." Two folk epic traditions merge in his passionate statement—Odysseus become Magarac in South Chicago.

The hero of *The Odyssey of Kostas Volakis* has none of the epic qualities of Angelo Varinakis. Instead of making steel and feeling kinship with the mythical Magarac, he helps to run a modest restaurant. Unlike Varinakis he does not object when his daughter Rhodanthe falls in love with and marries the "Norseman," Edward Hellstrom. Nevertheless, despite Kostas Volakis's lack of heroic qualities, the novel depends on archetypes for much more than the odyssey, the saga, of a family.

No doubt the single most significant event is the fratricide—the killing of Manuel by Alex. "The newspapers called it the 'Cain-Abel' murder, and for a few days it vied with the war for space on the front pages" (p. 186). Petrakis prepares the reader for the ritual action by a careful depiction of Alex as a moody youth beset by emotional disturbance including oedipal feelings toward his mother. She, in turn, overprotects and smothers him with a castrating love that abets his unmanning. On the night of his sister's wedding, Alex in desperation picks up a woman, accompanies her to her room, but cannot perform. Later he blames both his mother and his father, crying: "You have crippled me! I'm not a man!" (p. 180). In his anguish and self-pity he forgets what trouble his juvenile delinquency has caused the family; he forgets that he once nearly killed Manuel by throwing him down the stairs. Alex now tells his father: "You tore off chunks of my body and ate my flesh!" (p. 181). Kostas in turn disowns him, saying: "I wish you had died in her womb!" It is then that Alex starts for his father with a poker, only to be stopped by his brother Manuel, whom he inadvertently kills.

The archetypes of odyssey and oedipal displacement overshadow the lesser archetypes in the novel. In Crete, Blind Limakis had sung a departure song for Kostas and Katerina—the fiddler descended, as Petrakis states, from the lyre-players who sailed to Troy with Agamemnon. The figure of the epic lover appears in several of Petrakis's stories. Here in *The Odyssey of Kostas Volakis* it is Captain Haritos. At eighty, with a patch over one eye, he says: "I have loved women all over the world. I loved each one as I had her, spawned God only knows how many bastards, and afterwards was as unsatisfied as before" (p. 177). Finally the Greek woman as harpy also appears. Petrakis wastes no mercy on the gossips Mrs. Pappas and Mrs. Barbaroulis, having Kostas Volakis regard them as "malignant harpies." The more fully developed termagent, however, is Constantina, who marries Doctor Barbaris. Ironically he had prided himself for his choice, thinking it is a "damned smart move in getting a good Greek woman from the old country, raised to revere a man and obey his every word" (p. 193). By having Constantina blossom into a vicious fury, Petrakis demolishes the view commonly held by many male chauvinists that a wife from Greece will be docile compared to Greek girls "spoiled" by American notions of equality. The fiery Constantina threatens to divorce Doctor Barbaris and take every penny that he has—until she gets pregnant and has a son, named Themistocles, to whom the happy father recites verses from the *Iliad*.

Petrakis makes use of several archetypes in the stories of *Pericles on 31st Street* (1965).[6] He adapts a classical myth, for example, in "The Ballad of Daphne and Apollo." In the original story Apollo loves Daphne, the daughter of Peneus the river god. Apollo pursues her, but she determines to remain innocent. To punish her Apollo turns Daphne into a laurel tree; thus forever will she stand but never love. The two ill-met lovers in Petrakis's version are Daphne Callistos and Apollo Gerakis. He plays a guitar in the tavern of Ali Pasha where Janco, the narrator, tends bar. Apollo, in his mid-thirties, knows Greek mountain dances, island melodies, and bucolic love songs of Zakynthos and Thessaly. As he plays, a "line of wild old men" dance—a bacchic atmosphere which Daphne Callistos joins one midnight. She asks Ali Pasha for a job as singer and she gets it. Wearing a tight black dress, she has a "careless insolence" about her as she sings first a lament and then a bawdy song that suggests abandon and fertility. "In such a way," Janco thinks, "must the wild nymphs have sung in the festivals of Dionysus before the satyrs playing their pipes made of reeds."[7] He notices that Ali Pasha already seems to lust for her. As Janco tells his friend Apollo, she is "from disaster" and on her way "to catastrophe."

Unfortunately the prophecy runs true. Apollo Gerakis and Daphne Callistos become lovers; she thinks him mad to love her honestly, he thinks her beautiful. Ali Pasha, whose namesake was notorious for his passion and violence, jealously spreads ugly rumors about Daphne's past. Apollo broods about her past and wants to protect her from patrons who tip Daphne and touch her. He rages: "I do not want the woman I love pawed by pigs!"[8] As time passes and Apollo goes more insane with jealousy, the situation for Daphne becomes more untenable. She states mournfully, "All my life seems a long, bawdy song." Instead of leaving as she threatens she kills herself with Ali Pasha's gun. A pall settles upon the tavern. Ali Pasha drinks savagely alone, feeling guilty; the once wild old men are "only sad and futile ghosts"; and Apollo plays even sadder laments that evoke the dead past, life being "a song and a harp and a legend that will never die."[9]

Characters named Matsoukas appear in the short story "Matsoukas" and in the novel *A Dream of Kings* in which he is the protagonist. The first Matsoukas materializes as the personification of death. It is about closing time for Lambos, the old storekeeper, when a stranger enters and claims he has arrived to give him rest. Matsoukas, the stranger, knows Lambos's name and the fact that a supermarket has ruined him. Matsoukas waits, and Lambos chides him, saying it is "not polite to enter a man's store at closing time and eat a pickle and sit around like you are in a coffeehouse." As he climbs the steps Lambos dies. The brief allegory depicts death as a rest-bringing Greek named Matsoukas . . . and when death came, "all snapped squarely and forever into darkness."[10]

The character of Leonidas Matsoukas in what is perhaps Petrakis's best known novel, *A Dream of Kings*, is a fully developed hero reminiscent of types as disparate as Zorba and Job. Unlike the other Matsoukas who represents death, Leonidas Matsoukas has a ravenous appetite for life—for food, drink, sex, humor—all of which he pursues with minimal financial means. His friend Cicero, the gambling-house dealer, tells Matsoukas: "The gods have chosen you for eternal disaster, but you take every act that has been prepared for your punishment and turn it into some kind of triumph."[11] Although not an Odysseus, Matsoukas is rarely ever at a loss when confronted by unusual problems, with one great ex-

ception—when Youssouf the Turkish bouncer nearly kills him in a
fight incited by Matsoukas's own arrogance. "Let me live," he begs
the Turk. "For the sake of my son" (p. 170). At church one Sunday
his son Stavros, afflicted by a mysterious disease, suffers a spasm,
following which Matsoukas like a modern Job criticizes God. "Once
you could apportion heaven and hell," he says, "but that is true no
longer. Error and chance rule the world" (p. 91). Matsoukas whispers softly to God: "Man have mercy on you," thus putting Him,
so to speak, in His place (p. 92).

In another adaptation, "The Shearing of Samson," the castrating
power of love afflicts the forty-year old Samson Leventis, owner of
the Zorah Wholesale Produce Company on Halsted Street.[12] The
last name, Leventis, which means a *splendid man*, befits one who
represents the biblical Samson. Like his prototype Leventis is very
strong: he can "open a crate of produce by shattering the wood
with his fist" (p. 46). He also has abundant hair, curled "like a
horse's nape over the collar of his shirt." Samson Leventis can out-
drink and outdance any man at the Parthenon coffeehouse where
the bouzouki plays every Saturday night. All goes smoothly until
one day he announces to his friends that he loves the Widow Delilah, who owns the Sorek Bakery on Harrison Street. This modern
Delilah, instead of serving the Philistines, is devoted to neatness,
decorum, and art. Once she has her *pallikar* in tow as a husband,
she invites his friends Anastis and Krokas to dinner. They are
shocked by what they see: Samson in a "white shirt with a tie
looped around his throat as if it were a noose" (p. 57–58). His once
shaggy hair is but a short stubble. From Delilah's "ears hung silver
earrings in the shape of slim glistening knives" (p. 59). Throughout the tense meal she keeps admonishing Samson about the right
fork, spoon, and so on. Krokas invites Samson to the Parthenon
that Saturday night to hear a new bouzouki player from New York,
but Delilah announces that she and Samson have opera tickets for
that evening. Poor Samson! Anastis and Krokas hurry off to the
Parthenon coffeehouse to get drunk on *mastiha*.

The archetype of the son in search of his father informs the plot
of "The Bastards of Thanos."[13] Poet, wanderer, and lecher, old
Thanos lies waiting for death while composing his last poem. He
demands of the attending priest some sign from God before he
will accept communion. Like Leonidas Matsoukas, Thanos speaks
harshly about God as an enemy of pleasure and fertility. "I would
not trade a single folly or vice of my life," he tells the priest, "for

an eternity of redemption. Your paradise is duller than the land-scape of your dismal and surrendered face" (p. 90). Thanos the hedonist has loved hundreds of women all over the world, "in the rocking beds of a hundred ports." A tall youth in seaman's jacket visits him in the hospital, declaring that for six years he, Petros, has been searching for his father, Thanos the poet. His mother was Magdalena of Athens. "I am your bastard son" (p. 93). After a while the dying father urges the tall youth to go because a "hundred scented lovely girls" are waiting for him in a "hundred gilded ports" (p. 97). Moved by the miracle of acquiring a son so close to his end, Thanos wonders how many more bastard sons might there be: "Perhaps as many as fifty or more androgynous mongrels of my rampaging journeys, devoted to life and drink and love as I have been, a virile host to carry on after I am gone, hurling my unrepentant seed into myriad races and through endless generations!" (p. 99). The priest is shocked, but gives Thanos the last rites that he now desires.

The author's most extended adaptation occurs in the novel *In the Land of Morning* (1973).[14] Its plot generally follows the *Agamemnon* of the Oresteia. The adaptation by Petrakis is limited when compared with that of Eugene O'Neill in *Mourning Becomes Electra*. Alex Rifakis is the war-weary Orestes who returns to Chicago from Viet Nam to find the makings of a tragedy at home. Greek Town is ruled by Antonio Gallos, a gangster who is owner of the Temple of Apollo. The word *gallos* means *turkey* in Greek. He in effect has killed Alex's father by winning away his small grocery and his meager savings gambling. Thus Alex, the son, must bear the burden of the inevitable vengeance. Gallos is the murderous Aegisthus who must be punished. The problem is compounded for Alex by the fact that his mother, Asmene, has become Gallos's mistress. She as Clytemnestra is another one of Petrakis's voluptuous widows. Alex's sister Eunice, as Electra, fumes at her mother's betrayal of her father. Like Orin in *Mourning Becomes Electra* Eunice through her diary is keeping a record of events. An important departure from previous versions, including the original, is the manner by which Gallos (Aegisthus) gets killed. The act of vengeance does not flow directly from Alex, but from the baker Nick Zervas, a friend of Alex's father, whom the hated Gallos had once humiliated and beaten. Together they go to the gangster's private chambers in the Temple of Apollo in order to wreak the vengeance. They surprise Gallos in his tub, and Zervas, not Alex, stabs him to death. His mother Asmene arrives for her appointed love tryst with Gallos. Alex wants to kill her, too, but he cannot. Instead he leaves Chicago for Phoenix, where he will begin rebuilding his life. He leaves Asmene and Eunice behind, "doomed to share the dreary unwinding of their lives, growing into ancient, hopeless figures that only death could liberate."[15] Perhaps, in time, Alex might escape the curse that haunts the Rifakis family.

Throughout his fiction Petrakis alludes constantly to the Greek heritage and to Greek customs. For example the arranged marriage that used to be the general rule figures in both *Lion at My Heart* and "The Waves of Night." In the novel the young girl Marika is examined by the rich old Mr. Gastris as a bride to be purchased. In the story Father Manos is approached for guidance by Angela Fotakis, who tells him: "They have found a man willing to marry me."[16] She wants a much younger husband. Of Greek hospitality Tony, the narrator of *Lion at My Heart*, says: "Hospitality, which is like a religion to a Greek, at least a Greek like Pa, demanded that a guest be well taken care of."[17] In this novel the ultranationalist is Simonakis. He serves as the polar extreme to Mike Varinakis, who breaks away to marry an Irish girl. His brother Tony is lightheartedly regarded by his classmates as a descendant of Plato and Aristotle.

The Odyssey of Kostas Volakis alludes to various ethnic conventions. Early in the story the hero's wife Katerina attacks Kostas for having married her only for the dowry and not for love. His Parthenon Restaurant prospers, among other reasons, for its being next to the Macedonian Funeral Parlor. "The Greek custom of serving food to relatives and friends of the deceased made the location of the Parthenon and the Macedonian a compatible one."[18] Both the classical myths and ancient Greek history provide Christian names for many a character in Petrakis's fiction; this is a common practice in the Greek-American community. Kostas Volakis calls his first son Aeneas after the Trojan wanderer. Another convention alluded to in *The Odyssey* is the venerable superstition of the "evil eye," a power for evil which differs from the inherited curse of the Greek tragedies because it takes effect instantly from the malevolent glance of the dispenser. The return to a Spartan code, according to a character named Sarantis, will solve the problems of the great depression. Doctor Barbaris tells Kostas: "Cretan, I envy you. Hercules in an apron."[19]

There are other important allusions to the Hellenic tradition.

The Greek wedding of Dr. Barbaris and Constantina is described in some detail. Similes such as "like a wily Odysseus" and as "bombastic as Zeus" add an ethnic coloration to many a passage. The pejorative use of the term *Turk* recurs from time to time, as in "Courtship of the Blue Widow." Old Mantaris condemns the young Mike Larakis for his attentions to the widow Angela. "You are a Turk," Mantaris cries, "bent upon pillage and rape!"[20] On two separate occasions Petrakis uses a similar set of allusions in describing a woman. For Vasili in "The Journal of a Wife-Beater" his wife Nitsa is "a Goddess, a fierce Diana, a cyclonic Juno!"[21] In *A Dream of Kings* Matsoukas arouses the aging Telecles by urging him to regard himself "as a God swept by wild desire" and of woman as "a Goddess, a lovely Diana, a cyclonic Juno!" In the story "Chrisoula" a man named Petros works for the gangster Gallos, who has a leading role in *In the Land of Morning*. When Petros is shot by rival mobsters, his body is taken "to be washed and anointed and dressed. And in the old ways of their people to be decked with basil and mint."[22] One of Petrakis's finest stories recounts the death of the "Karaghiozis tradition" when one of its greatest practitioners tries to bring his puppetry art to America, tries to pass on the art to his son, but fails. These and other examples of ethnic custom abound in Petrakis.

The perdurable theme of the gap in generations goes back to the mythical titan Cronus, who deposed his father Uranus and was himself deposed by Zeus and thrown into Tartarus. In the fiction of Petrakis the conflict usually occurs between first and second generation Greek-Americans. Sometimes but not always the ethnic factor creates the tension. At the very start of *Lion at My Heart* the ethnic conflict is established when Mike Varinakis, the son, plans to bring Sheila Cleary home at Thanksgiving to meet his father. "That old country crap is for the birds," Mike says. "If you love a girl, it don't make any difference whether she is damn Greek or not."[23] The father Angelo counters bitterly: "My son brings home girl from Irish house. Greek girl is not good enough" (p. 16). A similar conflict develops in Tom T. Chamales's *Go Naked in the World*, in which Greek father and son break apart over a non-Greek girl; but the issue is less ethnic than on the girl's having been a prostitute. In *Lion at My Heart* it is the total Greek heritage which looms between the two antagonists. At one point Sheila says: "Where do you Greeks get off? You think you have the only heroes" (p. 163). The idea of heroism is vital both to Angelo Varinakis's self-conception and to what his other son, Tony, thinks of him. Tony goes to college to become a teacher; he marries a Greek girl Marika, and he witnesses at close hand the fierce domestic squabble; and he, as the narrator, explains why his father could not bear to realize that the old heroes were gone.

> That Ajax and Achilles and Odysseus no longer hurled lances and howled their great war cries before the ramparts of Troy. He could not suffer to live quietly in our time of dwarfs. For him the fury and fire of the mills, the blazing furnaces, the flashing rolls were once again the battlegrounds of Troy and Thermopylae and Salamis. He was of a race of mighty men belonging to another age. His spirit as much flame as the spirits of Hector and Achilles and Odysseus and all the valiant men who lived like lions on this dark and unfathomable earth. (p. 238)

By the time of this explanatory eulogy, however, Angelo Varinakis has become a tainted and diminished hero in the reader's eyes. The lion has cursed and disowned a fine son; he has damned the priest, who tries to bring him to his senses; and he has inhumanly gloated when his Irish daughter-in-law gives birth to a stillborn and deformed child. These are not the actions of an honorable man, no matter what his reasons.

In *The Odyssey of Kostas Volakis* the causes for the generation gap are primarily psychological and not ethnic. From the day of his birth Alex, the second son, is doomed to be the black sheep of the family. His mother's labor was long and painful. She soon loses her milk. Alex is sickly and irascible. In his lingering grief over the death of Aeneas, his first born, Kostas takes no interest in Alex; thus the preconditions are established early for the chasm between father and son. When Manuel, the third son, arrives, Alex is very jealous. He fights constantly with his sister Rhodanthe. He grows up moody, asthmatic, and mentally disturbed; not only was he a steady bedwetter, but he had fits and uttered senseless banshee cries. Despite his troublemaking Alex's mother Katerina defends him against Kostas. One day Alex nearly kills Manuel. Kostas, to punish him, calls him "a monster" and beats him with a yardstick. In a burst of feeling Katerina cries to Kostas: "You poisoned his blood before his birth!" Then she warns him: "If you touch this boy [Alex] again, I will kill you while you sleep!"[24]

The bad blood between father and son thickens as Alex grows

older and therefore capable of greater evil. He brings a modicum of disgrace upon the Volakis name when he runs away from home; twice he returns by himself, but two other times the police have to find and return him. He reacts perversely and maliciously at Manuel's more normal success with girls. Alex sneers: "The young King Manuel surrounded by his court" (p. 137). The gulf between them makes it impossible for Kostas Volakis to help when Alex genuinely needs paternal guidance and solace. Striving hard for manhood, Alex suffers a cruel blow when he is rejected for military service because of a slight scar on his lung. He drinks more and more. Kostas condemns him: "Drunken bum! Loafer!" (p. 154). By now Alex hates his father with a vengeance; and his personal problems worsen. He suffers a further shattering blow when he finds himself impotent. When he blames his parents, the ensuing altercation leads to the murder of his brother Manuel. Alex attempts patricide but achieves fratricide. The reader's interest hereafter centers on whether or not Kostas Volakis will relent in his vow never to visit his son in prison. Years later he does, and the generation gap at long last begins to close. "He is my son, Kostas thought and felt a strange stirring of compassion in his heart. He has the face of a stranger, but he is my son" (p. 267).

Several of Petrakis's short stories depend on various conflicts between the generations for their plots. In "The Legacy of Leontis" a fifty-eight-year old Greek, Leontis Marnas, marries Angeliki, who is only twenty-four. It does not take his wife long to cuckold him. The very next spring a son is born to the couple. In Leontis's store works a quiet youth named Thomas Sarris. Having a weak heart, Leontis keeps telling Angeliki that she should marry Thomas after his death. The "strange sparkle in her eyes" when the youth is mentioned makes us suspect that he has fathered her son. We are certain when, as Leontis dies, Angeliki entreats him: "You must not die before you forgive me!"[25] Leontis, however, never hears her plea.

Some stories by Petrakis involve minor conflicts between parents and offspring. Such gaps imply a certain amount of irreconcilability. That is not the case in "Pa and the Sad Turkeys," even though the son thinks of his father as a "gorilla" and his father calls him a "hoodlum." In "The Song of Rhodanthe" a Greek girl is being harried by her father to marry. Rhodanthe is twenty-seven. Much to her father's dismay, she rejects all the old suitors and waits for a young man with "a wild dark curl across his forehead" who "whis-

tles and makes the earth burst into song."[26] The passage of time
and not ethnicity creates the problem in "A Hand for Tomorrow."
The small grocery of Kostas Stavrakas has remained unchanged
for thirty years. His son Nick wants to modernize the store and
says his father is the laughingstock of the street. The sons of Max
Feldman, Kostas's friend, knocked down their father's tailor shop
and built a drive-in dry cleaner. In the end Kostas gives in to his
son's plans to remodel. "Maybe we are the selfish ones," he says to
Max.[27] "Homecoming" has a character named Alex whose mother
is dying. He has come to Chicago from California to see her; but,
restless and lost, he stays only one night and then because of his
sister's curse. "You bastard," she cries, "do you think the lousy fifty
bucks you send each month buys you off everything else?"[28] One
of the most powerful stories by Petrakis, "Dark Eye," does have an
ethnic base for the schism between a Greek son and his parents.
The father is a Karaghiozis, "a puppetmaster of the shadow puppets once so popular throughout Greece." Tradition demanded
that the father pass on the art to his son. In America where he
hopes to practice the Karaghiozis, the father suffers a double defeat: he has no audience to appreciate him, and his son cannot
learn because the "huge dark eye" of the puppet terrifies him. His
father tells him, "Get out, little bastard."[29] When the boy blurts out
to his mother that he wishes his father dead, she beats him and
explains what great renown he had in the old country. Bent on
self-destruction, he drinks and rages to forget his grief and loss.
Years later, when both parents are dead, the boy, who is the narrator, throws the cardboard figures of the Karaghiozis into the fur-
nace.

The main conflict of the novel *In the Land of Morning* concerns
the unbridgeable gap between the returned veteran Alex and his
mother Asmene, the lover of his father's "murderer." Petrakis's adaptation of the Oresteia stops short of having the vengeful son and
daughter destroy their doomed mother. Equally doomed is the
Electra figure of Eunice, devoured by envy and hatred of her
mother. In contrast to Asmene's physical opulence, Eunice is austere and dry, suffering from systemic arthritis. At one point Father
Naoum takes her hand and finds it "stony and cold as the hand of
a corpse." She is a "symbol of death in life"—an image that foreshadows the dire events ahead. So consumed is Eunice with hatred
for Asmene that on the very night of Alex's return she yells: "Goddam her!"[30] Such is the depth of her separation.

Priests, widows, restaurant owners, war heroes, gamblers, old men, fools—these and other types make up the crowded gallery of Petrakis's characters. The fact that the author's own father was a priest, Father Mark Petrakis, provides him with a rich authentic background for his fictional clergymen. At times Petrakis's attitude toward the church as an institution is acerbic, its elders rent by petty and vicious squabbles. Petrakis portrays both the strengths and human frailties of his men of God. In his autobiography, *Stelmark*, he includes the church: "Greek parents, Greek language, Greek food, Greek school, and Greek church."[31] With respect to the last, Petrakis enjoyed a special vantage because of his father's position as the priest. Father Petrakis was "no ivory-tower cleric," the son writes. When he wore his traditional vestments he had an "irrevocable dignity about him," and he moved with the "majesty of a Byzantine king." For the church service by unspoken consent the oldest sat in front, then the middle-aged, then the young. Petrakis describes the customarily huge Sunday dinner after church service when his mother, the *papadia*, performed the "miracle of the multiplying loaves and fishes"—she managed to feed as many as twenty-five people with a chicken-and-rice pilaf. In time Father Petrakis ran into serious trouble with his board of trustees over the issue of moving the church from what had become an all-black section. Petrakis devotes a chapter of *Stelmark* to the bitter controversy; in it he speaks of "one crafty faction" fighting another in a spirit far removed from Christian charity. With such intimate knowledge of the affairs of the Greek Orthodox church, it is no wonder that Petrakis creates a number of fictional priests and writes about them with authority.

Such a priest is Father Kontoyiannis ("Short John") in his first novel, *Lion at My Heart*. In the story Mrs. Bratsos, the mother of Marika, does not want her daughter's wedding in St. Sophia because Father Kontoyiannis is not in great favor compared with the priest of Annunciation. A leaflet has been circulated denouncing him as a libertine and gambler; and in response he admits to human frailties and venal sins but denies the mortal ones. His parish is not wealthy, his church not lavish. The ceiling, as Petrakis writes, "had been painted long ago by an unfrocked priest who had later gone mad." So hostile is his congregation that once Angelo Varinakis, the lion, hits a big butcher who spits at the priest's feet. Later in the novel a climactic scene occurs, a moment of truth, when Father Kontoyiannis intercedes in reaction to Angelo's cursing of his Irish daughter-in-law. "Let girl burn," he cries while Sheila's giving birth to a dead child. Then Angelo turns to Father Kontoyiannis and curses him too. "Goddam priest who stand before church, before God, and spit own sin."[32] The priest confesses that yes, he does go to a woman—a frailty in a priest but not in a man; and he strikes back at Angelo Varinakis with revelations from the confessional. He accuses Angelo of adultery with a Sicilian tart, and of how he almost killed Komarski who tried to take her away from him. The priest mentions "all the wild and driven whores" that his wife *did* know about. Like a "great stricken Judas you fought to raise your sons with all the mighty affection you had denied her."[33] Varinakis is chastened by the charge, but Father Kontoyiannis as also defeated. After the wedding of Tony and Marika, he will retire and go to "a monastery on the side of Lania, the mountain of many sheep, not far from where I was born."[34]

Another priest, Father Marlas, appears in *The Odyssey of Kostas Volakis*. He helps the new immigrants Kostas and Katerina adjust to Chicago. Life is very difficult and lonely for them, as they work eighteen hours a day in Glavas's restaurant. Father Marlas invites the couple to attend church and meet other Greeks. Glavas hopes to chase the priest away, growling: "This is no monastery where we can spend hours on our knees."[35] It is a great moment in Katerina's life when, pregnant with her first child, she is permitted to attend church on Sunday morning. Father Marlas also helps Kostas by giving him lessons in English three times a week. The priest lives with his grumpy, opinionated mother in the basement of the building adjoining the church. She bewails her fate and his, feeling that her son does not enjoy himself as a priest. Better had he been a gangster with fine clothes, women, and other luxuries. Father Marlas merely admits to carnal desire, whereas Father Kontoyiannis had said he went to a woman. In the course of the novel Father Marlas's mother dies. During the depression he and Dr. Barbaris minister to the poor. The priest calls the doctor an anarchist who "works more diligently than any saint in tending to the suffering of the people." During World War II Father Marlas has to comfort those whose sons do not return. In his church he holds a special service for Greek-American soldiers who are killed or missing in action. He officiates at the wedding of Rhodanthe and Edward Hellstrom. Toward the end when tragedy has twice befallen Kostas Volakis, he asks Father Marlas: "Is there any hope that I will find Ithaca?" And the saddened priest replies: "Everyman's life is an odyssey. It does not matter if the body remains rooted to one place for it is the heart and the spirit that journey to Ithaca."[36]

In "The Miracle" a tired old priest, unnamed, is restored to faith by the death-bed confession of Barbaroulis, an irreverent rake. He is one of Petrakis's several satyrs and hedonists, "a grizzled and growling veteran of three wars and a thousand tumbled women."[37] After forty years of service the priest feels he is failing God because his heart is not in his work. In despair he visits his friend Barbaroulis at the Little Macedonia coffeehouse where they banter about death, the devil, God, and each other. The priest calls him "Saint Barbaroulis" of "The Holy Order of Mastiha" who might have been a good deacon of the church. Returning the compliment, Barbaroulis says the priest would have made a good wencher. Then one night the priest is summoned to his friend's death bed. The *miracle* of the title takes the unexpected form of a last-minute confession by Barbaroulis. He has known a thousand men and women well, he says, but he has loved only one: "A priest who reflects the face of his God."[38]

In the humorous story "The Journal of a Wife-Beater" the girl Nitsa is the niece of Father Antoniou. Her husband Vasili, a stupid sexist, believes in "improving" his wife by beating her. Instead of having the broken television set repaired and doing other nice things for her, he hits her. Much to his surprise, Nitsa strikes back, giving him blow for blow. Vasili bitterly complains to Father Antoniou. In a conversation heavily laden with irony the priest pretends to be on Vasili's side, knowing only too well that Vasili deserves his comeuppance. When he attempts another beating to end once and for all his wife's mutiny, Nitsa bounds after him with a cleaver; he falls down the stairs and ends in the hospital with a possible concussion. Vasili now admires Nitsa. As he writes in his journal: "I had fancied myself married to a mortal woman and instead was united to a Goddess, a fierce Diana, a cyclonic Juno!"[39]

Petrakis takes a potshot at boards of trustees of the church in *A Dream of Kings*, reminding us thereby that his father had troubles with such a board as described in *Stelmark*. His protagonist Matsoukas owes a gambling debt of 483 dollars to Falconis the bookie. Falconis wishes he could belong to the Mafia so he could punish Matsoukas properly. Alas, he says, "the Greeks are incapable of such unity and dedication." Matsoukas counters, "Join the Board of Trustees of some of the Hellenic churches."[40] They include men who emulate the tactics of Falconis's Sicilian idols.

At times Matsoukas acts like a Job and criticizes God for His cruelty. In another instance, pursuing one of his wild plans, Matsoukas seeks an audience with Bishop Zenoitis who is renowned for the way he thunders against life insurance—it makes widows "secretly jubilant, impatient for death to call, 'Haul ho!' for the coffined remains." At the archdiocese Matsoukas is stopped from seeing the bishop so he describes his scheme to a young deacon instead: that the church cremate one thousand corpses, get a small surplus rocket from the U.S. government, fill a special urn, and blast off from either Soldier Field in Chicago or Yankee Stadium in New York, with the grandstand packed, to send the satellite "whirling forever around the earth in God's pasture for a truly celestial interment!" All other denominations will be envious of the Greek Orthodox church. Matsoukas cries, "We will be the first faith into space!"[41] The young deacon, frightened for his life, hurriedly crosses himself and escapes from the "madman" who comes with such a plan.

In "The Bastards of Thanos" the priest hopes for a miracle to restore the faith of the dying old lecher, Thanos. That sign from God appears in the unexpected person of Petros, one of the countless bastard sons that Thanos fancies he has spawned throughout the world. The *waves* mentioned in the title story "The Waves of Night" refer to the routine duties of Father Manos. He, like the priest of "The Miracle," suffers the agony of a fading faith. At fifty-nine he is weary of the prison of his routine. "There was the peculiarly Greek conception of the priest having to spin like a whirling dervish to fit the parishioners' vacillating moods and needs."[42] Father Manos tries to maintain a balance so he can survive. He knows that Father Peter at St. George's is caught between two rabid factions, that Father Theodore of St. Dionysios is under attack for having gambled and drunk. The constant bickering, the malice, the reckless rivalry of groups, the vanity of the wealthy, the resentment of the poor—"Our priests are forced to wear the mask of clowns and fools, the savage Father Grivas of Holy Trinity Church often cried" (p. 187). These and other attitudes toward the church emerge in a long story that dramatizes a week of crisis in the life of Father Manos. At the end he, too, by a simple act of devotion, has some of his faith restored.

We see Father Manos preparing for the Sunday service. He puts on the stiharion, the long robe, the stole, belt, and cuffs. He enters the sanctuary where, to this modern day of liberation, no women are permitted. From the Holy Table he takes up a large wooden crucifix. Then, to face his congregation, he comes out to the soleas, the elevated section between the sanctuary and the main part of the church. After the service Father Manos waits to see those who are waiting for him: a drunk asking for money, who is promised a basket of food; a man named Yalukis, who wants the priest to speak to his son Sam about his refusing to serve because of Viet Nam; and Angela Fotakis, a girl over thirty, whose parents have found an older man to marry her. Father Manos counsels her that youth can also be cruel. After the service he eats at the bountiful Lantzounis table. As in the case of other priests, Petrakis shows him to be sexually frustrated. Father Manos after food and wine has an urge to pat the slender behind of Aspasia Lantzounis. Also, he has confiscated from an eighth grader a magazine with photographs of nude women; and he sometimes imagines himself resting on a soft bosom. Then he looks at his wrinkled hands. "They seemed desiccated and bloodless like the hands of the saints in the icons" (p. 198).

At four o'clock that Sunday afternoon Father Manos officiates at a baptism, which is followed by a reception at the St. Regis Hotel. The girl is Greek, the father is non-Greek, but rich; his being manager of a lucrative Ford agency had helped "to obliterate the parental wrath." At 8 o'clock Father Manos speaks before the Daughters of Sparta. Later he receives a phone call from Mercy Hospital where the nine-year-old son of Peter Kramos is dying of leukemia. The child dies while taking communion. Raging with grief, Peter Kramos beats Father Manos, screaming, "Goddam you priest bastard! Goddam your God! Goddam animals who let my son die!" (p. 207). When the priest gets home, in pain, he too wonders why God let the boy die. The next time he eats with Father Grivas at the Hellenic Café he expresses his spiritual doubts. They drink and talk. Father Grivas attacks other priests for being toadies before "pimping merchants obsessed with spoils while children burn in Viet Nam!" (p. 216). When Father Manos says he can no longer find God, his bitter friend thinks he has finally awakened to the absurdity of the religious charade in which they are involved. "Hate alone," Father Grivas says, "keeps me alive" (p. 219).

On Saturday morning Father Manos sees Bishop Okas in order to confess his doubts. He tells the bishop that a great fear comes to him in the night . . . more of the *waves* of life and death. Bishop Okas seeks to reassure him, and says that "life is a jungle," but that through it runs "the road of faith" (p. 226). Since man cannot save himself, all he can do is keep the faith alive until Christ returns. The next morning in church the old sexton, Janco, whose simple duty is to open the door, comes to Father Manos. He is terrified, the crooked-limbed gerontion says, of committing "some terrible indiscretion before his priest and his God" (p. 230). Father Manos, himself in spiritual pain, understands. He manages to console Janco. Both have tears in their eyes.

Father Naoum in the novel *In the Land of Morning* has a fifteen-year-old son, George, who allegedly spends his ample time away from home "in some basement corner smoking hashish with a group of his cronies."[43] The priest hates not only beatniks but also the Hellenic Hour on television, including the "pompous idiocies of the program host, Banopoulos." The programs themselves are "abominable and inept exercises in hyperbole" (p. 32). Because his wife Lambrini is too fat to love, Father Naoum occasionally desires a parish widow or a mature unattached woman. This era of sexual freedom bothers him; he finds family loyalties gone, the youth embittered by much including the Viet Nam war. Father Naoum has a daughter, Ellie, whose husband Jim was killed in that war. She has a baby son, Paul. The neighborhood in which Father Naoum lives has deteriorated badly, into a "bleak landscape of desolate yards . . . littered alleys where rapacious rats and cats foraged after scraps among the cans of garbage" (p. 37). The old priest and his parish are dying at the same time. Father Naoum has to serve those Greeks who remained in a "ménage of taverns, flophouses, missions and seedy cafés, beset by the evils of gambling, prostitution, and assaults" (p. 38).

The protagonist, Alex Rifakis, eventually falls in love with Ellie. Although she is "moist and seminal," she is one of Petrakis's less volatile widows. Father Naoum takes her to a dance; seen from the priest's eyes, it provides the reader with a variety of attitudes toward a variety of people. Father Naoum's son and his friends arrive in "scarlet and yellow shirts, striped bell-bottom trousers and white tennis shoes studded with stars." Alex, Asmene, and Eunice come too. Father Naoum wants Asmene, a seamstress, to make new vestments for him. He knows of her affair with Gallos. During the dance Father Naoum dwells on classical analogy, "that Tsokas [one of the celebrants] was actually Apollo, his dancing possessed of a fleet and divine grace." He makes further analogies: "The exquisite dark-haired beauty in line behind him was Artemis, goddess of hunting and the moon, renewed once more. The walrus-moustached old man at her heels was wily and concupiscient Zeus on the spoor of nubile prey. And the quartet of women standing along the hall, their faces turned in unison toward the dancers, were the Caryatides, descended from the Acropolis to guard the evening's revel" (p. 122). Echoing the outrage of Father Grivas in an earlier story, Father Naoum decries the decline of the Greek race—the "dark, brutish-visaged Greeks" who eat like carnivores and swill dissolutely, a "race of turtles," a species of shallow mediocrity composed of "Small merchants, fools, schemers, gross youth, addle-headed girls, all hedonists, insensitive" (p. 124).

Father Naoum has a presentiment of tragedy when he goes to the Macedonian, a restaurant founded by Avram Dalgounis who is now ninety-six. Asmene Rifakis enters and buys a bottle of wine for her love tryst with Gallos. Avram vengefully hisses at her, "Cursed fam-i-lee!" Father Naoum, though a Christian, seems to put some stock in pagan magic. He tends to agree that the Rifakis family is out of balance. He recalls Kyra Petrou who has accused a woman of being a Striges, a "witch-woman." She in turn had screamed a blood curse on Kyrou Petrou that resulted in disaster. The Daflos was another doomed family. Father Naoum thinks: "Somewhere in the obscure old-country village past of the Rifakis family, a curse had been inflicted upon them, a curse Avram Dalgounis had remembered" (p. 168). Father Naoum has the last word, expresses the tonal idea, at the end of the novel when the fated tragedy has run its course. His daughter Ellie and Alex have left for Phoenix (no doubt to rise from the ashes of their past). The aged priest now recalls his own youth; and he stands once more on the doorstep of his life, "in the land of morning."

Far from Father Naoum's jungle of taverns, flophouses, missions, and seedy cafés are the clerics in *The Hour of the Bell*, set in Greece when the Greek revolution opens in 1821.[44] They are not simple parish priests but leaders of the Christian faith during the nation's bloody rebirth. Nearly seventy, Father Markos has lived long enough to know that good and evil exist in both Greek and Turk. He has a close friend in a Turk, Ahmed Bajaki. After a brief visit elsewhere he returns to his home town of Kravasaras to find out that the aroused Greeks have killed the Turks, including Ahmed. Father Markos laments the cruelty in all; and he praises the good—a striving for reconciliation that smashes on the crimes of war. The fanatic monk, Papalikos (Father Wolf), stands for the extreme of anti-Turkish hatred. He favors genocide. "Mercy is not a word the cursed Musselmen understand!" he roars. "Fire and sword are their religion and by fire and the sword must they be scourged!"[45] Archbishop Germanos, who raised the banner of revolt at Aghia Lavra, cautions against the resort to "senseless massacre." Instead of idealizing his Greeks during their holy war for independence, Petrakis shows them capable of both the highs and the lows of human behavior.

As with Greek priests, Petrakis has also exploited the varied dramatic possibilities of Greek widows. In neither case, however, has he built upon popular superstition and folklore that sometimes attend both types. For example it is considered bad luck by some Greeks to encounter a priest on the street; a person so doing hurriedly crosses himself and escapes as fast as he can. This superstition may have its origin in the fact that the priest often has been the bearer of ill tidings. Given the charge to break the news, he is also the one to comfort the bereaved and otherwise saddened. Father Kontoyiannis plays the role of messenger in *Lion at My Heart*. He arrives very late at the Varinakis home to say that Sheila is in the hospital and bleeding. Her time of birth is premature. Angelo's anger is not directed at the priest; he is already furious at his son Mike for having married an Irish girl. Rather than answer the emergency, Angelo cries: "I go to hell first."[46]

In the fiction of Petrakis all widows are voluptuous. They are depicted as sexually desirable, more so than other women, including wives. Liberated from their marriage vows by death, and seasoned veterans in bed, widows possess pent-up emotions that turn volcanic when released by a wild lover. In some aspects of Greek folklore, however, the widow is an outcast, a pariah, a vessel through whom Satan wreaks his vengeance upon the village. The widow, if young and beautiful, serves as the proverbial temptress whether she wants to be or not. She is taboo for the married men who lust for her. Their wives fear, hate, and often envy her freedom. For these reasons Nikos Kazantzakis dooms the widow in *Zorba the Greek*. In a grim and cruel scene the townspeople stone her to death.

No such dire fate befalls the Greek widows in Petrakis. The first in his fiction, Aphrodite, has a very minor role in *The Odyssey of Kostas Volakis*. She is one of his three Greek widows who own bakeries. Kostas Volakis sees her at the coffeehouse on New Year's Eve. Ordinarily women are not welcome in Greek coffeehouses, much less allowed to dance there provocatively. "The widow Aphrodite,"

Petrakis writes, "laughed loudly and slapped her massive breasts."[47] Before the assembled men she brags of her physical strength.

If the breasts of the widow Aphrodite are massive, those of the widow Angela are "like great cabbages." She appears in the comical short story "Courtship of the Blue Widow." For two years she has mourned the death of her husband, a Spartan and "a giant of a man who worked in produce." No pun seems to be intended by the reference to her breasts as cabbages. Old Mantaris the grocer wants to protect the luscious Widow Angela from the "pillage and rape" of her canny suitor, Mike Larakis. Mantaris calls him a Turk, but introduces him to Angela anyway. The two have a date. For a week Mike plays the shy and lonely comforter. Then one rainy night Angela invites him in for coffee. They listen to music and drink wine. Just as Mike has her melting, the buzzer rings and old Mantaris comes—to deliver groceries that the widow has not ordered. Atop the bag is a cabbage. She suddenly turns cold, wearing her virtue "like a coat of armor." Frustrated, Mike Larakis leaves for Crotty's Bar where he knows a cigarette girl. "To hell with the Widow Angela."[48] All the while he has suspected that she has not been too faithful in her grief; for example, when she had earlier taken him to a small dark restaurant, she had "knocked off that wine like a champion."

Another widow whose husband has been dead for two years is Katerina in "The Return of Katerina." She lives with her father-in-law Lycurgus (namesake of the stern Spartan lawgiver) above their tavern. He wants to retire, hating the idea of Katerina's working in a "smoky room of boisterous men," but she wants to keep the place. After two years of visiting her dead husband's grave, she becomes restless, snappish, envious of lovers in the park. Lycurgus cannot understand why Katerina is so often cross, but Zakinthos does: "She needs a lover."[49] He himself has been a fighter and lecher all his life—a type of character that Petrakis admires. Yet Lycurgus calls him an "animal out of darkness" and kicks him out. Then summer arrives, and with it a group of young blond Norsemen. One of them returns every evening thereafter to see Katerina. She turns radiant, joyous, blossoming anew. It is autumn, and she leaves the tavern to spend two weeks in the country. She returns late one night after closing to report: "This is my husband, Edwin Larsen." Furious, Lycurgus throws them all out. In leaving Zakinthos tells him that he does not weep only for his son. "You weep for yourself."[50]

In *A Dream of Kings* the Widow Anthoula owns a bakery whose kitchen door is visible from the only window in the "office" of Leonidas Matsoukas. From the very beginning she is the object of his lust. So intent is his gaze upon her that he feels Anthoula senses his "muted desire." She usually wears a sleeveless white shift with probably nothing underneath. An old woman named Barbounis, who hates Matsoukas, does the selling in the front part of the store. She derides his taking so long to buy "one raisin cookie." Matsoukas's passion rises when he sees Anthoula. He compliments her *kouloura*. She is "chaste" to him, "her dark eyes seemly with a virtue she has spun from the cloth of her sorrow on the loom of her loneliness."[51] Matsoukas next sees her in church when he has his sick son Stavros in his arms. The boy suffers a spasm. Looking at Anthoula, Matsoukas wishes he could be a "maddened centaur abducting a Lapith bride." The time comes when Matsoukas succeeds in seducing the Widow Anthoula; he performs with "rampant artifice and guile" a fornication described in epic terms—"holding her thighs like the frame of a chariot, he drove forward and down." Illicit love with the widow, however, does not swerve Matsoukas from his obsessive purpose, which is to take Stavros to Greece for a possible cure. When she learns of his going, the Widow Anthoula curses him with cries of "Pervert! Fairy! Queer!" Matsoukas in turn advises her to pray Zeus send her Apollo, "for no mortal man can fill your insatiable tank."[52]

As previously noted, the Widow Delilah in "The Shearing of Samson" owns a bakery, marries Samson Leventis, and reduces him from a lion to a lamb. Because of the severity of the theme (Delilah demands neatness and decorum) Petrakis plays down her physical attributes. She does have thick black hair, ivory skin, dark bright eyes, and majestic breasts. In "Chrisoula" Petros, an enforcer for Antonio Gallos, is killed in gangland fashion, leaving Chrisoula to mourn for him throughout the winter. When spring arrives, she feels a resurgence in her body. Again Chrisoula wants a "wild laughing lover" for her bed. "She came to understand in the lonely passage of those long spring nights that the time of love was brief and that vows of eternal fidelity faltered before the yearnings of her body. There was nothing the dead could offer the living but lament."[53]

The novel *In the Land of Morning* has two widows with prominent roles. Asmene Rifakis was widowed by the death of her husband after he had lost his grocery store in a gambling match with the racketeer Gallos. The young husband of Ellie, daughter of Father

Naoum, was killed in Viet Nam. The two women are brought into significant relationship by Alex Rifakis, the returned veteran who is son of the one and the lover of the other. It is he, too, who feels driven to avenge upon Gallos the death of his father. The Widow Asmene, pictured as a hard and determined woman, has become the mistress of Gallos, who toward the end has decided to sell his properties, marry Asmene, and retire from the underworld. Thus Alex in helping to kill Gallos helps to murder his future stepfather. As for his mother Asmene, Alex sees a "curious opulence about her body, some indefinable fulfillment." He also feels the "immensity" of her strength. In the embrace of arrival, "he felt her breasts, the nipples big and hard as thumbs, the muscles under the slight ripple of fat across her belly, the mound at her loins."[54] Alex expresses an oedipal tendency when he notices "the glitter of her tongue" and wonders "suddenly, disturbingly, how swift and cunning her mouth might be in love." How different is his "sparrow-like" sister Eunice, from whose mouth issues the "thin, sour scent of her breath."

The sensuous qualities of the Widow Ellie are more subdued, gentle, and loveable. As the daughter of Father Naoum, she lacks the fascination of the hoyden. Petrakis stresses her "gentleness of spirit," not her body. Her lover is to be Alex Rifakis, like herself a victim of melancholia. Under the circumstances—his father dead, his mother the mistress of his killer—Alex can hardly match the Homeric sexual power of a Leonidas Matsoukas. Or of an Alexis Zorba, made famous by Kazantzakis. Indeed, when Alex performs rather poorly as he and Ellie first make love, he has a chance to say during the conversation that he feels sorry for the "poor damn Greeks and Zorba." "Every Greek male, whatever his temperament, has to live up to that image of a man living only for wine, dancing, and love."[55] The emotional wounds of war will take much time to heal in Alex. His dream, as he tells Ellie, is to find a little farm somewhere and grow things on the land. Their affair continues until the climax when Zervas, accompanied by Alex, kills Antonio Gallos in his apartment at the Temple of Apollo. Alex leaves for Phoenix. Early in the new year Ellie and her son Paul will pay him a visit. By loving him, she will help Alex recover from his new wounds.

The truism "when Greek meets Greek, they start a restaurant" is only partly true. Restaurants have indeed been very important for the small-business sector of the Greek-American experience.

Petrakis himself, as he reveals in *Stelmark*, owned a shabby lunchroom with a partner for a year or so. Having once been a barn, the place had a lingering smell of horses. His trade came mostly from the factories and the railroads—hoboes and drifters off the freights as well, "men driven restlessly by their secret furies." During that year, Petrakis writes, he "lost his innocence" and learned a great deal. Finally the lunchroom was sold by a ratty broker named Pericles to two Greeks who hated each other. The broker reemerges as Aristotle in *A Dream of Kings*. All the restaurants in Petrakis are shabby with the exception of the Temple of Apollo; but that is owned, not by a decent Greek, but by the gangster and blackguard Gallos.

Petrakis's first rounded description of a Greek restaurant occurs in *The Odyssey of Kostas Volakis*. Glavas takes Kostas and Katerina to his restaurant, the Mt. Olympus, where they are to wash dishes and do other menial chores. The gloomy Glavas complains that he has to cook food "fit for the palates of kings and gods and serve it to beggars and boors." He calls his customers even worse names: donkeys, gorillas, baboons. "A restaurant is like a zoo," he tells Kostas. "The animals grunt and tear and rend their food. Don't get too close or you may lose a finger."[56] Despite its Olympian name, the restaurant has a kitchen whose "stench" makes Kostas sick. The rats who frequent the place are big enough to kill cats; twice they have bitten Glavas. He tells Kostas, "Ali Pasha, the Turkish sultan, is foraging with his harem. They are the real owners here. Glavas only pays the rent."[57] Later Kostas Volakis has his own restaurant, which prospers.

The setting for "Pa and the Sad Turkeys" is a "drab lunchroom in a factory district." The young Greek narrator is as cynical about restaurants as Glavas. He implies that Greek partners will steal from each other. As the son narrates, his Pa is conned by Sam Anastis into buying a crate of turkeys for the bargain price of twelve cents a pound. Anastis "was a renegade wholesale meatman specializing in animals that died natural deaths." Pa gets eighty pounds for only $7.50. All night long he and his partner Uncle Louie boil the turkeys, "fretting around the pots like a pair of mad chefs." The smell is awful. With his bonanza Pa makes up a week's menu of turkey "specials." Mock-epic humor results from the venture: Uncle Louie eats some turkey, collapses to the floor, and is taken by stretcher and ambulance to the hospital. Doctor Samyotas orders Pa: "Go bury those turkeys!"[58] Pa is very sad that he has almost killed his brother. When Sam Anastis comes in to ask if the turkeys are roasted yet, Pa forces a sandwich upon him; and the son hears a "cry of lament and despair from the kitchen." He runs off to get a bet down on the last race at Jamaica.

Vasili Makris, the villain of "The Journal of a Wife-Beater," runs a restaurant on Dart Street. Petrakis attributes to this fictional street the many Greek establishments on the real Halsted Street. Both at home and at work Vasili is a pronounced sexist and penny pincher. Although he is rich, he forces Nitsa's father, a house painter, to pay the one thousand dollar wedding cost. Nitsa and Vasili honeymoon at the nearby Mortimer Hotel so that he can return to the restaurant each night at closing and count the cash. He tries to beat Nitsa to keep her "happy and contented," as his beaten mother had allegedly been. "Women are by nature," Vasili writes, "as emotionally unstable as dogs under the mad light of a full moon."[59] He learns soon enough that he has married a strong woman.

The Athenian Lunch in Petrakis's *A Dream of Kings* is one of his shabbiest restaurants, with a battered pie case, dented and tarnished coffee urns, a worn counter, stained table cloths, and so on. For a good commission Matsoukas schemes to sell it for Javaras, the owner. The broker is the "well fed wolf" Aristotle who was "fined last year for selling tickets to Greece on a steamship that didn't exist."[60] The potential buyer is the dapper Mr. Cascabouris, who must be tricked into making the purchase. To do so, Matsoukas arranges with the union leader Orchowski to fill the place with members getting a free lunch. Bedlam ensues after the union men arrive; even Matsoukas helps to serve the meal. Ironically Cascabouris rejects the proposed deal because, with so much business and work, in three months he would be dead.

Other Greeks in Petrakis's fiction own sleazy restaurants: Nick Manos in "Rosemary," and Alexis Krokas in "The Shearing of Samson." Manos's is located near a whorehouse. Only the Temple of Apollo, owned by Gallos, has enough class to attract celebrities and politicians. Its appointments glitter with gross elegance, attracting "an abundance of tourists afflicted by the mania for things Greek." Gallos himself cuts a resplendent figure as he greets his customers and kisses the hands of women in a courtly fashion. The kitchen is very clean; Gallos inspects it like a general. Although its name invokes the god of light and wisdom, the Temple of Apollo is a fountainhead of corruption.

The gamblers who move about in Petrakis's fiction need not be inspired by the legendary Nick the Greek. In *Stelmark* the author devotes a chapter to his own gambling sickness while a youth. He details the exquisite excitement, the frantic hope, the despair. He often cuts class to visit the bookie joint. Petrakis the gamester begs money with which to gamble; he sells his books, even his brother's suit. He tells of a real person who also figures in his fiction—Gero Kampana—"for seventy-five of his ninety years on earth, he had been abstemious in all facets of his life but gambling."[61] In time Petrakis overcomes his obsession, but he leaves the field with some unexpected winnings: the knowledge and the memories which he puts to creative use in his work.

Among his other virtues or faults, Matsoukas in *A Dream of Kings* is a compulsive gambler. His one good friend, Cicero, is a dealer in the gambling house owned by Falconis. Anxious to raise money for his projected trip to Greece, Matsoukas gambles every chance he has. Well meaning, he always tries to pay back his debts. Petrakis captures the sinister romanticism of Falconis's gambling parlor:

> It was Nepheloccygia, the city of birds, the "Cloud-cuckoo-borough," of Aristophanes. All were gathered in this room, the owl, jay, lark, thyme-finch, ring-dove, chicken and cuckoo, the feathered company of dark-winged dreamers, pigeons of the scratch sheet tip and sparrows of the fifty-cents-across-the-board parley. Around them lurked the falcons and the hawks, the ticket writers and spotters perched on high stools behind the long counter, their heads poised sharply as beaks.[62]

The novel has two dramatic gambling episodes. In the first Matsoukas demonstrates his skill at poker; in the second, as a result of his cheating with "busters," he is nearly killed by Youssouf the bouncer. Both events occur in Falconis's gambling house. In the "inner room" Matsoukas joins a stud-poker game being played for relatively high stakes. Among the participants are Fatsas and Roumbakakis, the fig king. Petrakis describes the beautiful fingers of Cicero, the dealer, his "flesh gleaming like marble in moonlight, holding the deck as a king might hold his scepter, with a grave and leisured grace."[63] For forty minutes Matsoukas studies the game; near him sits old Gero Kampana, ninety years old now, blind and deaf, who periodically stirs and cries, "New deal!" He is the real life personage who is mentioned in *Stelmark* as having played poker for 75 years. Matsoukas wins $670. When the fig king accuses him of cheating, Matsoukas retorts that poker is a skill, "a game of deception, strategy, mathematics, and psychology," and not a game with such elements as chance, alibis, frets, and frowns.

Despite his usually benign chicanery, Matsoukas has the pride not to cheat in gambling. At last, however, he is driven to do so by a desperate need to change his luck. Events have gone very badly for him; he has just broken bitterly and finally with his mistress, Anthoula. Both his wife Caliope and his mother-in-law hate him. Thus back he runs to Falconis, this time with the busters, a pair of loaded dice. Matsoukas wins, but his arch enemy Youssouf spots the cheating. Falconis angrily erases his old debt and banishes Matsoukas forever. The incident provides Youssouf with the excuse to fight him to the death, so intense has been the ethnic-based hatred between them. Although Matsoukas had once won a belt as a wrestler, he is now no match for the powerful Turk. Defeated, Matsoukas has to confront his bitter moment of truth and beg for his life.

The most complete plunge by Petrakis into the gambling world occurs in his fictionalized account of the great one himself, *Nick the Greek* (1979).[64] Nick was a Cretan whose real name was Nicholas Andrea Dandolos. Petrakis begins with a prologue, dated December 1966, wherein a narrator describes Nick's funeral in Las Vegas, the town he made famous. The author then reverts to September 1919 when Nick arrived in Chicago as a Greek immigrant from Smyrna. He gambles away then wins back $25,000 lent him by his godfather with which to organize a business. He lives above the No-worry Club, a gambling joint owned by Elias Korakas and his wife Lambri.

Once beaten by clever Greek gamblers, all "high rollers," Nick undergoes a rigid tutelage at the hands of Nestor, the old master, and then goes forth to battle the giants. Among them is New York gangster Arnold Rosenberg, who wins $500,000 from him. One theme that runs through the novel is the tension between Nick's love for Marina and his destiny to be the legend we know. Another is the pervasive and violent competition between rival gangsters to control Chicago's underworld—a fact of life in the 1920s. The powerful Angelo Genna uses a claim forced upon Nick as a means of gunning down a rival mobster.

At its deeper levels *Nick the Greek* reveals what playing for high stakes does to the human personality, how it strips and hones it to its barest essence. The story of life itself can be told in the metaphors of gambling (until the final cash-in of our collective chips), and perhaps no better and more poignant example can be had than the triumph and tragedy of Nicholas Andrea Dandolos.

Other Greek types play lesser roles in Petrakis's work. Mothers-in-law are invariably bitches, as is, especially, that of Matsoukas; wives are little, if any, better. The author develops no Greek-American war heroes, as Chamales does, by having them actually involved in warfare. His Greeks in uniform are either going to war or returning; what happens to them as veterans is more vital to plot and theme than what they did on distant battlefields. Besides restaurants, bakeries, coffeehouses, and bookie joints run by Greeks, Petrakis mentions a produce company, a funeral parlor, grocery stores, a candy store, the Hellenic Hour on television, and a music shop that fronts for Falconis's gambling den. The Greek wrestler Zahundas is cited in both "The Wooing of Ariadne" and *A Dream of Kings*. Among professionals, only Dr. Barbaris in *The Odyssey of Kostas Volakis* has an extended role to play.

In *Stelmark* Petrakis recalls the Cretans he knew as a child, among them the "white-haired old men from Sfakia dancing on the holidays."[65] The author invests most of his octogenarian and older persons with an epic grandeur that may be deemed both Odyssean and Zorbaesque. A powerful vitalism brings them toward death bursting with exotic memories. The oldest of the grand old men is Avram Dalgounis, who at ninety-six revives and levels an ancient curse upon the Rifakis family. Next, at ninety, is Gero Kampana, who wasted seventy-five of his years on the game of poker. Captain Haritos, now eighty, has been a wandering lover and maker of bastards, as has the dying lecher Thanos in "The Bastards of Thanos." In another story the character Zakinthos is a "veteran of 10,000 drinking bouts and three wars." In "Dark Eye" the tragic puppetmaster of the Karaghiozis drinks himself to death. Old grooms for young brides and old priests in vanishing parishes appear in the fiction—as do perhaps the most exotic elders of all, the retired bodyguards and hit men of Antonio Gallos—big-game hunters who murdered with grace and skill.

Harry Mark Petrakis has depended heavily on the Greek experience in America for his characters, themes, settings, and plots. By writing so abundantly about Chicago's Greek Town, he becomes an urban regionalist whose local color derives from a nearly autonomous ethnic enclave. It is truly remarkable that an ethnic novelist should succeed so well at a time when in the shrunken fiction market the slick, the esoteric, and the vulgar are touted. The first novels of Petrakis appeared on best-seller lists long before ethnic, native, and minority studies grew popular; and now that such studies are standard offerings in many universities, Harry Mark Petrakis will undoubtedly receive increased critical attention. His major achievement to date may well be his large gallery of Greek-American characters; and among those the most appealing and enduring may be the comic. As a group his Greeks are genuine ethnic types who reflect the diaspora and subsequent progress in their adopted land. Some move as archetypes enriched by resemblance to ancient antecedents, but most of them speak for themselves. The whole corpus of Petrakis exemplifies the continuing viability of the ethnic dimension in American literature.

12

PRIVATE EYES AND VICTIMS

To APPLY THE WORD *mystery* to *Oedipus Rex* perhaps reduces the stature of the great tragedy and gives to the genre of detection an undeserved status. The fact is that Oedipus had to find the criminal whose rash and unnatural deeds brought the blight upon Thebes. Step by step the powerful drama unfolds the truth, and Oedipus recognizes in a shattering climax that the seeker and the sought are one—himself. Unfortunately the detective or mystery story today too often means a potboiler filled with sensationalism, stock characters, excessive violence, lurid sex, and foul language. Many of them also tend to stereotype the modern Greek as greasy, stupid, perverted, sneaky, repulsive, and so on. These are bigoted attitudes not taken very seriously in fiction that is not highly regarded. Other mysteries, of course, both here and abroad, brilliantly achieve the true excellence of literature. From the days of Poe to Agatha Christie, the genre has brought countless hours of pleasure to millions of readers.

Most of the American mysteries with Greek characters appeared during and after the sixties. Although some of the ethnic images they conveyed were negative, the Greek-American community paid no attention to them. These novels perpetuated a practice that was initiated in the early thirties by three writers: Dashiell Hammett, Ellery Queen, and James M. Cain. Queen and Cain both employ Greeks as murder victims; one is a rich New York art collector, the other a poor restaurant owner. A number of more recent mysteries have Greeks as gangsters. In this type of novel the first Greek may well be Joel Cairo in Hammett's famous classic, *The Maltese Falcon* (1929).[1] One needs to say *may* because the author is not entirely clear about Cairo's nationality. Most of the time he refers to Cairo as "the Levantine," an appellation more geographic than ethnic. Nor is the name *Joel* likely to represent a Greek name Anglicized. However, other evidence points firmly to the fact that Hammett intended Cairo to be of Greek descent.

Early in the story Sam Spade, the tough detective, has occasion to disarm and knock Cairo unconscious. In going through his pockets, he finds "a much-visaed Greek passport bearing Cairo's name and portrait" (p. 42). After Spade's partner has been mysteriously killed, Lieutenant Dundy takes Cairo to headquarters for questioning as a suspect. Then Spade asks Cairo if Dundy had beaten him, and he answers yes. Indignant, Cairo says, "I shall certainly take the matter up with the Consulate General of Greece and with an attorney." Perhaps the most conclusive evidence of his nationality comes from Caspar Gutman, the "fat man" who also seeks the fabulously valuable Maltese falcon. Sam Spade has the bejeweled statuette. Gutman wants to know how much Joel Cairo has offered him for it. When he learns the sum is ten thousand dollars, he scoffs, "Ten thousand, and dollars, mind you, not even pounds. That's the Greek for you. Humph!" (p. 96).

Caspar Gutman recounts to Spade the history and the value of the Maltese falcon. The foot-high bird, crammed with precious jewels, is worth untold millions on the gem market. Coming up to the present time, Gutman mentions another Greek, an art dealer.

For seventy years, sir, this marvelous item was, as you might say, a football in the gutters of Paris—until 1931 when a Greek dealer named Charilaos Konstantinides found it in an obscure shop. It didn't take Charilaos long to learn what it was and to acquire it. No thickness of enamel could conceal value from his eyes and nose. Well, sir, Charilaos was the man who traced most of its history and who identified it as what it actually was. (p. 112)

Seventeen years have passed since then. Gutman found the Greek dealer reluctant to convert his treasure into money, perhaps hoping to do business with a wealthy order descended from the original owners, the Order of the Hospital of St. John of Jerusalem, later called the Knights of Rhodes. The fat man continues: "One year to the very day after he [Konstantinides] had acquired it . . . I picked up the *Times* in London and read that his establishment had been burglarized and he had been murdered. I was in Paris the next day" (p. 113). What Gutman tells Spade makes an interesting detail: it seems that Charilaos is the first Greek in American literature to be a murder victim. He is not, by any means, the last.

The Maltese Falcon may also be the first work in which the legendary gambler Nick the Greek is mentioned. Another murder victim in the story is Floyd Thursby, a gunman. The police detective Tom Polhaus fills in Sam Spade about Thursby's unsavory past in St. Louis, New York, and Chicago, where he became the bodyguard for a mobster named Dixie Monahan. The detective informs Spade, "That was when Dixie was almost as big a shot as Nick the Greek in Chicago gambling" (p. 127). Neither Nick the Greek nor Konstantinides looms large in the plot; the only Greek to play an important role is Cairo.

Another avid seeker for the falcon, Cairo has arrived in San Francisco from Constantinople along with Gutman and a mystery woman, Brigid O'Shaughnessy. We see him first when he enters Sam Spade's office to offer him five thousand dollars for the statuette—supposedly on behalf of the rightful owner.

Cairo and Miss O'Shaughnessy have been sent to San Francisco by Gutman to find the Maltese falcon. Sam Spade becomes involved when she hires him—ostensibly to look for her missing sister. Actually she and the others want to enlist Spade's help in re the bird. Three murders occur, including that of Miles Archer, Spade's partner. During the revelations at the end it turns out that Brigid O'Shaughnessy killed Archer while Gutman's gunman, a boy named Wilmer, killed both Thursby and a Captain Jacobi who managed to bring the falcon to Spade's office where, badly wounded, he died. Joel Cairo flits in and out of the action. When he threatens Spade, the detective disarms him and searches through his pockets. Cairo is more comical than sinister. Unlike O'Shaughnessy, Gutman, and Wilmer, he neither kills nor orders anyone's death. At the conclusion, Sam Spade has the police go after the whole group of jewel thieves and is surprised that Brigid O'Shaughnessy killed Archer. Wilmer kills Gutman because the fat man had agreed to hand him over as the murderer. Ironically, too, the Maltese falcon over which they conspire, struggle, and die is a fake.

In *The Maltese Falcon* Dashiell Hammett has an important character often referred to as the fat man. Hammett goes from fat to thin in his popular next novel, *The Thin Man* (1933), named after the murder victim.[2] Hammett's new detective is Nick Charles, a Greek whose real last name is Charalambides. His wife Nora says: "He's an old Greek fool, but I'm used to him" (p. 218). On two other occasions Nora calls Nick a "Greek louse." He himself reveals his nationality early in the story when Dorothy, the damsel in distress, comes to him for help. Nora says, "She's got so much confidence in you, Nicky." He replies: "Everybody trusts Greeks" (p. 210). He also explains what happened to his father's long name upon reaching America. "When the old man came over, the mugg that put him through Ellis Island said Charalambides was too long—too much trouble to write—and whittled it down to Charles. It was all right with the old man; they could have called him X so they let him in" (p. 218). The characters of Sam Spade and Nick Charles differ widely. Spade is an active detective whereas Charles has been retired for six years, "since 1927," he says. Spade is tough and violent, but Charles is suave, urbane, rich, upper class. Spade is a loner; Charles is married to Nora, whose father willed them much property. Charles retired from sleuthing in order to manage the estate.

Nick and his wife live in San Francisco but have come East to New York for the Christmas season. The girl Dorothy Wynant barges in on Nick at a speakeasy and asks about the location of her stepfather, Clyde, who had once been a client of the detective. From that moment on Charles becomes increasingly involved; and three murders later he solves the case with a brilliant display of skill. The murder victims are Julia Wolf, Wynant's confidential secretary; Arthur Nunheim, her friend; and Clyde Wynant himself, the thin man for whom the novel is named. The killer of all three is Herbert Macauley, Wynant's lawyer, who has used his powers of attorney to embezzle large amounts of money. He murders Wolf and Nunheim when they discover evidence of his game. That game, as Nick Charles soon suspects, includes the previous murder of Clyde Wynant in order to fleece his rich estate.

A minor mystery that remains unsolved is why Dashiell Hammett has his protagonist, Nick Charles, be a Greek in the first place, unless he felt that doing so added a touch of the exotic to his whodunit. Toward the end he stresses the Greekness of his hero when Nora says, "Explain that to me, Mr. Charalambides" (p. 368). For in fact Nick Charles is a Greek in name only. Like many a Hemingway hero, he seems always to have a drink in his hand; but the drink is never *ouzo*, *raki*, or *mastiha*. Except for the name-shortening at Ellis Island, his Greek background is not mentioned. We get no ethnic past. Other than a vague reference to his father, there are no allusions to his family. Nick and Nora eat out a lot, but not at any Greek restaurant. Even in anger, Charles never utters an expletive in his native tongue, as one might expect a real Greek to do. Nevertheless Hammett clearly intends him to be regarded as one, for whatever his reasons. In addition, the film vogue begun by *The Thin Man* brought together William Powell and Myrna Loy as a mystery-comedy team. As one might expect, the Hollywood producers did not exploit the Greekness of their suave leading man.

Not of Greek descent but more famous as a private eye is Ellery Queen in *The Greek Coffin Mystery* (1932).[3] In this early Queen whodunit, a wealthy Greek art dealer and collector, Georg Khalkis, dies at his home on 54th Street in New York City. "It goes without saying that when Georg Khalkis dies of heart failure no one, least of all Ellery Queen, suspected that this was the opening motif in a symphony of murder."[4] The mystery opens with the burial of Khalkis, who was blind, in a private church cemetery next to his ancestral home on 54th Street near Madison Avenue. Queen has the Khalkis family as parishioners of this church for "almost two hundred years," a curious fact in itself: a wealthy venerable Greek family dating to colonial days, but not Greek Orthodox. This is possible, but it needs explanation.

Faulkner in *The Sound and the Fury* has his idiot in Benjy, and Ellery Queen has his in Demmy, the nickname for Demetrios Khalkis, cousin of the decedent. Other Greeks in the novel include Delphina Sloane, Khalkis's sister married to Gilbert Sloane, manager of the Khalkis Galleries; Alan Cheney, her son; and Trikkala, the Greek interpreter. The rest of the cast in this relatively long novel is non-Greek; and the novel has no ethnic details or coloring whatsoever. Apparently the name *Khalkis* like that of *Charalambides* is Greek for exotic purposes only.

No sooner does the funeral party return to the house than Woodruff, the lawyer, discovers that the iron box containing the new Khalkis will has been stolen from the safe. When cross-examined, the lawyer reveals that Gilbert Sloane was dropped as a beneficiary and another person's name, not known to him, inserted by Khalkis. Where is the will, who took it, and why? All preliminary investigation fails, so Ellery Queen, the son of Inspector Queen, enters the case to apply his "ability to combine pure reason with practical criminology" in order to find the solution. All other detectives, district attorneys, sergeants, and assorted minions of the law appear crude beside his cool calculations and deductions. Ellery's first conclusion: the iron box with the will must have been left in *"the coffin itself, with Khalkis' corpse in it!"*[5] They plan to disinter the coffin.

All the principals gather for the unusual event. When they open the coffin they discover another body lies on that of Georg Khalkis, a putrescent body all blue and blotched! Pushy newsmen hounding the police for a story are here as well. Ellery Queen uncovers the identity of the second corpse as that of Albert Grimshaw, a forger newly released from Sing Sing. Questions and answers continue for page after page. Inspector Queen calls for Trikkala, "that Greek interpreter" who hangs around the Criminal Courts Building, in order to quiz the idiot, Demmy. The inspector orders autopsies on both corpses to determine the time and cause of death. Trikkala, when he arrives, turns out to be a "roly-poly, greasy individual," who immediately questions Demmy concerning his movements during the fatal night and morning after. The imbecile Demmy, it turns out, dressed Khalkis daily according to strict schedule. Also, he goes to a psychiatrist twice a month. Trikkala gets nothing very useful from him. The author seems to be casting suspicion on the nephew, Alan Cheney, a drunk.

In time Ellery Queen, who is brash and very literate, announces the killer of the convict Grimshaw—Georg Khalkis. Years before, apparently, Grimshaw had brought Khalkis a Leonardo da Vinci painting stolen in Europe, which the Greek dealer, having lost most of his fortune, sold while Grimshaw was in Sing Sing. Released, he accosted Khalkis for blackmail money; and rather than pay, Khalkis killed him. The excitement in turn killed him—leaving the mystery of the altered will, the suspected relatives and associates, and Ellery Queen searching for answers. Soon, however, Queen's supposition collapses, and the real murderer is still undetected. So the plot goes, back and forth, with shifting clues and evidence, until Queen begins to fit the puzzle together toward the end. He finds the Khalkis will was burned. Gilbert Sloane's real name, it turns out, is Gilbert Grimshaw; he is brother of the murder victim. Gilbert commits suicide, and that concludes book 1.

The final book opens with Delphina Sloane telling Inspector Queen (1) that Gilbert, her husband, did not murder anyone, and (2) that his death was murder, not suicide. These truths become evident just before Ellery Queen's typical summing up when, as a result of a shootout, the criminal masterminding all the trouble, Assistant District Attorney Pepper (blackmailer, thief, murderer), now lies dead. One of those originally suspected, Alan Cheney, has been exonerated and will now manage the Khalkis fortune and the Khalkis Galleries.

Not long after *The Greek Coffin Mystery* and Hammett's *The Thin Man*, James M. Cain published a tale of crime and punishment called *The Postman Always Rings Twice* (1934)[6] Whereas Hammett has a Greek private eye in Nick Charles, and Queen has the rich Khalkis, Cain in the character of Nick Papadakis has an impecunious Greek murder victim. With his wife Cora, a non-Greek, he owns the Twin Oaks Tavern, a "roadside sandwich joint" that consists of a lunchroom above which they live. They also have a filling station and a "half dozen shacks they called an auto court." They seem to be getting along well until a drifter arrives by the name of Frank Chambers. Actually the Greek's wife hates him, a feeling that contributes much to plot motivation.

The story is told from the first-person point of view by Chambers. Not only does this technique provide the usual internal account of the action, it also helps to effect a very dramatic and, more or less, surprise ending. The character of Papadakis, though not the protagonist, plays a major role since it is around him that the evil of others swirls. He is its focus and ultimate victim. He emerges as a friendly outgoing person to whom the narrator, however, ascribes certain traits that are negative and stereotypical. Some expression of negative details may be needed in the plot in order to justify his wife Cora's duplicity in his killing. When the cuckolding of Nick begins, Cora tells Chambers: "And you're hard all over. Big and tall and hard. And your hair is light. You're not a little soft greasy guy with black kinky hair that he puts bay rum on every night" (p. 15). Nick Papadakis is obtuse, childlike, dumb. He cannot see what's going on right under his nose. And the author gives him a distinct Greek accent, a departure in dialogue from previous authors using Greek-Americans.

Nick says *Hokay* for *Okay*. When he describes the clean air where he lives he says: "Nice, a clear, alla time nice a clear" (p. 2). Of course Cain does not give Papadakis much chance to speak: early in the action Nick Papadakis is dead, having had his skull cracked with a wrench by his wife's lover.

The liaison between Cora and Chambers, the drifter given a job by Papadakis, begins immediately. At the outset he asks: "How come you married this Greek, anyway?" (p. 5). Although Papadakis does all he can to please the young stranger, Chambers plans to deceive him. The narrator makes the Greek simpleminded and sentimental about his American wife, as if it were a special triumph on his part to have such a treasure. Nick says, "She is my little

white bird. She is my little white dove." He entertains Cora and
Chambers by singing and playing his guitar, and by giving them
wine. "He poured some out of the bottle, but it was sweet Greek
wine, and made me sick to my stomach" (p. 7). In fact, Chambers
vomits, but not only because of the wine. He vomits because he
wants Cora so badly.

He gets her in no time. Their first attempt to murder Nick Papadakis fails. Cora answers her new lover's question about why she
married the Greek. "You spend two years in a Los Angeles hash
house and you'll take the first guy that's got a gold watch" (p. 13).
Cora's bitterness is turned upon herself. Her life has been shabby;
and she feels shabby now, explaining she can no longer stand being
touched by a greasy Greek. Frank Chambers to her is not greasy,
but Papadakis is.

Chambers leaves for a while after Cora clobbers but does not kill
her husband. Recovered, Papadakis runs into Chambers again and
greets him warmly. "Well Frank, you old son a gun, where you
been, put her there, why you run away from me just a time I hurt
my head I need you most?" (p. 35). On the morrow Nick wants
them all to attend a fiesta in Santa Barbara. An example of pride
is Nick's showing Chambers his private scrapbook that holds his
naturalization certificate, his marriage certificate, license to do
business, a picture of himself in the Greek army, pictures of him
and Cora when they got married, and other items. "Over the naturalization certificate he had a couple of American flags, and an
eagle, and over the Greek Army picture he had crossed Greek
flags, and another eagle, and over his wedding certificate he had a
couple of turtle doves on a twig" (pp. 38–39). Unfortunately for
Papadakis, his little turtledove Cora still has murder in her heart.
The renewed urge to kill him rises abruptly when Cora tells Chambers that the scrapbook has a purpose. "*It's to show to his children!*"
she cries. Then she says, "I can't have no greasy Greek child,
Frank. I can't, that's all. The only one I can have a child by is you.
I wish you were some good. You're smart, but you're no good"
(p. 41). They both know that, but they love each other anyway.

They murder Nick Papadakis on the way to Santa Barbara, making it seem like an auto accident caused by drunken driving. They
stop next to a gorge with a five-hundred-foot drop. At an oppor-
tune moment Chambers hits Papadakis over the head with a
wrench; then he and Cora push the car down. He rips Cora's
clothes and punches her in the eye to make it seem she also got

hurt in the accident. At the coroner's inquest the verdict, as Chambers put it, is that "Nick Papadakis came to his death as a result of an automobile accident on the Malibu Lake Road, caused in whole or in part by criminal conduct on the part of me and Cora." It was "recommended that we be held for the action of the grand jury" (p. 63). A detective named Sackett, who has looked up Chambers's criminal record, keeps pressure on him to confess to murdering the Greek. "Out with it, Chambers. Why did you stick with Papadakis for six months?" And later, "Come on, Chambers. You and that woman murdered this Greek, and the sooner you own up to it the better it'll be for you" (p. 68). During the conversation Sackett gives Chambers an even stronger motive than the murderer was aware of: besides the property for which Papadakis had paid $14,000 in cash, there was something else the Greek had. "*That little $10,000 accident policy that Papadakis carried on his life*" (p. 70). He bought the policy after their first attempt to kill him. Despite the detective's correct surmise, Chambers and Cora go free.

Richer by $10,000 and more, they attend Papadakis's funeral held at a little Greek church. The two killers are proud of themselves, especially Chambers. "We got away clean," he says, "and got $10,000 for doing the job. So God kissed us on the brow, did he? Then the devil went to bed with us, and believe you me, kid, he sleeps pretty good." What Chambers does not know is, as the title of the novel affirms, "The postman always rings twice." That is, if Death or Nemesis or Fate fails to get you the first time, he will get you the next. The ironic ending, when the "postman" does ring again, happens as a result of a totally unpremeditated auto accident. In this one Cora is killed, and Frank Chambers is convicted on totally circumstantial evidence—that and a note left behind by Cora which detailed how and why they had killed Nick Papadakis. The detective Sackett had it all figured out. "We murdered the Greek to get the money, and then I married her, and murdered her so I could have it all myself." What really sunk him, Chambers writes, was that note that Cora put in the cash register so he would get it in the morning but forgot to tell him. He never saw it. "It was the sweetest note in the world, but it had in it about us killing the Greek, and that did the work" (p. 138). The jury was out only five minutes. After the guilty verdict, Frank Chambers waits on death row, and writes his story. Its being available for anyone to read proves that he is already dead.

The Postman Always Rings Twice, of all the mysteries examined here, expresses the most bigotry against a Greek even though that Greek, Papadakis, emerges in a sympathetic light. He, the murder victim, is a far better person that either of his killers. In a novel by Nelson Algren, *Never Come Morning* (1942), some ethnic hostility occurs in a story about Poles on West Division Street, Chicago.[7] The protagonist is an unsavory character, Lefty Bruno Bicek, a prize fighter and bum. Among his ring victims he numbers the Greek "Christopher"—but he is not the Greek that Bruno kills in a brutal and senseless manner. The circumstance itself is sordid, even without the murder. A "club" of bald-headed Poles meets in a warehouse to fornicate with Steffi, Bicek's friend. They will fornicate again that night even though she is menstruating. Outside the warehouse a line of men has formed, each to await his turn. "As he [Bruno] listened a heavy-shouldered Greek, looking like Grand Avenue and Halsted Street, shouldered his way in ahead of the second man in line. Bruno looked at the situation blankly."[8] He tries to scare the young Greek off by saying the "heat" will soon be along, but the intruder does not scare. Then Bruno orders, "Beat it, Sheeny, this is a white man's party." The line of Poles with shaven heads looks on, the girl Steffi shouts "Next!" from inside, and the Greek puts his back against a telephone pole as the fight nears. It is no contest. The Greek boy quickly goes down, smashed by Bruno Bicek's blows; and when the boy is on all fours, Bruno kicks his head like a football. The neck snaps, the Greek dies. This murder hangs over the Polish prize fighter until the end of the novel when, just after a final ring victory, the cop Temzara reaches Bruno Bicek on the rubbing table and says, "Got you for the Greek, Lefthander. Two witnesses. One boy seen the body 'n the other seen you do it."[9]

Still another Greek is murder victim and gangster in *Banyon* (1971), the "novelization" of an episode in the NBC–TV series.[10] Its front page proclaims: "The private eye of the Thirties returns" and "In the tradition of Dashiell Hammett and Raymond Chandler." There is more of Sam Spade than of Nick Charles in Miles Banyon—more muscle and less charm. Throughout most of the short novel Banyon searches for Victor Pappas, gangster and "onetime czar of coastal corruption" (West Coast), only to find his body in the swimming pool of his rich wooded estate. "The body was that of a man, fully dressed except for his jacket. Banyon kneeled. Tugging on the body, he turned it over onto its back. He recognized the dead man immediately. It was Victor Pappas."[11] No explanation is given of how a Greek could rise so high in the under-world as to be a "one-time czar" of the West Coast. For two previous killings Banyon tends to blame Pappas, who has been recently released from prison. But now, the question is who killed Victor Pappas? Banyon proceeds to solve the puzzle. The man responsible for all the killings is Lee Jennings, a radio announcer who wanted to kill his wife Diane and have it seem as if Pappas were to blame. Jennings had hired Harry Sprague, a friend of Banyon's, to do the actual murders. The novel has no ethnic dimension and little value as literature. *Banyon*, however, exemplifies a volume in a series, such as *Nick Carter* and more recently *Kojak*.

Lieutenant Theo Kojak against all the creeps of New York City could well be the overriding theme of both the popular television series and the novelizations based upon the programs. Pocket Books published *Siege* as the first in a growing number of *Kojak* potboilers that capitalize on the renown of the program's star, Telly Savalas.[12] Another Greek-American on *Kojak* is George Savalas, a brother, who plays the role of Stavros. It is Lieutenant Kojak, however, who is the protagonist and who establishes another version of a relatively old archetype, the sleuth. In this respect he differs greatly from Nick Charles, the Greek detective created by Hammett two generations ago.

The Greek ethnicity of both Charles and Kojak is minimal. Now and then a *Kojak* episode will draw upon its hero's heritage. The significance of these two detectives as culture heroes lies in the differing types of investigator whom they represent. Nick Charles is an ex-detective, now rich, comfortable, and happily married, who is reluctantly drawn into the solution of a crime. In speech and manners he is highly cultivated, witty, and blasé compared to Kojak, who uses the talk of the street, the argot of the criminals that he regularly apprehends. Sometimes he tends to be sadistic. Even as a working detective Nick Charles was private, on his own, whereas Kojak has the entire New York City police department at his disposal. He operates from his precinct station—set up like a military command post; we never get to see his domestic life, living quarters, his personal side, so to speak, except on those rare occasions when an episode touches him personally. Conversely *The Thin Man* begins in the Charles apartment where Nick lives with his wife Nora and their little dog, Asta. They belong to the smart set of the twenties when the talk is all wit and sophistication, at least in their circles. Nick Charles invariably sets out to solve a mystery by ratiocination and a minimum of violence, and with some help from Nora he always manages to succeed. Of the long series of *Kojak* television episodes and books only some are genuine whodunits, while many involve stratagems to overcome criminals already known. For example, as the blurb for *Siege* reads: "A sporting goods store becomes an arsenal when three armed robbers hold six hostages at gunpoint and sixty cops at bay. Their demand—safe conduct to the airport and a fully staffed plane within two hours. Their obstacle—Kojak's plan. But, even for Kojak two hours isn't much time." Such a problem would not even begin to challenge the investigative talents of Nick Charles. By the same token, *The Thin Man* by Dashiell Hammett is a minor classic of detective writing, whereas the novelizations of the *Kojak* programs make no effort to be excellent.

The ethnic importance of both the television and the literary *Kojak* lies elsewhere, in the fact that a fictional Greek character and a real Greek actor, Telly Savalas, can emerge so strongly as culture heroes for all Americans. This national prominence of Savalas naturally creates much ethnic pride among Greek-Americans. More than that, Savalas openly accepts his heritage, and gives a break whenever he can to struggling Greek actors and actresses. In an earlier period when the Greeks were fighting against odds for a place in the American sun, their greatest symbol of ethnic pride was Jimmy Londos, the wrestler. Wherever he fought, life-size posters showed him, the world champion, in stance ready to grapple with his new challenger. Today, when the Greeks have achieved their place, not the shrewd wrestler but the suave, sophisticated, and affluent Telly Savalas looms larger than life in everyone's imagination, Moreover, his smiling figure has stood five stories high in the huge whiskey advertisements with the suggestive caption "Feel the Velvet, baby!"

An extremely rich Greek as murder victim is Nikos Karados in Hugh Pentecost's *Girl Watcher's Funeral* (1969).[13] "Nikos Karados was murdered in New York's plush Hotel Beaumont, surrounded by the people who had the most to lose by his death. Possessing a fortune astronomical even for a Greek tycoon, he was noted for his generosity as well as for his ruthlessness."[14] Karados is the girl-watcher of the title. Afraid of sex because he is prone to heart attacks, he watches beautiful women as they model exquisite clothes made by designers whom he finances.

Karados has determined that Max Lazar sweep the world of

fashion with his creations. Before the Beaumont Hotel showing which will launch Max, Karados dies of "natural-unnatural causes." During an attack of angina pectoris, he reaches for his nitroglycerine tablets. His current secretary, Jan Morse, slips one into his mouth, but he dies despite her strenuous efforts to revive him. Soda mints have been substituted for the nitroglycerine.[15]

Timothy Gallivan, Karados's lawyer, reveals that the rich mogul not only left something for all his friends but that he also provided for parties immediately after his death. Furthermore, Gallivan indicates that Max Lazar's fashion show will go on as scheduled. When Rosey Lewis, a journalist and public-relations man for Karados, is pushed out a window nineteen stories up, it is very clear to Pierre Chambrun, the cultivated hotel manager, that the killer must be quickly found. During the great war, Nikos Karados had funneled huge amounts of money to the French resistance when Chambrun had been one of its leaders. He must now find and punish the murderer.

With the help of a Greek named George Pappas, Gallivan throws suspicion on Jan Morse. Mark Haskell, the narrator and Chambrun's agent in tracking down the killer, tries to follow this lead. He is sadistically struck by Mike Faraday, a millionaire who has been having an affair with Jan Morse. But just as things seem to point to her, a new clue surfaces. One of the models reveals she was given a dress by a manufacturer of a cheap line, which Rosey Lewis, now dead, had recognized as a copy of Max Lazar's creations. The killer had obviously pirated Lazar's line to Bernard Dreyfus—dress manufacturer, Nazi collaborator, and enemy of Nikos Karados.

When Max Lazar decides to postpone his showing despite Gallivan's wishes, Haskell informs Dreyfus. Pierre Chambrun arranges to listen in on all incoming calls; and he hears Dreyfus contact Gallivan, who assures him that the show will go on. Gallivan's dreadful sellout has been caused by his bid for the kind of power enjoyed by Karados. Haskell goes to the Karados yacht to retrieve Jan Morse, but they are prevented from leaving by Captain George Pappas. He has joined forces with Gallivan, whom he expects aboard soon. They will dump Haskell overboard, but not Jan Morse (for whom Gallivan has a yen). At the end a switch happily brings Chambrun and the police instead of Gallivan. They arrest Pappas, and the case is solved.

Of the two Greeks in the novel, Nikos Karados is characterized positively and George Pappas negatively. The sinister element in Karados emerges only when someone attempts to frustrate his wishes. His wealth and power transcend that of any Greek ship-owner. Pappas, though a fellow Greek, betrays Karados and brags that over the years he has stolen a great deal of money from him.

Among the other unsavory Greeks from the underworld is Bri-dey-the-Greek in Mickey Spillane's *The Erection Set* (1972).[16] Its title reflects the novel's sexuality and elaborate structure of mystery and mayhem. Spillane's literary gimmickry shows in the effeminate moniker *Bridey* attributed to an international hit man, an artist in murder, a slick sadist with an ice pick. He either kills outright or tortures his victims to the degree needed to extract information for his employer. "A little nothing of a guy who could be buried in a crowd of two thought he was still one of the grand gang of anonymous killers. A first-class ice-pick man who could cripple or murder on order" (p. 101).

The person thus pondering is Spillane's superagent Dogeron Kelly—a Mike Hammer under another name. He has returned from cloak-and-dagger work in Europe to contest his evil cousins who have just inherited Barrin Industries. All he wants, Dog Kelly claims, is the $10,000 left him in the will. But he also buys away from Cross McMillan, his antagonist, a vast property at Mondo Beach for $250,000. More of a plot is needed, and it develops from Dog Kelly's real intention: to break up a big narcotics operation on behalf of the United States government. He ruminates about why The Turk, a drug king, has sent killers after him. If it were mur-der, The Turk would not have used Bridey-the-Greek. Kelly would be the example. Markham, the second killer, would hold Kelly un-der the gun while Bridey would do the butchering. "*Right side par-alyzed, Turk? Or maybe from the waist down? You want, I can make it so that only his head swivels around. He can't even pee without somebody holds his dick and somebody else squeezes his bladder. Like that sex opera-tion, a vase-something, you know? All the way it can go with one slice and not only babies don't he get but no fun either*" (p. 101).

The tough tone exhibited here is the hallmark of Dog Kelly, the hero of *The Erection Set*, Spillane's twenty-first Signet paperback. Kelly's true role does not emerge before the final explosive action. Bridey-the-Greek and his partner Markham think their boss, The Turk, wants them to kill El Lobo, a leader in the world narcotics traffic, who has decided to quit. They and other syndicate figures threaten Dog Kelly because they believe he has absconded with a

haul of heroin worth $70 million. He has the heroin, as his pur-
suers surmise, but not to enrich himself; instead it is to help destroy the drug syndicate. Kelly had killed the real El Lobo ten years
earlier, and had assumed El Lobo's identity as a cover to strike
down the syndicate at the proper time.

Before the final revelations, Dogeron Kelly shows a remarkable
facility in self-defense, great sexual prowess, and a savagery beyond belief. Waylaying Markham in the men's room, Kelly slams
his face against the "two-inch dirty ceramic" of the toilet bowl and
his teeth break "like dry matsos in a splatter of blood that speckled
the stagnant water like obscene curds" (p. 104). Kelly is even
rougher on Bridey-the-Greek. He breaks every one of his fingers
and pins him to the floor by driving the ice pick through his testi-
cles. Later both Markham and the Greek are found murdered because they failed in their mission to kill Dog Kelley. "The same .22
caliber gun had killed both of them, but Bridey had tried to scramble out and it took four shots to pull him down. The last was
through the back of the head and he lay face down halfway out
the open window leading onto a fire escape" (p. 169). That was the
end of Bridey, the Greek killer and ice-pick virtuoso.

The Greek as loan shark for the Mafia is the Greek (no other
name given) in George V. Higgins's *The Digger's Game* (1973).[17] Told
primarily in dialogue, the novel perhaps sets a record for the number of times the word *fuck* is used. In the past the Greek has been
a very small juice man—getting back six for five dollars—but now
the Don has allowed him to collect larger amounts. Among them
is eighteen thousand dollars owed by the Digger, Jerry Doherty,
proprietor of a bar and a petty racketeer. He got into this terrible
bind by gambling and losing in Las Vegas. Against his better judgment, he took advantage of an air flight organized by his friends
in the mob. The flap of the jacket states:

> This is how a slick (Beacon Street) setup like the Regent
> Sportsman's club, Inc., works. It's an air charter operation:
> package tours to top casinos. What its clients—respectable
> businessmen hooked on gambling—don't know is that in ad-
> dition to the front man, a seemingly respectable ex-stock-
> broker, one of the partners, is a Mafia connection and the
> third, put in by the Mob, is "the Greek," the loan shark who
> collects the markers.

The enterprise is smooth, neat, and lucrative until the Digger loses his bundle and the Greek begins to pressure him to pay up—principal plus the *vigorish*.

At forty-one the Greek is a health addict. His muscles are hard and his stomach flat. As he says, he has self-respect. He wants to move out to the country with his family and start a chicken farm because America's going to the dogs. He refuses to wear fancy clothes. The Greek has a reputation for keeping his word; on the other hand, he cannot afford to be lenient with anyone—if the word got out, he would have an extremely difficult time collecting from the others—not to mention his trouble with the Mafia Don. Now he has trouble both with the Don and with the Digger.

The Greek falls out with his partners, Schabb and Torrey, because they feel he cannot be controlled. For example he foolishly charges the Digger more than the Digger thinks is proper, especially among friends. Their difference over the eighteen thousand dollars could lead to violence, which in turn could destroy their profitable shuttle to Vegas. Unable to raise the money any other way, the Digger organizes a theft of furs on behalf of their owner, so he can collect insurance. On another front Schabb and Torrey, both hit men, get permission from the Don to kill the Greek, on grounds that he is too independent. They all agree they erred when they gave the Greek responsibility for collecting on big markers. Now Schabb and Torrey suggest the Greek's operations be handed over to Bloom. The Don agrees. But, the Greek is not as easy to kill as they imagine. "Schabb saw the Greek crouch. He saw the Greek's right hand flash back toward his belt, then forward again with a revolver."[18] It is the Greek who kills Torrey and not the other way around. As a result of the trouble, he gives up the big piece of the juice racket and returns to his "old business," making small loans to relatively poor people, like workers at the G.E. plant. As for the Digger, one of the men on his heist, Harrington, calls up the FBI to say he can exchange incriminating evidence about the thieves for the twenty-five-thousand-dollar reward being offered by the fur company. *The Digger's Game*, without having offered any aspects of Greek ethnicity, ends with the implication that the Digger will soon be arrested.

Among Greek-American authors only Harry Mark Petrakis and Nicholas Gage have fictionalized the Greek gangster. Some real Greeks, of course, are alleged to hold high positions in the underworld rackets. Gage's imaginary Greek mobster is Takis in the novel *Bones of Contention* (1974).[19] The author has been an investigative reporter for the *New York Times*. His writings on the mob include *The Mafia Is Not an Equal Opportunity Employer* and *Mafia, U.S.A.* He also dramatizes the jet-set world of the Greek shipowners in *The Bourlotas Fortune* (1975), to show that greed, corruption, and other evils can exist in high places as well as low. Gage's title *Bones of Contention* derives from the underworld argot "make their bones," meaning that novitiates for the Mafia must "prove their mettle" in order to be "connected" and enjoy both the discipline and the protection of the "family." Two brothers, Vinnie and Angelo Zamparra, who seek the connection from the Old Man, the Don, must dispose of two stolen paintings which have been stored for six years.

The role played by Takis, a minor Greek hoodlum, consists merely of giving information about the two paintings to the FBI agent Martin Visco. Takis calls Martin from the Bergen County Jail in New Jersey to propose a deal. Narcotic agents have arrested him during a raid in an apartment where they find eight hundred grams of *babanya* on a Brazilian and four thousand dollars on Takis, "so they say I was there for a buy," the Greek complains. On his word that he has some new and possibly valuable information, Martin goes to the jail to speak with him. It turns out that Takis had been asked by a fellow petty hoodlum named Oscar Schlitten if he knew any Greek shipowners willing to buy stolen paintings. "Takis, you gotta hand it to you Greeks. Rich or poor you know how to enjoy life—food, women, art. Like take Pericles, he spent half the money in ancient Athens to build the Acropolis and nobody's been able to top it since. I never met a Greek who didn't appreciate the better things in life" (p. 32). All this is spoken primarily to entice Takis into finding a Greek shipowner rich and dishonest enough to purchase the paintings.

After listening to Schlitten, Takis says he has on occasion "had an *ouzo* with a Greek shipowner or two." One of the paintings is a Rubens, the other by a Dutch artist. Martin tells Takis he will return the next day with two thousand dollars for a previous favor done the FBI, and Takis will pursue the matter and continue to provide information gathered on the street. What he actually does is to arrange a meeting between Oscar Schlitten and Martin's FBI partner posing as a go-between for rich collectors willing to buy stolen items. After this initial contact, Takis the stoolie makes no further appearance in the novel. The story ends with the Old Man, the Mafia head, having the two paintings burned. As he says, they are *too hot.*

The main Greek character in *The Rocksburg Railroad Murders* (1972) and in subsequent whodunits by K. C. Constantine is Myron Valcanas, who has to be sobered up to perform his duties as a lawyer.[20] Drunk or sober, Valcanas makes caustic comments and usually contributes a vital idea or two that helps effect the solution. The novels by Constantine feature Police Chief Mario Balzic, "a hokey, untypical detective who works from a bedrock of compassion and shrewd common sense."[21] An unnamed Greek in the story, who owns a newspaper store, is convicted on an obscenity charge by Froggy, a rackets connected politician. Valcanas is hired by the family of Tommy Parilla, a young psycho killer, who hated his father for being a deserter. He kills his stepfather John Andrasko under the illusion it is his real father. Then he kills a top Mafia bagman. Chief Balzic finds Valcanas playing cards in the rear of the Rocksburg Bowl; and they agree that Parilla should get a psychiatric examination.

Valcanas speaks bitterly about thieves and liars in high places, and is especially critical of the then Vice-President Spiro Agnew for his approval of the fascist military junta in Greece. "Mr. Vice President, I'd say, how do you pronounce democracy in Greek? Then I'd ask him how many political prisoners are being held incommunicado in Greek jails." Valcanas is also furious about the junta's banning of books like *Tom Sawyer*. "The colonels have it all their way now, but I give them about three more years."[22] In having Valcanas speak this way, Constantine proves to be prophetic. The book appeared in 1972, and in two years the Greek democracy desired by Mo Valcanas was restored; and the fascist colonels he condemned had lost their power. His young client loses his life.

In a subsequent mystery by Constantine, *The Man Who Liked to Look at Himself* (1973), Chief Mario Balzic has Mo Valcanas defend Mickey Sammara against the charge that he killed Frank Gallic, a partner in the rod and gun club that rents and leases farms for hunting trips.[23] On one of these Pennsylvania farms a dog has dug up a human bone—a curious fact since Gallic has been missing for a whole year. Mickey Sammara and his sister, Tina, run a meat discount house. She was Gallic's fiancée. When her brother is arrested, Chief Balzic swings into action to find the real murderer and solve the mystery.

Valcanas, asked to help, is his usual alcoholic self: seedy, jovial, clever, and acerbic. He arrives on the scene "in the shuffling gait of one whose nerve ends have long since been burned ragged by alcohol" (p. 95). When asked by a state trooper about his black eye, Valcanas blames a woman. "In the South," he explains, "they call it reckless eyeballing, and you can get thirty days for it. Ten years if you're a nigger. Since I'm only a Greek, all I got was some knuckles. Only in saloons is justice so swift" (p. 95). When he and Chief Balzic discuss Tina Sammara, Valcanas delivers a judgment on some Italian and Greek girls.

"Offhand, I'd say she [Tina] was one of those puritanical Italian females, the kind that looks like they ought to be great in the hay until some poor sap gets in there and finds out he's trying to make love with somebody that should'ave been a nun. I know a lot of Greek females like that, and to my mind, there's no worse breed than a Mediterranean body parading around under a Victorian head." (p. 102)

Tina's puritanism has much to do with the mystery and its solution. On various "hunting trips" Gallic with his friends Janeski and Peluzzi went to Canada, Mexico, and Alaska for whores and other girls, and with them Gallic made pornographic movies. The key to solving his murder would be the movies with the girl who was last with Gallic. That turns out to be his fiancée, Tina Sammara. She had gone to Gallic's place unexpectedly and had discovered that Gallic was homosexual. In her fury she killed Gallic, cut him up, and buried him. Mo Valcanas's client, Mickey, is released.

The Greek lawyer also contributes to the solution of the murder mystery in Constantine's next novel, *The Blank Page* (1974).[24] In it Chief Mario Balzic investigates the murder of a college student. A quiet withdrawn girl, she had hired another student to write her papers. He is an ex-gymnast turned poet; and he kills her because he identifies himself with her. If lost like himself, she is better off dead.

As usual Valcanas stumbles about one degree away from alcoholic stupor, yet with his mind alert and brilliant. He can hardly recognize his friends in the bar, among them Chief Balzic and Father Marrazo. The priest patiently listens to Valcanas's speech peppered with obscenities. They discuss the murder. The girl was not strangled, raped, or robbed; but the killer merely left a "blank piece of paper on her stomach." They ponder the puzzle until Valcanas recalls Hemingway and concludes the killer found himself in the same dead end: he was unable to write. Thus he points the way to the ultimate solution. In a backhanded compliment to Mo Valcanas, his intelligence, and his alcoholism, Father Marrazo refers to a study done by a psychiatrist about the fact that "of all America's Nobel prize winners in literature, only one, Pearl Buck, wasn't a heavy drinker or an alcoholic" (p. 83). O'Neill, Sinclair Lewis, Hemingway, Steinbeck, Faulkner—they all fit the type. "Liberty, equality, oblivion," Valcanas cries as he empties his glass and totters out the door. Chief Balzic tells the priest not to worry. "I've seen him [Valcanas] in court slightly less juiced, making jerks out of assistant D.A.'s. Why don't you talk to one of them about it?" (p. 84).

A later mystery by Constantine, *A Fix Like This* (1975), also uses the alcohol-soaked talents of Valcanas.[25] The novel begins with Chief Balzic at the hospital to investigate the stabbing of an obese Italian named Manditti—a runner for the local mob. At the usual impasse in the plot Balzic seeks out Mo Valcanas for help. This time he finds Valcanas at the bowling alley playing cards with Gervasi, the owner. Balzic wants "to talk to the Greek for a couple minutes." Gervasi is glad to let him go. "This Greek's killing me today," he says. Balzic asks him a point of law: how much is a wife's testimony against her husband worth if she volunteers? Valcanas, brilliant as usual, for two free drinks gives the chief a well qualified answer. He also advises him on what to do next in trying to solve the case; and when Balzic buys him only one drink, Valcanas curses him in Greek. He makes no further appearance in the novel, and the reader never learns if Chief Balzic buys him the other drink.

Thomas Tryon's strange novel, *Harvest Home* (1974), shifts the murder scene from Pennsylvania to Connecticut.[26] The story lacks an ethnic dimension reflecting modern Greek customs but the ancient Hellenic tradition provides the rituals and the motives for the dreadful things that happen. A Greek-American artist by the name of Ned Constantine quits his New York City advertising agency and, with his wife Beth and daughter Kate, moves to the remote and archaic village of Cornwall Coombe. Ned is a Catholic Greek, not an Orthodox; and perhaps for that reason the story carries no contemporary ethnicity. The murders of Cornwall Coombe do not constitute the usual fare of whodunits; nor is Ned Constantine a professional detective. As a stranger in Cornwall Coombs he begins to puzzle over various cryptic remarks and odd actions of the natives. The locals are mostly farmers whose main crop is corn. They live a year governed by seasonal rituals strictly observed. All the lesser rites lead to the Harvest Home in the fall, when the "corn is made," the seven-year cycle starts anew, and the Earth Mother is appeased. She either makes life bountiful or brings about a Great Waste.

At first everything seems quiet and idyllic—a lovely New England town nestled in a valley, far from the madding crowds of Manhattan. Then an idiot child, Missy Penrose, points at Ned a finger dipped in chicken blood and speaks what sounds like a warning. Later he sees an apparition known as the Ghost of Soakes's Lonesome. The Widow Fortune deals in herbs, potions, and folk medicine. She cures Kate of her asthma. She takes a proprietary interest in Ned's family for reasons that become shockingly clear at the end. As summer turns into fall, and he enters more of the town's life, Ned becomes certain of some underlying horror ruling the valley. He wants to learn, for example, why no one but the wild Soakes clan can enter the neighboring wilderness of Soakes's Lonesome. A dissident who did, Jack Stump, had his tongue cut out so he could not tell what he found: a human skull in a hollow tree. Ned also finds the skull, and he wonders even more about the many deaths reported to him. About Gracie Everdeen, who allegedly committed suicide by leaping off Lost Whistle Bridge; and Clemmon Fortune, supposedly killed by gashing himself with an axe; and Loren McCutcheon, dead from over drinking; and Roger Penrose, dead after allegedly falling from a horse. None of them dead for the reasons given, but from something else.

Ned's search for answers leads him into frightful knowledge and personal danger. At the final ritual, Harvest Home, the women of Cornwall Coombe initiate the Harvest Lord and Corn Maiden to reign for the next seven years. The youth chosen for the new period, Worthy Pettinger, refuses to serve, curses the corn, and gets executed for his heresy. The wife of the man chosen to replace Worthy, Justin Hooke, hangs herself. A lusty temptress, Tamar Penrose, admits she killed Gracie Everdeen for desecrating their ritual; then she successfully arouses Ned to perform with her sexually, an act which she later reports as a rape. Tamar, during her pain and ecstacy, moans to "my Greek, my Lord," saying, "Plow me, plow me" (p. 336). By this time Ned has alienated himself from Cornwall Coombe and from Beth, who sides with the local women against him. He finally pieces everything together and learns the truth: the women of the town, pursuing the "old ways," have built their lives according to the Eleusinian mysteries of ancient Greece. "Back in the old days there was a cult of women who worshiped a goddess called Demeter. She was the earth goddess" (p. 361). What the women did never became known; and every breach of secrecy "resulted in death." Theirs was a deity of grain— just as in Cornwall Coombe the women chose a Harvest Lord and a Corn Maiden who on Harvest Home "made the corn." In effect this was a fertility rite to guarantee bountiful crops.

What the guarantee demands Ned Constantine learns by escaping from his confinement and secretly, he thinks, spying upon the rites of Harvest Home in Soakes's Lonesome. Justin Hooke, the Harvest Lord, is aroused to "make the corn" with the Corn Maiden, to fornicate with her, to "plant the seed," and the Maiden is none other than—Beth, Ned's wife. Human sacrifice follows. Justin Hooke, drugged and spent, will be executed to make way for the new Harvest Lord, already chosen. As Ned cries out, strong hands bind him, then oblivion. The final brief chapter with quiet but grisly details informs the reader of the terrible fate which has befallen Ned Constantine. His wife Beth is pregnant from the Harvest Lord's seed. Ned himself, though not killed outright, has been blinded and had his tongue cut out. The Eleusinian mysteries of Cornwall Coombe, in Connecticut, will go on forever.

William Brashler brings us back to a more believable scene in *City Dogs* (1976), set in the seamy side of Chicago's new Uptown.[27] There lives a creepy Greek named Gus Koutsos, night clerk at the Vicklen Hotel. The protagonist is a fifty-seven-year-old down-and-out Pole named Harry Lum. The murder victim is Deborah Cortez, "girl friend" of an Italian pimp, Jimmy del Corso. The two detectives assigned to find the beast who knifed and threw Deborah out the hotel window are Johnny McMahon (Irish) and Gene Farber. *City Dogs* reeks with ethnicity, none of it wholesome. Deborah conducted her business in and out of the Vicklen Hotel; so the detectives come to question Gus Koutsos, "a paunchy middle-aged Greek" well known to the Chicago Police Department. Farber suspects Koutsos as a kingpin of vice and other petty crimes in the neighborhood. "Farber had done his homework on Koutsos, an immigrant first arrested for torching a restaurant in the old Greektown strip on Halsted, no conviction, but later one for robbery, then petty theft, then possession and sale of stolen property the police believed he got from small-time Mafia types" (pp. 31–32).

When the detective Farber questions him, Koutsos claims he knows nothing about the murder of Deborah Cortez. The Greek gives Farber the keys to search the hotel rooms for evidence. The Greek night clerk disappears for much of the action; then suddenly he emerges as the prime suspect. As time passes, other crimes and criminals in Uptown occupy the cops, and the Deborah Cortez case is pushed aside; yet all the while "Farber was convinced in his own mind that the answer to the whole thing was probably contained solely in the hotel night clerk, the bastard Greek whom they could smell all the way back to the station but who moaned and complained that he was the cleanest thing out of Greece since Plato" (p. 266).

The solution to the mystery comes swiftly when Farber and McMahon, with the help of Detective Rojas, discover what actually occurred at the Vicklen Hotel. Gus Koutsos fenced stolen goods there to patrons. Rojas explains, "Anyone takes a room here for more than a week and he gets a discount so long as he buys a piece of equipment from the Greek" (p. 267). The case breaks when a complainant, Harris, tells Rojas he bought a radio—not from Koutsos but from a prostitute in the hotel, Deborah Cortez. So the Greek killed her and threw her five floors down. "It's one thing to mess around doing pussy," Rojas says, "but it's another to take business from the man in charge." Farber and McMahon drive up to the new Greek Town, around Lawrence and Western, and arrest Koutsos at home.

The character of Gus Koutsos hits rock bottom as far as the Greek-American image is concerned, being alleged vice king, arsonist, fencer of stolen goods, and murderer. He is also very dirty, paunchy, and stupid, he wears very loud shirts and sports an ill-fitting toupee. Other ethnic types in *City Dogs* (an Italian is a pimp) fare little better. It would appear that some authors of the seamier whodunits, like Cain, Spillane, and Brashler, feel they can freely use ethnic slurs because their creeps, crooks, and killers reek with bigoted attitudes. These attitudes form part of the evil they portray. The question arises, however, of the degree of slander needed to make a point—beyond which point the ethnic slur becomes sensationalism only; or, in perhaps an extreme case, deliberately to foster bigotry. On the whole the modern Greek character enjoys a balanced treatment in the popular murder mystery. With respect to imprint on the public mind, hardly anyone has heard of a Koutsos, whereas Kojak has become a household word standing for law and order.

13

THRILLERS SET IN GREECE

M ODERN GREECE and her islands have long been a favored
setting for adventure, mystery, and spy novels among American,
British, and continental authors. Many stories begin in the United
States, like the romances of George Horton, and then shift to
Greece to be developed and finally resolved. To judge from the
books themselves, the Greek terrain suits many types of action,
from the romantic to the gothic. The popular tourism of Greece
brings together throngs of people—strange, cosmopolitan, and
often sinister. For some writers the Greeks themselves are both
dramatic and exotic. The strategic position of Greece as crossroads
for three continents makes her a natural setting for novels that
exploit power struggles, espionage, and illegal traffic. Finally the
very antiquity of Greece resonates with memory and mystery enriched by archetypes from myth, classical literature, and history.

Since World War II at least eighteen assorted thrillers set in
Greece have been written by American authors. They continue a
literary interest begun by the Philhellenic poets and travelers of
the nineteenth century. For many of these voyagers the "sad relic"
was a land whose inhabitants might or might not have lingering
traces of classical greatness. The travelers went to Greece and returned to record their impressions. Later in the century the novelists found Greece a useful setting for melodramatic romances
wherein the stock heroine, the stock villain, and the stock hero
played their predetermined roles. Out of the wild and misty
mountains rode a new stereotype—the Greek or Turkish brigand—
and he threatened, killed, stole, and abducted fair damsels for his
harem and held others not so fair for ransom. In our time Greece
remains a lively subject for social studies and is still a favored setting for fiction, be it historical novels, war stories, tales of adventure, or thrillers.

Seven of the eighteen are spy stories in which the bad guys are
usually Soviet agents and the good are led to victory by a charismatic American hero. Two of them deal with internal traitors, and

one is a spoof that ridicules the CIA. Three of the thrillers mingle murder with possession of valuable artifacts. Treasure hunts that require dangerous deep-sea diving dominate two plots, while two others provide adventure and menace for female readers who want livelier fare than Nancy Drew. One concerns domestic intrigue and another, opposition to the fascist Greek junta. As one might expect, the Athens area accounts for a large block of settings, five; and the Greek islands account for six. The action of four novels occurs in the mountains of northern Greece, one in the Peloponnesus, and the remaining two primarily in Turkey.

Nearly all the American heroes have Greek friends or foes who play essential roles. One protagonist who goes to the Levant and meets Greeks is Major Hugh North in Van Wyck Mason's *Dardanelles Derelict* (1949).[1] Major North drinks in the Three Moons Café owned by Vasil, a Greek, in the Balata section of Istanbul. An American agent named Stoddard comes to him with the problem posed by the death of another agent, Phoebus Skoularis. Vasil is a "beetle-browed Levantine Greek" who speaks with a slight Smyrna accent. Mason's image of him is both negative and gratuitous since his ugliness is purely decorative. He has no part of the action—but "because of a huge and pointed nose, flaring gray mustaches and tiny, bright black eyes, Vasil suggested nothing so much as a vicious and gargantuan rat" (p. 11). The most important Greek character in the novel is the dead spy. He seems to be the key to solving what is called the "Mata Hari business." From a Soviet agent Major North learns that Skoularis was buried in Vaisal; and he goes there in company with enemy agents to exhume the body. The mystery approaches solution at the Greek Orthodox cemetery of Vaisal, for Mata Hari means "Eye of the Morning," and Major North with a pencil point picks the contact lenses from the corpse's "chill flesh." One of the lenses holds a secret message, the name of a "supreme enemy of the people," according to the Russian. The rest of the cloak-and-dagger operations involves no Greeks, only Greece as a nation. Owing to Major North's brilliance as an agent, the Soviet Union rescinds an ultimatum that could have precipitated war with the United States.

Among deadly Greek beauties Lili Lamaris ranks near the top, in a novel in which narcotics money supports espionage—and in which another rich and powerful Greek shipowner plays a central role. Clearly the rich Greek shipowner has become an archetype or stock figure in modern world literature. The novel is *Assignment*

Lili Lamaris (1959) in the *Assignment* series of thrillers by Edward S. Aarons.[2] His secret agent, Sam Durell, goes to Rome, where he learns that Purdy Kent, another agent, has had his throat cut while "coddling the monster" through Lili, their only link. Durell works for the CIA. American money spent on drugs has been funding an army of foreign spies working against American agents. Durell must locate and destroy this dangerous syndicate.

As his boss Harvey Shedlock informs him, Lili Lamaris is the daughter of Dante Lamaris, a shipowner on the scale of Onassis and Niarchos. Until her retirement three months earlier, she was "the hottest entertainment attraction on the continent" as a ballerina (p. 11). Lili fell in love with Mitch Martin, once the kingpin of narcotics peddlers in New York City, reputed to have fled to Europe with a million dollars. Her father Dante was a naturalized American of Greek descent "who spent most of his time in Europe, on the Riviera or in offices in Athens, from where he directed the web of commerce that rated him as one of the ten wealthiest men in the world" (p. 16). When the story begins Lili Lamaris is in a villa in San Eufemia, a fishing village halfway to Naples. "There was a classic beauty in her profile and the slim youthful lines of her figure. The face, however, was a mask devoted to her art; he [Durell] could not read anything in it." During his briefing Durell learned she was a Radcliffe graduate (no ordinary *femme fatale*), "then tutored by Mensilov, the ballet master and impressario, in New York" (p. 24).

Why she fell for Martin is inexplicable. In the complicated plot Durell faces various contradictions between appearances and reality. An important false lead is the apparent innocence, the vulnerability, of Lili herself. Another is the initial conception of Dante Lamaris as a worried father who desires only to rescue his misled daughter from the evil clutches of an international gangster. Later, in a flashback, the reader learns how Martin took her virginity— "in the warm shadows of the walled garden, on the grass, like a common woman of the waterfront, she reveled in his brutality and the pain and the joy of it" (p. 73). Characters appear whose true relationship to the mystery is typically withheld until the denouement. Durell goes from Italy to Geneva, Switzerland, and then to the castle of a Dr. Koenig in Obersdorf, Bavaria, drawn there by the movements of Dante Lamaris and other major suspects. The main fact surmised by Durell at this point is that Dante Lamaris, the powerful shipowner, also runs the spy ring that Durell has been assigned to destroy.

At the castle in Obersdorf all the records of the spy operations are kept in "the dungeons, below the wine cellar." There Durell will find the tables of organization, plus "the lists of agents, paymasters, petty informers; the pattern of narcotics distribution, the depots, the dossiers on them all" (p. 163). There, also, the final shocking truth emerges. The real shape of conspiracy and murder is Lili Lamaris. Before his eyes, at the moment of truth, she transforms from butterfly to viper. Threatened by exposure, she stabs Martin. The former Radcliffe girl and famed ballerina is "beautiful as before—but different. Gone was her look of bewildered innocence. Her air of tragic confusion had given way to something else, to someone who carried herself with determined pride and a kind of feline ferocity" (p. 167). Lili heads the entire spy ring. She is not an addict as presumed, but an actress. She has used everyone, including her father.

The explanation given to Sam Durell is that Lili Lamaris hated her father Dante, regarding him as evil. In addition, Lili felt that the West did not appreciate her art, but in Moscow her art was appreciated. Therefore she agreed on behalf of the enemy to head a spying and narcotics organization to implicate Dante and to destroy him. It appears that Mitch Martin has tried to doublecross the organization, and so she killed him. Lili Lamaris then fires a rifle at Sam Durell. Martin shoots and kills Lili, then dies. The case is over. Durell sadly looks at her on the snow, gone, but "her face was still a lovely mask of innocence" (p. 173). Another Greek beauty has met her doom in the high tragedy of a paperback thriller.

A greedy Greek millionaire is one of the treacherous cabal that the legendary dime-novel hero Nick Carter has to subdue in *Seven against Greece* (1967).[3] Carter's character has evolved so that for some time now he has been featured as "Killmaster," coded N3 as an AXE agent for American Intelligence. The cold war provided many plots for the thriller series; it was inevitable that one should have a Greek setting. The story begins in Washington with Carter being briefed about a problem caused by the death of an agent in Greece who was investigating a Red Chinese–funded spy operation, the Golden Island Promotions. The Greek front man is Papadorus, a shipowner who is supposedly a billionaire but who has actually lost his money; and his empire survives only because the Chinese find it a useful means of enlarging their worldwide spy apparatus. "His freighters would be landing Chinese spies and saboteurs in ports around the world every day while Papadorus continued to live the good life in his villas and on his yachts" (p. 118). Papadorus has become a pawn of General Lin who, with Gorgas, the Cypriote terrorist, and assorted allies, plans to ship hordes of agents to America, murder statesmen, topple governments, and gain world domination. Gorgas heads a movement known as the Sons of Prometheus. The real brains of the conspiracy is Princess Electra, a Greek as lethal as she is lovely.

Nick Carter arrives in Athens to undergo peril after peril until, at the end, he once again saves the world from destruction. He receives aid from a number of good Greeks including Leonidas: "Uncombed thick black hair, the head of a horse. A real tiger when he was younger, still robust from the look of him. Good man against the Germans and later against the Communists. Bit of a black marketeer in the old days. Not greedy, just made his nest egg. Worth every dollar of it, too, as far as U.S. Intelligence was concerned" (p. 18). Nick Carter is nothing if not a superpatriotic, superreactionary agent of American imperialism. Toward the end of *Seven against Greece* he uses Leonidas and his caique to infiltrate the Golden Island spy operation on Baos Island. During the foray Carter blows up the installation, but Leonidas is killed.

In Piraeus Nick Carter, disguised as Thomas "Pedro" Evans, meets the whore Xenia Mitropoleos, a tall, voluptuous, and beautiful widow who has one peculiarity. "She never slept with a man on Monday," the day she heard of her husband's death on Cyprus. When two thugs try to kill Carter, Xenia the "furious *hetaera*" drives them off with a skillet; later, she breaks her never-on-Monday rule and goes to bed with him. What Xenia "had learned from corrupt skippers of Arab dhowz and coastal steamers" she is willing to use in pleasing Nick, "the great-thighed American" (p. 36). Toward the novel's climax he rescues Xenia when Gorgas the mad terrorist has abducted and tied her, nude, to a column of the Parthenon which he intends to blow up. Before Gorgas can push the detonator, Nick Carter kills him. He also kills Electra: "The heavy knife caught the Princess in the throat and went into her windpipe up to the hilt" (p. 139). Often in contemporary thrillers the hero's reward for a caper's success is a vacation with a beautiful playmate. In Carter's case a yacht awaits him at the harbor, "equipped with enough steaks, wine and Scotch whisky for a month's cruise." And in the cockpit, waving at the big American as he walks down the dock, is "a dark-haired beauty named Xenia, whose grave dark eyes glowed with promise" (p. 158).

The Nick Carter type of agent in the Assault series by Alan Caillou is Cabot Cain with an MS in psychology from Harvard.[4] The fifth volume in the series, *Assault on Agathon* (1972), takes him to Greece, where he matches deadly wits with a Greek guerrilla leader. Caillon is wrong historically when he has a character tell Cain that the British executed Agathon on Christmas 1941. The German Nazis completely occupied Greece long before that date; and the ELAS, which the author calls terrorists and thugs, was the military arm of the EAM, the major Greek resistance movement. To the Nazis, of course, the Greek guerrillas were terrorists, thugs, and Bolsheviks.

The two major Greek characters are Maria Christophorous, another lethal beauty; and Agathon, the guerrilla. The rich widow says, "Two shipping magnates and one industrialist, and they all worked themselves into early graves and left me all their fortunes" (p. 23). An agent, she works as Athens representative for Colonel Matthias Fenrek, head of an Interpol department. Maria has driven north to Yugoslavia in search of Fenrek, who disappeared while investigating a series of bank robberies. She urgently calls upon Cabot Cain to help her find Fenrek and solve the riddle of the robberies. Interpol in Paris tells Cain about the Greek terrorist Agathon, who committed a brutal murder in Florina, Greece. A student of Greek history, Cain believes that the terrorist took the name of Felas Agathon, a Greek general who fought the Turks in 1474 and who was buried in Serigrad. Acting on a surmise, Cain and Maria go to Serigrad with the hope that Agathon might be holding Fenrek there.

Cain's deduction proves correct: the Agathon gang has Fenrek in a house owned by the Kolettis family—Greeks in Yugoslavia— whose son alone remains. To create a diversion Cain sets fire to a stable, then enters the house. Whereas Nick Carter killed an enemy by deftly snapping the hyoid bone, Cain disables a man by hitting the "superficial cervical nerve" on his neck with the point of his middle knuckle. Cain and Maria rescue Fenrek. The "son" of the Kolettis family is, actually, Otho Kolettis, otherwise known as Agathon. The problem is to find him and stop the robberies. Fenrek in this regard provides a clue because his Greek captors had mentioned "Athene's tears." Cain knows it as a spring in the Macedonian mountains that bubbles up near a cluster of rocks, the Athene's Hearth, close to the village of Evropas. Five members of the Agathon gang, just escaped from a Trieste jail, are presumed by Cain to be heading for the same area. Fenrek informs him about a leak in the highest echelon of Interpol. Later in the story, while still trying to unravel the mystery of the robberies and various killings, Cain joins up with a Greek woman, Helen Poulardis, assumed to belong to Agathon's gang. At a hotel room in Salonika they prepare for love when Cain falsely states that he works for Agathon; and the beautiful girl cries: "Please don't kill me" (p. 130). Helen, nude in bed, tells him all she knows about the old ELAS hoard of money in a Swiss account, the numbers of which are a bone of contention between Agathon and Cernik. A sinister new figure enters the plot: the mysterious *wife* of Cernik.

Ethnic touches surface here and there in the story. Helen has "an excellent figure, small-breasted, full-hipped in the Greek fashion"; and upon meeting Fenrek at a noisy café, Cain thinks "the Greeks have a great horror of silence except during the afternoon time of siesta" (p. 140). From a Captain Tsamados of the Greek police he learns that Helen Poulardis had been one of the twenty-five thousand children abducted by ELAS into the Iron Curtain countries; and that Maria Christophorous belongs to the cult of Anastenaridos—a link with Macedonia's ancient past whose members "claim mystical healing powers" and "walk barefoot on burning embers once a year, on May twenty-first, feast day of St. Helena and St. Constantine" (p. 141). Fenrek and Cain speculate that Cernik and Agathon may be planning a second ELAS revolt; thus the money in Switzerland would be used to finance the new effort to overthrow the Greek government. Or would the gang members fight over the money, for whatever cause? Helen Poulardis has stolen the money that was in the safekeeping of Gravena, one of the old ELAS gang—money taken in one of the bank robberies. She has deposited the hoard in Switzerland.

While Fenrek and Cain are eating in a café, Maria Christophorous brings the news that Helen Poulardis is dead. Stricken, Cabot Cain determines to drive to Evropas that very night to assault Agathon, Cernik, or whoever committed the killing. He, Fenrek, and Maria leave in his Jensen. They reach the village of Evropas where Cain is "captured" by an armed band. Their leader, Agathon, looks like the "conventional, stylized picture of a pirate—or a fanatical

Greek guerrilla" (p. 158). Agathon had not seen Cernik (the Bulgarian). The summer villa where they go is comfortable, with "an original Cassalis, one of Greece's newest and finest painters." Cain and Agathon talk. Things are not going well with Agathon's plan to mount a new revolution. He needs to know who Cernik's wife is because she has the money—$10 million.

A battle breaks out in the surrounding hills, "the old wars being fought all over again" (p. 175). Cain and his friends sneak out the cellar, while outside the battle goes on, to enter the villa where Cain gets the drop on Klaus Cernik. They find Agathon dying. "He was still alive, but the blood was seeping out of a long, deep cut across his belly, the Bulgar's terrible stomach wound that kills, but infinitely slowly, and with agonizing pain" (p. 180). Cain unbinds Fernek's bleeding hands. As Cernik tries to escape, they fight, and Cain kills him by breaking his neck. The Bulgar was trying to get the whole ten million for himself.

With both Agathon and Cernik dead, the huge sum of money might never be claimed. Outside, Cain learns that Maria has been shot. Maria confesses what Cabot Cain already suspects: she has been the highly placed Interpol traitor, she was Cernik's wife, she killed Helen Poulardis, and all the time she was Fenrek's mistress. Cain promises her not to tell Fenrek. As she dies, Maria explains all—especially how she schemed to get the money for Klaus, her husband. In a while Fenrek arrives to find her dead. "He picked Maria's body up gently in his arms, and moved off with her over the ancient, broken stones, the stones that had known Athene, and Artemis, and Persephone, and Aphrodite, and Callisto, the most beautiful of them all" (p. 191).

By now one's impression of the rich Greek shipowner is that any money corrupts him, but that huge amounts of money corrupt him absolutely. A corollary seems to follow: that the rich daughters of such moguls, girls like Marpessa Andruledarkis and Lili Lamaris, are sexy beyond belief and evil beyond any redemption. The excesses of character and action common in the thriller easily lend the genre to parody and satire. A novel that spoofs spy thrillers, and incidentally ends in Greece, is *E Pluribus Bang!* (1970) by David Lippincott.[5] It pokes fun at the presidency, the Department of State, the CIA, and assorted flunkies of the federal government. George Ramsey Kirk, the thirty-ninth president of the United States, murders a Secret Service agent whom he surprises in bed with his wife Ginger, a notorious flirt. The first lady has ducked a state dinner in order to effect her liaison. In this way begins a comic novel which goes from farcical episode to episode, until the CIA sends a secret agent to the Greek town of Lindos, on Rhodes. There he is given a parcel to deliver, but he chooses to cross over a stream at a dam rather than a bridge as instructed. While on the dam he discovers the package contains a bomb; the result is that he tosses the bomb into the lake, he gets killed, the dam bursts, and the ensuing flood drowns 832 people. Another brilliant snafu by the Central Intelligence Agency.

The American agent, Toby Raymond, has for contacts in Lindos a Greek named Birbilos and a Turk named Mekne. All spies on Rhodes, including the Chinese, dress like shepherds in baggy trousers and wool vests. "His eyes were a dead giveaway, of course, but the poor man insisted on eating his grape leaves with chopsticks" (pp. 75–76). For Birbilos, a heavy drinker of retsina, the coming of Raymond to Lindos means a possible loss of his CIA job. "You trying to cut a poor Greek out of his job? You came to cut the budget, eh?" The Turk assures Birbilos that is not the case. Mekne tells Raymond that Rhodes is important only as an "easy way to slip into Turkey without being caught" (p. 76). His good humor returned, Birbilos says that the spies qua shepherds are not good for the sheep. "With this many shepherds on a small island, the sheep look better than the women" (p. 76).

Despite the joking, a dreadful fate soon befalls Raymond: while delivering a battered case to a farmer named Pistra, who would give him the details of his real mission, he blows himself up and causes a disastrous flood. Birbilos runs down the slope to retrieve the dead American's shoes. Mekne says they are Hush Puppies. "Very good for running" (p. 79). The Turk manages to escape to Turkey, but the police capture Birbilos. The CIA orders Aronkia, head of Greek Intelligence, to give Birbilos a cyanide pill. President Kirk's military aide says: "The Greeks. Those poor Greeks. First the Communist threat, then the Junta, then the 'seventy-one drought. Now this." The President mutters, "Ever since Spiro," and disappears into his office (pp. 81–82).

Another American author, Leo Katcher, has written two mystery thrillers set in Greece—*The Blind Cave* (1966) and *Hot Pursuit* (1971). The hero of the first is Richard Landon, the CIA's man in Athens, whose desperate mission is to find plutonium missing from one of America's satellites.[6] The hero of *Hot Pursuit* is the dehumanized Captain Robert Braden, an American trained in guerrilla tactics. He rescues a child kidnaped by the Communists during the Greek civil war. Landon in *The Blind Cave* is ordered by Washington to cruise the Greek islands on the luxury liner *Aurora*. To recover the plutonium he must work with the Soviets, whom he hates for having killed his wife; and with Harvey Pennell of the State Department, whom he hates for having once betrayed him. Before the voyage he lunches near the Parthenon with Stavros, a polished, sneaky, dwarfish, erudite, polylingual, greedy, pock-marked stoolpigeon and man of affairs. At another restaurant later, feeling condemned, he eats a Greek dish called *gevetch*. Landon has been made to feel that he will be the bait to attract the malefactors.

What Lisbon was in World War II, Landon believes, Athens has become for the Cold War—a hotbed for international espionage. The Athenians themselves are night people. "Darkness acts upon them like alcohol, freeing them of inhibitions, loosening all the bonds of work and duty" (p. 20). Landon is warned not to leave the *Aurora* for his mission. But of course he does. A Greek in the CIA, Aleko Pappas, is there to help him. "He was a Greek-American or an American-Greek, you could take your choice. He'd been born in Salonika and brought to the United States— 'Atlantic City, New Joisey'—when he was eight" (p. 34). Aleko speaks English "with disdain for number, gender, and tense." On the *Aurora* with them is a major suspect, a Swiss engineer named Peter Wallace.

To Landon the cruise of the Greek islands means constant peril and continual searching. Before they arrive at Rhodes Aleko Pappas is killed. A Greek guide, Paola Lambros, shows interest in Landon. On Crete, during a side trip to the Palace of Knossos, Wallace abducts him and urges him to help use the plutonium to destroy the Communists by allowing the United States a first strike nuclear attack. On Rhodes the guide Paola gives him a thin metal plate wrapped in a paper having four numbers and the word *Chronos*; but Landon loses both after a blow on the head knocks him out. Nobody can be trusted, not even the CIA.

The cruise takes him to Istanbul, Delos, Mykonos, and then back to Athens. An imposter posing as a British agent, but working for Wallace, had killed Aleko Pappas. In Istanbul, Landon is questioned by communists, among them the girl Paola Lambros. She turns out to be the daughter of Yorghis Lambros, an "EDA commander" killed in the civil war. "My father was killed by the fascists," she says. "He was fighting to free Greece" (p. 130). On My-konos he meets with his own Harvey Pennell and the Soviet agent, Colonel Danovich. The soviets are as baffled by the lost plutonium as everyone else. Landon learns that the plate taken from him was titanium, which mixed with plutonium could produce an atomic bomb. The word *Chronos* stood for a Greek-owned ship registered in Liberia with its home port in Piraeus. Landon thinks he has one last chance to learn the truth—Stavros, but Stavros has been stabbed. Before Stavros dies, he whispers that "the woman knows."

Who is the woman? Landon finds a Mrs. Harris dead in her apartment, killed shortly after Stavros. Finally the CIA with Lan-don's help solves the mystery. They pinpoint the Greek island where the atomic warheads are set to ride up in missiles. The ulti-mate culprit is *not* Wallace but Roberts, Landon's own superior and top intelligence official in Washington. Vassos, a Greek demolition expert, blows up the control room in time. Roberts, as the story ends, commits suicide.

Leo Katcher's other Greek novel, *Hot Pursuit*, "is based on a true happening during the Greek civil war in the late 1940's."[7] In his preface Katcher comments on how "cruel, brutish and bitter" that struggle was, with mass murder at Vlasti and Orestikon to equal that later at Hue and My Lai. The Greek military participated in these horrors. The story begins with the hero, Robert Braden, being ordered to join a government pursuit party out of Vlasti, which has been attacked by Communist guerrillas who abducted children. Does Stalin not know that the Mediterranean belonged to the United States? Braden is picked because he fought with the Greek partisans during the resistance, and thus he knows the lan-guage and the wild terrain.

Along with Braden goes Nasso, a friend and hardened fighter from the days when they battled the Nazis together. With politics altered, he now fights the communists. President Truman had sent forces to Greece under General Van Fleet. Now an "outsider," as the Nazis had been, Braden regards himself strictly a mercenary (not an antifascist) and, as he thinks, "All soldiers are germ car-riers, but mercenaries are professional Typhoid Marys." He does not express this self-condemnation to Nasso, but the reader un-derstands: he has dirty business to perform, under orders; and he senses that, like the Nazis before him, being "under orders" may be his only comfort and defense. In a jeep loaded with explosives they head north to destroy sanctuaries used by the Communist bands.

As they near Vlasti they find a dead man, Patrissou, who "sold produce to the camp." The camp itself is a shambles. Swenson, the UNRRA man, cannot understand the reason for the attack on their "peace mission," but Braden does. "Peace" is not the proper frame of reference. "No one told him [Swenson] this was a country where you tore the wings off the angel of mercy." They find eight bodies in Vlasti. Hurriedly Braden, Nasso, and Joannis leave for their unit in the woods. Among them is a woman, Elena—former lover of Braden's.

Despite its attempt at political realism, *Hot Pursuit* employs the common stereotypes of the thriller. Braden's superficial self-analysis results from a dehumanized cynicism that sees no justice for his cause, only victory. His enemies, the communists, are evil because the Pentagon so decrees them. He leads his avenging band through a terrain that bristles with perils worse than those faced by Natty Bumppo in Cooper's novels. Natty is a Deerslayer, while Braden is a Manslayer—and, despite a few qualms, he loves his expertise. Within his band, he correctly suspects, lurks a traitor who must be unmasked. Much of the story's suspense derives from this situation. The role of the damsel in distress falls upon Elena. In her resistance days she too had been a guerrilla. Now she is prepared to kill for her son, Alex, whom the communists have kidnapped.

Braden's band trails the communist bandits who attacked Vlasti. In retaliation Braden wreaks havoc on the village of Orestikon. After they rescue a group of eight kidnaped Greek children in Albania, they are themselves pursued back into Greece—by a communist band led by Braden's former protegé and friend, now traitor—Nasso. The harsh rules of the game demand that Braden and Nasso hunt each other down, man to man. Braden wins. Before Nasso dies, he reveals that Alex is Braden's son. Spiritually drained beyond love and redemption, Robert Braden leaves for another mission.

The several Greek characters remain shadowy and undeveloped in Aaron Marc Stein's *I Fear the Greeks* (1966).[8] Matt Erridge is working for an Arab potentate in Cairo, whom he calls Sonof, when his mother decides to visit Greece. On his way there someone first steals his bag, then his clothes; and eventually both are returned. A Greek named Kostya Leonidas follows him around for some unknown reason. For that matter, so does the man in brown who stole his bag in Cairo. Erridge's mother picks up a friend, Mrs. Grymm, who sees a body falling past her window of their hotel, the Queen's Palace. The murder victim is the man in brown. Did Leonidas kill him? If so, for what reason? The hotel manager and his helpers seem to know what is going on, but Erridge does not. He determines to find out. By now he has observed the Greeks. He has drunk a lot of *ouzo*. He has seen the terrible traffic of Athens. He has observed the hotel people's reluctance to notify the police. "They were all Greeks, and the less a Greek has to mess with the fuzz, the better he likes it" (p. 101).

Erridge's mother and Mrs. Grymm take him along on a trip to the Peloponnesus. They are, of course, followed. They pick up two hippie hitch-hikers, Jake and Roy. The party drives beyond Corinth to a seacoast town. Events now move quickly to their conclusion. Early the next morning Erridge's mother disappears. Erridge sees a yacht in the harbor observing him. On it he finds his Arab employer Sonof. He is driven to a villa in the hills, where agents of Sonof tie him up in the dungeon—along with the hitchhikers Jake and Roy. All three soon escape.

The solution to the mystery involves a conspiracy on the part of Sonof's many brothers to wrest power from him. To plan their moves, the brothers converge on the Greek villa. When Erridge left Cairo for Athens, Sonof suspected that he had betrayed him to his brothers. The man in brown pushed from the hotel balcony was Hamid, one of Sonof's agents. Who killed Hamid? Mrs. Grymm. In cahoots with the disloyal brothers, she is selling them guns. At the end the Greek police arrest her and send all the Arabs away from Greece. Erridge gets Mom back, who gets a Greek policeman as a lover. In view of the plot, *I Fear the Arabs* would have been a more fitting title.

The antiquity of Greece with its priceless artifacts creates the aura for three mysteries in which possession of such objects provides the plot. The stolen treasure in Phyllis A. Whitney's *Seven Tears for Apollo* (1963) is the statue of a boy, "the son of the nymph, Rhoda, beloved of Apollo."[9] The novel has a heroine, Dorcas Brandt, an American girl whose great grandmother came from the Peloponnesus. Dorcas flees to Greece in search of sanctuary after the death of her Greek-Italian husband, Gino Nikkaris. She and her daughter Beth are pursued for mysterious reasons, by persons who apparently have unfinished business with her deceased husband. Twice her quarters have been rifled in her absence. Dorcas travels as secretary to a writer friend, Fernanda Farrar. She feels the mystery will be cleared when she speaks with the widow of a museum worker, Markos Dimitriou. The dead Markos had once given Dorcas one thousand dollars to get away from her husband, the evil Gino, who had caused her nervous breakdown. For a guide on Rhodes Fernanda has chosen Johnny Orion, a young and helpful American high-school teacher who likes to spend his summers in Greece.

After a sight-seeing tour Dorcas returns to the hotel apprehensive that Beth has been left with a Greek maid, Vanda Petrus (who turns out to be Gino's sister). She has carefully unpacked all the luggage—an excellent way of making a thorough search. In reading to Beth, Dorcas finds a letter from Greece addressed to Gino Nikkaris.

"*The bride of Apollo mourns her loss. Done is the fearful deed. Gone the Princess from her Castle. At the hour of devils shadow lies upon the grave. Dolorosa, dolorosa, dolorosa*" (p. 69). She notices at the lower right-hand corner a small figure of an owl with large round eyes. The coded letter she cannot fathom, but on two occasions Dorcas had seen chalk marks in circles, like an owl's eyes. The mystery deepens, and she feels threatened. *Shadow, grave, dolorosa* are words that imply danger and possible death.

A rich former actress, Xenia Katalonos, invites Fernanda to tea, an act that means she wants something. Vanda Petrus reveals to Dorcas that Constantine Katalonos, Xenia's second husband, is not dead but in hiding. A sculptor, he felt a slave to his rich wife. At one point Madame Xenia reveals to Dorcas that the owl eyes are Constantine's signature. After many complications the plot unravels and leaves Dorcas finally free and happy.

What she suspects about her husband Gino is true—that at the time of his death he was dealing in stolen rarities for very rich clients. He had arranged to get the statue of the boy from the museum and have it replaced with a copy made by Constantine Katalonos. A series of revelations solves the mystery for Dorcas. A great burden hangs over her in the fact that Beth has been abducted and held as hostage—as it turns out, by her husband Gino and his accomplice, Fernanda Farrar. Gino did not die in the plane crash that supposedly killed him, but Constantine did. On the basis of clues in the cryptic letter Dorcas manages to find and confront her husband, who claims that all he wants is the statue. At a crucial moment, however, toward the end, he demands both Beth and the statue. With the help of Stavros, Madame Xenia's chauffeur, Gino is foiled. Beth is safely returned to Dorcas and the genuine statue safely returned to the museum.

A golden Hittite treasure sparks the action in *Death of a Hittite* (1969) by Sylvia Angus.[10] The setting is actually Jerjilikoy, Turkey, but the moving force is Menides Mitrou, a Greek millionaire who wants to add a Hittite antiquity to his already famous collection of art and artifacts recovered from sunken ships in the Mediterranean. The protagonist is David Gavin, an American journalist who joins a Hittite archaeological expedition to Jerjilikoy in order to help prepare a series of articles. Headed by Dr. "Steve" Stephenson, the expedition appears to be haunted by the mysteries of a previous one. Fifty years earlier, Stephenson as a youth has been a member of Dr. Werner Rausch's expedition to the same Jerjilikoy site. One member of the Rausch expedition, Wilhelm Ochst (whose parents were the financial backers) disappeared, as did a spectacular Hittite treasure.

Gavin thinks that Stephenson hid the treasure and then murdered Wilhelm Ochst; but later he suspects Benjamin Wyndham, an English archaeologist and rival with Gavin for Stephenson's daughter, Ann. In Munich Gavin gets a confession from Dr. Rausch that he killed Ochst fifty years before because he had slept with Rausch's wife and did not revere archaeology. Stephenson at Jerjilikoy has aimed to find Ochst's body, remove it, and preserve Rausch's reputation. At Jerjilikoy Gavin foils Wyndham's attempt to force Nazim Bey, the old foreman at Rausch's dig, to reveal the whereabouts of the golden treasure. Conspiring with Wyndham are Alexander and some other Greek thugs, employed by Menides Mitrou. Mitrou, of course, is beyond the Turkish authorities. "He sits like a fat spider among his treasure, but he sits in Greece. The Turkish government can't get at him especially now, with all the hatred that the Cyprus situation has whipped up" (p. 189).

Wyndham, Alexander, and the other Greek thugs are captured as they attack Nazim Bey, who hid the treasure years earlier. Bey reveals the hiding place since by doing so he saves Stephenson's honor. When it is unearthed, Stephenson passes off Ochst's body as that of an ancient Hittite, saves Rauch's reputation, and returns to London. The Hittite treasure will be housed in the museum in Turkey. And Gavin, now married to Ann, prepares to travel to Yucatan for another series of articles. Alexander, the Greek thug, is characterized as a cruel villain. On the other hand, "Menides Mitrou was a millionaire, a Greek millionaire. Everyone who read gossip columns knew of him, his yacht, his fabulous parties, his famous art collection, his treasure hunts for sunken ships in the Mediterranean. If Mitrou were after the Jerjilikoy treasure, money would be no object" (pp. 178–79). In this description one recollects the style of life associated with Aristotle Onassis and the other "Golden Greeks" who vied with each other for wealth, fame, and power.

In Jean Muir's *The Smiling Medusa* (1969) the treasure at issue is a pair of priceless antique Sèvres vases, originally intended for the czar of Russia as a gift from Napoleon.[11] The heroine of this young adult novel is Suzy Benson of Kansas City, who goes to the island of Hydra to claim a house left her in her grandfather's will. Suzy has a Greek heritage through her mother (a Kalasidis) and speaks Greek fluently. She is also steeped in Greek myths and other lore. In mentioning her Aunt Clio, Suzy thinks: "To be without kin is a cursed thing to a Greek so the thought of this waiting aunt was important" (p. 2). Her mother had run away from Hydra, years before, with an American student. Aunt Clio, according to Suzy's father, had what "you Hydriotes would call the Devil's Beauty" (p. 3). Suzy now ponders that remark as she finally meets her aunt. The reception is unusually cold. More than that, a man named Costa Dedes is murdered; in his pocket the police find a piece of paper with her name and address. Suzy Benson is very puzzled.

Of Aunt Clio she thinks: "Medea, maybe? Or Clytemnestra? Something out of tragic drama" (p. 21). Clio represents the venerable and once powerful Kalasidis family of shipowners, traders, and adventurers. Suzy meets Marko, who works around the place, and Dimitriou, her aunt's brother. She has not yet seen Nikko, the child to whom she sends CARE packages. Suzy the next morning walks down a steep cliff trail to the sea. There a servant, Fanni, brings her fruit juice and shows her the spot where the body of Socrates Kalasidis had been found. Later, a boy for a fee gives her a message from the dying Costa Dedes: a warning about danger in her house. Suzy sees Craig Hunter, a man she had met on the boat to Hydra. At the taverna Hunter introduces her to Wing Amory, a girl who was renting a room from Dedes, the murder victim.

After arranging to go skindiving with Hunter, Suzy leaves for Nikko's house. The boy's grandfather says "The house is honored" when she arrives. They all sit outside as evening falls. Nikko points to the rocks along the shore and proclaims: "That's where the Gorgons live" (p. 46). Suzy has now met a satyr (Dimitrios), a sea god (Hunter), and the Gorgons. Medusa was killed by Perseus, but the two other Gorgons still live, according to the local legend. When Nikko learns that Suzy owns and stays in the Kalasidis house, he crosses himself as protection from the devil. Suzy wonders why. At home she hears beautiful piano music and meets, for the first time, Aunt Clio's son, Georgeos Kalasidis. "His reckless air sat gracefully upon him. So did the ironical cast to his face. Yet he must be a bad one or his grandfather would not have cut him off so completely" (pp. 50–51). Suzy Benson feels she has displaced both her aunt and cousin by coming to claim the ancestral estate. Something more has to be wrong.

In showing her around the house, Dimitrios takes her to a storage room. Among other valuable dust-covered objects are the two Sèvres vases. As Suzy learns, the Kalasidis, before the war, traded with both France and Russia. Clio and Dimitrios belong to the Petres family. "Our histories," he tells Suzy, "revolve exclusively around boudoirs and wine shops. But a-ah, the heroic exploits we have undertaken there! They stagger the imagination!" (p. 68). Later that day, she goes down to the sea and the outcropping of rocks where Nikko said the Gorgons still live. Suzy hopes to find "the Medusa face in profile." While she stands, a knife passes by her head. She turns and runs in terror toward the house.

Suzy Benson sees Craig Hunter regularly for several days. She worries about his knowing Wing Amory, a temptress who goes around the island "looking dirty, indolent, and incredibly beautiful" (p. 75). Captain Zachariou continues to investigate the murder of Costa Dedes. Some suspicion still falls upon Suzy because of the paper with her name and address. She also finds herself unwelcome at the home of Nikko Mihaelis. She still does not know why Hydra regards the Kalasidis to be damned, doomed, or possessed. Are they a murdering clan? What about Wing Amory, who almost pushes Suzy off the cliff, and who would have succeeded had not Nikko appeared? If Suzy dies, Georgi Kalasidis would inherit the estate; and then Wing could marry him and set herself up for life.

These appearances are false clues that hide the truth. Georgi shocks Aunt Clio by accepting a paying job as a bouzouki player in a local taverna. By this time Suzy Benson has fallen in love with him. She wonders what Craig Hunter might do out of jealousy. At the taverna she entreats Georgi to return home, or at least attend a grand party that Aunt Clio has planned. From Georgi she learns a vital part of the family mystery. As she has begun to surmise, he is not a Kalasidis, which explains why his grandfather cut him from the will. Years before, Clio had had an affair with Mihaelis, Nikko's father. "That fool Dimitrios let it slip. He was the only person Clio had told. Unfortunately, Dimitrios never can resist saying outrageous things." When her husband, Socrates Kalasidis, heard about it, he ordered Georgi out of his sight, walked down to the harbor, "shot Mihaelis and then he came back to the cove and shot himself" (p. 121).

Even this past tragedy, however, does not account for the current violence, which goes on to include the near-rape of Suzy Benson by Craig Hunter, the attempted murder of Nikko, and the actual murder of Aunt Clio. At a cave near the Medusa rocks, Suzy finds the Sèvres vases being readied for shipment out of Hydra. Craig Hunter has made replicas which are stored in the Kalasidis house. Both Wing Amory and Dimitrios Petres (the satyr type) were part of the plot to steal and sell the priceless antiques but had not counted on any murder. Dimitrios helps during the solution of the mystery. Craig and Marko, the man around the house, go to jail. Suzy Benson now feels kindly toward the deceased Aunt Clio, since both she and Costa Dedes had been killed by the evil Craig Hunter. Suzy will marry Georgi and, presumably, will live happily ever after.

The pattern of a young American girl going to Greece and facing both mystery and danger is repeated in *House of Athena* (1970) by Janice M. Bennett.[12] After her graduation Christine Shaw leaves Massachusetts to visit Greece; then she stays on as a companion for Athena Christopherou. The Greek girl is eighteen, tiny, and paralyzed from an automobile accident. She is also extremely rich. The Christopherou wealth derives from "shipping, vineyards, and other lucrative enterprises." Her uncle is Dimitrios; her aunt, Helena; her womanizing cousin, Andreas. Both of Athena's parents died in the accident. The little rich girl seems to be at the mercy of her kin.

To make Athena happier Christine takes her shopping. They have a wonderful time visiting the Acropolis, eating out, and driving to the Piraeus shipyards where Dimitrios has his office. Christine wins permission from Dimitrios, the administrator of her estate, to teach Athena how to use crutches. At their return Christine and Athena go swimming, and Andreas challenges the American girl to a game of tennis. The old folks argue constantly over Andreas, still unmarried at twenty-six, who has a tendency to be profligate. For some reason Dimitrios, Christine feels, is frightening his wife and niece and trying to destroy his son Andreas. Another source of domestic conflict is the vineyards which Andreas loves but which Dimitrios wants to sell.

Andreas professes love for Christine, and she finds him very attractive. They visit the vineyards on the occasion of a wedding there. She meets a youth, Apollo, who is later revealed to be an accomplice of Dimitrios in his scheme to secure Athena's vast fortune. Christine, for reasons she cannot yet fathom, is in danger. When a ramp collapses, she falls and suffers two broken ribs. Another ominous incident occurs on the Christopherou yacht when their trip aboard is cut short by Athena's seasickness, brought on by a touch of poison. If Athena dies (she does not) Andreas gets his beloved vineyards and Dimitrios gets the bulk of her fortune.

Christine in desperation cables her brother, Garth, a lawyer, to come from America. She and Athena drive to Delphi, then race back to the airport chased by Apollo, who has perhaps been hired to kill them. Garth arrives and learns the details. They return to the Christopherou house in order to confront Andreas or Dimitrios or both. She accuses Andreas about the ramp, the poison, Apollo. Andreas expresses shock and bewilderment. Christine has been wrong again: it is Dimitrios. Garth later calls Andreas at the farm; he has made Apollo admit everything. Later Andreas arrives home with some tragic news about Dimitrios. "He's dead—the Mercedes went off the road" (p. 188). Everyone is finally free of his evil domination. "You know why he had to get rid of you, don't you?" Andreas asks Christine. "He was losing power over us. Athena was fighting back, even mother was defying him" (p. 189). Dimitrios's flunky was Apollo. Apollo had also tampered with the tie rods on the Mercedes, not knowing that Dimitrios would use the car. Andreas and Christine will start anew—married.

Precious objects already found and then stolen figure in some novels, while others are based on priceless rarities still being sought. The search for new treasure through dangerous diving missions occurs in two mysteries set in Greece. An expedition to find a galleon loaded with artifacts motivates the characters in Edmund Keeley's *Voyage to a Dark Island* (1972).[13] As in the author's other novels, the principals are Americans in Greece: Malone, a womanizing Irishman who aspires in vain to join the classics department at Harvard; Valerie, his snobbish Bostonian wife; and the narrator, an old friend of both. To prove himself a leader despite academic failure, Malone organizes a perilous diving mission off Antikythera, one of the Greek islands. On board his yacht are two Greek sailors, Achilles and Kosta, their girls, the cook Vassili, and several others. The eventual tragedy is foreshadowed by the initial trouble caused by the presence of the women.

The expedition begins in the waning of a *meltemi*, a northern storm that makes the Greek girls sick. At Monemvasia the group is joined by a young agent of the Greek archaeological service. The two Greek divers are at opposite poles politically. Achilles and the archaeologist, Alexi Nicolaou, argue over the merits of the junta colonels, with Alexi damning them for having dismissed competent intellectuals from their posts.

That Greece, despite her squabbles, is a country that non-Greeks can love is indicated by what Keeley writes about Brewster, one of the mission members, who originally came to Greece "as to a jungle—for a minimum of two years' suffering" which he owed to a Midwestern religious sect that sent him there to convert the heathens. "Somewhere along the line he started falling in love: first with Greece in general, then with the sea around Kavalla, then with the daughter of a local caique captain, finally with the firewater they made in the villages by boiling and distilling what was left over in the presses after the wine ran off" (pp. 26–27).

Malone's yacht and party reach their destination, Antikythera, to find the weather too risky for diving. They practice some dives in order to pass the time. From local gossip and legend they learn that a bronze horse may be part of the lost treasure they are seeking. Achilles and an Englishman, Newell-Morgan, go down first. The Greek diver comes up half dead, but Newell-Morgan fails to surface. The tragedy is compounded when Malone and Kosta also go down and fail to return. The narrator and Brewster follow. They discover Newell-Morgan's body but not the others. They bring the body up then argue about its disposition. Achilles tries to assume command, to call off any further search for either the bodies or the treasure; but the narrator is determined to dive down again for a last look. At 230 feet he finds the fabled bronze horse, and atop it, Malone's body caught by his cartridge belt. Nearby is the drowned Kosta. The disastrous expedition ends when the three victims are buried at sea. The fabulous bronze horse remains on the bottom knee-deep in the sand.

A more successful treasure hunt in Greek waters occurs in *The White Hand of Athene* (1974) by Jim Thorne, himself an adventurer whose travels and exploits remind one of Richard Harding Davis and Lowell Thomas.[14] Thorne has an expertise in underwater archaeology. His hero, Jib Gordon, is not unlike the author himself; and Gordon writes books. The novel begins in New York City, at a Greek restaurant called The Sea Net, whose owner, Martin Tossis, proposes that he recover the missing hand of the statue Athene off the island of Vomos. Born on Vomos, he came to New York when he was twelve. Now he will finance the entire expedition so he can share in the world's applause when they find Athene's hand. Gordon accepts.

Gordon and Tossis leave for Athens. The statue of Athene stands in the Louvre in Paris. Tossis recounts what happened when the French ensign DuValle "saw the Greek sailor throw the hand into the sea not more than a few hundred feet from the shore," adding that the hand "was broken off deliberately so the French would not take the statue as a gift for King Louis XVIII" (p. 9). They reach Athens. Although he is anxious to begin the search, Tossis cautions him about the Greeks' use of time. They promise to do something *amessos*, meaning immediately. "Unfortunately, it also covers time lapses of a few hours, a few days, or a few weeks" (p. 11). They need a permit from Admiral Voucharas, who is in charge of marine activity, but must wait six days to see him.

That gives him time to locate two experienced divers, both of them Americans, and to romance a 21-year old Greek actress, Sophia Christopher. Sophia readily sleeps with Jib. As pictured in fast-paced potboilers, lovely Greek girls are pushovers for blonde American heroes like Jib Gordon. He needs the instant erotic triumph in order to conform to the stereotype that he represents. Sophia reveals an old trauma—at the age of twelve she was taken in incest by her father. She now loves Jib truly after wanting to hurt all men. They make promises to each other before he sails for Vomos.

After a month Jib Gordon finds the submerged ruins of Emborium, City of Commerce, a Minoan center which vanished in 2450 B.C. It becomes clear that Martin Tossis brought him to Vomos under false pretenses when he takes from a musty trunk a *fake* hand of Athene that he plans to use to win world renown. Gordon refuses to cooperate in the conspiracy. The local curator, Dr. Vosalis, finds it hard to believe such a charge against Tossis, the island's leading benefactor. Jib thinks that Tossis may have hidden the hand in a crypt at the catacombs. Suddenly the heavy door of the catacombs slams shut. For twelve hours he fights in panic, is burned by a lantern, is nibbled at by a rat, and finally escapes through a narrow tunnel. His friends find and help him away to recuperate.

Sophia's mother commits suicide. Only her Turkish suitor, Alin Amir, is there to aid Sophia. Unfortunately she loses her job. Seeing her destitute, Alin Amir offers her a job in his night club if she will go to Turkey and be his mistress. The offer tempts her, but she loves Gordon. The Turk gives her two weeks to decide. Tossis has been intercepting and destroying Sophia's letters. Her disillusionment with love deepens, she distrusts all men. Tossis wants Sophia for himself.

Gordon discovers that his coworker Paul Thornton is pouring oil into his compressed air tank in order to murder him. They fight, and Gordon nearly kills him; later, they turn Paul over to the police. For two weeks Gordon and Bill Crydell furiously work on Emborium. "Daily they brought up artifacts from different cultures and different ages—Byzantine, Roman, Greek; amphoras, lamps, perfume jars, crockery" (p. 120). One day they find a great treasure —a sacrificial bowl from the Stone Age, made of a rock not indigenous to Greece. Immediately famous, Jib Gordon accepts an offer from England's *Today* magazine to write up the story.

There is still Martin Tossis to deal with. Jib Gordon gets the fake hand of Athene from a retarded boy, Costa, who happens to find it; and Tossis tries to kill Jib in order not to be exposed. While Tossis and his ally Nikol chase him they run into an old German mine. Both of Jib's pursuers are blown to bits. More secure now, and more affluent, he seeks out Sophia who has gone to Turkey with Alin Amir. He risks arrest entering the country illegally, only to find Sophia dead from an overdose of heroin. The novel ends with Jib Gordon sadly remembering her, as he is on his way to New York and a new assignment. "The state of Mississippi had hired him to search for and raise a Civil War ironclad gunboat named the *Cairo*. The ship had been downed in the cold, murky depths of the Yazoo River" (p. 147).

A mystery that merely uses Greece but develops no Greek characters is Mary Reisner's *Mirror of Delusion* (1965).[15] The protagonist is Charlotte Clarke, an American who is traveling companion to the rich Justine Eaton, an invalid, who needs her while her husband George paints Greek scenes. The *delusion* of the title applies to Charlotte, who mistakingly comes to believe that George is trying to murder Justine. But Justine is attempting to kill George instead of the other way around. The novel deserves a brief mention for two reasons: its Greek setting and its interesting description of the taverna Laïny which the Eaton party patronizes.

> Built against the back wall [of an open courtyard] was a green-painted wooden shed, in which was laid out an array of raw fish on beds of ice, whole lobsters, clams, joints of meat, salads, sections of melons, and other fruit, and bottles of Greek wine. At the back of the shed was a kitchen range over which a white-capped cook presided. With the assistance of a sympathetic waiter, the customers made their choice, and the fish and vegetables were then handed over to the cook, while the party found seats in the courtyard. (p. 39)

The novel ends with Justine Eaton dead, after her confession, and Charlotte and George in love with each other.

James Jones, the celebrated author of *From Here to Eternity*, wrote the thriller *A Touch of Danger* late in his career (1973).[16] His aging hero, Lobo Davies, leaves Piraeus by boat for the island of Tsatsos on a month's vacation paid for by Freddy Tarkoff, his last client. Lobo's assignment had been to retrieve from a Greek lawyer the $130,000 he had embezzled from several natives, including Sonny and Jane Duval. Most of Jones's Greek characters are villainous in one way or another. Even his cleaning woman riles him, sniffing at his "one bag as if it had dead rats in it." Although Tsatsos is supposed to be a resort island catering to both hippies and the very rich, Lobo is always eating "lamb-stew guk" at the various tavernas. He romantically pursues the Countess Chantal von Anders. She speaks with a distinct German accent—a fact explained by a bizarre comment: "The same was true of all the older, poorer Greeks on the islands that had been occupied." How the brief German occupation created such a linguistic change is not explained. Sonny Duval points out Girgis Stourkos as the "local pusher." What mostly gets pushed on Tsatsos is hashish as well as a little heroin, as far as users are concerned. The most important operation, not initially revealed, is a heroin base brought from Turkey and processed on the island. What concerns Lobo Davies more than narcotics are the two murders that occur.

He is hired first by his friend Chantal, who is being blackmailed by Girgis. After Lobo stops the blackmail by confronting the Greek pusher, he spends his days in the taverns, on the caique *Daisy Mae*, owned by Sonny, or in bed with women. He meets Jim Kirk, captain of the *Agoraphobe*, owned by a Mr. Kronitis. "Mr. Leonid Kronitis. A Greek. A very rich Greek. Owned ships. Not like Onassis, or Niarchos. But still very big" (p. 77). Kronitis exudes the usual mysterious aura of the "rich Greek shipowner." He has great potential for both good and evil. At first Lobo Davies suspects that Kronitis may be engaged in the hashish smuggling ring, but this is puzzling because no vast sums are involved.

Actually, it is Kronitis's underlings such as Girgis who handle the hashish. Girgis seduces tourist girls and local wives—Jane Duval in particular. Lobo Davies meets a loveable beachcomber named Sweet Marie who has slept with everybody on Tsatsos. He, however, abstains. From a Pete Gruner, who perhaps is a "nark," Lobo hears of a possible activity much more serious than the hashish: the running into Tsatsos from Turkey of the raw morphine base for heroin. The action picks up for Lobo when the corpse of Girgis is found with the head brutally severed. Kronitis hires him to hunt down the killer.

All sorts of people might want Girgis dead. A Greek named Steve owns a machete that might have done the grisly deed—a false clue, since Steve is not guilty. Jim Kirk could have killed Girgis as a rival in the hash trade, but he did not. Lobo Davies proceeds with little commitment until a second murder—that of Sweet Marie. He regrets not having accepted her erotic offers; now it is too late, and he is angry. Soon the solution is at hand. Duval murdered both Girgis Stourkos and Sweet Marie owing to jealousy and revenge because both in their way had stolen his wife Jane from him. Sonny beheaded Girgis because he had been one of her lovers; and he killed Sweet Marie because she and Jane had a lesbian affair.

Leonid Kronitis does indeed operate a heroin ring. With his boat his men intercept Turkish ships that bring the morphine base to be processed at his villa. Much to Lobo's surprise, however, the supreme head of the operation is none other than Freddy Tarkoff, his client, friend, and benefactor.

The legend of the Greek shipowner takes a giant step forward in Sidney Sheldon's *The Other Side of Midnight* (1973).[17] A murder trial in Athens gives Constantin Demiris, the shipowner, a chance to wreak vengeance on a couple who have betrayed him. Larry Douglas, his pilot, has fallen in love with his French mistress, Noelle Page. Larry cheats on his wife Catherine while Noelle cheats on Demiris, a vindictive billionaire. The two lovers are tried in an Athens court for the alleged murder of Larry's wife. The novel begins with "Prologue, Athens: 1947" describing men emotionally involved with Noelle Page, all of whom are heading for Athens to attend her trial. The novel itself is a long flashback dramatizing the lives of the principals up to the trial and after. The description of the leading character, Demiris, does not exactly fit Aristotle Onassis; yet it fully represents the stereotype of the rich Greek shipowner.

Although married to the attractive daughter of a Greek banker, Demiris sleeps with numerous "motion picture stars, the wives of his best friends, a fifteen-year-old novelist, freshly bereaved widows, and it was even rumored that he had once been propositioned by a group of nuns who needed a new convent" (p. 241). Such a man is indeed a hero of our time. The books about him do not touch the essence of Constantin Demiris, for he is a deeply private man despite his fame. "The reporters who chronicled his life were permitted to see only his geniality and charm, the sophisticated urbane man of the world. They never suspected that beneath the surface, Demiris was a killer, a gutter-fighter whose instinct was to go for the jugular vein" (p. 242).

The word *ruthless* is often applied to the fictional Greek shipowner. Demiris's private joy is to destroy ruthlessly anybody who betrays, slights, or otherwise opposes him. Such a fate befalls Noelle Page when she is unfaithful to him. She and Larry Douglas love each other so desperately that they plot to murder his wife Catherine. Larry and she have violent quarrels; he asks for a divorce, but she refuses. After the murder plan is under way (Noelle once killed someone in Paris), Larry pretends reconciliation with Catherine so that he can lure her to Joannina and kill her there. He leads her without a guide into the dangerous part of some caves, then abandons her to hordes of vicious bats. Her sanity snaps in the "black tomb of horror." She disappears, no body is ever found, and both Noelle Page and Larry Douglas, on the basis of circumstantial evidence, are indicted for her murder. Unknown to her, the celebrated Greek lawyer defending her, Napoleon Chotas, has been bribed by Demiris. The lure offered Chotas: millions in fees for handling the legal business of the Demiris empire. Chotas accepts, and he cleverly allows the circumstantial evidence to build up against Noelle and Douglas. When their case appears lost, and execution faces the two defendants, Chotas proposes that they plead guilty as charged in order to receive lighter sentences, the implication being that the judges have been bribed. They do plead guilty. Too late, when they hear the death sentence, they realize that the judges had *not* been bribed. Demiris has tricked them. They die before a firing squad. Catherine is not dead, but insane, and immured in a convent.

The recent politics of Greece informs the mystery thriller *The Judas Sleep* (1975) by Jan Roberts.[18] The time is 1973, and the action involves the fascist regime of the colonels led by George Papadopoulos. A former British agent with the Greek resistance, Richard Burns, gets an urgent call from an old friend, MacDonald, to meet him in New York. Burns owns art galleries in Greece and London; and one of his client artists, Stavros Alexandratos, served with him in the underground. Stavros allegedly died in an automobile accident, but MacDonald shows Burns a new Stavros painting. The mystery: does Stavros still live, or did he die as reported? Also at issue, and sought by various adventurers, is a cache of gold given the Greek partisans by the British. To find Stavros means, also, to find the treasure. The gold means nothing to Burns, but Stavros does.

A Greek in New York, Maria Fowler, sends Eleni Harper after Burns to Greece in order to keep him from finding Stavros. The two women are engaged in the business of helping the new democratic Greek resistance. An unsavory Greek entrepreneur, Kostandis, serves a secret fascist cabal in also seeking Stavros. Stavros has become a legendary figure around whom the Greek people can rally. Burns suspects even his friend MacDonald and the CIA because of alleged American complicity in the coup d'etat staged by the military junta. Once in Athens, Eleni Harper loses no time finding Burns—a contact that swiftly develops into a genuine love affair. The affair also complicates his mission, about which he has been dubious from the start. His return to Greece revives painful memories. Yet he must learn the truth about Stavros Alexandratos. Wall signs read STAVROS LIVES.

Kostandis is the hit-man dispatched by a fascist cabal to kill Stavros. After the defeat of Hitler, the evil Kostandis worked for Dr.

Murer, who helped war criminals escape by changing their physiognomies. Murer learned his surgical art in Nazi concentration camps where he sadistically tortured and disfigured inmates. He still serves fascism, this time the cabal that plans to replace the Greek colonels.

Kostandis is one of the few Greek characters in fiction who are homosexuals. For his paramour he has a delectable Turkish boy, Youssef. Unfortunately for Kostandis, he keeps failing the generals who employ him to get Stavros; and they pay Youssef to kill him. Kostandis has been described as a "ripe melon," but when Youssef's knife penetrates his stomach, "it sank in with the ease of a warm knife entering a tub of lard. Kostandis took a long time to die, and he died knowing he'd been betrayed" (p. 208). Whether melon or lard, Kostandis symbolizes the political dregs of Greek society.

The man whom Burns regards as the political hope for the restoration of Greek democracy is Andreas Papandreou. To frustrate his forthcoming electoral victory the colonels mounted their coup. A partisan named Mino complains to Burns about the current political situation.

> Greece's best men and women are either in prison camps, dead or in exile. Our political thinkers, our artists, our musicians, our scholars . . . dead or silenced. The King sits in his comfortable villa in Italy and spends his time going to parties and night clubs. Which is all right with us as nobody wants him back anyway. Neither the colonels nor the people. Thank God Papandreou is free, for around him is built our hopes and our struggle. With him we have the chance to return to democracy and parliamentary rule. (pp. 112–13)

With these sentiments Richard Burns, the British art dealer and former guerrilla, fully agrees.

The novel speeds to its conclusion after Burns helps to rescue Eleni Harper from Dr. Murer. By this time Burns knows that Eleni is Mrs. Alexandratos, the wife of Stavros. She has claimed, however, that he died, which fact allows her freedom to love anew. Nevertheless Eleni now leads Burns to meet Stavros in the awesome region of the Meteora in northern Greece, at Kalambaka in Macedonia. The "incredible formation of rocky spires," more than 1800 feet high, formerly held twenty-three fourteenth-century stone monasteries, and could once be reached only by rope-drawn nets and ladders. Eleni drives Burns to one of the six remaining

structures. A monk takes them to a room where a "tall, robed figure" stands at work before an easel. "Stavros!" Burns whispers, but
the man is not Stavros. "The burning black eyes were sunken, and
the cheeks were hollow. Deep creases ran down from the sides of
the nose to the ends of full lips that held a gentle smile. The monk
spoke, saying, 'I am his brother, Vassos.'" And he adds, "*Yassou,*
Apollo," using the code name that Burns went by during the resistance (p. 226).

Vassos explains that he paints the new pictures that others attribute to Stavros, and thus he keeps Stavros alive. "Stavros has a personal hold on the morale and imagination of our people, and the
forces that would destroy Greece fear both him and his hold" (p.
229). Neither his friends nor his enemies must know the truth.
Burns knows because Eleni trusts him to keep the secret. The
Greeks have hubris, Vassos says, pride—"their pride in the knowledge that the fight goes on." After lunch Burns and Eleni drive
down to the village of Kalambaka where, at the Hotel Odession,
they learn that they were followed by a Greek named Nikos Frangidakis, who wants the gold. To thwart Frangidakis and his man
Tony, they pretend to find the treasure at an abandoned monastery; after filling a sack with rocks they plan an ambush for Frangidakis that succeeds. The traitors to Stavros and his cause are captured, but Frangidakis and Tony escape and try to descend the
sheer cliff by a rope net. The net breaks, and they die. That night
Burns and the beautiful Eleni sleep in the monastery. Later, at the
Athens airport, the CIA agent Caldwell comes to see them off. The
political fate of Greece still hangs in the balance. The secret
learned at the Meteora will not be revealed. When Caldwell anxiously and "unofficially" asks: "Is Stavros alive . . . or isn't he?"
Burns puts him off a moment, then replies: "As long as there's a
Greece, Stavros is alive" (p. 248).

From matters purely adventurous to the seriously political, the
thrillers set in Greece have been a busy industry for American writers. Even the ruins of Greece with their lost treasures yield themes
and structures for suspenseful novels. Being so old a country,
Greece provides naturally romantic and often gothic settings that
authors can exploit without having to invent much. Manmade ca-
tastrophes and horrors should not torment such a beautiful sunny
land; but they do, and very often in modern times. Many observers
feel that Greece's geographic location creates the internal turmoil
as Great Powers contend for domination, for alleged strategic pur-

poses. If Athens were indeed the "Lisbon of the Cold War," as one of these authors asserts, then foreign agents and spies did scurry about on Greek soil their shabby missions to perform. The new myth of the fabulous Greek shipowner, a postwar phenomenon, widens the range of Greek character from lowly shepherd to an ambiguous and often evil personage more powerful than kings, popes, and presidents. The vast numbers of American tourists who have crowded Greece in recent years also must influence the publication of thrillers set in a nation that they have also experienced. They are part of the ready market toward whom such books can be aimed.

꜒꜖꜒꜖꜒꜖꜒꜖

14

꜒꜖꜒꜖꜒꜖꜒꜖

CHILDREN'S LITERATURE

A GLANCE at any of the several standard indexes and bibliographies of children's books reveals an extensive use of ethnic and minority characters. The writers of such books, which are needed for schools, public libraries, and homes, have a whole world of nations to be brought into the ken of their young readers. Each national background requires its particular personae; and since the United States, through immigration, has drawn so heavily from everywhere, children's books that are set here are also filled with ethnic types. Another observation follows—that many children's books with modern Greek characters parallel, at the juvenile level, adult books of the same general nature. For example, a host of nineteenth-century travelers visited Greece and wrote about the country and its people. In some children's fiction, youthful travelers also trek to Greece for adventure and education. Later works parallel adult books in such situations and themes as the Greek immigrant, growing up Greek-American, the young Greek war hero, mysteries set in Greece, and tales of magic and the supernatural.

The double aim of entertaining while teaching pertains to the popular nineteenth-century Peter Parley books with their combination of fantasy, whimsy, and fact. *The Balloon Travels of Robert Merry and His Young Friends* (1863) was written by Samuel Griswold Goodrich and purportedly edited by Peter Parley.[1] This early instance of science fiction involves a balloon trip. A group of students leaves Boston to see the world, including Greece. Robert Merry, the leader, plans to write a new book on geography and history, and the voyage will give him fresh and exciting knowledge. The relatively new mode of travel lets the balloonist look down upon countries like a map, to study them from a clear vantage. The idea of balloon flights fascinated both devotees of the sport and general readers. Mark Twain has Tom Sawyer soar to strange lands in that fashion in *Tom Sawyer Abroad* (1878), but Tom's balloon crosses North Africa and misses Greece.

Robert Merry in *The Balloon Travels* has no difficulty in convincing Ellen, James, Peter, Laura, and Seth to accompany him. He admits the journey to be "a little dangerous perhaps, but think of the pleasure we shall have," and away they go, excited and brave. Eventually they reach Greece after floating across Ireland, England, France, Spain, and Italy. "Oh, how delightful it is!" exclaims Laura. "And this is Greece!" (p. 204). They see the Ionian Islands first, and Ithaca, home of Ulysses. Merry relates events about ancient Greece, Homer, the Trojan war. James wants to know about Greece's "present condition," and he is told: "At present they are governed by a young king, named Otho" (p. 212). When they land their balloon on the Acropolis, they pause long enough for a historic discourse about Athens, the royal palace, the old Greek gods, the battle at Marathon, and various classical myths. Unfortunately they do not meet one real modern Greek during their sojourn. Their most exciting and dangerous experience occurs later, when they encounter some real history: a battle of the Crimean war. A bullet forces the balloon to land inside a Russian fort; after repairs they continue their travels and in time return to Boston.

Two years after *The Balloon Travels* appeared Daniel C. Eddy's *Walter in Athens* (1865), the last volume in the Walter's Tour of the East series for young readers.[2] The author describes his purpose: "Moral teaching has been blended with geography and history, and the aim has been to impart a knowledge of the customs and manners of Eastern people living in Oriental lands." What the "moral teaching" amounts to is an expression of snobbery on Walter's part—an effort to demonstrate the superiority over the backward Greeks of the Protestant American way of life. Walter, before going to Greece, had studied Egypt, Jerusalem, Samaria, Damascas, and Constantinople. He belongs to a group with whom he can talk and share experiences. They now have the opportunity to learn a good deal about the country, its geography and its people. The visitors express what can only be regarded as negative preconceived notions, or at least judgments based on hasty examination. Like many other tourists before them, they are impressed by Greece's glorious past but find the present poor and shabby, the people "degenerated."

Young Walter's party leaves Constantinople on a French steamer bound for Athens. When Walter asks about the gods and myths, he is told that many ancient nations developed mythological systems. For the most part, Roman names are now used for the Greek gods, according to Mr. Percy, a leader of the group. At Piraeus, the port that Themistocles chose for Athens, Percy bargains for a boat with "a stout, honest looking boatman, who had a clean felucca"; and though he at first asked "an exorbitant sum," the boatman came down when he realized the party could not be swindled (p. 66). The boats in the harbor appear less neat and trim than those at Constantinople. The party sees Greek field workers; others sit by the roadside, dressed in peculiar costume. Walter is disappointed in the modern Greeks, and when asked what kind of "race" he expected to find, he replies:

> Why, I have heard so much about the Greeks, and lecturers and public men who have spoken at the lyceum in Cambridge, have said so much about the noble Greeks, the classic Greeks, the heroic Greeks, that I thought I should find a people looking different from other people—a noble, manly-looking race, but instead of that I find a puny, slouchy, dwarfed-looking class of toilers in the field. My romantic notions are having a fall. (p. 68)

On the coach to Athens they note the rudeness of the farming tools. The modern Greeks have the refinement and culture of neither Cambridge nor ancient Greece. Even their horses, as Walter says, are not as good "as ours at home." They wish they had Pegasus.

Several chapters are devoted to sightseeing; the detailed commentary is intended to instruct the reader. Walter's curious party finds the classical ruins of Athens more interesting than the present "miserable" city. One member of the group asserts he would not live there "if you gave me the whole place, and half of Greece besides" (p. 85). They visit the Theseum, the temple of Zeus, the theater of Bacchus, the Acropolis, the Parthenon, the court of Areopagus, the burial place of Socrates, and other historic sites. They receive a lengthy discourse on the philosophers, poets, and orators of ancient Greece, together with a judgment in which the ancients are regarded as theoretical, impractical, lacking a sense of experimentation. The Greek of old was "feeble as a child" but great in "universals and generalities"—a view that makes one wonder how they developed their city-states, conducted a busy commerce, defeated the Persians, and built the Parthenon.

In their discussion the visitors mention a Professor Koeppen's views on the effects of climate on character traits; he relates the

Greek's "bright, creative imagination" and his "high sense of beauty" to his scenic environment, to the "brilliant tints" of the rainbow. The Goths, Danes, and Anglo-Saxons, with their "cold and cloudy skies," admired "the immense gray and gloomy piles of their Christian churches, the vaulted aisles of their convents, and their battlemented castles. The Greeks . . . were fond of light and life; they consecrated darkness and death to the austere deities of the infernal regions, and called the Furies the sable sisters of night!" (p. 132). Despite the climate the boys would not like to live in Athens. They prefer Boston, the "Athens of America."

The visitors see the king and queen of Greece passing in a carriage. King Otho is despotic and unpopular; the people regard him and his Bavarians as foreigners. Mr. Tenant, a member of the group, quotes from an American traveler and writer: "No satisfaction is there with their present puppet of a king, none with their theatre-show of a church. Witnessing every kind of perversion in both, rejecting both alike in indignant scorn, the young men of Greece 'bide their time.' By a spirited press and an ever-thronged café they utter their indignation at present corruption, their pantings for a brighter day to come" (p. 142). Tenant quotes the writer's attack on King Otho for building "an immense, tasteless, marble palace" with drachmas squeezed from the poverty-stricken masses. The king's soldiers are eating out the "heart of the land" merely to gratify his royal vanity. Tenant's authority argues on the basis of their presumed character that the Greeks would prefer the American form of government to a monarchy. "The besetting sins of the Greek, his credulity, fickleness, dishonesty, are not such as demand an armed force to keep them under restraint. While his kindheartedness, his good-nature, his spirit of hope, his child-like love of pleasure, would respond at once to the paternal sway of a government like our own" (p. 144). Still quoting, Tenant describes the corruption in King Otho's government. High officials take bribes, criminals go unpunished, the land is not tilled, "and, worst of all, the government espouses the cause of an utterly effete superstition."

The author, Daniel C. Eddy, had stressed the "moral instruction" to be derived from Walter's travels in foreign lands. A typical gem of wisdom about the modern Greeks occurs when Walter asks: "Do you suppose that we should become indolent as the Greeks are, if we should come here to live?" The answer is "perhaps." In a further comment Walter finds the Greeks inefficient and inactive as well. Tenant agrees: "They are, and we should probably catch their bad habits if we were to stay here for a long time. Evil company always produces bad results" (p. 147). At least one member of the group, Harry St. Clair, notes that the Greeks have beautiful faces, but he is told that other things are more important than "good looks." After more sightseeing, the young travelers leave; and despite the flaws of the modern Greeks, they depart reluctantly because there is still much to visit and "learn"—to learn even more completely the author's "moral lesson," or so it appears, that Americans have traits of character superior to those of uncouth and indolent foreigners.

The Greeks get a more favorable report from Oliver Optic, pseudonym for William Taylor Adams, in his book of travel and adventure *Cross and Crescent; or, Young America in Turkey and Greece* (1873).[3] The voyagers are on a cruise with their teachers. Having left Turkey via the Bosporus, they approach Greece which appears "like the meanest country in the world, though its scenery is bold and rugged" (p. 310). At Piraeus they are inspected by a Greek customs official dressed in the gaudy Albanian costume, the *fustanella*. While still on board the students listen to a lecture on Greece given by Professor Mapps—actually an outline of Greek history and culture from the ancients to the moderns. He makes the point that even as subjects of the Ottoman empire the Greeks managed to achieve a great deal.

> They were so much superior to the Turks in mental capacity, that the direction of affairs had to be intrusted to native leaders in various parts of the country, and towards the end of the last century, many Greeks at Constantinople had risen to eminent positions as interpreters, physicians, and even as hospodars in the Moldavian and Wallachian provinces. Others had become wealthy merchants and bankers in the principal cities of the empire. (p. 327)

The lecturer feels sorry that the newly liberated Greeks were saddled with a monarchy by the great powers of Europe. Both King Otho and his queen were "tyrants and oppressors" who deservedly lost their throne in the popular revolt of 1862. Professor Mapps joins those American observers who felt that four hundred years of Turkish enslavement did not turn the Greeks into moral degenerates. "The modern Greek seems to have most of the characteristics of his ancestors of two thousand years ago. The Greek still has dark hair, brown complexion, and sparkling eyes; is still lively, quick to understand, adroit, eloquent, curious, and eager for novelty" (p. 328). Like their forebears the Greeks are mariners.

Unfortunately the young scholars have little chance to mingle with their hosts because their visit to Athens and vicinity is brief. In fact, in a book of 347 pages only 34 are devoted to the Greek encounter. The boys of the "Academy Squadron," as the student group is called, go to the Acropolis where they hear another lecture. Later, at famed Salamis, Mapps talks about the Persian wars. The boys also visit Eleusis, the "holy city" of the Greeks. Their last stop on Greek soil, before leaving for Italy, is the island of Syra. Although some of them wish for more extensive Greek travels, and more contact with the people, their elders fear to take them into the hinterland "on account of the brigands" (p. 333).

Like all immigrant groups, the Greeks met with both disdain and approval, or at least tolerance, from the very beginning of their arrival. Many American observers during the progressive era protested the child labor that was rampant and shameful, and that often affected young immigrants. In "The Greek Bootblack" (*Survey*, September 16, 1911) Leola Benedict Terhune deplores the semislave conditions under which countless Greek boys are exploited, often by their own relatives.[4] When asked their age, the indentured bootblacks always reply at least seventeen, a fact that prompts the author to say "there seems to be an entire absence of Greek numerals between ten and seventeen." Terhune urges that "this immense army of lads" must be rescued for they are "doomed to ignorance by the unscrupulous greed of their masters"—who give their wards no time to attend school (p. 854).

A much happier note is struck by Myron Levoy in a children's story, also set in the early years of the century, about an aged Greek "rags man," in "Andreas and the Magic Bells," living on the lower east side of New York.[5] Old Andreas Kastanakis drives along the streets buying and reselling used clothes to poor people along the way. The rags are sold for paper or shredded into stuffing for sofas and mattresses. A time comes when the poor horse clops along head down and listless. Nothing the worried Andreas does can revive him. Andreas takes Socrates first to Dr. Withers, the veterinarian, who advises more plentiful and more varied feed. Still the horse clops with bent head. For eighteen years they have worked together on the same streets. "When Andreas had arrived from Greece with just enough money for a horse and wagon, he had picked out Socrates from all the other horses because he had looked so sad and noble. But now Socrates only looked sad" (p. 35).

Mario, the Italian vegetable man, urges Andreas to groom Socrates to the point where the old horse would feel young at heart. Andreas grooms him daily but nothing happens. One day as they pass Petruscu's Antiques, the sound of tiny bells suddenly makes Socrates raise his head! Andreas tries bell after bell from the Rumanian's shop, but none of them work. Then Petrescu suggests that Socrates is bewitched, maybe by gypsies, and he needs special bells. Magic bells. All the bells in the shop fail until Socrates hears the slight tinkling sound from three tiny bells on a wooden toy cart pulled by Petrescu's two-year-old grandson. They are the magic bells. Their story is told by children and adults alike all over the lower east side.

The theme of growing up Greek-American is dramatized with verve and humor in *Demo of 70th Street* (1971) by Harry S. George.[6] Again, as in Levoy's tale of Greeks in New York, the time reverts to the early 1900s when daring little boys hitched rides on horse-drawn trolleys. Such a boy is Demosthenes Demetracopoulos, called Demo by everyone except his father. Because of his illustrious namesake, Demo tries to improve his speech with pebbles in his mouth—and nearly chokes to death! Nineteen additional episodes describe his experience with both his family and with neighborhood friends of varied ethnic origins. With money stolen from his mother he buys a toy gun and goes around with Willie, a German boy, shooting blanks. For a school pageant he wears an *evzone* costume in which he feels painfully conspicuous until he sees other pupils wearing Bohemian, Russian, Polish, Italian, and German garb. One spring day Demo and his pals help Nicky Prodromidis get back his pushmobile that was grabbed by a gang from Avenue A. From their Greek teacher, Mr. Demetriades, Demo and his two sisters learn about the Greek myths; and when he dozes, they make fun of him. Demo and his family have a happy Greek Easter, with his mother beating everyone at cracking eggs.

Demo and a mean boy named Freckles blacken each other's eyes. His parents refuse to pay for a watermelon which the boys accidentally drop and then devour. Demo's block gang, the Spartans, have a skirmish with Freckles's gang, the Terrors. From the rooftop of the building Demo flies a kite that he loses to his enemies who "sling" it, and later the kite flies off free. The Olympia coffeehouse is raided by the police, and Demo's father is briefly arrested on the suspicion that the Greeks are gambling for money. A Greek from Aliquippa visits New York, takes Demo's family to the fabulous Hippodrome, and becomes engaged to his sister Athena. The fun, excitement, and fuss of the wedding follow. Later Demo's mother nags his father into getting his citizenship papers. On Christmas day Demo and his sisters wake up to see their first Christmas tree—even though such ritualistic objects did not exist in the Greek religion. The final two chapters describe "the Big Snow Fight," the beginning and the end, between the Spartans and the Terrors. The battle rages to mock epic proportions, to conclude a book filled with ethnic details, fine touches of humor, and mementoes of a nostalgic past.

The scene shifts to a Greek household of 1909, living in troubled Turkey, in Demetra Vaka Brown's fine novel *Delarah* (1943).[7] A young Greek girl, Alcmene, has in Delarah a Turkish girlfriend for the first time in her life. For the protected Delarah their association means a change in personality and an intellectual awakening, in a period when the Young Turks stage a revolt to overthrow the old order. In the chaos and peril the families of the two girls must escape Turkey or perish. The setting for *Delarah* is the island of Prinkipo in the Sea of Marmora, not far from Constantinople. While picking figs on her father's rich estate, Alcmene Floros sees a carriage coming driven by a Turkish gentleman, and beside him demurely sits a small girl. The man is Ali Pasha, one of the closest advisers to Sultan Abdul Hamid, and the girl is his daughter Delarah. Kimon Floros, a Greek banker, finds it astonishing and even dangerous for such a high-placed Turk to break custom and visit his home.

Left to entertain the Turkish girl, Alcmene proudly says her namesake was the mother of Hercules; but Delarah has never heard of Hercules, nor of demigods. To her there is but "one God, Allah, and Mohammed is his prophet." She avers after hearing the myth that Hercules must have been a slave, for only slaves perform such labors. Alcmene is surprised that the name *Delarah* has no precedent in ancient mythology. She mentions the gods of Olympus "when Greece was the greatest country in the world," which statement Delarah quickly regards as foolishness—clearly "Turkey is the greatest country in the world" (p. 5). She expects a slave to pick some figs for them, but Alcmene herself shins up the tree as if she were "a man-child," and not a well-mannered girl. Delarah can eat all she wants, but Alcmene can have only two. She finds the Turkish girl ignorant but lovely, and wants badly to see her again. Kimon Floros emphatically declares, "Certainly not," but admits to his wife Helen that little Delarah *is* lovely. That night Alcmene adds to her regular prayers: "Please, dear God, make papa and mamma think differently; for I do want to see Delarah again" (p. 9).

The next day Alcmene wakes up "full of puzzlement." She tells her father that when in France they speak French, in Germany, German, and in England, English; but, though they live in Turkey, they speak no Turkish. The paradox reveals their cultured and cosmopolitan household, as well as the gulf between Greeks and Turks. Alcmene, until the day before, had never spoken with a Turkish child. Kimon Floros explains how the Turks since 1453, when they captured Constantinople, have kept to their own way of living. They are neither Christian nor European, but Oriental. In their houses the women live apart from the men. Her father tells Alcmene how the Turks managed to conquer the Byzantine empire. She admits that she prayed for her parents to invite Delarah again. "If more invitations follow," Kimon Floros declares to his wife, "you will certainly have to take her to Paris, and put an end to this" (p. 13).

The next morning, dressed in a trim sailor's suit, Alcmene goes by carriage to Ali Pasha's house, to the women's quarters surrounded by a high wall. Delarah, excited and joyous, greets Alcmene in the Turkish fashion and kisses her. Alcmene thinks the women present mean a party in progress, but Delarah says they are slaves. In a large room they meet the Validé Hanoum, mother of Ali Pasha, and "first lady" of the household. Alcmene kisses her hand; then, at Delarah's suggestion, she puts her hand on her own head to be under the Hanoum's protection. Delarah translates, speaking to her grandmother in French. Alcmene speaks Greek, French, German, English, and Italian—but the sound of Turkish is the strangest of all. The girls profess their love for each other. Alcmene explains about the Greek gods and myths, Delarah explains Turkish expressions. A slave brings them sherbets and cakes. Delarah eats immoderately; and she is worried when warned she may become fat. When she takes her daily nap, Alcmene goes to the beautiful garden hoping to learn more Turkish from a slave. Delarah soon reawakens. Her new Greek friend uses the metaphor of "a pair of winged sandals" in her head to describe imagination—a quality of rare value that she feels Delarah will have to acquire.

Alcmene learns that *karvalto* means the midday eating time, that *témena* is a Turkish salutation, and that *peck gusel* means *very pretty*— a compliment paid her for reciting some poetry. Delarah is astonished at how smart Alcmene is. Earlier, Ali Pasha had told Delarah that Greeks read books and make a lot of money. The formal lunch goes according to revered Turkish custom. Because Alcmene cannot devour the huge helpings, the Turkish women feel she is starving; the impression given is that rich Greeks eat cautiously, whereas rich Turks are gluttons and soon get fat. Among the women is an exquisite young lady who Delarah says is Nazip Hanoum—"my father's youngest wife." She has a baby dressed like a miniature general, wearing on his cap a "small piece of garlic and a blue stone" as protection against the evil eye. Greeks also use garlic as a philactery. Alcmene is allowed to hold the baby, who smiles—a good sign. Slaves do everything for Delarah, so she has no need for self-reliance; when Alcmene says that she likes to play with her dog and chase a hoop, Delarah replies she would order a slave to chase her hoop if she had one. Instead of reading stories, she calls for her storyteller. They play with Delarah's great doll collection for two hours. When Alcmene has to leave, Delarah cries and wants her to visit again and again.

At home, Alcmene describes everything she encountered in the Turkish home, including the promise made to Delarah by her grandmother that Alcmene would return. That settled it. Alcmene and her mother would leave for Paris immediately to escape Ali Pasha's friendship. Yet that very night the unwelcome pasha comes to thank Kimon Floros for the great joy Alcmene has brought Delarah and his entire family. To Delarah, Alcmene is "Little Heart," a term of endearment not easily bestowed, especially upon a Greek. Much to Kimon Floros's annoyance, the powerful Turk is determined to bring Alcmene and Delarah even closer together. He brushes aside all excuses, then takes the Greek banker into his confidence. Ali Pasha, though rich and well-favored, fears for his life. He serves Abdul Hamid, a despotic sultan who detests progress, has a widespread spy system, and forbids Turkish children like Delarah to be taught by foreign women. "I cannot put her into an English, French, or even an American school here. Neither the sultan nor the priests would permit it" (p. 35).

Very humble, the distraught pasha explains that he, Kimon Floros, is the only chance Delarah has for an education. "I, a man of the ruling class, am begging you, a man of the conquered race, as a charity, to allow my child to share in your child's education" (p. 35). The pathos and honesty of Ali Pasha leave the Greek banker little choice but to agree. What decided the pasha's move was the good omen witnessed the day when Alcmene held his infant son. From now on Delarah, who they believe is not known to the sultan's spies, will take her lessons with Alcmene each morning. Maybe it is for the best, since Alcmene has been lonely. In fact, as Helen Floros says, Alcmene may "remake the Turkish child, and Ali Pasha will find himself with a changeling in his household" (p. 37).

Delarah is as puzzled by the Floros home as Alcmene was with Ali Pasha's. The Greeks have no *selamlik* for the men, and no women's quarters. At the table Delarah is denied second helpings. And a *man*, Kimon Floros, eats with them! A problem arises with Delarah's attitude, "I have finished with learning. I am twelve years old" (p. 39). She has no concept of the mind as something that requires education. The teacher, Madame Gerard, fails at first to interest Delarah in her language, literature, and geography assignments. "With dignity she left her seat at the table, stretched herself upon the chaise lounge, and went to sleep" (p. 44). Although twelve, Delarah has never been in the sea; so she must learn how to swim. She also has to dress herself, a thought that makes her wail: "I might as well be a slave." Delarah can dance and sing in French, but she resents learning from books. "We are rich," she says. "In three years the effendi, my father, will marry me to a young man, also rich. So why put things in my head?" (p. 49). Alcmene replies that only education can prepare them for life. For her part, she is making great strides in Turkish.

The summer of enchantment for the two girls moves along, and Delarah has begun to learn. Saturdays are spent at her house, much to Alcmene's joy. Slowly Delarah begins to use her imagination. The Floros handyman, Spyros, builds a kennel for Pir, Alcmene's dog, near the cliff fronting the sea. She has her father get them a rope ladder that they can drop down and climb—as the monks do on Mount Athos. They might need the ladder, Alcmene says, in case they are pursued by pirates. Delarah prefers to use the stairs near the bathhouse. When Ali Pasha spends three days in Stamboul, he takes Delarah with him; before she leaves the two girls take a vow under the Virgin Pine Tree that they will "dig the foundations" of their character. For Alcmene the vow means she will become a stoic. To rid herself of craving honey sweets, *bourecks*, Alcmene deliberately eats too many in order to get sick. Her father accuses her of stealing and gluttony before she explains her motives; and then he smiles, deeply moved by his "stoic." She reports her experience to Delarah, who admits she tried to think and "dig her foundations," but nothing came of it; so it seems "the good Allah meant me to be like the flowers, just living and blossoming" (p. 67).

One Saturday at her friend's house, Alcmene finds Delarah obsessed with a beautiful new doll whom they name Star Hanoum. Alcmene gets cross with Delarah. Then the Turkish girl has a bright idea: to marry off Star Hanoum to a man doll, for such a beautiful creature should not die unmarried. But where to find a man doll? Delarah's cousin from Smyrna, Kiamilé, suggests they find one at the store, get it on approval, marry him to Star Hanoum, then take him back. Delarah protests. She wants the whole *dughum*, the wedding ceremony, which lasts six days. They bring home a suitable doll from Achilles, the Greek shopkeeper. They spend a magical six days acting out the *dughum* for Star Hanoum and her bridegroom. In the process Alcmene learns all about a formal Turkish wedding. For having borrowed the doll, they pay Achilles all the money they have—five pennies. Later, Delarah has the two Turkish pounds needed to buy Star Hanoum's "husband," but Achilles has sold him to an Armenian family that has a sick daughter, Sourpouy. In an act of great generosity, Delarah gives her beloved Star Hanoum to the girl so that the doll will be happy, and not die a "widow hanoum."

Following up on this training in Christian charity, Alcmene maneuvers Delarah into donating *all* her beloved dolls to the Greek orphanage at the church of St. Demetrius. Every Saturday she is to give away as a prize two of her dolls to deserving orphans. At first the prospect stuns her, but her mood changes to elation when she sees how happy the orphans are. Delarah's reluctant generosity impels Alcmene to present her, as the "best little girl of the week," with a French copy of *Robinson Crusoe* to read. "Not only do I have to give my dolls away," she complains, "but now for my reward I have to work?" (p. 103). She thinks that reading will make her old and wrinkled. She does not want to be wise, only happy. In addition to everything else, Delarah has to become accustomed to the Greek name that Alcmene's mother has given her—Daphne Mousouros. The Floros family may take her to Vienna with them if her father approves; and she will have to travel as a Greek. Otherwise she cannot leave Turkey. When she learns who Daphne was in mythology, Delarah says she would prefer "to belong to Apollo, rather than furnish crowns of glory" (p. 93).

Meanwhile, portents of trouble multiply; an insurrection by the Young Turks movement, led by regular army officers, appears imminent. The moment does not seem propitious to Kimon Floros for Alcmene's being invited by Ali Pasha to witness Sultan Abdul Hamid at his prayers, and then to lunch at the royal palace. For Alcmene to adventure to Stamboul is as fabulous as the Arabian Nights—the opportunity rare for any little girl and for a Greek, unthinkable. During the whole journey Alcmene must speak Turkish only since, as Kimon Floros warns, "the ignorant and fanatical Turks do not approve of Christian children being treated as their equals." Despite the risks Alcmene excitedly packs and goes to Delarah's house where her friend, unused to such objects, calls the suitcase a "baby coffin." They go by steamer to Constantinople, then by closed carriage to the city mansion of Ali Pasha. They are taken by a royal carriage to the Yildiz Kiosk, the palace of Sultan Abdul Hamid built high above the Bosphorus. At the mosque there they witness the colorful pageantry of the monarch attending to prayers. A huge crowd watches and waits, all under scrutiny of spies and the Albanian guard, his trusted mercenaries. To Alcmene, who catches a glimpse of him, the sultan looks old and sad. With the crowd she shouts, *Padishahin chok tasha!* "Long live the sultan!" (p. 112).

Alcmene meets the lovely sultana, the sultan's young wife, and her daughter, the Princess Malkhatoun. The three girls discuss clothes, customs, and Paris. They eat a huge luncheon. When Delarah and the slaves fall asleep, the princess eagerly seizes her chance to talk with Alcmene. She asks questions, bursting with curiosity about the world outside the palace. She reveals her mother to be very unhappy because the sultan's other wives treat her badly—she has only one child, and a girl at that. From what Princess Malkhatoun says, the impression is once again given that life even for the most favored Turkish women is backward, emotionally bleak, intellectually vacuous—in short, a form of slavery.

At Alcmene's suggestion Princess Malkhatoun and she embark upon an adventure within the palace walls. They escape the surveillance of the eunuchs who act as guardians of the women.

Among some vines they find a rusted doorway. Unknown to them they have entered the sultan's private garden; and they encounter the sultan himself. Since they surprise him in the men's quarters, he whips out a pistol, fearing assassins; then he understands, recognizes his own daughter, and asks them many questions. Sultan Abdul Hamid is fascinated by Alcmene's boldness, her lack of fear, her innocence, her compassion. Princess Malkhatoun, however, makes the mistake of praising Alcmene's knowlege, derived from travels with her parents and from her education. When she admits that she, too, craves to learn, her father the sultan turns furious and malevolent, and orders his Albanian guards: "Conduct Princess Malkhatoun and her guest to the women's quarters" (p. 134).

At home Alcmene relates to her parents all that happened. They are secretly shocked at how close she came to being shot by the sultan. Kimon and Helen Floros discuss the political dangers stemming from the Young Turks. When Delarah next visits, she exults in having read *Robinson Crusoe*. Alcmene prays for two miracles: one, "Make Delarah and me sisters" (p. 139). Two, melt Sultan Abdul Hamid's heart and permit Princess Malkhatoun to learn. The two girls love each other more than ever. Their relationship deepens as the storm clouds gather. Much of the remaining story deals with the effect of public events on Alcmene and Delarah. Kimon Floros brings twenty armed Cephalonians to guard their house. Sultan Abdul Hamid, much to everyone's surprise, grants the new constitution demanded by the Young Turks.

Elated by the lack of violence, Ali Pasha arranges for Alcmene and Delarah to go to Constantinople "to witness the great ceremony of elections" the next day. There the girls are put into the care of Muchtar, a secretary of the ministry. Huge crowds mill about, drunk with the "new freedom." In an altercation Muchtar gets beaten, and he dies. The girls almost panic, until Alcmene gathers her wits and wends her way to the patriarchate of the Eastern Orthodox church. The patriarch feeds the tired girls; then he has a carriage deliver them to Ali Pasha's house. The episode proves something very important to Delarah: she has not been brought up to take care of herself in case of trouble. Kimon Floros is proud of Alcmene's bravery and intelligence, as is the patriarch, who wants to give her the medal of merit.

October brings back the governesses and the school lessons. Delarah learns to use the rope ladder, and to like it. The girls decide on a secret signal—the bray of a donkey—should they need the

ladder at night. In November when Ali Pasha closes down his summer place, Delarah stays with the Floros family except for week-
ends. She begins to acquire Greek. When for some reason Delarah
does not come one week, Kimon Floros takes Alcmene to Stamboul
to see the festivities at the opening of the new parliament. An extraordinary event happens when a trunk arrives at the Floros bank
containing the fortune of Ali Pasha—priceless shawls, a box of jewels, securities, and English bank notes—and a letter explaining
that the Young Turks may confiscate the whole lot. Ali Pasha wants
the Greek banker to take care of his family with the money, should
he be killed.

Under the pressure of events Delarah proves herself as resourceful as Alcmene; she arranges the escape of Princess Malkhatoun from the Young Turks. They want to dispatch her to Anatolia. Now she, too, enters the fearful household of Kimon Floros.
"For much less than that [aiding and abetting escapees] Greeks
had been destroyed and their fortunes confiscated" (p. 211).
Among other changes in temperament, Delarah loses her interest
in food. At all costs, now, they must get Princess Malkhatoun out
of Turkey. Kimon Floros will secure from the Greek minister an
emergency passport for her. Henceforth she will be a Greek girl.
Soldiers arrive to arrest Ali Pasha; Delarah invents a story about
his being rolled away in a barrel. Like Alcmene she has learned to
cope with trouble. Yet guards are placed at Ali Pasha's house. The
prospect of being poor looms ahead for Delarah's household. The
reason why the soldiers cannot find Ali Pasha is explained: his
mother, the Validé Hanoun, has had him shaved and dressed like
an old woman wearing the *tchit-tcharf*, the shroud-like garment for
outdoors; and by a ruse the Validé, Ali Pasha, and Delarah all escape the house together and head for the estate of Kimon Floros.
They ride to Prinkipo among the third-class passengers on a
steamer. On the island Turkish mobs have begun to attack the
homes of rich Greeks.

On Prinkipo no carriages are available for Delarah and her
father to reach the Floros house. Delarah and Ali Pasha walk the
long distance in the rain. He is dressed as a poor Armenian. More
trouble awaits them; a mob of looters is trying to penetrate the
Floros mansion. Again Delarah proves resourceful. She goes by
the seashore, next to the cliff, and finds the rope ladder which she
and Alcmene had used for imaginary escapes from pirates. Before
climbing, she says a final farewell to Ali Pasha, her father. He tells

her that henceforth she will belong to the Floros family as Alcmene's sister—thus the miracle the girls had prayed for has come
to be. Ali Pasha disappears into the night, while Delarah enters her
new life as a Greek girl named Daphne Mousouros. Technically
she is the younger sister of Helen Floros, Alcmene's mother.

The former Princess Malkhatoun, now Dorothea Vlastos, is to
pose as the niece of Kimon Floros. Ravenous for knowledge, she
has already begun to read and to learn Greek. Now the Floros
family has three lovely daughters. *Delarah* concludes happily with
the entire family successfully leaving Turkey for Paris on the Oriental Express. The miracle of Delarah's liberation has occurred.
She has become, like Alcmene Floros, a vibrant, self-reliant, and
accomplished young lady.

The subtleties and tensions of *Delarah* are absent from *The Spear
of Ulysses* (1941) by Alison Baigrie Alessios.[8] The setting is Ithaca;
the protagonist, an eleven-year-old boy, Pavlo. He and his friend
Lambro have a series of small adventures capped by their finding
a valuable bronze spear from the days of Homer. The boys enjoy
an idyll of youth on their beloved island. They visit the farm of
Yoryi, who sells goat milk on the streets; and they hear wonderful
stories: from a shepherd about a treasure at the castle of Ulysses,
from their maid about the women of Suli who leapt to their deaths
to avoid Turkish captivity. They also visit the old prison at Dafni
where an inmate gives Pavlo an antique coin and reveals where he
hid the spear that could have once belonged to the great Ulysses.
From that moment on the boys ardently wish to find it.

Pavlo survives the fasting of Lent when Greeks can eat no meat,
no cheese, no olives. At school the boys learn about their religion
and the struggle of their forefathers to win their freedom—about
the *Armatoloi*, the *pallikars*, and the *klephts*, all fighters for Greece.
The children enjoy Greek Easter with all its rituals, including the
cracking and eating of red dyed eggs. Pavlo and Lambro then visit
the island of Zante. They sightsee and sail and listen to stories.
They explore the currant orchards and take part in the harvest.
Back on their island the boys with the cousins along trudge to
Yoryi's farm where they learn about flax and cotton. Pavlo's father,
Patera, arrives on his ship, much to the boy's great joy. They all
plan a trip to Athens, but before that Patera helps them organize
a search for the lost spear of Ulysses. Pavlo finds it. They donate
both the spear and the antique coin to the museum in Athens.
They sightsee in the grand and venerable city. Having returned to

Ithaca, Pavlo eagerly waits for the letter from the museum; and when it comes the letter says "it had been definitely established that the spearhead was of the sort of bronze used in Homeric times," but that nobody knows if it actually belonged to Ulysses (p. 212). "The coin is a rare one of the same period, and will be given its proper place" (p. 213). To reward Pavlo and Lambro, Patera will take them to America.

Many of the Anatolian Greeks who left Turkey during the catastrophe of 1922 settled in a new village named Pyrgos near Mt. Athos, the Holy Mountain. In that region of Greece are set two delightful books by Joice M. NanKivell, *Tales of Christophilos* (1954) and *Again Christophilos* (1959).[9] The author lived in Pyrgos both as a Quaker relief official and as a doctor to the villagers and the monks. She gathered firsthand the tales which she reproduces in a simple, concrete, and evocative style. The first volume contains fourteen tales, the second ten. They represent the writer as an archaeologist of the mind who garners a literary treasure from the rich and vibrant memory of the Greek folk. Both young and old readers will find recorded much information about the customs and mores of the modern Greeks.

In her introduction the author states, "I knew the village and all the people, and Christophilos, and some monks." She adds: "All the Tales of Christophilos are told by villagers, and by simple monks. You will find other versions of many of them in the books and records of the Holy Mountain; but they will be different from these which have been passed from mouth to mouth, and are what the people believe." All the tales are highly readable. Their titles follow a pattern established by the first, "Christophilos and the Pig," followed by "—and the Shark," and so on, with the rest of the list in the first book being Ship, Oars, Petticoat, Witch, Athos Legends, Pascal Lamb, Silver Ducks, Man Blessed to Go, Rug Miser, Yaryar [Granny], Eggs, and Herbalist. *Again Christophilos* adds ten other items to the list.

The folktales reproduced by NanKivell are too numerous for detailed examination here, but some of the themes may be noted to suggest their scope and depth. Christophilos is an agent in them all: the taming and raising of a little wild pig, initially suckled by a dog; the saving of a monk from a shark by the sacrifice of a young goat; the rescue of a ship's passengers in a storm by the ringing of a warning bell; the getting of a new shirt as a reward for finding a pair of oars; the lifting of a curse allegedly caused by the evil eye;

the use of a witch's charm to convince a selfish reluctant man to marry a poor aging woman; the giving of stories and advice by an old monk rather than badly needed bread; the exchange of a pair of silver earrings to help a neighbor lift a curse; the revelation of sainthood by the color of a dead man's bones; the pride of owning a rug too priceless for anyone to buy; the saving of a dying grandmother by a pilgrimage to a distant ikon; the finding of a scarce egg to satisfy the last wish of a holy hermit; the purchase of a fine little donkey by a happy young man, Christophilos.

The subtitle of NanKivell's *Again Christophilos* is "more folk tales from Athos, the Holy Mountain and old-world." The tales begin with "Christophilos and the Owl," and their themes include: the utilization of monks to cure illnesses; the value of a saint's relics to frustrate evil; the barter of honey for fish desired by the monks; the mischievous antics of goblins called *kalikantzaroi*; the effort to pass off wolf meat as wild pig; the mistaking of a bee sting for a snake bite; a miser's hoard of paper drachmas used by rats for their nest; the effects of bitter blood in a woman who saves everything; the foiling of a rich old widower who wants to marry a young girl against her will; and the gift of a female sheep, unwanted on Athos, that bears four lambs for Christophilos.

In many embattled countries of World War II the children often committed deeds as heroic as those of their elders. The youth section of the Greek resistance, the EPON, organized hundreds of thousands to help harass and finally defeat the Nazi invaders. Among them were the legendary *saltadoroi*, youths who leaped upon German supply trucks to take food, arms, medicine, and other badly needed material. During the bloody civil war that followed the liberation, the Greek children again suffered the customary perils and deprivation; and toward the end of hostilities the defeated left and communist movement "rescued" many thousands of children from "Anglo-American imperialism" and took them north for an allegedly better chance in socialist countries. Even before that the royalists led by Queen Frederika "rescued" thousands of Greek children from the embattled areas to save them from "Communist indoctrination." Unhappily the children were the pawns of great contending forces. In a novel by Robert Shaffer called *The Lost Ones* (1956), the bad guys are the "*andarte-bandits*" and the good guys the Americans sent by Truman to help the Royalists.[10] The return to power of the Royalists "meant that everyone who had belonged to any group opposed to the monarchy was suddenly in disfavor and believed to be Communistic" (p. 155).

The protagonist is a young American boy, Peter Barrett, whose father is a captain in the military mission headed by General Van Fleet. Other principals include Ting, also an American boy; Arno, a large boxer dog; and Alexis, a Greek foster child of fourteen who lives with the Barretts. It turns out that Alexis had been among a group of twenty children abducted by the "*andarte-bandits.*" He had managed to escape, but his sister Irene had remained with the group—a fact that makes him moody and sad. The hope remains, however, that she is alive and may be in a position to be rescued. It also turns out, by a great coincidence, that the dog Arno had once belonged to Alexis and Irene. Peter and Ting undertake to learn the location of the lost sister. From the Red Cross they find out that her group of abductees had been brought back by a unit of the Greek army; and Irene could very well be at one of the camps for refugee children organized by Queen Frederika. A complication arises when the Barretts must clear Alexis of false charges of holding subversive ideas. If guilty, he would be sent to the island of Leros for punishment and the "cleansing" of his views. The solution to finding Irene, as one of the "lost ones," occurs with the help of Arno at the Children's Home in Nauplia. A girl there by the name of Irene Aristides is flown to Athens where she and her brother Alexis are reunited. For his heroism at the siege of Konitsa Alexis receives from "Her Majesty, Frederika, Queen of the Hellenes," a medal of honor "for his outstanding service to the Kingdom of Greece."

Another novel that describes the mass abduction of children—and a boy's role in it—is James Forman's *Ring the Judas Bell* (1965).[11] The Greek village of Serifos, nestled among the Macedonian mountains, is controlled by the revolutionary partisans. Nicholas Lanaras at fifteen is caught between the pacifism of his father, the local priest, and the harsh violent realities of life. The bell of the title has in its metal one of the coins given Judas.

Nicholos loves the sheep that he tends and protects on the mountainside. He fears both the Andartes, the partisans, and the fierce wolves. He hates the Andartes because during the resistance, which they led, the Germans killed his mother as a hostage. To justify the boy's intense feeling, the author makes it almost seem terrible for the Greeks to have fought the Nazis, forgetting that most of the hostages died as heroes. Nor does Forman state the real political issues that divided the Greek people—for example the demand by the British that King Paul be restored to his throne. The young Nicholos shares Winston Churchill's view that the Greek partisans are communist bandits who want to destroy if they cannot rule. Politics aside, the plot develops much tension and suspense when the Andartes sweep into Serifos and kidnap the children, among them Nicholos and his older sister Angela. She likes Thanos, one of the Andartes, whom she finally joins.

Before she does, she and about twenty other children from Serifos are taken to a refugee camp across the border in Albania. They are hardly settled when Nicholos and Angela escape. They trudge across snows first to nearby Yugoslavia (where Angela kills a woman who wants to betray them) and then back to Greece, to Florina. In the course of the difficult journey Nicholos matures. The violence and death confirm him in the role he must play as a man—that of one, like his father, who seeks to promote peace, understanding, and love. With the help of the children Nicholos raises the Judas bell to the chapel tower from whence it fell during a bombardment.

A wartime book for children with an implicit plea for brotherhood among all peoples is *Strangers No Longer* (1943) by Annie Barclay Kerr.[12] Her thirteen chapters dramatize episodes in the lives of various ethnic types. In one of them, "A Little House for God," a young Greek boy, Lambros Linardos, has become a problem for his teachers and his widowed mother. He seems to have lost interest in school; he consorts with rowdies, and he plays tricks on his sister Helen. When chastised for breaking some Greek custom he retorts: "I don't have to be like the old Greeks. I'm an American" (p. 82). His mother Penelope has moved away from a city with a Greek church because her brother Metax disapproved of her job in a factory. She now wonders what ill effects the absence of a Greek environment is having on Lambros.

Something unknown to her is keeping him out late after school. To learn the secret Penelope seeks help first from her daughter and then from a worker at the church, Mr. Blake. It turns out that Lambros has been visiting the workship of a Norwegian carpenter, Mr. Peterson. The Greek boy is "crazy to learn carpentry" (p. 87). Furthermore he wants to construct something to surprise his mother and sister—a cupboard for the one and bookshelves for the other. The friendship between the older man and Lambros results in Mr. Peterson's setting up a shop in the church basement for classes in carpentry. Other boys participate with great enthusiasm. Soon a sign appears outside the door: OLD FURNITURE REPAIRED—PRICES REASONABLE. Even more important, Lambros and his young friends build a children's chapel, a "little house for God," in one of the vacant rooms. Lambros is chosen to make the pulpit. On the day of dedication the boys and girls conduct the entire service. The story ends with Lambros Linardos coming out of the chapel after meditation, his face "illumed as are the faces of those who talk with God" (p. 93).

An American author now living in Greece, Edward Fenton has translated two war stories written by Alki Zei primarily for young readers. They are *Wildcat under Glass* (1968) and *Petro's War* (1972). Among his own work Fenton has written in *Aleko's Island* (1948) a fine story about a Greek boy, his goat Lesbia, and his important archaeological find.[13] The time of the action is immediately after World War II, presumably the spring and summer of 1946. The ruins of Aleko's house still stand, reminding him of the bomb that killed both his parents. For young boys and girls on Mytilene the capital city of Athens looms in the distance as a Mecca where they could seek their fortunes. Beyond Athens lies the even more distant and more fabulous goal of America.

Aleko, a poor orphan who lives with his grandmother, loves the island and his wild and impetuous she-goat, Lesbia. When she gets lost again, the irate guardian orders that she be sold at the *agora*, the marketplace. Aleko goes to town for that purpose with his friend Stelio. At the *agora* the irrepressible Lesbia creates a disturbance, has a *barbouni* (a red mullet) thrown at her, and runs off. No Lesbia, hence no sale. At home where she arrives before him, Aleko fancies that he "could see the wicked look of triumph in her hard, glittering eyes" (p. 53).

During a picnic on "Clean Monday," the first day of Lent, Lesbia manages again to wander off; and her young master after a frantic search finds her "right in the middle of the bomb crater in the next field, near the shattered stump of an ancient olive tree which the force of the bomb had completely uprooted" (p. 71). Lesbia is digging at something which turns out to be a bronze artifact about three inches tall. It is that of a boy "with an oddly shaped conical cap," and on his shoulders he "carried a fat young lamb." The object is perfect.

The rest of *Aleko's Island* deals with the effects of the boy's invaluable find. Stelio, his best friend, says the treasure can bring in enough money to take them to Athens. A rich lady, Kyria Alexandra, wants badly to buy it. Another rich lady, Kyria Papamichaelides, offers him a very large sum. The teacher, Kyr' Iannis, wants to keep the bronze shepherd boy, ostensibly to have photographs made and sent to Athens; but Aleko suspects his motives. The *nomarch* himself, the governor, arrives to try claiming it on behalf of the island. Aleko carefully hides the relic, much to the annoyance of his grandmother, who calls him wicked. One day he arrives home to overhear her consummating a sale of his statuette—a betrayal that impels him to run away.

With his goat Lesbia along he meets up with an itinerant painter, Mr. Eleftheros, or "Free Man." The stranger, who travels from place to place, shares his *feta* cheese, dark bread, olives, and *retsina* wine. The three of them leave on foot for the other side of Mytilene. Those they encounter regard them as father and son. Already the bronze shepherd, a lucky talisman, has secured for Aleko a friend in Eleftheros and a taste for the free life. The older man sees in the bronze "a second Aleko," a Greek boy of the distant past. On the opposite shore of the island Eleftheros paints murals on the white-washed walls of the Kaffenion of the Good Heart— the Burning of Troy, the wanderings of Ulysses, and, finally, a picture of Aleko as a barefoot boy with the goat Lesbia on his shoulders.

During the Easter feast a jeep arrives bearing the teacher Kyr' Iannis and an American archaeologist, Mr. Gotch. He declares the bronze shepherd to be a votive piece and the first of its kind to be uncovered on Mytilene. The lamb to be sacrificed was "dedicated to the god Hermes who protected all shepherds and their animals." If Aleko lets the museum have the bronze, Mr. Gotch will speak to the authorities about Aleko's education to become an archaeologist. His grandmother will also be well provided. Although his free life appeals to Aleko, the painter Eleftheros advises him to accept the offer, for the real meaning of freedom is "to keep what is important and let the rest go." Aleko does accept, and he returns to his own town a hero. The nomarch makes a speech just before the boy embarks for Athens on the boat *Thessalonika*. In leaving, he realizes how much he loves and will miss his island, its people, and his perky goat Lesbia.

For the simple entertainment of nine- or ten-year-olds Edward Fenton has also published *An Island for a Pelican* (1963).[14] The small Aegean island has 366 churches built by sailors to honor

Saint Nicholas, who allegedly saved them from death at sea. One day the boy Vassili finds a strange bird, a pelican, who decides to stay rather than fly on to Africa. Named Petros, the pelican becomes a tourist attraction along with the many churches and the windmills. Visitors who like being photographed with Petros crowd the island and make it prosper, much to the envy of neighbors. Then one day the famous pelican is kidnaped; and nothing helps to get him back, not even appeals to Athens, until Vassili rows by himself across the sea, finds Petros, and brings him home where he belongs.

Fourteen brief but interesting stories for young people comprise the collection *Racing the Red Sail* (1947) by Alice Geer Kelsey.[15] The author writes in her foreword that the stories, which grew from her relief work and travel during 1945, "show the boys and girls of Greece as they are today, meeting life with a gallant disregard of hard times" (p. xii). To show her concern for them she donates all royalties from the sale of her book to the Near East Foundation "for its work with the children of Greece."

Nicola lives in the island city of Upper Syra. From the roof of his house he scans the sea for a red sail to show the approach of his father's boat. Strong winds delay him on Delos, but he must return to fetch brushwood from the hills so the baker can work his oven. In his father's absence Nicola with his friend Spiros and two donkeys undertakes to collect the brush himself. This the two boys do, and when the donkeys are loaded they notice down in the harbor a little boat with a red sail. They race the sail and arrive at the quay "just as Nicola's father jumped ashore to pass the heavy rope through the iron ring to hold the boat fast" (p. 13).

Other boys and girls do other nice and often unusual things. Mitsos of Athens is a Boy Scout whose leader announces a treasure hunt—for members of the troop to find the oldest clock in their neighborhood. The search is also a lesson in local history, for the answer is the Clock of Andronicus, a sundial in the Tower of the Winds constructed by the Romans. Another story, "Candles at Midnight," describes the rites of Greek Easter on Mount Lycabettus, as witnessed by ten-year-old Costas Papadopoulos. Down the slope he runs with a lighted candle for his home. Manoli, a young Cretan, in "The Skeleton Windmill," works briefly for an American ship in port and receives in payment what he dearly wants—some canvas "to fit a sail to each of the five pairs of empty arms" of their dormant windmill (p. 53). The happy boy asks that he sleep near

the windmill that night to hear it singing again. In "Even an Octopus" little Popi thinks the live creature ugly, but changes her
mind when her mother, a fine weaver, shows her a pillow top in
which she has worked a Cretan design copied from a vase found
at Knossos. After one glance Popi says: "Even an octopus can be
beautiful." Aristocles is a lame boy who needs five thousand drachmas for leg braces so he can walk upright. He proves his worth as
a fisherman to himself and to others in "A Fisherman of Eleusis."
He will soon earn more than enough for his needs.

In a touching story, "Mari from Menidi," two young sisters, Agatha and Penelope, have a problem in having to manage the house
after the death of their mother. They are "daughters of a once-
wealthy Greek government official" who cannot lower themselves
by accepting just any work. Therefore Agatha poses as a servant
girl, Mari from Menidi, and spends an exciting day selling bunches
of lavender on the streets of Athens. In "Constantine" a blind boy
of that name will be taught braille through the kindness of a Greek
lady, Kyria Angelopoulou. On the island of Euboea, in "Michali's
Bell," a cobbler always rings the bell because he and others brought
it from their village in Asia Minor when the Turks drove out the
Greeks in 1923. In "Under the Shining Rocks" a group of Greek
children experiment with the acoustics of the theater ruins at Delphi. Michael and Phrosi of Delphi become friends with Nina and
Aleko of Athens. Other stories deal with Stavros, who brings home
wheat spilled from trucks on the quay; with young King Otho, who
allegedly taught the Greeks to like potatoes; with Theodora, who
decides to plant sesame seeds rather than eat them; and with Nicolas and Cleo, who learn that visitors come to Philippi to examine
"the place where Saint Paul gave Greece the greatest treasure it
ever had—the story of Jesus."

Another story for young readers that deserves mention is *Nikos
& the Sea God* (1963) by Hardie Gramatky.[16] Nikos, a boy, also lives
on a Greek island, and he, like Vasili, has a pelican for a friend.
After hearing from his Aunt Mara about the ancient Greek gods
and myths, Nikos names his pelican Icarus. In the island's museum
he studies old vases and notices a picture of Poseidon, god of the
sea. One night when the winds howl Nikos thinks that he actually
sees Poseidon. The boy talks about his vision. Some laugh at him,
especially when he fishes without making a catch. Then one day
he pulls out of the water an old Greek vase, "as old as the Gods
themselves, perhaps," with a picture of Poseidon holding a fish. A

crisis erupts when Aunt Mara needs a doctor, and the regular doctor is absent. Despite a violent storm Nikos and his pelican sail out to intercept a cruise ship; and again he imagines that he sees Poseidon. The ship's doctor helps Aunt Mara get well—and thereafter she tells visitors about the time when Nikos saw Poseidon.

Picture books for children that combine photography and text represent most of the nations of the world, including Greece. Usually the text embodies a simple plot with enough suspense to lure the reader on from page to page. An excellent example is *The Flower of Vassiliki* (1968) by Yolla Niclas.[17] The setting for both photography and story is the small Cretan village of Vassiliki, named after *vassilikos*, or basil, a flower considered holy by the Greeks. According to legend, its fragrant scent led to the hidden cross of Christ. Thereafter it was believed "that the flowers cast a spell of faith and hope upon everyone who touches them." They allegedly bring good fortune to Kyria Sofia, who has lost her husband and who now has a desperate time alone with four young children. Her problem is resolved when Maria, her eldest daughter, becomes the foster child of some kind people in the United States. The whole village is happy for Kyria Sofia and her family. Maria wishes she could give her foster mother a bouquet of *vassilikos* for she, too, might have "a special wish that would come true with the help of the holy flower."

Just as Nick Carter and other American secret agents go to Greece on suspenseful capers, so do the Bobbsey twins and other young sleuths and adventurers. Some are drawn there by mysteries that originate in the United States, while others are caught up while touring the country. All juvenile sleuths seem to have in common a keen desire to mix in other people's affairs. Without such curiosity they cannot exercise their fine ability to solve tough and dangerous cases. In the opening paragraph of *Mystery of the Hidden Hand* (1963), set on the island of Rhodes, Phyllis A. Whitney writes: "Neither Gale nor Warren had any idea of the strange events that would soon involve them in unexpected adventure."[18] They visit the Greek island to see their Aunt Marjorie, who is married to Alexandros Castelis, owner of the Hotel Hermes in which they stay. Through the hall and up the stairs a black-hooded figure floats; and in one of the rooms a grim Greek lady stirs in bed. She has returned to Rhodes from America seeking revenge for an old hurt.

Gale Tyler and her brother Warren meet the angry lady in the hall. Together they notice mirror signals coming from a house some blocks away. The woman, who smells of geraniums, calls it the "house of my enemy." For the young sleuths the adventure has begun. The author in her typical fashion weaves a complicated web that eventually unravels in a fairly simple solution. In *Mystery of the Hidden Hand* two lines of action stemming from the past merge to create a critical situation for the principals. The irate woman is Geneva Lambrou. Before she left for the United States, where she married a Greek-American, she worked as a maid in the mansion of a sculptor, Thanos Castelis. He discharged her when she accidentally discovered he had kept for himself a beautiful marble hand that belonged in the museum, a vital part of an archaeological find he had made. While out on a caique a sudden squall dumped Geneva and her sister into the sea, and the latter drowned—a tragedy for which Geneva blamed Thanos Castelis. She has returned to Rhodes, now a widow, with a plan to discredit him.

The second line of action involves a counter plan by the sculptor's grandchildren, Nicos and Tassoula, to have the marble hand brought to the museum in such a way as not to implicate Thanos. The arrival and intervention of their American cousins threaten for a while to wreck their benevolent purpose; and the wreckage becomes doubly probable when Mrs. Lambrou also wants the hand to use as a weapon against her enemy. The black-hooded figure in the hall was Tassoula pretending to be a ballerina. Nicos takes the hand from its hiding place, buries it at a likely site, then conspires with Gale and Tassoula to have Warren "find" it and give it to the museum as a discovery all his own. Mrs. Lambrou steals the hand from them, however. Gale then informs Thanos Castelis about the whole problem, and he in turn tells the museum authorities that he kept the hand for a time, perhaps too long, before relinquishing it to them. They understand, and all is forgiven. During the novel Tassoula learns that her real talent is not ballet, in which her famous sister, Lexine, excels. Thanos has been insisting that Nicos become a sculptor like himself, but now realizes that his grandson's true interest is in running the Pegasus pottery shop which the family owns. In the end, even Geneva Lambrou admits the error of her ways and joins the group as a friend.

In an afterword Phyllis A. Whitney notes that she went to Rhodes where she did the research for the novel. By having the children visit various landmarks she is able to give much information about the island's long past and about Greek customs of the present. These facts are what a typical observant tourist would want to learn; thus, in part, the story serves to educate young readers about history and geography while entertaining them with a mystifying series of events. As much as possible Whitney makes the visits to landmarks relevant to the plot itself. The children explore an old Venetian castle, they examine the spot where the Colossus of Rhodes once stood, and they visit the exciting Valley of the Butterflies.

In another mystery from a series, *The Bobbsey Twins and the Greek Hat Mystery* (1964), the action begins in the United States, then moves to Greece for development, climax, and solution.[19] In their hometown of Lakeport the older of the two sets of twins, Nan and Bert, find a box of *baklava* dropped from a bicycle. After going home, in order to seek the owner, they call the Greek bakery on Main Street to learn the box belongs to Mr. Karilis, who owns a fur shop downtown. The twins return the *baklava* to the Greek furrier. Karilis tells them about Greece. His brother Yannis runs a small factory in Athens. He shows the Bobbsey children a carton of fur hats just received from his brother's factory. Young Freddie Bobbsey puts on one of the hats and discovers something stiff in the lining: a piece of paper with a figure resembling two horns, and under them the words *tessera epta*, meaning *four seven*. All are puzzled. The mystery of the Greek hat has begun.

They check through the remaining hats but find nothing; then the cryptic label itself disappears, possibly destroyed by the foreman Jim. Along with Mr. Karilis's mail arrives a letter from his brother in Athens. A bale of valuable furs has been stolen. Mr. Karilis explains to the children that he packs and ships to Greece the paws and other bits of fur which are leftover when coats are made. These remnants are cut into strips and sewn together into larger pieces called "plates," then shipped back by his brother for fur coats and hats. Without the lost bale Mr. Karilis's workers would lose their jobs. According to the letter, Yannis the brother "sent a workman named Thanos in the truck to Piraeus to pick up the fur from the ship. He got the bale but never came back to the factory!" (p. 11). The Bobbsey children indicate a lively curiosity about Greece. The furrier tells them a little about Piraeus, the port of Athens; and that afternoon Mrs. Karilis shows them informative slides. Most of them concern Crete, the ruins of Knossos, and the "bull dancers"; one shows a large piece of stone on a hill that re-

minds them of the bull's horns they saw on the paper in the fur
hat. Too bad the mystery was in Greece, Bert Bobbsey had said,
otherwise they could have fun "working on the case."

In no time at all their chance to continue work materializes; for
their father asks: "How would you all like to go to Greece?" Mr.
Bobbsey has been corresponding with a shipbuilder named Gorzako in Athens. "They had been consulting about lumber to be
used in building a new ship. Now Mr. Gorzako had invited Mr.
Bobbsey to bring his family to Greece as his guests" (p. 22). A century earlier, in 1863, Robert Merry and his young friends had
crossed the Atlantic on their educational journey via balloon. Now
in 1964 the Bobbsey twins cross by jet; and although the solving of
a mystery is their game, they also learn some history and geography. Even before they leave, their teacher in school tells them
about the Olympic games as well as the Pythian held at Delphi and
the Isthmian held near Corinth. After school the children pretend
they are Olympian athletes and hold their own races.

The action moves rapidly in the usual Bobbsey Twins fashion,
without much characterization or detailed description, and no
deep thought to perplex adolescent minds. Before the children
land in Athens they see the Parthenon beneath them. They are
met at the airport by Georgos, sent by Mr. Gorzako to pick them
up in a Volkswagon bus. At the Gorzako house they are introduced
to Aliki and Mihalis, children about their own age. After dinner
Nan Bobbsey notices strings of beads on various tables in the living
room. "They were made of jade, amber, and other stones, and
each one ended in a silken tassel" (p. 34). Mr. Gorzako explains
that they are worrybeads, or *komboloia* in Greek, and very popular.
When one's hands are busy, "one has no time to worry." The next
day Mr. Gorzako takes them to the Acropolis. The word in ancient
times meant "fortification," he says; but the one in Athens is the
most famous because on it "are the ruins of three buildings, the
Parthenon, the Propylaea, and the Erectheion" (p. 35). The Bobbsey children tell their host about Mr. Karilis's brother Yannis and
ask to be taken to his fur factory. Now in Greece they have a mystery to solve.

From Yannis they get a description of Thanos, the fur thief:
short, plump, with thick eyebrows. Perhaps he has returned to
Crete, his place of origin. The Bobbseys learn Greek words like
efcharisto, thank you, and *parakalo*, please. They are told that "dry
Greece" means the mainland while "wet Greece" means the is-

lands. Mr. Gorzako arranges a trip to Crete for them, and he warns them not to take out any antiquities. At the ruins of Knossos they hear about the myth of the Minotaur, of Theseus and Ariadne. They see the throne of King Minos, the oldest one in Europe. They even find a rare artifact—"a tiny bronze chariot drawn by two little bronze horses" (p. 45). At the museum Mr. Telides shows them other Cretan objects of art. Their own find will be examined by an expert. Bert Bobbsey asks about fur factories and learns one is nearby. When they go there, a man bars the way who fits the description of Thanos. Later, after the police have come and gone, Bert chases the thief who had hidden behind the building. Thanos escapes when Bert crashes into a donkey loaded with pottery. The factory manager, Dimitris, had told the police that nobody else was in the building. The Bobbseys return to Athens without solving the mystery; and Bert gets a phone call from Yannis urging him not to find Thanos. "It's too dangerous! I have received a warning!" (p. 59).

The American and Greek children play *koutso*, the Greek equivalent of hopscotch. Then they play tag and "statues," during which they freeze in various attitudes such as the discus thrower. Mr. Gorzako has the children taken on a round of sightseeing trips; and everywhere they go they find increasingly vital clues to the mystery. On the way to Delphi they discover the truck, now wrecked, that was stolen from Yannis Karilis by Thanos. They examine a large mountain cave which they feel is being used by smugglers of antiquities. The ferry ticket to Corinth is like the piece of paper that Bert Bobbsey had found in the truck, indicating that Thanos and his accomplices might have also used the ferry. They then voyage to Mykonos and Delos looking for a boat named *The Bull*. At Delos they catch up with Thanos, a rather plump man whose "thick eyebrows met over his little beady eyes" (p. 150). From the opposite side of a cove the adventurous children watch the thieves loading *The Bull* for the trip to Piraeus where their stolen antiquities will leave Greece. The Bobbseys return to Piraeus where again they search for *The Bull*. Little Flossie Bobbsey spots it. With the police they chase an old car with Thanos and a companion in it—Dimitris, "the man who had let them into the fur factory on Crete" (p. 165). In a warehouse, where the police question Thanos and Dimitris, Nan finds the same kind of label—with the drawing of a bull's horns and the words *tessera okto*—they had found at the Karilis factory at Lakeport. Freddie Bobbsey notices something strange—a bale of fur slit open and containing a large marble foot—a stolen relic. The solution to the puzzle is that the thieves are sending antiquities out of Greece in bales of fur plates. With Bert's help the police capture the culprits. The Bobbsey Twins have solved another mystery.

The most famous of girl detectives, Nancy Drew, does not caper in Greece but in Istanbul, yet in *The Mysterious Mannequin* (1970) she does patronize a Greek restaurant. Her friend Bess exclaims at one point: "Nancy, I don't think we should go to the Greek restaurant. Suppose that awful burglar decides to have lunch there too? Oh, Nancy, I have a feeling you'll be in real danger if you go there."[20] The mystery concerns a Turkish rug-dealer, Farouk Tahmasp, who had disappeared two years earlier. He had been a client of Nancy's father, Carson Drew. At the Drew house arrives a package containing a prayer rug. The restaurant which Nancy and her friends visit is in a section of town "where most of the people speak Greek" (p. 67). Called the Akurzal Lokanta, the Greek restaurant is apparently owned by a Turk—a situation not improbable since many Greek and Turkish dishes are similar. No other Greek references exist in the story. The prayer rug contains a secret message that the shrewd Nancy Drew is able to unravel. *Find the mannequin. I love her. Bring her to Istanbul.* Farouk Tahmasp sent the rug. In America he and a girl called Aisha had been engaged, but he had to leave when falsely accused of smuggling. In the end the young lovers, Aisha and Farouk, are reunited—thanks to Nancy Drew.

Rhodes is used to demonstrate the close connection between Greek tourism and literature in *A Present from Petros* (1961).[21] The biographical item about the author, Claire Huchet Bishop, states: "During a recent stay in Greece she fell in love with the country, and the young guide and his donkey she knew there were her inspiration for Petros and Kyrios in A Present from Petros." The story begins with a potential disaster for the poor Papapoulas family when the father, while painting a boat, suffers a compound fracture of both legs. With the summer season at hand he cannot pursue his usual job of guiding tourists around Rhodes. The task of necessity reverts to Petros, even though he is only eleven, and to his pet donkey Kyrios, who is young and untrained. Nevertheless Petros insists on trying to take his father's place.

The Greek guides and their donkeys line up at the dock waiting for boat passengers to disembark. Petros would not have been hired had not a young American girl, Susan Spencer, noticed him and Kyrios standing alone. Petros's grandfather also has not secured a client. At Susan's insistence the Spencers ride up the hill on the two donkeys instead of in the car sent by the hotel. So delighted is she with the spirited Kyrios that Mr. Spencer, who is a famous writer, decides to hire Petros and his donkey for the entire summer.

On the island Susan's father gets the inspiration to write, a fact that leaves her much in the care of Petros and his family. He wants to learn English, while she wants to learn Greek. After much pondering about what gift can adequately show his appreciation, Petros has the idea of taking Susan to a special place for a picnic. Grandpa Cosmas and the doctor accompany them. "They stopped at a farm to buy goat cheese, homemade dark bread, ripe black olives, honey, peaches and grapes, and, for the animals, carrots, a rare treat in Rhodes" (p. 60). They eat in a cool spot; then Petros leads Susan on a hike to what seems to her a mysterious place. Petros stops, claps his hands, and a cloud of butterflies rises to fill the air! Again and again they clap their hands, and each time a great cloud of butterflies rises and falls. He has brought Susan to a phenomenon of nature, to the Valley of the Butterflies. As an extra special gift, he selects one of the most beautiful and places it asleep on her dress just above her heart. The gift pleases her very much. Later in the story, Susan Spencer writes from America that the butterfly stayed on her dress all the way home, and that she will keep it in a transparent plastic bag, forever. Furthermore, her father will write about *petaloudes*, the Greek for *butterflies*. Susan is learning Greek because they plan a return trip to Greece. All this news makes Petros and his family very happy.

Depending upon their content, Greek folktales can also be regarded as children's literature. An early adult collection is *Fairy Tales of Modern Greece* (1930) by Gianakoulis and MacPherson.[22] The prolific children's writer of Greek descent, Aliki Likouris Brandenberg, has rendered into English a fine Greek folktale in *Three Gold Pieces* (1967).[23] The story contains advice of value to young people about to enter the great adventure of life. "Once upon a time in a Greek village, there lived a very poor man named Yannis." Disheartened, he leaves his wife and son to seek his fortune. After walking for three weeks he reaches Constantinople where he finds a job as servant to a wealthy old man. Yannis receives food and lodging, but the master keeps his pay. Someday he will give Yannis the money in one large sum.

Ten years pass, and Yannis gets his pay: three gold pieces for all that work, all those years. He does not complain, however. Then the old man wants to sell Yannis "a good piece of advice" for one of the gold pieces. Yannis readily returns the coin, receiving this homily: "*Never ask about something that is not your concern.*" For a second gold piece Yannis is advised: "*Never leave a path you have taken.*" And for his third and last coin: "*Suppress your evening anger until morning.*" As one might expect, each bit of advice works out to Yannis's advantage.

Penniless, he leaves the old man, walking until he comes to a high tree. High on a branch sits a Moor who is sticking gold pieces to the leaves. Yannis, remembering the first homily, does not ask the Moor why. The Moor calls him back, and says for 107 years he has been sticking gold pieces to the leaves. Yannis is the first passerby who does not ask why. "It was not my concern," Yannis replies. Pleased, the Moor shakes the tree, letting gold coins fall for Yannis to keep.

Some days later he meets three men leading a long line of mules. Yannis rides on one of them. They reach an inn. Instead of going inside and eating with his fellow travelers, he stays outside, remembering: "*Never leave a path you have taken.*" Again the advice proves invaluable; while the men are eating, an earthquake destroys the inn and kills them all. Yannis goes on with the mules which are now his to take home.

Three days later Yannis reaches his village. Ten years have passed, and, full of joy, he knocks at his own door. He decides not to reveal himself immediately to his wife but to ask, as a stranger, if he can rest his mules. "I cannot ask you into the house," his wife says. "But there in the yard is a shed where you may rest." Then he sees a man enter the house, and his joy turns to rage. Tired of waiting, his wife has taken another man. Yannis grabs his gun and starts for the door—but he remembers the third injunction: "*Suppress your evening anger until morning.*" He does so, and morning comes. Yannis sees a young man leave. "I am going now, Mother dear," he says. "I will send you some beans for lunch." Yannis gasps with astonishment: the man he almost killed the night before is *his own son*, now grown up. Yannis has his family, the gold, the mules— enough wealth for all to live in comfort the rest of their lives.

Another rendering of an older Greek tale by an American writer is Eve Merriam's *That Noodle-head Epaminondas* (1968).[24] The lad by that Greek name has grandparents living on the other side of a hill. Given a piece of cake to take home, he holds it too tightly and it crumbles. "The way to carry a cake," his mother says, "is to wrap it all up in leaves and put it in your hat and then put your hat on your head and come along home" (p. 13). He follows this rule the next time his grandparents give him something to take home; the trouble is that the gift is butter. Thus begins a series of misapplied directives that proves Epaminondas to be a fool. The butter wrapped in leaves on his head naturally melts all over him in the hot sun. His mother's advice about how to carry butter he applies to a puppy, the result being that he freezes the poor creature in a cold brook. The new advice about leashing a dog and dragging it along Epaminondas applies to a freshly baked loaf of bread. He ruins the bread by dragging it through the dust. His mother decides to visit her parents, and she warns Epaminondas: "I've got six mince pies cooling on the doorstep and you be *careful how you step on those pies!*" (p. 30). Naturally he is careful, for he steps "right-in-the-middle-of-each-one!" (p. 31). Seeing the footprints, his mother declares he will never have the sense he was born with, but she loves him anyway. Epaminondas, being very literal, will never forget that she loves him.

Neither the Bobbsey Twins nor the Nancy Drew series professes to have aesthetic value, other than to intrigue young readers through vicarious adventures. *What the Gulls Were Singing* (1967), by Phyllis Reynolds Naylor, does have such value in that it attempts to reveal subtle relationships among a group of youngsters who are growing up.[25] The author pauses to describe objects and to develop character. The ethnic interest centers around the Greek boy Nico, who has come to America to live with the Buckley family. The story dramatizes Marilyn Buckley's summer at the ocean; an only girl in the family, she wants someone to belong to her specially. Her older brother Peter now teases too much, but maybe Nico can be the one with whom she can share secrets. That summer she learns about love from various people. Even the gulls have something to tell her. "Their cries came to symbolize for Marilyn that each person—even the old, wrinkled ferris-wheel man—is unique and worthy of love."[26]

What the Gulls Were Singing begins when the Buckleys move into an old gabled house they have purchased on the Maryland seashore where the author also spends her summer. Marilyn and her brothers gleefully explore the creaky mansion. They believe the place is haunted. The family awaits a new arrival. "A few more days and Nico would be here. None of the family had ever seen him. Nico was from Greece. If all went well, Father would adopt him and he would become one of the Buckleys" (p. 16). Among the beach characters Marilyn meets is Cassandra, a self-styled gypsy who gathers and sells driftwood. Other characters enter the action when the Buckleys advertise for summer boarders. Nico arrives by plane from Greece. About thirteen, he is a year and a half older than Peter, Marilyn's older brother. She likes Nico's olive black eyes and large white teeth. Part of the novel's exposition necessarily concerns Marilyn's discovery of the new environment and the Greek visitor. She wonders if she will be his special friend. From the start it appears that Nico likes his new family; and he likes the ocean setting even though a group of young surfers make fun of him.

Several mysterious occurrences happen at the old seashore house—a strange tapping in the wall, a boarder named Julius Green digs in the sand at night, secret relationships come to light. The arrogant surfers again express their juvenile bigotry. They ask Marilyn, "Where's your Greek boy friend?" Another one jeers and calls Nico "cheap labor" for the Buckleys (p. 56). A great hurricane reminds Nico of an earthquake that he read about in Volos; the boarding house loses its porch and living-room wall and has to be repaired. The Buckleys are discouraged until several artists reserve rooms at their place. On the Fourth of July, Nico learns about fireworks and other customs and he says that Greek Independence Day falls in March. "The children wear blue and white clothes— the color of our flag—and there are parades. But we do not have fireworks. We save those for Easter" (p. 62). He explains about bells ringing, fireworks going off, candles burning, and celebrants cracking boiled eggs. Marilyn wants to crack eggs next Easter. She ponders why Cassandra avoids being liked by someone special, why she seeks solitude and her own company.

Another bit of bigotry surfaces when Nico contributes some drachma coins toward the purchase of a birthday gift for Mrs. Buckley. At an auction the children buy a large papier-mâché octopus. The auctioneer looks at the Greek coins and frowns: "What's this? Spic money, huh?" (p. 77). The term *spic* puzzles and disturbs Nico; and Mrs. Buckley tells him about "foolish people" who call Negroes, Greeks, and others bad names.

The novel revolves around Marilyn and what the summer teaches her about love. She learns that love is related to human need; for example, her retarded little brother Ricky needs more love than others because of his condition. She sees, too, that Nico keeps surfing with the nasty boys even though they make fun of him. Toward the end of the story Nico tells Marilyn that to swim with them is a challenge; to avoid their laughter he tries to surf even better. When he gets tired of hearing nice things, he goes to play with his enemies. Marilyn claims that she understands. And all the while the gulls are singing, and what they sing means different things to different people.

The summer goes on. Nico dances Greek for his American friends. They put on a play, *Cinderella*, and make $21.17 to be used for the house repairs. The children keep an inquisitive eye on Julius, Cassandra, Miss Tugberry and her goat, and the painter Ward Evans, who does a beautiful portrait of Cassandra. And of course the surfers keep pestering them. Marilyn wants Nico to belong to her, and she learns that he belongs only to himself. A tiff develops between Peter Buckley and Nico over a homing pigeon that Peter buys. Inadvertently Nico leaves the cage door unlocked; the pigeon escapes; and Peter cries: "You creep! You lousy creep!" (p. 152). Marilyn fears this hostility will drive Nico away from them; instead it draws Nico even deeper into the family. The children make progress with the "secret in the sand" when they unearth a bottle that contains a coded message. Decoded, the message reads *Can you be the same Julius Green? Alice is gone.* On the back of the bottle is a label directing the finder to receive a reward in room 209 of their house—the room of Julius Green. Led by Miss Tugberry, the children confront him and request an explanation.

Thirty-three years before he had been a lifeguard at the beach. He met a lovely girl named Alice, and they fell in love; but her parents did not like him, maybe because he had less schooling than she. Alice lived in what is now the Buckley house. Unable to see Alice openly, Julius and she left messages in the sand near an old stump. They planned to get married, but Alice's parents whisked her away to another city. "I never heard from her again." He now wonders who else knows about the hiding place and the code. "And who in the world would ever recognize me after all these years?" (p. 116). The answer comes later in the story from Cassandra. She was born in the Buckley house, she grew up on the beach, and her mother was the Alice that Julius had loved and lost so long ago. Cassandra recognized Julius from an old photograph of her mother's, and she knew about the old stump and the code and the bottle left in the sand. She wanted to puzzle Julius a bit before revealing that she was the daughter of the girl he had once known and loved.

Nico, the boy from Greece, is thoroughly involved in all these happenings. And so is Marilyn, who gathers meanings that help solve her own problem of relating to others. She also has a harrowing adventure when she hides on a fishing boat that goes out to sea. The angry fishermen disrupt their plans to return her to the pier. When a northeaster comes up, Nico remarks: "Poseidon is angry and makes the oceans roar" (p. 151). In a week school will reopen and the Buckley family will close up Cliff House and go home to Wheaton. "Nico would either go with them or fly back to Greece" (p. 152). Marilyn, who assumes he will leave because of his tiff with Peter over the lost pigeon, is pleasantly surprised when Nico replies: "I want to stay. I have decided. I am going to be Nicolas Panagiotis Buckley. How does that sound?" (p. 155) Marilyn shrieks and runs to the house with the good news.

The decision regarding Nico made, *What the Gulls Are Singing* concludes with the wedding in Cliff House of Cassandra and Ward Evans. Nico has found a home in which love abounds. The protagonist, Marilyn, comes to understand that love goes deeper than mere possession, of having someone belong to you. Love is also allowance for the other person to belong to himself. Even the tapping in the wall is explained: it is Miss Tugberry's goat beneath the house chewing on a rope hanging from a hidden laundry chute. When Marilyn, Peter, and Nico go to Cassandra's small beach house to close it down for the winter, they are accosted by the surfers, who claim it as their own. The boys fight. Again the delinquents call Nico a "greaseball." And they say: "All Greeks have sticky fingers" (p. 179). During the fight the police arrive and apprehend two of the troublemakers. One yells back at Nico: "You stinkin' Greek! You dirty, rotten Greek!" But Nico, more mature now in these matters, takes it in stride. He tells Marilyn he is not an apple to get rotten. "So I am only Greek, and of that I am glad" (p. 183). It is then that Nico explains why he still plays with the surfers, and she understands. They all depart Cliff House until next summer, and the gulls "sing" along the shore. "The night was alive with moving stars and crashing ocean, and Nicolas Panagiotis Buckley and his brothers and sister sat outside in the darkness and listened and looked and wondered" (p. 191).

The Greek ethnicity in children's literature, as we have seen, parallels to some extent that to be found in adult fiction. Many young Greeks appear in adult fiction as the offspring of immigrant parents; and they have been noted in previous chapters. Many other young Greeks appear in books which are set in ancient Greece. Three examples of this type are *Niko Sculptor's Apprentice* (1957) by Isabelle Lawrence, *Theras and His Town* (1961) by Caroline Dale Snedeker, and *Greek Slave Boy* (1968) by Lillian Carroll.[27] Both the Christian and the Byzantine eras also provide colorful and significant characters for children's books. Added to the titles cited here and to those written abroad, the children's literature involving Greeks would fill a large shelf. As in the case of nineteenth-century volumes like *The Balloon Travels of Robert Merry and His Young Friends*, they tend to combine adventure with learning about Greece and Greek civilization. Whether based on myth or on history, they introduce young readers to some of the essential features of Hellenism.

꙰꙰꙰꙰꙰꙰꙰

15

꙰꙰꙰꙰꙰꙰꙰

FREAKS AND OTHER HELLIONS

Modern Greeks who are freaked-out, weird cultists, oddly possessed, mad, or otherwise abnormal exist in the American fiction of this age of anxiety. That allegedly clear and logical Greek mind of the ancients allowed for belief in mythological monsters, cryptic oracles, mystic rites, assorted seers, and the supernatural. Mary Renault is only one of many authors who utilize themes and characters from the venerable Hellenic tradition. Both Jack Williamson and Barbara Michaels, for example, use the Ariadne archetype. Williamson's *The Age of Wizardry* (1964) retells the myth of Theseus and his epic struggle to rid the world of the Dark One, the power of the Cretan Minos and his dreaded Minotaur.[1] Both Williamson and Michaels, too, allude to the legend of Atlantis, the lost empire mentioned by Plato. In the foreword to his fantasy, Williamson writes about the Atlantis myth as fiction—until Heinrich Schliemann uncovered, first, the ruins of Troy at Hissarlik, then "the Palace of Minos at Knossos in Crete." Further excavations at Mycenae and Tiryns "have filled out the picture of a reality more amazing than the legend of Atlantis and the myths of the Greeks" (p. 6). The strength of Theseus in *The Age of Wizardry* wins out against the combined dark and mystical forces of the Minoans. When he severs the head of Keke, Ariadne's beautiful dove, the head turns into the "dark, skeletal visage of Daedalus." A dwarfish wizard becomes the brazen giant Talos. For Theseus the lovely Ariadne at the end renounces the power of wizardry.

In *The Sea King's Daughter* (1975) Barbara Michaels presents a heroine named Ariadne whose father, an archaeologist, seeks a fleet of Minoan ships sunk in the harbor of a Greek island, the alleged location of Atlantis. A major character, Kore, practices sorcery until the "game" gets out of hand.[2] The Greek in Ira Levin's *Rosemary's Baby* (1967) arrives on time to validate the satanic birth.[3] John Fowles, an English author, places the action of *The Magus* (1975) on the Greek island of Phraxos whose residents revive a lost magical cult.[4] From these aberrant beings it is only a short distance to the fanciful leaps and constructs of science fiction. Here, too, Greek characters play a role.

An American girl in Michaels's *The Sea King's Daughter* is drawn to the island of Thera by a father who has been away from home for twenty years. In the meantime Sandy (Ariadne) Bishop's mother married Jim Bishop, who is Sandy's stepfather. She had received gifts addressed to "Ariadne Frederick." Mother had explained that her father, Professor Frederick, loved only his work, nothing else. One of his gifts to Sandy was a statue of the princess Ariadne, who was thought to live on Crete about 1500 B.C. At her dentist's office Sandy reads an article that severely attacks her father's belief that the ruins of Atlantis are still there, buried in the sea north of Crete. Minoan houses had been unearthed on Thera, an island in the Santorini group. Sandy reminisces about finding Spanish coins from a wrecked galleon, made while diving with her stepfather off the Florida coast.

Seeing her photograph in the *National Geographic*, her father, Frederick, visits her with the proposal to come with him to Thera where he will dig and she can dive. Her diving would be illegal, but the reward is finding the lost Atlantis. She agrees, and after being graduated from college, she leaves for Greece. Sandy recalls the Cretan myth of King Minos, the Minotaur, Theseus, and Ariadne. She sightsees on Crete before sailing for Thera. She also practices her Greek. Climbing to the hotel on the island she meets Jim Sanchez, who works for a rival archaeologist, Sir Christopher. Frederick palms her off as his secretary. He wants it kept secret that she will dive for him professionally. What he seeks specifically are the "Minoan ships, the trading fleet of the sea king himself. They are there," Frederick states, "in the water, where they sank over three thousand years ago."[5]

After they swim to the underwater spot where he expects to find them, Sandy dresses and walks about the town of Zoa. She meets Sanchez with whom she talks, drinks ouzo, and watches a religious procession. She notices a very striking woman, gaudily dressed, like some ancient priestess. The people call her Potnia, the old word for the Minoan goddess. She lives in a nearby villa with its elderly owner. When Frederick shows up and sees her, he wanders off, shaken, into the darkness.

Back at their rented house, Sandy questions her father about the woman. She resembled someone he knew, he says, long ago. They discuss the diving; she will begin the next day. To convince her of "something down there," Frederick shows her part of a gold inlaid dagger. Sandy dives and finds the awesome abyss, the "outer caldera," as her father calls it. On Sunday she sees Jim Sanchez. Later she meets Sir Christopher. Among other things, they discuss the imminence of a volcano. He mentions the great Thera eruption of 1450 that was greater than Krakatoa. From him Sandy learns some important facts about Frederick. The two of them and a German, Durkheim, had studied archaeology together at Oxford; then they worked in Crete before the Nazi invasion. They joined the underground, but things went badly. The Germans captured and executed Durkheim, the liaison officer. Durkheim was Jim Sanchez's uncle. Sir Christopher, who knows that Sandy is Frederick's daughter, warns her to be careful when diving. After a huge meal, Sandy and Sanchez hike to the hills, nap, and begin to make love when a rider on horseback showers them with pebbles. Falling rocks badly hurt Sanchez, who protects Sandy with his body. The man on horseback, she thinks, is "the one who lives in the villa on the headland." When she tells Frederick the man is a German, a colonel, Frederick grows pale and almost faints.

The next day, while Sandy and Sanchez sit in the plaza, the gaudy "priestess" says: "Ariadne . . . Welcome back" (p. 124). The woman's name is Kore, which in Greek means maiden. During their strange conversation Kore says: "Thera is the home of *vrykolas*, the vampire. Sometimes the men do not work the fields because there are ghosts. And you have seen . . . how they are afraid of me. Perhaps they think I am *vrykolas*, an old harmless woman like me" (p. 126).

She wears bracelets on each arm—"coils of gold that went halfway up her forearms and ended in serpents' heads." The serpents have ruby eyes that flash. Kore calls Sandy the "sea king's daughter," and though coming to warn her away, Kore now thinks she should stay. "Give my greetings to Minos" (p. 128). Sir Christopher explains that she has used their code names from the days of the resistance. He was Daedalus, Durkheim was Poseidon, and Minos was her father. Sanchez now also knows that Sandy is actually Ariadne, the daughter of Frederick. Later Sandy discusses Kore with him. He explains that Kore was another name for Persephone, daughter of Demeter, whom Pluto, the king of Hell, stole. Sandy knows the myth. Kore, the woman of Thera, regards herself as a snake goddess. She is terrifying the peasents by "pretending to have occult powers" (p. 133). The last Minos, according to Frederick, was a Greek whose daughter was Ariadne, priestess of the mother goddess. The name *Ariadne* means "Most Holy."

Sandy dives, watched by the villa man. She finds a lovely amphora that spurs her on. In town she meets Sanchez, who knows about her search. He wants to dive with her. For some reason the people on Thera are disturbed—probably by Kore. Sanchez says about her: "And the Greeks have several words for women like Kore, who went over to the enemy" (p. 141). She needs magical powers for her own protection. On her way home Sandy hears the thundering hooves of a horseman. "The Greeks believed in monsters," she recalls. "My imagination re-created the flying figures of horse and rider, and added shadowy snake-haired forms, flapping black bat wings" (p. 143). The next time she dives she finds another amphora, but she gets cut on some metal, bleeds a lot, swims, faints, and is rescued by the mystery man of the villa, the German colonel. She revives on a bed in the villa; her savior, called Jürgen, is there along with Kore, who nurses her. Kore chides her, a "mermaiden," for being careless. Drowsy, Sandy hears an incantation: "And when you sleep, she will awaken, she who has slept so long and found a vessel of rebirth. O Most Holy, guardian of the dancing floor, daughter and maiden, awaken to your ancient heritage and live again!" (pp. 156–57). Sandy has been drugged by Kore, who means to turn her into the reincarnated Ariadne of old.

Sandy's friend Jim Sanchez visits her at the villa. They talk. When Jürgen sees Sanchez, he drops an armful of books and leaves pale and shaken in "mindless, headlong flight." Jürgen is clearly the man who killed his uncle in Crete during the war. "It was duty!" Kore defends him. His last name is Keller. He feels strong guilt, saying he believes in Nemesis—retribution. The two young people, Sandy and Jim, wonder why all these old associates have converged upon Thera. Alone with her, Keller advises Sandy to leave Thera, escape the "web," for her own safety. He appears to be under Kore's domination. In the afternoon Kore plies Sandy with a thick wine. Keller demurs at this, and gives her an antidote. Then shots ring out, meant for Keller. Kore gets a rifle to ward off further trouble. Not long after, an angry Frederick pushes himself past the servant girl and insists upon taking Sandy home. Sandy refuses. Frederick has brought help in the persons of Sanchez and Sir Christopher. But Sandy stands her ground and will return when she feels ready.

During dinner mild tremors sway the chandelier. Afterwards,

Sandy reads more about Ariadne and her dancing, whose function was perhaps to deliver victims for human sacrifice. Before Theseus killed the Minotaur, Athens had to provide yearly victims to appease the monster. Sandy sleeps, dreams, and wakes to find her feet red and scraped, as if she had run "barefoot, across a rough, hard surface." Sandy now thinks she has figured out Kore. "She had resurrected some antique cult and was playing high priestess, with half the women of the village dancing—literally—to her tune" (p. 199). Sandy was to be Kore, the maiden of the myth, and who was this Kore of the villa to be? With Jim Sanchez present, Keller reveals that the young man's uncle found the Minoan ships in the harbor two years before the war. He found them spread out in all their glory after a severe storm—then another storm promptly buried them again. The uncle told Keller and presumably Frederick, and now Frederick wants to rediscover the old find. Keller, however, feels that the ships are gone.

Suddenly the volcano erupts, accompanied by a quake. Terror seizes Sandy. Falling ash fills the sky. She and Sanchez rush to the wrecked house and help Frederick, who is hurt. He wants his books. Sandy helps him up to Keller and Kore's villa which is still intact, then runs to the village, where Sanchez says the people have turned ugly. They need a scapegoat. Back at the villa again, Sandy explores the place. Sanchez arrives to report the attitude of the villagers: with Kore to choose the victim, they want to perform the rite of human sacrifice to appease the angry gods. Sandy wonders what role Kore has reserved for her. Through the women, Kore controls the town. Is Kore sane? Keller tells Jim Sanchez that his uncle did not fall into German hands by accident. He was betrayed by someone whom he trusted like a brother. And that man might kill now in order to keep "the secret of his shame."

Thus the novel moves towards its conclusion with a strong element of suspense. The women of Thera who have been indoctrinated by Kore seize both Sandy (Ariadne) and Jim Sanchez, prepare the fire, and ready them for human sacrifice. They are beyond her control, Kore states. They have misunderstood her and take the old Minoan ritual literally; whereas, as she claims, "It was a game, a little game. . . . Oh, yes, I pretended to believe; at times I pretended so well I almost did believe" (p. 231). They did make sacrifices—but only "a chicken, a goat." Not human beings as the women now seek. Kore redeems herself in Sandy's eyes when she manages to make the women flee.

Her father, Frederick, also redeems himself, when the danger to Sandy and Sanchez appears in the form of Sir Christopher. To make the Minoan ships in the harbor *his* great find, he had betrayed Durkheim (Sanchez's uncle) to the Nazis then under Keller. Keller had to execute Durkheim; but he vowed that Sir Christopher would never find the Minoan treasure. Frederick, who also knew of the ships, had brought over Sandy to dive for them. It was Sir Christopher who had tried to frighten her off. Now, at last, Frederick helps to frustrate and arrest Sir Christopher. Sandy and Jim Sanchez marry and remember that strange time on the Greek island of Thera. She still wonders a little about the magic.

A satanic Greek has a small but vital part in that well-concocted witch's brew, *Rosemary's Baby* (1967), by Ira Levin.[6] In the story the young housewife Rosemary becomes the antithetical Madonna with Child, in that her baby is the only begotten Son of Satan sent by His Holy (or Unholy) Father to do for Him what Jesus Christ did for God. The divine birth occurs not in a stable with manger but in the Bramford, an old New York apartment building peopled by a coven of satanists. The Greek bearing gifts for Rosemary's Baby is Argyrou Stavropoulos. He is "a robust, handsome, dark-skinned man in a snow-white suit and white shoes. He carries a large box wrapped in light blue paper patterned with Teddy bears and candy canes. Musical sounds came from it" (p. 212). Stavropoulos represents either the Devil himself or an important archangel. He reminds the celebrants of a prophecy regarding the exact date of birth, June 25th, as distant as possible from Christ's birthday. Stavropoulos asks, "Didn't Edmond Lautréamont predict June twenty-fifth three hundred years ago?" (p. 213). Other than to be present to see Rosemary's Baby, the Son of Satan, Stavropoulos plays no role. The novel's unsettling conclusion belongs to Rosemary: as the archetypical mother she gradually accepts her little Adrian and intends to love and raise Him like any other child.

In and out of reality roams the modern Greek character. The Greek as a freaked-out culture hero finds a vivid representation in Gnossos Pappadopoulis, the protagonist of Richard Fariña's *Been Down So Long It Looks Like Up to Me* (1966).[7] Just as Jay Gatsby revealed a truth of the twenties and Tom Joad the thirties, Gnossos stands for the sixties and its varied alienations. "He's a shaggy-haired, pot-puffing product of the Great Society, an amoral collegiate hipster who loathes convention, lusts for kicks and is determined, above all else, never to lose his cool. He's the guy who has been down so long it looks like up." The book's blurb lists mescaline trips, campus riots, sacrilegious rites, the New Left, and sex. Not mentioned are humor, insight, bravado, a style bordering on Shandyism, and satire. The legend of Gnossos whaling through life with rucksack and drugs received a tragic underscoring by Fariña's sudden death. "On the night of April 30, 1966," according to an editor's note, "returning from a party celebrating the hard-cover publication of his book, Richard Fariña was thrown from the back of a motorcycle and killed." Of Irish and Spanish parentage, he was married to the sister of Joan Baez, the folksinger and political activist.

Fariña chose a Greek for his hero and called him Gnossos Pappadopoulis. Gnossos suggests Gnostic, the seeker of knowledge, the archetypical *knower*. What he knows, in essence, is the mystique of the new freedom, the code language of the hipster aristocracy. He is also the poet as *maker*, who makes the scenes that define his nature. The novel opens with Gnossos, the modern Odysseus, returning to Lairville (Ithaca?), New York, after a year's wanderings throughout the godforsaken land. Once again he has survived its perils. Unlike his mythical prototype, however, Gnossos comes back to a triple betrayal, so chaotic is this barbaric America. "Home to Athené, where Penelope has lain in an exalted ecstasy of infidelity, where Telemachus hates his father and aims a kick at his groin, where old, patient Argus trots out to greet his weary master and drives his fangs into a cramped leg, infecting with the froth of some feral, hydrophobic horror. Oh welcome" (p. 17). The madman is home, Fariña writes, the satyr dressed in hobnails, "smelling of venison and rabbits, the anise odor of some Oriental liquor on his breath" (p. 17). Gnossos being Greek, the liquor is ouzo. He comes glowing in legend, for rumors have him dead of thirst "at the bottom of Bright Angel Trail, eyes gnawed out by wild Grand Canyon burros; fallen upon by tattooed pachucos and burned to death in the New Mexico night by a thousand cigarettes dipped in aqua regia; eaten by a shark in San Francisco Bay, a leg washed up in Venice West; G. Alonzo Oeuf has him frozen blue in the Adirondacks"—these in lieu of Cyclops and Circe, Scylla and Charybdis. Back to Athené, to Mentor University. Actually the time is not yet that of Lyndon Johnson's Great Society; it is 1958, the days of Dwight Eisenhower and Richard Nixon, but the feverish spirit of alienation carries over well into the sixties.

Farina clearly establishes the time when he lists the contents of

Gnossos's rucksack. He also uses the contents as a means of characterizing his hero and suggesting his way of living—to make any mother despair for her "lost" son. Wearing his parka, his "portable womb," Gnossos shuffles up Academe Avenue, his rucksack packed "thickly"

> with the only possessions and necessities of his life: a Captain Midnight Code-O-Graph, one hundred and sixty-nine silver dollars, a current 1958 calendar, eight vials of paregoric, a plastic sack of exotic seeds, a packet of grapevine leaves in a special humidor, a jar of feta, sections of wire coathanger to be used as shish kebab skewers, a boy scout shirt, two cinnamon sticks, a bottle-cap from Dr. Brown's Cel-Ray Tonic, a change of Fruit-of-the Loom underwear from a foraging at Bloomingdales, an extra pair of corduroy pants, a 1920's baseball cap, a Hohner F. harmonica, six venison loin chops, and an arbitrary number of recently severed and salted rabbits feet. (p. 18)

A modern Odysseus, a "furry Pooh Bear," as Fariña calls him—but also shades of Cooper's Natty Bumppo, shades of Huck Finn, shades of plain Hobo, yet all of these with a fundamental difference: Gnossos, despite his style, pursues an Ivy League degree. Instead of fleeing the encroachments of civilization, he wallows in its pleasures. In the affluent society much can be afforded even by its most disaffected sons and daughters. The rucksack is full.

Be that as it may, Gnossos Pappadopoulis is a fascinating character and literary creation. He leads others by being most deeply committed to his compulsions. Gone a year on his "great adventure," he rejoins his peers: Fitzgore, Heffalump, Mojo, Heap, Oeuf, and other rogues. Gnossos's first act is to rent a room from a girl named Pamela Watson-May, in a house that also contains the alcoholic Rajamuttus, a couple from an old place of massacre, Benares. Although Pamela is all bones, Gnossos plans to seduce her. He asks for Metaxa which she does not have. After a meek knock on the door, his old friend Fitzgore enters, shocked to see "Paps" restored from the dead. They will share the room. More exposition follows. Fitzgore tells Gnossos about people and events during his long absence. Together they visit a campus hangout, the Plato Pit, where Gnossos loses no time in making one of his famous scenes, with some justice. The waitress refuses to accept his silver dollar as money; and when she calls him "sonny" Gnossos terrifies

her with a horrendous threat. "I am the King fucking MONTE-
ZUMA," he screams, "and *this* is the coin of my kingdom!" If she
fails to honor the symbol of his realm, he continues, he will have
her heart torn out, at the top of a pyramid. "And I will eat it RAW!"
(p. 32) From the start the reader knows that Gnossos is capable of
being a maniac and, on other occasions, sophomoric.

In his room Gnossos smoothly slips into his next scene: he fornicates with Pamela Watson-May before the photo of her fiancé. At
the Plato Pit he had frightened the waitress with a wild threat; now
he terrifies Pamela by laying her without a contraceptive. Like
Odysseus Gnossos tells lies, artfully fabricates, amuses. For scene
three he cleverly tries to con the dean out of paying his late registration fee. Gnossos pays with five silver dollars. Then an artist
friend of his, Calvin Blacknesse, takes him to the country in his
Saab, to his home; there Gnossos eats dinner, takes mescaline, and
poses for a sketch. On the return to the campus Calvin lets Gnossos
off at Guido's Grill where, after much badinage, he steals the show
by taking from his rucksack a Captain Midnight Code-O-Graph.
Later, Gnossos and Heffalump break into Dean Magnolia's office;
there, with a hammer, he smashes into dust and sand the dean's
collection of mineralogical specimens, crystal, shale, semi-precious
quartz—all in sweet revenge for the late registration fee. Of such
stuff is the modern Odysseus made.

Through much smart, heavily allusive prose the plot moves
ahead. Two apparent drug pushers named Heap and Mojo revitalize Gnossos's old "Cuban connection," bring him a special mixture
of marijuana and hashish, and invite him to a loft party. That evening, at his pad, Pamela Watson-May arrives, intending to kill
Gnossos with a thrown knife; it barely misses him but impales his
rucksack to the French doors. Her fiancé Simon has committed
suicide, by sucking an exhaust pipe, because she told him that she
loves Gnossos. Pamela gives Gnossos a knee in the groin, breaks
Fitzgore's new copper hunting horn, bleats like a lamb, and stumbles out the door. Gnossos later finds the Code-O-Graph in a bed
of rabbit's feet. "While he was turning it over in his hands it discharged its secret little Captain Midnight spring with a sudden
boing, shuddered, and lay lifeless forever" (p. 99). A symbolic
death.

After a flashback to Las Vegas and a rabbit hunt on a composer's
farm, Gnossos and cronies attend the loft pot party mentioned by
Mojo, in the town of Dryad. Directly from the party they go to the

Black Elks downtown in a stolen Anglia; everyone there remembers Gnossos, though he has been gone a year. He passes out some of the Mojo mixture to his black friends. They call him Sophocles. With him from the loft is Kristin McLeod, who calls him Pooh Bear. Cool rock, talk, drinks, and grass. Gnossos takes Kristin to his pad, where they talk and drink retsina from his rucksack. After dropping her off at her dormitory, Gnossos returns the stolen Anglia to the loft party, to stay around till dawn among the dwindling highs; then home to sleep and then to wake, telling Fitzgore: "I'm in love!" The recognition transforms Gnossos into a Pan, a satyr; and it inspires him to take a bath. From Kresge's he buys "a bottle of Revlon bubble bath, two giant-size Yardley lavender bath soaps, a tortoise shell comb, and a back brush for stray pimples." To prepare a feast for his new lady love, Kristin, Gnossos brings to his room a rucksack filled with foods. "More vine leaves, unpolished brown rice, marinated olives, ground round, fertilized eggs, organic lemons, tarragon, bay leaves, garlic, Spanish onions, okra, resin wine, cruets of orange extract," not to mention the cosmetics (p. 146).

Three friends await him there, to be joined soon by Fitzgore and Agneau. Gnossos, who has long been constipated, finally enjoys a "visceral event," one which ironically contributes to his epic stature.

Gnossos pours bottles of oil and salt into the steaming tub for his bath. "He slipped on Fitzgore's skin-diving goggles and descended, looking for treasure, a tiny Poseidon or Aphrodite clip-clopping along in the microcosm" (p. 152). After the bath he impales seasoned lamb on coathanger skewers to cook above the flames. Then he waits and waits for Kristin. She wakes him from a nap when she arrives; they eat the food cooked carefully by Gnossos, "secret recipe, brought with Momma Pappadopoulis from the old country" (p. 157). After all his preparation Kristin demurs, claiming to be a virgin; then, changing her mind, she agrees to fornicate. But before they start, the alcoholic Rajamuttus enter the unlocked door and stay. "Tomorrow," Kristin promises before running up to her dormitory room so as not to be marked late.

Thus concludes the first part of Fariña's feisty novel. The second begins with G. Alonzo Oeuf, the perennial student and campus rebel, inviting Gnossos to join the latest plot: to take over the university. To indicate the significance of their victory Oeuf tells him that Sandoz, a trustee, has just won the proxy fight at Sandoz laboratory. "Largest manufacturer of synthetic mescaline in the world"

(p. 177). If Gnossos helps win the independents, and the school falls into Oeuf's hands, he can stay around indefinitely for the drugs and sex. He claims to have the clap. Gnossos refuses the mission and the bribe. Just as he is about to leave, most of his cronies pile into Oeuf's room for a meeting. Outside the door Heffalump awaits him with momentous news: Pamela Watson-May, though recently bereaved by Simon's suicide, soon will marry Mojo the pusher. They reach the chapel in time to see the wedding party disperse. Pamela tosses her bridal spray of St.-John's-wort into Gnossos's lap. Again, as he soon learns, the fates have cast him as a loser. Heffalump informs him that Pamela is sole heiress to the Watson-May holdings—billions in oil. Mojo the creep is "home-free," but it could have been Gnossos just as well.

The marriage between Pamela and Mojo has the immediate effect of devastating Fitzgore. It turns out that he sought the money himself—and he introduced Mojo to her. Gnossos finds their room a shambles and Fitzgore half-dead from various overdoses. Fitzgore now says that he planned the whole loft drug party just to get Pamela; but Pamela liked Mojo. That night Gnossos fornicates with Kristin McLeod, the fake virgin. They make love often and in sundry places during the growing warmth of spring. Kristin's father is a conservative and adviser to the president. "Militant, paranoic, just about everything," Kristin says, stating the generation gap; and Gnossos adds: "He thinks there's a Negro-Jewish plot, man, to take over the republic" (p. 192). Even the name Gnossos Pappadopoulis would give him some kind of attack. Thus possible marriage with Kristin would present some problems.

A letter by Gnossos appears in the Mentor *Daily Sun* protesting the rigid rules about the presence of women in men's dormitories. His phone rings with congratulations. Heffalump wants Gnossos to accompany him to Cuba over spring vacation, but he has Kristin. She is absent from her dorm all night, absent from classes all day, and Gnossos wonders and worries. Kristin finally returns in the midst of the hectic planning for a student demonstration. Sulking, Gnossos locks himself in the john where he smokes a joint and, for an hour, reads the *Anatomy of Melancholy*. His problem is Kristin's credibility; he reeks with pot and doubts. Then, suddenly, they both feel a strange and horrifying presence, a demonic invasion of their room.

"The monkey," she sobs passionately, "it wants to kill me" (p. 207). After a bourbon at Guido's, which does not help, Gnossos takes the hysterical Kristin to her dormitory. And he, fearing the demon could cut his throat by mistake, goes to spend the night with Calvin Blacknesse and his family—a weird night, with Gnossos unable to sleep. He walks outside in loin cloth only, followed to the bank of a stream by Calvin's wife Beth. She warns him about Calvin, whom she hates; her "Brahmin specter of a husband" is scanning photographs of monkeys, practicing occult powers, sending forth demons. Beth makes a move to seduce Gnossos, but leaves him puzzled; and he walks back to his pad less afraid, even of Proctor Slug waiting in his prowl car taking notes. So far Gnossos has agonized over everything except his studies. Yet not once has he lost his cool. That plus a certain perverse integrity seem to be his leading virtues.

More plotting ensues with Oeuf's minions working against the college administration, with Kristin involved and trying to avoid Gnossos. With revenge on his mind, he cuts off the protective tip of a contraceptive with a pair of scissors. Back at his pad they argue heatedly, she hits him with a martini pitcher, draws blood, melts; and then he goes to bed with her. Leaving Kristin a note, he decides to go with Heffalump and friends to Cuba—to abandon her, an eye for an eye, or one betrayal deserves another. While passing through Washington on their way to Miami, Gnossos makes another typical scene: he phones Kristin's high-powered father to say that he has probably knocked up his daughter. "Ought to be a good-looking kid, actually, Greek, lots of curly hair, dark. My name is Pappadopoulis" (p. 226).

Their journey south is mad like other mad and hipster journeys in American fiction—for example, *On the Road* and other beat works by Jack Kerouac. Gnossos enlarges his scope as imp, scamp, bastard, and whatnot. Under his hand, "The Impala did 111 miles an hour on the straight, 120 coming out of a downhill grade" (p. 226). At the monument they ridicule George Washington. In Richmond Gnossos hurls two sugar jars through the window of a restaurant refusing to serve them because Heffalump is black. Gnossos later finds Heffalump weeping in the men's room of a black restaurant. A suspicious pain starts in the lower part of Gnossos's abdomen. He fills his rucksack with oranges from a Florida orchard. "In Miami there was an ecstatically painful burning sensation when he went to the bathroom, and he had to lean against the wall to steady himself" (p. 231). The group boards the S.S. *Florida* for the voyage to Havana.

Gnossos confesses to Heffalump what he did to Kristin, so the baby, if she has one, will bring them closer together. They meet Aquavitus, a Mafia drug peddler, who has business with Heffalump. When Gnossos realizes he has the clap, Oeuf's clap through Kristin and the cut condom, he threatens to jump into the sea but is held back. Next morning they reach Havana. For three days Gnossos stays in bed. He will not see a doctor but will wait until they return to Athené. Heffalump suggests they remain in Cuba for the vast "bread" available to them in drugs. Suddenly an armored car discharges soldiers who begin firing in all directions. When it ends, Heffalump has "a hole the size of a thumbtack in his Adam's apple. His eyes were wide open and twisted crosswise. There was blood soaking his kinky hair. Gnossos threw up his arms and wailed a single, faltering cry that rang in the afternoon like the peal of a shattering bell" (p. 247). A prized friend is dead. The dead boy's girl leaves two hundred dollars for Gnossos to bury Heffalump. Gnossos writes a brief poem and tosses it into the grave, along with "the last of the severed rabbits' feet, a bottlecap from Dr. Brown's Cel-Ray Tonic, a piece of moldy feta, loose pot seeds to flourish in the tropical heat, a vial of paregoric and his Hohner F" (p. 249). Heffalump's real name was Abraham Jackson White.

Before leaving Cuba, Gnossos attends a psychedelic session with Louie Motherball, the Buddha. He sells souvenirs in Havana, pays for the funeral, buys aureomycin for his clap, wins nearly fifteen hundred dollars in a card game, and takes an executive flight to Idlewild Airport on his way back to the university. He finds a note of condolence from Irma Rajamuttu, whose husband has a job in London. Gnossos arrives at Athené in time for The Demonstration. He goes to the arts quad and hears the thousands assembled there. "The sky beyond flickered with violence, the undersides of clouds danced in reflected flame" (p. 259). Photographers recognize Gnossos, crowd around him. "That Greek," says one, "the nut from Lairville." His beating them off with his rucksack starts a rhythmic beating generally. Demonstrators hustle him to a platform—hosts of anarchists everywhere itching to blow all to pieces. "A now steaming Pappadopoulis was rushed through their midst" by friends and leaders like Oeuf, Kristin, and Youngblood so that he could control the crowd before they burned down the university. Before he agrees to try, Gnossos gets Oeuf to give him forty minutes with Kristin after the demonstration. "For fully five minutes he was Lindbergh at Orly, MacArthur on Wall Street, Ulanova at the Bolshoi, Sinatra at the Paramount" (p. 263). He succeeds— by an inspired and obscene gesture. The crowd responds with joy, giving Oeuf the time to cool them even more and lead them in an orderly march to the president's mansion.

That Gnossos's intentions toward Kristin are vengeful, for giving him gonorrhea, becomes evident when he drives her in the bor- rowed Anglia to a clearing near the closed Dairy Queen out of town. Using superior strength he gags her and ties her hands be- hind her back. He forces her face down on the seat, her panties off. "He was sitting on the small of her back as he opened the box. Inside was a glycerin suppository filled with Motherball's uncut horse [heroin]. He poised the pellet like a small torpedo between thumb and forefinger, then used it precisely as it was meant to be used, adding little for old times' sake but tender care" (p. 267). "Welcome to Limbo," he tells the hapless girl, freeing her from her bonds as the drug takes effect, "hope you enjoy your stay."

For seven days Gnossos lives off nature on "David Grün's idyllic hill," then sees in a paper brought by the children that Oeuf has acceded to the presidency of Mentor University after President Magnolia's accidental death. Gnossos returns hurriedly to his apartment to find Proctor Slug waiting for him. "He had a dossier under his arm and was rattling the heroin-filled castanets. There was an unmistakable odor of monkey-fumes in the air" (p. 268). Two sergeants enter; but instead of arresting him they hand him an envelope with PERSONAL written on it. When Gnossos opens it, he sees GREETINGS from the United States Army. Signed by the chairman of the Athené draft board, "and although Gnossos had never seen Oeuf's pudgy signature before, he reflected how like him it was" (p. 269). Gnossos gives up his beloved rucksack. With one shrewd move Oeuf has saved him from prison and got him off the campus for good. Oeuf's climb to power will be further sweet- ened by Kristin McLeod as his wife.

What keeps Gnossos Pappadopoulis a true hellion as well as a loser seems to be a deep streak of viciousness stemming from com- pulsive vengeance. He has other flaws, of course, in that he too perfectly represents "today's turned-on, hung-up youth" lost in cynicism, drugs, and sex. To what extent Gnossos is also a Greek depends upon one's opinion of how Greek an American Greek has to be. That Richard Fariña makes his bizarre culture hero a Greek must be a backhanded compliment to his ethnic heritage. On the whole, though, Fariña's knowledge of modern Hellenism, and indirectly that of Gnossos, does not go much beyond food and drink. The allusions to mythology and classical Greece are common knowledge. Gnossos on various occasions drinks Metaxa, retsina, and ouzo; he eats lamb kebab, *dolma, feta*, marinated olives, and a few other familiar items; but not the more obscure foods that are known by actual Greeks. He has no knowledge of any Greek-American community.

The Greek as picaresque hero slouches through Charles Tekeyan's *The Revelations of a Disappearing Man* (1971).[8] He is Al Harris, short for Aristotle Harisiades, who reminds one of another archetypical loser of our times, Tommy Wilhelm in Saul Bellow's *Seize the Day*. Whereas Tommy, or Wilky as his father calls him, is the urban Jew who represents the Freudian Thanatos syndrome, Aristotle goes down essentially the same drain as the wandering Greek—the modern Odysseus whose Ithaca is the kingdom of despair and death. The dustjacket states: "He drops in and out of a number of activities—college, marriage, assorted occupations and various young women—each time discovering that whatever seems to promise freedom is just a new form of imprisonment, and everything that appears to be an end in itself is just another pointless beginning." He finally withdraws into a cynicism that offers no hope.

The first sentence of the novel reads: "I was frying pork chops when Rachel told me she'd like to get a divorce" (p. 1). A dramatic beginning in the style of " 'Hell,' said the duchess." The mood for the downhill slide of Aristotle Harisiades is established. A week after his wife's announcement she writes him from Miami. She has absconded with their son Alan, who eats only when his father feeds him. Al bemoans his fate with Ray, a Greek buddy from college days, also divorced. At Ray's suggestion Al Harris begins auditing classes at Riverside University. Ray's also there two nights a week working on his master's degree. In a philosophy class he meets a brilliant girl whom he invites to his apartment; but she refuses to satisfy his sexual needs. She explains: "Sexual activity deprives me of it [her individuality], makes me like everyone else, a foul-smelling beast" (p. 127). Cold comfort for a lonely deprived Greek.

At Christmas he meets an old friend, a black handyman who has totally forgotten him. Al is convinced his son Alan has also forgotten him. One day he finds himself in the cemetery where his cousin is buried—his other self, also named Aristotle Harisiades, killed in the war. "The words on the stone are all in Greek, like the other stones around it, and I can't read Greek" (p. 21). There he meets a German girl who is putting flowers on her mother's grave.

An aura of weirdness surrounds Al Harris and permeates his world. Karla runs an art gallery filled with her father's paintings that never sell. Karla wants him to eat roses. "She eats them after we make love. She says eating them changes love-making from a selfish thing to a beautiful noble act" (p. 42). A couple come to the gallery one day and buy twelve paintings at one thousand dollars each. That Karla has a strong death wish emerges from more than her frequenting of cemeteries and wakes; she dies from an apparent heart attack, but Al Harris suspects suicide from an overdose of opium. With the two thousand dollars Karla had given him as his "commission," he goes to Miami to see his wife and son. But he soon returns to New York, convinced he and Rachel cannot live together, and that having Alan was the only great thing he has done.

Back in Manhattan he meets the Leather Girl. She wears a leather suit she has made, nothing else, and demands that he sink his teeth into her when they fornicate. The nameless girl takes Al to an orgy on Park Avenue, to an apartment filled with leather-clothed revelers. Against his will he allows the butler to assault him in the men's room—a homosexual act that partly pleases him. He learns that the Leather Girl is bisexual; at the party she has sex all night long with both men and women. Because he asks questions, she leaves. He ponders if the leather suit can really protect her from the fate that she fears.

Years pass, Rachel remarries, and Alan turns ten. Aristotle Harisiades starts for California; but his used car breaks down fifty miles from New York and he accepts a job as car salesman in a town called White Church. At first he claims he is not a car salesman, but the agency owner says, "If you're Greek you can sell anything." He ruminates:

I wanted to answer: Greeks are no better or worse than anyone else at selling things. For centuries, as a matter of fact, they haven't been able to sell the world the fact that they are the same people who lived in Greece twenty-five hundred years ago and had that great civilization. Today everyone thinks Greeks are some kind of dark Irishman.

But instead I merely said, "I wish you'd quit calling me Greek. I'm as Greek as you are; when I see Greeks who have come here from Greece, they look as foreign to me as they do to you. I'm so American I'm almost a WASP. In fact I'm more than that. There's an Englishman inside of me trying to come out. I'll be speaking with a British accent soon. And let me tell you this: My ancestors were Etruscans, Saxons, Phoenicians, and Ionians. And most of the time I don't even feel I'm an earthling. I feel I came here from another planet and have no relation to anyone in this world. So don't ever call me a Greek again." (p. 78)

The car dealer tells Aristotle Harisiades that he admires his spirit of independence.

Al Harris sells cars because, although disdaining honesty, he appears to be honest; and he regularly visits Alan. He befriends a rough ugly woman who practically rapes him. His stepfather, a dentist, dies, and he blames his mother for having killed him. It seems that a perverse addiction to the truth behind the appearance keeps making him obnoxious to everyone. He demolishes even the illusions that he has to live by, and ends up alienated, contrary, hypersensitive, and hopelessly unhappy. A deeply introspective person, he flounders for the correct decisions. In rationalizing an impulse to remarry, he thinks that perhaps he could get along with a foreign girl—European, perhaps Greek. "Might go as far as Greece. Rather not shack up with a Greek girl though. I'm an American and I don't want to act like the immigrants who came here and could only think of mating with their own kind. Also, girls in Greece are mostly puritans, and those that aren't are whores. I like a woman to be neither and at the same time both" (p. 108). Instead of Greece he goes to Kennedy Airport to find a wife among the international arrivals. No luck there.

His quixotic adventures continue. They include his marrying Bibi, a girl of Swedish descent. Years pass, and he's back at Riverside University finishing work for a degree. Then he plans to attend the seminary, except that he realizes he is an atheist who not only denies the existence of God but also regards Him as a "cruel idiot." Another problem with Aristotle: he often sees both sides of questions, confusing both others and himself. He wants to become "the first Minister of Extrication, telling people over and over to be aware of the illusions of religion and to escape from the self-deceptions of faith" (p. 153). A parallel would be to work for General Motors in order to destroy the automobile as idea and object.

At the university, before he is graduated, he meets an English girl, Jill, who wants both to write and to make love. He evades her. He cannot read the "gibberish" on his diploma, but takes pride in his name. "A true name, Aristotle Harisiades. Beautiful and almost endless" (p. 167). The next big event, forced upon him by his wife Bibi, is a steamship trip to Europe. She wants badly to visit Sweden. On the way, among other things, Bibi says she wants to get pregnant; but Aristotle objects on grounds the world is too rotten. They reach England. In London, while Bibi sleeps in the hotel room, he slips out to roam around the vast strange city. He runs into Nigel who had previously wanted to "guide" him to a sex show. Because Aristotle is Greek, Nigel offers to bring him a "lovely boy." They go to a gambling house but Aristotle refuses to enter. Later he pays ten dollars to an English hooker who kicks him out because he fondles her breasts; thus he bungles his first act of infidelity.

After a couple of more days in London, Aristotle and Bibi go to Paris. They make love in a hotel. They sightsee. Bibi shops. Aristotle Harisiades walks about Paris as a sardonic innocent abroad—more cynical than ever. He meets an Algerian who speaks Greek. They drink Greek wine, but Aristotle dislikes it. "Tasted like benzine. A person had to be crazy to drink wine from Greece when he was in Paris" (p. 267). He learns that the Algerian has a lovely daughter for whom he acts as procurer, and he asks three hundred dollars for a week's bliss. The girl, Angela, is only thirteen. Aristotle walks away with their curses in his ears.

The next stop is Germany, which he deems the enemy country. The train passes through to Denmark; then to Stockholm, and Bibi's fatherland. Aristotle at Bibi's home meets her family and feels inferior because the women do heavy farm work better than he can. He drives the tractor into a ditch. He hates using the outhouse. For him the Swedish farm becomes a prison. One morning he receives a letter from his mother who asks if Sweden has any Greeks and a Greek church. He writes enigmatic postcards to her and to his old boss, the car dealer. Bibi's anguish grows that they are not having any children. His refusal to make her pregnant stems from his despair over the sorrows inflicted upon mankind. "*Circumstances* are cruel, our *needs* are cruel, *methods* are cruel, *results* are cruel" (p. 296). He complains not for himself, but for the *billions* of others who suffer life. Angry, Bibi rips into pieces before his eyes a letter from his son Alan. His marriage over, Aristotle Harisiades packs and leaves for New York alone.

There he resumes his friendship with the English girl Jill, only to find that she has become the lover of a rich lesbian. Aristotle punches the lesbian in the belly and leaves. When he meets Alan, they do not hit it off very well. He gets a job at the university keeping buildings in repair. That his boss is committing adultery repulses him so much he quits. Nearly penniless, he looks around for another job. Inadvertently he becomes a lecturer and makes money speaking on the need for women to stand up for their rights. He is "very popular with unfeminine feminists" (p. 336). Everyone including his ex-wife respects him. Alan has a scholarship at Riverside University. Taking the time to write, Aristotle sells his first story since he was nineteen. A publisher wants him to write a novel. His mother tells him she will be buried with her *second* husband, so there is room for Aristotle to use the second plot at his father's grave. He resents her planning his future resting place. "Damn it, I'm going to outlive this woman, and I'm going to buy a mountain somewhere to be buried on someday!" (p. 344).

The novel he writes is rejected because of its style: it is written like a telegram that never reveals the message. He meets Diane, a girl for whom any touch means excruciating pain. Aristotle has sex after chloroforming her; it makes him feel he is copulating with a corpse. The novel ends with Aristotle detaching himself from society: he disappears into Central Park where he lives most of the time, foiling muggings, and proud he has made it a safer place.

Despite the fact that Aristotle Harisiades is a Greek, he thinks of himself as thoroughly American. He has no real contact with the thriving Greek-American community of New York City. He disdains his mother's suggestion to attend a Greek church. He will not consider marrying a girl from Greece because girls there are either puritans or whores; and he prefers a synthesis of both—a paradox. Unlike Wilky in *Seize the Day* Aristotle gets rich through an absurdist fantasy-fraud: he manages to have cashiers at restaurants and elsewhere treat one dollar bills as twenties, hence his change is his never-ending profit. Being rich, he finds himself respected. "A Greek benevolent organization to which I contributed a thousand dollars has invited me to talk at its next meeting" (p. 336). Although rich Aristotle Harisiades withdraws at the end into his strong Thanatos syndrome. Whereas Bellow's lost hero weeps for himself at someone else's funeral, Aristotle ends up haunting Central Park, invisible to all who once knew him. There he thinks of the planet dying. "The sun will finally explode and this planet, along with many other planets, will go to pieces with it. And if the sun doesn't explode and merely turns cold, then the earth will turn into solid ice and no life on it will be possible. In any case, people are doomed" (p. 354). Bereft of wife, of son, of job, of lovers, of friends, Aristotle Harisiades lives in Central Park as his "estate," where he feeds squirrels and waits for death, the final disappearance.

The highly placed Greek politician as latent fascist dictator appears in the fictionalized character of Spiro T. Agnew in Herbert Mitgang's *Get These Men Out of the Hot Sun* (1972).[9] The main thrust of the satire is the election of Agnew to the presidency in 1976. Whatever punch or perverse humor the novel might have had was deflected by the harsh realities of Watergate. Long before 1976, the year of Agnew's imagined takeover, both he and Richard Nixon had resigned their respective positions. Because Mitgang uses the names of real people, his implied predictions about their future miss their mark so completely that art cannot save the book from oblivion. For example the author writes: "Early in 1976, Messrs. Haldeman, Kleindienst, and Klein of the President's communications *apparat* began to panic. The President [Nixon] was in no condition to face the leaders of his own party, let alone the press" (p. 22). By then, of course, the real president was Gerald Ford.

In the novel, with Nixon nonfunctional for reasons of health, the even more conservative half-Greek Spiro T. Agnew seems destined to win the Republican nomination. He does so by a brilliant political ploy—the use of "ethnic astronauts." Agnew supervises "the monthly space shots . . . under the Super-Apollo manned exploration series" (p. 72). The appeal to the electorate is simply electrifying. "Apollo 52," the novel states, "was beautifully executed by a team of Greek-American, Swedish-American, and German-American astronauts" (p. 74). Mitgang manages to bring in Agnew's rightist views of the early 1970s in a projection for 1976. A Greek politician named Licata says of him: "Agnew never, never raised his voice about the dictatorship in my Greece of thugs and political prisoners. A word, a phrase, a sentence—this is what the underground and the exiles hoped for. But it never comes" (p. 95). In reality the Greek fascist junta of Papadopoulos and company had disappeared by 1976. In the novel, however, Licata and two former agents in Greece, Pringle and Durham, meet in Manhattan to plan the assassination of Agnew as a first step toward the destruction of Agnewism. The aging antifascist killers, who once fought the Nazi occupation, thus hope once again to change the course of history.

The fictional Agnew of Mitgang's fantasy becomes president of the United States. The former agent Pringle ostensibly goes over to him. The crypto-assassin prepares his weapon: a converted Waterman pen filled with explosives. When he is called to help revise parts of the inaugural address, Pringle, alone with his intended victim, tries to kill him. But the pen as weapon merely fizzles and Agnew is unharmed. Secret Service men pump bullets into Pringle. "Without a word he slumped and fell, the first and last critic of the new Administration" (p. 201). Nothing can now stop Agnew from turning the United States, like Greece, into a fascist totalitarian state. Luckily for both nations, real events took an opposite course from that predicted by Mitgang in his mad novel about mad, and evil, men.

From these earth-bound fantasies Greek characters in science fiction soar into various celestial realms on the power of the literary imagination. In the Hellenic tradition the first science-fiction elements undoubtedly occur in mythology where the gods, the demigods, the monsters, and mortals under divine influence perform incredible deeds. One needs to mention only Medusa and Medea. Homer's *Odyssey* offers many examples with the epic hero himself undergoing physical changes by grace of the goddess Athena. Plato's *Republic* initiated a vast industry of science fictionizing (including the "Man from Atlantis" on television) by his citing of a lost continent beyond the Hesperides.

A prolific writer of science fiction, Robert Silverberg, has Greeks in two of his many works. In *To Live Again* (1969), a Greek named John Roditis, an "immigrant shoemaker's son," rises to head a financial empire of the future.[10] A student of Homer, a dynamic and strong-willed man, he keeps his body lean and muscular. In this futuristic world Roditis has had transplanted to his brain a number of personae including that of Anton Kozak, a sculptor. Roditis is now trying to get approval to receive another persona transplant, that of Paul Kaufmann, recently dead, a financial wizard and a ruthlessly powerful man. Competing with Roditis is Mark Kaufmann, Paul's grandson. From the contested persona can flow obvious benefits to its recipient.

Francesco Santoliguido, the administrator of the Scheffing Institute which performs the transplants, must approve the selection of the living person who will get the persona of Paul Kaufmann. He hesitates to give it to Roditis because the young Mark Kaufmann strongly objects; nor can he give the persona to Mark because the transfer of persona to relatives is illegal. When a *dybbuk* (a persona who has taken over a living personality) is discovered by Risa Kaufmann, Mark's daughter, the invading persona is erased; but the invaded body, Martin St. John, cannot be invested with his own personality again. Therefore Santoliguido decides to give the Paul Kaufmann persona to St. John's body. But Roditis gets his weak assistant, Charles Noyes, to destroy by chemical disintegration the Kaufmann persona in St. John. Noyes has been helped by Elena Volterra, Mark Kaufmann's mistress.

In the meantime Mark has illegally had the Paul Kaufmann persona transplanted in himself by bribing one of the Scheffing Institute employes. Mark succeeds in getting Charles Noyes to confess that Martin St. John was killed at the instigation of Roditis. Roditis is tried and escapes death; but he will be treated through psychology to remove his aggression. Risa Kaufmann, although only sixteen, seduces a Scheffing Institute worker, threatens she will charge him with rape, and hence forces him to transplant Roditis's persona (up to his sentence) in her. As the novel closes, Mark, enhanced by the Paul Kaufmann persona, and Risa, quoting Homer, are scheming to cut chunks out of the Roditis empire to enlarge their own holdings. Santoliguido has agreed to store Paul Kaufmann's persona, and that of Roditis will supposedly never be transplanted because of his crime.

In Robert Silverberg's *Up the Line* (1969), the narrator is in the time-traveling business, and he uses the term *up the line* to mean time past.[11] "Now I have been up the line. I have seen those who wait for me in the millenia gone by. My past hugs me as a hump" (p. 1). Sam, the black guru and narrator's friend, works part time in the Time Service, as a courier. The narrator wants to be smuggled up the line to Byzantium, but first he must join the Time Service, which he does. Name on application: Judson Daniel Elliott III. The year is 2059. Sam the guru vouches for Jud; and he is accepted on the Byzantine run—ostensibly to improve his knowledge of Byzantine culture.

Jud undergoes training as a novice Time Serviceman who will shunt tourists around the past. The setting is called Under New Orleans. The "sniffer palace girls" put on an exhibition of biological acrobatics. "They had learned the steps in Knossos, where they watched Minos' dancers perform, and had simply adapted the movements to modern tastes by grafting in the copulations at the right moments" (p. 59). To begin his duty as a Time Service Courier, Jud Elliott goes to Istanbul where he is told that only a Greek can respond fully to Byzantium. Now Elliott admits that he is a Greek, explaining: "My mother's name was originally Passilidis. She was born in Athens. My maternal grandfather was mayor of Sparta. On his mother's side he was descended from the Markezinis family." (p. 65) The Greek to whom he is speaking, Spiros Protopolos, cries, "You are my brother!" It turns out that "six of the nine other Time Couriers assigned to the Byzantium run were Greeks by nationality or descent." Jud's surprise that one of the couriers was named Gompers elicits the remark that Gompers's grandmother "was pure Hellene." Before he undertakes his first time run Jud receives a "hypnosleep course" in Byzantine Greek. When he wakes up he can order a meal, buy a tunic, and "seduce a virgin in Byzantine argot," not to mention "some phrases that could make the mosaics of Haghia Sophia peel from the walls in shame." The voyager out of time-now gets more and more excited as his first Byzantine run approaches. He and another Courier will lead a group of eight tourists there; all have taken the hypnocourse in Byzantine Greek.

Constantinople, in the year 408. The visitors from time-now go sightseeing, study the period, enjoy themselves, and move forward to their next stop, 532 A.D. Two weeks later they all return to 2059. Jud receives the highest rating as an apprentice courier. Protopolos tells him his next trip will be as assistant to Metaxas. For his vacation Jud decides to time-jump to post-Byzantine Istanbul rather than visit Crete or Mykonos. He receives the proper clothing from the wardrobe department, plus the gold and silver currency of the sixteenth century. He also gets hypnosleep courses in Turkish and Arabic; but he must pretend to be "a Portuguese national who had been kidnapped on the high seas by Algerian pirates when ten years old, and raised a Moslem in Algiers" (p. 82).

Judson arrives at Istanbul on August 14, 1559. There in the Turkish environment he meets his beloved black guru Sam, or one of the four versions of Sam, this one being hostile to him. He quickly leaves and goes up the line to 1550, watches them construct Suleiman's mosque, and returns to time-now for his second trip to Byzantium as a courier. His chief for the voyage is Themistokles Metaxas:

Metaxas was bantam-sized, maybe 1.5 meters tall. His skull was triangular, flat on top and pointed at the chin. His hair, thick and curly, was going gray. I guess he was about fifty years old. He had small glossy dark eyes, heavy brows, and a big sharp slab of a nose. He kept his lips curled inward so that he didn't seem to have lips at all. There was no fat on him anywhere. He was unusually strong. His voice was low and compelling. (p. 88)

The narrator feels Metaxas has both charisma and chutzpah. "For him the whole universe revolved around Themistokles Metaxas; the Benchley Effect had been invented solely to enable Themistokles Metaxas to walk through the ages. If he ever died, the cosmos would crumble" (p. 88). It appears that Metaxas is a racketeer, a plunderer, who prefers being an active courier to heading the entire Courier Service; he owns a villa in "the suburbs of the early twelfth century," and he has "a variety of small and large illegalities" up the line. Metaxas is bawdy to boot, for he tells Jud that he has not lived until he has fornicated with one of his own ancestors.

From Metaxas the novice Jud learns that a good courier assembles "a portrait of the past" for his clients. He learns arrogance from Metaxas, the "oldest, smartest, slickest and most corrupt" of all the couriers. Every tour, apparently, turns into a sexual feast. Not only are tour members available to him, but also women of the past. Metaxas, for example, wants to put Jud Elliott with the empress of Byzantium, Justinian's wife. Most of the couriers have slept with her. For the hero, serving as a courier in the Time Service means the gaining of knowledge by direct research and new dimensions of pleasure. In addition Jud uses his access to time-past to establish his own genealogy as far back as 700 A.D. On his first foray into his family's past he meets and lusts for his own grandmother, Katina Passilidis!

As he finds her up the line she is not, of course, the "withered, shrunken, palsied little woman" he knew back in the real-time year of 2049, when she was in her seventies and he was fourteen. On his layoff Katina reverts back to the year 1997, in the city of Sparta, when she is twenty-three or twenty-four. "She was beautiful, the way the girls on the Minoan murals are beautiful. Dark, very dark, with black hair, olive skin, dark eyes. Peasant strength to her. She didn't expose her breasts the way the fashionable mustachioed receptionist had done, but her thin blouse wasn't very concealing. They were high and round. Her hips were broad. She was lush, fertile, abundant" (p. 108).

He naturally lusts for her, a "fantastically desirable woman," but he does not copulate with her. Nor with his mother, Diana, whom he meets as a nude five-year old! He admires her neat slit. His maternal grandfather, Konstantin Passilidis, is mayor of Sparta. While there Jud Elliott begins to realize he has begun a genealogical quest. He does not reveal to Passilidis that they are related. The mayor says of his background, "In Byzantium we were of the Ducas family" (p. 112). Later they were the Markezinis family. All of this information fascinates Jud immensely, especially since the Ducases were illustrious in Byzantium. He had seen Constantine rise to the imperial throne. Jud Elliot, too, was a Ducas.

On another time jaunt he seeks out his Ducas forbears in the year 1205. They are exiles in the Epirus town of Argyrokastro. He then goes down the line to the sixteenth century seeking the Markezinis estate. With his grandfather Passilidis he poses as an American correspondent who wants to write about the Spartan mayor's career. To Gregory Markezinis, his "great-great-great-multi-great grandfather," he poses as "a wealthy young Cypriote of Byzantine descent who was traveling the world in search of pleasure and adventure" (p. 115). Greek hospitality at the Passilidis home consists of an excellent lunch of boiled lamb, *pastitsio*, and retsina wine. "My grandmother poured us more wine, and I stole a quick, guilty peek at her full, swaying breasts. My mother climbed on my knee and made little trilling noises" (p. 113). At the Markezinis estate Greek hospitality consists not only of food but also a very talented slave girl as bed mate. The year is 1556 A.D. He pleases Gregory Markezinis by describing the Indians that the Spaniards found in the New World.

Of the two schools of thought regarding the conduct of time-tours, the leisurely Capistrano and the Metaxas, Jud prefers the latter which means "to construct an elaborate mosaic of events, hitting the same high spots but also twenty or thirty or forty lesser events," spending half an hour here and two hours there. The entire novel is an often serious, often comical and even bawdy play on Time. The allusions to the real history of Byzantium required considerable research by Robert Silverberg; the liberties taken derive from the added dimension which the fantasy allows.

Up the Line is replete with time-trips, sightseeing, major historical

characters, meetings with ancestors, description of places, observation of events, dialogues, coincidences of various kinds, para-
doxes, and a running plot of sorts, from Jud Elliott's point of view,
which includes a romance with the lovely Pulcheria Ducas: "She
had a supple, liquid Mediterranean beauty; her eyes were dark
and large and glossy, with long lashes, and her skin was light olive
in hue, and her lips were full and her nose aquiline, and her bearing was elegant and aristocratic. Her robes of white silk revealed
the outlines of high, sumptuous breasts, curving flanks, voluptuous buttocks. She was all the women I had ever desired, united
into one ideal form" (p. 134).

Jud Elliott has no qualms about sleeping with someone else's
ancestors—with Eudocia, for example, who belongs to Metaxas's
genealogy; but he demurs from the remotely incestuous mingling
with his own. On a layoff he visits Metaxas in his twelfth-century
villa in the suburbs of Constantinople. Metaxas has made a time-
now identity for himself "ten centuries up the line." Two other
Greek couriers there, Kolettis and Pappas, have praised Jud to Metaxas. The wily Themistokles Metaxas is taking the fullest advantage of the miraculous Benchley Effect that makes Time Travel
possible. He has to be careful, though, not to make after the fact
changes while in time-past that seriously tend to alter the recorded
events of history. Research while in the past is allowable, and revi-
sionist books appear regularly. The "law" prohibits the transporting of any "tangible object" from up the line, a prohibition policed
by an ubiquitous Time Patrol. At the villa of Metaxas, Jud sleeps
once with the passionate Eudocia.

What he does with Eudocia is actually strictly forbidden by Time
Patrol rules. "We are not permitted to strike up friendships, get
into long philosophical discussions, or have sexual intercourse with
inhabitants of previous eras" (p. 161). From the legal point of view,
therefore, it is wrong for Jud to lust so hard for Pulcheria Ducas;
as far as the incest taboo is concerned, he cannot see any reason
strong enough to abstain from Pulcheria, his grandmother many
times removed. The fear of punishment makes him hold back. "If
the Time Patrol caught me sexing around with my multi-great-
grandmother, they'd certainly fire me from the Time Service,
might imprison me, might even try to invoke the death penalty for
first degree time-crime on the grounds that I had tried to become
my own ancestor. I was terrified of the possibilities" (p. 162).

Despite his fears the passion for Pucheria Ducas intensifies. In an effort to drown his feeling, Jud surreptiously joins the Black Death tour and later contrives to fornicate with the Empress Theodora. Nothing helps. The longing for Pulcheria changes him from an inspired Metaxian courier to a bored and listless mediocrity. He has a difficult tour, he has trouble with a fellow courier named Capistrano, and he violently lays a tourist, Miss Pistil. In romantic despair he abandons his wretched tour and shunts himself with his times to the year 1105, to seek out Pulcheria Ducas. With the help of Metaxas he meets her under the cover name of George Markezinis of Epirus. After the Byzantine soirée, when Leo her husband sleeps, Judson and Pulcheria make forbidden love.

During the brief three minutes of manipulated time that he has been gone, a member of the tour, Conrad Sauerbend, has disappeared. Item One reads, "a Courier must remain aware of the location of all of the tourists in his care at all times" (p. 201). Panic begins to grow in him because the Time Patrol will ask about Sauerbend; and in the replay they will not only find him shunting unlawfully up the line but also committing transtemporal incest with his ancestral grandmother. In trying to find Sauerbend loose with his tourist's time, Jud spawns an alter ego "by the Paradox of Duplication"—another time-crime. Metaxas and other courier friends make an elaborate effort to track down Sauerbend before the Time Patrol learns of the trouble. The searchers include Pappas, Kolettis, and Plastiras. When his friends learn that Jud has stupidly duplicated himself, they lose respect for him. Yet they split up to search through different eras for Sauerbend.

Strange things happen to Pulcheria's identity. In another time-slot Judson discovers a likeness to her as the whoring wife of Conrad Sauerbend, who is living as a tavern keeper named Heracles Photis! Judson and his other self work out a schedule whereby their time-lines do not get ensnared. When Pulcheria reverts to her Ducas self, the two Juds can take turns copulating with her without her knowing the difference. In the end Jud with Metaxas's help restores Sauerbend to his original status in the same tour from which he vanished in an effort to become a smuggler up the line. Just when Jud feels he has everything under control, his friend Sam the black guru warns him that the Time Patrol is after him. Sam cries: "Get your things together and clear out of here, fast! You've got to hide, maybe three, four thousand years back, somewhere. Hurry it up!" (p. 243). Jud learns from Sam that he has become a nonperson who has retroactively ceased to exist. As long as he remains *up the line* he is "protected by the Paradox of Transit Displacement," but the minute he returns to now-time, he will be automatically obliterated—which is what has already occurred to his alter ego. The novel ends with the banished Judson Elliott living a thousand years before Christ, in what may be the remnant "of the old Hittite empire," where the farmers treat him like a god, where he yearns for the lost Pulcheria, where he now dictates his memoirs, and waits for the end, should the Time Patrol find him. "Why, it could even come right in the middle of a sentence, and I'd . . . " Thus ends *Up the Line* with its fantasy of time manipulation, complicated plot, tongue-in-cheek humor, and assorted Greek characters who shunt back and forth through past and present. The ethnicity they evince remains general and historical, not domestic and concrete. They spring full-grown from the literary imagination.

Among other Greeks in science fiction are two sisters, Athena and Aphrodite (not the goddesses but Greek-Americans), in Pamela Sargent's chilling tale "Matthew." [12] The time is the future, when a genocidal virus intended for India and Africa spreads throughout the world dooming all mankind. Only a rare few of those still living can procreate; thus each new birth is regarded as sensational. The people exist by grace of the remaining computers that work to provide food, drink, and other sustenance. The narrator, David Feinberg, sired the boy Matthew with Athena, a tall Greek wench "with red-gold hair" and nice long legs. Her sister Aphrodite, unlike the goddess of love, is ugly, acne-scarred, and bucktoothed. Matthew was born without arms. A genius, he communicates with a counterpart in the Soviet Union named Yuri; and together they compute the conclusion that man will soon be extinct. At the end Matthew dies by falling from a cliff in Maine, hearing the voices of children who do not exist. In "Matthew," therefore, two Greek women named for Olympian goddesses live and suffer the knowledge of the coming end of man—of man self-destroyed.

In another frightening tale, *This Immortal* (1966) by Roger Zelazny, the protagonist is Conrad (Konstantin) Nomikos. [13] The time is the distant future, after mankind has suffered the catastrophe of the Three Days, an atomic war. Earth has areas called the Hot Places that cause mutations. In fact, Earth seems to be at the mercy of other beings. Many of the earthlings now are expatriates living on Taler and want to reclaim their former planet. Nomikos serves as Commissioner of Arts, Monuments, and Archives; but in the past he had also been called Kallikanzaros and Karaghiosis, a warrior and defender of Earth. His most valued female friend is Cassandra, who lives on the island of Kos. One of his projects is to dismantle the pyramids of Egypt. A quiet terror pervades the story, with details of the dreadful situation given offhand, as though natural and familiar. For example, Nomikos fights a wild boar that has mutated to a larger size than an elephant. In the end he, a futuristic Greek, inherits the Earth to own and rule. He does not particularly relish the idea.

Whether archetypes out of myth or individuals with chronic or lesser disorders, the foregoing Greek characters reflect the interest of contemporary authors in the bizarre, the occult, the gothic, and the fantastic. Some of these Greeks represent too esoteric a theme to touch our lives directly and forcefully. They may exercise our minds somewhat, but they do not involve our emotions. For example, we read Silverberg's *Up the Line* to see how he sustains and exploits his "happy idea" about time-travel based upon the Benchley Effect. We may also compare and contrast his novel with *The Time Machine* by H. G. Wells. A book like that of Fariña, however, touches us much more personally. A whole generation of shaggy-haired, pot-smoking, bad-mouthed, dissident youth patterned themselves on the likes of Gnossos Pappadopoulis—or he on them. The kind of social and historic warning that Gnossos implies for America has not been fully understood. In and out of Fariña's novel, therefore, Gnossos remains a dynamic, disturbing character. He exists for future social crises and their writers to revive and multiply.

16

COUNTRY FULL OF GREEKS

I N THE IMPLACABLE ONRUSH of American literature new novels continue to be published, some with Greek characters in various roles: hero, villain, victim, lover, foil, archetype, either major or minor, static or dynamic. A number of such works dramatize a neglected past period or episode; others respond to current literary fads, or crackle with artifice and slick topicality for a quick dollar; and still others with varying degrees of originality deal with familiar types and themes. As amply shown, to write about Greek characters in fiction often means to record a segment of American history and culture from a specialized ethnic viewpoint, at a time when the multilingual, multicultural, and other ethnic emphases are growing throughout our educational system. The Greek immigrant, for his part, has had an effect upon the total American experience; and, conversely, his arrival, struggle, and acculturation in the United States have greatly influenced him and his succeeding generations.

Today's Americans of Greek descent, like those of most other nationalities, fill positions in every walk of life. Since the mid-sixties a new influx of Greek immigrants has arrived to enlarge and revitalize Greek Town, U.S.A. The modern Greeks cannot be stereotyped by class, style of life, geography, or profession. The novels and stories already cited reflect many physical and intellectual occupations, from proletarian to upper middle class. With the exception of Greek shipping tycoons, few fictional Greeks are represented as belonging to the super rich who seriously influence finance, industry, and government. Even the fictional Greek billionaire cannot be compared with the real-life Rockefellers, Fords, Mellons, and Morgans as symbols of American economic and political power. Nor does the immediate future promise to alter the rich Greek's status in this regard. The Greek characters remaining to be examined appear either in very recent works, or they belong in categories not hitherto explored. Some reflect new regions and occupations not exploited in earlier fiction, while others go back in time to the Greek revolution of 1821–28. As a group they illustrate how Greek ethnicity in its various forms continues to flourish in American literature.

The Greek revolution provides the historical milieu for *The Missolonghi Manuscript* (1968) in which Frederic Prokosch recreates on the basis of research the "memoirs" of Lord Byron.[1] Some of the Greeks that Prokosch limns as associates of Byron are humble and unknown; others are famous and actual revolutionary heroes. The real Byron in *Don Juan* gives a highly romantic picture of the brigand Lambro. Needless to say, the Byronic hero and Byron himself remain literary forces throughout the nineteenth century. The fictional Byron in the Prokosch book starts his memoirs on a rainy day in Missolonghi. He interweaves past and present in the relating of his experiences. Among the Greeks who attend him personally are his man Tita, his page Loukas, and Christophoros, who ferries him and his friends across the lagoon.

Byron has come to Greece for self-renewal and peace, but finds himself fighting for a people who may not yet be capable of freedom. The Greeks are "a cozening, pilfering populace." The Suliote soldiers he commands are "a drunken and avaricious bevy of ruffians." Even his Italian friend Pietro buys bolts of cloth at Byron's expense without informing him. Both Loukas and Pietro contract a fever, and Byron is also unwell. "Dyspeptic, dizzy, and distinctly *peculiar*" (p. 41). The wicked and equivocal Prince Mavrocordato arrives and talks with him. Byron has trouble with the superstitions of the Greeks when they refuse to unload supplies on a holiday. In retrospect Byron recounts his trip to Epirus, to Yannina, to see the bloody tyrant Ali Pasha. Now in Missolonghi, Byron prepares his forces for an attack upon Lepanto, and he ponders the meaning to him of modern Greece.

I feel myself being sucked into a deeper and unknown Greece and being metamorphosed into a Greek, sad and sensual, tinged with the barbaric. A dreadful Greek duplicity is beginning to seep through me. The Greece of Pericles is dead but the Greece of Odysseus is still alive, with its smell of salted fish, resinous wine and dyed leather. I catch a whiff of a still older and pre-Athenian Greece in the smell of burning oil and freshly slaughtered goats, of the ships fresh from Ithaca and the sweating sailors as they drag their ships up the long red beach. (p. 63)

Prokosch has deftly caught Byron's "flavor" of Greece, his *feeling* for the adopted land of his death. Inevitably the narrative mentions Mrs. Macri and her three daughters, Mariana, Katinka, and Theresa. The beautiful Theresa, immortalized as the "Maid of Athens," is only twelve years old, but beloved of Byron. Already she possesses enough wit to banter about wicked poets falling in love with little girls. Byron sits in the garden writing *Childe Harold*. Then he goes swimming at Piraeus with his young friend Nicolo, who resembles Theresa in his fine good looks. Half the bathers are nude. The "memoirs" reveal Byron's sexual ambivalence in that he wants both Theresa and Nicolo, but gorges himself in the Athenian brothels.

The ethnic and personal material comes between long sessions depicting Byron's earlier life in England and elsewhere. His Hellenism keeps surfacing because in Missolonghi he is writing, talking with friends and visitors, and preparing for battle. Byron discusses his tangled love-life with Prince Mavrocordato. More long patches of autobiography follow with less reference to events at Missolonghi. Byron hopes for action at Lepanto. Over dinner Mavrocordato tells Byron that some elements in Athens want to make him King of Greece. "Monarch of Hellas! The crowned ruler of the land of Plato!" (p. 218). Byron regards the "gnome-like smile" on his friend's lips, and regards Mavrocordato as "an insidious, very cruel little man." March comes and goes with Byron "horribly weak." He has grown very thin and suspects that he is the victim of the Evil Eye. The Turkish fleet arrives to blockade Missolonghi. Byron receives a letter from Mavrocordato claiming that Karaiskakis, a rival chieftain, is conniving with Kolokotronis against him. Events prove the rumors true. The rebels under Karaiskakis seize the "fortress of Vasiladi at the mouth of the harbour." Byron recounts conversations about Greece with Trelawny and others, and tells how he loves Greece and longs for her liberty. He quit Italy for Greece to fight the Turks; and now at Missolonghi he hopes to realize his dream, but his fever worsens. Other signs are bad: an eagle falls from the sky; a million locusts scream; a pregnant sow dies on the beach. Byron refuses the leeches of Dr. Bruno. His memoirs now devolve upon his earlier arrival in Greece. Like earlier travelers he notes the depravity among the "black-eyed Greeks" caused by Turkish tyranny. Byron is dismayed but not disheartened. Knowing his wealth, the Greeks fawn before him. Yet Byron finds much to admire, including their physical beauty.

He recalls meeting his page, Loukas Chalandritsanos, whose

family had been large landowners in Patras. "He was fifteen years old. His face was like Apollo's. His eyes were extremely blue, which is a rarity among the Greeks, and his hair was touched with copper; also a rarity among the Greeks. His body was like a lamp, it exuded a gentle glow, as though a flame were burning under his lion-tawny skin" (p. 324). Now the boy Loukas brings more black hyacinths to the weakening Byron. Finally, in his memoirs, he reaches Missolonghi the previous 4th of January. Two doctors now attend him, both urging him to be bled, but he still refuses. A series of final impressions appears in Byron's faltering hand: three drunken Suliotes under the moon, a Turkish sword dropped to the floor, the doctors, the "blackamoor" weeping, then no more. The last entry is dated April 19, 1824.

The most impressive of the recent fiction about the Greek revolution is Harry Mark Petrakis's *The Hour of the Bell* (1976), the first novel of a projected trilogy.[2] It covers the beginnings of rebellion from the autumn of 1820 until the next September. The copious plot of fifty-one principal characters and assorted events, on both land and sea, culminates in the seige and massacre of Tripolitza— when the Greeks prove themselves as cruel as the Turks from whom they seek freedom. The title refers to a church bell buried unused in a Greek cemetery for a century because the Turkish pasha ordered that it never be rung. But it does ring, in the Greek imagination—and now its hour has arrived. Petrakis provides useful maps, a cast of the leading characters, and a detailed "Calendar of the Greek War of Independence." To gain a modicum of objectivity and aesthetic distance, he has the most central segments of the action reported by Xanthos, a scribe from Zante who serves the great leader Theodoros Kolokotronis.

The following events of 1821 are listed by Petrakis as the historical foundation of the novel.

"Prince Alexander Ipsilantis invades the Danubian provinces and proclaims the revolution.

"Meeting of archons and clerics under Metropolitan Germanos at the monastery of Aghia Lavra.

"Revolt breaks out across Greece.

"Fall of Kalamata to Petrobey Mavromichalis.

"Hanging of Greek patriarch in Constantinople and massacre of Christians in Asia Minor.

"Islands of Spetzia, Psara and Hydra join the revolt.

"Surrender of Monemvasia.

"Surrender of Navarino and massacre of Turks.

"Destruction and massacre of Turks at Tripolitza.

"Meeting of the First National Assembly at Epidaurus."

The first event listed for the next year, 1822, is "Destruction and massacre of Greeks at Chios" (p. xiii).

That the Greek revolution succeeded against the might of the Ottoman empire was indeed a miracle, given the rivalries among the Greek chieftains which in turn often reflected the contending ambitions of the great powers. The freedom of the Greeks was less valued than these ambitions, which would have been pursued by other than revolutionary means had not the Greeks rebelled. At times in *The Hour of the Bell* the Greeks themselves do serious damage to their cause by their own petty ambitions, greed, and squabbles. At times the hunger for spoils equals if not exceeds the thirst for liberty. Even love turns ugly and disruptive when a love-crazed Cretan youth kills a heroic Cretan warrior in a jealous rage. The isolation of the *klephtic* bands, the difficulty of communicating between land and sea, the long and separate development of sub-ethnic peoples (Maniat versus Cretan, for example), the natural class hiatus between rich and poor, between merchants and peasants—these and other political, geographic, and cultural differences, not to mention the Turkish foe, made the Greek revolution unusually complicated, drawn-out, and bloody. That the revolution succeeded in freeing at least some of the "Greek lands" testified to the proposition that the modern Greek, like the ancient, can still transcend his *self* for the good of his *patrida*, his Greece.

For the broad scope of action that Petrakis undertakes to record, he needs a large cast of characters. With their long and unfamiliar names he runs the risk of having them blur and blend together in the reader's mind. Yet they must be included if the panoramic view is to be maintained. There are the real-life historical figures, such as the two Princes Ipsilantis, Petrobey Mavromichalis, Archbishop Germanos, Theodoros Kolokotronis, Alexander Mavrokordatos, Athanasios Diakos, Bouboulina, and Ali Pasha; revolutionary clergy such as Father Markos, Papalikos, Father Verganis, and Brother Apostolos; various captains and warriors, Kostas Makrydis, Vorogrivas, Boukouvalas, Balalas, Lambros Kasandonis, Kyriakos, Makrakis, Kringas, and so on; sea captains and fighters, Admiral Tombazis, Konstantine Kanaris, Leonidas Kontos, and Demetrios Papanikolis; Greek women besides Bouboulina, Ephrosene Kitsos, Lascarina, Aspasia Kontos, Gianoula, and Voula Psychoundakis; the leader of Albanian mercenaries, Elmas Bey; and Turks such as Ahmed Bajaki, Mehemet Selik, and Khurshid. These and other principal characters in *The Hour of the Bell* do more than swell a progress; they represent necessary types and play roles of varying importance to the plot.

The climactic seige of Tripolitza and the massacre of its Turkish inhabitants by the Greeks reveal the basic theme of *The Hour of the Bell*—that the bloody struggle for freedom brings out the best and the worst in people—that being free is not necessarily the same as being human. For months the Greek forces under Prince Demetrios Ipsilantis have beseiged Tripolitza with the plan of starving the Turks into surrender. As time passes and hunger mounts, the scribe Xanthos notices the increasing barter at the night gates, with Greeks exchanging bread and other foodstuffs for jewels and other prospective booty. To grab the rich spoils of Tripolitza the brave captains itch to hurl their soldiers against the battlements. Even the "crafty Bouboulina," the patriotic pirate, boldly goes inside the walls and retrieves great quantities of gems. The barter becomes a thriving open bazaar when Prince Ipsilantis leaves the scene for a foray elsewhere. Then, suddenly, the Greeks under Kolokotronis storm and conquer the city.

The scribe Xanthos is appalled by the senseless massacre that ensues; nor is he convinced that the gratuitous slaughter of women and children is needed by a Greek soldier's comment that the Greeks are only paying back the Turks in kind. As Xanthos tells the dying *pallikar* Balalas, "I am convinced butchers are butchers whether they are Turks who massacre Greeks at Kydonies or Greeks who massacre Turks at Tripolitza" (p. 343). When Xanthos tries to save a lovely and innocent Moslem girl, a maddened hunchback (symbol of a twisted soul) savagely attacks him and murders her. And later, when he begins to teach a group of Greek children about the "evils of ignorance, the malignance of power, the corrosions of greed, envy, vanity, ambition; the eviscerations of war, throttling mercy and compassion, despoiling men's dreams so they became the gutted shipwrecks of nightmares," they do not listen (p. 355). Instead they listen to a thrush singing nearby. "The thrush was Greece," Petrakis writes, "its song an unfoldment of the lovely, eternal and inextinguishable land" (p. 356).

Another novel of the Greek revolution, *Island of the Winds* (1976) by Athena G. Dallas-Damis, dwells more specifically with the Turkish massacre of Chios that occurred in March of 1822.[3] For the cover of her novel the author chose Chudiakov's painting *The Massacre*. In that atrocity the Turks slaughtered an estimated seventy thousand Chiotes. "During the Summer and Fall of 1972 and 1973," the author writes, "I lived with the villagers of Chios, most of them descendants of the survivors of the great massacre of 1822."[4] The research and writing meant a return to her own roots. Although the supreme event is the massacre itself, the plot of *Island of the Winds* also involves the trials and perils of a Greek woman, Helena. At eighteen she marries Stratis, a sea captain whose mother detests her. In a relatively short time Stratis abandons her and her twin boys. One of them, Joseph, is kidnaped by the Turks. With her other child, Jason, she escapes back to Chios. Twenty years pass. Only then does she tell Jason about his lost twin brother, that he "was alive somewhere in that country he despised . . . that his own flesh and blood was a part of the yoke that strangled the Christians" (p. 38). By this time the Greek lands stirred with rumors and portents of rebellion. Jason dreams of finding his lost brother now that independence seems at hand. The brother Joseph, in time, returns to Chios as Youssef, a Janissary who participates in the massacre. Because he remembers *Titika*, a kitten, Helena is positive that Youssef is her own Joseph. He just misses saving Jason, whom Turkish soldiers kill. At the end, when Chios begins to live again after the holocaust, Helena has another Jason, a grandson born to Youssef and a Greek girl, Joanna. The winds still blow without mercy, the fierce *meltemi* of the Aegean.

In a recent biographical novel, *The Greek Treasure* (1975), Irving Stone re-creates the love and adventure story of the famed archaeologist Heinrich Schliemann and the Greek girl who became his wife, Sophia Engastromenos.[5] Together they searched "for the ancient city of Troy and the royal tombs of Mycenae." He had become an American citizen in order to get a divorce from his Russian wife. Sophia was only seventeen, Schliemann forty-seven, when her relative Bishop Vimpos of Athens arranged the marriage. *The Greek Treasure* dramatizes their historic discoveries in Stone's excessive detail. The book's jacket states: "Sophia became a trained archaeologist. She suffered from the blazing sun, the bitter cold, the chilling rain, her husband's impetuous nature, the calumny heaped upon them; but survived to go back to work the next time there was a historic site to be uncovered and great treasures to be taken from the earth."

The lengthy novel begins in Sophia's household when Schliemann, her suitor, first arrives. Though a poor girl Sophia had attended the best Greek school for girls, the Arsakeion. From the start Schliemann talks about his plans to dig for ancient Troy. His views contradict those of eminent Greek authorities. Having access to the extensive Schliemann correspondence, Stone quotes liberally from his letters. Both Sophia and Henry are steeped in Homer. They marry, have a daughter. In Constantinople they receive permission to excavate, then arrive at the site. They hire diggers from the Anatolian Greek town of Renkoi. The man who oversees the digging for Troy is Georgios Sarkis, who may be thinking: "What am I, an Armenian, doing here as a Turkish official, overseeing a German-Russian-American man and a Greek girl engaged in a folly that will turn up nothing?" (p. 140). What the Schliemanns did find has long been history, and Irving Stone has done his usual thorough if pedestrian job of telling the story. Sophia's first child, Andromache, does well; but Sophia's next conception ends in a miscarriage. Stone interweaves personal domestic matters with the more significant historical facts—the remarkable discovery of not one city of Troy, but nine, testifying to the factual basis of Homeric and later ancient Greek literature. Toward the end Stone writes: "Henry Schliemann, dead just before his sixty-ninth birthday, had run his life span. He had fulfilled himself. Homer's Troy, Pausanias's royal tombs at Mycenae, the treasury at Orchomenos, the palace at Tiryns . . . " (p. 471). The Greek girl who became his wife, Sophia Engastromenos, had seen it all happen during the more than two decades of life with him—now, as his widow, the custodian and sharer of his fame.

The theme of growing up Greek-American persists in our fiction, more strongly in some novels than in others. The hero of Richard Bradford's *Red Sky at Morning* (1968), Joshua Arnold, has a Greek friend in William Stenopolous, Jr., "a chunky, brown-haired boy who looked as Greek as Eric the Red."[6] For William, or "Steenie" as he is called, to be a junior seems rather odd, since Greek fathers as a rule do not name sons after themselves. The Arnolds live in Mobile where the father runs a shipyard until he leaves for the navy at the start of World War II. Josh and his mother go to their summer place in Sagrado, New Mexico, to live out the war. The mother has a drinking problem worsened by the loss of her southern aristocratic friends. Josh as a teenager enters a new environment of wild mountains, Mexican-Americans, rural school, and a Greek classmate, Steenie. The Greek boy's father is Dr. Stenopolous, a harried obstetrician. Steenie's sharp sense of humor and mild deviltry complement Josh's own temperament. The boys are precocious wits. They have a mutual friend, Marcia Davidson, who is also a wit.

The three friends attend school together in Sagrado. They attend an annual fiesta where they eat *burritos*, gossip, and talk about sex and other subjects. Since the story belongs to Josh, Steenie moves only on its periphery, providing some comedy and company for a number of episodes. Much of the novel deals with Josh's going from being an enemy to becoming a friend of Chango Lopez. But the main source of concern for Josh is his father's absence in the Navy, and finally his death in action. At times Josh stays over at Steenie's house. "Mrs. Stenopolous didn't mind; for a woman with only one child, she was the most harried mother I've ever seen. I think it came from having everything she planned—meals, parties, small chores, sleep—interrupted by frantic calls from women in labor" (p. 165). She tells Josh: "I've given this advice to my son, and I'll give it to you: Never marry an obstetrician. It's hell on earth" (p. 166). The thought had never crossed his mind.

Being the son of an obstetrician, Steenie has access to very informative and exciting books on sex and the human body—material which he gladly relays to his friends. As the boys reach age, the war intervenes to dominate their lives. Josh and Steenie both leave Sagrado to serve their country in uniform.

The process of growing up Greek-American is much more fully developed by Charles E. Jarvis in *Zeus Has Two Urns* (1976).[7] He writes about a twelve-year-old boy, Socrates Genos, living in the Greek section of Lowell, Massachusetts, on the Merrimack River. The story opens in December during the early 1930s. The prose is self-conscious, at times stilted. The boy's father, who owns a restaurant, blames the Depression on the bloated greedy rich. Jarvis briefly describes Cabot City's Greek Town. Of the Greek church he says, "It was a masterpiece of Byzantine beauty and served as a living symbol to all the Greeks of Cabot City that theirs was an ancient and solid faith" (p. 9). Socrates's mother dispatches him with a dish of macaroni for an old blind man named Tiflos. The word *tiflos* means *blind* in Greek. Tiflos in turn sends Socrates for cigarettes to the grocery owned by Ligdas; there he discovers the "misshapen, wrinkled old man" fondling a little girl. Shocked, Socrates runs away to buy the cigarettes elsewhere.

Seeing him quiet at home, Mrs. Genos suspects that her son has been caught by the *mati*, the evil eye. The idea displeases him, for it means that Mrs. Magisa would be called to exorcise the offending spirit away from him. The word *magisa* means *sorceress* in Greek. Her equipment consists "of a glass of water, a small container of olive oil, and incense." The author proceeds to elaborate on her method of exorcism. "If the eyebrows [of the victim] were not smoothly set but looked ruffled, and if there were even a hint of paleness, the presence of an evil spirit was immediately suspected" (p. 15). Following this first step, Mrs. Magisa would place three drops of olive oil into the water, and if the drops "touched each other and evolved into one large drop, there was no doubt that the victim had been bewitched." To exorcise the demon, Mrs. Magisa would light the incense and wait for the smoke to rise upward; then "place the burning incense between herself and the bedeviled one and commence to chase away the evil spirit." She concluded the rite by simultaneously sprinkling and spitting on the victim's face. "Yet not being content with this, Mrs. Magisa would also blow incense smoke at the bespattered person's face. Thus the combination of water, oil, spit, and smoke joined by Mrs. Magisa's mysterious mumblings created a force that no evil spirit was able to withstand" (p. 16). Socrates convinces his mother that he has no need of the exorcism.

Out on Columbus Street, Socrates watches Mr. Kotopolos, a chicken-dealer, haggle with a customer over the price of a rooster. Socrates consorts with his two friends, Mitso and Spiro. At a debris-cluttered canal the boys see floating a roll of money tied by a rubber band. While they try to retrieve it, Officer Tom Drinan appears on a bridge; and of him Jarvis writes: "He was a simple Irishman thrown into a maelstrom of Greeks and at first he was unable to construct any order or regularity surrounding these frightfully energetic people" (p. 29). The sight of him, the *kliteras*, sends the boys running off. The author explains that the money belongs to a Nicholas Argeris, who dropped it on his way to the bank. The money finally disappears, and Argeris laments the loss of his small fortune. "Oh, America, oh, Columbus that brought me to this land! Oh, the hours and days I sweated to save this money!" (p. 32). Oh the folly!

Christmas comes for Socrates and Cabot City. Jarvis describes the boy's attendance at the Greek parochial school, in his sixth and last year. The author recounts the domestic routine of the Genos family. Constantine Genos talks about his migrating to America and to Cabot City. The children romp in the new snow. They skate. In the presence of George Stemas, an indigent friend, they discuss their Christmas presents; and when they prevail upon George to mention his gifts, he angrily says he got only "three onions and five potatoes." And he runs off ashamed.

Soon after the holidays, Cabot City girds for an election the first Monday of March. The Irish predominate in a population made up of Greeks, Irish, French, old Yankees, Poles, Syrians, Portuguese, and Turks. Roland "Mattress" Boudreau wins over Irish Jim "Boozer" Bailey. A Greek named Gianno wins a political bet from Manoli, and receives as spoils "a huge serving of *kokoretsi*, a concoction of lamb's liver, heart, and spleen, spicily prepared in the best Greek cooking tradition" (p. 61). Socrates and his friends explore the city dump. They stir up hordes of rats. The worst flood in history swells the Merit River. The Genos family has a problem paying the rent. Socrates discovers that Officer Drinan drinks bootleg wine in his father's Sparta Restaurant.

Summer arrives with new excitements for Socrates. To their restaurant comes "the broad, almost square figure of Demetrios Pallas, professional wrestling champion of the Merit Valley." Hating the mills, Pallas became a wrestler, a "symbol of Greek pride, Greek strength, and Greek achievement to all of the Hellenes of Cabot City" (p. 81). He fights mostly in small cities like Lawrence and Manchester. That Friday he takes on a Frenchman from Manchester. At the match gather the gamblers.

> Paul Manetis was the king of the Greek gamblers in Cabot City and, although the large, hard working segment of Greeks regarded him as a black sheep, still they could not completely damn and ostracize him. This they could not do, for outside of his gambling, he was a neat, quiet-voiced, well mannered human being. Paul Manetis was a difficult man to dislike; he was a symbol of tact and courtesy with the women, children, and men of Columbus Village. (p. 87)

Several pages are devoted to the epic match between Pallas the "Greek Lion" and Giguere the "French Tiger." The chicken man Kotopolos secretly bets on the Frenchman, Manetis on the Greek. The match, ending in a draw, leaves Pallas still the champion.

That summer of the Depression, Socrates and his friends hike outside of Cabot City. One day they hurl stones at a bull. At the farm of Mr. Fotos, a fellow Greek, they frighten a horse into having an erection. At home Socrates finds his older sister Diana resisting the idea of quitting high school in order to work in a shoe shop. Socrates leaves his tense home for the Boys Club, which is patronized mainly by Greek-American youth—"suffused with Greek voices, Greek words, and Greek temperaments" (p. 115). Yet he changes his mind and walks toward the huge looming factories; and there he prays to God that Diana may remain in school.

In the summer and fall of 1932 the campaign between Hoover and Roosevelt stirs the people of Cabot City, including the Greeks. Roosevelt is going to visit them to make a campaign speech! In the excitement of the impending event Socrates bumps into Peisistratus Zacharias, head of the "Diogenes Democratic Club." Its members raise a Greek flag in support of Roosevelt. In his brief address the candidate alludes "to the tragic spectacle of a once mighty textile empire that was allowed to sicken and decay with no medicine offered to it by the indifferent doctor in the White House" (p. 127). That night in their homes the Greeks say, "*Tha mas sosi.*" "He will save us" (p. 131).

Another Christmas season approaches. Socrates now attends public school where he must adjust to a new situation. In Miss Slattery's class he sometimes forgets and answers in Greek. Next to him sits a dull-witted Greek boy, a pest, named Peter Vlakas. The word *vlakas* in Greek means *dunce*. Rather than study, Vlakas plays with girls. Caught, he gets severely reprimanded both at school and at home. Much to Socrates's joy, Vlakas moves to another room where he can no longer beg answers from him. The Genos family feels great pride over Socrates's excellent report card. To reward him, his mother gives him money for a new woolen cap.

The inauguration of Roosevelt as the new president does not immediately help the Genos family. Jarvis describes Cabot City as a cemetery filled with dead industries. "These vast crypts were the hulking, looming mills that grimly huddled in the textile wasteland by the river, and the bones they housed were the myriads of looms and spindles that were riveted in the rot and the decay of the dying world around them." Socrates contracts pneumonia but recovers. Owing to lack of sufficient business his parents in June decide to close their restaurant. When Leander returns home from New York, he gets a job on a flood-control project on the Merit River, but he quits after two weeks. His malingering, sickness, and eventual death compound with stark tragedy the poverty and despair in the house. "Leander Genos died on a Sunday, on a warm April morning that promised an early spring." Socrates wonders what will happen next. To be poor in the Depression is bad enough; to be poor and Greek is even worse.

The rich Greek shipowner as a character continues to be a popular stereotype in fiction. Just as traffic in munitions created the phenomenon of Sir Basil Zaharoff, so traffic in war, oil, and other commodities created the more recent phenomenon of the Greek shipowners. Book titles about them use words like *golden* and *fabulous*. They are stamped upon the world's consciousness as one of the greatest success stories of all time. Perhaps the best researched and most honest of the many novels about the Greek shipowners is Nicholas Gage's *The Bourlotas Fortune* (1976).[8] What Gage writes has a solid basis in the factual history of the shipping industry, with special emphasis on the Greek component. He also includes a considerable amount of Greek ethnicity in the text. *Bourlotas*, for example, means *fire-ship*. The great-great-grandfather of the protagonist, Kosmas Bourlotas, sacrificed his coveted boat, the *Saint Nicholas*, as a fire-ship to destroy a powerful Turkish flagship during the Greek revolution. The family surname derives from that heroic action. In the aura of this legend Kosmas Bourlotas builds a financial empire and enjoys the style of living of an actual tycoon such as Onassis.

The rise of the Greek shipowner devolves in the broadest sense from the venerable Greek maritime tradition that dates to pre-Homeric times. The Bourlotas family saga begins on the island of Chios, in the early nineteenth century, when sea captains enjoyed high status. Born in 1896, Kosmas Bourlotas at an early age follows other Greeks to London, then the center of world shipping. He enters that world as a clerk in the marine brokerage firm of Durstyn and Bromage. Kosmas engages in many business and private transactions as he gains wealth, power, and influence. His career acquires an American flavor in 1941 when he and other Greek shipping magnates leave war-torn London for the relative safety of New York. Gage describes their role in the successful prosecution of the war. He relates the well-known story of the surplus Liberty ships, the registration of the Greek ships in countries like Panama, the problems with maritime unions, the boom created by the Korean war, and much else. The notorious rivalry between Onassis and Niarchos has a fictional parallel in the bitter rivalry between Bourlotas and Malitas. Gage's Greeks run the gamut of good and evil, in both their business and their private lives. The back cover of the Bantam edition describes the leading characters: "Kosmas Bourlotas—born into poverty, he burned with ambition for money, sex, and family dynasty. Chrysanthi Bourlotas—a regal Aegean girl, wife to Kosmas, and mother of two strange children. Demosthenes Malitas—the Machiavelli of the Greek shipping world. Jason Venetis—a power-hungry sadist whose lusts were endless. Daphne Sarantis—a profligate daughter with a talent for love."[9] Given these ingredients, *The Bourlotas Fortune* is a reliable report on the era of the "Golden Greeks."

The character of Eli Chaconas represents the Greek as Hollywood screenwriter in Edwin Gilbert's *The Squirrel Cage* (1947).[10] When a New York playwright, Tony Willard, arrives at the Milikan Studios to turn his play *The Dark City* into a film, he receives office space in the writers' building that is called, among other things, the "Squirrel Cage." The novel attacks the Hollywood establishment as bitterly as does *The Day of the Locust* by Nathanael West. The novitiate Willard finds himself among craven opportunists, stool pigeons, brain pickers, paranoic red-baiters, brown nosers, and assorted rats. Among them, too, are several decent human beings. Eli Chaconas, a well-established writer with a long list of credits, belongs to Willard's small group of friends. His role in the story has no ethnic dimension and has little significance beyond showing what compromises with integrity the highly paid Hollywood writers have to make.

The post–World War II atmosphere reeks with the fear of communism that resulted in the celebrated case of the Hollywood Ten. The big studios regard the Screen Writers Guild as the dangerous "red menace" for demanding "a minimum weekly wage of $187.50." When Tony Willard first meets Chaconas, he is not surprised to learn he had once been a truck driver. Chaconas still looks like one.

> He had, in his youth, worked for a trucking company transporting produce from New Jersey to New York, and now he wrote screen stories about rugged men who drove trucks at night while their wives betrayed them in highway motels. Thus, if a story demanded characters of the virile, tough-talking type, Chaconas was summoned to write the screen play. As a result, Eli talked and dressed like the species he portrayed, an eccentricity which paid him fifteen hundred dollars a week. Despite this obvious masquerade Chaconas was a sincere man

and a talented one. Tony felt that he would have become the author of first-rate works had he not been burdened with a wife, three children, and a dozen impecunious relatives. (p. 52)

Tony Willard quickly loses his job because he falls for a beautiful stool-pigeon who slanders and betrays him; but Eli Chaconas knows how to survive and still remain a "good guy."

An old Greek mechanic gives fatherly advice to Will Redfern, who loves a Greek girl, in Gerald Warner Brace's *Bell's Landing* (1955).[11] Bell's Landing is the family mansion on the North Shore above Boston. The "elderly Cretan gentleman," Constant Sardis, is also a philosopher. Their friendship begins when young Will gets a job in the same garage; and it becomes closer when he falls in love with one of Pop's four granddaughters, Sally Anthonakis. The love, however, does not extend much beyond an initial coupling during which she loses her virginity. Her actual aggressiveness in the matter contradicts the cliché that Greek girls expect to remain virgins until they are safely married.

Circumstances keep Will and Sally apart, with neither one of them apparently able to love strongly enough to transcend the obstacles. The result is a bittersweet relationship that leads nowhere. He goes off to war in the navy; she marries a man whom she merely likes. Will later asks her to run off with him, but Sally refuses. She and her husband leave Massachusetts for Mexico, where he thinks conditions are better for writing. After Will's aunt dies, he is willed Bell's Landing; and he has a new girl, Betsy, who prevails upon him not to sell the old place. Among the memories that now will haunt him is the Greek girl, Sally.

A Greek oldtimer living in Cope's Corner, next to the artist's colony of Olympia, Pennsylvania, fits the description of Nick Kolassi, a former stonemason, in Edmund Schiddel's *The Devil in Bucks County* (1959).[12] One of the story lines involves the Connells' driving some squatters, the Gipes, off their land. It was not known that they lived on land owned by someone else until the Connells searched their deed. Kolassi, after the meeting at the Connells, goes to the Gipes to relay the decision made. The author has Kolassi and his wife talk a kind of Greek-American shorthand. "So what's 'a gonna do?" she asks. "Is a Connells gonna buy out Gipes?" And he replies, "Shuddup, old lady, go to bed" (p. 88).

Kolassi seems to touch the lives of most of the local citizens. He is a familiar figure to a Colonel Stackhouse who sees him wandering down the road. Kolassi "walked unsteadily, weaving from one side of the road to the other" (p. 93). Nick Kolassi has been living in Cope's Corner long enough to be able to pass judgment on later arrivals, to be a maker of public opinion. At one point the author writes: "The Kolassis were suspicious of artists and detested the Eks, but they nodded to them, condescendingly, pitying them for their lack of central heat and storm sashes" (p. 126). He as an oldster likes to tell newcomers how the Corner has grown and, had he known, he could have made a killing had he bought up cheap land as recently as ten years back, "such as the Gipes occupied, which today could be sold for premium prices." On another occasion Kolassi tries to play Cupid by urging a friend, Clay Harmon, to become interested in Eleanor Marko, who had been immediately abandoned by her husband. Kolassi is a busybody, for he observes what others do and then gossips. He lives on the edge, so to speak, of the adultery and other aberrant behavior in the area. Forgive and bear each other's frailties, the novel seems to say, and life will endure.

Some modern Greeks like Fariña's Gnossos Pappadopoulis, as we have seen, represent the severely alienated American of the sixties. Other Greeks aid and abet the same type of lost anguished souls—victims trapped in the affluent society. This tangential role is played by a Greek in *Last Exit to Brooklyn* (1965) by Hubert Selby, Jr.[13] The Greek, Alex, owns an all-night diner near the Brooklyn Army Base. The word *scatah* (shit), used from the first paragraph on, constitutes the novel's only Greek ethnic reference. Alex himself is characterized as one who relates to all the weird and way-out patrons of his joint. Drunks and bums frequent the diner; they banter words and jokes with him. He sits on a stool at the end of the counter, smoking, talking, advising, warning, and saying "scatah." Sexual perversion saturates the story. Car thieves, junkies, and former convicts patronize "the Greeks," as it is called. Throughout the story freaky people do sadistic things to each other. For business reasons Alex tolerates the freaks and losers; they swarm around him and his establishment in what has been called a vision of hell, a hell that is spiritual and psychological. But Alex seems unaffected by the horror that swirls about him.

No account of Greek-American characters, fictional or otherwise, would be complete without a further reference to gambling. The marble-topped tables with their ouzo glasses, cups of Turkish coffee, and playing cards were fixtures of the traditional Greek coffeehouse. These *kaffenia* served as cozy men's clubs for early immigrants, and many still operate in the remaining Greek Towns of America. Sometimes the local ethnic racketeer used the coffeehouse as a hangout from which to conduct policy and other shady business. Young gamesters met there to pore over the Racing Form and ponder the odds.

The greatest gambler of all, Nick the Greek, has already been the subject of two books, the most recent a novel by Petrakis. His well-known career went from rags to riches to rags. Cy Rice's biography of this phenomenon, *Nick the Greek* (1969), reads more like a romance than a piece of factual prose.[14] If the Hellene who travels has Odysseus in his consciousness, the Hellene who gambles does so in the aura of Nick the Greek. Two sobriquets attached to Nick's name are King of the Gamblers and the Last of the Gentlemen Gamblers. Nick the Greek established his fame during the twenties, along with legendary figures in other fields— Red Grange, Rudolph Valentino, Charles A. Lindbergh, Bill Tilden, Bobby Jones, Babe Ruth, F. Scott Fitzgerald, Al Capone, Jack Dempsey, Jimmy Londos. During his lifetime, various writers have estimated, he won and lost as much as a half billion dollars. "Nicholas Dandolos reigned as undisputed gambling monarch of the world from 1928 until 1949" (p. 177). He gave millions to charities, friends, and beggars. But he died broke in 1966 at the age of eighty-four.

Cy Rice's portrait of Nicholas Andrea Dandolos, Nick the Greek, reveals a most extraordinary and complicated individual. His reputation rests upon his exploits as a gambler. A medical phenomenon, he could play poker for days on end without fatigue or fluctuation of blood pressure. Rice narrates from taped interviews that, as Nick rose from obscurity to notoriety, gambling with him had the same social status as dancing with the Prince of Wales. He gambled with cards and dice or at the track not only for money but also for excitement. Among his close friends were leading celebrities of show business, politics, business, royalty, and the underworld. With the aid of a phenomenal memory, he could quote the classical philosophers and poets at length. He had an aptness for aphorism.

During Las Vegas's early growth as a gambling capital, Nick the Greek was the town's leading attraction; tourists came to catch a glimpse of him at the gaming tables. "He became the arbiter in gambling disputes," and his decisions, Rice writes, "were accepted with the validity of an edict from the higher courts" (p. 178). Some observers suspected at times that Nick the Greek was financed by the crime syndicate, but Rice claims that he was able to play for high stakes with his own money. No-limit dice and poker games were his specialty. Twice he tried to dethrone New York gangster Arnold Rothstein from his position of gambling king, and twice he lost. "There was $797,000 on the table," Rice writes, "the biggest pot in the history of stud poker" (p. 141). Rothstein won, but soon afterward he was gunned down in gangland fashion, and the title King of the Gamblers passed to Nick the Greek.

Rice credits Nick with elevating the game of dice from the back alleys to plush palaces. Although a gambler, he deeply respected learning and helped many a student through college. He knew many beautiful women, but his true mistress was Lady Luck, who remained faithful to him long after he had become a living legend. Then, fickle in the end, she allowed him to die in poverty.

It is not likely that there will ever be another Nick the Greek. The social conditions that made him have passed into history. The new age of laws, taxes, and computerized percentages leaves no room for the dash, skill, and stamina of a Nick the Greek. On the other hand, it offers broad scope for the talents of a Jimmy the Greek, well-known columnist, syndicated oracle, odds-maker of Las Vegas, and author of his own life story, *Jimmy the Greek* (1975).[15] The odds are that he, too, will become a legend.

Fictional Greeks who are strikers, labor leaders, and revolutionaries are relatively rare; as such, they do not compare with the real-life Greeks who engaged in labor and leftist activities. Many early immigrants served unwittingly as strikebreakers. Later they joined the unions and even became strike leaders. Perhaps the most notable of these is Louis Tikas, the martyr of the Ludlow massacre, whose story is vividly told by Helen Zeese Papanikolas in *Toil and Rage in a New Land* (1970), published in a special issue of the *Utah Historical Quarterly*.[16] Other Greeks died in the San Francisco general strike, in the Republic Steel strike, and elsewhere. For a time Greeks were influential in such unions as the furriers and the hotel and restaurant workers. Leftist Greeks supported the *Greek-American Tribune*, a Marxist newspaper; they also maintained, in the larger cities, local lodges of the International Workers Order, a fraternal and insurance organization. The protagonist of Elmer Grossberg's *Farewell, My Son* is a Greek communist. Greek-American writers who have depicted working-class types and political radicals include Theano Papazoglou-Margaris in her short stories, Mary Vardoulakis in *Gold in the Streets*, Jim Dilles in *The Good Thief*, Elia Kazan in *The Arrangement*, and Harry Mark Petrakis in *Lion at My Heart*.

Another reference to a Greek unionist appears in Julian Moynahan's *Pairing Off* (1969), although the labor theme is secondary to the theme of mating and happiness.[17] Louis Doxiades, a union leader, plays Cupid for the protagonist, Myles McCormick, who works in the Boston Free Library with a young Greek girl named Angelina Stratis. Angelina is a brilliant girl of seventeen, who has an I.Q. of 145 and was "Girls' Latin School Salutatorian and vice-president of the Athenian Club, 1958" (p. 12). She is a brunette "with clearly separated breasts under her tight red jersey, with race-horse legs and big sooty eyes." Myles feels that she should be in college, but her stubborn father offers her the choice of the family spa or her present job at the library. When a friend of Myles dies, he is paid a visit by Angelina and Lou Doxiades, who is her uncle and regards her as a genius who should be attending the Sorbonne.

Myles admires Doxiades and jokingly thinks he is "Aristotle Onassis' man in the Boston shipping world" (p. 119). To some extent Doxiades is a man of mystery who calls himself "a close student of society in all its strange and fascinating forms." "I am a Greek," he says. "I was born there, in Thessalonika. If I wish to join the Boston establishment I must analyze it, see what makes it tick" (p. 120). He refuses to remain among the "hoipolloi" like John Stratis, Angelina's father. Doxiades says the Irish have moved up in society; the Italians are coming up, and will be followed by the Armenians and then the Albanians.

After the funeral Myles McCormick quits his job and decides to return to Ireland. Before leaving, he recalls an earlier youthful imaginary dialogue with himself on the subject of pairing off, which he sees as "the fate of mankind." Disgruntled with life and not paired off with anyone, he waits for his flight at the airport, where he meets Lou Doxiades in the cocktail lounge. Lou is on standby for a flight, and Myles invites him to visit Ireland with him. As they drink and talk, Lou spots a bulky man watching them. Lou asks Myles to help him by hiding in the fifth stall of the men's room and pushing out hard at the signal, "Be reasonable, Leo." Myles does so, and together the two of them overpower a Greek thug sent by Albert Korones to beat up Doxiades. The mystery concerns a "jurisdictional labour dispute with petty gangster overtones," Lou explains to Myles.

> I run a small dignified operation bringing in waiters from Athens to work around town. I do the leg work rounding them up and fixing them up with visas. They sign into my union local when they get here, and they're all experienced men so there's no sweat and no sweating. Albert Korones has set up what we call a paper local and he wants to steal my waiters. First he tried to buy me into his racket and now he's trying to muscle me out of my legitimate work. But he's a born loser. (p. 233)

Myles says the whole business sounds pretty Greek to him, and Lou replies that in Boston being a waiter tends to be a "Greek thing."

In Ireland Myles and Lou go to castles and other historical places. "I dig the antiques," Lou tells Myles. "In Greece though, I never get a chance to look around. I'm usually too busy signing up waiters and chasing tail" (p. 239). Now he acts like an enthusiastic tour guide. They visit a graveyard because Myles wants to bury his friend's ashes with his own ancestors. Lou Doxiades leaves him alone and goes to a pub for a few drinks. At the graveyard, sitting on the wall, Myles finds an old friend, a beautiful girl named Eithne Gallagher waiting for him. "Your friend Lou kept at me with telegrams," she tells him. "'Come dance with us in Ireland. Myles is your man.'" (p. 248).

Myles calls Lou his "favourite native of the human race" when Eithne says Lou has gone native. It turns out that the Greek entrepreneur has not gone to a pub, but has instead secretly waited to witness the reunion between Myles and Eithne. "Behind them someone began making owl noises. Louis Doxiades stood outside the wall." Myles then laughs and says, "Louis Doxiades, the old panderer himself, Uncle Eros," and adds, "He thinks we should moan at each other through a chink in the wall, like Pyramus and Thisbe" (p. 251). Myles did Lou a favor at the airport, now Lou returned the favor by bringing him together with Eithne.

Another Greek entrepreneur, in Denison Hatch's *Cedarhurst Alley* (1971), is obese but dapper Boros Niforos, the owner of Nif-T-Novelty Company in Far Rockaway.[18] He sells the protagonist, Hendon Chait, helium for an army-surplus barrage balloon. His father on his sixty-fifth birthday gives Hendon the deed to Summerleas, an eighty-thousand-dollar house in "the Long Island commuter town of Cedarhurst, less than an hour from Manhattan" (p. 1). It turns out that the house lies in the main landing pattern of John F. Kennedy Airport. The huge jets go by at six hundred feet, one after the other, day and night. Very shortly their youngest daughter becomes withdrawn, autistic. They are told of several similar cases. Disturbed, they move back to New York and try to sell their house in Cedarhurst.

Various realtors try, but the most they are offered is about half what Summerleas is worth. Furthermore, they run into trouble with neighbors, one of them the owner of an exclusive golf club. Hendon must not sell to Jews or blacks. Julie's father, a pilot, says they live in Cedarhurst Alley, the name given to a low approach to the airport. By chance Hendon sees in the *Sunday Times* a small ad offering surplus U.S. government barrage balloons. Hendon decides to float a balloon over Summerleas and thus stop the jets from flying over. His lawyer, Bill Kindersley, advises him to do it big or not at all, to take a full page ad in the *Times* stating his grievances and giving fair warning. Bill cites a precedent in which a North Carolina farmer sued the government for damages due to noise and was awarded two thousand dollars by the U.S. Court of Claims. The balloon arrives from the Heidelberger Sales Company. It will be launched the Saturday before Labor Day. Heidelberger advises Hendon to get the helium from the Nif-T-Novelty Company, but warns: "Beware of Niforos; he'll charm the birds off the trees and the pants off your wife" (p. 66).

Boros Niforos is as lovable a dandy as Louis Doxiades in *Pairing Off*. He drives up to inspect the job of providing about ten thousand cubic feet of helium for Hendon's balloon. Only thirteen people on the entire East coast have two-telephone cars, and Boros Niforos is one of them. He has "exquisitely white but uneven teeth"—a Greek "with little pop eyes," balding, and hair in swirls. Of immense girth, he resembles "an up-ended version of the Goodyear blimp" (p. 65). Refined and articulate, Boros Niforos represents the immigrant on his way up the social ladder.

A strange man, really, huge and hulking in his immaculate blue silk suit. He was undoubtedly self-made. Self-made men yearn to be part of the Establishment but they seldom make it. Even though Niforos could do business with the Establishment, mingle freely with it, go to its parties and live in its communities, he would always be the Establishment's favorite Greek; just as Jack Javitz is everybody's favorite Jew and Daniel Patrick Moynahan is everybody's favorite Irishman. If Niforos kept his nose clean, and sent his kids to the right schools, they could become Establishment. (p. 70)

If Niforos gets involved in a radical stunt like B-Day, Balloon Day, his children would not become Establishment; for he as an immigrant might be clapped into jail as a troublemaker. Hendon S. Chait *is* Establishment—white, moneyed, Mayflower. Not only will Niforos help, however, but he will donate the helium to the "very worthy cause." Niforos has his own plans that involve no flights between nearby cities, but trains that go 150 miles per hour as in Europe and Japan. Hendon, Niforos, and the lawyer Kindersley form a triumvirate against the airlines. Niforos suggests Hendon use a coupon in his *New York Times* ad so the general public can help finance the antinoise crusade. Hendon agrees. To light up the balloon Niforos suggests Christmas tree lights, with an electric wire up the anchor line. "The Nif-T-Novelty Company is very big in Christmas decorations" (p. 90). As the launch approaches, Niforos proves himself more and more amazing as an entrepreneur. The huge crowd that gathers must be fed—by the Nif-T-Delicatessen, in which Niforos holds a partnership. Explaining, he tells Hendon "you know what they say about Greeks: put two Greeks together and they start an argument; put three together and they start a restaurant" (p. 104).

To avert trouble with the law Boros Niforos alerts his friends on the Nassau County Police, a brilliant move to let them in on B–Day. The big jets keep flying over, making everybody wince. He secures a battery of telephones, saying: "I was Nassau County coordinator for the governor's campaign. For me, the phone company works overtime" (p. 125). Of course the barrage balloon, once up, seriously hampers air traffic into New York City. The president calls and threatens to bring in the army. Thousands gather and wait. Headlines appear in all the papers. The FBI seizes Hendon Chait, then releases him—a celebrity. Four different government agencies are investigating his past, all to no avail.

The spectacle of B-Day results in a national television special sponsored by Gulf Oil. Mrs. Barbara Niforos arrives for the gala evening. Niforos looks unkempt after a night of poker. A Greek bouzouki band plays for the vast crowd. At the refreshment tent most of the people "were downing ouzo and Metaxa; there was even a small run on retsina, a resin-flavored Greek wine that tastes rather like Montgomery Ward paint thinner." Hendon likes the Greek hors d'oeuvres, and the music that stirs his glands. The beautiful Barbara Niforos entertains the crowd with Greek songs about Piraeus and her homeland and happiness. She is a "gloriously stunning girl" who sings in a language no one speaks but which everyone understands. She sings *Never on Sunday* with a naughty glint in her eyes. Then Barbara and Boros Niforos dance. "They moved in perfect half-time to the rhythm, doing the slow sensuous leaps that punctuate Greek dancing." They drink Metaxa in rhythm and throw the empty glass "over their shoulders against the tent walls."

The celebration ends with the alarming news that the 101st Airborne is on the way. Hendon and Niforos bring the balloon down to five hundred feet. The paratroopers as they drop look like white mushrooms in the sky. They land. Will they shoot down the balloon? No, a new F–111 swing-wing fighter swerves toward it then sharply away; and the balloon is fatally stricken. "He blew a hole in the balloon with his jet," Boros says. "A superb piece of flying. He blew a hole in the balloon and all the helium is leaking out. Project B–Day is coming down on our heads! And he did it without firing a shot!" (p. 191). Dejected over the apparent defeat, Boros Niforos gives a farewell speech for the benefit of the press. Already the big jets have resumed flights overhead, even lower and noiser than earlier. Boros leaves Hendon Chait with a Turkish "gulè, gulè" that means "Go laughingly" (p. 203). Yet all is not lost. Mail trucks begin to arrive loaded with heavy sacks. They are filled with contributions. By the end of the month Hendon receives 600,000 letters with roughly $2,700,000. Elated, he thinks he may run for president, and make some needed reforms. *Cedarhurst Alley*, one may note, was published long before the attempt to keep the supersonic Concorde fron landing in New York. Perhaps the real protesters should have used balloons.

Of the nonthrillers and nonmysteries set in Greece, one of the most charming is May Sarton's *Joanna and Ulysses* (1963).[19] From her home in New Hampshire the author in her foreword writes a letter to Joanna, back in Greece, who told her the story she now reproduces. "What I did not tell you," Sarton avers, "was that I too once fell in love with a donkey, a donkey for whom I could do nothing, who was kept shut up in a dark barn in New Hampshire. So your story had for me a particular resonance" (p. 7). The story begins when a thirty-year-old Athenian girl, Joanna, leaves her widowed father behind and goes to the volcanic island of Santorini for a month's vacation. An artist, she cannot produce; a woman, she cannot love; healthy, she generally has ennui. Joanna has been too committed to a father who needs her too much, who himself suffers from the effects of war and of personal loss.

Santorini helps Joanna to be reborn as an artist and a woman, the most effective cause being Ulysses, a little dying donkey that she buys and restores to health. Immediately upon her arrival, she notices the pitiful creature on the quay, cannot stand his suffering, and buys him for the large sum of eight hundred drachmas. She buys a salve for his sores. As the days pass the "strange" Athenian lady with the decrepit donkey becomes the talk of Santorini. Joanna loads her easel, canvas, and other equipment upon the obedient animal and goes off for sites to paint. She shows spirit and anger at those who scoff and otherwise impede her endeavor; but slowly the people veer to her side, and turn friendly. During the brief month Joanna meets several who touch her more deeply than others: Nicholas, a young boy who asks provocative questions; Zarian, "a particularly handsome young man," to whom she almost gives Ulysses upon leaving; and, back at Piraeus, a friend named Christopher who finds a truck to take Joanna and Ulysses back home to Athens. There, for a time, she tries to hide the donkey in the basement.

Joanna's father finds out and is furious at first. Then a number of significant facts emerge. The most important for Joanna is that, as a result of her care and love for Ulysses, she escaped from her old self and entered a new one. Upon examining her new paintings, her father, much to her surprise and joy, declares her to be a real artist. A new and frank bond grows between them; and a new life dawns: they move to Mykonos.

The Greek as very minor character, of whom quite a few exist here and there, reappears in Irwin Shaw's *Rich Man, Poor Man* (1970).[20] The "poor" Thomas Jordache injures Quayles, a syndicate-connected boxer, and has to run for his life. His friend and manager Schultzy gives him money and urges him to go cross-country to New York by bus. Thomas must leave the United States or be killed.

> The softest thing is getting a job on a ship. When you get to New York go to a hotel called the Aegean. It's on West Eighteenth Street. It's full of Greek sailors. Ask for the manager. He's got a long Greek name, but everybody calls him Pappy.

He handles jobs for freighters that don't fly the American flag. Tell him I sent you and I want you out of the country fast. He won't ask questions. (p. 460)

In New York the fugitive Jordache holes up in the Aegean Hotel for eight days, with Pappy bringing his meals personally. Pappy disguises Thomas as an old Norwegian seaman and assigns him to the *Elga Andersen*, of Greek ownership. The ship's crew has many nationalities. The worst of them is Falconetti, whom Thomas smashes in a fight. Back in New York again, he stays with Pappy at the Aegean. The heat is still on. Pappy does errands for him, and brings him food, drink, a woman, and his brother Rudolph. Other than that, neither Pappy nor any other Greek does anything for the Jordaches in *Rich Man, Poor Man*.

An experimental novel set in Greece is James Merrill's *The (Diblos) Notebook* (1965), a finished work in the form of an unfinished first rough draft.[21] The effort compares with other recent experiments that self-consciously exploit the mechanics or craft of writing. Two other examples that come to mind are John Barth's "Lost in the Funhouse" and Joyce Carol Oates's "How I Contemplated the World from the Detroit House of Correction and Began My Life Over Again."[22] The content is explained in the subtitle of the Oates fiction as "Notes for an essay for an English class at Baldwin Country Day School," and the reader himself must re-create the story from the notes. Barth's gimmick combines the telling of a story with a concurrent lecture on the craft of writing, from such minutiae as the use of italics to the final intended effect. In *The (Diblos) Notebook*, whose title is still tentative, Merrill more closely approximates the method of Oates than of Barth. He gives us his preliminary notes toward a novel rather than the novel itself. Since the plot is ambiguous, let me quote the jacket as a cogent synopsis:

A young writer keeps a notebook, which records at one and the same time a series of happenings on the Greek island of Diblos in which he is deeply involved, and his attempts to transform these happenings into a novel. Everything which might be found in such a notebook is used here with great cunning: the false starts which end in the middle of a thought; the endless revisions, cancelled out in the search for the right word or phrase; the many approaches and back trackings as the writer seeks an entrance to the materials through several possible doors; the musings on how the material is to be treated; the wrestlings with the problem of appearance and assumed reality.

The narrator is the half-brother of Orson, who is the note-book's central figure. A youngish Greek-American man of let-ters, of vast enthusiasm and energy, Orson has gone back to Greece in search of his roots. The "novel" will begin seven years earlier, when the narrator pays his first visit to Diblos and Orson is establishing a liaison with a cultured, intelligent, older woman of the island, Dora. The younger brother sets down the bare bones of their story as part of the notebook kept on his second visit to Diblos seven years later. At one point, abruptly, we are given a "fair copy" of Part Three of his novel, which describes the experiences of Dora and Orson in America, their marriage and eventual separation. Then, back to Diblos, an encounter between the two brothers—the writer and his main character—forces both notebook and "novel" to a strange but logical conclusion.[23]

The writing itself, the detail, contains vivid images and sharp insights, with ethnic touches to flavor both settings and characters. With a poet's feeling the author notes the colors of the Greek is-land. As for Orson: "I was born 35 years ago in Asia Minor of Greek parents. My father, a goatherd, fell in love with a beautiful etc. Dead of cancer. Poverty. New York. Mother remarried, lives in Texas. A step-father, a half-brother" (p. 3). The Greek flag is blue and white. A caïque is a seaworthy boat. A classical theater is at Epidaurus. A dog is named Kanella (Cinnamon). One feature of being Greek is that one never directs an offcolor remark to one's mother. The Greeks hold a *panagyri*, a festival or picnic. "Tiny glasses of ouzo were served, followed by tumblers of cold water & rose-flavored jam on spoons" (p. 68). As for Greek children— "Pose a Greek child for a snapshot, his shoulders lift like wings, his arms stiffen at his side, and he smiles" (p. 69). These and other ethnic tidbits add color to the Diblos "note-books." If the finished novel ever appears, a more nearly definitive scholarly statement can be made regarding its ethnic and aesthetic value.

Two rhetorical questions—"How do you make fiction? The writer must use himself, but how does he lose himself?"—begin Sylvia Wright's group of three stories, A *Shark-infested Rice Pudding* (1969).[24] The first of them, "Fathers and Mothers," is a finished-unfinished first draft about a domestic tragedy—the bringing to America of a Greek father-in-law to receive cobalt treatments that unfortunately fail to delay death. The major characters have no names other than *daughter-in-law, mother, father-in-law, husband,* and *baby*. The non-Greek daughter-in-law writes a series of episodes that are connected by the condition of the dying patient, a Greek painter with Paris, Athens, and famous people in his past.

Mother is actually the narrator's Greek mother-in-law; and some of the ethnicity in the story derives from the contrast between what she knew in Greece and what she learns in America, especially about the running of a household. She "discovers" supermarkets, television, electric gadgets, Halloween, pizza. Another source of ethnicity is her husband's longing to return to the leisurely routine of Athens. He misses the daily walk to the *kiosque* for his paper, the *koulouria* with his coffee, the fellow Chiots with whom he shares stories. When he speaks he often uses a sign language that his daughter-in-law cannot understand. She studies Greek, takes care of the baby, and waits for her father-in-law to die. The parents return to Greece. The story ends with the narrator's missing the funeral but arriving in time for the memorial service held forty days later. By Greek custom the period of mourning ends at that time.

Nicholas Delbanco's first novel, *The Martlet's Tale* (1966), begins and ends on the island of Rhodes with the middle section set in Athens.[25] The episodic plot revolves around the fortune allegedly secreted by a dying old lady, Orsetta Procopirios. The style features numerous pithy vignettes, cameo appearances, cryptic comments, broken images, non sequiturs, slick ironies, flashbacks, and other literary devices. A calf has been fattened for Orsetta's eightieth birthday a few months away, but her strength rapidly wanes. "There were three sons: Manos, the youngest, the fat man standing outside; Triphon, the eldest, living in America now; and Apelis, the father of Sotiris" (p. 17). All these men have lusted for their rich mother's hoard. She has given them nothing but false clues. The doctors allow Orsetta's wish to be moved from the hospital to her seaside mansion in Charaki. There, as she nears the end, she tells Sotiris the secret of her wealth but wants him not to dig for it until after she dies.

With the slow dying of Orsetta as his structure, the author weaves an intricate web of relationships among those affected. He uses many ethnic allusions and transliterations of Greek words for color and tone. One of the more important flashbacks narrates Apelis Procopirios's stay in the United States, an example of a *failed* immigrant. "Bewildered, twenty-three, Apelis had gone to Pittsburgh, and lived there seven years. When, by 1935, with the worst hunger passed, he held onto a job it was as a house handyman, a servant to the rich" (p. 115). Apelis returns to Rhodes where he organizes some very successful garment shops. Given the coveted secret by his grandmother, Sotiris runs off to Athens to escape the covetous pressure of his elders. In the big, busy, and decadent city he enjoys some sensual experiences. He evades the police search instigated by Apelis, his father. The section on Athens concludes: "Orsetta Procopirios, lying on her back, looked up at the ceiling, saw it, did not see it, and was dead" (p. 158).

The third and final section of *The Martlet's Tale* brings Sotiris back to Rhodes for Orsetta's birthday feast, now altered to her funeral. Apelis foresees legal troubles because she left no will. He doubts if the uncles (his brothers) would agree to let Sotiris, his son, have all her money, providing that she actually has the money and that she revealed its correct location. The last pages intersperse details about the burial rites with behavior of the various major and minor characters. Parts of the funeral liturgy are reproduced as chanted by the two priests. At this point the narrative is fragmented to give a montage effect. Sotiris walks behind his father in the funeral procession. "A bird spiralled through sky" (p. 223). A martlet bird, for whatever the information is worth, has no feet, sleeps on the wind, and dies when and if it lands on earth.

Another novel set in Greece which is not a thriller rife with shock and violence is Thomas Doulis's *The Quarries of Sicily* (1969).[26] In it a young American, Gordon Warrington, "has discovered the writing of an elderly Greek genius and made it his life's work. He has lived on the small Greek island of Chios for five years, as admirer, translator, friend, and would-be biographer of the master. Now a film producer arrives to discuss a $2 million film to be based on one of the old man's books."[27] This quotation from the *Book-of-the-Month Club News* states in part the gist of the novel. That a young American goes to Greece where he has unexpected adventures recalls the same plot technique used by George Horton at the turn of the century. Horton's novels employ much peril and melodrama, whereas *The Quarries of Sicily* has less action and more substance.

At the port of Chios the *T.S.S. Kolokotronis*, named for the Greek revolutionary hero, will soon arrive, bringing an American film producer, Hy Gainsborough. Gordon Warrington waits for him at a coffeehouse on the quay where he talks with Niko, an old waiter. In power now are the fascist colonels, led by George Papadopou-

los. Democracy has been crushed, the press censored, private life
invaded, and, Gordon feels, culture has been set back at least a
decade. Niko reveals that Stamos Patrinos, Gordon's idol, has been
stifled by both the political and the literary establishment in Athens. Only because of Gordon's interest and work on the manuscripts has Patrinos's reputation begun to rise. Niko and other
Chiotes highly respect Gordon for making their local genius
known to the world. He ponders the nature of the modern Greeks:

> In the preface to *Greece* by William Miller, Gordon read the
> perpetual complaint of the Greek scholar and philhellene:
> trying to say something final about contemporary Greece was
> a task resembling the web of Penelope—"what was set down
> as the existing situation in the manuscript may require modi-
> fication in the proof sheets and contradiction before publica-
> tion." That was written in 1928, and Gordon could attest to its
> truth almost forty years later. The Greeks, he had discovered
> in his almost five years in their country, were a restless, willful,
> and gifted people, ready at any time to ignore something of
> great value merely because they had tired of it. (p. 14)

As a case in point, the works of Patrinos were ignored in Greece
until foreigners abroad praised *The Quarries of Sicily*, which Gordon translated and had published in both England and America.
Now, as the *Kolokotronis* appears, a new phase may begin in Patrinos's resurrection—even greater renown via the film. During his
conversation with Gainsborough Gordon explains why the Greeks
blame the CIA for the fascist regime. To Gordon's dismay, Gainsborough's conception of the film threatens to vulgarize the novel—
the film will "contain a cornucopia of great characters and clashing
ideologies." Gainsborough sees it as only an antiwar story, whereas
it contains much more: it concerns the Athens that wants "to dominate the world, initially for the best of motives, but eventually for
the worst of motives" (p. 26). The story is also about the disastrous
Athenian invasion of Sicily during the Peloponnesian wars, after
which Athens rapidly declines.

In the harbor they see the *Navarino III*, the flagship of Basil Pelekoudas, described as "the biggest shipowner in the world," and a
Chiote. Gordon admits to Gainsborough that he has been having
problems writing his own novel. They agree to meet the next day
and pay a visit to Stamos Patrinos. Gordon returns to his apartment where he finds Margo, his mistress, waiting for him. She is a

Greek-American girl, also from Pennsylvania like himself, now married to Gino Favloglou. Their talk provides more exposition and foreshadowing. They mention Madame Chrysanthe Raphides, who nurses a great hatred for Patrinos, for reasons that Gordon feels are political but suspects go deeper—to a time when perhaps the two were lovers. Also mentioned by Margo is the offer to produce the film of *The Quarries* by the great Carlo Patriarchi. Patriarchi has the art, but Gainsborough has the money, thus posing a critical choice that Gordon may soon have to make. He wonders how much Madame Raphides will do to scuttle the entire project.

Gordon and Margo also talk about modern Greek music. The Greeks are "too political a race" to believe in art for art's sake. Gordon recalls the great battle over language when the liberals favored the demotic and the reactionaries the *katharevousa*, the purist speech of the academy. Musical instruments now help to identify one's politics. The guitar (Ionian Islands), the clarinet (northern peasant areas), the lyre (other islands), the *oud* (Greeks from Turkey)—all for tradition and conservatism. "The bouzouki, however, was the instrument of the worker, the proletarian, the sailor, the frequenter of clubs, the urban man" (p. 38). Thus is explained Margo's comment that whenever Platon Favloglou hears the bouzouki, "he sees Communist ideology everywhere." Even sex, Gordon muses, may have some basis in politics. How else would a doctrinaire view the actions of Margo? "Spoiled Greek-American daughter-in-law of wealthy shipowner, disaffected by the reactionary attitudes of the family she has married into, attempts to hold onto her self-respect by indulging in an affair with a dedicated, politically neutral American, an admirer, student, and translator of a Greek leftist. Eros in a search for psychic equilibrium?"

As Gordon goes to meet Gainsborough, for a visit to the home of Patrinos, the author recounts how five years earlier Gordon had learned Greek, "discovered" Patrinos, and had gone to Chios to begin their fruitful literary association. Although Margo is his mistress, he also likes the daughter of Patrinos, Rhea. Patrinos reveals that he has a new work-in-progress. More important at the moment is that Gainsborough does indeed fail to grasp the deeper meanings of *The Quarries of Sicily*. No doubt the film as he sees it— sensational and topical—would enhance the reputation of Patrinos; but it would probably lack the power and the beauty of the novel.

At the mansion of Madame Raphides Gordon meets the Favlog-

loi and a visiting writer from Athens, the rightist Sophocles Sa-
pounas. In her early sixties Madame Raphides is still very impressive. Her sister Nina had been Patrinos's first wife. The Favloglou
whom Gordon cuckolds, Gino, is also there. "The elder Favloglou,
it seemed, had developed an interest in the film, not in an aesthetic
sense, certainly, but as an area for investment" (p. 95). In that respect Madame Raphides fishes for information about the plans for
The Quarries of Sicily. Gordon vehemently defends Patrinos against
the charge, leveled by Madame Raphides and supported by Sa-
pounas, that Patrinos is a Communist. Even Platon, the magnate,
claims that he fears only men of action, not idealists like Patrinos.
As a matter of fact, Gordon knows, "Stamos was hated by both the
Royalists and the Communists" (p. 101). A free thinker, Patrinos
had something in his vast achievement to offend everyone. Gainsborough is distressed to find Patrinos so controversial. The evening with Madame Raphides ends on a mysterious question posed
by Gino Favloglou: where did Stamos Patrinos get the 500,000 to
700,000 drachmas needed to pay in cash for his house and surrounding land? Gainsborough has a dreadful moment—fearing
the money had come from Soviet Russia.

The character Alcibiades creates friction between Gordon and
Gainsborough; Gordon regards the Athenian traitor as central to
The Quarries of Sicily, but Gainsborough does not.

> If Alcibiades were in, so were ideas Patrinos considered cru-
> cial and important for audiences, particularly those in America
> [relevant to the Viet Nam War]. With Alcibiades came dema-
> gogic speeches, came greed in idealistic phraseology, came the
> illogic that seemed so rational, came—finally—a hypocrisy
> that was doubly threatening, dangerous both to the listener
> who believed it and to the hypocrite who soon began believing
> himself. (p. 108)

Patrinos defends reason against the irrational that leads to wars in
Sicily and Viet Nam. Gordon also disagrees with Gainsborough
over the use of Spain as a setting for the film. Why not Sicily?

Gordon takes the time to inform Gainsborough about the para-
doxical literary career of Patrinos. He mentions various titles and
their fates, such as the early play *Alcibiades* that created lifelong
enemies for its author. He spent years in virtual exile—very much
like Nikos Kazantzakis, of whom Patrinos reminds one in various
important respects. They talk of Nina, the sister of Madame Ra-

phides who married Patrinos; and Gordon still wonders what happened among the three to cause Madame Raphides's undying
hatred. In fact, Margo tells Gordon that Madame Raphides has
talked Platon Favloglou out of backing *The Quarries of Sicily*. Nor
would *any* "Greek money" be available after Platon's refusal.

With this new problem in mind, Gordon goes to see Stamos Patrinos, at whose home he talks to Rhea because the master is out.
Rhea mentions a secret weapon that her father could use to get the
money from the Favloglou, but she does not know exactly what it
is. It seems from what Rhea saw as a child that Basil Pelekoudas,
the shipowner, had given them their present house out of respect
for Patrinos. She hands Gordon the finished manuscript of her
father's latest book—*The Lizard God*—dedicated to Gordon Warrington. The volume puzzles and dismays Gordon, for it negates
all the positive values hitherto held by Patrinos. *The Lizard God* is a
vision without faith, without hope, whose protagonist, Claudius
Nicanor, realizes that "every temple man builds will fall and the
lizards will fight to the death on all our consecrated altars." Patrinos, it seems, has "reverted to the enemy" (p. 133).

Margo, on the other hand, loves *The Lizard God*. She argues with
Gordon, whose idol has become just another prophet of despair.
He confronts Patrinos with his disillusionment; and the old Greek
writer declares that the book, in effect, wrote itself, so strongly was
he seized by the creative process. To be honest with himself and
his art, he had to write the book. In talking with Patrinos, Gordon
admits the problems with his own novel. His elder advises him to
let "the beasts" run loose for awhile, that perhaps he has them too
tightly locked up. Patrinos convinces Gordon that he, Gordon,
lives an alienated life without being aware of the alienation. Since
he is gathering material for a definitive biography of Patrinos,
Gordon questions him about his wife Nina and Madame Raphides.
Gordon promises to translate and publish *The Lizard God*. Patrinos
reveals that the present Madame Raphides, Nina's sister, was his
mistress for two years in Paris. Nina would not agree to a divorce.
These and other details are contained in a box to be opened after
Patrinos dies. Gordon and Rhea kiss.

Mentioning to Platon Favloglou the "Paris years" of scandal (if
published in the biography), Gordon blackmails the tycoon into
changing his mind about backing *The Quarries of Sicily*. He brings
the contract, which includes one hundred thousand dollars for Patrinos himself, to the author for his signature. Gordon, Patrinos,

and Rhea discuss the pros and cons of letting Gainsborough produce the film. The decision rests with Patrinos to choose Gainsborough or the better artist, Carlo Patriarchi. In the end Patrinos
takes Patriarchi—a Sicilian with a Greek name. "The purest of
Greek" (p. 174).

Novels such as *The Quarries of Sicily* refer the reader to the geographic and cultural roots of the Greek experience that flourished,
modified and often anguished, on the rich American soil. Owing
to the great Depression, that soil is arid and seemingly cursed in
The Tyrants (1977), Charles E. Jarvis' sequel to his earlier *Zeus Has
Two Urns*.[28] The two novels juxtapose time and place, yet differ by
concentrating on different characters—the first on the Greek boy,
Socrates Genos, the second on the *kafetzi* (coffeehouse owner) and
politician, Peisistratus Zacharias, and on Bishop Marterios, a powerful Greek Orthodox bishop who is eventually dethroned. Both
novels feature the same visit to Cabot City (Lowell, Massachusetts)
of Franklin D. Roosevelt during his first run for the presidency.
The vast textile mills along the Merrimack River, called both Merit
and Boott in the fiction, lie idle, in silent and bitter testimony to
the temporary failure of the American Dream. The ethnic dimension in *The Tyrants* does not embrace heritage and customs, except
for background details to explain the effort of the Greeks to gain
political power. In dramatizing the bitter struggle to oust Bishop
Marterios, the novel faithfully reflects the historic and long-per-
sisting schism in Greek Towns everywhere between the Royalists
and the Venizelists. The Greek immigrants imported virulent controversy along with their beloved olive oil, olives, *retsina*, and *feta*
cheese.

Jarvis begins *The Tyrants* with a description of how the textile
mills affect the Greeks of Cabot City. The aspiring politician,
"Strati" Zacharias, leads the discussion to the Irish who control city
hall. They, too, he says, were once despised as peasants and out-
casts; but they came in large numbers and eventually realized their
potential power. "So they organized; they combined their large
number of votes with their ability to talk fast and often, until finally, at the turn of this century, Cabot City, hitherto Yankee-held
and Yankee-led, had its first Irish-Catholic mayor" (p. 11). In the
current mayoral election, the incumbent, Jim Bailey, is trying to
ward off a strong challenge from Leo Boudreau, who represents
the ethnic/political ambitions of the French-Canadians. If the
Greeks had an organization, they could swing the election one way

or the other. Despite a speech in comic broken English from Zacharias, Bailey loses to Boudreau.

The spring of the great presidential election year arrives in Cabot City. Spurred on by Zacharias, the Greeks after much debate set up the Diogenes Democratic Club. The main opposition comes from the rich Greek bootlegger Panos Maskatis. A Republican, he detests Roosevelt because his victory would end prohibition and put all bootleggers out of business. Although Maskatis leaves the meeting livid with anger, Zacharias still hopes to get some of his money for the new club. He thinks of Maskatis as a *bastard* and a *Turk*. A big moment for the Diogenes Democratic Club arrives with the visit of Roosevelt, who speaks to a huge crowd from the train. This event is seen in *Zeus Has Two Urns* from the viewpoint of the boy Socrates. Zacharias and his troupe manage to raise their banner near enough up front to be noticed by the candidate.

The Greeks of Cabot City celebrate Roosevelt's victory "in true Olympian style." They eat, talk, drink, and sing.

> The entire world of Greek food lay before them and all the odors that it emitted rendered the air into an overpowering typhoon of garlic and well cooked, almost burned meat. There was *souvlakia* (lamb on the stick), with garlic; there were stuffed peppers, with garlic; there was roast chicken, with garlic; there was baked fish, with garlic; there was roast pork, with garlic; there was a cataract of soups, all with garlic. And there was a huge platter in the middle of the table that contained what looked like farina; but it was really the dessert: garlic pudding. This avalanche of food that rolled toward them was hurried on its course by a variety of beverages that were all brewed within one hundred feet of their feast. (p. 64)

The occasion elicits stories and reminiscences, among them a reference to an important episode in early Greek-American history—the return to their homeland of many immigrants to serve with the Greek Army during the Balkan wars of 1912–13. Some, like the character Manoli, left from Cabot City and returned to resume "their transplanted existence," and those who had not served "always regarded these ex-soldiers with deference and a kind of subtle awe" (p. 66).

From the New Deal of Roosevelt come a series of agencies designed to help put the unemployed back to work. Led by Peisistratus Zacharias, the Greeks make their initial political move and secure their share of the available jobs and patronage. Since the 1930s, of course, the city of Lowell has had several mayors of Greek descent, including a Greek woman; and the commonwealth itself has had a governor of Greek descent, Michael Dukakis. The second half of *The Tyrants*, however, deals not with politics as such but with the religious politics that bitterly splits the Greek community. In this ethnic combat Zacharias is again very involved, since to dominate the board of Saint Sophia Church would clearly give him the broad base that he needs. An Irish architect, Kevin Shanahan, had built for the Greeks a cathedral copied from the venerable Saint Sophia of Constantinople. To it came Bishop Marterios, a renegade and a refugee who "had remained unshakable in his refusal to stop using the pulpit in Greece as a political spear aimed at the heart of Eleutherios Venizelos" (p. 90).

Since Cabot City (Lowell) has emerged as the leading Greek-American center of Boott Valley (Merrimack), whoever heads its cathedral wields great power over the entire region. What had seemed a special honor to have a real bishop eventually turns into a nightmare. Bishop Marterios fills pulpits with satellite priests, some of whom are incompetent and morally unfit. The bishop's counterpart in New York City "accused Marterios of simony, the selling of ordinations for the aggrandizement of his personal wealth" (p. 94). Eventually Zacharios succeeds in getting the president of the church board to move to replace Bishop Marterios with a young Father Silas of Boston. Two fiercely hostile factions rend the community of Saint Sophia. At first the adherents of Marterios seize the church, are driven out by a court order, then are violently repulsed when they return in force. The defiant bishop is physically attacked and loses his scepter. Defeated, he leaves Cabot City, as does his replacement, Father Silas. His rival in New York is also recalled. A new prelate arrives in America, who in time unites all the churches under one supreme archdiocese. "Thus would the religious war fought in Cabot City," Jarvis writes, "prove the monumental step toward the unification of the Greek Orthodox Church in the United States" (p. 147).

The final chapter of *The Tyrants* sums up the political career of Peisistratus Zacharias who, by his support of Jim Bailey, helps to forge the powerful Irish-Greek alliance that runs Cabot City. As his reward Zacharias is appointed chief assistant to the director of the public works department. When the city receives federal projects, he as King of the Greeks, with ten thousand votes in his pocket, is able to dispense jobs to his compatriots. He tells them: "We will no longer be the damn Greeks, the stupid Greeks. We will be a force to be reckoned with and the city hall doors will be wide open to us!" (p. 158). Years pass. Zacharias hires someone else to run his coffeehouse while he wields his clout. "Like that tyrant of Ancient Athens, Peisistratus, he would bestow gifts and goods to the populace, but always with the colossal conviction that he alone had the power and the wisdom to set a straight course" (p. 160). At last he too, like Bishop Marterios, is toppled.

This novel by Jarvis illustrates that by the 1930s the Greek-American minority had already achieved some measure of social and political integration. During that same turbulent decade President Franklin D. Roosevelt reminded the nation that we, the people, are all descendants of immigrants, thereby widening awareness of the multiethnic basis of our society. In the 1930s, for a character like Zacharias, the American Dream materializes as political clout insured by ten thousand Greek votes. Perhaps nothing could be more American than to be a Zacharias functioning as a cog in the real machinery of our political system, and perhaps nothing could be more Greek than to have Zacharias compared with Peisistratus. The romanticism of Byronic philhellenism that helped to liberate Greece remains for the modern Greek a valued passion to recall. From it and the popular struggle flowed the Greek revolution, nationhood, the heroes of land and sea now long celebrated in poetry, fiction, and song. From the romanticism of the American Dream has flowed the establishment within the United States of a strong, energetic, often prosperous, often exciting Greek community.

≈≈≈≈≈≈≈
17
≈≈≈≈≈≈≈

CONCLUSION

THE GREEK EXPERIENCE in American fiction has required sixteen chapters of comment and resumé to record, even though Greek-Americans number hardly more than two million. The resumés are not plot summaries as such, since they deal mainly with Greek characters and not others. They provide the concrete details for the term *ethnic experience*. Ethnic groups of greater size have their own extensive reflection in novels, short stories, and plays. Libraries are filled with interesting but often neglected works that illuminate vital fragments of ethnic behavior, which, when added up, give much reality to the abstraction *America*. Now that the ethnic dimension in American literature and native studies have become increasingly popular subjects in education, scholars of ethnic origins have begun to investigate the ways in which their particular ethnicity factor operates in American fiction. Their research and criticism appear in journals such as *MELUS*, whose title is an abbreviation of *Multi-Ethnic Literature of the United States*.

From the foregoing sixteen chapters one may well conclude that the Hellenic tradition is thriving in American publications. Indeed, a rather astonishing list of authors, most of them non-Greek, have used Greek characters in both major and minor roles for a wide variety of dramatic and thematic purposes. Several years ago *Hellenes and Hellions* had its beginning in curiosity about whether modern Greeks are stereotyped by fiction writers or not. After all, the early immigrants were often greeted with bigotry, ridicule, trickery, and violence. They were called *ginees*, *wops*, greaseballs, and other derogatory names. Yet no generalized or recurrent stereotype has surfaced among the many assorted Greek villains. For that matter, the positive Greek hero also follows no set pattern. When thoroughly Americanized and middle class, he is hardly Greek at all, except in name. Of all the fictional Greeks, the most stereotyped is the "fabulous Greek shipowner" with his vast wealth, power, villas, art collections, chicanery, and mistresses.

Many Greeks do, of course, own restaurants; but a common occupation does not necessarily make them all the same.

With the question of ethnic stereotyping out of the way, the work of *Hellenes and Hellions* went on to become as complete a survey as possible of the many functions of Greeks in our literature. The bulk of relevant material found was totally unexpected, since existing bibliographies revealed only the tip of the proverbial iceberg. It is difficult to determine how much should be made of the ethnic dimension in the overall achievement of our literature. On the other hand, such a dimension does exist both as subject matter and aesthetic form—for the many ethnic components of our society—and it is beginning to receive serious critical attention.

The recording of the Greek experience in *Hellenes and Hellions* has itself been an experience, a voyage of discovery to find relevant books and the ethnicity they contained. The effort has educated the author, first, with respect to his own Hellenism. Some aspects of that new knowledge had almost the force of revelation. For example, the rebirth of modern Greece meant different things to different Americans. For some the Greek Revolution caused disruption of established trade relations with the Ottoman Empire. Indeed, some travelers to the Levant favored the affluent Turks, although Moslems, to the impoverished though Christian Greeks. For various church missions, revived Greece became a target-area for conversion from Greek Orthodoxy to Protestantism. Perhaps the most prevalent attitude of American travelers toward Greece was the assumption that Greeks were degenerate. By that they meant sneaky, dishonest, uneducated, and unclean. The most negative blamed the basic Greek nature for this condition, which offered little hope that the Greeks could govern themselves or escape from their "barbaric" religion. The most positive blamed the alleged degeneracy on four hundred years of Turkish domination. In time, these Philhellenes believed, the Greeks might once again show some resemblance to their illustrious ancestors.

A second benefit of the necessary research was the opportunity to examine the work of worthy but forgotten writers, among them George Horton and Demetra Vaka Brown. In recent years, as evidenced in *MELUS* and elsewhere, the buried literature of native Indians has undergone a somewhat similar process of rediscovery. The result of such findings can only be the further enrichment of our culture, the widening of our awareness, and perhaps even the deepening of our compassion. It was a pleasant revelation to learn that George Horton, a latter-day philhellene, had filled a sizable shelf with books about modern Greeks. Unlike earlier philhellenes such as Dr. Samuel Gridley Howe, who felt the need to defend the Greek character, Horton accepts that character without apology and delights in explaining it to others. His prose books *In Argolis* and *Home of Nymphs and Vampires* stand as durable and enjoyable accounts of Greece. His novel *The Tempting of Father Anthony* transcends in aesthetic quality his several romances and deserves to be reprinted as a minor classic. To discover even one such classic for American literature seems reward enough for the labor of writing *Hellenes and Hellions*.

However, one may cite a number of other works that deserve similar recovery to make them accessible to a new generation of readers. Surely the immense industry of Demetra Vaka should not go forever unnoticed; yet her autobiography still languishes as installments in separate issues of *Athene*, and apparently nobody reads her books. In her prose Vaka undertook to introduce the peoples of the Levant to Western readers. Of Greek descent, she championed, in works like *Haremlik*, the liberation of Turkish women from their oppressed social status. Time has tarnished the topicality of polemics written during World War I that sought to expose German machinations in the Levant. Yet it cannot diminish the charm of *Delarah*, a novel about two girls, one Greek and one Turkish, bound together by mutual peril, understanding, and love. Indirectly, Vaka pleads in *Delarah* for reconciliation between these rival cultures, Christian and Moslem; yet, in the end, she favors the Christian by having Delarah flee her Turkish heritage and take a Greek name. Not only does the novel deserve a reprint, but Demetra Vaka herself deserves a full and well-researched biography.

The writing of *Hellenes and Hellions* unearthed more incidental knowledge about Greek fictional characters than can be mentioned here. Jack London, like Melville before and Eugene O'Neill after him, liked to universalize his themes by the use of ethnic types. It amused my lecture audiences to hear that London, in one of his stories, depicted a Greek belly dancer in the Klondike during the Gold Rush. The first novel with a Greek immigrant as protagonist, *Mr. Achilles* (1912), not only pits him against some Chicago criminals but also allows him a chance to extol his Hellenic tradition. The novel, though not great literature, gives a sympathetic picture of a Greek fruit peddler during a time of widespread bigotry and xenophobia.

As the reader of *Hellenes and Hellions* knows, interspersed throughout the text are examples of firsts that involve Greek characters, one of the most interesting being Hammett's Nick Charles in *The Thin Man*. The first of a long line of famous private eyes is a Greek whose name is Charalambides. Why Hammett has Greeks in his fiction is not aesthetically clear, except that perhaps they lend color, exoticism, and mystery to his plots.

Still another incidental bit of knowledge concerns soldiers such as Kantaylis in *The Big War* and Reynolds in *Never So Few*. Just as classical figures like Odysseus, Achilles, Philip, and Alexander established ancient archetypes of the warrior, so also Kantaylis and Reynolds symbolize the latest type of soldier—tough, amoral, often sadistic, never protesting the death-dealing institution of war. These are only some of the many increments of knowledge garnered by the research for *Hellenes and Hellions*.

That authors of Greek descent should employ Greek characters seems natural enough, but what proved surprising was the large number of non-Greek authors who used such characters. We can certainly attribute much of the nineteenth-century awareness of Hellenism to the classical education then prevalent. In our own time, although the teaching of Greek and Latin has diminished, the many immortal works from those two illustrious cultures are still very much alive, still very potent influences. But they do not directly explain why Carson McCullers has created Antonapoulos in *The Heart Is a Lonely Hunter* or why Robert Penn Warren has used Pappy in *The Cave*, or why Greeks have appeared as characters in dozens of other contemporary novels. Then one might ask, why not? Their ethnic tradition is replete with myths, legends, archetypes, great events, weird cults, wild humor, and dark tragedies; name a proclivity of thought or action and the Greek may have a name for it. If there exists a wandering Jew, he has a counterpart in the wandering Greek, romantic, often passionate, restless for experience. Like David daring to confront Goliath, the Greek has on three historic occasions challenged powers far beyond his own: first, the Persian Empire, that gave the world Thermopylae, Marathon, and Salamis; second, the Ottoman Empire, the revolt from which restored nationhood; and, third, the Nazi occupation, during which the Greek resistance set an early example for other oppressed peoples. The above may be some of the underlying reasons why so many non-Greek authors have used Greeks in their fiction.

The degree of ethnicity shown by these characters varies from author to author. As has been noted, many of them are Greek in name only. A few non-Greek writers, from Horton to Auslander, attempt to round out their characters with concrete ethnic detail. A novel on Tarpon Springs like *The Islanders* begins to compare in such detail with *The Wing and the Thorn* by Roxanne Cotsakis. The reason may be that Tarpon Springs itself, the setting, is so thoroughly a Greek enclave that verisimilitude depends upon ethnic realism. Some writers of Greek descent, of course, eschew the use of fellow Greeks in at least part of their fiction. No matter what his origin, every writer is free to respond to whatever inspiration motivates him. That so many Greek-American authors do employ ethnic characters, actions, and situations means they are following the simple dictum of writing about what they know best—families, friends, themselves. In doing so they collectively preserve a system of ethnic customs, rites, beliefs, values, sacraments, prejudices, folk traditions, remedies, and much else that may eventually disappear, or remain as mere quaintness, in the inveterate process of cultural homogeneity. The composing of *Hellenes and Hellions* has, it is hoped, performed the service of documenting much of this material and citing sources where even more of it may be found.

Another service may well be in informing the Greek-American community that so much fiction about modern Greeks does exist, and that a great deal of it is worth reading. We are in a literary period when many scholars are publishing or preparing studies on ethnic image and self-image. It would be difficult to find common denominators in the ethnic self-image created by Greek writers. The picture seems too fragmented, the characters too varied, their natures too disparate in spite of their general drive to succeed, to survive, to be happy.

Depending upon place of parental origin, a Greek is more than a Greek; he is also a Macedonian, a Cretan, a Thracian, an Athenian, a Spartan, an Epirote, a Cypriot, a Maniat, not to mention the particular village or island of his ancestors. Once in America he eventually breaks away from Greek Town and spreads throughout the city and suburbs.

Not overly religious, he does not allow the Orthodox Church to govern his secular behavior; yet he has built beautiful and plush churches in this affluent period. Very often the old bromide is still true, "When Greek meets Greek, they start a restaurant." But equally true has been the Greek's avid movement into the professions, into other types of business, and lately into politics and government.

Such a trend toward individuality occurs both in reality and in fiction. Therefore, if the question is asked, Do the Greek writers create their own stereotype? the answer would have to be no. Some of them do have a certain style, a predilection, a habitual mode of conception. The most visible Greek writer, Harry Mark Petrakis, tends to supercharge his characters, to give them enormous appetites for experience, to make them bigger than life. Yet one cannot say that excessive vitality constitutes a stereotype. We do not have, for example, a tribe or cult inspired by the rogue Zorba.

The better novels contain much of real value for the student of immigrant/ethnic literature. New critical terms besides *ethnicity factor* have begun to enter our working vocabulary. Another term is *interface*, which is defined in *MELUS* by Joseph T. Skerrett in a manner quite relevant to *Hellenes and Hellions*.

> An interface is what happens when two systems meet. A culture is a system; a poem is a system; every critical commentary or interpretation is a system (or part of one).
>
> An interface is engendered when Greek meets Greek, but a more exemplary interface occurs when Greek meets Turk. Between two Greeks the dialogue is likely to be familiar, casual, comfortable, phatic. But when Greek meets Turk, both are likely to do and say things that reach beyond their individual systems to make the new and unfamiliar relationship work.
>
> The dialogue engendered by an interface embodies a new level of relationships between the two systems involved. Something happens in this dialogue: something new comes into existence. Without altering the integrity of either system, Greek and Turk have their consciousness enlarged.
>
> This is surely a primary goal of an ethnically sensitive American literary criticism.[1]

When Greek meets Turk, one may add, the quality of their encounter may depend upon awareness of the hatreds, massacres, and wars that have marred their mutual past. On the other hand, a Greek might say, "I'm *filled* with awareness of all that, but yet I've never met a Turk I didn't like." Such a situation indicates that interface of *systems* can be both subtle and complicated.

Those fictional characters who are essentially Greek in name only can hardly be said to interface at all. Their actions have no ethnic significance, except the general impression they leave with the reader. A mass killer with a Jewish name hurts all Jews; a black rapist hurts all blacks. Charlie Stavros in John Updike's *Rabbit Redux*, a Greek, is a "good guy" who provides therapeutic sex for his best friend's wife. Pappy in Robert Penn Warren's *The Cave*, though not very ethnic, nevertheless helps to support a positive image of Greek-Americans.

A true interface results from a meaningful encounter between two systems, as broadly defined by Skerrett. The participants must be conscious of the clash of cultures and act in accordance with the inner logic of their predicament. Thus Petrakis, in both his first short story, "Pericles on 31st Street," and his first novel, *Lion at My Heart*, depends upon a genuine ethnic interface for plot and theme. In the one a Greek challenges a non-Greek landlord and wins; in the other, a Greek father damns his son for marrying an Irish girl.

Most of Petrakis's fiction, however, depends upon Greek Town for setting, character, plot, and theme. The impression left is that of a rather hermetic community with relatively few outside contacts. In this romantic and exotic world his Greeks are often free to grow—as Kurt Vonnegut, Jr., says—to be fourteen feet tall. The reader has to draw his own conclusions about the ethnic significance of these often tragic, often comical, often mad Greeks. What they mean to American culture is not defined through an intimate interface with that culture.

All the fiction mentioned in *Hellenes and Hellions*, good and bad, contributes to the total tally of Greek characters created by American writers. At some point quantity perhaps turns into quality, and we wonder again why such a small ethnic minority should enjoy such a large presence in our literature. Interest in this and related questions has developed at a time when the ethnic, racial, and native aspects of our literature are getting the scholarly and critical attention they deserve. Scholars representing other groups may find *Hellenes and Hellions* useful as a means of assessing their own ethnic presence in our fiction.

In a more detailed and concrete way, the ethnicity factor expands for the formal critic the area of his expertise. Much has already been said or implied about the value to history, sociology, and psychology of the immigrant/ethnic novel. Works such as *My Antonia, Giants in the Earth, The Jungle, Call It Sleep, Christ in Con-*

crete, and *Pocho* dramatize the immigrant experience far more vividly than any prose can do. More specifically, however, the ethnicity factor can serve a number of important aesthetic needs.

For the structuralist critic the fact of being Greek provides the basic form, the Platonic shape, that organizes all the parts into a final complete and organic whole. Ariadne Thompson's *The Octagonal Heart* is an excellent example of how "structure follows ethnicity," as a Greek girl determines to marry the non-Greek of her desire. The quality of being Greek serves for the novel essentially the same structural purpose as "journey to the Promised Land" serves for Steinbeck's *The Grapes of Wrath*. The novel is further structured and enriched by the author's nostalgia for a world long gone. Another fine example of ethnic structuralism is George Christy's *All I Could See from Where I Stood*, in which the boy Stephanos, from beginning almost to the end, reacts strenuously to the family pressure to remain Greek.

To the extent that tension, mood, characterization, archetype, and symbol are formal attributes the ethnicity factor must be included alongside other such attributes in the making and meaning of fiction. Just to mention the first, *tension*, the following are some of its recurrent sources in the immigrant/ethnic novel: the hypnotic lure of the American Dream, the trauma of departing from loved ones, the perilous journey, the first impressions of the New World, the problems of initial adjustment, the nostalgia for the mother country, the encounters with bigotry, the alienation, the pressure to Americanize, the guilt of betraying one's heritage, the monomania to succeed, the clash between "foreign" parents and American-born children, the changing, more liberated status of women, and the internal hang-ups and psychic flaws exacerbated by one or more of the above factors.

The writing of *Hellenes and Hellions* has in many ways been fun, in some filled with anguish, and in others often quite tiring labor. A scholar can dive into the vast sea of books and come up, like a Greek sponger, with his own precious conchs and pearls. Every scholar knows with what joy he greets a valuable and unexpected find that adds immeasurably to his endeavor. A modicum of anguish remains as a result of failure to track down a promising lead. Was it a wrong bit of information or did James O'Neill, the father of Eugene, really act in a play called *When Greek Meets Greek*? After many years on this kind of a project a researcher has to say, "This is it, enough. Whatever remains can be done in an addendum, an article, or left for others." One then pushes away the typewriter, pauses to rest a moment, stacks the manuscript neatly, admires its bulk, and begins to wonder what has been done, say, by the Armenians.

NOTES*

CHAPTER ONE

1. Terence Spencer, *Fair Greece, Sad Relic* (New York, 1973). Some of the same attitudes are expressed in *The Greek Phoenix* (New York, 1972) by Joseph Braddock, another English author. The page numbers in the text refer to Spencer.

2. Theodore Saloutos, *The Greeks in the United States* (Cambridge, Mass., 1964).

3. See Epaminondas P. Panagopoulos, *New Smyrna* (Gainesville, 1966).

4. Stephen A. Larrabee, *Hellas Observed* (New York, 1957).

5. Ibid., dust jacket.

6. Ibid., p. 3.

7. Ibid., p. 6.

8. Alexander Papas, and Marios Byron Raizis, *American Poets and the Greek Revolution* (Thessaloniki, 1971).

9. Fitz-Greene Halleck, *The Poetical Works of Fitz-Greene Halleck*, ed. James Grant Wilson (1869; reprint ed., New York, 1969), p. 17.

10. Some but not all of these works are discussed by Larrabee.

11. Quoted in Isaac Goldberg, *Major Noah: American-Jewish Pioneer* (Philadelphia, 1936), p. 185.

12. Ibid.

13. Ibid., p. 184.

14. William S. Cardell, *Story of Jack Halyard, the Sailor Boy; or, the Virtuous Family* (Philadelphia, 1825).

15. Larrabee, p. 53.

16. Ibid.

17. Samuel Gridley Howe, *An Historical Sketch of the Greek Revolution* (New York, 1828).

18. Ibid., p. xxii.

19. Ibid., p. vi.

20. Ibid., xxii.

21. Henry A. V. Post, *A Visit to Greece and Constantinople* (London, 1830).

22. Nathaniel Parker Willis, *Pencillings by the Way*, 3 vols. (London, 1835), 2:2.

23. The literary prominence given to Bozzaris may obscure the fact that the Greek revolution produced many legendary heroes and martyrs.

24. John L. Stephens, *Incidents of Travel in Greece, Turkey, Russia, and Poland* (Edinburgh, 1839).

25. Walter Colton, *Visit To Constantinople and Athens* (New York, 1836). The edition used here is *Land and Lee in the Bosphorus and Aegean*, ed. Henry T. Cheever (1851).

---

*Page numbers following quoted material in the text refer to the immediately cited source unless otherwise noted.

26. William Cullen Bryant, *Letters from the East* (New York, 1869), p. 219.

27. J. Ross Browne, *Yusef, or The Journey of the Frangi* (New York, 1853), p. 87.

28. David F. Dorr, *A Colored Man Round the World* (Cleveland, 1858).

29. S. G. W. Benjamin, *The Turk and the Greek* (New York, 1867).

30. Samuel Gridley Howe, *The Cretan Refugees and Their American Helpers* (Boston, 1868).

31. Larrabee, p. 294.

32. Ibid., p. 274.

33. Herman Melville, *Journal up the Straits*, ed. Raymond Weaver (New York, 1935).

34. Larrabee, p. 277.

35. Herman Melville, *Clarel*, ed. Walter E. Bezanson (New York, 1960).

36. Ibid., p. x.

37. Walt Whitman, *Leaves of Grass* (New York, 1931), pp. 409–15.

38. Mark Twain, *The Innocents Abroad* (New York, 1922).

39. Edmond About, *The King of the Mountains*, trans. Mary L. Booth (Boston, 1861).

40. Anthony Hope, *Phroso* (New York, 1899).

41. Stephanos Theodoros Xenos, *Andronike, The Heroine of the Greek Revolution*, trans. Edwin A. Grosvenor (Boston, 1897).

42. Hallie Ermine Rives, *The Castaway* (Indianapolis, 1904).

43. A recent novel based on Byron's life is Frederick Prokosch's *The Missolonghi Manuscript*, a tough-minded and bold version that depicts Byron's bisexual proclivities. See ch. 16 for a summary.

CHAPTER TWO

1. Lillian Gilkes, *Cora Crane* (Bloomington, 1960), p. 111.

2. Ibid., p. 671.

3. Stephen Crane, "Death and the Child," in *The Complete Short Stories and Sketches of Stephen Crane*, ed. Thomas A. Gullason (Garden City, 1963), pp. 392–408.

4. Id., *Active Service*, in *The Complete Novels of Stephen Crane*, ed. Thomas A. Gullason (Garden City, 1967).

5. Demetrios M. Michalaros, "George Horton and His Work," *Athene* 7 (Summer 1946):7.

6. George Horton, "Aphroessa," in *Poems of an Exile* (Indianapolis, 1931), pp. 187–248.

7. Id., "To My Wife," ibid., p. 16.

8. Id., *Constantine: A Tale of Greece under King Otho* (Chicago, 1897).

9. Id., *A Fair Brigand* (Chicago, 1899).

10. Id., *Like Another Helen* (Indianapolis, 1900).

11. Id., *The Tempting of Father Anthony* (Chicago, 1901).

12. Id., *In Argolis* (Chicago, 1902).

13. Id., *Home of Nymphs and Vampires* (Indianapolis, 1929).

14. Id., *In Argolis*, p. viii.

15. Ibid., p. xi.

16. Id., *The Monk's Treasure* (Indianapolis, 1905).

17. Michalaros, "George Horton and His Work," p. 5.

18. C. J. Lampos, "Three Novels of George Horton," *Athene* 7 (Summer 1946):14.

19. Kenneth Brown and Demetra Vaka, *The First Secretary* (New York, 1907).

20. Demetra Vaka, *Bribed to Be Born* (New York, 1951).

21. See ch. 14 for a discussion of *Delarah.*

22. Vaka, *Bribed to Be Born,* p. 23.

23. Kenneth Brown, "Demetra Vaka," *Athene* 9 (Spring 1948):16.

24. Delarof served as governor of Alaska from 1783 to 1790. See Hubert Bancroft, *History of Alaska* (New York, 1959).

25. Jack London, *The God of His Fathers* (Garden City, 1925), p. 17.

26. Ibid., "The Scorn of Women," pp. 252–99.

27. Saloutos, *The Greeks in the United States,* p. 275.

28. London, "The Scorn of Women," p. 252.

29. Id., *The Mutiny of the Elsinore* (New York, 1914).

30. Jeannette Lee, *Mr. Achilles* (New York, 1912).

31. Samuel Hopkins Adams, *Our Square and the People in It* (Freeport, 1970).

32. For the most recent account of the Greek experience in the United States, see Charles C. Moskos, Jr., *Greek Americans: Struggle and Success* (Englewood Cliffs, N.J., 1979).

CHAPTER THREE

1. Seraphim G. Canoutas, *Christopher Columbus: A Greek Nobleman* (New York, 1943).

2. Henry Pratt Fairchild, *Greek Immigration to the United States* (New York, 1911). Later in his life Fairchild supported many Greek causes as a dedicated philhellene.

3. Saloutos, *The Greeks in the United States,* p. viii.

4. Ibid., p. 391.

5. Demetrios A. Michalaros, *Sonnets of an Immigrant* (Chicago, 1930).

6. Elia Kazan, *America America* (New York, 1962).

7. Kazan reports on the subsequent life of Stavros Topouzoglou in his next novel, *The Arrangement.* See ch. 9.

8. Grace E. Marshall, *Eternal Greece* (Rochester, 1938).

9. Mary Vardoulakis, *Gold in the Streets* (New York, 1945).

10. Elmer Grossberg, *Farewell, My Son* (New York, 1946).

11. George Demetrios, *When Greek Meets Greek* (1947; reprint ed., Freeport, N.Y., 1970).

12. Joseph Hatton's *When Greek Meets Greek* is a sentimental romance set during the French revolution and serialized over several months in the mid-1890s by *Leslie's Weekly.* James O'Neill, the father of Eugene, acted in a play of that name. Sir Reginal Leeper's *When Greek Meets Greek* (London, 1950) recounts his experiences during the Greek civil war, 1945–47. Samuel Selvon's "When Greek Meets Greek" is included in *Stories from the Caribbean,* ed. Andrew Salkey (New York, 1968).

13. Jim Dilles, *The Good Thief* (New York, 1959).

14. Theano Papazoglou-Margaris, *Eftihia and Other Stories* (Chicago, 1939).

15. Ibid., "Eftihia," p. 19.

16. Ibid., "The Waitress," p. 85.

17. Ibid., "Our Neighbor," p. 103.
18. Ibid., "The Fiancée of the Prince of Wales," p. 118.
19. Id., *A Tear for Uncle Jimmy* (Athens, 1958).
20. Ibid., "A Tear for Uncle Jimmy," p. 19.
21. Ibid., "Roots," p. 16.
22. Ibid., "Amen," p. 34.
23. Ibid., "In the Fog," p. 59–60.
24. Ibid., "This is America," p. 80.
25. Ibid., "Refuge," p. 115.
26. Ibid., p. 116.
27. Ibid., "The Spark Dies Out," p. 123.
28. Ibid., p. 129.
29. Id., *The Chronicle of Halsted Street* (Athens, 1962).
30. Id., *The Travels of Uncle Plato* (Athens, 1972).
31. Paul Gallico, *Further Confessions of a Story Teller* (Garden City, 1961), pp. 303–16.

CHAPTER FOUR

1. Thomas Doulis, *Disaster and Fiction: Modern Greek Fiction and the Impact of the Asia Minor Disaster of 1922* (Berkeley, 1977).
2. Ernest Hemingway, *In Our Time* (1924; reprint ed., New York, 1958), p. 10.
3. William White, ed., *By-Line: Ernest Hemingway* (New York, 1967), p. 51.
4. Marjorie Housepian, *The Smyrna Affair* (New York, 1971).
5. Richard Reinhardt, *The Ashes of Smyrna* (New York, 1971).
6. McKinlay Kantor, "That Greek Dog," in *The Best American Short Stories, 1942*, ed. Martha Foley (Boston, 1942), pp. 141–55.
7. F. Scott Fitzgerald, *The Great Gatsby* (New York, 1925).
8. Henry Dan Piper, *F. Scott Fitzgerald: A Candid Portrait* (New York, 1962), p. 332.
9. Ernest Hemingway, *The Sun Also Rises* (New York, 1926).
10. James T. Farrell, "The Benefits of American Life," in *The Short Stories of James T. Farrell* (New York, 1934), pp. 302–11.
11. Charles Caldwell Dobie, *San Francisco Adventure* (Freeport, N.Y., 1969).
12. Maxwell Anderson, *Winterset* (1935), act 1, sc. 3.
13. William Saroyan, *The Time of Your Life* (New York, 1939), act 2.
14. Ibid.
15. Id., *Love's Old Sweet Song*, in *Three Plays* (New York, 1940).
16. Ibid., p. 15.
17. Id., "Laughing Sam," in *Little Children* (New York, 1937), pp. 3–12.
18. Id., "The Crusader," ibid., pp. 203–18.
19. Id., "The Only Guy in Town," ibid., pp. 85–98.
20. Id., "The Struggle of Jim Patros with Death," in *Dear Baby* (New York, 1944), pp. 53–60.
21. Ruth McKenney, *My Sister Eileen* (New York, 1938).
22. Joseph Fields and Jerome Chodorov, *My Sister Eileen* (New York, 1938), act 1.
23. Sterling North, *Seven Against the Years* (New York, 1939).

24. Edward Newhouse, "Manny Hirsch," in *Anything Can Happen* (New York, 1941).

25. Philip Freund, "The Young Greek and the Creole," in *The Young Greek and the Creole* (New York, 1944), pp. 95–112.

CHAPTER FIVE

1. Ariadne Thompson, *The Octagonal Heart* (Indianapolis, 1956).
2. Dean Brelis, *My New Found Land* (Boston, 1963).
3. George Christy, *All I Could See from Where I Stood* (Indianapolis, 1963).
4. A. I. Bezzerides, *Thieves' Market* (New York, 1949).
5. Thalia Selz, "The Education of a Queen," *Partisan Review* 28 (1961):552–73, 669–87.
6. Id., "The Death of Anna," *Virginia Quarterly Review* 33 (Spring 1957):262–69.
7. Grace Metalious, *Peyton Place* (New York, 1956).
8. Ibid., p. 134.
9. Ibid., p. 142.
10. Id., *Return to Peyton Place* (New York, 1959), p. 114.
11. Id., *The Tight White Collar* (New York, 1960).
12. Konstantinos Lardas, *A Tree of Man* (Privately printed, n.p., 1968).
13. Id., "The Devil Child," *Atlantic Monthly*, July 1961, pp. 55–56.
14. Ibid., p. 56.
15. Id., "The Bird." *Prairie Schooner* 44 (Winter 1969–70):386.
16. Ibid.
17. Id., "The Broken Wings," *South Dakota Review* 10 (Spring 1972):5–15.
18. Id., "The Usurpation." *Literary Review* 13 (Winter 1969–70):224–35.
19. Id., "The Cypress Trees, the Sun," *Hawaii Review* 1 (Spring 1973):79–86.
20. Ibid., p. 85.
21. Id., "How Beautiful, the Feet," *Descant* 15 (Winter 1971): 9–22.
22. H. L. Mountzoures, *The Empire of Things* (New York, 1968).
23. Id., *The Bridge* (New York, 1972).

CHAPTER SIX

1. See ch. 7.
2. Roxanne Cotsakis, *The Wing and the Thorn* (Atlanta, 1952).
3. Thomas Wolfe, *Look Homeward, Angel* (New York, 1929).
4. Ibid., p. 150.
5. Ibid., p. 280.
6. Id., *Of Time and the River* (New York, 1935).
7. Id., *The Web and the Rock* (New York, 1937).
8. Ibid., p. 52.
9. Carson McCullers, *The Heart Is a Lonely Hunter* (New York, 1967).
10. Robert Penn Warren, *The Cave* (New York, 1959).
11. Shirley Ann Grau, *The Keepers of the House* (New York, 1964), p. 259.

12. Ibid., p. 287.

13. Cotsakis, *The Wing and the Thorn*, p. 8.

14. Daphne Athas, *Entering Ephesus* (New York, 1971), dust jacket.

CHAPTER SEVEN

1. Jennie E. Harris, "Sponge Fishermen of Tarpon Springs," *National Geographic* 91 (January 1947):119–36.

2. George Th. Frantzis, *Strangers at Ithaca: The Story of Tarpon Springs* (St. Petersburg, Fla., 1962), pp. 192–93.

3. Eileen Elita Doering, "A Charm of the Gulf of Mexico Sponge Fishers," *Journal of American Folk-Lore* 52 (1939):123.

4. Both of these articles are cited in Wayne Charles Miller, ed., *A Comprehensive Bibliography for the Study of American Minorities*, 2 vols. (New York, 1976), 1:549.

5. Ahmad Kamal, *Full Fathom Five* (Garden City, 1948).

6. Joseph Auslander and Audrey Wurdeman, *The Islanders* (New York, 1951).

7. Frantzis, *Strangers at Ithaca*, p. 102.

8. Auslander and Wurdeman, *The Islanders*, p. 8.

9. Ibid., p. 2.

10. Frantzis, *Strangers at Ithaca*, p. 107.

11. Auslander and Wurdeman, *The Islanders*, pp. 14–15.

12. Ibid., p. 17.

13. Frantzis, *Strangers at Ithaca*, p. 107.

14. Auslander and Wurdeman, *The Islanders*, p. 13.

15. Harris, "Sponge Fishermen of Tarpon Springs," p. 119.

16. Ibid.

17. Don Tracy, *Bazzaris* (New York, 1965).

18. Frantzis, *Strangers at Ithaca*, p. 60.

19. Ibid., p. 62.

20. Tracy, *Bazzaris*, p. 187.

21. Elia Kazan, *Acts of Love* (New York, 1978).

CHAPTER EIGHT

1. Harry Mark Petrakis, *The Hour of the Bell* (Garden City, 1976).

2. Colin Forbes, *The Heights of Zervos* (New York, 1970).

3. Alistair MacLean, *The Guns of Navarone* (Garden City, 1956).

4. Leon Uris, *The Angry Hills* (New York, 1955).

5. For a novel about an Australian soldier in Greece, see George Johnstone, *Closer to the Sun* (New York, 1960).

6. Uris, *The Angry Hills*, p. 190.

7. Theodore Vrettos, *Hammer on the Sea* (Boston, 1965).

8. Glenway Wescott, *Apartment in Athens* (New York, 1945).

9. George N. Rumanes, *The Man with the Black Worrybeads* (New York, 1973).

10. Alexander Karanikas, "Throuffi," *Texas Quarterly* 13 (Autumn 1970):38–50.

11. Tom T. Chamales, *Never So Few* (New York, 1957).

12. Wayne Charles Miller, *An Armed America—Its Face in Fiction: A History of the American Military Novel* (New York, 1970).

13. Anton Myrer, *The Big War* (New York, 1965).

14. Tom T. Chamales, *Go Naked in the World* (New York, 1959).

15. Ernest Hemingway, *A Farewell to Arms* (1929; reprint ed., New York, 1953), p. 270.

16. Chamales, *Go Naked in the World*, p. 166.

17. Thomas Doulis, *Path for Our Valor* (New York, 1963).

CHAPTER NINE

1. Xaviera Hollander, *The Happy Hooker* (New York, 1972), pp. 196–97.

2. Janet Baker, *I Am Sexual* (New York, 1970).

3. Ibid., p. 10.

4. Ibid., p. 11.

5. Cy Rice, *Nick the Greek* (New York, 1969), 35.

6. Ibid.

7. Harry Mark Petrakis, *A Dream of Kings* (New York, 1966), p. 125.

8. Id., *In the Land of Morning* (New York, 1973), p. 61.

9. Edmund Keeley, *The Libation* (New York, 1958).

10. Ibid., dust jacket.

11. Id., *The Gold-Hatted Lover* (New York, 1961).

12. Id., *The Imposter* (New York, 1970).

13. Ibid., pp. 98–99.

14. Elsie Lee, *The Passions of Medora Graeme* (New York, 1972).

15. Ibid., p. 29.

16. Elia Kazan, *The Arrangement* (New York, 1967).

17. John Updike, *Rabbit Redux* (New York, 1971).

18. Anatole Broyard, "Updike Goes All out at Last," *New York Times*, November 5, 1971.

19. Updike, *Rabbit Redux*, p. 42.

20. Peter Sourian, *Miri* (New York, 1957). The New American Library edition (1959) is used here.

21. John D. Spooner, *Three Cheers for War in General* (Boston, 1968).

22. George Revelli, *Sweet Marpessa* (New York, 1973).

23. C. L. Sulzberger, *The Tooth Merchant* (New York, 1973).

CHAPTER TEN

1. Demetrios A. Michalaros, "Editor's Note," *Athene* 3 (March–April 1942):24.

2. Peter Gray, "Threnody for Stelios," *Athene* 3 (January 1942):6–9.

3. Peter Gray, "The Swallow," *Athene* 3 (July 1942):10–13.

4. E. L. Elsworth, "Adventure in April," *Athene* 3 (July 1942):18–21, 32.

5. George B. Soorlis, "Shambles," *Athene* 12 (Winter 1952):18–19, 36–38, 48.

6. Jane Lianos, "The Liberated." *Athene* 11 (Spring 1950):13–14, 41.

7. Ibid., p. 13.

8. Theodore P. Vasilopoulos, "A Messenger," *Athene* 13 (Winter 1953):36–39.

9. Peter Bien, "The Scholarship," *Athene* 17 (Summer 1956):21–23, 44.

10. F. P. Zachariou, "Papa and the Turkish Language," *Athene* 7 (Spring 1946):10, 34.

11. John Belasco, "Robbery at the Acropolis," *Athene* 3 (March–April 1942):24–27; 3 (May 1942):24–27.

12. Ibid., 3 (May 1942):25.

13. Ibid., p. 27.

14. John Belasco, "Atlas Takes Over," *Athene* 18 (Spring 1957):38–39, 41; 18 (Summer 1957):46–47, 49.

15. Ibid., 18 (Spring 1957):38.

16. Ibid., p. 41.

17. Nicklas Frankel, as told to M. R. McLaren, "From Turkish Slave to American Chef," *Athene* 19 (Winter 1959):21–23; 20 (Autumn 1959):43–48.

18. Ibid., 19 (Winter 1959):21.

19. Ibid., 19 (Autumn 1959):45.

20. Jewel Drinkamer, "The Heart's Tongue," *Athene* 5 (September 1944):12.

21. Ibid.

22. Ibid.

23. C. J. Lampos, "The Atomic Bomb and Greek Fire," *Athene* 7 (Summer 1946):37–39.

24. Ibid., p. 60.

25. Paul Nord, "Napoleon Kalmer," *Athene* 55 (Spring 1954): 14–16, 36–37.

26. N. Nicolai, " . . . And a Time to Love!", *Athene* 21 (Summer 1960):27–29; 21 (Autumn 1960):30–32, 60–61.

27. Alexander Karanikas, "Shortcut to Riverdale," *Athene* 15 (Autumn 1954): 109–14.

28. Theano Papazoglou-Margaris, "Theia Giannitsa," trans. S. Koutsos, *Athene* 22 (Autumn 1961):55–56.

29. Theano Papazoglou-Margaris, "The Nymphs of Lake Michigan," trans. Vivian M. Kallen, *Athene* 24 (Autumn 1963):15–16, 62.

CHAPTER ELEVEN

1. Harry Mark Petrakis, *Lion at My Heart* (Boston, 1959). The works considered in this chapter are by Petrakis unless otherwise noted.

2. *A Dream of Kings* (New York, 1966).

3. *Stelmark* (New York, 1970).

4. Ibid., p. 11.

5. *The Odyssey of Kostas Volakis* (New York, 1963), p. 1.

6. *Pericles on 31st Street* (Chicago, 1965).

7. "The Ballad of Daphne and Apollo," ibid., p. 57.

8. Ibid., p. 64.

9. Ibid., p. 70.

10. "Matsoukas," ibid., p. 156.

11. *A Dream of Kings*, p. 108.

12. "The Shearing of Samson," in *The Waves of Night* (New York, 1969), pp. 45–63.

13. "The Bastards of Thanos," ibid., pp. 87–100.
14. *In the Land of Morning* (New York, 1973).
15. Ibid., p. 282.
16. *Lion at My Heart*, p. 194.
17. Ibid., p. 20.
18. *The Odyssey of Kostas Volakis*, pp. 47–48.
19. Ibid., p. 113.
20. "Courtship of the Blue Widow," in *Pericles on 31st Street*, p. 27.
21. "The Journal of a Wife-Beater," ibid., p. 169.
22. "Chrisoula," in *The Waves of Night*, p. 145.
23. *Lion at My Heart*, p. 9.
24. *The Odyssey of Kostas Volakis*, p. 86.
25. "The Legacy of Leontis," in *Pericles on 31st Street*, p. 53.
26. "The Song of Rhodanthe," ibid., p. 173.
27. "A Hand for Tomorrow," ibid., p. 192.
28. "Homecoming," in *The Waves of Night*, p. 167.
29. "Dark Eye," ibid., p. 177.
30. *In the Land of Morning*, p. 28.
31. *Stelmark*, p. 26.
32. *Lion at My Heart*, p. 23.
33. Ibid., p. 205.
34. Ibid., p. 232.
35. *The Odyssey of Kostas Volakis*, p. 17.
36. Ibid., p. 25.
37. "The Miracle," in *Pericles on 31st Street*, p. 18.
38. Ibid., p. 24.
39. "The Journal of a Wife-Beater," ibid., p. 169.
40. *A Dream of Kings*, p. 28.
41. Ibid., p. 48.
42. "The Waves of Night," p. 186.
43. *In the Land of Morning*, p. 31.
44. *The Hour of the Bell* (Garden City, 1976).
45. Ibid., p. 313.
46. *Lion at My Heart*, p. 197.
47. *The Odyssey of Kostas Volakis*, p. 206.
48. "Courtship of the Blue Widow," p. 42.
49. "The Return of Katerina," in *Pericles on 31st Street*, p. 103.
50. Ibid., p. 109.
51. *A Dream of Kings*, p. 23.
52. Ibid., p. 164.
53. "Chrisoula," p. 146.
54. *In the Land of Morning*, p. 21.
55. Ibid., p. 137.
56. *The Odyssey of Kostas Volakis*, pp. 11–12.
57. Ibid., p. 14.
58. "Pa and the Sad Turkeys," in *Pericles on 31st Street*, p. 82.
59. "The Journal of a Wife-Beater," p. 163.
60. *A Dream of Kings*, p. 63.
61. *Stelmark*, p. 117.

62. *A Dream of Kings*, pp. 29–30.
63. Ibid., 35.
64. *Nick the Greek* (Garden City, 1979). For more on Nick the Greek, see ch. 16.
65. *Stelmark*, p. 12.

CHAPTER TWELVE

1. Dashiell Hammett, *The Maltese Falcon* (1929; reprint ed., New York, 1964).
2. Id., *The Thin Man* (1933; reprint ed., New York, 1964).
3. Ellery Queen, *The Greek Coffin Mystery* (New York, 1942).
4. Ibid., p. 3.
5. Ibid., p. 37.
6. James M. Cain, *The Postman Always Rings Twice* (1934; reprint ed., New York, 1946). The Fiction Book Club Edition (1946) is used here.
7. Nelson Algren, *Never Come Morning* (1942; reprint ed., New York, 1963). The Harper Colophon Books edition (1963) is used here.
8. Ibid., p. 72.
9. Ibid., p. 283.
10. William Johnston, *Banyon*, based on screenplay by Ed Adamson (New York, 1971).
11. Ibid., p. 123.
12. Victor Miller, *Siege*, based on the Kojak television series episode *Siege of Terror* by Robert Heverly (New York, 1974).
13. Hugh Pentecost, *Girl Watcher's Funeral* (New York, 1969).
14. Ibid., dust jacket.
15. Ibid., pp. 5–6.
16. Mickey Spillane, *The Erection Set* (New York, 1972).
17. George V. Higgins, *The Digger's Game* (New York, 1973).
18. Ibid., p. 201.
19. Nicholas Gage, *Bones of Contention* (New York, 1974).
20. K. C. Constantine, *The Rocksburg Railroad Murders* (New York, 1972).
21. Ibid., dust jacket.
22. Ibid., pp. 113–14.
23. Id., *The Man Who Liked to Look at Himself* (New York, 1973).
24. Id., *The Blank Page* (New York, 1974).
25. Id., *A Fix Like This* (Roslyn, 1975).
26. Thomas Tryon, *Harvest Home* (New York, 1973).
27. William Brashler, *City Dogs* (New York, 1976).

CHAPTER THIRTEEN

1. Van Wyck Mason, *Dardanelles Derelict* (Garden City, 1949).
2. Edward S. Aarons, *Assignment Lili Lamaris* (Greenwich, 1959).
3. Nick Carter, *Seven Against Greece* (New York, 1967).
4. Alan Caillou, *Assault on Agathon* (New York, 1972).
5. David Lippincott, *E Pluribus Bang!* (New York, 1970).

6. Leo Katcher, *The Blind Cave* (New York, 1966).
7. Id., *Hot Pursuit* (New York, 1971).
8. Aaron Marc Stein, *I Fear the Greeks* (Garden City, 1966).
9. Phyllis A. Whitney, *Seven Tears for Apollo* (New York, 1963).
10. Sylvia Angus, *Death of a Hittite* (New York, 1969).
11. Jean Muir, *The Smiling Medusa* (New York, 1969).
12. Janice M. Bennett, *House of Athena* (New York, 1970).
13. Edmund Keeley, *Voyage to a Dark Island* (New York, 1972).
14. Jim Thorne, *The White Hand of Athene* (New York, 1974).
15. Mary Reisner, *Mirror of Delusion* (New York, 1965).
16. James Jones, *A Touch of Danger* (Garden City, 1973).
17. Sidney Sheldon, *The Other Side of Midnight* (New York, 1973).
18. Jan Roberts, *The Judas Sleep* (New York, 1975).

CHAPTER FOURTEEN

1. Samuel Griswold Goodrich, *The Balloon Travels of Robert Merry and His Young Friends*, ed. Peter Parley (New York, 1863).
2. Daniel C. Eddy, *Walter in Athens* (New York, 1865).
3. William Taylor Adams [Oliver Optic]. *Cross and Crescent: or, Young America in Turkey and Greece* (Boston, 1873).
4. Leola Benedict Terhune, "The Greek Bootblack," *Survey*, September 16, 1911, pp. 852–54.
5. Myron Levoy, "Andreas and the Magic Bells," in *The Witch of Fourth Street* (New York, 1972), pp. 29–45.
6. Harry S. George, *Demo of 70th Street* (New York, 1971).
7. Demetra Vaka Brown, *Delarah* (Chicago, 1943).
8. Alison Baigre Alessios, *The Spear of Ulysses* (New York, 1941).
9. Joice M. NanKivell, *Tales of Christophilos* (Boston, 1954), *Again Christophilos* (Boston, 1959).
10. Robert Shaffer, *The Lost Ones* (New York, 1956).
11. James Forman, *Ring the Judas Bell* (New York, 1965).
12. Annie Barclay Kerr, "A Little House for God," in *Strangers No Longer* (New York, 1943).
13. Edward Fenton, *Aleko's Island* (Garden City, 1948).
14. Id., *An Island for a Pelican* (Garden City, 1963).
15. Alice Geer Kelsey, *Racing the Red Sail* (New York, 1947).
16. Hardie Gramatky, *Nikos & the Sea God* (New York, 1963).
17. Yolla Niclas, *The Flower of Vassiliki* (New York, 1968).
18. Phyllis A. Whitney, *Mystery of the Hidden Hand* (Philadelphia, 1963).
19. Laura Lee Hope, *The Bobbsey Twins and the Greek Hat Mystery* (New York, 1964).
20. Carolyn Keene, *The Mysterious Mannequin* (New York, 1970), 68.
21. Claire Huchet Bishop, *A Present from Petros* (New York, 1961).
22. Theodore Gianakoulis and Georgia H. McPherson, *Fairy Tales of Modern Greece* (New York, 1930).
23. Aliki Brandenberg. *Three Gold Pieces* (New York, 1967).
24. Eve Merriam, *That Noodle-head Epaminondas* (New York, 1968).

25. Phyllis Reynolds Naylor, *What the Gulls Were Singing* (Chicago, 1967).
26. Ibid., dust jacket.
27. Isabelle Lawrence, *Niko Sculptor's Apprentice* (New York, 1957); Caroline Dale Snedeker, *Theras and His Town* (Garden City, 1961); Lillian Carroll, *Greek Slave Boy* (New York, 1968).

CHAPTER FIFTEEN

1. Jack Williamson, *The Age of Wizardry* (New York, 1964).
2. Barbara Michaels, *The Sea King's Daughter* (New York, 1975).
3. Ira Levin, *Rosemary's Baby* (1967; reprint ed., New York, 1968). The Dell reprint is used here.
4. John Fowles, *The Magus* (Boston, 1965).
5. Michaels, *The Sea King's Daughter*, p. 59.
6. Levin, *Rosemary's Baby*.
7. Richard Fariña, *Been Down So Long It Looks Like Up to Me* (1966; reprint ed., New York, 1974). The Dell reprint is used here.
8. Charles Tekeyan, *The Revelations of a Disappearing Man* (Garden City, 1971).
9. Herbert Mitgang, *Get These Men Out of the Hot Sun* (New York, 1972).
10. Robert Silverberg, *To Live Again* (Garden City, 1969).
11. Robert Silverberg, *Up the Line* (New York, 1969).
12. Pamela Sargent, "Matthew," in *Ten Tomorrows*, ed. Roger Elwood (Greenwich, 1973), pp. 75–90.
13. Roger Zelazny, *This Immortal* (New York, 1966).

CHAPTER SIXTEEN

1. Frederic Prokosch, *The Missolonghi Manuscript* (New York, 1968).
2. Harry Mark Petrakis, *The Hour of the Bell* (Garden City, 1976).
3. Athena Dallas-Damis, *Island of the Winds* (New Rochelle, 1976).
4. "Author's Notes," Ibid., n.p.
5. Irving Stone, *The Greek Treasure* (Garden City, 1975).
6. Richard Bradford, *Red Sky at Morning* (Philadelphia, 1968), p. 43.
7. Charles E. Jarvis, *Zeus Has Two Urns* (Lowell, 1976).
8. Nicholas Gage, *The Bourlotas Fortune* (New York, 1976).
9. Ibid., dust jacket.
10. Edwin Gilbert, *The Squirrel Cage* (Garden City, 1947).
11. Gerald Warner Brace, *Bell's Landing* (New York, 1955).
12. Edmund Schiddel, *The Devil in Bucks County* (New York, 1959).
13. Hubert Selby, Jr., *Last Exit to Brooklyn* (New York, 1965).
14. Cy Rice, *Nick the Greek* (New York, 1969). The novel *Nick the Greek* (1979) by Petrakis is cited in ch. 11.
15. Jimmy Snyder, *Jimmy the Greek* (Chicago, 1975).
16. Helen Zeese Papanikolas, *Toil and Rage in a New Land* (Salt Lake City, 1970).
17. Julian Moynahan, *Pairing Off* (New York, 1969).
18. Denison Hatch, *Cedarhurst Alley* (New York, 1971).

19. May Sarton, *Joanna and Ulysses* (New York, 1963).

20. Irwin Shaw, *Rich Man, Poor Man* (New York, 1970).

21. James Merrill, *The (Diblos) Notebook* (New York, 1965).

22. John Barth, *Lost in the Funhouse* (Garden City, 1968); Joyce Carol Oates, "How I Contemplated the World from the Detroit House of Correction and Began My Life over Again." *TriQuarterly* 15 (Spring 1969):5–21.

23. Merrill, *The (Diblos) Notebook*, dust jacket.

24. Sylvia Wright, *A Shark-infested Rice Pudding* (Garden City, 1969).

25. Nicholas Delbanco, *The Martlet's Tale* (Philadelphia, 1966).

26. Thomas Doulis, *The Quarries of Sicily* (New York, 1969).

27. Ibid., dust jacket.

28. Charles E. Jarvis, *The Tyrants* (Lowell, Mass., 1977).

CHAPTER SEVENTEEN

1. Joseph T. Skerrett, "The dialogue engendered when two systems meet," *MELUS* 5 (Summer 1978):3–4.

BIBLIOGRAPHY

Aarons, Edward S. *Assignment Lili Lamaris*. Greenwich: Fawcett, Publications, 1959.

About, Edmond. *The King of the Mountains*. Translated by Mary L. Booth. Boston: J. E. Tilton, 1861.

Adams, Samuel Hopkins. *Our Square and the People in It*. Freeport, N.Y.: Books for Libraries Press, 1970.

Adams, William Taylor [Oliver Optic]. *Cross and Crescent; or, Young America in Turkey and Greece*. Boston: Lee & Shephard, 1873.

Alessios, Alison Baigre. *The Spear of Ulysses*. New York: Longmans, Green, 1951.

Algren, Nelson. *Never Come Morning*. New York: Harper & Brothers, 1942. Reprint ed., Harper Colophon Books, 1963.

Aliki. *Three Gold Pieces*. New York: Pantheon Books, 1967.

Anderson, Maxwell. *Winterset*. In *Four Verse Plays*. New York: Harcourt, Brace & World, 1959.

Angus, Sylvia. *Death of a Hittite*. New York: Macmillan, 1969.

Athas, Daphne. *Cora*. New York: Viking Press, 1978.

———. *Entering Ephesus*. New York: Viking Press, 1971.

Auslander, Joseph, and Wurdeman, Audrey. *The Islanders*. New York: Longmans, Green, 1951.

Ayrton, Elisabeth. *Silence in Crete*. New York: William Morrow, 1964.

Baker, Janet. *I Am Sexual*. New York: Belmont Tower Books, 1970.

Bancroft, Hubert. *History of Alaska*. New York: Antiquarian Press, 1959.

Barth, John. *Lost in the Funhouse*. Garden City: Doubleday, 1968.

Belasco, John. "Atlas Takes Over." *Athene* 18 (Spring 1957):38–39, 41; 18 (Summer 1957), 46–47, 49.

———. "Robbery at the Acropolis," *Athene* 3 (March–April, 1942):24–27; 3 (May 1942):24–27.

Benjamin, S. G. W. *The Turk and the Greek*. New York: Hurd & Houghton, 1867.

Bennett, Janice M. *House of Athena*. New York: Ace Publishing Co., 1970.

Bezzerides, A. I. *Thieves' Market.* New York: Charles Scribner's Sons, 1949.

Bien, Peter. "The Scholarship." *Athene* 18 (Summer 1956):21–23, 44.

Bishop, Claire Huchet. *A Present from Petros.* New York: Viking Press, 1961.

Brace, Gerald Warner. *Bell's Landing.* New York: W. W. Norton, 1955.

Braddock, Joseph. *The Greek Phoenix.* New York: Coward, McCann & Geoghegan, 1973.

Bradford, Richard. *Red Sky at Morning.* Philadelphia: J. B. Lippincott, 1968.

Brashler, William. *City Dogs.* New York: Harper & Row, 1976.

Brelis, Dean. *My New Found Land.* Boston: Houghton Mifflin, 1963.

Brown, Demetra Vaka. *Bribed to be Born.* New York: Exposition Press, 1951.

———. *Delarah.* Chicago: Ziff-Davis Publishing Co., 1943.

Brown, Demetra Vaka, and Brown, Kenneth. *The First Secretary.* New York: B. W. Dodge, 1907.

Browne, J. Ross. *Yusef, or The Journey of the Frangi.* New York: Harper & Brothers, 1853.

Broyard, Anatole. "Updike Goes All Out at Last." *New York Times,* November 5, 1971.

Bryant, William Cullen. *Letters from the East.* New York: G. P. Putnam & Son, 1869.

Buchanan, Georgia Gianakos. *Paved with Gold.* New York: Vantage Press, 1979.

Caillou, Alan. *Assault on Agathon.* New York: Avon Books, 1972.

Cain, James M. *The Postman Always Rings Twice.* New York: Alfred A. Knopf, 1934.

Canoutas, Seraphim G. *Christopher Columbus: A Greek Nobleman.* New York: St. Mark's Press, 1943.

Cardell, William S. *Story of Jack Halyard, the Sailor Boy; or, the Virtuous Family.* New York: Wilder & Campbell, 1825.

Carroll, Lillian. *Greek Slave Boy.* New York: Scholastic Book Services, 1968.

Carter, Nick. *Seven Against Greece.* New York: Award Books, 1967.

Chamales, Tom T. *Go Naked in the World.* New York: Charles Scribner's Sons, 1959.

———. *Never So Few.* New York: Charles Scribner's Sons, 1957.

Christy, George. *All I Could See from Where I Stood*. Indianapolis: Bobbs-Merrill, 1963.

Colton, Walter. *Visit to Constantinople and Athens*. New York: Leavitt, Lord & Co., 1836. Reprinted under title *Land and Lee in the Bosphorus and Aegean*. Edited by Henry T. Cheever. New York: A. S. Barnes & Co., 1851.

Constantine, K. C. *The Blank Page*. New York: Saturday Review Press, 1974.

———. *A Fix Like This*. Roslyn: Detective Book Club, 1975.

———. *The Man Who Liked to Look at Himself*. New York: Saturday Review Press, 1973.

———. *The Rocksburg Railroad Murders*. New York: Saturday Review Press, 1972.

Cotsakis, Roxanne. *The Wing and the Thorn*. Atlanta: Tupper & Love, 1952.

Crane, Stephen. *The Complete Novels of Stephen Crane*. Edited by Thomas A. Gullason. Garden City: Doubleday, 1967.

———. *The Complete Short Stories and Sketches of Stephen Crane*. Edited by Thomas A. Gullason. Garden City: Doubleday, 1963.

Dallas-Damis, Athena. *Island of the Winds*. New Rochelle: Caratzas Brothers, 1976.

———. *Windswept*. New Rochelle: Caratzas Brothers, 1979.

Delbanco, Nicholas. *The Martlet's Tale*. Philadelphia: J. B. Lippincott, 1966.

Demetrios, George. *When I Was a Boy in Greece*. Boston: Lothrop, Lee & Shepard, 1913.

———. *When Greek Meets Greek*. Boston: Houghton Mifflin, 1947.

Dilles, Jim. *The Good Thief*. New York: Thomas Y. Crowell, 1959.

Dobie, Charles Caldwell. "All or Nothing." *Arrested Moment and Other Stories*. New York: John Day, 1927.

———. *San Francisco Adventures*. Freeport: Books for Libraries Press, 1969.

Doering, Eileen Elita. "A Charm of the Gulf of Mexico Sponge Fishers." *Journal of American Folk-Lore* 52 (1939):123.

Dorr, David F. *A Colored Man Round the World*. Cleveland, 1858.

Doulis, Thomas. *Disaster and Fiction: Modern Greek Fiction and the Impact of the Asia Minor Disaster of 1922*. Berkeley: University of California Press, 1977.

———. *Path for Our Valor*. New York: Simon & Schuster, 1963.

———. *The Quarries of Sicily*. New York: Crown Publishers, 1969.

Drinkamer, Jewel. "The Heart's Tongue." *Athene* 5 (September 1944):12.

Eddy, Daniel D. *Walter in Athens.* New York: Thomas Y. Crowell, 1865.

Elsworth, E. L. "Adventure in April." *Athene* 3 (July 1942):18–21, 32.

Fariña, Richard. *Been Down So Long It Looks Like Up to Me.* New York: Random House, 1966.

Farrell, James T. "The Benefits of American Life." In *The Short Stories of James T. Farrell.* New York: Vanguard Press, 1934.

Fenton, Edward. *Aleko's Island.* Garden City: Junior Literary Guild and Doubleday, 1948.

———. *An Island for a Pelican.* Garden City: Doubleday, 1963.

Fields, Joseph, and Chodorov, Jerome. *My Sister Eileen.* New York: Random House, 1941.

Fitzgerald, F. Scott. *The Great Gatsby.* New York: Charles Scribner's Sons, 1925.

Forman, James. *Ring the Judas Bell.* New York: Bell Books/Farrar, Straus & Giroux, 1965.

Fowles, John. *The Magus.* Boston: Little, Brown, 1965.

Frankel, Nicklas. As Told to M. R. McLaren. "From Turkish Slave to American Chef." *Athene* 19 (Winter 1959):21–23; 20 (Autumn 1959):43–48.

Frantzis, George Th. *Strangers at Ithaca: The Story of Tarpon Springs.* St. Petersburg: Great Outdoors Publishing Co., 1962.

Freund, Philip. "Young Greek and the Creole." In *Young Greek and the Creole and Other Stories.* New York: Pilgrim, 1944.

Gage, Nicholas. *Bones of Contention.* New York: Berkeley Publishing Corp., 1974.

———. *The Bourlotas Fortune.* New York: Bantam Books, 1976.

Gallico, Paul. "The Hat." In *Further Confessions of a Story Teller.* Garden City: Doubleday, 1961.

George, Harry S. *Demo of 70th Street.* New York: H. Z. Walck, 1971.

Gianakoulis, Theodore, and MacPherson, Georgia H. *Fairy Tales of Modern Greece.* New York: E. P. Dutton, 1930.

Gilbert, Edwin. *The Squirrel Cage.* Garden City: Doubleday, 1947.

Gilkes, Lillian. *Cora Crane.* Bloomington: Indiana University Press, 1960.

Goldberg, Isaac. *Major Noah: American-Jewish Pioneer.* Philadelphia: Jewish Publication Society of America, 1936.

Goodrich, Samuel Griswold. *The Balloon Travels of Robert Merry and His Young Friends.* Edited by Peter Parley. New York: Sheldon & Co., 1863.

Gramatky, Hardie. *Nikos & the Sea God.* New York: G. P. Putnam's Sons, 1963.

Grau, Shirley Ann. *The Keepers of the House.* New York: Alfred A. Knopf, 1964.

Gray, Peter. "The Swallow," *Athene* 3 (July 1942):10–13, 31, 32.

———. "Threnody for Stelios," *Athene* 3 (January 1942):6–9.

Gringo, Harry [Henry A. Wise]. *Scampavias from Gibel Tarek to Stamboul.* New York: Charles Scribner, 1857.

Grossberg, Elmer. *Farewell, My Son.* New York: Messner, 1946.

Halleck, Fitz-Greene. *The Poetical Works of Fitz-Greene Halleck.* Edited by James Grant Wilson. 1869. Reprint. New York: AMS Press, 1969.

Hammett, Dashiell. *The Maltese Falcon.* 1929. Reprint. New York: Vintage Books, 1964.

———. *The Thin Man.* 1933. Reprint. New York: Vintage Books, 1964.

Harris, Jennie E. "Sponge Fishermen of Tarpon Springs," *National Geographic,* 91 (January 1947):119–36.

Hatch, Denison. *Cedarhurst Alley.* New York: Pocket Books, 1971.

Hemingway, Ernest. *A Farewell to Arms.* 1929. Reprint. New York: Charles Scribner's Sons, 1953.

———. *In Our Time.* 1923. Reprint, New York: Charles Scribner's Sons, 1958.

———. *The Sun Also Rises.* 1926. Reprint. New York: Charles Scribner's Sons, 1970.

Higgins, George V. *The Digger's Game.* New York: Alfred A. Knopf, 1973.

Hollander, Xaviera. *The Happy Hooker.* New York: Dell Publishing Co., 1972.

Hope, Anthony. *Phroso.* New York: American News Co., 1899.

Hope, Laura Lee. *The Bobbsey Twins and the Greek Hat Mystery.* New York: Grosset & Dunlap, 1964.

Horton, George. *Constantine: A Tale of Greece Under King Otho.* Chicago: Way & Williams, 1897.

———. *A Fair Brigand.* Chicago and New York: Herbert S. Stone & Co., 1899.

———. *Home of Nymphs and Vampires: The Isles of Greece.* Indianapolis: Bobbs-Merrill, 1929.

——. *In Argolis*. Chicago: A. C. McClurg & Co., 1902.

——. *Like Another Helen*. Indianapolis: Bowen-Merrill, 1900, 1901.

——. *The Monk's Treasure*. Indianapolis: Bobbs-Merrill, 1905.

——. *Poems of an Exile*. Indianpolis: Bobbs-Merrill, 1931.

——. *The Tempting of Father Anthony*. Chicago: A. C. McClurg & Co., 1901.

Housepian, Marjorie. *The Smyrna Affair*. New York: Harcourt Brace Jovanovich, 1971.

Howe, Samuel Gridley. *An Historical Sketch of the Greek Revolution*. New York: White, Gallaher & White, 1828.

——. *The Cretan Refugees and Their American Helpers*. Boston: Lee & Shepard, 1868.

Jameson, Harris P. *For Sully's Sake*. New York: Carlton Press, 1970.

Jarvis, Charles E. *Zeus Has Two Urns*. Lowell, Mass.: Apollo Books, 1976.

——. *The Tyrants*. Lowell, Mass.: Ithaca Press, 1977.

Johnston, William. *Banyon*. Based on a screenplay by Ed Adamson. New York: Warner Paperback Library, 1971.

Johnstone, George. *Closer to the Sun*. New York: William Morrow, 1960.

Jones, James. *A Touch of Danger*. Garden City: Doubleday, 1973.

Kamal, Ahmad. *Full Fathom Five*. Garden City: Doubleday, 1948.

Kantor, McKinlay. "That Greek Dog." In *The Best American Short Stories, 1942*. Edited by Martha Foley. Boston: Houghton Mifflin, 1942.

Karanikas, Alexander. "Shortcut to Riverdale." *Athene* 15 (Autumn 1954):109–14.

——. "Throuffi," *Texas Quarterly* 13 (Autumn 1970):38–50.

Karanikas, Alexander, and Karanikas, Helen. *Elias Venezis*. New York: Twayne Publishers, 1966.

Katcher, Leo. *The Blind Cave*. New York: Viking Press, 1966.

——. *Hot Pursuit*. New York: Atheneum Press, 1971.

Kazan, Elia. *America America*. New York: Stein & Day, 1962.

——. *The Arrangement*. New York: Stein & Day, 1967.

——. *Acts of Love*. New York: Alfred A. Knopf, 1978.

Keeley, Edmund. *The Gold-Hatted Lover*. New York: Modern Literary Editions, 1961.

——. *The Imposter*. New York: Modern Literary Editions, 1970.

——. *The Libation*. New York: Modern Literary Editions, 1958.

——. *Voyage to a Dark Island*. New York: Curtis Books, 1972.

Keene, Carolyn. *The Mysterious Mannequin.* New York: Grosset & Dunlap, 1970.

Kelsey, Alice Geer. *Racing the Red Sail.* New York: Longmans, Green, 1947.

Kerr, Annie Barclay. "Little House for God." In *Strangers No Longer.* New York: Friendship, 1943.

Lampos, C. J. "The Atomic Bomb and Greek Fire," *Athene* 7 (Summer 1946): 37–39, 58, 60.

Lardas, Konstantinos. "The Bird." *Prairie Schooner* 44 (Winter 1969–70):383–92.

———. "The Broken Wings," *South Dakota Review* 10 (Spring 1972):5–15.

———. "The Cypress Trees, the Sun," *Hawaii Review* 1 (Spring 1973):79–86.

———. "The Devil Child," *Atlantic Monthly* 208 (July 1961): 55–56.

———. "How Beautiful, the Feet," *Descant* 15 (Winter 1971):9–22.

———. *A Tree of Man.* Privately printed, 1968.

———. "The Usurpation," *Literary Review* 13 (Winter 1969–70):224–35.

Larrabee, Stephen A. *Hellas Observed.* New York: New York University Press, 1957.

Lawrence, Isabelle. *Niko Sculptor's Apprentice.* New York: Viking Press, 1948.

Lee, Elsie. *The Passions of Medora Graeme.* New York: Dell Publishing Co., 1972.

Lee, Jeannette. *Mr. Achilles.* New York: Dodd, Mead & Co., 1912.

Levin, Ira. *Rosemary's Baby.* New York: Random House, 1967.

Levoy, Myron. "Andreas and the Magic Bells." In *The Witch of Fourth Street.* New York: Harper & Row, 1972.

Lianos, Jane. "The Liberated," *Athene* 11 (Spring 1950):13–14, 41.

Lippincott, David. *E Pluribus Bang!* New York: Viking Press, 1970.

London, Jack. *The God of His Fathers.* Garden City: Garden City Publishing Co., 1925.

———. *The Mutiny of the Elsinore.* New York: Macmillan, 1914.

MacPherson, Georgia H., and Gianakoulis, Theodore. *Fairy Tales of Modern Greece.* New York: E. P. Dutton, 1930.

Marshall, Grace E. *Eternal Greece.* Rochester: DuBois Press, 1938.

Mason, Van Wyck. *Dardanelles Derelict.* Garden City: Doubleday, 1949.

McCullers, Carson. *The Heart Is a Lonely Hunter.* 1940. Reprint. New York: Bantam Books, 1967.

McKenney, Ruth. *My Sister Eileen*. New York: Harcourt, Brace, 1938.

Melville, Herman. *Clarel*. Edited by Walter E. Bezanson. New York: Hendricks House, 1960.

———. *Journal up the Straits*. Edited by Raymond Weaver. New York: Colophon, 1935.

Merriam, Eve. *That Noodle-head Epaminondas*. New York: Scholastic Book Services, 1968.

Merrill, James. *The (Diblos) Notebook*. New York: Atheneum Press, 1965.

Metalious, Grace. *Peyton Place*. New York: Julian Messner, 1956.

———. *Return to Peyton Place*. New York: Julian Messner, 1959.

———. *The Tight White Collar*. New York: Julian Messner, 1960.

Michaels, Barbara. *The Sea King's Daughter*. New York: Dodd, Mead & Co., 1975.

Michalaros, Demetrios A. *Athene* 3 (March–April 1942):24.

———. *The Minoan*. Chicago: Athene Editions, 1958.

———. *Sonnets of an Immigrant*. Chicago: American Hellenic Publishing Co., 1930.

Miller, Victor B. *Siege*. Based on the Kojak television episode *Siege of Terror* by Robert Heverly. New York: Pocket Books, 1974.

Miller, Wayne Charles. *An Armed America—Its Face in Fiction: A History of the American Military Novel*. New York: New York University Press, 1970.

———, ed. *A Comprehensive Bibliography for the Study of American Minorities*. 2 vols. New York: New York University Press, 1976. Vol. 1.

Mitgang, Herbert. *Get These Men out of the Hot Sun*. New York: Arbor House, 1974.

Moskos, Charles C., Jr. *Greek Americans: Struggle and Success*. Englewood Cliffs, N.J.: Prentice-Hall, 1979.

Mountzoures, H. L. *The Empire of Things and Other Stories*. New York: Charles Scribner's Sons, 1968.

———. *The Bridge*. New York: Charles Scribner's Sons, 1972.

Moynahan, Julian. *Pairing Off*. New York: William Morrow, 1968.

Muir, Jean. *The Smiling Medusa*. New York: Dodd, Mead & Co., 1969.

Myrer, Anton. *The Big War*. New York: Dell Publishing Co., 1965.

NanKivell, Joice M. *Tales of Christophilos*. Boston: Houghton, Mifflin, 1954.

———. *Again Christophilos*. Boston: Houghton, Mifflin, 1959.

Naylor, Phyllis Reynolds. *What the Gulls Were Singing.* Chicago: Follett, 1967.

Nevins, Allan. *American Social History as Recorded by British Travellers.* New York: Henry Holt, 1931.

Newhouse, Edward. "Manny Hirsch." *Anything Can Happen.* New York: Harcourt, Brace, 1941.

Niclas, Yolla. *The Flower of Vassiliki.* New York: Seabury Press, 1968.

Nicolai, N. ". . . And a Time to Love!" *Athene* 21 (Summer 1960):27–29; 21 (Autumn 1960):30–32, 60–61.

Nord, Paul. "Napoleon Kalmer," *Athene* 15 (Spring 1954): 14–16.

North, Sterling. *Seven Against the Years.* New York: Macmillan, 1939.

Oates, Joyce Carol. "How I Contemplated the World from the Detroit House of Correction and Began My Life over Again," *TriQuarterly* 15 (Spring 1969):5–21.

Panagopoulos, Epaminondas P. *New Smyrna: An Eighteenth Century Greek Odyssey.* Gainsville: University of Florida Press, 1966.

Papanikolas, Helen Zeese. "Toil and Rage in a New Land: The Greek Immigrants in Utah," *Utah Historical Quarterly* 38 (Spring 1970):97–203.

Papas, Alexander, and Raizis, Marios Byron. *American Poets and the Greek Revolution (1821–1828): A Study in Byronic Philhellenism.* Thessaloniki: Institute for Balkan Studies, 1971.

Papazoglou-Margaris, Theano. *The Chronicle of Halsted Street.* Athens: G. Fix, 1962.

———. *Eftihia and Other Stories.* Chicago: Modern Thought, 1939.

———. "The Nymphs of Lake Michigan." Translated by Vivian M. Kallen. *Athene* 24 (Autumn 1963):15–16, 62.

———. *A Tear for Uncle Jimmy.* Athens: Diphros, 1958.

———. "Theia Giannitsa." Translated by S. Koutsos. *Athene* 22 (Autumn 1961):55–56.

———. *The Travels of Uncle Plato.* Athens: Star, 1972.

Pentecost, Hugh. *Girl Watcher's Funeral.* New York: Dodd, Mead, 1969.

Petrakis, Harry Mark. *A Dream of Kings.* New York: David McKay, 1966.

———. *The Hour of the Bell.* Garden City: Doubleday, 1976.

———. *In the Land of Morning.* New York: David McKay, 1973.

———. *Lion at My Heart.* Boston: Atlantic Monthly Press/Little, Brown & Co., 1959.

———. *Nick the Greek.* Garden City: Doubleday, 1979.

————. *The Odyssey of Kostas Volakis*. New York: David McKay, 1963.

————. *Pericles on 31st Street*. Chicago: Quadrangle Books, 1965.

————. *Stelmark: A Family Recollection*. New York: David McKay, 1970.

————. *The Waves of Night*. New York: David McKay, 1969.

Piper, Henry Dan. *F. Scott Fitzgerald: A Candid Portrait*. New York: Holt, Rinehart & Winston, 1962.

Post, Henry A. V. *A Visit to Greece and Constantinople*. New York: Sleight & Robinson, Printers, 1830.

Prokosch, Frederic. *The Missolonghi Manuscript*. New York: Farrar, Straus & Giroux, 1968.

Queen, Ellery. *The Greek Coffin Mystery*. New York: Pocket Books, 1942.

Reinhardt, Richard. *The Ashes of Smyrna*. New York: Harper & Row, 1971.

Reisner, Mary. *Mirror of Delusion*. New York: Belmont Publications, 1965.

Remde, Harry. *The Thirteenth Island*. Boston: Peripatetic, 1946.

Revelli, George. *Sweet Marpessa*. New York: Bantam Books, 1973.

Rice, Cy. *Nick the Greek*. New York: Funk & Wagnalls, 1969.

Rives, Hallie Ermine. *The Castaway*. Indianapolis: Bobbs-Merrill, 1904.

Roberts, Jan. *The Judas Sleep*. New York: Saturday Review Press, 1975.

Rumanes, George N. *The Man with the Black Worrybeads*. New York: A. Arthur Fields Books, 1973.

Saloutos, Theodore. *The Greeks in the United States*. Cambridge, Mass.: Harvard University Press, 1964.

Sargent, Pamela. "Matthew." *Ten Tomorrows*. Edited by Roger Elwood. Greenwich: Fawcett Publications, 1973.

Saroyan, William. *Little Children*. New York: Harcourt, Brace, 1937.

————. *Three Plays*. New York: Harcourt, Brace, 1940.

————. *Dear Baby*. New York: Harcourt, Brace, 1944.

Sarton, May. *Joanna and Ulysses*. New York: W. W. Norton & Company, 1963.

Schiddel, Edmund. *The Devil in Bucks County*. New York: Simon & Schuster, 1959.

Selby, Jr., Hubert. *Last Exit to Brooklyn*. New York: Grove Press, 1965.

Selz, Thalia. "The Death of Anna," *Virginia Quarterly Review* 33 (Spring 1957):262–69.

————. "The Education of a Queen." *Partisan Review* 28 (1961): 552–73, 669–87.

Shaffer, Robert. *The Lost Ones.* New York: Henry Holt, 1956.

Shaw, Irwin. *Rich Man, Poor Man.* New York: Delacorte Press, 1970.

Sheldon, Sidney. *The Other Side of Midnight.* New York: Dell Publishing Co., 1973.

Silverberg, Robert. *To Live Again.* Garden City: Doubleday, 1969.

————. *Up the Line.* New York: Ballantine Books, 1969.

Skerrett, Joseph T. "The dialogue engendered when two systems meet." *MELUS* 5 (Summer 1978), 3–4.

Snedeker, Caroline Dale. *Theras and His Town.* Garden City: Doubleday, 1961.

Snyder, Jimmy. *Jimmy the Greek.* Chicago: Playboy Press 1975.

Soorlis, George B. "Shambles," *Athene* 12 (Winter 1952):18–19, 36–38, 48.

Sourian, Peter. *Miri.* New York: Pantheon Book, 1957; New American Library, 1959.

Spencer, Terence. *Fair Greece, Sad Relic.* 1954. Reprint. New York: Octagon Books, 1973.

Spillane, Mickey. *The Erection Set.* New York: E. P. Dutton, 1972.

Spooner, John D. *Three Cheers for War in General.* Boston: Little, Brown, 1968.

Stein, Aaron Marc. *I Fear the Greeks.* Garden City: Doubleday, 1966.

Stephens, J. L. *Incidents of Travel in Greece, Turkey, Russia, and Poland.* Edinburgh: William & Robert Chambers, 1839.

Stone, Irving. *The Greek Treasure.* Garden City: Doubleday, 1975.

Sulzberger, C. L. *The Tooth Merchant.* New York: Quadrangle Books, 1973.

Tekeyan, Charles. *The Revelations of a Disappearing Man.* Garden City: Doubleday, 1971.

Terhune, Leola Benedict. "The Greek Bootblack." *Survey,* 16 September 1911, 852–54.

Thompson, Ariadne. *The Octagonal Heart.* Indianapolis: Bobbs-Merrill, 1956.

Thorne, Jim. *The White Hand of Athene.* New York: Pinnacle Books, 1974.

Tracy, Don. *Bazzaris.* New York: Ravenna Books, Trident Press, 1965.

Tryon, Thomas. *Harvest Home.* New York: Alfred A. Knopf, 1973.

Twain, Mark. *Innocents Abroad.* New York: Gabriel Wells, 1922.

Updike, John. *Rabbit Redux.* New York: Alfred A. Knopf, 1971.

Uris, Leon M. *The Angry Hills.* New York: Random House, 1955.

Vardoulakis, Mary. *Gold in the Streets.* New York: Dodd, Mead, 1945.

Vasilopoulos, Theodore P. "A Messenger." *Athene* 13 (Winter 1953):36–39.

Vrettos, Theodore. *Hammer on the Sea.* Boston: Little, Brown, 1965.

Warren, Robert Penn. *The Cave.* New York: Random House, 1959.

Wescott, Glenway. *Apartment in Athens.* New York: Harper & Brothers, 1945.

Willis, Nathaniel Parker. *Pencillings by the Way.* 3 vols. London: John Macrone, 1835. vol. 2.

White, William, ed. *By-Line: Ernest Hemingway.* New York: Charles Scribner's Sons, 1967.

Whitman, Walt. *Leaves of Grass.* New York: Aventine Press, 1931.

Whitney, Phyllis A. *Seven Tears for Apollo.* New York: Appleton-Century-Crofts, 1963.

———. *Mystery of the Hidden Hand.* Philadelphia: Westminster Press, 1963.

Williamson, Jack. *The Age of Wizardry.* New York: Lancer Books, 1964.

Wolfe, Thomas. *Look Homeward, Angel.* New York: Charles Scribner's Sons, 1929.

———. *Of Time and the River.* New York: Charles Scribner's Sons, 1935.

———. *The Web and the Rock.* New York: Harper Brothers, 1937.

Wright, Sylvia. *A Shark-infested Rice Pudding.* Garden City: Doubleday, 1969.

Xenos, Stephanos Theodoros. *Andronike, The Heroine of the Greek Revolution.* Translated by Edwin A. Grosvenor. Boston: Little, Brown, 1897.

Zachariou. F. P. "Papa and the Turkish Language," *Athene* 7 (Spring 1946):10, 34.

Zei, Alki. *Wildcat Under Glass.* New York: Holt, Rinehart, & Winston, 1968.

———. *Petros' War.* New York: E. P. Dutton, 1972.

Zelazny, Roger. *This Immortal.* New York: Ace Books, 1966.

INDEX

THE AUTHOR

ALEXANDER KARANIKAS has taught English at the University of Illinois since 1954. He won a Friends of Literature award for *Tillers of a Myth*, a critical study of the Southern Agrarians. With his wife Helen he wrote a biography of Elias Venezis, a Greek novelist. He has published two collections of poetry. Long active in the Greek-American community, he cochaired a national bicentennial symposium on The Greek Experience in America, sponsored by the Modern Greek Studies Association. His poems, articles, and short stories have appeared in various journals and magazines.

P6